MASTERING MANAGEMENT 2.0

FINANCIAL TIMES

MASTERING
MANAGEMENT 2.0

**Your Single-Source Guide to Becoming a
Master of Management**

Executive editor **James Pickford**

FINANCIAL TIMES
Prentice Hall

London New York San Francisco Toronto Sydney Tokyo Singapore
Hong Kong Cape Town Madrid Paris Milan Munich Amsterdam

PEARSON EDUCATION LIMITED

Head Office:
Edinburgh Gate
Harlow CM20 2JE
Tel: +44 (0)1279 623623
Fax: +44 (0)1279 431059

London Office:
128 Long Acre, London WC2E 9AN
Tel: +44 (0)020 7447 2000
Fax: +44 (0)020 7240 5771
Website: www.business-minds.com

First published in Great Britain in 2001

© Compilation: Pearson Education Limited 2001

Note: Licences have been granted by individual authors/organizations for articles through-out this publication. Please refer to the respective articles for copyright notice.

ISBN: 0 273 65491 8

British Library Cataloguing in Publication Data
A CIP catalogue record for this book can be obtained from the British Library.

10 9 8 7 6 5 4 3 2 1

Typeset by Land & Unwin, Northamptonshire
Printed and bound in Italy

The Publishers' policy is to use paper manufactured from sustainable forests.

Contents

Introduction

In October 2000 the *Financial Times* newspaper launched Mastering Management, a series of 15 weekly supplements explaining the theory and practice of management. Written by experts from leading business schools around the world, the series guided readers through the fundamental concepts of management science, and brought them up-to-date with the latest developments in what is a fast-changing field. This book contains the complete text of Mastering Management as it appeared in the *Financial Times*.

For most of the past century, general managers in large companies could pick up almost everything they needed to know about management in the day-to-day course of their careers. As they climbed the corporate ladder, young managers would spend time in different departments. They would supplement their technical knowledge of production and business processes with broader skills. Ultimately, they would be able to make "big-picture" decisions about the organization's structure and strategy, thanks to their accumulated understanding of the business.

In the 21st century, large corporations are too complex for managers to amass such a breadth of knowledge. Gaining mastery of one area, such as operations or corporate finance, takes several years. It is no longer feasible to design a career path that demands all managers pass through all departments.

Although individual managers have a high level of specialist skill, they no longer have the broad knowledge they need to take on greater responsibility. When they make long-term decisions, chief executives need to draw on an informed perspective about the full range of business activities. Just as important, a chief executive needs to express a vision of the company's future that all employees find credible and inspiring.

To acquire these skills, they must undertake an MBA or try to find their way through a bewildering proliferation of management books and journals.

Mastering Management 2.0 aims to offer an antidote. As a primer in the core concepts of management, it is organized into 10 parts: the state of management today; enterprise and innovation; strategy; global business; business and society; the organization and human resources; skills of management; marketing; finance and accounting; production and operations. Seasoned readers of the *Financial Times* will remember the Mastering Management series and book of 1995, *Mastering Management 2.0* covers some of the same areas, but brings a new set of academic perspectives and updates them for a different business environment.

The biggest of those differences has been the emergence of the internet and e-business. Some might argue that its importance should dictate an 11th part devoted entirely to the subject. To hive the internet off, however, is to miss the point. Its influence on management is such that it can only be properly examined as an integrated part of each sub-discipline. Where relevant, therefore, the authors have attempted to identify the specific, long-term effects of e-business in their field of expertise.

Many distinguished academics and experts have contributed to *Mastering Management 2.0*, from a diverse collection of business schools, including Wharton, London Business School, Harvard, Insead, Columbia, the Tuck School at Dartmouth, IMD, Templeton College, Oxford, IESE and Saïd Business School.

Mastering Management 2.0 is no substitute for an MBA degree, but it will serve as a guide through some of the important issues managers face. By studying the lessons of this book, we hope that readers will gain sufficient knowledge of the theory to see benefits in their own practice.

James Pickford, *Executive editor, FT Mastering*

The state of
management today

1

Contents

Introduction to Part 1

Mastering Management begins with three chapters charting the current state of management and speculating on its future. Despite the rapid development of business schools and the spread of management education, the pace of change in the past 30 years has often outstripped the ability of management thinkers to identify and explain the most important issues facing business. When established practices have been found wanting, managers have sought help from management theory. The writers in this part examine the successes and failures of management. They outline its history, and propose views on the forces governing change in the future.

Thriving on the
chaos of the future

Daniel Muzyka considers how cherished management practices have been exposed as inadequate and suggests what will be needed for the next decade.

Dr Daniel F. Muzyka is dean of the Faculty of Commerce and Business Administration at the University of British Columbia (Vancouver), where he is also a professor of management. He was formerly IAF Professor of Entrepreneurship at Insead.

How can we describe the last few decades in business? For those of us who have witnessed developments since the 1960s, the words of Charles Dickens come to mind: "It was the best of times, it was the worst of times." The past few decades have not only given rise to discussion of chaos and uncertainty, but have given new meaning to these words.

For managers, the time has been one that has tested and exposed the inadequacies of many cherished assumptions and practices. For entrepreneurs, these turbulent times have led to significant opportunities. For those of us monitoring and trying to make sense of the scene, it has been at once interesting, challenging, humbling, and exciting.

As humans, we search for ways to communicate and clarify what is happening around us. There are many characterizations of the evolving environment that border on the banal. Take two examples. The internet created a "new economy" straining against the "old economy." (We are beginning to realize these distinctions are overblown.) The introduction of the personal computer would "liberate" people from central structures and would decentralize the economy. (We are more decentralized in some ways, but have become increasingly dependent upon centralized standards and suppliers.) While these events have created opportunities, none of the characterizations has endured, nor have they had the impact expected. Their failure begs the question: "What is going on?"

Modern times revisited

So what fuels our turbulent times? Are they more turbulent? There are simple and complex answers to the first question. Accelerating human discovery has led the parade, fueled by a growing population, the emergence of new economic regions, and the growing acceptance of Adam Smith's gospel around the planet. This has led to a doubling of scientific knowledge every 17 years, according to a 1997 study.

Another force we can point to is the changing expectations of this growing population. Clearly, there is a greater sense of self-determination, an expectation of rewards and recognition for efforts expended, and a growing appetite for a better life. These forces are interacting in complex ways to move and change markets, businesses, and the economic fortunes of regions.

We have enhanced the ability of these forces to affect us by removing many of the barriers that protected us in our various corners of the world. The global village has been realized through communications, burgeoning airline networks, and significantly reduced economic (Gatt) and social barriers (Nafta, the EU) to commerce and integrated financial markets. Financial resources are readily available globally and move quickly. Shocks can roll through the global economy with frightening speed and opportunities originate from many different points. To those who espoused globalization in the 1960s, I simply say, "Be careful what you wish."

Combined with shocks traveling through the system, we find people both more important and more willing to move around. The irony is that automation, on which so many productivity gains have been built, requires people to create and sustain it. Individuals are more important because of the knowledge they possess and the fact that more of our economy is based on services: the production assets are people and not machines. At the same time, labor mobility in many parts of the world, or at least the opportunity for it, has increased.

Labor is often more willing to travel or move for a number of reasons. First, our expectations of what life should offer have changed. Modern communication and air travel make it easy to shop around and compare lifestyles. Second, the loyalty that joined the person to the corporation has broken down. As corporations have evolved new models for changing times, they have experimented with extensive downsizing and re-engineering. Such practices, in particular the

Conditions that existed in the past are less likely to lead to successful **prediction** than ever before

wholesale elimination of jobs, have fundamentally altered the bonds between a corporation and its staff. People will often stay less for reasons of loyalty and more for the value they perceive their association will generate for them.

The combined impact of these factors makes forecasting the future harder: the conditions that existed in the past are less likely to lead to successful prediction than ever before. In the end, the world is more turbulent than in past decades.

Is there any prospect for a reduction in turbulence and uncertainty? The answer is a clear "no." We haven't begun to see the effect of discoveries in areas such as quantum computing and the human genome. In recent years, Moore's law, which predicts a doubling in computer chip capacity every 18 months, was surpassed and we are beginning to make headway with some formerly intractable diseases, such as some cancers.

Yet we have clearly not settled socio-economic questions that confront the new global economy: "How do we deal with the growing rift between rich and poor?"; "How do we fund key social needs in an era of low taxation and reduced government?"; "How do we ensure equity of business treatment of the population and consumers in all countries?"; and "How do we create sustainable economic growth?". These still lie ahead of us and addressing them is critical if we are to build a sustainable relationship between corporate and social needs.

Business reality

So, what is different about business? The reality is that opportunities, in the form of business products and services, don't last as long. Opportunities are neither equally available, nor available in the same way for everyone. Increased complexity is at the heart of this. For instance, people have many ways of managing

The reality is that **opportunities**, in the form of products and services, do not last as long

their schedules, whether it is a diary, hand-held device, database on the web, or personal computer software. It is safe to say that many substitutes exist and more will evolve.

Another reality is that business is generally more "atomistic" and the boundaries more open and flexible. What does this mean? Companies are being created to exploit more focussed opportunities and working around a smaller set of activities while subcontracting many more. The value chains of some companies look like a piece of Swiss cheese, with the holes filled by suppliers and partners.

This is driven by the difficulty of being competitive in all business activities and the fact that flexibility is gained through subcontracting or strategic partnerships. This trend has led to a position where many e-commerce retailers never even touch a product; their inward and outward supply chains are totally outsourced.

Business is certainly more ephemeral. Research by population ecologists, who study corporate mortality rates, has suggested shortening lifetimes for organizations. Businesses might never have been planned to last forever, but today's environment guarantees obsolescence on an increased scale. This means we move with increasing haste to create and exploit value, or we increase our ability to exploit opportunities.

Management practice

How have these considerations altered management practice, particularly over the past decade? Consider a few developments.

Opportunity reigns

It is clear that management is more focussed on the opportunities available and what is likely to follow. As one executive said: "I wouldn't value a company strongly on what it sells today or even the growth potential in these products, but what

future options its current competencies and customers create for future opportunities." Executives of high-tech companies speak more about the customer or "market space" they are exploiting than the size of their organizations or production facilities. They worry more about becoming out of date than running out of cash.

There is also more focus on reviewing opportunities from different sources within the organization. The widespread call by corporate executives for entrepreneurship has its roots in seeking broader opportunities. Managers no longer depend solely upon product development staff to come up with the goods; they rely upon everyone being empowered to present opportunities.

Options abound

The word "option" is now heard much more in the halls of the larger corporations. Since business opportunities are evolving more quickly and it is more difficult to establish through analysis exactly which opportunities to pursue, managers must learn to choose between and work with options. Investments in one innovation and market may be considered by adopting the venture capitalists' technique of investing in the choice to pursue the business further. (Venture capitalists typically invest in "rounds" of investment, future rounds being dependent upon the successful completion of earlier rounds.) This option model of investment lowers risk and improves potential.

Since information is not readily available, and there is a cost in losing an opportunity if you wait for full data to be available, managers must also rely on intelligent experimentation. Often several parallel experiments are undertaken. For this tactic to be successful, it must be combined with a higher tolerance for smaller failures and a true willingness to observe and learn from the experience.

Resources redefined

In a world where financing is available (witness the explosion in venture capital, investment capital, and cross-border deals) and ownership of traditional assets such as factories can cause inflexibility, we have to look more critically for resources on which to base new opportunity or competitive advantage.

Some resources, such as a skill or competency, may be the source of a distinctive competitive advantage. Others may be "nice", but of little importance in a more turbulent world. A large corporate bank account or "state-of-the-art" factory may be of little value, especially if they can be readily copied or acquired by others. In the end, no matter what resources we possess, it is our ability to employ them and to re-employ them that is of most use.

Speed required

As is implied by earlier points, speed of execution is more important than quality of execution, especially when combined with an iterative approach to development. Corporations are embracing a reality that entrepreneurs who have limited resources have long known: that the best place to test any product is in the hands of the consumer.

As one successful entrepreneur noted: "Better and cheaper are fine, as long as it is faster."

One group of engineers I worked with made an observation that stuck with me, an observation that may finally provide a chance for everyone to use some calculus. To quote one of the engineers: "Mastering the first derivative is no longer sufficient; it is the second derivative that counts in economic competition."

Translated, this means that if you want to be a successful competitor, it is no longer your ability to demonstrate speed that is important, but your ability to accelerate quickly to capture opportunity. I've known start-ups that established new markets, developed, but then permitted others to catch them because of their inability to "ramp up" quickly.

Networking abounds

The capability to build, manage, and exchange value in networks is key. Networks of individuals and teams help identify and exploit opportunity. Evolving networks of suppliers and distributors help realize products and services and help activate the business value chain. Networks of companies help build successful economic regions. A person's own network helps to build a career. It is clear that navigating and working in networks provides a flexible and reliable foundation for business growth.

Adaptation required

Building businesses that can continuously transform themselves to identify and exploit opportunities is not easy. However, this is what is required for a sustainable corporation. Managers are learning how to build systems and processes that permit organizations to maintain flexibility and exploit opportunity that is both planned and unplanned. A continuous stream of biographies and chronicles of businesses has been addressing how to build organizations that are dynamic and adaptive. In the end, it is clear that structure is very flexible and serves strategy and opportunities, not the reverse.

People achieve

New ideas of how to motivate and deploy people have developed. A new contract is evolving that involves the exchange of value. Individuals need to be encouraged and permitted to achieve: to perform to their highest potential, for their benefit and that of the employer.

Organizations are encouraging staff to craft more flexible, value-laden, and specific rules governing their relationships. They are helping people chase opportunities and are then allowing individuals to share in the value they create through more abundant options. Furthermore, they are encouraging people to undertake initiatives to learn and extend themselves, as well the company. They are permitting people to become involved in a way that promotes achievement and opportunity. In the end, treating people as willing participants in corporate organizations pays off.

Management research

So, with all of this accelerating change going on, where has management theory and research been? What is the impact on the "science" of management? Where is the future in management theory and research?

Those who observe and structure thinking

We have learned about the power of **networks**: they are more robust and effective than assumed

about the economy, business, and management have made significant discoveries. Modern times have been trying and testing researchers as much as managers. In many areas, such as economics, sociology, and psychology, there has been a growing appreciation of the impact of uncertainty on models and behaviors. Many business disciplines, such as marketing and production, have seen dramatic changes in prescriptions for managers and the introduction of "dynamic models." For instance, logistics and production have moved from set-piece models of efficient production to flexible manufacturing aimed at meeting customer needs as well as providing efficiency.

Organizational behavior has moved from an emphasis on the structural aspects of functional and cross-functional organizations to more flexible models, including enhanced consideration of short-term, high-performance teams.

Other than the effect of uncertainty, what have theorists learned? We could add the central role of opportunity and the need to ensure its effective search and development, no matter what the source of the opportunity. We have also learned more about the power of networks: they are more robust, effective, and efficient than first assumed. Finally, we are beginning to understand the balance needed between pure organizational efficiency and the demand to provide additional resources to promote adaptation. Resources are required to provide "slack" in the system, thus allowing innovation to build capabilities and to promote flexibility.

Changing analogies hint at the shift in management models. Many fields have moved away from physical analogies using structure to biological analogies stressing evolution. Management theorists are beginning to understand that truly predictive models are hard to come by. The shift is in some ways no less dramatic than the way particle physics moved from atoms in defined orbits to quantum mechanics, with its central role for uncertainty.

Some of the shift has involved research into entrepreneurial business. For people with a foot in both traditional studies of business functions and the emerging study of entrepreneurship, the past decade has been amusing. Many of the ideas concerning models of opportunity, business organization, and resource allocation have gone from being "fringe" models to accepted practice. For instance, the entrepreneurs' and venture capitalists' model of incremental investment has become received wisdom for business investment.

So, have management researchers been leading management through the change or following management? The answer is a profound "yes." There are areas where researchers have played major roles (for example, derivatives and activity-based costing), and there are other areas where practitioners have taken the lead (business transformation).

While it may sound self-serving, management researchers and business schools do have a significant place in this evolving world. Business schools have important roles in recording, crystallizing, and structuring models of management. They are a major "node" in the knowledge network. They also maintain their role of preparing new generations for business and bear an increased responsibility for renewing knowledge through postgraduate programs.

Having said all that, business researchers and educators must cut the physical and mental distance between themselves and business, increase direct dialog with business, and reduce the time taken for ideas to reach managers. Researchers must be willing, like managers, to develop models in a co-operative and iterative way, with active experimentation and evolution of ideas in the field. There will be more "action research" and "action learning," so enabling researchers to create new models by working more closely with managers.

Looking ahead

What is important for the successful business executive of the next decade? Let me end by suggesting three ideas. First, beware of *l'idée du jour*. What is happening is not new, but a logical extension of what has happened before. You might even want to find opportunity based on the fad-driven myopia of others. Second, maintain the entrepreneur's comportment: continuous optimism, a focus on opportunity rather than problems, and personal flexibility (leave room to change your mind). Third, constantly renew your skills and knowledge.

Providing time for reflection in this exciting, demanding world is important and reading and reviewing have a core role to play. This book provides a convenient, effective, and efficient means to do this.

The new battlegrounds
for capitalism

Japanese and European models of capitalism have lost out to the Anglo-Saxon. **Ben Hunt** finds shareholder value driving companies across the world.

Ben Hunt is head of New World Research, a financial research company. He is editor of a number of management books and was previously director at Brightwater Research and Editing.

The conflict between capitalism and socialism came to an end a decade ago, only to see a new one rising from its ashes. Business and academia alike began to argue that capitalism was in fact many capitalisms, each with its own economies, social systems, cultural values, and management styles. Anglo-Saxon capitalism, which had evolved in the UK and US, was distinct from the version found in Japan and Germany, occasionally referred to as the Rhenish model. Indeed, the former was frequently viewed as inferior. In the 1980s and early 1990s, Japan was admired for its management styles and operational practices. Many US and UK manufacturers tried to emulate Japanese methods such as just-in-time inventory control and employee involvement.

Box 1 **Winds of change in Japan**

■ **1997** Sony shrank its company board to 10 directors from 38, and was one of the first Japanese corporations to do so

■ **1999** Sumitomo Bank and Sakura Bank, traditionally part of different *keiretsu*, announced a merger

■ **1999** Nissan said it would cut 14 percent of its global workforce, including 16,500 jobs in Japan, as well as cutting its supplier network and selling noncore assets

■ **1999** Nippon Telephone and Telegraph announced job cuts of 20,000 over three years; Mitsubushi planned to cut 10,000 jobs by early 2004

■ **2000** Merger and Acquisition Consulting launched the first domestic hostile takeover in Japan. It bid ¥14bn for Shoei Corporation, a real-estate and electronic components group linked to the Fuyo group

Box 2 Changes in the governance environment

Characteristics of "Rhenish" business

- Sales, market share, and headcount dominate performance measures
- Interlocking patterns of ownership and close banking relationships
- Undeveloped market for corporate control
- Employees are most important stakeholders
- Large company boards
- Salary-based management pay

Examples of recent change

- Greater attention paid to financial markets
- Selling of cross-shareholdings, bond financing, and growth of equity culture

- Emergence of hostile bids
- End of lifetime-employment systems; downsizing
- Shrinking board size
- Legal reform

Anglo-Saxon practices emulated

- Managing for shareholder value
- Higher role ascribed to corporate finance and shareholder value
- See above
- More flexible approach to labor
- Greater accountability and transparency
- Introduction of stock options to compensation packages

Today, however, something new is happening. After a decade in which Rhenish capitalism, to varying degrees, has been struggling, both Japanese and German corporations are restructuring and reforming along the lines of their US and UK counterparts (*see* Boxes 1 and 2). The argument that Japan and continental Europe have to catch up in areas such as shareholder value and corporate governance, not to mention information technology, has been won. Moreover, Japanese business is coming to terms with the fact that US corporations and others have beaten them at their own game. By designing and building in customer-facing processes to all aspects of their business, US companies have extended Japanese management styles beyond the shop floor.

Although there is scope for disagreement over the depth of reform taking place, it is significant that multinationals everywhere champion similar objectives. Increasingly, shareholder value is the measure of corporate performance and corporations are willing to use similar tools, such as downsizing, to reach performance goals. Overall, it is hard to dispute that management styles around the world are locked into a similar trajectory and, in the process, are becoming more homogeneous.

Global business framework

The dominant view is that the restructuring and reform process has something to do with market and financial pressures, increasingly at the global level. The rise of Anglo-Saxon practices, such as decentralization and greater focus on core competences, is, in this interpretation, the product of a more competitive climate where corporations everywhere shed inefficient fat and obey the logic of the financial markets. In Japan, for example, such measures are adopted, or need to be adopted, because companies are inefficient, unprofitable, and need to become more focussed on the market.

There are merits to this interpretation, but it does not explain recent change. In the Anglo-Saxon context, it is true that companies choose restructuring to shore up flagging profit rates. But equally, so have companies with strong balance sheets. Furthermore, many of the strategies or restructuring measures have taken place more or less continuously through different business cycles in the last 20 years. Downsizing, for instance, has continued since the early 1980s, but intensified in the 1990s, a time of record corporate profitability in the Anglo-Saxon nations.

Similarly, parallel strategies and restructuring methods can be seen in nations with varying states of economic health. Explaining change with reference to market or competitive pressure is therefore not a helpful explanation of why these particular strategies are becoming dominant.

It is useful to place change in a wider context. The starting point is that the dominant framework in which business operates has changed dramatically in the past two decades. Post-war "corporatist" relationships between the state, business, and labor, always weak in the US, were dismantled during the 1980s in the Anglo-Saxon world. Reforming labor relations led to industrial and corporate restructuring in the 1980s. In the 1990s, the corporatist framework continued to erode, allowing organizational freedom, efficiency, and flexibility. Gradually, another framework was built around corporate governance. Here, the focus shifted to shareholder value, management accountability, and transparency. Japan and continental Europe are still faced with the tensions of both frameworks, while Anglo-Saxon nations have made the change.

The new framework differs qualitatively from its predecessor. First, it encourages market-driven strategy. Decisions become more based on change in the marketplace. Second, it carves a new role for management. In particular, it encourages a move away from "autocratic" leadership and hierarchies, toward decentralization. To illustrate these points further, it is instructive to examine the rise of market-based performance measures such as shareholder value, changing patterns of growth and investment, decentralization, and the rise of internal markets. These measures are seen in Japan and continental Europe.

Market-based performance measures

The shift toward market-based strategy is reflected in managing for shareholder value and customer relationship management. The dominance of shareholder value as the prime corporate performance measurement seems assured everywhere, at least in theory. Managers of large corporations are increasingly likely to use the price of a company's stock as the main guide to allocating resources and making decisions. The incorporation of stock options into management compensation packages creates an important incentive. Whereas in the past, strategies such as reinvestment in the core business, staff retention, and size were measures of success, today the efficient management of capital has become a benchmark for comparison. Other business objectives or "drivers of value," such as sales, are assessed by whether they create shareholder value.

The second important corporate performance measure is customer satisfaction. There is an increasing tendency to allow customers to dictate how organizations are managed. Leading companies organize along customer-driven processes, rather than tasks driven by internal hierarchies. Manufacturers have long used just-in-time for better response to customer needs (one of many examples of a crossover between Japanese management practices and the rest of the world). A further trend has been for global manufacturers to expand customer services and even rebrand themselves as services companies.

Firms have striven to incorporate customer feedback into product innovation and research and development, so ensuring products will be launched more successfully. Management performance and pay are increasingly tied to customer satisfaction, especially in service industries. Levels of customer complaints – and an organization's ability to respond – are viewed as benchmarks of success or failure.

There are many reasons for using these measures, not least, for shareholder value, the rising power of institutional investors in financial markets. However, market pressures cannot be the most important driver. Managing for shareholder value, for instance, is built on the premise that capital should be viewed by managers as a scarce resource. This has motivated companies to return capital to shareholders by buying back shares.

However, such a view has become popular at a time when financial markets and Anglo-Saxon economies are characterized by high levels of liquidity and relatively easy access to capital. Institutional investors may demand higher returns than other financiers, such as banks, but this is a measure of institutional pressure rather than market forces such as supply and demand.

Market-based measures of performance have

risen to prominence partly because notions of what companies and managers are for have changed. In the 1970s, a "corporatist" consensus governed relations between business, state, and workforce. Although there was conflict between these groups for much of the post-war period, this consensus existed around wider economic aims – growth, stable employment, rising living standards, and so on. With the collapse of this consensus, there has been a reversion to market-based criteria to judge business success. By default, company objectives have narrowed and become more focussed on serving constituents, or stakeholders, in the marketplace.

Accompanying this shift has been a rethinking of the role of company management and boards. Traditionally, managers have had autonomy to pursue objectives. For example, in the US, post-war arrangements between managers and shareholders were explicitly built on the concept of "trusteeship," where managers of companies were widely viewed as custodians of the public good. This trust, however, began to break down in the late 1980s and 1990s in the Anglo-Saxon world, when it was argued that shareholders require far greater transparency and accountability in the workings of boardrooms. In the emerging corporate governance framework, various codes of conduct began to replace relationships of assumed trust.

Growth and investment

The transition from one framework to another can also be seen in dominant patterns of growth and investment. Corporations, now including those in Japan and continental Europe, increasingly favor forms of growth that do not tie up resources for significant amounts of time but can increase shareholder value. This is one of the most important reasons for acquisition-led growth rather than organic growth, or reinvestment in the core business. It is also an important reason for the recent increase in strategic alliances. These allow companies to access new markets, skill bases, and technologies through pooling resources, without committing long-term investment.

A more short-term outlook is often attributed to market pressures. Long-term investment, under the auspices of a long-term plan, is now said to be near impossible. According to conventional wisdom, this is because, with markets moving so fast, it is much harder for businesses to stick to a goal for any length of time. Too much change is likely to happen in between, making the plans redundant. This is increasingly viewed as a problem across the board, but especially in research-intensive industries such as pharmaceuticals. In this context, investing in the core business is more likely to be viewed as a problem rather than a desirable choice.

However, it is more accurate to see the transition as a result of more deep-seated changes in the changing framework of business. Before the 1990s, investment was seen as an important driver of economic growth and prosperity. Government often played a role in promoting investment. In the 1980s, corporations still tended to use surplus capital to diversify and/or invest in the core business. In the 1990s, by contrast, companies have concentrated more on their core competences (either by shrinking product portfolios or recognizing key processes where they truly add value in the marketplace).

At the same time, they have returned excess capital to shareholders by buying back shares. Reinvestment has been heavily channeled into information technology in the US and UK, which has increased operational efficiency. This trend is well documented in the US. In a significant development in the UK, during 1999–2000 information technology became the single biggest recipient of investment in the manufacturing sector for the first time.

The drive to decentralization

The restructuring of company hierarchies and demise of autocratic management styles are clearly seen in management literature. Large corporations in the past suffered under the weight of dozens of management layers, which had the effect of slowing decision making. This was part of a more general business model that placed emphasis on heavy reinvestment and the retention of employees.

More recently, companies have stripped out layers of middle management in a bid to cut bureaucracy and speed up decision making, as well as shrinking company boards – a process now seen in Japan.

In the last ten years, large corporations have extended an earlier process of decentralization, by turning subsidiaries into separate profit centres. Increasingly, in internal markets, these units cross-sell to each other, compete as separate entities, and are subject to external competition for the business of the parent.

The management writer William E. Halal has written extensively on internal markets. As well as pointing to efficiency gains, he has said that: "The hope that participation, team spirit, inspiring leadership, and other vague ideas can create dynamic action among tens of thousands of people in the typical organization is little more than pious thinking." This indicates an important development: companies that feel they cannot create enterprise through the coherence of their culture, or management leadership, resort to further decentralization and market principles to generate "dynamic action."

In this context, the emergence of internal markets can be seen as related to changing relationships between managers and employees. In Japan, for example, loyalties among employees to companies that once offered jobs for life, a feature of an older framework, have weakened greatly. Japanese managers are looking to encourage entrepreneurship among employees as a replacement for these relationships.

Conclusion

Today's business framework brings a number of distinct advantages for companies everywhere. Corporations can use various tools to make their organization and operations more flexible and manage capital more efficiently. Anglo-Saxon companies that have used these tools have recorded record profit rates in the last decade.

It also brings new challenges. The challenge for managers everywhere is that a market-oriented approach, with short-term measures of growth, makes it difficult to sustain long-term vision. At the same time, corporate governance requirements leave managers and boards grappling with new roles in managing large corporations. Business in the near future will continue to be dominated by an adjustment to these new circumstances.

Further reading

Dore, R. (2000) *Stock Market Capitalism: Welfare Capitalism*, Oxford: Oxford University Press.

Hasegawa, H. and Hook, G. D. (eds) (1998) *Japanese Business Management: restructuring for low growth and globalization*, London: Routledge.

O'Sullivan, M. (2000) *Contests for Corporate Control*, Oxford: Oxford University Press.

Managers face
up to the new era

Thinking of companies as well-oiled machines makes robots out of workers. **Leonard Greenhalgh** sees the future in managing relationships instead.

Leonard Greenhalgh is a professor of management at the Amos Tuck School of Business Administration and academic director at Duke Corporate Education.

It is clear that the twenty-first century represents a new era for business. Today, successful management involves rethinking methods laid down in the twentieth century and developing approaches that are better suited to the new opportunities and constraints. The past two decades have created challenges for which existing knowledge is inadequate. Consider the examples in Box 1.

These changes call for corresponding changes in the role of the manager. Gone is the notion of the corporate leader as the person who supplied the vision, decided on the appropriate strategy and tactics to achieve that vision, then assigned tasks of implementation to a hierarchy of subordinates.

Also gone is the notion of worker-as-robot, someone who didn't think but merely performed as instructed. Such notions have been replaced by decentralized rather than top-down decision making, empowered rather than mindless subordinates, teamwork rather than individualistic performance, and customers or clients – rather than top management – as the drivers of decisions.

Successful management involves adapting to the new order. Companies in California's Silicon Valley were first to discover that the new generation of knowledge workers don't think of themselves as "subordinates": they consider themselves independent professionals who can be given a general goal and be left to accomplish it without "micromanagement." They look to managers to facilitate their achievement rather than to direct and control their work.

Top managers no longer judge middle managers simply by the efficiency of the unit they manage. Criteria now include the ability to work with managers of other units at the same level and the ability to maintain groupings of work associates striving to increase value for the client or customer. This has been true of consulting companies such as Accenture for some time, and other organizations are catching on quickly.

Box 1 **Challenges for the new order**

- Domestic businesses of any significance have become rare. They are now global, drawing on supply chains that transcend national boundaries and serving customers worldwide.
- Homogeneous workforces and customer bases have become heterogeneous. As a result, a crucial component of managerial competence is the ability to benefit from diversity and to market to the full spectrum of customers.
- Industries have shifted from making products to providing services. As a result, the value of many items that seem like products (such as computers) is in the service that they provide (word processing).
- Start-up companies are more important in bringing products and services to market, in response to the acceleration of technological advancement. Young, technologically competent workers are drawn to these vibrant workplaces, making it harder for other companies to recruit and retain them.
- Worker rights once protected only by unions are now protected by laws and public opinion. For example, companies that violate civil rights stand to lose far more from consumer boycotts than from fines.

- Quality standards that used to apply to luxury goods are now expected of all goods and services. In the new era, quality arises from work done by the lowest-level employees rather than from the intervention of a separate quality department.
- Business was once separate from the environmental movement. Now, businesses must consider environmental responsibilities throughout a product's lifecycle, just as they have to think about profits.
- Employees who used to be valued for their skills are now valued for their knowledge. Knowledge workers have different ties to organizations – sometimes none – and need to be managed differently.
- Large institutional investors, who used to be silent when executives were overpaid and corporate performance was lagging, are exerting their influence on how organizations are managed.
- Free-standing organizations have given way to extended enterprises. These are boundary-less systems of networked companies, each contributing a distinctive competency. Lone companies no longer compete with other companies: instead, value-chain partnerships compete with each other.

The ability of a company to control operations is no longer adequate: managing relationships has become just as important.

To complicate matters, managers' jobs have become less secure. Companies have delayered, re-engineered, restructured, and right-sized. In becoming lean, organizations – General Electric being a prime example – have eliminated middle management positions that didn't add value.

This approach has removed much of the status, power, and upward mobility of the managerial role. So managers in the new era need to view career progression as something different from "climbing the corporate ladder." Promotion, in the new sense, means being entrusted with more responsibility rather than the traditional move to a bigger office, a better title, or a special parking place.

There has been resistance to change among middle managers: Jack Welch was quoted as referring to GE's "cement layer." Although perhaps regrettable, resistance is understandable. Many people achieved their positions because they did a good job under the old system. But there's no turning back the clock. Corporations can't survive using the old ways. So, the message for managers is that they need to adapt or stand aside.

The **lean approach** has removed status, power, and upward mobility from the managerial role

Misguided models of management

Some of the resistance comes from a reliance on "conventional wisdom," which is outdated. One problem is that managerial thinking has been overly influenced by misapplied economic theory. Economics is useful in understanding how markets should operate, but is limited when applied to a particular organization and the behavior of employees.

An organization, at its core, consists of people managing people; economics was never intended to address such things as relationships and individual behavior. Unfortunately, the misapplication of economic theory has distorted past generations' views of management and organizations, mainly because it skews thinking about relationships. As a result, conventional management wisdom embodies misunderstandings about how to achieve organizational effectiveness, as well as bad advice about managing people.

Economic theory isn't the only thing that has been misused. Much of the problem with management thinking can be traced to the inappropriate use of imagery from the physical sciences. When an organization is productive and coordinated, westerners tend to describe it as "a well-oiled machine." But machine imagery has serious drawbacks.

Parts of a machine carry out unvarying tasks and are regulated by control systems to optimize their efficiency. The inputs are raw materials and energy. The outputs are whatever gets delivered. The throughput is a set of mechanical processes (routines, flows, and procedures) predetermined by the designer. The machine is impersonal, is highly adapted to its current role, and has only one way of doing things.

When this metaphor is applied to organizations, workers are seen as cogs in a machine, each carrying out a prescribed task. It doesn't matter who carries out a task, but the task must be done exactly as prescribed. Thus, each role is designed to optimize efficiency and workers are interchangeable as long as they are proficient at the task. This creates the role of "worker-as-robot" and causes relationship problems that sap competitive advantage.

Managers' roles are almost as constrained by this guiding metaphor. Their mission is machine monitoring and maintenance – to ensure that everything goes to plan. Within this system, managers are organized into a hierarchy with the most comprehensive responsibilities at the top and the most task-specific at the bottom. At any level, the manager's job is to "control operations" – to ensure the machine runs smoothly.

The problem with a machine is that, once built, it is fixed. It doesn't adapt to change. And the machine can never be better than its design. Yet, in reality, organizations are human systems that don't follow mechanistic laws.

Empowered workers, rather than hierarchical system designers, are in the best position to achieve continuous improvement, responsiveness to customers, quality, and efficiency. They make these efforts when they feel they are members of an organizational community, not when they feel like cogs in a machine. Effectiveness is determined by the quality of the relationships managers create.

The shortcomings of the traditional knowledge base are evident when we consider that few conventional organizations have ever achieved greatness; those that have usually excelled in spite of their structure rather than because of it.

For example, Jack Welch – the chief executive at the top of the *Financial Times* survey of admired corporate leaders – is revered because he defied conventional wisdom in transforming the ultimate conventional organization, General Electric.

The shortcomings of conventional approaches to management are also evident when you ask westerners to provide examples of high-performing systems – situations in which they were drawn into the excitement of a group operating at the limits of achievement. They almost invariably pick examples outside conventional business: the crew of a racing yacht, strangers striving to cope with disaster, or a surgical team.

When businesses are described as high-performing systems, the examples are almost invariably start-up companies. In these unconventional structures, egalitarian groups work extraordinarily hard and achieve astonishing results. People may be working harder than in the worst sweatshop, but the work is not drudgery: it's exhilarating.

Participants tend to have strong bonds, commitment, and unstructured, flexible roles. They all share a sense of commonwealth – the knowledge that if the enterprise prospers, it is to everyone's advantage and credit. You do not see these people watching the clock; you are more likely to hear them saying they work only 80 hours a week because they can't manage to work even longer.

New emphasis

If high-performing systems are a rarity, something must be wrong with our knowledge about organizing. We seem to be good at using technology, creating infrastructure, and optimizing assets, systems, and processes. Where we fall short is in managing business relationships – between people, within and between groups, and within and between organizations.

Let's look at some examples of how inadequate attention to managing relationships has undermined managerial effectiveness and competitive advantage.

Alarming numbers of lower-level workers hate their jobs. In the US, the anthem of the working class is a country-and-western ballad called "Take This Job and Shove It." The attitude of these workers is a far cry from that of some of their Asian counterparts, who begin each day singing the company song while doing group calisthenics.

Yet, US workers' resentment should not be surprising if we consider their managers' relationship to them. Rank-and-file workers are paid by the hour, whereas managers are on a salary. This makes the rank and file rented labor rather than members of the organizational community. They are a "factor of production" to be severed as soon as they lower profitability. They are managed by people referred to as superiors, in a caste structure managers have set up. They are banished from managerial enclaves and allotted their own caste-specific dining rooms, parking lots, and lavatories.

They could have been treated as equals, performing a different but nevertheless essential role, yet they are not; as a result, they toil without enthusiasm, loyalty, or dedication. Blind to the problematic relationship they have created, managers attribute workers' lackluster attitude to personality and character.

Relationships shaped to fit hierarchies are equally problematic. Managers create organization charts to make accountability explicit. In conventional organizations, this involves division into functional units. To match accountability with control, communication and co-ordination are forced to be vertical rather than lateral (a result of applying military principles to civilian hierarchies).

This means subordinates receive instructions only from their superiors and provide progress reports, suggestions, and feedback only upward. They don't co-ordinate with other units, departments, or divisions: that's the superior's job. These communication firewalls, coupled with a tendency of divisions to disparage other groups, create vertical schisms that high-level managers ruefully describe as organizational "chimneys" or "silos," without ever owning up to having created them.

The failure of incentives

The problem with the structures westerners create can also be seen in the dismal success rate of mergers and acquisitions. A survey of 31 of the largest companies by Arthur Andersen revealed that two-thirds of the combinations generated negative effects and the primary problems involved poor integration. Badly handled acquisitions encourage employees to leave, yet companies often attribute this to market problems rather than relationships. Offering financial incentives to stay distorts pay structures, creates feelings of inequity, and reduces profitability. Such expensive tactics deal with the symptoms without addressing the underlying problem.

Financial incentives are never good substitutes for strong relationships, and often undermine them. For example, merit systems that reward people who outperform others are intended to stimulate excellence and effort, but they usually make people compete who ought to be co-operating. This happens because there are two ways of doing better: make yourself look better, or make your peers look worse. If there's an incentive to become the top performer, then

Financial incentives are never substitutes for **relationships**, and often undermine them

there's a disincentive to co-operate: why would anyone, acting rationally, do anything to improve a competitor's performance?

Recognizing this problem, some managers use team-based rather than individual incentives; but all this does is move the problem up one level, killing off collaboration between teams. Of course, it's possible to design incentives so as to minimize the risk of unintended side effects, but this is seldom done. Managers should keep in mind that most high-performing systems have no merit system at all: people excel because they are committed to the communal goal; their motivation arises from relationships, not self-interest.

The worst relationships are often those between unions and management. Too often, management construes the union as an enemy, and treats it as such. But just think about this. What is the union? It's the company's own workers. Reciprocal distrust and hostility keep managers and workers in a state of perpetual disharmony. It's no different, in essence, from what happens in politically troubled areas such as the Middle East and Northern Ireland.

In the latter cases, most people think it's time to break the destructive cycle and try to heal the relationship strains. Yet these same people seem to accept internecine conflict within organizations as normal and not as evidence of managerial failure. It is worth noting that Jaguar was only able to reverse its decline when it changed its historically adversarial relationship with the union.

External relationships

Managers also don't pay enough attention to relationships beyond the organization's walls. For example, they have been taught to value customer loyalty. There's an economic motive for doing so: it costs a lot more to attract a new customer than to retain an existing one. But most companies don't treat customers as though the relationship is important.

In the western car industry, for example, manufacturers have spent millions trying to create a positive image among customers, but then they turn over the selling process to dealerships, which have the freedom – and an incentive – to exploit their customers. It doesn't work when companies talk as though relationships matter, then act as though they don't.

Similarly, manufacturers say they want to develop partnerships with buyers downstream in their value chain. Yet when their product or service becomes scarce, they auction it off. This may make economic sense, but it doesn't make sense in relationships. The choice to auction tells your customer that you don't care whether they get their needs met or come up empty-handed: all you're interested in is profit. The way you manage the relationship belies what you said about wanting to be a partner.

Relationships are managed no better upstream in the value chain. Large western manufacturers tend to exploit suppliers to the extent possible given the power differential. For example, the *Financial Times* reported that Chrysler will be squeezing its suppliers so that it can pinch off the flow of red ink. The suppliers consider this unfair, because it wasn't their fault that Chrysler got in trouble. Chrysler's resurgence after its last crisis is widely attributed to the efforts of its suppliers, but Chrysler isn't looking back, by all accounts.

Exploiting dependency creates strains with suppliers that may one day prove to have been short-sighted. In the new era, competitive advantage can derive from any point in the value chain, and this is particularly true of the car industry, in which outsourced subassemblies can be an important source of innovation as well as efficiency. So a value-chain partner isn't just someone to be exploited during hard times. Suppliers, it turns out, have long memories.

Legal cultures

Managers' disregard for relationships between companies is also evident in the western preoccupation with written contracts. These documents are supposed to confirm and clarify the agreement that was made to meet each other's needs, reflecting a relationship created for mutual gain.

In practice, however, contracts become a substitute for agreements.

The contrast between US and Japanese contracts highlights this. In Japan, contracts are very short, because all they do is confirm the companies' commitment to work together. US contracts are long and detailed, specifying as many contingencies as the lawyers can foresee.

The problem with the latter approach is that business conditions now change quickly: new competitors enter the market, technology evolves, the political and regulatory environment changes, and currencies fluctuate. Terms agreed when the contract was drafted may not make sense when it comes to implementation. Japanese businesses revise the terms of agreement as conditions change; US businesses are stuck with what they signed and their relationships are strained by having to live with an unbalanced deal.

The challenge of the new era

Understanding and managing relationships isn't that difficult: managers do rather well at it outside business contexts. But within the business domain, we simply haven't given relationships the attention they deserve. Economic theorists assume relationships are adversarial as people compete and pursue their own interests. Organization theorists have looked primarily at structural and exchange relationships, deriving a rather sterile, and often divisive, view. But the elegance of economic and sociological models comes at the expense of managerial effectiveness and competitive advantage.

If we could draw the right lesson from why much of the best young talent is drawn to start-ups, it wouldn't be about becoming a dotcom millionaire. That's a lure for some, but it doesn't explain why young people put in hours that would be intolerable elsewhere. Naturally occurring communities, rather than hierarchies, have the greatest potential to be high-performing organizations.

When organizations are communal, managers have different roles. Their main objective is to preserve cohesion and stability. They need to make people feel included and to prevent coalitions within the group ("in-groups") from destructively excluding nonmembers ("out-groups"). More specifically, managers should foster, coach, protect, and support, rather than plan, organize, direct, and control.

More broadly, mastering management in the new era involves developing a different view of what an organization is. Managers need to visualize a system of relationships radiating through their own organization to other organizations in its value chain. These business relationships enable the organization to achieve consensus, to implement strategy, to tie in strategic partners, and to achieve market dominance. Effective managers in the new era don't establish and manage relationships to be nice. They do it because strategic success depends on it.

Further reading

Greenhalgh, L. (2001) *Managing Strategic Relationships*, New York: Free Press.

Helgesen, S. (1995) *The Web of Inclusion*, New York: Currency/Doubleday.

Lewis, J.D. (2000) *Trusted Partners*, New York: Free Press.

Slater, R. (1999) *Jack Welch and the GE Way*, New York: McGraw-Hill.

Enterprise and innovation

2

Contents

Introduction to Part 2

At the beginning of the 21st century, corporations no longer hold individuals in thrall to a lifelong career path. The 1980s era of restructuring and downsizing broke the bonds of loyalty between a company and its employees, and people have since learnt to forge their own career paths, picking up skills in different places and depending more on their own initiative. At the same time, technological advances have created opportunities for new products and services.

In this environment, entrepreneurship has blossomed. This part looks at how people can strike out on their own in new business ventures. How is capital raised? How should a business plan be structured and presented? What is the process by which a company floats itself on the stock market? Finally, authors examine how the lessons of entrepreneurship have not been lost on big business. "Intraventuring" is now seen as essential for maintaining a company's level of innovation.

Be prepared for when
opportunity knocks

Business opportunities are becoming more fleeting and difficult to grasp. **Daniel Muzyka** explains why and what you can do to prepare for them.

Dr Daniel F. Muzyka is dean of the Faculty of Commerce and Business Administration at the University of British Columbia (Vancouver), where he is also a professor of management.

Opportunity has taken a front seat in management thinking. The reasons are simple: opportunities no longer last as long or function as predictably. In a world of accelerated technological development, world trade, and globalization, companies need to search for opportunities if they are to renew their product or service lines. Not surprisingly, competition often arises from the least likely quarters and may involve whole new approaches to customer needs.

Several things have been learned about opportunities recently; most interestingly, that they are often more complicated and subtle than first imagined. Furthermore, they are not necessarily embodied in products but in other aspects related to producing the product or service (such as skills required, knowledge, and access to customers).

Opportunities don't always present themselves clearly or in an orderly way: sometimes they appear when salespeople meet customers, or when suppliers discuss their product lines with operations managers. In addition, many "large" opportunities are the result of seemingly small products, services, or initial prototypes. One should be careful in judging any opportunity as "unworthy" or "too small" if it is associated with other values such as introducing into the organization skills, broader networks, or personnel. Finally, it is often necessary to develop an opportunity with a network of individuals and organizations. Opportunities that one can simply pick up and execute single-handed are few and far between.

Even large, successful multinational corporations must adopt new approaches to identifying and seizing much larger numbers of opportunities to adapt and grow. Companies need not only to provide for new technological and product development, but must also mobilize and reward staff in the identification and pursuit of new opportunity. This is a characteristic that has long distinguished adaptive companies such as 3M.

Box 1 Warnings to e-business

It is a fallacy to suggest that somehow digital business should not be governed by economics, business strategy, and investment finance. While e-business has helped us redefine certain limits in business practice (such as speed and market leverage), it has not obviated the need for a return on investment, the need to manage cash flow and working capital, and the strategic need to create competitive advantage.

Economics@Real.World

E-business opportunities are not exempt from needing to make a profit. There has unfortunately been a strong focus on revenue models without much consideration of how a profit would be achieved. Entrepreneurs should be concerned about profit.

Giving it away

Many e-businesses, especially those in retail, suffer from a low-price entry strategy. Their plans are predicated on prices that, it is argued, will prove irresistible to consumers. However, entrepreneurs should be careful not to give away their products. This has become particularly evident during the crash of various online retailers. When they were "forced" to become profitable, they were required to raise their prices. When they did raise their prices, customers disappeared. It is clear there was little value to customers beyond price in several of these cases.

Penetrating new markets

E-business management teams often fail to appreciate that every consumer in a marketplace will not necessarily switch over to the internet for their needs immediately. Winning customer confidence takes time and changing consumption patterns can take even longer. There has been significant "cash burn" on some e-businesses that have tried to enter markets.

Limits to growth

How many sites are you proposing? What will be the upper limit on web usage in various consumer groups? How many sites will people visit regularly? Is there a danger of further dividing the market by creating yet more speciality websites?

Adding value

Many e-businesses assume that value is added for the consumer simply by e-delivery. The fact that consumers of a similar kind are flocking to another website and that people are becoming increasingly focussed on the internet does not necessarily imply that a given consumer looks for given needs on the internet. Be clear about how much value is added beyond that from "information" or "access."

Leveraging everyone else

Look carefully at where money is being generated. Many business opportunities ride on the same underlying revenue model: advertising. In a world where advertising on the web is becoming ubiquitous and advertisers are increasingly concerned about efficacy, how far can one justify another e-commerce business on the strength of other people's value-added?

Managers need to increase their opportunity "bandwidth" and rely on both investment in new product development by organizational units and the "random" development of opportunity by individuals and teams throughout the organization.

If organizations are to witness more opportunity, they must equip a broader group of people to search for, identify, and be willing to capture chances. For people to pursue opportunity, there needs to be a shared sense of what it is; in effect, they must possess models of opportunity. Creating such a shared sense is not necessarily something organizations see as a priority.

Some perspectives

The identification, selection, and pursuit of opportunity are natural human activities. The first lesson is that there is no "pool" of available opportunity. There is no "law of conservation of opportunity." The identification and pursuit of opportunity are conscious activities that require effort. Some opportunities, though technically achievable, are not captured for years.

Another lesson is that opportunity is not the same for everyone. Louis Pasteur was quoted as saying: "Chance favors the prepared mind." Opportunity is much the same. One rarely identifies a good opportunity in an unfamiliar field, both in an individual and a corporate sense. Some companies have looked at the degree to which products and services have been profitable if both the technology and the customers are new.

Results tend to show that the ability to exploit existing knowledge of either the customer or the technology gives a better perspective on opportunities. Asymmetric knowledge and skills, combined with differences in networks, often account for differences in the perception and quality of execution in capturing opportunity.

Related to this last point are two additional lessons in opportunity:

- being first mover is not always most important;
- not every market comes down to "winner takes all."

First-mover advantage has been much discussed, particularly when combined with the notion that the first and fastest will take the whole market. Some technologies appear to be natural (near) monopolies because they provide common platforms (such as Microsoft's operating system), but they are not necessarily the first product introduced. Sometimes it is better to be a "fast follower," building on knowledge provided by the first mover, and a number two in the market that exploits superior knowledge or capabilities.

At a recent lecture at a business school, I sat through presentation after presentation where newly minted MBAs preached that their business concept would succeed given that they invented the concept first. While listening, I was reflecting that most of the early inventors of spreadsheet languages have disappeared. I further reflected that some of the early providers of PCs don't exist any longer or are suffering.

Opportunities either arise from or create real customer need. Understanding customers is essential for successful development of entrepreneurial opportunities. The ability to excite customers about a product or service is a fundamental part of this development. It is not the ability to sift through reports from experts who suggest that "all you need is 2 percent" of this "fast-growing market" that results in the perception of real opportunities. Understanding customer need and how you can create and fill that need is crucial to triggering customer purchase and loyalty.

Understanding customer needs at a fundamental level has distinguished many successful service businesses as they compete with established enterprises. Examples in the airline business include Virgin Atlantic and Southwest Airlines. They are successful because they understood the unmet customer need first and customer requirements second. They were then were able to combine this with a fundamental understanding of the economics of the business.

There are two observations about opportunity that are not always popular. First, opportunity does not last forever. Customer needs and technological opportunities move on. The mark of successful, long-run growth enterprises is that they are constantly searching for ways to build on existing opportunities as well as working to develop new ones.

The second observation is that many profitable, successful opportunities are both simple and boring. It goes with a phrase heard regularly from contented long-run entrepreneurs: Boring is beautiful! Boring businesses attract less attention from analysts and are often last to receive the attention of those attempting to introduce technological improvements. One person became very successful as a producer of hamburger buns in the UK in the 1980s. Even though baking was well established, the segment had not been exploited. This may be very successful but not necessarily terribly exciting as a "new-age" business.

Three initial tests

Though it is hard to generalize, managers should test their favored opportunity against three conditions: balance, profit, and risk.

Ask the people **proposing** an idea whether they think it is worth their time and effort

First, the company should demonstrate a "balanced desire" to pursue opportunity. Successful opportunities should have a number of characteristics. Opportunity is pursued by individuals and teams who are more likely to be successful at things they feel are useful and interesting, even if this is not rational. Ask people proposing an idea whether they feel it is worth their time and effort. Managers should also assess other factors:

- the value to customers of a new product or service;
- an organization's ability to produce and deliver a product;
- access to resources (primarily financial) to capture an opportunity.

Selecting the opportunities that are balanced in these respects is important. Venture capitalists, for instance, value the ability to implement an opportunity above all. They will take a B-grade economic opportunity implemented by an A-grade team over an A-grade opportunity implemented by a B-grade team. The presence of the necessary skills and attitudes ranks high on their list. Venture capitalists will assess the leadership potential and track record of the entrepreneur and the management team, as well as their functional capabilities. Larger organizations do the same thing when pursuing opportunities internally.

Second, the presence of a reasonable business and profit model is important. Do you understand where and how you make money? Is profit (not just revenue) realized in reasonable time? It is the discipline of understanding and arguing the business model that is captured in writing a business plan. Many successful business models are profitable due to several factors.

For example, one successful entrepreneurial business developed a chain of stores in small shopping centers outside towns. The stores generated good revenue (though not extraordinary). However, the development of the land just outside town created significant returns as additional stores were built.

Third, have you undertaken a reasonable risk analysis? The meaning of "reasonable" is important here, because detailed risk analysis is not likely to be effective or efficient: things change too quickly. If you wait for all the data to be available, the opportunity is gone. Having said this, it is still reasonable to assume that a full understanding of the "differential" risks in an opportunity have been thought through.

Differential risks are not generic, that is, not in the category of the "economy declining" or "industry weakness." Often, the key measures of financial risk in ventures are expressed in "time to break-even" and "time to payback." The longer one waits, whatever the nominal internal rate of return, the higher the risk exposure.

Evaluation

After weighing up the opportunity in these terms, assessment should turn to three dimensions: the scale, the scope, and the span of the opportunity. Scale refers to the potential size of the opportunity. Scope refers to its value, both in the short run (for example, gross margins or value-added) and in the long run (for example, access to more opportunities in the future). Span refers to how long it is likely to last.

One might think of the value of the opportunity as expressed by the combined value of the three items. An opportunity may have a great deal of potential if it isn't very large in scale, but has high margins that last a long time. Also, if the scale is very large and the value-added extensive, the opportunity may be good even if it does not last as long.

The following questions give some indication of the scale presented by an opportunity:

- Is the potential customer group easily identifiable and large?
- Is value to the customer high?
- Are competitive offerings not meeting customers' needs?
- Is the overall industry in growth or being redefined?

Box 2 **Common errors**

There are several common mistakes that limit the success and ultimate potential of opportunities.

Fads

Don't jump into the pool just because everyone else has. Fads are wonderful distractions that are not meant for everyone. Even experienced venture capitalists have fallen victim in large numbers. When everyone gets excited about a particular opportunity, it becomes difficult to justify why you have not complied with the trend and given in by investing in a particular area. In fact, there may be less risk in investing rather than not investing. By not investing, you may be criticized for "missing the boat," even though the boat might have sunk.

Adaptation

Most successful entrepreneurs will admit that what they end up producing and selling is generally very different from their original concept. It is through the process of development, testing, and early introduction that one realizes the "true" opportunity. Always be willing to adapt. This is one reason that inventors (that is, people who produce inventions rather than opportunities) are often not successful entrepreneurs. Simply stated, they are not willing to adapt their original inventions to meet real or evolving customer need.

Miscalculating competition

Another common flaw is not fully to appreciate the nature and degree of competition. While a product or service may be "first in category," it is often substituting for an old application or service, or competing for time with other consumer activities. Be careful to recognize full competition or other substitutes.

Low-price entry

Finally, be clear about the value you are providing and do not fall victim to a low-price entry strategy. Offering customers low prices may seem to make sense, but it often sends the wrong signal about the value of a product or service, wakes up competition, and can put the business at risk from low cash flow. Furthermore, customers feel resentful when prices are raised right after they adopt a product or service. This is a trap into which many inexperienced entrepreneurs have fallen.

Scope may be measured by gross margin and whether the opportunity creates capabilities and follow-on opportunities. The span may be assessed by a variety of measures, including the strength and vindictiveness of competitors; the ability to create post-entry barriers; and the inherent length/position of the technologies in their lifecycle.

All of these may determine how long the opportunity may last. For instance, an opportunity that involves the construction of significant barriers (post-entry barriers) or areas of cost, which must be confronted by subsequent entrants, is one that will stand longer. Also, opportunities that exist in a broader market where potential competition is not very aggressive tend to last longer or have a longer span.

Few opportunities are extraordinary on all three measures. A new toy may have extraordinary scale and scope (high margins). It may, how-

ever, only last one season. A pollution control service may have extraordinarily high scope (when the problem occurs, someone may pay virtually anything for immediate service), but there may be limited potential (only so many pollution incidents in a given period). The opportunity may, however, last for quite a while.

Finally, many an opportunity has been lost to an organization because it was not expressed in a context that could be appreciated by others. Given the biases and irrationality that are often present in human relationships, it remains for the proposer to be aware of the perspectives and needs of potential stakeholders. Be careful to present the idea in a way that is intelligible to the receiving party, and that allows you to express your understanding of their needs and sensitivities with regard to opportunity. Importantly, opportunities are often better accepted if one acknowledges their weaknesses up front.

Conclusion

The pursuit of opportunity is fundamental to business. Whether a business will survive in the long run has significantly less to do with the resources it controls and significantly more to do with the opportunity it can create or access.

Realizing opportunity requires heightened awareness of the need for opportunity among all people in an organization and their understanding of what sorts of opportunity make sense. Employees need to develop reasonable models of what constitutes opportunity in their industry. This demands experimentation and education. It also requires shared learning about what does not constitute an opportunity, in other words, what the traps are in identifying opportunity.

Getting to "yes"
with the business plan

Joe Tabet is adjunct professor of entrepreneurship at Insead and senior vice president of business creation at GorillaPark.

Albert Angehrn is professor of information technology and entrepreneurship, and director of the Center for Advanced Learning Technologies at Insead.

Competition for venture capital is fierce and investors look hard at web start-ups, making a good business plan essential. **Joe Tabet** and **Albert Angehrn** offer their advice.

The new economy has revolutionized the way we are doing business and the way businesses are created. Underlying the changes is the way venture capital has made it possible to finance an idea or a team even before there is any product or patent. In 1999, "gold rush entrepreneurship" flourished and was fed by an abundance of funding. However, the times when anyone could get financed are over; investors are looking for well-structured, credible projects. Negative sentiment to internet start-ups means e-business plans need to be at least as solid as traditional business plans.

This article aims to help entrepreneurs wanting to start a business. The objective is not to provide a template for a business plan, but to give hints, based on the experience of those who have already done it, be they entrepreneurs or investors. Writing a business plan develops understanding and provides a focus on the essentials. It may seem a time-consuming, even painful, exercise, but the returns are worth the effort.

Structure

The business plan summarizes a project in a way that makes it understandable and attractive to potential investors, business partners, or employees. It should contain a clear message for the target audience and has to be tailored, in the same way that a curriculum vitae needs to be modified to match each job position. The business plan has three objectives:

- To give a clear, understandable description of the opportunity.
- To provide convincing arguments that make the opportunity credible.
- To formulate a direct request to investors, strategic partners, or potential employees.

Keep in mind that the first review of a business plan is an elimination process, rather than a selection process. The challenge is to stimulate readers' curiosity and allow them to read the plan easily. Venture capital companies have to go through many proposals, all competing for the same money: you miss out important details at your peril (*see* Box 1). The objective should be to get an invitation to make a detailed presentation, which is the real selection process.

Three types of document should be prepared: an "elevator pitch," an executive summary, and the business plan.

The elevator pitch is a one-paragraph description of the business, presented as if you were in an elevator with an investor. You would have 30 seconds to stimulate interest. The pitch can be printed on a business card or a flyer. The executive summary is what readers should remember. It should be no longer than four pages and can be sent to initial contacts.

Finally, the business plan gives the details in no more than 20 pages, or 30 slides for a presentation. Longer documents force readers to make their own selection, which may not be in your favor. It is more difficult to write a short document than a long one. By getting to the essentials, you will gain a better understanding of the important issues.

Contents

The business plan should start with a clear value proposition. What matters to the reader is the value your business will create. A clear value proposition will answer the following:

- What kind of business are you in?
- What do you provide and how?
- Who are your target customers?

The plan should clearly identify the problem, not only the solution. Many projects are too solution driven; success resides in a good understanding of the problem. First confirm the need, then build the product. Show you understand the problem and your solution will be more convincing.

Be focussed. With an e-business plan, it is no longer necessary to point out that the number of internet users will be growing exponentially and that the market will be worth billions in 2005. Avoid industry description and focus on the business. Define the target market and provide a relevant description, with figures that show the size of the market. Projects that bet on capturing a small fraction of a huge market, which may in theory represent billions, are unlikely to fly. If this principle worked "we should all be selling tea in China."

Highlight the "so what." If you want readers to reach your conclusions, rather than their own, you need to steer them. It is not enough to describe facts. Different readers may draw different conclusions. For example, the fact that some people don't wear shoes doesn't indicate whether there is a huge potential market for shoes or no market at all.

Show some evidence of market acceptance, in particular with a new product or concept. Consumer behavior is hard to predict. A common pitfall is to assume customers will behave in the way you expect. Reality is different and common sense is the least accurate way to predict people's attitudes.

Describe the implementation approach. A good idea is unlikely to be unique. If it's good, expect a few other people to be thinking about it. If it's really good, you may find others working on it already. The difference is in execution. This is the real challenge. Even if the idea is not unique, you can make a difference in the way you implement it – this is what investors are looking for.

Be coherent with figures. There will never be accurate figures until the business is underway and even then some pieces may be missing. However, it is always possible to use comparisons, benchmarks, and reference points. Use them to estimate market size, market share, and profit margins. Unless you really miss the point, you should be much better positioned than anyone else to find the best figures. If it is difficult to find estimates, potential investors are even less likely to find better estimates.

At first, investors will not be able to check the figures. They would rather look at the coherence of figures and check that they are consistent with the strategy. If a key factor for success is to reach critical mass rapidly, focus on customer acquisition and put in the resources up front to do that. A timid approach, taking a percentage of revenue for marketing, is unlikely to match a jump-start strategy.

The format

Use an easy-to-read format, be creative in composing the document, but don't go to extremes. Find a balance: complicated documents are irritating and flat text with long paragraphs is boring. Think about the way people read a newspaper: they check the headlines first and focus on interesting stories. Readers of business plans are no different. They like catchy titles, tend to read in diagonals, and have a short attention span. So, make it easy to get the essentials. Use margins for quotes or comments and appropriate graphics. End with the points you want people to remember.

Don't use small type and never exceed 30 pages, including appendices. If readers want more, they can ask; if they want less, they don't know what to leave out. Keep in mind that the file may have to be sent by e-mail. Large files take time to download, particularly in hotel rooms.

What to include

Use a simple style, common vocabulary, and avoid abbreviations. Use analogies, without being too vague. (For example, don't say you want to be the Amazon for Africa.) Describe the business in a way that makes it easy to understand. It is not enough to say you want to build a reference portal for mobile phone users; you may need to explain what your business is about and how you will be doing it. As a general rule, start with the "most important," then go to the details and finally go back to the important again.

Business description

First, describe the need to be addressed and the market opportunity it represents. Next, explain how this need will be met. Then show how you want to implement the idea, the business approach. Illustrate the product or service with examples. Use customer scenarios or storyboards to explain how it will work. Always take the client's perspective and never expect them to do something you wouldn't.

Team and organization

Draw the organization chart as it should be at maturity, not to fit the current team. Highlight the team's capabilities and don't hesitate to identify gaps. This shows awareness of future needs. Mention the strategy for recruiting other key people and the top executives who are willing to join the team once financing is found. (However, this may not be taken seriously because it doesn't show commitment.)

An advisory board adds credibility, in particular if it is composed of well-known experts. Nevertheless, be careful with name dropping; the world is small and serious investors are diligent. In summary, show the competencies you already have, but stay realistic, humble, and credible.

Your team is your most valuable asset; choose people very carefully. They will determine the success of the business. The team is the first element investors look at.

Competitive analysis

It is a mistake not to include a thorough analysis of potential competition. If there is no direct

If two companies are offering a **similar service**, there are probably a dozen preparing to launch

competitor, look for alternatives or substitutes for the product. If there is no competition it is not necessarily a positive point; in fact it may be very negative, because there is no market for the idea.

Once competition has been covered, show the differentiating points. Avoid the line of "better, cheaper, and faster." Keep in mind that what you see of existing competition is only the tip of the iceberg. If two companies are already offering a similar service, there are probably a dozen preparing to launch. Also take into consideration the schedule competitors may be following. For example, if you want to offer features that competitors are not offering, but it will take six months before you start up, competitors – particularly on the web – might by then have added those features.

Don't underestimate competitors' ability to catch up and don't forget bricks-and-mortar companies moving online. Geographic barriers are not always high, but have to be taken seriously if the business has multinational ambitions. Scheduling needs care; if your ambition is to cover several countries, speed is vital. If you aim to launch in one country in year 1, another two countries in year 2, and arrive in the next three large markets in year 3, it will be difficult convincing investors that the final markets will wait. Just think about the web three years ago and the speed at which applications are transferred.

Marketing strategy

Marketing and sales are strategic components of any business. Focus on how this will be done and remember that the marketing approach may provide a competitive advantage. It has to match strategy and objectives. If the business relies on building a critical mass of customers, initial investment in client acquisition should be a priority.

Estimate marketing costs in terms of the costs of customer acquisition, rather than fixed budgets or percentage of revenues. Use reference points and comparisons to estimate the average cost of acquiring a new customer in your business category.

Implementation and logistics

The most important determinant for success is the ability to execute. Implementation is the real differentiator. This includes all aspects, from the choice of technology to customer service. On the web, first-mover advantage has proved to be insufficient to dominate the market. The game is about speed and scalability. The first one to scale up is most likely to keep the competitive edge.

As e-businesses become more interdependent, it is vital to find a place in the industry value chain. Strategic alliances are critical and can be very valuable at an early stage. With a smart approach, possible competitors can turn into allies or collaborators.

Evaluating the business

Attributing value to a young business is not easy. The variability is very wide and methods used by investors keep on changing. Traditional ratios are in most cases impossible to calculate. The use of comparisons often helps. Evaluation can still be very difficult, in particular for novel applications. At a later stage, profit making will be the bottom line and traditional methods become much easier to apply. At the idea stage, venture capitalists tend to use very simple formulae to evaluate potential, such as:

$$\text{Potential size} = \begin{array}{l} \text{market size} \\ \times \text{market growth} \\ \times \text{your contribution} \end{array}$$

No matter what the valuation is, think of the business as a way of creating assets. The assets can be anything that contributes to the value of the company. Influence the choice of valuation method by defining some measurable assets that can be used. Assets are always a mix of tangible and intangible, such as goodwill or brand name, or human capital and intellectual property. A customer (or supplier) base can also represent a measurable asset.

In choosing a particular asset, make sure your implementation gives absolute priority to maximizing this asset's value and how to measure it.

As a general guideline for early-stage valuation, here are some rules:

1 An idea is worth nothing if it remains an idea.

2 Nothing can be protected, even with a million patents.

3 Take the money when it's available; windows of opportunity are narrow.

4 All evaluation methods are good; none makes sense.

5 Time is money; don't waste it on negotiation.

6 Focus on the investors' value-added and not on valuation.

Always include a section analyzing the risks that may affect the business. An accurate assessment of risks will help convince investors that you are fully aware of the threats the business may face. It also shows that you are prepared and capable of responding to the challenge.

Don't forget to state clearly what is expected from the target audience. The conclusion should include your funding request. You can also include a bullet-point summary to help the readers find what they have to take away. Remember, attention span is short, retention is low, and the memory decay curve is steep.

Conclusion

- Use the business plan as a communication tool.
- Be simple, realistic, and use common sense.
- Don't look for funding, but for raising interest.
- At the first stage, success is to get to the second round.
- Be ready to support any statement with detailed information.

In search of capital
for the young business

Benoît Leleux is the
S. Schmidheiny Professor
of Entrepreneurship and
Finance at IMD, Lausanne.

From business angels to stock markets, there is a great range of finance sources. **Benoît Leleux** proposes ways of deciding which are best for the entrepreneur.

Valuable entrepreneurial opportunities should finance themselves. In a world of perfect information and endless financial and managerial resources, it would seem natural that a worthy investment would find its ideal financier easily. Unfortunately, the world of entrepreneurship is not one of complete information and predictability, nor are there endless resources: it is constrained and laden with uncertainties. Further, growth is an integral part of entrepreneurial activities and a major consumer of resources, both human and financial.

The combination of higher risk and uncertainty, small scale and superior growth potential is a potent cocktail, but one that can leave the fundraising entrepreneur with a world-class hangover. So, what are the central issues faced when financing the growing company?

Resource gaps and bundles

Many entrepreneurial ventures suffer from an imbalance between the resources needed to capitalize on opportunities and what is available. The gap includes cash but also management skills, distribution channels, networks, and technology. Using the term "resourcing" rather than "financing" acknowledges that high-growth companies face many constraints, not just a lack of money. Understanding resource requirements is a critical first step in assembling a deal.

Whereas mature companies can segment their needs and buy in resources (such as consultants, lawyers, shelf space, and so on), young, high-growth companies often face what is called a "bundled offer." For example, they may neither be able to develop their own marketing channels, nor have the credibility to sign agreements with companies with established channels. Raising venture capital may not only provide financial resources but also open the door to channels that would

Higher risk and superior **growth potential** can leave the entrepreneur with a world-class hangover

otherwise inaccessible. Financing is not an end in itself, but a means used to satisfy a company's needs, such as locking in critical partners, or gaining visibility for a product launch.

Resources needed by the growing business go far beyond financial requirements. Risk and growth interact, for example, to create difficulties in recruiting the people required in such circumstances. Quality people need to be brought in, yet financial resources are heavily constrained. Designing pay packages becomes an important task.

Resourcing the entrepreneurial business, irrespective of size, becomes a multi-faceted exercise where financial elements have to be balanced against nonfinancial dimensions that are equally critical. Without the means to shop around for each individual need, entrepreneurs have to be creative in assembling the key elements at a smaller cost and scale.

Dimensions of financing

There are 12 characteristics of financing sources that need investigating by entrepreneurs when optimizing a resource package. These have financial and nonfinancial dimensions (*see* Box 1).

Required rates of returns vary depending on the ability of each source to manage the risk. Similarly, the costs of raising funds vary greatly,

from relatively insignificant costs in the case of friends, to a cut of 10 to 20 percent in the case of public offerings of equity. Investors also differ in the extent to which they can continue financing the growth of the company, how much collateral they require, how comfortable they are with risk, and the signal their investment may send to other investors.

On the nonfinancial dimensions, investors differ as to how fast they make decisions (which may be critical), their industry knowledge and management skills, their flexibility, and how involved they get with the company management.

Financing types and resource maps

With these criteria in mind, it is possible to map the circumstances under which a particular source is most likely to invest. Figure 1 shows a model of financing types determined by the company's stage of development. It indicates that there is a significant overlap in financing sources at each stage.

Early money is used to develop a "proof of concept" for the product or service. With such a proof in hand, a start-up round of financing can attract a significantly enlarged pool of capital suppliers. A number of debt suppliers will be added to the seed-stage equity providers.

The simplified model only goes so far, however. To determine the relevant mix of resources, it is necessary to analyze in more detail the offer made by each source. The 12 dimensions of the resource framework were described earlier. To help entrepreneurs identify appropriate sources of financing, Table 1 lists the relative score (with

FIGURE 1 Financing types by stage of development

	SEED	START-UP	1ST ROUND	2ND ROUND	LATE STAGE

Insider money

Friends and family

Angels

Venture capital

Strategic partners

Public equity

Mezzanine/late-stage funds

Supplier and trade credit

Commercial loans

Asset-based lenders

Public debt

Commercial paper

10 being high) of each major source of financing on these 12 dimensions.

In the friends and family category, investors rely primarily on trust and friendship to counter information asymmetries. They are often limited in resources (money, skills, networks, industry knowledge) and the business relationship can create tensions with relatives, especially when things don't go well.

Beyond the immediate family circle, there are others willing and able to invest in entrepreneurial companies. They are known as angels or informal private equity investors and include entrepreneurs, professionals (lawyers, doctors, consultants, and so on), and wealthy families.

These people invest for a variety of reasons, including being proxy to entrepreneurial thrills, or as diversification in an investment portfolio.

TABLE 1 Resource maps scores for major financing sources

	Range of values							
Source of financing	Venture capital	Angels	Friends & family	Public equity	Trade credit	Asset loans	Gov't	John's project
Cost of money	8–10	6–8	5–8	2–5	0–2	1–3	0–3	**5–9**
Fund-raising expenses	0–2	4–6	3–6	7–10	0–2	3–5	6–9	**1–5**
Depth of pocket	7–9	5–7	3–5	8–10	0–3	1–4	1–4	**6–9**
Collateral requirements	0–2	1–3	1–3	0–3	2–5	7–10	0–3	**0–2**
Risk-bearing abilities	7–10	6–8	3–6	5–8	0–2	0–3	3–6	**7–10**
Reputation and signaling	8–10	5–7	0–3	5–8	0–3	0–3	0–2	**3–6**
Management skills	7–10	5–7	0–4	0–5	0–2	0–3	0–3	**7–10**
Speed of decision	7–9	5–7	3–5	3–6	6–9	7–10	6–10	**7–10**
Industry/product knowledge	7–9	5–7	1–5	1–4	6–9	5–8	0–3	**7–10**
Flexibility	7–9	6–8	5–8	1–4	0–3	0–3	0–3	**7–10**
Other resources	7–9	5–7	2–5	1–4	0–3	0–3	1–4	**7–9**
Control tendencies	7–9	5–7	3–6	1–3	0–2	0–2	1–4	**2–5**

Angels: informal venture capital investors; Asset loans: asset-based lending; Government: public financing programs; John's project: see below

They also bring different levels of resources, ranging from none to a high degree of industry knowledge and extensive networks.

Private equity investors operate mainly at the early stages of the company, when their more limited resources can buy larger ownership stakes. Their required rates of return are in line with those required for these stages of development, often falling at the lower end of the scale when nonfinancial benefits exist.

Angels have also taken advantage of the internet to develop a more organized approach to finding deals: formal networks provide direct access to them for entrepreneurs. Networks include AceNet, FindYourAngel.com, and UniversityAngels.com.

Venture capital firms, or professional equity investors, raise money from institutions, individuals, or even public entities to target equity investments in companies at all stages of development, from seed to buyouts and bridge financing. Funds can also specialize by stage of development and by industry. Whereas a significant percentage of investments by venture capitalists in the US are committed to early-stage deals, their European counterparts target mostly late-stage deals.

Venture capitalists share a professional approach to investments, running extensive due diligence and bringing internal and external expertise when needed. Known for having a hard-nosed approach, they are ready to take on risk and provide expertise. Established venture capitalists carry powerful reputations and their presence will send a strong signal to other potential investors.

In the "depth of pocket" category, nothing beats public markets with their ability to raise large amounts of money repeatedly. Public markets provide a well-organized forum for fundraising activities. The share price provides a good way of evaluating managers' actions and may allow the company to fund acquisitions.

Unfortunately, the process of going public is convoluted and expensive, requiring extensive disclosures and the costs associated with using reputable advisers. In addition, it imposes disclosure costs for as long as the company remains publicly owned. Government regulation can also be intrusive because it is designed to protect the public from unscrupulous managers.

Availability of public equity markets differs markedly by country: whereas the US has cultivated the notion of "public venture capital," with investors willing to capitalize companies very early on, European investors have proved more conservative and less willing to take on equity risks. The wave of new markets in Europe since 1996 has met the demand for growth-oriented investment opportunities.

John's project

The two frameworks presented above help in the design of appropriate financing plans by structuring what is otherwise perceived as an art form. To move from these frameworks to actual deal structures, one must start by mapping the company's resource requirements.

To illustrate the process, consider the situation faced by John, a 30-year-old entrepreneur trying to launch an internet-based charter plane reservation system for the corporate market.

He has a background in business administration and consulting, having helped some companies establish commercial websites, but he has limited experience in the aviation market. John has $90,000 of his own capital, not including the second mortgage he could get on his house, worth another $90,000.

John has developed a working prototype of the website that would provide business travelers with a quick and efficient way to tap into the private plane charter market. He has set up the company and has a web registration. What is missing are relationships with charter plane companies, full development of the site, and an aggressive marketing campaign to make the service known to business travelers and charter plane companies. He estimates his funding needs at $1.5m, two-thirds of which will be spent on marketing.

John's company is stuck somewhere between the seed and the start-up stage. With signed commitments from service providers (charter plane companies), a more polished product, and a solid business plan, John's project would be labeled more squarely a pure start-up.

Based on the financing types shown in Figure

At an early stage, business angels and **venture capitalists** should constitute the main investors

1, this stage of development calls mainly for equity financing, given the level of risk faced and the lack of information about viability. Practically, this means insider seed money, friends and family, angels, venture capitalists, strategic partners, or the public equity markets.

John needs to evaluate his portfolio of resource needs. Besides money, he lacks connections to the plane rental industry and the charter companies, as well as knowledge of that sector. Speed of decision is of the essence, since there is, according to him, a clear first-mover advantage in this business. With little money to spend in searching for investors, and little collateral to offer beyond his house, fundraising expenses should be as low as possible.

On the other hand, further rounds of fundraising may be required, so depth of pocket is important as well as flexibility. At this stage, the project risk remains very high and investors must be willing to bear it. With all these non-monetary needs, the cost of the money may be less relevant since the project seems to have significant potential for profit. John knows he would resent intrusion into management, so an arm's-length relationship is preferred.

With these resource requirements in hand, let us check which financing sources match the project's needs. Friends and family are short on depth of pocket, risk-bearing abilities, reputation and signaling, management skills, speed of decision, industry knowledge, and other resources, and long on control tendencies. Not the best match, but they may still provide the base on which to build the rest of the deal.

High net worth individuals may provide a better fit, particularly if they have the right backgrounds. They can provide the management expertise and industry knowledge, while remaining flexible and making decisions fast. As long as control tendencies are kept in check, angels could provide many of the skills and resources needed.

Venture capitalists would also make strong candidates for John's venture. Their reputation can help attract other investors and key personnel, and their expertise would be useful. Of course, they will be expensive and intrusive, but their ability to move fast and motivate others can be critical at an early stage. Public equity markets would fail to provide the necessary expertise in many areas, would be too costly, and would take too long to raise the money.

Strategic partners may be another option, as long as it is recognized that they may not help solve the management problem and that their investment may later jeopardize the independence of the company. On the positive side, they may be able to provide technical expertise and relatively cheap capital to bring the project to market fast.

What would be John's ideal financing package? At this early stage, business angels with industry experience and venture capitalists should constitute the main investors, with strategic partners as a supplementary benefit. The objective is not to obtain the absolute lowest-cost package but one that offers the most desirable balance of resources, now and for the immediate future.

Conclusion

With these tools in hand, individuals should be better able to chart a course through the jungle of start-up financing. However, they will never eliminate the need to expend efforts in reaching the final financing plan. They offer the maps and machete to direct guerrilla financing efforts, but they will not fight the battles for you. It is in those fights that the drive and spirit of the true entrepreneur will reveal themselves.

This article is based on "Resource Maps and Financial Ecotypes: A Visual Approach to Resourcing the Entrepreneurial Business," *Babson Entrepreneurial Review*, Spring 1999.

Further reading

Birley, S., Leleux, B. et al. (1996) "Trade-Offs in the Investment Decisions of European Venture Capitalists," *Journal of Business Venturing*, 11.

Brav, A. and Gompers, P.A. (1997) "Myth or Reality? The Long-Run Underperformance of Initial Public Offerings: Evidence from Venture and Non-Venture Capital-Backed Companies," *Journal of Finance*, 52(5).

Gompers, P. and Lerner, J. (1997) "Money Chasing Deals? The Impact of Fund Inflows on Private Equity Valuations," *Journal of Financial Economics*, 55.

Gompers, P. and Lerner, J. (1999) *The Venture Capital Cycle*, Cambridge, MA: MIT Press.

An insider guide
to going public

The number of companies going public has reached record levels. **Michael Horvath** explains the process behind an IPO.

Michael Horvath is an associate professor at the Tuck School of Business at Dartmouth. He co-founded Kana Communications, a software company that was taken public by Goldman Sachs in 1999.

Initial public offerings (IPO) reached record levels in 1999. In the US alone, a record 510 companies sold shares to the public markets in an IPO, raising just under $70bn. However, despite the resulting heightened awareness of IPOs, the process by which a privately held company transforms itself into a publicly traded company is still a mystery to many managers. This article aims to demystify the process. Although different rules apply in other countries, the underlying strategic considerations are similar to those in the US.

Legal aspects

The process of going public in the US is governed by a combination of institutional tradition and government regulation. In the wake of the 1929 stock market collapse, the US Congress enacted the Securities Act of 1933, otherwise known as the "truth in securities" law, to govern the issue of shares to public markets. The two main objectives of the act were to require issuing corporations to provide investors with detailed information and to prohibit deceit and fraud in the sale of securities.

The first objective is accomplished by requiring issuing corporations to register with the Securities and Exchange Commission (SEC). The SEC does not verify information; it merely disseminates it to interested investors. (One can view filed registrations at www.sec.gov.) The second objective is accomplished by the courts; investors have legal redress in the event that they suffer losses and can prove that a company provided incomplete or inaccurate information to the SEC.

The Securities Exchange Act of 1934 requires a public company to post corporate performance data to shareholders. Companies with more than $10m in assets whose securities are held by more than 500 shareholders must file annual and other periodic reports with the SEC,

Before 1999, practice dictated that companies had to show **profits** before going public

which makes them available to the public through its Electronic Data Gathering, Analysis, and Retrieval (EDGAR) database. The 1934 act also regulates events such as proxy solicitations for shareholder voting, tender offers for significant shareholders, and insider trading.

Since regular financial reporting may not have been a high priority for the privately held company, going public may mean beefing up the finance department. If a company's managers cannot close its books within a week or two of a quarter's end, then they are not ready for the public markets.

When to go public and why

If a company is like most of those filing for an IPO today, it will have survived on periodic infusions of venture capital. The timing of the "next round" is probably an oft-discussed topic among managers and directors. When public markets in 1999 were so accepting of technology companies that had yet to show a profit, start-ups frequently chose to go public rather than take a "mezzanine" or later-stage round of venture funding.

Yet, 1999 may have been an anomalous year. Before then, practice dictated that companies show at least two quarters of profits before going public. By this standard, most companies that went public in 1999 should not have done so. In fact, US markets are now showing evidence of heightened selectivity regarding IPOs. In the second quarter of 2000, 97 filed IPOs were pulled and another 38 postponed. In particular, there were noticeably fewer loss-making dotcoms.

The main reason to undertake an IPO is to raise funds for expansion. One can think of the IPO as another trip to the well of capital, except this time a company will draw from the vast public capital markets. Private equity placements amounted to just $36bn in 1999, roughly half the sum raised through IPOs. Furthermore, the pri-

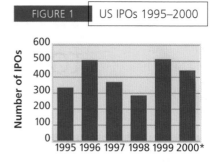

FIGURE 1 — US IPOs 1995–2000

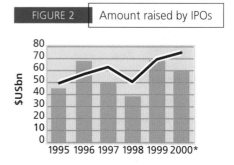

FIGURE 2 — Amount raised by IPOs

Source: based on SEC S-1 filings
* Full-year 2000 estimate based on data to September 25, 2000

vate equity funds were spread over 4,000 start-up companies, compared with the 510 companies that issued publicly traded shares (*see* Figure 1).

The second reason to go public is to benefit from widening the shareholder base. The shares a company sells in an IPO go to hundreds if not thousands of investors, providing (in ideal market conditions) a stable base for the company's valuation.

The principal purchasers of IPO shares, especially in the technology sectors, are institutional money managers with mandates to diversify their funds' holdings across a broad selection of companies within a fairly tight industry focus. When there are few publicly traded companies in a relatively new sector such as optical networks or internet infrastructure, every new issue is an opportunity to diversify further while hoping to catch the next Oracle in its infancy.

Creating liquidity is a close third in the list of benefits of going public. Having a liquid or tradeable stock benefits a company directly if it is pursuing acquisitions. More importantly, liquidity benefits existing shareholders: the founders, early investors, and employees with stock options can sell their shares more easily. However, the SEC regulates this with rule 144, concerning the sale of restricted or unregistered shares by company insiders (those with management-level knowledge of their company) and affiliates.

The company typically registers with the SEC only those shares being offered in the IPO. These usually amount to between 10 and 20 percent of the total number of shares held by insiders before the IPO. The SEC does not register insider shares. Unregistered shares may be sold, but rule 144 permits insiders to trade limited numbers of shares in only a short window following the release of quarterly financial information to all investors.

Further, insider selling under rule 144 is public knowledge and is widely discussed by financial sites on the web. Large trades by key insiders can send stock prices into unpleasant gyrations, so insiders get lessons in how and when to sell from corporate lawyers and their underwriters in an effort to minimize these.

Mechanics of an IPO

There are five distinct phases to an IPO, all of which need to be planned in detail well ahead of time:

- selecting an underwriter (one or two months);
- registering with the SEC and writing the prospectus (two to three months);
- staging a "road show" of presentations to investors (two to four weeks);
- pricing shares and beginning to trade (24 hours);
- the lock-up period following the IPO (typically 180 days).

Assuming a company has attracted the interest of underwriting investment banks, the first step requires managers to choose an underwriter (*see* Table 1). Just as choosing the right venture capitalist was important earlier, choosing the right underwriter can establish a company as a winner in the public markets.

Underwriters take anything from 4 to 9 percent of the proceeds of the offering, with 7 percent being the average. However, it would be a

| TABLE 1 | Major US underwriters in 1999 |

Lead underwriter	Number of IPOs	% total IPOs
Credit Suisse First Boston	56	11.0
Goldman Sachs	54	10.6
FleetBoston Robertson Stephens	44	8.6
Morgan Stanley Dean Witter	41	8.0
Donaldson, Lufkin & Jenrette	35	6.9
Merrill Lynch	30	5.9
Lehman Brothers	28	5.5
Bear Stearns	25	4.9
Deutsche Banc Alex Brown	25	4.9
Hambrecht & Quist	23	4.5
All others	149	29.2
Total	510	100.0

Source: based on SEC S-1 filings

mistake to choose an underwriter purely on this figure. Underwriters have reputations to uphold and the best ones are picky about which companies they take public and typically command a higher percentage fee. If they pick a certain company, some of this reputation rubs off in the form of a more successful IPO and a stronger market performance for its shares, at least for a while.

The role of the underwriter is complex and far-reaching. The lead underwriter, in association with a syndicate of other investment banks, helps with SEC hurdles and facilitates presentations to institutional investors.

The underwriter communicates directly with institutional purchasers of the stock and keeps the order book for the IPO shares. In consultation with the company's management, the underwriter sets the final offer price on the eve of the IPO. After trading begins, the underwriter is crucial in maintaining price stability, usually through analyst recommendations and sometimes by serving as the chief market maker for the stock.

Commonly, the underwriters take the company public under a "firm commitment" offering, which legally binds them to buy the company's shares in the IPO. As mentioned, underwriters are paid in the form of a percentage take of the offering. In practice, underwriters buy all the shares from the company at a discount of, say, 7 percent of the final offer price, then sell the shares to fill their order book at the offer price and pocket the difference.

The underwriters typically request, and are granted, an "overallotment" or "green shoe" option. This specifies a number of shares, typically 10 to 15 percent of the IPO offering, that they have the option of purchasing from the company at the underwriter's discount for 30 to 45 days after the IPO.

Overallotment shares allow underwriters to fill excess demand, thus keeping their institutional investors or wealthy private clients happy and eager to come back for their next IPO. The benefit to the company is that extra capital is raised in the IPO; on the other hand, if the stock price rises substantially on the first day of trading, selling more stock at the underwriter's discount can be painful.

The process of pulling together the registration statement for the SEC, called an S-1, is laborious. The S-1 reveals nearly all aspects of the company to prospective investors. The underwriter helps assure it is correctly presented, but managers have to provide the content. The company also has to write its prospectus with the underwriter. The underwriter will distribute the prospectus to potential investors in an effort to entice them. Luckily, the S-1 statement provides most of the content for the prospectus.

The S-1 is filed with the SEC, complete with an offering price range per share and the number of shares being offered. However, the final decision on pricing and size is made the night before the IPO. The SEC reviews the registration statement and may issue comments or ask for revisions and an amended S-1. It is not uncommon for companies to file three or four amended S-1s, since any change in company operations or opportunities between the time they initially file and the day of the IPO must be publicly disclosed in the S-1.

After the SEC approves a company's S-1, the underwriter can print the prospectus and the company is ready for the road show. The underwriter ideally has contacts among institutional money managers who might be interested in purchasing the company's shares. But the company's managers still have to shake their hands,

Going public before a company has a strong **competitive** position may make it more difficult to gain market share

give their pitch, and answer questions. One of the criteria by which one should choose an underwriter is the caliber of institutions on the road show. Be sure to ask about this during the courting phase.

Following each investor presentation, the lead underwriter takes the temperature of the audience and records indications of interest in an order book. Final decisions on price and quantity are based on this order book. The pricing phase lasts less than 24 hours and typically comes down to a telephone call with the underwriter.

If the company has a bright future and is doing its IPO during an exuberant time in the market, it is not uncommon for its book to be oversubscribed by 20 to 30 times. Oversubscribed issues may get a small price increase and more shares may be offered, meaning more capital will be raised. Poorly subscribed issues may be cut back or may get scrubbed altogether. On IPO day, the company's shares begin trading typically a few hours after the market opens, once a market maker has been able to gather enough selling and buying interest to determine an initial bid–ask spread.

While outside holders of registered securities in the company are free to buy and sell after the IPO, holders of unregistered securities are typically "locked up." This period is dictated by the underwriters rather than the SEC and the underwriter's intentions for a lock-up period should be discussed at an early stage. The norm is 180 days, during which holders of unregistered shares are prohibited from selling or hedging their shares.

The lock-up is intended to prevent a stock overhang, where supply exceeds demand at the current market price. After all, insider holdings typically far exceed the size of the IPO offering and the cost basis of insider shares is typically far below the IPO price. In practice, however, lock-ups merely tend to delay overhang rather than prevent it altogether. When lock-ups expire and insiders finally become free to sell, the company's stock price may disconnect from fundamentals until the overhang can be absorbed.

Mergers and acquisitions can also muddy the lock-up accounting. Typically, insiders are subject to a lock-up following the change of control that can last for three months or longer. Again, this is determined by the investment banks.

Strategy and the IPO

As with everything else in business, there are strategic issues concerning the IPO. Chief among these is the timing in relation to the company's development. An IPO has broader implications than merely providing capital. "Going public" implies both selling publicly traded shares and revealing once-private information about a company's finances, products, customers, and management.

Competitors and analysts will peruse the S-1 statement and quarterly reports. While an IPO may have been on the cards for a company for several quarters, going public before it has a sufficiently strong competitive position may only make it more difficult to gain market share.

Further, an IPO requires managers to jump through hoops at the SEC and give the road show for investors while still running their business. From the time it chooses its investment bank underwriter until 25 days after the IPO, the company is in its "quiet period," when any released information that may be construed as hyping the company's stock may result in an SEC-mandated delay for the IPO. Online retailer Webvan was a high-profile case of this in 1999: its IPO was delayed after a journalist gained access to a road show presentation and heard details not in the S-1 being offered to the audience.

One should also remember that just as with venture capital funds, it is never a good idea to try to raise money in an IPO when cash balances are low. Sudden downturns in the market just prior to the IPO day may result in a postponement of the offering and the accompanying possibility of having to file an amended S-1 and issue a new prospectus. It is not uncommon for start-ups to raise venture capital just prior to their IPO, at or near the same valuation proposed by the underwriters, simply to strengthen their balance sheet. Some venture funds specialize in this.

Another strategic issue concerns raising additional capital after the IPO by a secondary offering. In a secondary offering, a company registers additional shares with the SEC and sells them at market prices following another, more selective road show. Since secondary offerings typically occur one or more quarters after the IPO, markets have more information to use in valuing the company and this can often mean more working capital can be raised with less dilution for existing shareholders.

Since underwriters on the secondary offering are usually amenable to having insider shares as part of the offering, secondaries are also a means of giving insiders liquidity before the IPO lock-up expires. However, since the markets become aware of the secondary well before it happens, it is likely that the company's stock price will come under pressure before the secondary offering date as investors react to the dilution in their valuation. The lead underwriter usually gets a right of first refusal on secondary offerings, so managers should be sure to discuss this aspect with the candidate investment banks before making a selection. A private placement with a single investor is a way of securing additional capital that circumvents SEC registration.

A final strategic issue concerns a company's valuation and how hard it should negotiate before selecting an underwriter. It is imperative that managers have at least preliminary valuation discussions with the underwriters vying to do their IPO, because choosing an underwriter with a strong difference of opinion on the company's valuation could spell disaster. Once the process gets as far as the road show, it is very difficult to renegotiate valuation with the underwriter and the IPO pricing range is unlikely to

Picking an underwriter with a strong **difference of opinion** on the company's value could spell disaster respond much to stronger than expected market demand shown by an oversubscribed order book.

Underpricing in IPOs is the norm. In the third quarter of 2000, the first-day price gain from the issue price averaged 39 percent. But this is a hotly debated topic within the SEC and among academic economists, who have come up with explanations based on the uncertainty of the issue or favoritism on the part of underwriters. On the one hand, a higher valuation is to the company's advantage because it raises more working capital. On the other hand, if the company becomes a "hot stock" following a healthy first-day price gain, this may help to ensure still higher prices for insiders when their lock-up expires and they can finally sell.

Going out

For many start-up companies in the run-down, one-room offices of the world, the IPO looms as a tantalizing finish to a long and competitive race. But in fact the IPO is a means to an end rather than an end in itself.

Once through the IPO process, the organization faces the same challenges, but the coffers are fuller and you can watch your valuation change second-by-second on a stock ticker rather than every 9 to 12 months with each successive venture round.

The important thing to remember is that the same factors that made a company successful when it was privately held are likely to prolong success as a publicly traded company. In the long run, the stock price should reflect success, not define it.

Further reading

Ernst & Young (1999) *The Ernst & Young LLP Guide to the IPO Value Journey,* New York: Wiley.

Websites with IPO advice

www.nasdaq.com/about/going_public.stm
www.iporesources.org
www.ipoguys.com

Websites with current data and company reports

www.ipomaven.com
www.ipo.com
www.ipomonitor.com

Don't hesitate
to innovate

Established companies find it hard to cope with emerging technologies. It need not be so, say **George Day** and **Paul Schoemaker.**

George S. Day is Geoffrey T. Boisi Professor, co-director of the Mack Center for the Management of Technological Innovation, and a professor of marketing at the Wharton School, University of Pennsylvania.

Paul J.H. Schoemaker is research director of merging technologies management research and an adjunct professor of marketing at the Wharton School, University of Pennsylvania. He is chief executive of Decision Strategies International Inc.

Disruptive innovations, spawned by developments in emerging technologies such as the internet, intelligent sensors, genomics, nanotechnology, digital ink, mutant materials, and file-sharing software, have the potential to consume industries and make existing strategies obsolete. Conventional wisdom holds that large established companies are likely to lose out to smaller attackers when they try exploiting these breakthroughs. Yet why should incumbents encounter so much difficulty? Can they overcome their handicaps? Companies such as GE, Intel, Schwab, and Microsoft have embraced disruptive innovations. What can we learn from their examples?

Established companies control substantial resources: established infrastructure and processes, scale and scope, valuable brand names, entrenched relationships, and deep pockets. They can and do spend heavily on technology development and market research, although most of this money is devoted to evolutionary innovations that make their current offerings perform better in ways their customers already value.

For all their advantages, incumbents are often impotent when it comes to disruptive innovations. Their size slows them down, and past commitments restrict their flexibility. Equity markets expect continued growth in earnings, while start-ups are valued for their prospects and rewarded with large market capitalizations they can use to fund innovation. Incumbents are disadvantaged by their structures, capabilities, and outlook. Their finely honed instincts, established ways of thinking, and embedded skills make it tough to deal with a disruptive innovation that requires a different approach.

Many of the problems that befuddle incumbents are rooted in the technological uncertainties, ambiguous customer signals, and immature competitive structures of markets for disruptive innovations. As recently as 1995, interactive television dominated corporate radar screens as the hottest new electronic marketplace. This technology soon faded as the internet revealed the power of networks. Which of the technologies now reaching critical mass in the laboratories will become the hot innovations of the future? Few companies can avoid asking themselves how well they will capitalize on these future disruptions.

Pitfalls for incumbents

Disruptive innovations, posing the threat to their existing capabilities, make established companies prone to stick with what is familiar for too long. Even if this is avoided, incumbents are often unwilling to make a strong commitment and find it difficult to persist in the face of uncertainty and adversity. Although these dangers are related, they occur at different points in the decision process and require different remedies.

Trap 1: delay

When faced with uncertainty, it is tempting to wait. A watching brief may be assigned to an internal team that monitors families of technologies. Whether there is any value in these moves depends on whether there is a credible champion who can see beyond the imperfections of the first costly version: early electronic watches were bulky and personal digital appliances were devalued by the limitations of the Apple Newton. It is natural to underestimate developing technologies or new approaches because they don't measure up to the familiar alternative, or appear suitable only for narrow applications. Other developments may be easy to dismiss on the grounds that their small markets will not meet the growth needs of large companies. Yet, all large markets were once in an embryonic state with their origins in limited applications.

Trap 2: sticking with the familiar

Choice of technology is often clouded by uncertainty about whether technical hurdles can be overcome and which standard or architecture will prevail. When there are competing choices, companies are likely to base their decision on the technology path that feels most familiar. For example, various US newspapers merged their classified recruitment advertising into a common database (Careerpath.com), without much

change in approach (unlike Monster.com). Established companies typically search in areas close to their current expertise, and may not have the capability to appraise the options properly. Their instincts may be to seek a proprietary position to lock in customers, because that worked in their core market. Such a move makes customers suspicious, especially in today's open systems environment.

Trap 3: reluctance to commit

Established companies seldom commit wholeheartedly to a disruptive innovation. Instead, they are more likely to enter in stages. Many plausible reasons explain their hesitation.

First, managers are concerned about cannibalizing profitable products or encountering resistance from channel partners. Even if this is not an issue, prospects may appear less attractive than current business, making it difficult to justify investments. Encyclopaedia Britannica was slow to move to CD-Rom and lost 70 percent of its revenue between 1990 and 1997. As one classic study showed, of 27 companies confronted with a threatening technology, only four entered aggressively and three never participated at all. One reason is that managers are focussed on existing customers, and new technologies may seem applicable only to small market segments they don't serve or understand. This makes them vulnerable to attacks by outsiders who use the disruptive innovation as their platform.

Finally, successful organizations are not naturally ambidextrous, so they cannot balance the demands of familiar markets with the alien requirements of a disruptive innovation.

These four explanations reinforce each other to impair decision making, erode enthusiasm, and cause managers to hesitate. Such afflictions do not inhibit new entrants.

Trap 4: lack of persistence

Established companies being held to earnings forecasts have little patience with adverse results. US newspaper giant Knight-Ridder, owner of more than 30 titles, is a case in point. When its early forays into television in 1978 and cable in 1983 met setbacks, the company sold the business. Success may require patience. It took

Gannett a decade of losses to make *USA Today* a winner. Yet, missed forecasts and dashed hopes are inevitable with disruptive innovation: demand may not materialize as expected, competitors may crowd into the market, or the technology may veer in an unexpected direction. Initial enthusiasm may be replaced with skepticism about the innovation becoming profitable. The result is that companies often withdraw from early probes and don't come back until the innovation is proven by others. At this point it is too late to achieve leadership.

Avoiding the pitfalls

While awareness of the pitfalls described can help avoid them, the best defense is a good offense. Here, there are four proven approaches: widening peripheral vision, creating a learning culture, staying flexible in strategic ways, and providing organizational autonomy. These solutions do not correspond one to one with each trap, but rather address several of them at a time. Think of them as ingredients from which an approach can be fashioned that fits your needs.

Signals from the edge

Disruptive innovations signal their arrival long before they bloom. Some signs may be clear to those who look; others can only be seen by the prepared mind. As the philosopher Kant noted, we can only see what we are prepared to see. Weak signals usually come from the periphery, where previously unknown competitors are making inroads, unfamiliar customers are early adopters, and different standards are emerging. But the periphery is noisy, with numerous tangential technologies that may or may not be relevant. Background noise surrounds the converging entertainment, telecommunications, information, cable, and computer sectors. Here, a myriad of technologies such as interactive TV, web TV, DVD, desktop video, and satellite transmission combine to create new products. Background noise to one company may be a strong signal to another.

The first step in deciding which signals and trends to scan is to define the significant tech-

The first step in deciding which signals and trends to scan is to define the **significant technologies**

nologies. This requires shifting the focus from the characteristics of products to features that provide benefits. For example, customers did not want X-rays as such, but they did need more accurate images of tissues and bones to help spot problems. Companies also can study users who are ahead of the curve to see the promise of a new technology, or work jointly with lead users (in, say, industrial markets) on the next generation of products.

Once features are defined, the next question is how well the innovation can deliver features that meet customer needs and budgets, relative to competing technologies. This entails more than a linear extrapolation into the future. First, remember the typical S-shaped curve plotting the relationship between performance and development expenditure: initially, there is little sign of progress, but then performance rises steeply for relatively little effort before leveling off.

Once a technology trajectory has been projected, the challenge is to estimate the rate of adoption and potential market size. When it is not yet apparent who customers will be and even early users have yet to experience the product, such estimates are difficult. Traditional market research is seldom applicable to embryonic markets. Sample surveys, concept tests, and conjoint analysis were designed for well-defined problems in existing markets. A different approach is needed when the concept is ill-formed, the technology is barely ready, and questions of cost, availability, and performance are unresolved. People may not know whether they want holographic TV, but they can assess how much more they value its benefits relative to present offerings.

Xerox's strategy for estimating the potential market for fax machines in the 1970s illustrates how customer benefits and functionality can be used to estimate markets. Managers measured the extent and the frequency of urgent written messages, their time sensitivity, and the form and size of the message. Then they contrasted the promise of fax with mail, telephone, express delivery, and so on. With this approach, Xerox foresaw a business market of a million units. In hindsight, this number proved too low, but was then larger than people expected.

In summary, choosing how to assess the market for a disruptive innovation should be guided by three principles. First, paint the big picture: this is not the time to ask for carefully calibrated results. The issue is simply whether the market is big enough to support development. Next, use multiple methods. While any one market research method will be limited or flawed in some respect, a combination may yield conclusions that are directionally sound. Finally, focus on needs not products: prospective customers may not be able to visualize radical products, but they can be eloquent about their problems and changing needs.

Building a learning capacity

A second way to avoid the pitfalls of disruptive innovations is to keep learning. The challenge here is collective, not just individual. Without learning, noisy information flowing from the periphery will create confusion, not insight. Information must be absorbed, communicated, and intensively discussed so its implications are understood. The organization must possess or acquire several attributes:

- openness to diverse views, within and across departments;
- willingness to challenge deep-seated assumptions;
- a climate that encourages experimentation and rewards "well-intentioned" failure.

Entrenched attitudes may impede thinking needed to grasp discontinuities and surprises. Changing is not easy because attitudes are grounded in experience, reinforced by commitments and protected by inertia. Before prevailing thinking can be challenged, it should be described by making the views and assumptions of managers clear. Scenario planning can help challenge deep-rooted mentalities.

Adapting to the vagaries of disruptive innovations requires experiment and an openness to learning from failures. Sometimes experiment requires a willingness to create diverse solutions, by endorsing parallel development activities. For example, Intel was researching Risc chips even as complex microprocessors were being emphasized; and Shell is developing renewable energy sources, from solar to wind to geothermal.

It may also mean introducing prototypes into a market segment. Learning from this quickly is vital, followed by modifying the product, and trying again in a process of successive approximation. This is how Motorola entered the cellular phone market, and GE tackled the scanning business.

Maintain strategic flexibility

A paradox of disruptive innovation is that although it is prudent to make limited investments, sometimes a strong commitment leads to success. One way to reduce this dilemma is to increase organizational flexibility, so lowering the cost of making a commitment and the cost of reversing direction. This is similar to using flexible rather than fixed manufacturing systems. Commitment might seem to be the opposite of flexibility and you may not be able to have it both ways. However, only if the commitment is irreversible does it destroy flexibility.

Microsoft is a prime example of a company maintaining flexibility. Its much-celebrated "turn on a dime" response when confronted with Netscape's web browser is just one instance. Microsoft was placing many bets as early as 1988. At that time, Apple was at its peak with its superior graphical interface for the Macintosh making Microsoft's DOS look like a distant second. However, Microsoft was operating on several fronts. On the one hand, it was developing Windows; on another, it was pushing OS/2, which it developed with IBM. At the same time, Microsoft was introducing application software, including Excel and Word, for both Windows and Macintosh. Lastly, Microsoft was in partnership with SCO, the largest provider of Unix for the PC.

Microsoft had developed a strong hand of cards to play in a variety of worlds that might emerge. In hindsight, its portfolio of options was commensurate with the uncertainties then

> Putting a **new business** in a cocoon will enable it to do things differently from the parent

surrounding hardware and software development. Questions of standards, features, channels, and delivery modes (PCs versus servers) were still to be settled. In addition to developing a robust hand, Microsoft developed a culture that could quickly change strategy.

Organizational separation

The fourth strategy to avoid the pitfalls of large incumbents is to hive off the disruptive business into a separate unit. The more the initiative can operate from a smaller, entrepreneurial mindset, the less it will be held back by the inertia, controls, risk avoidance, and big-company thinking that lead to the pitfalls discussed above. By creating an isolated nursery, the company protects the new venture from infection by microbes that, while not dangerous to the large company, can be deadly to the new.

Many large companies set up a separate unit dedicated to new ideas. Examples include GM's Saturn division, IBM's PC unit, or Roche's Genentech investment. The objective of putting the new business in a cocoon is to enable the new group to do things differently while still permitting the transfer of resources and ideas from the parent. This also permits separate objectives, recognition of long development cycles, and continuing cash drains, as well as different criteria so the performance of managers in the rest of the organization is not jeopardized. Above all, it creates flexibility.

There are many degrees of separation. Some companies take the approach as far as to create spinoffs. These may be complete companies with their own stock, board, and management teams, in which the parent retains some ownership. Such equity carve-outs have been pursued by Thermo Electron, Safeguard Scientifics, Enron, Genzyme, and The Limited. This approach offers access to capital (via a public stock offering), strategic value from the corporate center, operating independence, development of executive talent in smaller units, and greater motivation for key personnel through stock options and operating freedom.

Kodak's experience with electronic imaging highlights the strategic importance of separation (in whatever form). Originally, electronic imaging activities were dispersed among Kodak's chemical imaging facilities. This had a number of bad consequences. Managers of the film business continually interfered with electronic imaging projects, which were perceived as threatening the existing customer base. The company policy that all engineers be paid the same meant Kodak could not compete for highly paid electronic engineers. Because digital imaging projects were scattered throughout the company, there was no cohesive vision and limited accountability for performance.

When George Fisher moved from Motorola to become chief executive, he put all digital imaging projects in one autonomous division and told managers to launch products. In a departure from a traditional "go it alone" strategy, he also initiated alliances to develop projects jointly.

Separation also implies willingness to cannibalize the core business. Indeed, a new venture may absorb the parent. This happened when Charles E. Schwab entered online brokerage. The Schwab website let investors trade securities for $30. By 1998, it was the dominant online broker. Meanwhile, customers of Schwab's discount brokerage were paying an average of $65 a trade, but getting personal service. As online trading boomed, the tensions from forcing customers to choose between service and price mounted. The decision was made that all trades would be made at $30, despite the damage to revenue. Not only did this help Schwab compete with online rivals, but its ability to deliver personalized information to customers at low cost made Schwab a bigger threat to full-service brokers.

> There should be diversity of opinion to **challenge** attitudes and precedents

Conclusions

How can established companies compete, survive, and succeed in industries that are being created or transformed by disruptive innovations? Success requires support from senior management, separation of the new, flexibility, and a willingness to take risks and learn from experiments. There should be a diversity of opinion to challenge dominant attitudes and misleading precedents, so avoiding myopic views of new ventures. The best innovators think broadly and will entertain a wide range of possibilities before they converge on a solution.

These prescriptions need considerable tailoring to match each disruptive innovation and the organization involved. Indeed, the purpose of a template for a high-commitment organization is to enable it to cope with the tension of uncertainty while achieving commitment to the choices made. The main point is that managing disruptive innovations constitutes a different game for established companies, with its own traps and solutions. We have identified the major pitfalls and remedies from empirical experience and academic studies of the underlying causes. We are a long way from understanding the intricacies of these pitfalls and ways to avoid them, but the broad outlines of common mistakes and practical solutions are becoming apparent.

Further reading

Christiansen, C.M. (1997) *The Innovator's Dilemma*, Cambridge, MA: Harvard Business School Press.

Day, G. (ed.), Schoemaker, P.J.H. and Gunther, R.E. (2000) *Wharton on Managing Emerging Technologies*, New York: Wiley.

Moore, G.A. (2000) *Living on the Fault Line*, New York: HarperBusiness.

Corporate ventures:
maximizing gains

Ian C. MacMillan is Sullivan Professor of Management and academic director of the Snider Entrepreneurial Center at the Wharton School of the University of Pennsylvania.

Managers of entrepreneurial ventures in established companies need to demonstrate leadership qualities. **Ian MacMillan** and **Rita McGrath** discuss how it's done.

Managers of entrepreneurial ventures launched from within established companies face a special set of challenges. Key among these is that, as the corporate venture takes shape, the manager needs to assume leadership responsibilities to succeed – and this includes managing failure. No one else can. This article maps out the critical activities and the most important responsibilities for the venture manager.

A tight proposition

The venture manager's first challenge is to convert each idea into a powerful, practical, business proposition that can be understood easily by the people responsible for executing it. The business proposition for a corporate venture needs to have three properties:

Rita Gunther McGrath is associate professor at the Graduate School of Business, Columbia University.

- it must be simple;
- it must be actionable;
- it must resonate with people.

When it comes to simplicity, managers should ask themselves whether they can write it on a business card and still convey its purpose. This makes the business proposition easy to comprehend and communicate. The proposition for Canon's personal copier exemplifies this principle: "Take to market a copier that is small, inexpensive and reliable enough for personal use on a secretary's desk." And the Japanese music equipment manufacturer Yamaha replaced the idea of being a company that only manufactured pianofortes with the terse proposition: "Sell keyboards."

The phrasing of the business proposition is all important. It is good to start by finding a direct link with the market and the customer, and simpler propositions are more powerful. Consider this statement from the US online auction site Priceline.com: "Customer: name your own price, any time, anywhere." Employees can mobilize around it, focus on it, and talk about it. Such images can be phrases, like those of Yamaha and Priceline.com. They can be pictures or symbols, metaphors or analogies – anything that makes it easy for people to understand the basic challenges of execution.

Absorb uncertainty

It is important for managers to help those involved in the project cope with uncertainty or they will find it hard to be decisive. Unfortunately, it is now more expensive for companies to be slow than it is for them to be wrong. The project leader must make uncertainty less daunting and create among colleagues the self-confidence that allows them to act without seeking detailed managerial permission. In particular, the project manager should prevent employees from being overwhelmed by the complexities of the project. How? By setting a clear framework in which they can take action.

In other words, the venture manager might say to the team members: "Assume X is going to happen. If you work on this assumption and I'm wrong, it's not your problem, but mine. I may come to you later and say I was wrong and we now have to assume Y is going to happen, but for now, you should assume I am right." The importance of this practice is that it liberates team members from the paralysis caused by uncertainty and frees their creativity.

The manager is left to cope with the uncertainty, of course, but then the business of thinking as an entrepreneur is all about coping with uncertain situations. In fact, a manager seldom has to be right all the time, just right enough often enough. Further, a competent, confident, and resilient team can usually cope with the differences between the framework set by a manager and events as they unfold.

Crucially, leaders must recognize when there is a need to absorb uncertainty so that others can get on with implementation. Furthermore, they need to accept that the leader is the one who can most afford to be wrong!

What does absorbing uncertainty mean? Leaders should ensure that team members have enough guidelines and latitude for setting their own priorities – what is important and what can wait. They should make sure people know what they are expected to prepare for – how soon, how big, with what level of aggressiveness. A manager's best-guess directions can help considerably until more information becomes available.

Frame the challenge

Managers must frame the venture in such a way that others can implement it. They must use their knowledge of the capabilities of their team members and know how far those capabilities can be stretched to make the venture happen.

The Japanese company Canon provides a good illustration. In the early 1970s, one of Canon's executives, Dr Keizo Yamaji, noticed a set of needs for photocopying that were not being addressed by the incumbent Xerox – the market for just a few copies of short documents. Xerox offered machines designed to produce hundreds of copies of long documents.

Carefully assessing the skills of his engineering staff, Dr Yamaji stacked up their talents against what he thought was required to produce a so-called "personal copier." He was then able to give them this framework for action: "I want you to make me a copier. It can be no bigger than a large breadbox. It can't retail for more than $1,000 in the US. It must never need servicing and it must be ready in 18 months."

Dr Yamaji framed the project, but he didn't micromanage it. He regarded his biggest challenge as setting a task for his technical people that would push them to the limits of their capabilities, without pushing them beyond their limits. His personal judgment was crucial in matching the difficulty of the project to the skills of the employees.

Dr Yamaji described the results: "At first the engineers did what engineers always do – they whined! But then, guess what happened – they went out and did it. It was a little bigger, it cost a little more. While it did need servicing, it very seldom needed servicing and it took just under two years instead of 18 months. But I got my copier and the multibillion-dollar business that it represented."

Dr Yamaji realized that his obligation as a manager launching an entrepreneurial venture was to frame the challenge to match his people's capabilities – and then get out of their way so they could get on with it.

Check market acceptance

The lowest-cost route to successful implementation is to probe constantly for evidence that the market you have envisaged accepts the business case for the venture. One successful entrepreneur will not launch a new industrial effort until he has a preliminary order from at least one customer. He argues that if not even one potential customer wants it enough to risk a conditional order, then there must be better opportunities elsewhere.

This may be difficult to pull off, but if you can't get orders, can you get letters of intent? If you can't get letters of intent, can you get letters expressing interest? If you can't even get someone to write a letter expressing interest, then the proposition should be viewed with suspicion.

Secure "killer" deals

Success for most ventures depends on being able to make three to five deals with stakeholders whose commitment is crucial, such as suppliers, distributors, funding sources, employees, customers, and sometimes key supporters in the corporation. Managers should ensure they have identified the deals that will make or break the venture and that they are progressing well with these deals ahead of major investment commitments. Failure to do so can threaten the survival of the enterprise. Iridium, for example, spent billions of dollars before finding out that major companies would not sign up for its expensive, bulky satellite phones.

Importantly, managers should have a clear idea of when to walk away. If the right deal can't be found, why fatally burden the venture by being forced to underprice or overpay for supplies? Other ventures will surface in future.

Use imagination, not money

Entrepreneurial managers must recognize that they should minimize expenditure on assets and fixed costs until they have revenue streams to justify them. They should reduce initial investment as near to zero as possible. If possible, the initial assets should be bought second-hand, or better still leased. If the venture is launched and operated with parsimony, the project managers can afford to make some learning-rich mistakes as they figure out what the true opportunity is.

They should also try to initiate revenues ahead of cost flows. For instance, one entrepreneur succeeded in persuading a consortium of future customers to fund the development of a prototype.

Whenever possible, costs should be incurred depending on use, which avoids commitment to a fixed cost. Another entrepreneur, for example, remunerates her salesforce with a big percentage of profits on orders once customers have paid – she gets money in before paying out. Such tactics reduce the initial investment burden on which the venture must eventually generate returns.

Identify skill deficiencies

The success of the venture may rely heavily on new and unfamiliar skills and it is easy to underestimate the difficulty of securing and deploying them, or developing them. Witness the many dot-com start-ups that cannot find programmers to develop and operate their systems. If the first recruits are deficient in critical skills, the quality of the products launched will be inadequate and the first brave souls who order will be disappointed. Venture leaders cannot allow this to happen – they must ensure the right skills are developed and reliably in use before inflicting the offering on unsuspecting consumers.

Keep the focus on learning. Venture managers

The spirit of **planning** is to convert assumptions to knowledge ahead of investment should carefully document and test assumptions ahead of investment and then systematically redirect the venture as these assumptions are tested against experience. The spirit of planning is to aim to learn by converting assumptions to knowledge ahead of investment. There is no point in trying to stick to a plan based on assumptions that prove invalid.

Consider, for example, the prospects of the carbon-fiber products industry if the innovators had stuck to their original assumptions, applications in space satellite housings, instead of redeploying the technology to sports equipment. In particular, the first customers should be checked against those predicted in the business plan. This can reveal a lot about where the real market lies.

Early warning systems

Small changes in key assumptions or market variables can presage large disruptions in performance. As venture managers get wrapped up in day-to-day issues, they need to give someone responsibility for monitoring the most sensitive variables for early warning signals.

Manage disappointment

Every venture runs a real risk of failure, so the greatest challenge for the manager lies in managing disappointments. When failure occurs, the entire workforce stops and waits to see what managers are going to do. This is a testing time and managers' reaction to disappointment will greatly influence the commitment of the workforce to future entrepreneurial developments.

How can the venture be redirected to areas of greater opportunity? Two practices characterize the successful venture manager when dealing with failure. The first is constructive post-mortems. No one should be rewarded for making bad decisions and entrepreneurial leaders of successful venture programs should not forgive foolish failure. On the other hand, ventures in which the team has consistently made good decisions, but which failed as a result of circumstances beyond their control, deserve recognition and reward.

Managers should hold constructive post-mortems to distinguish between ventures that failed because of bad luck and those that failed because of bad decisions. They must publicly recognize good work concealed by overall failure.

The second practice is recouping some value from the exercise. Failed ventures can be analyzed for information, which can be profitably deployed elsewhere. In a failed foray by a financial services company into capturing consumer data, the company had developed powerful data compression technology. This asset could have been used by the parent company, but the potential was lost in the recriminations that followed the shut-down. Recouping value helps convey to project workers that it was the venture that failed, not them.

Conclusion

We conclude by suggesting some key questions that venture managers should ask themselves during the course of a project.

1 Has sufficient attention been paid to reducing uncertainty for the team?

2 Has the venture been framed adequately?

3 Is there a system to monitor market acceptance?

4 Is there a process to secure the deals that make or break the venture?

5 Are team members driving down fixed costs?

6 Have skill requirements been thoroughly assessed?

7 Is there a plan to keep the focus on learning?

8 How can post-mortems be constructive?

9 What are the plans for recouping failure?

This article draws from ideas contained in the authors' book, *The Entrepreneurial Mindset*.

Further reading

Collins, J.C. and Porras, J.I. (1994) *Built to Last*, New York: HarperBusiness.

MacMillan, I.C. and McGrath, R.G. (1995) "Discovery Driven Planning," *Harvard Business* Review, July–August, 44–54.

McGrath, R.G. and MacMillan, I.C. (2000) *The Entrepreneurial Mindset*, Cambridge, MA: Harvard Business School Press.

Strategy

3

Contents

Introduction to Part 3

All managers are involved in strategy. Decisions about what to produce, when to produce it and where to sell it are fundamental. However, strategy also involves looking at one's competitors and the wider economy, choosing alliances carefully, managing mergers and acquisitions, leadership and the human side of the organization. In this part, writers begin by working through the principles of strategy-making and implementation, before focusing the major strategic development in recent times: e-commerce. They show how, despite the stock market turmoil facing many of the biggest dotcoms, the internet can deliver real benefits to a company's operations and bottom line. The final essay in this series discusses a subject that is covered little in standard works on strategy: when and how should a company disengage parts of the company that add no value to the whole? Demergers will play a greater part in tomorrow's economy, and executives must learn how to handle them astutely.

Competitive strategy
to lure the investor

In the global fight for capital, companies must attract investors with better returns. **Richard Whittington** shows how managers can beat the averages.

Richard Whittington is a reader in strategy at the Saïd Business School, Oxford University.

Competition is more and more about competing for capital. Companies today find themselves competing not only with rivals in immediate product markets – Boeing versus Airbus, or AOL/Netscape versus Microsoft, for instance – but across industries. Furthermore, they compete for investors' support, and do so aggressively, across an increasingly international terrain.

One reason for this is the greater ease with which institutions and private investors can switch investments from one company to another, one industry to another, or one part of the world to another. They are armed with better and almost instantaneous information. Financial performance is increasingly transparent. The number of cross-border mergers and acquisitions is increasing and the internet feeds investors with continuous data on corporate assets. Companies have never been as easy to buy and sell.

So senior managers are under daily pressure to deliver superior performance. Failure may be quickly punished by dismissal, takeover, or even break-up. Recent high-profile victims of investor impatience include Eckhard Pfeiffer of Compaq, Douglas Ivester of Coca-Cola, and Durk Jager of Procter & Gamble. The dismissal of chief executive Derek Wanless was not enough to save failing British bank National Westminster from the Royal Bank of Scotland's hostile bid.

It is not just Anglo-Saxon managers and companies that fear impatient investors. The acquisitions of Mannesmann by Vodafone and IDC by Cable & Wireless show that hostile international bids are now acceptable even to investors in Germany and Japan. Few public companies are safe.

In a performance-hungry economy, good strategy is about persuading investors that your company offers superior prospects for financial returns. Strategists need to realize they are competing for investor support not just with rivals in their own industry, but with just about every investment opportunity around the world. It becomes imperative for managers to demonstrate both that they are operating in industries with good prospects and that, within these industries, their company is one of the best. This article introduces techniques for analyzing industry returns and determining how individual companies can beat industry averages.

Choose your industry

Industries vary widely in their average investor returns. Every year, *Fortune* magazine compares 41 industries according to the results of the largest 500 US corporations. Most revealing are the average annual rates of total returns to investors over 10 years. Table 1 takes a range of these industries, from the top, middle, and bottom. As it shows, returns can vary from an average 57.7 percent for computer peripherals companies (such as Seagate and EMC) to a miserly 2 percent for hotels, casinos, and resorts companies (such as Marriott and Trump). Even

TABLE 1	Ten-year return to investors (selected industries)

	1998–9 annual rate %
Computer peripherals	57.7
Securities	28.6
Soaps, cosmetics	21.4
Pharmaceuticals	20.6
Speciality retailers	20.5
Telecommunications	18.2
Entertainment	12.8
Food	11.4
Motor vehicles and parts	9.4
Petroleum refining	9.3
Health care	6.5
Hotels, casinos, and resorts	2.0
Median (all 41 industries)	12.8

Source: www.fortune.com

FIGURE 1	Investor turbulence 1998–2000

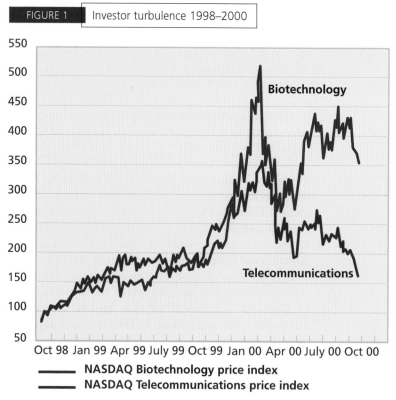

NASDAQ Biotechnology price index
NASDAQ Telecommunications price index

Source: Datastream

with such broadly defined industries, the long-run performance of top and bottom industries varies by a factor of nearly 30.

Investors can react rapidly to expectations of performance. Consider biotechnology and telecommunications stocks (Figure 1). The biotechnology index nearly trebled over a few months, then halved in a few weeks. Meanwhile, capital has leached out of industries with poor prospects such as steel and household products. Clearly, a good strategic move is to start in the right industry.

The data in Table 1 tell us about the past. We need to know about the future. Here, the analysis given by Harvard academic Michael Porter in his 1980 book *Competitive Strategy* provides an important tool for analyzing the potential profits of industries. According to him, industry prospects are determined by the interplay of five forces:

- bargaining power of buyers;
- bargaining power of suppliers;
- intensity of industry rivalry;
- threat of new entrants;
- threat of substitutes.

Estimating future trends in the five forces should give a good notion of how profits will turn out. The five forces are examined below in turn, with prospects for the focal industry at the center of the analysis.

Power of buyers

Powerful buyers have the potential always to squeeze their suppliers' margins. The buying power of Wal-Mart, the world's largest retailer, has exerted huge pressure on the prices of suppliers in the clothes, garden equipment, and toy industries. The power of buyers is increased and supplying industry profits decreased when:

- buying volumes are large and concentrated in a few hands;
- products are fairly standard, so competition is around price rather than features;
- buyers can integrate backwards, in other words, supplying the product or service themselves.

Power of suppliers

The tables are turned when it is the suppliers who have the power. Thus, Intel dominates the supply of microprocessors, at the expense of the personal computer industry's many assemblers. The factors that increase supplier power are the mirror image of those that increase buyer power. Suppliers are powerful when:

- supplier volumes are large and concentrated;
- products are highly differentiated, so it is hard for buyers to switch according to price;
- suppliers can integrate forwards, bypassing their buyers altogether.

Industry rivalry

Profits are depressed when industries are highly rivalrous – with incumbents competing fiercely on price, marketing, or innovation. The US airline market has suffered over the long term from constant competition on price or easily imitated schemes such as air miles. Industries tend to become highly rivalrous when:

- there are many competitors of a similar size, so they continuously fight for leadership;
- growth is slow, so competition is a zero-sum game, with one company's gains matched by another's losses;
- there is little scope for differentiation, so companies are locked in vicious price competition.

It can be seen that Michael Porter's vision of the interplay of buyer power, supplier power, and industry rivalry is like arm-wrestling. Profits depend on who has most bargaining muscle – buyers, suppliers, or industry in the middle. However, there are two other forces that put a ceiling on profits.

New entrants

The problem for many industries is that they are too easy to enter. It takes only about $2m to set up an operation capable of assembling 200,000 personal computers a year. The greater an industry's profits, the more likely it is to attract new entrants. As they enter, they spoil the game for everyone. The threat of new entrants is high where there are:

- low economies of scale, so entry can be incremental;

- low capital requirements, so the entry ticket price is small;
- few barriers in terms of government tariffs, regulations, or patents.

Substitutes

The threat of substitutes also dampens profit potential. This is not competition from new entrants, but from products or services that can meet similar needs. Profits in beverage packaging are capped because buyers can switch between steel, aluminum, and glass containers. The threat of substitutes is high where:

- costs are low, so switching involves little disruption to buyers;
- the price/performance ratio is similar; for instance, the alternative may not be as good but is cheaper.

Michael Porter's advice, therefore, is to pick industries where the forces are favorable. Good industries have few competitors, high bargaining power against buyers and suppliers, and little risk from entrants or substitutes. The message is clear: market power is good for profits. Although Porter called his book *Competitive Strategy*, he probably ought to have called it *Anti-Competitive Strategy*. The first step in competitive strategy is to choose an industry where you don't have to compete very hard.

Some say such faith in stable market power is outdated, with e-business start-ups and international competition disrupting markets and technologies. However, one should not give up on market power too quickly. Even in new markets, powerful players can rapidly emerge. Microsoft has 80 percent of the world's operating system market, Cisco Systems accounts for about three-quarters of the market for high-end internet routers, and Corning makes half of US optical fibers. These companies should reap the rewards of market dominance.

Beating the averages

Entering the right industry is only the first step. It is all very well to operate in an industry with good profit potential, but managers still have to offer investors a reason for backing them rather than competitors. Even in a good industry, investors will seek out companies that beat the industry averages.

In most industries, the distribution of company performance follows a bell curve. Returning to the *Fortune 500* data, consider the distribution of company performance within the US specialty retail industry, which is relatively successful. The largest group of companies achieves 10-year investor returns close to the average, between 11 and 20 percent (*see* Figure 2). But many companies beat the average substantially, some achieving over 30 percent. For example, Gap's annual rate was 39 percent. There are companies doing worse than average too: Toys 'R' Us had an negative rate of 5 percent. Clearly, investors will only be interested in companies with good prospects of superior returns.

To beat the averages, companies need something special. Here we can use the idea of "core

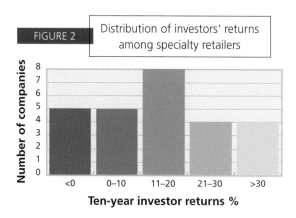

FIGURE 2 Distribution of investors' returns among specialty retailers

Number of companies (y-axis): 0–8
Ten-year investor returns % (x-axis): <0, 0–10, 11–20, 21–30, >30

Source: www.fortune.com

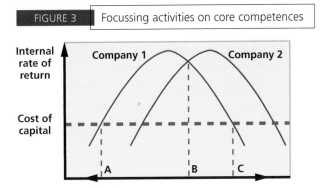

FIGURE 3 Focussing activities on core competences

competences," developed by management academics C.K. Prahalad and Gary Hamel, to help us understand what might underpin superior performance by a company.

For Prahalad and Hamel, a core competence typically involves a bundle of skills and technologies that enable a company to deliver fundamental benefit to customers. They cite Canon, which uses its skills in integrating microelectronics, optics, and precision mechanics to build superior cameras, fax machines, printers, and copiers. For a core competence to be an enduring source of competitive advantage, it should have three main features. First, it should be unique: if not, it is unlikely to command a premium. Second, it should be hard to imitate: the more a company integrates skills and technologies, the harder it is for competitors to match. Finally, there should be no substitutes for its products.

In a sense, core competences are again about power, but the roots of this power lie deep within the company. A company with a core competence that is unique, hard to imitate, and hard to substitute is a monopolist too. And from the point of view of investors, a company with strong core competences is valuable because it is tough to compete against.

The notion of core competences has a radical implication for strategy: a company should focus on doing only what is close to its core competence. For Canon, for instance, personal computers might seem a logical extension of its presence in office equipment, but, making little use of the company's integrating skills, they are distant from its core competence. From this point of view, diversification or integration up and down the value chain should be met with suspicion.

The focussing effect of core competence thinking is illustrated by the profit potential profiles in Figure 3. The horizontal axis measures the scope of a company's possible activities. The vertical axis measures potential profitability in these activities (assuming no other company is doing them). Take Company 1. Its profitability is likely to be highest at the center of its core competence. Conventional finance theory tells us, however, that it should do all activities that at least match its cost of capital, in other words the full range between points A and C on the horizontal axis.

But once combined with a true concern for investors, core competence thinking challenges this logic. To keep it simple, assume Company 1 is competing for capital with just one other company, Company 2. Company 2 also has a humpbacked distribution of profitability, but its core competence is to the right of Company 1's. This means there are activities Company 2 can do more profitably than Company 1, even within the same industry.

As far as investors are concerned, they would rather give the capital to Company 2 to do these activities than to Company 1, regardless of whether Company 1 could beat the cost of capital in them. In other words, according to core competence thinking, Company 1 should restrict itself only to activities in the range A to B. If one extends the competition for investor support to many companies, then clearly the range of appropriate activities for Company 1 is likely to become even more restrictive. A company can only beat the averages if it stays focussed on activities that it does better than the competition.

The essence of competitive strategy, then, is

putting the company in a position to offer investors superior future returns. Superior returns are best achieved by avoiding competition. So, first choose an industry that is not too competitive. Then stay focussed on what you do better than anyone else.

Further reading

Porter, M. (1980) *Competitive Strategy: Techniques for Analysing Industries and Competitors*, New York: Free Press.

Prahalad, C.K. and Hamel, G. (1990) "The Core Competence of the Corporation," *Harvard Business Review*, May–June, 79–91.

Whittington, R. (2000) *What is Strategy: and Does it Matter?* London: International Thompson.

The structures behind
global companies

Julian Birkinshaw is associate professor of strategic and international management at London Business School.

Balancing bureaucracy with the benefits of size is a problem for international companies. **Julian Birkinshaw** sets out the options for corporate structures.

Global companies have several advantages over their smaller local or regional counterparts. Sheer size gives them enormous economies of scale in manufacturing, in new product development, and in market coverage. Global reach allows them to tap into new ideas and opportunities wherever they may arise. And a presence in many countries gives them bargaining power over local governments, as well as flexibility in deciding where they will source products.

However, these benefits can also be liabilities. The reality is that global companies end up being perceived as complex, slow-moving, and bureaucratic. The challenge for top managers lies in minimizing these liabilities, while retaining the benefits of size. As Sir Martin Sorrell, chief executive of advertising group WPP, observed: "Every CEO wants the power of a global company with the heart and soul of an entrepreneurial company."

There are many ways of addressing this balancing act. One way is to work on culture, to get people to think entrepreneurially. Another way is through systems – reward systems, career management, and so on. A third way, and the focus of this article, is through structure – the basic lines of reporting and accountability that are typically drawn on an organization chart. The structure is never the whole story, it is just a way of dividing responsibilities among executives. It is meaningless unless supported by appropriate systems and a consistent culture. However, structure is still surprisingly informative about strategic priorities and the work going on, so it is as good a place to start as any.

Four global structures

How should a global company be organized? The answer depends on a host of factors, such as the number of businesses and countries in

FIGURE 1   Four models for global company structure

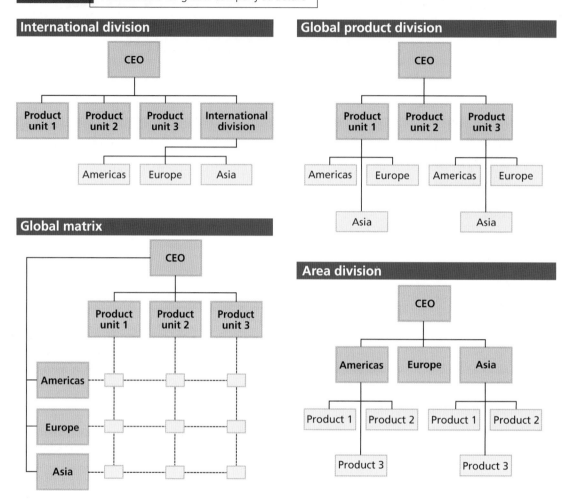

which it operates, the type of industry, the locations of its major customers, and its own heritage. At the risk of oversimplification, we can identify four models (*see* Figure 1).

The international division

Some companies are divided into business units or divisions, with each division responsible for its business in the home country. There is then a separate international division, which is responsible for all sales outside the home country. Many medium-sized companies with limited international sales are structured in this way.

Let's say there are four business units, each

one selling between 80 and 95 percent of its output to local customers. It makes sense for them to focus on their local business. But the rest of their output is sold abroad and that business needs to be managed in a different way, because there are tariff and trade issues, relationships with foreign partners or agents to manage, and so on. The international division is therefore set up to deal with all those issues. It typically does not make anything itself – it is just the international selling operation for the other four business units.

The international division is rare in large global companies. Most companies have moved on to one of the structures described below. It

The **global product division** is emerging as the most common structure among large companies

can sometimes be found as an exporting operation for small or emerging markets. Interestingly, it often still exists by name, in that there will be a senior executive of international operations who has an overview role, but no direct responsibility for international sales.

The global product division

The major line of authority in some companies lies with product managers, who have responsibility for their product line globally. For example, in General Electric there are a dozen global businesses – lighting, aircraft engines, plastics, and so on. Each has its own president, who is responsible for that business around the world. If GE's plastics business wanted to close a factory in Germany, for example, the country manager of Germany might voice concern, but it would be up to the plastics business president to make the decision.

The main advantage of the global product division is that it facilitates the co-ordination and integration of activities worldwide. The main disadvantage is that its standardized approach hinders the ability to respond to country-specific differences. Nonetheless, the global product division is emerging as the most common structure among large global companies. BP, BT, Siemens, Ericsson, Sara Lee, 3M, and many other global companies use this basic structure.

The area division

Here, the major line of authority lies with the country or region manager – for example, the president of Asia Pacific region, or the president of the German subsidiary. This individual has the final say on everything that goes on there. The main advantage of the area division is that it enables responsiveness to national markets because each country has its own dedicated resources. The corresponding disadvantage is that co-ordination across countries suffers,

which makes it difficult to achieve scale economies in development and production.

Good examples of the area division structure are now hard to find. Ten years ago many companies were organized in this way – Philips, Nestlé, Shell, Unilever, and others. Today, most of these have moved toward the global product division or some sort of hybrid between global product and area. Unilever, for example, is organized by geographic regions, but with strong product divisions in Europe and North America, and an industrial cleaning division, DiverseyLever, which is run as a pure global business.

The global matrix

The matrix is, in theory, a way of gaining all the benefits of the previous two structures, without their disadvantages. In the global matrix, a business manager reports to two bosses – a global business unit manager and a country manager. The country manager is responsible for ensuring that the company is responsive to local market needs. The global business unit manager ensures that activities are co-ordinated worldwide. The aim, in other words, is to achieve global integration and national responsiveness at the same time.

This is the theory; reality is rather different. Put yourself, for a second, in the shoes of the business manager responsible for chocolate products in France (working for, say, Nestlé or Mars). Your global business manager wants you to adopt a new global advertising campaign to save money and he wants you to close a factory and import the product from Germany. Your country manager wants you to create a new product line to compete with a very successful French competitor and is very much against closing the factory, for obvious reasons. The result is that you are torn in two directions and the only way to resolve the differences of opinion of your two bosses is through meetings – lots of them.

The matrix structure has a turbulent history. It emerged in the defense industry as a way of structuring cross-functional teams, and was adopted in the late 1970s by global companies as a way of reconciling the tension between product divisions and countries. However, most found it unworkable because of the decision-making gridlock it spawned. Dow, Citibank, and others famously dropped the matrix in the 1980s.

It was given a second lease of life in the early 1990s, largely through the efforts of ABB and its chief executive Percy Barnevik. ABB apparently found a way of making the matrix work and its approach was imitated by some other global companies such as Alfa Laval. But the problems of matrix management surfaced again and ABB has moved gradually away from a global matrix toward the increasingly popular global product division structure.

One point of clarification on the matrix. The above discussion refers to the balanced matrix in which one manager has two equally accountable bosses. This is the structure that is very hard to make work. A different proposition is the arrangement in which, for example, a manager reports directly to the product division, with a dotted-line relationship to the country manager. This then becomes a more traditional global product division or area division structure, though the terms "latent matrix" or "unbalanced matrix" are also used.

This overview highlights a couple of important points. First, there is no perfect structure – each has its own drawbacks. For most global companies it is a question of choosing the least-bad structure and then figuring out how to mitigate its greatest weaknesses. A common approach, for example, is to use the global product division structure, but to beef up country management in places such as China or India that need a high level of political presence and local responsiveness.

Second, organization structure, like so many other aspects of business, is hostage to fads and fashions. The matrix has gone in and out of favor a couple of times and many companies have moved in pendulum-like fashion between an area division and a global product division structure. In part this is healthy, because business demands are continually changing and reorganizing is a useful way of correcting the problems of one structure (even if it creates new problems). But in part it is also dangerous because, costs aside, what works for one company may well not work in another.

Current trends

In looking at contemporary trends, we should note that many "new" ideas have in fact been around in some form for decades. So, rather than claiming that these are truly new structures, it is better to see them as issues that global companies are grappling with at present.

The network organization

It is a common misconception to talk about the network organization as an alternative to one of the four structures described earlier. In reality, the network organization is best seen as an informal overlay that cuts across whatever formal structure is chosen.

Volvo Cars, for example, describes itself as a network organization because it has strong project groups that cut across functions, as well as cross-country teams. However, there is still a formal chain of command that lies with product divisions (the car platforms).

The network organization is a good idea, because it gets away from the strict chains of command or "silos" that obstruct fast and informed decision making.

However, it is worth remembering that there have always been network organizations, to the extent that individual managers communicated with colleagues in other areas. What is new is the emergence of tools and systems designed to build such networks. Cross-functional teams, global business teams, dotted-line reporting, project groups, and so on are all networking structures. Underlying them are computer systems, and employee transfer and rotation policies, all of which are designed to make networking easier.

Internal market

Another alluring concept that has been debated and used for perhaps a decade is the internal market. Like the network organization, this is an anti-hierarchy concept. Large companies, it can be argued, suffer from bloated overheads, too little accountability, and a system of resource allocation that is more akin to Soviet-style central planning than free-market capitalism. The alternative is to "bring the market inside the

Global customers cut across traditional global product units as well as countries

company," which equates to making everything into a profit center.

Volvo, for example, took all of its support activities and put them together as a separate company, Celero. Rather than just acting as a group of lazy corporate staffers, Celero's employees suddenly became businesspeople, selling their services to Volvo in a competitive market. Some companies have applied the internal market concept in a broader sense. Using Silicon Valley as the model, they have tried to make capital for new ideas available in a more decentralized way and to encourage the free flow of employees throughout the company.

Again, the internal market is not really an alternative to one of the traditional organization structures, because there still need to be clear lines of accountability on which internal market relationships are based. Instead, it is either used as a way of making staff activities more efficient, or as a principle by which the informal organization should work (rather like the network).

Global customers

Global companies have always done business with customers that are themselves global, but it is only in the last decade that such customers have started to push for global purchasing. For example, Ericsson used to sell telecoms equipment country by country to major customers such as Cable & Wireless or Telefonica, but now these relationships are managed at the global level. Similarly, Electrolux negotiates the sale of commercial refrigerators to BP through a single global account.

In such industries as banking, computers, consulting, automotive engineering, and even retailing, global customers are now a key segment. The ramifications of this shift are enormous because global customers cut across both traditional global product units and countries. Potentially, they end up becoming another dimension to the matrix.

Given the problems we have already noted with matrix management, the preferred solution is typically to give "global account" ownership to someone from the customer's home country (for example, Ericsson's global account manager for Telefonica would be in Spain). He or she would still report to the local sales executive, but would have the job of co-ordinating sales to that customer across all countries – difficult to do, but with the right level of support and incentives not impossible.

The effect of global customers on organization structure has yet to be fully realized. Most global companies are designating global account managers but leaving the core structure intact. However, we can expect to see companies with dedicated customer-facing groups. It is common in professional services companies, for example, to organize by industry sector (because knowledge is so specific to the industry being served), so it is a relatively small step to break an industry group into a number of customer units. This approach is not without problems, but it is the ultimate in customer orientation and may better reflect the relative importance of country versus customer to the success of the business.

Conclusions

It should be apparent that there is no simple or entirely satisfactory way of organizing the global company. This article has highlighted some important and emerging issues, but has really just scratched the surface of a complex subject. At the risk of gross simplification, therefore, it is worth highlighting themes that have withstood the test of time.

1 *Simple is better.* The pure matrix, with equal stress on two lines of accountability, does not work. Most global companies have moved to a global product division structure whereby the assets associated with a given product or business are under a single line of command. Philips, for example, struggled with various forms of matrix structure for 20 years and it is only in the last few years that it has killed off strong national organizations in favor of global product divisions.

2 *Accountability without authority.* The corollary of a single dominant structure is that the other "latent" dimensions of the matrix have to be managed

through more informal processes. Global account managers, for example, have accountability for the profitability of sales to their customer base, but they have to get their job done through influence and argument, rather than through having direct authority. Country managers and project managers face a similar challenge.

3 *Strong but informal horizontal relationships.* Again, this follows from the single dominant structure. If the global company is going to be effective in reconciling conflicting pressures, the informal part of the organization has to work well. Knowledge management, for example, is really all about improving information flows between parts of the organization. A lesson from this field is that knowledge transfers cannot be forced, they can only be encouraged by a supportive computer system and organization culture.

4 *Country managers in developing markets.* Despite observations about the declining role of the country manager, in developing countries this is still a key role. Political connections are central, local market conditions are new and fast-changing, and products often have to be tailored more to local demands. All these things require a strong "king of the country", much as was seen in the developed world 20 years ago.

Further reading

Arnold, D., Birkinshaw, J. and Toulan, O. (2000) *Implementing Global Account Management in Multinational Corporations*, MSI Working Paper 00-103 and London Business School working paper 57/99.

Bartlett, C.A. and Ghoshal, S. (1990) "Matrix Management: Not a Structure, a Frame of Mind," *Harvard Business Review*, June.

Birkinshaw, J. (2000) *Entrepreneurship in the Global Firm*, London: Sage.

Strategy must lie at
the heart of alliances

Companies go into alliances for many reasons, but the results are often not what they expect. **Benjamin Gomes-Casseres** explains why.

Benjamin Gomes-Casseres is a professor at Brandeis University's Graduate School of International Economics and Finance. He can be contacted at ben@alliance.strategy.com

A decade ago, IBM and Apple launched a much-touted strategic alliance, including investments in joint ventures and research. Together, they would take on Intel and Microsoft. It didn't happen. Eight years later the alliance faded away, leaving unfulfilled hopes, frayed relationships, and wasted effort.

Other alliances formed at high levels, often blessed with the designation "strategic," have also failed to deliver. Analysts argue over what caused each link-up to fail. Some blame egos and clashing cultures, others cite business conflicts and ruthless competition. Yet these cases often share one factor: amid the hype, the alliance came to be seen as an end in itself, rather than as a means toward a broader goal. The failures teach one clear lesson: what matters is the strategy behind the deal, not the deal itself.

For the same reason, many of today's digital alliances will fail. In many quarters, the new economy race to "get big fast" has been reinterpreted as "get hitched fast." If companies cannot gain market share and strategic dominance rapidly, the argument goes, they must find partners. For dotcom business development managers, this means: sign as many deals as you can, as soon as you can. In doing so, they forget the saying, "Marry in haste, repent at leisure."

Companies that succeed with alliances put strategy first and deal-making second. For example, Sun Microsystems has leveraged its capabilities impressively through a multitude of alliances. Some alliances survived for a long time, others were short-lived; some were narrowly focussed and a few broader. Sun's partners included Fujitsu, Toshiba, Oracle, Netscape/AOL, and IBM. But none of these partners or individual alliances accounts for Sun's success. Rather, the way Sun integrated alliances into a coherent strategy and managed them over time allowed it to get the most from partnerships.

A coherent alliance strategy also lay behind Intel's rise. Intel made its breakthrough in the alliance with IBM to develop the PC in 1980. Plus, Intel used astute licensing to build its dominance. Its first generation of microprocessors was licensed to several allies; later generations were licensed to fewer companies; today, Intel is the sole producer of its high-end processors. Intel's alliances were steps on a ladder. The real goal was creating and dominating processor standards.

Alliance strategy

So, while companies announce "strategic alliances" daily, many lack "alliance strategies." The difference is more than semantic: an alliance lacking strategy is doomed. A coherent alliance strategy has four elements:

- a business strategy to shape the logic and design of alliances;
- a dynamic view to guide the management of each alliance;
- a portfolio approach to enable co-ordination among alliances;
- an internal infrastructure to maximize the value of collaboration.

At the right time and when managed well, alliances create tremendous value; at the wrong time and when managed poorly, they can be costly.

Underlying logic

In principle, most managers would agree that an alliance needs to be backed by business strategy. Signing up as many partners as possible is not a strategy – worse, it can sap the company of energy.

Ideally, strategy dictates why each partner and structure is better than any other option, what the company expects, how risks will be managed, and how the new alliance will be co-ordinated with others. Even knowing this, companies make alliances without a clear strategy. Why?

The reason lies partly in the tendency of the deal's champions to see the alliance itself as a goal. Often, the opportunity for an alliance arises suddenly – perhaps prompted by an inquiry, a competitor's move, or a chief executive's conversations with a counterpart. Before they know it, companies are "doing the deal" rather than determining what kind of deal is best. Time to think can seem a luxury, but it is precisely because of the tendency to focus on the transaction that it is essential to examine how the alliance fits the business strategy.

Alliances have many goals, depending on the strategy.

Being clear on how the alliance fits business strategy is also important for measuring its performance. The true value of any alliance is usually not evident from the narrow costs and revenues of the collaboration, even when the alliance is a stand-alone joint venture. Because the alliance is part of a broader strategy, its effect must be measured in terms of its contribution to that strategy. Thus, we must also account for the opportunity costs of options foreclosed and for the qualitative benefits the alliance brings to the company.

Take the case of Fuji Xerox. This venture between Xerox and Fuji Photo Film was created to help Xerox sell copiers in Japan. Over time, Xerox's strategy and Fuji Xerox's capabilities evolved so that the venture became a supplier of products to Xerox globally and a partner in developing technologies. The joint venture was profitable, grew in size and issued modest dividends to Xerox. But its true value lay in how it helped Xerox beat back Japanese competition in the 1980s, halt its previous decline, and launch initiatives worldwide. The alliance's role in corporate strategy is much bigger than the partnership itself.

A dynamic approach

The example of Fuji Xerox also shows the value of a dynamic approach to managing alliances. Just as the broader strategy is more important than the individual deal, so too the evolution of the relationship over time is more important than the initial deal.

Alliances, by their very nature, are open-ended and ever-changing. If all the terms between two companies can be specified and agreed at the outset, there is no need for an alliance; a contract will do. In that sense, many digital "partnerships" are not that at all, but simply agreements to exchange links and so on. A true alliance is an organizational structure that enables control over future decisions to be shared and governs continual negotiations – it is a recognition that the initial agreement is incomplete. That is why success in alliances depends so much on governance structures and on the relationship between companies, including personal relationships between managers.

This tendency of alliances to change over time is often misinterpreted as a weakness. Managers complain about the high "divorce rate" in alliances and academics conduct statistical studies of their "instability." This misses the point: the goal of an alliance is not its survival, but the success of the alliance strategy. Sometimes, strategy will call for using alliances as transitory mechanisms. At other times, the strategy may involve launching several alliances at once to see which ones are worthy of further investment and which should be terminated. Such a strategy is no different from companies hedging their bets or pursuing parallel projects to develop products. The flexibility of alliances is often a strength, not a weakness.

The early history of personal digital assistants (PDAs) offers an illustration. In the early 1990s, many computer and telecommunications companies formed alliances to develop and market these hand-held devices. By 1994, Apple sold the Newton; AT&T offered the EO; and Lotus and HP made the LX series. Less than a decade later, none of these PDAs was still in the market and most of the alliances had ended. Does this signify failure? I think not. The field these companies were entering was uncertain and fluid. The alliances allowed participants to conduct market experiments quickly and at relatively low cost. This was their underlying strategy.

Alliance portfolios

The PDA strategies also show the value of careful design and management of a portfolio of alliances. The PDAs were produced using components from several companies and selling through many channels, so the alliances could

reinforce each other. Again, the effectiveness of an alliance strategy depends on a strategy that transcends the individual deal.

Some types of companies recognize the importance of a portfolio of allies. Business units that use multiple components will depend on many supply alliances, and business units that sell in multiple markets will use several allies to reach different customers. Alliances among national airlines are examples of this. Similarly, a portfolio of alliances is useful when a critical mass of "sponsors" is key to market acceptance, such as in establishing software standards.

But being involved in multiple alliances is not sufficient; the company must also manage the portfolio as a whole. Two alliances of a company, with two different partners, may either complement each other or they may conflict. The same is true, in spades, of a portfolio of many alliances. A poorly designed and managed network can entangle the company and waste managers' time.

Good co-ordination, on the other hand, can save resources and diversify options for growth. How are companies facing the challenges? Pharmaceutical company Eli Lilly has an office of alliance management that helps identify alliance candidates, evaluate deals, and train managers new to the field. This should lead to the company having a higher proportion of successful alliances, compared with companies adopting a more informal approach.

Internal support

Eli Lilly's system is not only important for co-ordinating a portfolio of allies, but also for upgrading its ability to manage alliances. In case after case, it has become clear that the internal organization of a company is critical to successful partnerships. Without a supportive infrastructure, every alliance will fail, no matter how ingenious the external deals.

All too often, however, alliances are seen as outside "core" operations and therefore less deserving of resources. In fact, relying on someone else to implement a piece of your strategy may require more, not less, management effort. Although companies typically choose to relegate to allies those functions they cannot do, or have no time to develop internally, forging and managing the relationship demands resources. Companies may overlook this and fail to provide the resources required for success.

A good alliance strategy therefore starts at home. The company must define a business logic for its alliances, keep an eye on the future, and manage the group of partners well. Moreover, it must align its organization and invest resources in the strategy.

Companies that are doing this (such as Corning, Xerox, Hewlett-Packard, Oracle, and Sun) are frequently cited for their "alliance capability." The essence of this capability is that alliances are made part of the everyday functioning of the company. They are not special deals relegated to a group of alliance experts.

Build capability

An alliance strategy is thus more than a strategic alliance. Managers need to construct processes that root alliances in strategy and recognize that alliances will work for some things but not others. Next, they need a way to manage change. The history of alliances shows you will not get everything you wanted; but you may well get much you didn't expect. The key is to grasp change, not ignore it.

With these elements in place, the number of deals will grow and need managing. This requires prioritizing among alliances and creating an organization to optimize the portfolio. And the importance of a supportive internal infrastructure will also become evident. Suddenly, alliances will begin to place substantial demands on resources, not least the attention of senior managers.

Companies will not survive if they try to do everything themselves. But they will not be served well by a headlong rush into multiple deals. Only a real alliance strategy will give them a fighting chance.

Further reading

Doz, Y. and Hamel, G. (1998) *Alliance Advantage*, Cambridge, MA: Harvard Business School Press.

Gomes-Casseres, B. (1994) "Group versus Group: How Alliance Networks Compete," *Harvard Business Review*, July–August, 62–74.

Gomes-Casseres, B. (1996) *The Alliance Revolution: The New Shape of Business Rivalry*, Cambridge, MA: Harvard University Press.

Kanter, R.M. (1994) "Collaborative Advantage: the Art of Alliances," *Harvard Business Review*, July–August, 96–108.

Websites

www.alliancestrategy.com
www.allianceanalyzt.com
www.strategic-alliances.org

Bringing some
discipline to M&A mania

Phanish Puranam is a doctoral candidate in the management department at the Wharton School, University of Pennsylvania.

Harbir Singh is Edward H. Bowman Professor of Management and chair of the management department at the Wharton School, University of Pennsylvania.

Maurizio Zollo is assistant professor of strategy at Insead.

Mergers and acquisitions are as likely to fail as to succeed. **Phanish Puranam**, **Harbir Singh**, and **Maurizio Zollo** aim to improve the chances of success.

Mergers and acquisitions (M&A) are among the most dramatic and visible manifestations of strategy at the corporate level. With a single deal, the strategic course of the organizations involved can be altered permanently. Capital market reactions may create enormous changes in shareholder value and the careers of individual managers at all levels may be profoundly affected.

The importance of M&A in corporate strategy can be ascribed to a single important fact: they allow the company's portfolio of resources to be transformed very quickly. Acquirers can gain immediate access to technology, products, distribution channels, personnel, and desirable cost and market positions.

The M&A phenomenon shows no signs of slowing and has even embraced the high-technology sectors where it was formerly rare. However, a harsh reality underlies this surge in activity, whether it be in high- or low-technology industries: about half of these transactions fail. The results are the same, whether measured in terms of capital market reactions, financial results, or employee retention.

Yet, these results do not imply that companies should abandon M&A. Indeed, the success rates are not substantially different from those for internal (organic) development and other forms of external development such as partnering.

Further, there is considerable variation in success rates: some acquirers seem to show a systematic capability for generating value from transactions, while others seem to destroy value just as systematically.

What can we learn from this mixed record? This article raises a set of fundamental issues that need to be addressed by managers undertaking M&A activities. The discussion covers strategic and implementation issues. It concludes by suggesting how M&A can be made a successful business process for a company, delivering deal after valuable deal.

Strategic issues

The 1990s saw a shift by corporate strategists toward resource-based thinking. In this view, companies are seen as bundles of productive resources and capabilities. These bundles generate competitive advantage for companies when they are difficult to replicate and also difficult to separate and trade in markets. An implication of such resource-based thinking is that for an acquisition to make economic sense for the acquirer, there have to be unique sources of value creation in the deal that are specific to the combination of acquirer and potential target.

To illustrate, no competitive advantage will accrue through buying a company that is worth the same to all potential acquirers. The situation is similar to an auction and ensures that the winning bidder will pay at least as much as the target is worth to it, or to any other bidder, hence the transaction is like exchanging cash for an equivalent amount of cash. If, however, Acquirer A values the target (correctly) at a higher amount than other potential acquirers, A will pay less than it values the target for, as the price only rises to the valuation of the second-highest bidder.

Acquisitions are made for a variety of reasons: to realize economies of scale and scope; to access resources such as technology, products, and distribution channels; to build critical mass in growth industries; to remove excess capacity and consolidate a mature industry; or to change the rules of competition as deregulation and technological change trigger convergence across industries.

However, unless each transaction is assessed for the unique value-creation potential of the combination, it is unlikely to generate competitive advantage for the acquiring company. Operationally, this amounts to managers asking what the key resources of the target company are in each transaction and how they will generate value when combined with the resources of the acquirer.

The answers from this kind of analysis are sometimes startling. Take the example of Cisco Systems, which stunned analysts in 1999 when it paid $7bn for Cerent, a start-up with $50m in

Managers can get caught in bidding wars or **ignore warnings** that emerge during due diligence

sales and no profits. Yet, when Cisco announced $1bn sales revenues from Cerent's products a scant nine months later, it became clear that the price reflected Cisco's ability to extract value from the unique combination of its manufacturing and distribution resources and Cerent's technology. When screening targets that display this degree of fit, acquisitive companies such as Cisco and Symantec may examine as many as a hundred potential targets for every one they finally acquire.

After target selection, there are important strategic issues to be faced during the next stages of bidding and negotiation. Typically, managers face two kinds of problem. First, good strategic information on the quality of the target company's resources is seldom available. Second, there is a tendency among decision makers to persist with an acquisition, in spite of information that it may not be the best course of action. The former problem typically manifests itself as a difficulty in valuing the target; while the latter problem comes up when managers get caught in bidding wars, or ignore warnings that emerge during due diligence.

There are no panaceas for these problems, but some measures may alleviate them. For example, it is useful to think of a "negotiation range." This is the range of valuations for the target that has its lower limit equal to the book value of the target and the upper limit (reservation price) set a little below the best projection for post-acquisition value creation (Figure 1).

Important intermediate valuation points are listed here approximately by increasing value:

- the current market value of the target;
- valuations of comparable transactions;
- discounted cash flow (DCF) valuations with post-acquisition synergies;
- valuations including option value of the target.

An acquirer who is disciplined will not revise the

FIGURE 1 | Negotiation range

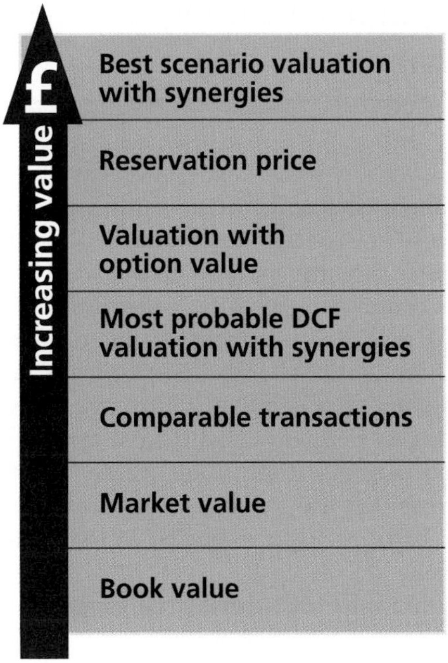

Increasing value f

| Best scenario valuation with synergies |
| Reservation price |
| Valuation with option value |
| Most probable DCF valuation with synergies |
| Comparable transactions |
| Market value |
| Book value |

negotiation range upward after negotiations have begun – after all, it is much more likely that information uncovered during negotiations will prove to be negative rather than positive.

Working out the negotiation range does two things. First, it drives home the fact that without accurate information on the quality of the target's resources, the valuation should be stated as a range, rather than an exact figure. Further, for each significant point in the negotiation range, there is a clear strategic rationale with some explicit assumptions. As negotiations on acquisition price proceed, it is easy to evaluate what assumptions are being challenged and in which direction. Second, the negotiation range tends to prevent managers persisting with the deal in the face of negative evidence. The upper bound represents a reservation price, at which a disciplined acquirer should walk away from the deal.

Implementation issues

Combining two distinct organizations with their respective structures, systems, and histories is a complex task, but it must be done if the strategy motivating the acquisition is to be implemented.

As stated earlier, resource-based thinking suggests that companies are bundles of productive resources. However, acquirers may not want to keep the whole bundle. The first task of acquisition implementation, therefore, is to decide which resources to retain and which to divest after the acquisition. Resource-based thinking suggests this can be difficult, because the resources that make up a company are closely tied to each other.

This can lead to unanticipated consequences. For instance, even if a target company is acquired primarily for its technical development team, separating it from the sales group can destroy a source of inputs that made the technical team valuable. Thus, knowing how to "deconstruct" the target company into organizational subunits and knowing what linkages to preserve are very important.

The second task is to "connect" resources in the target company with those in the acquiring company in a manner that generates the unique value that (should have) motivated the transaction. This includes decisions on the extent to which the target companies, or more precisely its organizational subunits, will retain their administrative identity after acquisition and the speed at which integration must take place.

What do these steps mean from the perspective of the company which is the target? Selective retention of resources amounts to corporate restructuring. Further, connecting resources in the two companies implies making changes in reporting relationships, monitoring, reward systems, and location.

In short, post-acquisition implementation by the acquirer invariably results in the target experiencing a great deal of change.

Organizational change can be stressful for employees and a source of demotivation. Indeed, "post-merger stress" is a recognized problem that may undermine the strategic logic behind the transaction. More importantly, change can damage the valuable resources that made the target company attractive in the first place.

Some resources, such as a good product design team, a skilled research team, a competent salesforce, or an efficient manufacturing unit, are valuable because they embody a group of people who have learned to work well together. These teams have "organizational routines" that work smoothly, time after time, to create productive outcomes. When personnel are lost, or the patterns of communication, reporting, and incentives are changed, these routines may be disrupted. Of course, not all valuable resources are based on organizational routines, but managers must discriminate between resources that are and those that are not.

Returning to the acquirer's perspective, the managerial task is to choose the resources to retain and connect them appropriately to the resources of the acquiring company. This has to be done in a way that minimizes the harmful consequences of change.

Solutions vary by context, but two examples illuminate approaches by acquirers in different sectors of the economy. NationsBank, before it merged with the Bank of America in 1998, had grown through a series of acquisitions. Nations-Bank created value in its acquisitions by replicating its own efficient systems and processes within the acquired organization. The resources it sought were location and customer relationships. Its acquisition "formula" was based on an established, routinized, and constantly honed post-acquisition integration process. The process was clearly and honestly described to the top management of the target company during negotiations and to the entire acquired organization on the day of the announcement.

Given its value creation strategy, Nations-Bank would invest considerable effort in planning the details of converting systems and processes, changes in reporting structures and incentive systems, and limiting redundancies. These changes would be implemented within weeks of announcement, so that each newly acquired unit became seamlessly integrated into a homogenous organizational framework.

Cisco Systems, another company that has grown through acquisitions, designs, makes, and sells telecommunications equipment such as the switches and routers that control the internet. Cisco creates value by combining the technological expertise of target companies with its own marketing, distribution, and manufacturing expertise.

The technical teams of **acquired companies** are often left unchanged

Like NationsBank, Cisco moves fast soon after the announcement and one of the first things it does is to ensure that the management information and communication infrastructure of the target company (including sales order processing, intranet, and telephones) is matched with its own. Like NationsBank, Cisco believes in early, honest, and clear communication to employees in the target company about their roles in the merged organization. But Cisco is buying resources that are based on highly tacit and rare technical knowledge, embedded in organizational routines.

To minimize disruption, the technical teams of acquired companies are often left unchanged in terms of composition, people they report to, and projects they work on. Usually, the technical and sales organizations of the target become a business unit within one of Cisco's lines of business. Thus, while Cisco aims to transform target company employees into "100 percent Cisco employees," it is careful not to change things that may disrupt the productive functioning of research and development teams.

These examples serve to illustrate the fact that careful thought is required in planning the implementation of the merger.

M&A as a process

Given the increased incidence of M&A, it is unlikely that a company will only ever make one acquisition. This is particularly true of companies whose strategy is built on growth through acquisition. What can such companies do to build and improve their acquisition management skills? Many successful acquirers treat M&A as a business process. This implies recognizing the sequence of activities that must take place in any given transaction and creating the organizational arrangements to ensure continuity and coordination across these tasks. The acquisition

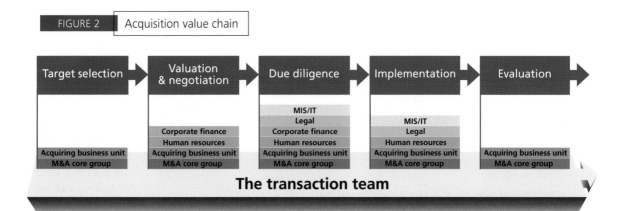

FIGURE 2 | Acquisition value chain

Target selection	Valuation & negotiation	Due diligence	Implementation	Evaluation
		MIS/IT		
		Legal	MIS/IT	
	Corporate finance	Corporate finance	Legal	
	Human resources	Human resources	Human resources	
Acquiring business unit	Acquiring business unit	Acquiring business unit	Acquiring business unit	Acquiring business unit
M&A core group	M&A core group	M&A core group	M&A core group	M&A core group

The transaction team

value chain is a useful device to prompt thinking about how M&A can be organized as a business process (Figure 2).

A trait of many acquisitive companies is to create a separate unit that specializes in managing acquisitions. The unit need not be large, but does require the presence of a core of dedicated personnel who develop acquisition management skills on many transactions. Such a group may also be involved in managing alliances and partnerships, which share some characteristics of the acquisition process, particularly in the selection and negotiation stages. Versions of this core M&A team exist in several active acquiring companies such as Cisco, Symantec, Intel, Hewlett, Packard, Sun Microsystems, and (formerly) at NationsBank.

In any given transaction, the transaction team comprises members of this core group and members from the part of the acquiring company that will house the acquired unit. In addition, experts from functions such as human resources, legal affairs, corporate finance, and information systems serve on this team for the phases of the acquisition that require their expertise.

Cisco and Symantec, for instance, have created "virtual" transaction teams of experts from

Key members of the **transaction team** will typically be party to every stage of the acquisition

various business functions. Such an innovation clearly makes sense in industries that suffer from chronic shortages of skilled personnel.

Key members of the transaction team, who come from the acquiring business unit and the M&A group, will typically be a party to every stage of the acquisition, beginning with target selection and ending with post-implementation evaluation. This ensures continuity and consistency at each stage, so pre-acquisition strategy is effectively implemented.

Having a core group that specializes in managing acquisitions allows tacit experience to accumulate within this team. However, research shows that a company can make the most of this experience if it invests in a process of "knowledge codification" – articulating the lessons learned from experience and setting them down in manuals to guide future transactions.

These "cookbook" manuals are valuable to future managers. However, the real value lies in the brainstorming and detailed analysis that take place after every transaction and precede codification. This generates a deeper understanding of the complex processes involved.

Conclusion

When a merger or acquisition fails, shareholder value is destroyed and society at large suffers if the productive resources in the target are destroyed or underused.

Managers can improve their prospects of success in the following ways:

1 Establishing a value range for the target that accounts for incomplete knowledge and guards against bias in making decisions.

2 Undertaking a transaction as a business process with defined stages.

3 Developing and retaining M&A expertise.

4 Being aware of the dangers in ignoring warning signs that emerge during negotiations.

5 Understanding when to walk away from a deal.

As understanding of the complexities of these processes increases, the success rates of mergers and acquisitions should rise.

Further reading

Collis, D.J. and Montgomery, C.A. (1995) "Competing on Resources: Strategy in the 1990s," *Harvard Business Review*, July–August, 118–28.

Haspeslagh, P.C. and Jamieson, D.B. (1991) *Managing Acquisitions*, New York: Free Press.

Zollo, M. (1999) "The Challenge of Learning to Integrate," *FT Mastering Strategy*, Dec 6.

The future looks fair
for electronic exchanges

Electronic exchanges have the power to transform supply chains, but **Eric Clemons** warns there are pitfalls.

Dr Eric K. Clemons is a professor of information strategy, systems, and economics at the Wharton School, University of Pennsylvania. He is a co-founder of Exchange Technology Corporation.

Business-to-business (B2B) markets are enormous, even if they are invisible to most consumers. Every item bought by a consumer represents a previous B2B transaction between the store and a wholesaler or manufacturer. Likewise, every sale by a manufacturer represents numerous purchases between the producer of the finished goods and a chain of upstream suppliers. The number and value of these transactions is a significant multiple of a country's gross national product. Optimistic entrepreneurs and venture capitalists have leapt in to support B2B transactions through electronic commerce. However, the recent collapse of B2B e-commerce share prices indicates that the market now understands that too few of the initial forays were based on solid business models or on understanding business needs.

To provide a valuable service at a profit, a business-to-business (B2B) venture must provide a structure that matches the needs of a market. For example, in an industry where there are many parties who differ in the valuation they place on a product, an exchange will be especially valuable. It allows participants to discover prices and allocates the product to the buyer willing to pay the highest price; this price discovery and the efficiency it engenders are among the most important benefits of an exchange.

Alternatively, an industry with few buyers and few sellers and where the buyer needs tightly scheduled delivery to maintain efficient production calls for a tightly coupled distribution system or channel between buyer and supplier. Just as important, an industry where production can be scheduled might support a tightly coupled channel, while an industry with unpredictable supply or demand may best be served by an exchange.

This article assesses structures for B2B e-commerce. It describes which are best operated as stand-alone businesses and which are best operated as service functions within existing businesses. Finally, it addresses the question of who is likely to profit from each structure.

Exchange structure

The most important characteristics of a structure for an e-commerce market are the number of buyers and sellers and the predictability of supply and demand. Predictable markets with few parties demand a different structure from markets with many participants and unpredictable supply and demand. Moreover, these differences suggest different strategies for developers of electronic markets hoping to operate at a profit.

Two exchanges provide good examples of different exchange structures: a global toy exchange and a global exchange for *sashimi*, Japanese raw fish dishes.

The *sashimi* exchange initially sounds trivial, yet the idea has real merit. Fresh *hamachi* (the high-grade tuna used to make *sashimi*) is valuable enough to justify rapid shipment to whichever regional buyer is willing to pay the highest price. Finding the highest bidder thus increases sellers' profits. This must happen quickly, to prevent loss of freshness and reduction in value. Since sellers represent the skippers of a large number of small fishing boats and buyers are fragmented and dispersed as well, bringing them together through an online global fish exchange benefits all parties.

Conversely, the idea of a toy exchange initially sounds clever. Sales of toys leading up to Christmas are enormous and toy sales are global in the sense that retailers are often western chain stores and producers are often Asian manufacturers.

However, there is a limited number of buyers for each toy market. US consumers frequently do not buy the same toys as British or French consumers, suggesting there are regional markets, rather than a single global market. Additionally, each year's bestsellers are different, making demand for toys time sensitive. Since demand changes, excess production for one season will generally be of little value in the next and thus will be liquidated at low prices; likewise, shortfalls in production cannot be rectified later, since

Christmas comes but once a year. After consideration, it is clear that toy distribution would see greater benefits from demand forecasting, production planning, and supply chain optimization rather than from an online toy exchange.

Alternative structures

Further study helps offer predictions about the ideal structure of markets for e-commerce to meet various forms of B2B demand. Structures available for e-commerce are:

- one-to-one: e-channel;
- one-to-many: e-market;
- many-to-many: e-exchange;
- parallel one-to-one: pseudo e-exchange.

One-to-one: e-channel

One-to-one e-channels are tightly coupled channels between a buyer and seller. This structure seeks to maximize co-ordination of production and consumption and to optimize channel performance. Supply should precisely meet demand and should match it precisely over time. There should be no excessive safety stocks or work-in-process inventory, nor should there be delays and shortfalls. Buyer and seller should co-ordinate their businesses like a well-choreographed ballet.

This structure has tended to emerge where there is a limited number of buyers (car makers, commercial airlines), a limited number of sellers (sheet steel suppliers, car makers), or both. E-channels are not generally stand-alone businesses, although they could be operated as such. More often they consist of inter-company communications systems, either bought from software vendors or developed from purpose-built linkages like those installed between Wal-Mart and its suppliers in the 1990s.

One-to-many: e-market

One-to-many e-markets allow a seller to serve numerous buyers, or a buyer to choose among numerous sellers, based largely on price. For example, insurance companies have learned to offer different prices based on each motorist's claims history, and credit-card issuers have learned to offer different prices to different consumers based on their expected finance charges and other contributions to profitability. In a similar way, airlines negotiate corporate travel packages with large customers and manufacturers have learned to offer different prices to buyers based on profits.

Once again, e-market systems are not generally stand-alone businesses, but rather are operated in-house by buyers or sellers with experience in managing customer relationships. Perhaps the best-known exceptions are in travel management, where companies such as travel group Rosenbluth International or American Express negotiate "relationship fares" between large corporate accounts and preferred carriers.

Many-to-many: e-exchange

The many-to-many e-exchange represents a market without a single control point and without explicit co-ordination. It does not rely upon planning, but allows the invisible hand of the market to substitute for explicit control. The market determines the price, by bidders with the best uses valuing the product the most and so bidding highest for it. The market allocates the product to the best uses and economic benefits will be maximized without explicit attempts to allocate supply, or even to determine what these best uses are.

This structure arises when there is a large number of buyers and sellers, when no single buyer or seller controls the market, and when unpredictability of supply or demand preclude scheduling production to achieve channel optimization. Moreover, this market structure is usually operated by a stand-alone provider who makes profits by bringing together a large, fragmented population of buyers and sellers.

Parallel one-to-one: pseudo e-exchange

The pseudo e-exchange is a set of tightly coupled channels, each of which provides a means for a buyer and a seller to co-ordinate production and consumption. Like the e-channel, it seeks to maximize co-ordination and to optimize channel performance. This structure benefits from the visible hand of explicit co-ordination. Again, supply should precisely meet demand, and should match it precisely over time, without excessive safety stocks or work-in-process inventory and without delivery delays or product shortfalls.

Unlike a true exchange, which seeks to maximize the effectiveness of the invisible hand in price discovery and allocation of scarce supply, this market is co-ordinated. Its principal benefits are that interaction, settlement, and clearing can be standardized, so buyers can share system development costs across an industry.

It emerges in two contexts: first, where a small set of buyers can use it to exercise control over a larger set of sellers, as in the automotive industry; second, in more concentrated markets, with a few large buyers dealing with a few large sellers. This second usage, which has been

---

Box 1 **A clear-cut case in the glass industry**

The glass industry provides an interesting illustration. Glass producers were initially enthusiastic about an exchange for selling excess glass. Previously they had produced larger batches than the customers' orders, given the high set-up cost, the risk of breakage, and the low cost of marginal extensions to production runs. Any excess production that was not sold could be ground down and reused.

Operators of a new exchange convinced producers that they could offer excess production through the exchange at prices that were low enough to attract customers and yet significantly higher than the value of recycling the glass. However, it did not take long for customers to realize that the product offered by the exchange was the same glass available through traditional ordering channels, but was being sold at an enormous discount.

Ultimately, glass producers came to dread customers figuring out that they could place an order, cancel it, and then use the exchange to buy the unsold "excess production" associated with their original order. This market called out for better supply chain management, not an exchange.

common in these early days of e-commerce, represents a mistake: a significant overestimation of the cost of the visible hand of explicit co-ordination, and thus a mistaken belief that an exchange will be more cost-effective than the existing channel structures. Here, optimistic entrepreneurs overestimate the distribution costs of current sales mechanisms and hope to command significant transaction fees by reducing the costs, which have already been controlled by investments in one-to-one e-channels.

The importance of alignment

It is crucial to match the structure of an e-commerce initiative with market needs. It is also crucial to understand the implications of an e-commerce market structure for the pricing and profitability of its participants. It is difficult to imagine a successful application of production management and supply chain optimization software for *sashimi*. Likewise, it is difficult to imagine a successful spot market for aircraft carriers.

However, while not all exchanges are good propositions, online exchanges can create opportunities. One new use of exchanges can be found in the emerging business of buying long-term contracts, selling short-term contracts, and profiting from the spread between long-term and short-term rates. For example, an exchange may have apartments that it leases for periods of several years and then subleases to people needing short-term lets. The same model underlies car rental and can be applied to areas where the internet can create a sufficiently large buyer population for expected demand to be predictable and constant.

The structure of a B2B e-commerce venture must be matched to its intended market and the needs of participants. Success also requires matching market structure and business function to value-creation and value-retention; someone has to operate the market at a profit for a successful business venture to result from a B2B e-commerce initiative.

Profitable e-channels

The value of an e-channel comes from optimizing interactions between buyers and sellers. This

Success requires matching **market structure** and business function to value-creation and retention

entails assuring that neither party has to keep excess safety stocks or work-in-progress inventory due to unpredictability in order flow; likewise, it assures that buyers' facilities are not idle due to late supplies and that suppliers are not idle due to unpredictable purchase orders. How can anyone make money out of this? For most suppliers, and for most large customers, the investment in channel optimization, like the past decade's investment in quality, will become a basic cost of doing business. A few companies will make money selling channel logistics and enterprise resource planning systems. Ultimately, however, e-channel optimization will be a strategic necessity. All buyers and sellers will deploy it and none will gain advantage from it. No systems vendor will have a monopoly share of the market.

Profitable e-markets

Customer relationship management (CRM) software allows companies to identify profitable accounts, provide the services they require, and do so at prices that are attractive to buyers and profitable for sellers. For many companies, CRM and relationship pricing will become a cost of doing business, just as supply chain management is in other industries. And, just as there are profitable opportunities for vendors of B2B supply chain systems, there are openings for CRM systems vendors. However, both supply chain systems and CRM systems will eventually become commodities – and less profitable for vendors.

A profitable e-exchange

The value of an e-exchange comes from bringing together the largest possible collection of buyers and sellers, facilitating price discovery, and assuring that goods are allocated to the buyer who can make the best possible use of the product. Exchange operators make money by charging some form of transaction fee, either a flat fee per transaction or a percentage of the transaction value.

Exchange operators will benefit from what in financial markets is called the "central market defense." That is, customers come to a market to make a transaction, as quickly as possible and with as little adverse affect on market prices as possible. In other words, buyers want to buy where there are sellers, so they can buy quickly and at a good price; likewise, sellers want to sell where there are buyers, for the same reason. The more participants a market attracts, the better it can serve these participants and the more participants will join. This suggests that first movers will enjoy some advantage and that it will enable them initially to charge higher prices, but because barriers to entry are low, profits will be limited. Experience from financial markets indicates that participants can readily tell when they are being overcharged for transaction services and that few things can destroy liquidity faster by driving it to an alternative trading venue.

A pseudo e-exchange

Pseudo exchanges have a value proposition, which is largely the same as that of supply chain management systems. They also offer economies of scale (Ford, GM, and Chrysler can invest in one system, not three) and standardization (suppliers can develop one interface, not three). However, it is important that operators can justify their development in terms of efficiency gains, rather than from using market power to restrain trade, intimidate suppliers, or in other unfair ways.

Conclusions

Supply chain optimization, sophisticated pricing strategies, and commercial exchanges will transform business interaction. Exchanges will allow hedging, risk management, and arbitrage, not only for commodity products (copper and aluminum) and near-commodity goods (spark plugs and pistons), but for capacity as well. Just as an energy futures contract is only a contract in the capability to perform certain classes of useful work, a stitching futures contract in clothing or a stamping futures contract in car making represents a contract for other forms of product transformation. Just as oil, sugar, and molasses have been arbitraged, so will aluminum and electricity.

E-commerce should primarily be about commerce, not the internet. An e-commerce venture is useful only if it attracts customers who will pay prices that cover all costs (including development costs and customer acquisition costs) and the owner of the venture retains a sufficient share of what they pay.

E-commerce offers opportunities, but there are many ways to fail:

- The structure may not match the needs of market participants or the characteristics of products.
- Exchange design may not capture liquidity from existing exchanges, or the fees demanded by operators may be too aggressive to capture or to retain business.
- An industry-wide exchange may appear to dominate suppliers or restrain trade, rather than focussing on efficiency gains for buyers and suppliers alike.

Further reading

Clemons, E. (2000) "Gauging the Power Play in the New Economy," *FT Mastering Risk*, June 13.
Sculley, A.B. and Woods, W.A. (2000) *B2B Exchanges*, Hamilton, Bermuda: ISI Publications.

Behavior is key to
web retailing strategy

Customer behavior should govern approaches to web retailing strategy, say **Eric Clemons** and **Michael Row**. They describe four types of relationship.

Eric K. Clemons is professor of information strategy, systems, and economics at the Wharton School, University of Pennsylvania.

Michael C. Row is a doctoral candidate in information strategy, systems, and economics at the Wharton School, University of Pennsylvania.

Consumer behavior should be the principal determinant of corporate e-commerce strategy. While technology will improve, consumer loyalty, for example, is likely to differ significantly between, say, online booksellers and providers of financial services. Two factors seem critical in predicting behavior and determining an appropriate e-commerce strategy.

First, what is the duration of the relationship between buyer and seller? That is, does the buyer have a relationship with a favorite seller, in which they come to learn about each other, or does the buyer search for a different electronic vendor for each interaction? The former suggests an opportunity for tuning offerings; the latter precludes stable relationships.

Second, what is the scope of goods and services linking buyer and seller? Does the consumer purchase a single good or service, or a bundle of related goods and services? The former suggests the consumer searches for the provider of the best individual goods and services, while the latter suggests a search for the best provider of a collection of goods and services.

Combining these indicates that different companies, in different industries, will find themselves in one or more of four competitive landscapes.

Consumers buying products that can be described as *opportunistic spot* purchases exhibit no loyalty: each purchase may be from a different vendor and there is no one-stop shopping. They may buy a ticket from British Airways one day and United the next, and book their hotels separately.

Opportunistic store markets occur when consumers exhibit no loyalty or relationship continuity to brands or stores. Unlike the spot market, however, they do use intermediaries to construct bundles of goods. They may shop at Sainsbury one day and Tesco another; they may use Amazon.com one day and Buy.com another.

Consumers buying in categories that may be described as *loyal links* exhibit continuity when choosing vendors and service providers, but have no desire to have bundles prepared for them. They may never leave home without their American Express cards, but see no reason for their card issuer to be their insurance provider or financial planner.

Finally, consumers buying in categories that may be described as *loyal chains* will have preferred providers. Additionally, they will count on these providers for a range of tightly coupled offerings. They may work with a financial consultant at Merrill Lynch who helps pick stocks, reminds them to draft a will and arranges guardians for their children, helps find a lawyer, and reviews their insurance. The integrated service is so effective they seldom consider switching providers or taking the time to provide these things for themselves.

The structure of these four markets is illustrated in Figure 1.

Each of these environments has a different competitive feel, requires a different strategy and use of different assets. This is as true in the physical world, where companies understand it pretty well, as it is in the dotcom world, where companies are struggling to develop profitable strategies.

Note that no e-commerce company occupies just one quadrant. There are, for instance, loyal link customers, and companies may pursue them with loyal link strategies, but in reality some customers may use a website for spot purchases and others may show great loyalty. The challenge for companies is to guide the consumer to the behavior matching the company's strategy; where this is not possible, companies should match the strategy to the customer's behavior. The approach given here may help managers discover the forces that determine their best strategy.

Opportunistic spot

Competition in opportunistic spot markets is based on price, since there is little loyalty to influence consumers' decisions. This brutal competition is exacerbated by nearly perfect web-based information. Thus, for standardized products such the latest *Harry Potter*, we observe both Amazon.com and BN.com selling at cost price. Where possible, companies try to soften competition by creating quality differences and ensuring consumers are aware of them. However, this branding must be based on real differences, since with nearly perfect information it is difficult to deceive consumers. There is a limited role for intermediaries. They may reduce risk in conducting transactions, but in most instances, consumers will buy from a set of trusted, well-known manufacturers and service providers.

The internet will be used for supply chain management and logistics to ensure the lowest cost structure and the lowest prices. It will also support access to information on consumers, both current and potential new accounts, to allow the most accurate setting of prices where differential pricing is required. That means that no applicant for insurance can be undercharged based on inaccurate risk assessment and no applicant for a credit card can be given too good a deal. In a market where no one can be overcharged without losing the account, there is little margin for error and little opportunity to recover

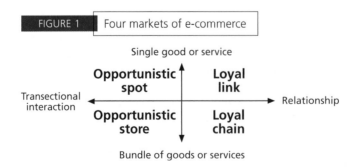

FIGURE 1 | Four markets of e-commerce

Single good or service

Opportunistic spot — Loyal link

Transectional interaction ←————————→ Relationship

Opportunistic store — Loyal chain

Bundle of goods or services

from undercharging anyone. The ability to predict the profitability of a new customer, and so to determine a price to offer, is called predictive pricing.

It is essential to recognize consumers exhibiting opportunistic spot market behavior and to develop an appropriate marketing and pricing strategy. For example, in markets that exhibit this behavior, buying market share is unwise since it can be acquired only temporarily; when prices are raised to cover losses, customers will flee. Similarly, a policy of offering selected items below cost as loss leaders to attract traffic will be unwise, because consumers may easily purchase loss leaders from one site and the rest of their items elsewhere. Only time will tell whether the market for books, CDs, or DVDs exhibits this behavior, so it is too early to assess the validity of Amazon.com's customer acquisition strategy or the promotional items of other web retailers.

Opportunistic store

In the absence of consumer loyalty, competition in opportunistic store markets again is based on price; however, it is the pricing of bundles rather than individual items that attracts consumers. Unlike spot markets, there are opportunities for intermediaries to add value, through logistical savings (shipping a box of books), or through assembly or integration (selling a package tour or designing a digital imaging platform where camera, printer, and computer work together).

In this scenario, intermediaries enjoy power over manufacturers because consumers select bundles with little attention to components. Thus, when filling an order for paper towels, a grocer will use the product with the highest margins. This pursuit of margins, in the absence of brand loyalty from customers, shifts economic power to intermediaries.

Manufacturers will attempt to use the web for branding, to create consumer awareness of product differences, and to weaken intermediaries' power. While it is dangerous to antagonize the existing channel in the opportunistic store scenario by trying to sell directly, branding offers manufacturers the ability to counter some of the power of intermediaries. As in the spot markets,

manufacturers will also use the internet to improve efficiency. Intermediaries will use the internet to create branding for their web stores, so weakening price competition. They will use customer information, as manufacturers did in spot markets, for predictive pricing.

As in spot markets, no consumer can consistently be overcharged, so it is difficult to recover from undercharging anyone. While loss leaders can work in these markets, since a customer may fill a basket or obtain a bundle of services, there is little loyalty to assure repeat business; thus, as in spot markets, buying market share is risky, since there is no assurance that initial losses can be recouped by overcharging for later purchases.

Of course, there may be reasons to buy share in a "scale-intensive" industry where volume is needed to bring down unit costs. Indeed, some aspects of online retailing, such as grocery shopping, may be extremely scale intensive, which could initially appear to justify buying share. However, without customer loyalty, the danger is that capital will be spent more on training users to accept online shopping and less on training users to accept your online shop.

Loyal link

Competition in loyal link markets is based on retaining the best customers through a careful blend of service and pricing. For the customer, relationship value and pricing improve over time. For example, anecdotal evidence suggests that online PC seller Dell has succeeded in creating loyal link behavior in customers, many of whom have bought several generations of computer from Dell.

In fact, no incumbent should ever lose desirable business to an attacker. If a less well-informed competitor were to attempt to persuade a loyal customer to transfer his or her business, the current supplier could decide whether or not to match the new offer. If the current supplier, with its detailed knowledge, were to choose not to match the new offer, the odds are that the new supplier is making an offer that is too low. Successful attempts to get customers to switch in loyal link markets probably represent pricing mistakes by the attacker. Relationship pricing and value work to soften pure price competition in loyal link markets.

Buying market share will work under certain conditions, since it is possible to learn enough to price effectively. However, buying market share is ineffective without loyalty, as online brokerage firms are discovering; so, it is critical to assess whether the company is operating in an opportunistic spot or loyal link market.

Using loss leaders in a link market will be unrewarding; offering online banking below cost to gain credit-card business is unlikely to succeed in a link market, where customers will pick the best hotel and the best air service, or the best online banking and the best credit offers, independently.

Systems will be used for branding and attracting customers and to support relationship pricing and relationship service to keep the best accounts. These markets may appear to have only a limited role for intermediaries; however, intermediaries enjoy an advantage in controlling customer information and may end up owning customer relationships.

Loyal chain

Competition in loyal chain markets, as in loyal link markets, is based on attracting and retaining the best customers and, as in loyal link, relationship value and relationship pricing improve over time. However, in chain markets, which are composed of a tightly coupled set of links, pricing to individual customers and the value they receive are determined by a bundle of goods and services.

Taking the earlier example of the digital imaging platform, it may not be necessary to replace all components when upgrading. However, if buying a higher-resolution camera and a faster laptop, it is helpful to know if the new computer and the old printer are compatible, otherwise the customer may experience an unpleasant surprise if picking and choosing components in a spot or link fashion. If the previous chain supplier is used to update the components, unpleasant surprises are likely to be avoided, since its vendor can be relied upon to provide components that are compatible with those bought before. Evidence suggests Amazon has succeeded in

---

> This shift in online power greatly increases the importance of **branding** for manufacturers

---

encouraging a degree of loyal chain behavior from its best customers, who value the book recommendations made to repeat buyers.

Loyal chain markets represent a power shift from producers to intermediaries. Online intermediaries can reconfigure the virtual store to show loyal purchasers the brands they wish to see; customers without a preference can be shown brands that earn the highest margins. Indeed, it is a small step from this relationship-based presentation to demanding rebates from manufacturers to ensure that their offerings will be shown to customers with no brand preference. While physical stores charge a fee for preferred locations such as displays near checkouts, they cannot reconfigure the store for each customer.

This shift in online power greatly increases the importance of branding for manufacturers, because a powerful brand is the best counter to pressure from retailers. It also suggests that, to the extent permitted by legislators, manufacturers should form consortia for web retailing. This would avoid loss of control to retailers, with significant information advantage. However, a broad consortium is needed since online markets reward scope and breadth.

Intermediaries may effectively buy market share through pricing low, enabling them to pursue informed relationship pricing over time. Likewise, they may use loss leaders to increase traffic through their website, selling other items to consumers interested in a complete bundle.

Systems play many roles in chain markets. Intermediaries will use them for branding, to attract customers, and for informed relationship pricing and service. Likewise, manufacturers will use the internet for branding, so limiting price pressure from online retailers. However, efficient markets still place significant price pressure on retailers, assuring the role of systems for logistics and other forms of cost control. Likewise, manufacturers and service providers will use the web for their own cost control.

Conclusions

Three observations are true across all four competitive landscapes:

- Only differences between brands, and consumer awareness of them, can blunt pure price competition in an efficient market.
- Cost control is important: efficient access to information makes it almost impossible to overcharge.
- As online information makes markets more efficient, predictive pricing will be used in spot and store markets, and relationship pricing in link and chain markets. Pricing strategies will be limited by adverse publicity that companies receive from charging different prices for the same goods.

Other conclusions follow from these:

- The role of buying market share will vary. In opportunistic markets, buyers will leave when you raise prices.
- Similarly, the role of loss leaders will vary. In spot and link markets, consumers will pick off loss leaders and do the rest of their shopping elsewhere. Once customer traffic has been acquired, there is a chance to sell extra items.

Copyright © Eric Clemons and Michael Row 2001

Further reading

Clemons, E.K. (1999) "When Should You Bypass the Middleman?," *FT Mastering Information Management*, February 22.

Schwartz, P. (1991) *The Art of the Long View*, New York: Doubleday.

The challenge of the
web-enabled business

Peter J. Brews is a
professor of management
at the Kenan-Flagler
Business School, University
of North Carolina at
Chapel Hill.

Using the internet and building intranets is not enough, says
Peter Brews. The best managers will use the web to
change the nature of their companies

Cisco Systems, the network equipment company, faced crisis in 1994. Explosive external growth and internal expansion had caused its systems to fail, almost bringing the company to a standstill. Senior managers feared that, unless the organization were redesigned to allow operations to be scaled up or down, the company's advance might end early and abruptly.

The answer was found in the network technology the company had pioneered. Using this technology, it created an internet-centered business model that increased efficiency, enhanced service capabilities, and empowered employees, while simultaneously improving response time and increasing customer satisfaction.

At the same time, Mexican cement company Cemex was undergoing a similar experience. Light years away from Silicon Valley and the pressures of the new economy, Cemex was using similar strategies to transform the business of cement and concrete in a way that continues to challenge competitors.

This article outlines how companies can become internet generation companies, by describing how Cisco and Cemex used network technologies to reorganize their business activities. As they discovered, the model of industrial organization established over the past century is fast becoming obsolete.

A superior model that organizes work around deeply networked communities is emerging, and the race is on to convert existing business operations to these more efficient, web-based infrastructures.

Internet generation companies

Managers of internet generation companies (IGCs) recognize the transforming and organizing potential of the internet, and employ network

The race is on to convert business operations to more efficient, **web-based** infrastructures

technology to connect everyone involved in the supply and purchase of their products or services. They view the internet as more than an electronic brochure through which customers order, or a medium merely permitting employees to communicate via e-mail. For them, it is the most important integrating device of the company and no facet of business is excluded.

Cisco: internet networking

At the core of Cisco's networking strategy are three portals: connection online, supplier system, and employee connection. Each portal provides interactive access to its users anywhere, at any time. In the case of online connection, it does so in 14 languages. As a publicly accessible extranet, it connects customers (existing or potential), potential employees, partners and resellers, and investors or those seeking general information. The supplier system is a password-protected intranet that connects Cisco, its suppliers, partners, and customers in a virtual supply chain.

Finally, the employee connection links all staff, enabling work to be done across the web. Executive information and decision support systems also operate through the employee connection. Box 1 shows some of the activities that are performed over the internet at Cisco.

The use of internet technologies lends Cisco several important advantages. Over 85 percent of orders are placed online without employee involvement. Suppliers and partners receive orders when they are placed. Customers track their orders online. Many lower-value-added activities required to install and maintain products have been outsourced.

More than 80 percent of service inquiries are handled electronically, many through web pages devoted to frequently asked questions. These are supported by artificial intelligence software that guides users to the information they seek. Customers provide electronic feedback on service

quality, which is tied back to business unit performance levels and employee remuneration. Customer satisfaction levels are repeatedly polled and monitored, automatically.

On their first day at Cisco, employees complete orientation, benefits selection, stock option plan registration, and other employment requirements online. No human resource staff are involved. Benefits changes are carried out in the same way. Other activities managed online include expense claims and distance learning. Cisco is paperless, with all internal information stored on servers, accessible on the web. Financial records are online and books close overnight. Cisco's 33,000 employees require the attention of only one human internal auditor – software does the rest.

By 1997, Cisco reported that its network structure had increased the speed and accuracy of orders, shipping, and deployment, and had dramatically increased supply chain efficiency. Selling and administrative costs also fell significantly. Further, while sales quadrupled, call center staff grew by only 10 percent and customer satisfaction increased from 3.4 to 4.2 on a five-point scale. Estimated savings of $1.5bn over three years were cited in late 1999.

Cemex: high-tech cement

Established in 1906, Mexican cement manufacturer Cemex's transition began in 1985. The new chief executive Lorenzo Zambrano began by building a telecommunications infrastructure to connect Cemex's plants. With fewer than 20 PCs, an unreliable state telephone service, and postal delays, Zambrano was unable to get the facts from plant managers.

So, the company bought satellite capacity over Mexico and a center was established in Texas to permit toll-free calls to the headquarters in Monterrey. Later, Mexican operations were connected to other parts of Latin America, and fiber-optic lines and microwave networks connected operations in Europe and the US. Short-wave radios linked plants in Venezuela. In less than 10 years and for under $200m, a network of 300 servers, 7,000 PCs and 80 workstations was built.

With connectivity established, Cemex turned to office and factory automation. A customized

Box 1 **Internet-enabled activities at Cisco**

Employee community

- Training and skills development
- Job postings and recruitment
- Development plans
- Performance reviews and pay
- Travel requests and planning
- Product training and education
- Expense claims
- Benefits selection and changes

Customer community

- Ordering
- Delivery tracking
- Product and service support
- Product and service-user training
- Satisfaction surveys and feedback
- Customized new product and services marketing

Management community

- Compilation, modification, and review of budgets
- Business planning and strategy development
- Financial, management accounting, reporting, review, and analysis
- Capital budgetting requests, discussion, and approval
- Sales and revenues forecasting

Supplier and partner community

- Demand scheduling and order placement
- Product and service change processes
- Product manufacturing status reports
- Service delivery and status reports
- Product or service delivery and installation information
- Education and training
- Centralized buying
- Supplies ordering from external vendors

system was built to feed an executive information system and the company's intranet. Zambrano no longer relies on employees for data. Instead, he logs on to check company-wide sales for the previous day, or to review the chemical composition of clinker in a kiln in Venezuela.

In the company's flagship Tepeaca plant, quality control is automated: samples flow automatically into a laboratory where clinker paste is dried into wafers and checked by laser. The plant is wired with sensors and process control computers, so operators can run close to capacity and still improve efficiency. Operating margins are double the industry average.

Cemex then used networks to drive innovation. In the company's second major business (the supply of ready-mix concrete) margins are high, but business difficult. Concrete must be poured within 90 minutes of loading to avoid spoiling. In Mexican cities, traffic congestion,

unexpected roadworks, and weather make deliveries a nightmare. Yet, by analyzing the volatile nature of orders and deliveries, the company was able to develop a system based on chaos theory that predicted concrete order rates by day, hour, and location. Fleets of trucks were equipped with dashboard computers and satellite global positioning systems to relay pouring status and location. The closest loaded trucks filled orders immediately.

Within six months, 98 percent of deliveries made in the congested Guadalajara test market arrived within 10 minutes of the promised time, prompting an on-time guarantee and a 5 percent rebate on orders more than 20 minutes late. Maintenance and fuel costs plummetted, truck deliveries rose from 4 to 10 a day, and loading was more uniformly distributed across plants. Irate customers no longer clog Cemex telephones, freeing people up for calls from customers.

Build bandwidth

How do other companies achieve similar gains? A company's ability to network is founded on the bandwidth connecting all its stakeholders – in other words, the network's ability to transfer information quickly.

First, hardware and software standards must be established. Servers and their operating systems must be specified, and database software, a management platform, and desktop office suite software chosen. For example, Cisco, Nortel, or Lucent might supply the network's basic plumbing; Hewlett-Packard, Sun Microsystems, IBM, or Dell provide servers; Oracle offers database management software; and Unix, Linux, and Windows NT are the main choices for server operating systems.

When internet-enabling a company, stakeholders under the company's direct control or those within easy reach are generally the first to be connected. Intranets are set up to connect employees and extranets are built to advertise products or services. Though these represent an important first step, the full potential of network technologies is only reached when applications move from passive information transmission and electronic brochures to interactive networks that empower communities to transact online.

Suppliers and strategic partners must also be included, but incorporating them presents difficult trade-offs. Supply chain integration often requires the company, its suppliers, and partners to adopt the same standards and protocols. Since confidential data on costs and operations are often shared, trust is essential.

Further, where suppliers or partners lack the resources or expertise to implement the changes quickly, a difficult question arises: should support be provided, or should suppliers be forced to rely solely on their own resources? And since building such complex relationships takes considerable time and effort, partners and suppliers must be carefully chosen: fewer, but deeper, strategic partnerships are likely.

Getting customers to migrate to internet-based infrastructures may present similar challenges. Many remain untouched by the internet. A company might choose to do business only with internet-proficient customers, or to maintain the old infrastructure while guiding customers toward the new ways of working: it might combine bricks-and-mortar shops with online sales. An intermediate strategy is also feasible: providing access points in traditional outlets for customers unable to access the internet elsewhere. As internet use expands, the defection to internet infrastructures will grow. Those with dual infrastructures remain exposed to the aggressive pricing of new entrants unencumbered by the costs of running parallel systems.

Industries and customers are thus not adopting network technologies uniformly or evenly and, though impressive, Cisco's network was built in a very favorable environment. The company's core business is network equipment and the industry is steeped in networking. Neither Cisco nor its partners existed in 1980, thus escaping the legacies of earlier business structures.

Web-enable operations

After building bandwidth, the next step is to web-enable existing operations. Activities and processes in every domain of business can be automated and web-enabled. Many processes and activities done by people will be committed to the web over the next few years.

A key early decision is determining which processes and activities are to be committed to standard solutions. For example, document imaging, service logistics, and call center software can all be standardized. This reduces complexity, cost, and support needs, while enhancing scalability. However, while the overall network and some applications are amenable to standard solutions, others require customized software to handle the complexity involved. Software development requires "suits" and "nerds" to communicate.

In these teams, business experts who understand fully the activity being automated specify the range and variety of combinations likely to be confronted, while IT specialists add the technical expertise to write and test programs.

This partnership between business and tech-

People will do what software cannot do: **create innovations** that transform the market

nology extends to the deployment of resources. While part of the budget should be centralized to provide the overall network architecture and infrastructure, business units and functions should be able to set priorities and budgets for their respective domains. This ensures that the overall (centralized) infrastructure remains of the highest quality with minimum redundancy and complexity, while business units determine and fund their specific (decentralized) needs. Intra-departmental competition for resources is also avoided. Further, business units and functions will devote more attention and resources to projects they conceive and implement.

At Cisco, IT spending by business unit and functional areas exceeds the centralized budget, and most IT staff develop applications for business functions or lines of business. Users set priorities and provide the money and business expertise, while the IT department hires technical staff and advises on each application.

In addition to substantial budgets and IT management, web-enabling requires sophisticated project management. Once the decision to convert a particular process is taken, a project plan must be developed. First, the existing process and its current operating costs must be established. Then, a decision regarding standardized versus customized software must be taken, and the business and IT resources required to achieve the conversion must be determined. Third, the savings expected from moving the process online must be estimated and compared with the projected conversion costs.

Finally, if the go-ahead is given, ways to measure the project's progress must be specified. Only under such conditions is web-enabling likely to succeed, activity by activity and process by process.

Once a process is web-enabled, maintenance and enhancement are required. At Cisco, a specific owner maintains and updates every web page. Most applications only remain viable for 18–24 months, so only quickly scalable applications are adopted. Moreover, automation is not a one-off event because the depth and reach of networked structures are not static after initial development. As computing power and bandwidth expand, so do the algorithms and structures that use them, page by page, layer by layer, and link by link.

Competing by networking

Once networking bandwidth is established and existing operations have been web-enabled, the third step to IGC status can be taken: employing network infrastructure to change the nature of competition. Using advanced software and network technologies, Cemex transformed operations in its ready-mix concrete business from a random delivery process to a complex logistics business. Competitors now need to match an infrastructure that controls trucks in citywide fleets by satellite.

Caterpillar is pursuing a similar strategy in the earth-moving equipment market. It is vital in this business to get spare parts quickly to stranded machines. Caterpillar possesses an efficient parts distribution capability, operated by an extensive intranet that links the company, factories, partners, dealers, distribution centers, customers, and mechanics worldwide. Existing operations are web-enabled as much as possible.

How will Caterpillar make the step to the third level? It is developing technology that automates the monitoring and replacement of spare parts. Sensors on its machines will signal the company via satellite when a component begins to fail, setting off a search for the nearest replacement part. At the same time, the machine's work schedule will be consulted to determine the best time for repairs before failure occurs.

Once the vehicle is operational, Caterpillar might offer guarantees against further failure. It thus transforms its competitive market from the manufacture of machines that occasionally break down and are speedily repaired, to the provision of high-value risk-management services, based on a sophisticated capability and delivered through an intranet.

Conclusion

To make the transition to the internet generation, a company must build bandwidth, then automate and web-enable existing operations. Finally, the freed-up people will do only what software cannot do: create innovations that transform the market in a way competitors cannot replicate and customers value. To prevent copying and so enhance sustainability, the innovation is embedded in the networked infrastructure.

Over the next decade, much of the business and operations infrastructure of the industrial world will be web-enabled. What will IGCs look like? They will not be the rigid hierarchies of industrial capitalism that pay fixed salaries for repetitive, mechanistic work. They will be flexible networks of entrepreneurial capitalism that unite communities around beneficial and automated productivity exchanges.

Readers wishing to participate in research that benchmarks the networking capability of their companies should e-mail Dr Brews at lyris@listserv.unc.edu, typing only "subscribe brewsresearch" in the message.

Further reading

Hartman, A.R., Sifonis, J. and Kador, J. (2000) *Net Ready: Strategies for Success in the E-conomy*, Maidenhead: McGraw-Hill.

Tapscott, D., Ticoll, D. and Lowy, A. (2000) *Digital Capital: Harnessing the Power of Business Webs*, Boston, MA: Harvard Business School Press.

Patel, K. and McCarthy, M.P. (2000) *Digital Transformation: The Essentials of e-Business Leadership*, Maidenhead: McGraw-Hill.

IT strategy in
the new economy

Michael J. Earl is a
professor of information
management at London
Business School.

Bringing technology strategy into line with business strategy was the challenge of the past decades, but now, says **Michael Earl**, the aim is to integrate internet thinking.

The proposition that information technology (IT) strategy should be aligned with business strategy has been a core theme of the past 20 years. In many ways, this was difficult to refute: investments should support real needs and the business should drive IT rather than the other way round. Application development priorities could be resolved more easily by applying a test of strategic fit. Perhaps most importantly of all, it became evident as companies began to depend on IT that a business strategy without a matching IT strategy was no strategy at all. So general managers as much as IT executives recognized the appeal and wisdom of "strategic alignment."

Unfortunately, there were problems. These included a lack of coherent or agreed business strategy in the first place, or a strategy that was forever changing, or a strategy-making process that was more emergent than structured. Even when a business strategy was settled, it was often difficult to interpret what it meant in terms of technology. Then, of course, there were implementation challenges. Alignment promised more then than it delivered.

From output to input

In the new economy, we can see that alignment is an antiquated concept. Quite simply, IT affects business strategy. It is an input to business strategy as well as an output. The internet, mobile communications, and future media present both threats and opportunities. So, business strategy that ignores how technology is changing markets, competition, and processes is a process for the old economy, not the new economy. This is what "e-everything" is about. A revised view of alignment is that it has to answer two questions: how does IT change business strategy and what IT investments does business strategy demand?

To be fair, these questions have been asked before, in particular when another technology arrived. We can call them the alignment question and the opportunity question. The opportunity question was asked infrequently and was posed haphazardly through local initiatives in companies. More crucially, it rarely asked what opportunities there were for creating new businesses (or losing old ones).

E-business is changing this. In particular, the appointment of directors of e-commerce and the formulation of e-commerce strategies recognize that IT is changing the ways companies do business. Indeed, in the past year, some boards have been asking a question not asked for a while: "What business are we in?" Then, as opportunities are identified and threats recognized, they ask a supplementary question: "Are we sure?" Formulating an e-business strategy recognizes that IT is an input as well as an output. So we are shifting from "alignment," with occasional opportunity, to "integration," where business strategy and IT strategy are independent and overlapping.

A warning here is that some companies still don't "get it," even if they are working on an e-business strategy. In 2000 I reviewed business strategy for a well-known company. It was a classic turnaround strategy that was full of bold recommendations – until it came to the appendix. This was a note on the e-commerce strategy; it hardly recognized the threats and opportunities of e-commerce. In this company, e-commerce was being treated as an opportunity rather than part of integration.

Clearly, just like IT itself, e-business cannot be treated and managed as an appendix. E-business is business and this is why companies who do "get it" see that IT strategy and business strategy are, in many ways, the same. We might call it an "information business strategy."

Toward a method

Companies often need a structure for developing strategy. One way to think is in terms of four tasks or elements that make up "information business strategy making": futurizing, assets, stimulants, and threats.

This "Fast" methodology is entirely inductive, but provides a way of addressing strategy-making in the new economy. The first element helps to confront the future.

Futurizing

Some companies, such as Swedish financial group Skandia, have created special teams to question what the future might bring. They often suggest identifying questions or highlighting important trends or significant uncertainties.

More perceptive chief executives realize, however, that this is not just raising an alarm about technology changing everything. It is about asking what is changing, threatening, or opportunity-rich at the intersection of new technologies and shifts in the business environment. The PEST (political, economic, social, technological) tool for environmental analysis applies in thinking about futures, but more thorough scenarios are likely to be where these variables interact.

So, some companies are constructing visions, stories, pictures, and dramas of what businesses might look like or what businesses could be created. This is the world of brainstorming, storyboards, and visions; the outputs can be good questions to ask, trends to watch, uncertainties to explore, experiments to begin, or "must do" ideas to develop.

The main points about "futurizing," as Skandia calls it, are explicitly to suggest that the future may not be an extrapolation of the past, that opportunities co-exist with threats, that uncertainty is inevitable, and that ignoring the future is more risky than trying to create it.

Assets

The second leg is to think of what competencies, capabilities, or assets might yield opportunities. I prefer to call this set "assets" because:

- they are potential sources of value creation;
- it suggests they should not be underestimated or left unexploited;
- often they are hidden until you think where potential might be realized through e-commerce.

For example, if your company has world-class fulfilment processes, then moving into e-commerce not only builds on this strength, but might also make this capability evident to the world. In other words, existing capabilities may have even more potential for value creation in the new economy. Jack Welch at General Electric has said that the company's achievements in its Six Sigma quality processes are now really paying off in e-business, where cost, speed, reliability, and quality matter.

As an example of underestimated assets, one conglomerate realized it had several partnership opportunities and, importantly, information threads between its businesses that might allow it to restructure part of the logistics industry. Likewise, many information-rich organizations have content that is valuable to traditional and emerging businesses.

Hidden assets can become evident in many ways. For example, an engineering company realized it had a valuable asset in its parts database when a business-to-business electronic market-maker approached it about building a business-to-business exchange. The database had taken 40 years to build and was now seen as an asset to protect as well as to exploit. In other words, when you re-examine a business as an information business or rethink it as a new-economy business, you may discover hidden assets.

Stimulants

The third element is suggested by companies that are trying to encourage entrepreneurial behavior. These efforts can be thought of as "stimulants."

We see organizations sprouting internal venture capital funds, incubator units, and e-business divisions. We see "white space" events, idea schemes, and venturing teams let loose deep down in organizations. Some companies are measuring how much of their capital budget is being allocated to new ventures and e-commerce. Some businesses are creating fast-track learning schemes to move people through venture capital units, incubator units, and back to the mainstream business: Bain & Co. and JP Morgan being examples.

The premise is that there are latent entrepreneurs and e-commerce ideas in companies; it is essential to break out of traditional practices; strategy is not all top-down, but should reach through all levels; and that it is time for action

and risk taking. It is the classic "let loose" cycle often employed when strategic change is on the agenda: stimulating everybody to think and act as a new business.

Threats

The final element is to think of threats, but not only as shock treatment. After all, if you see how a new entrant or rival can attack or destroy your business, why not attack first? This has been a philosophy at General Electric, where executive teams have been asked to think how their business could be destroyed by e-commerce. Threats stimulate survival instincts and can be more effective than looking for opportunities, which can seem optional.

The combination of these four Fast elements suggests that both IT personnel and business executives are involved, and that initiatives are prompted that involve multifunctional teams. In this way, business strategy and IT strategy are integrated. Indeed, if we learn from the dotcom world, multifunctional teams build and evolve the business with no demarcation between functions, skills, and strategies. This leads to redefining IT strategy and planning.

Research shows that developing IT strategy usually requires an injection of methods; the Fast methodology is proposed as appropriate for the new economy. However, the process of strategy formulation matters too, and that without attention paid to implementation, strategies can end up as just reports filed or presentations that are soon forgotten.

Discontinuity

The Fast methodology can seem to ignore process and implementation. However, Fast is more of a framework for ensuring that the right

Without attention paid to **implementation**, strategies can be just reports filed or presentations that soon are forgotten questions are asked and a mechanism for getting started. In practice, the aim is to ensure that the process issues of understanding, involvement, communication, and buy-in are addressed by engaging both IT and the business.

Traditional methods of IT strategy-making, whether framed as "alignment," "opportunity," or both, were periodic, formalized, long term, and driven by IT. They were discontinuous and easily lost momentum.

My current research indicates that new mechanisms of IT strategy-making are continuous, involve learning by doing, are short term, and are just a natural activity. Often strategy – integrated IT and business strategy – is revisited weekly; priorities are examined every Monday, and a limited number of projects is resourced and monitored by time, not cost. The strategic plan is a continuously rejigged portfolio of projects.

The pressure to launch, the need to respond to what is learned by doing, the uncertainty of new markets and models, and the fact that online business evolves in real time mean that the formal structures of traditional IT strategy-making are inappropriate.

Furthermore, because IT strategy-making in the new economy is business development, it is a team effort. The chief executive and technology director should be in frequent dialog. IT people are learning to work with marketing people and vice versa. Everyone realizes that doing something outperforms weeks of planning. So, Fast may get you started as a one-off activity, but after that, making strategy should become an evolving, continuous, ever-changing process.

New and old

However, in traditional companies, not everything is concerned with the new economy. "Integration" may be the watchword for IT strategy-making in e-business. Indeed, as the new replaces the old and "the business" and IT learn to work together better, it may apply to IT direction-setting across all the business. But for now, IT investments are needed to support the old business, and much of the organization will be working in old ways rather than acting as multifunctional development teams. So, there is a binary approach to IT strategy.

Most of the IT department is working on large infrastructure and application projects, still sorting out alignment and running business systems. Then there is often a new IT group that is closely related to the e-business division or located with that division or with e-business venture teams.

This arrangement may be transitory, using a separate, differentiated unit of organization or temporary teams to achieve rapid change. It makes sense because the model of new IT is quite different from that established over the past 40 years – just like the business models are radically different. And the pace or tempo is equally different. Speed is key in this race to learn (and unlearn) and win (or at least survive).

One consequence of this binary approach is that IT investment comprises two subsets (*see* Figure 1): the new business ("new economy") portfolio and the business as usual ("mainstream") portfolio. Over time, responsibility may be transferred from the new portfolio to the mainstream portfolio. Eventually, we may see the return to a single IT organization and one investment portfolio. The "new" will not be so new – but there are always advances in the pipeline, so a binary approach may be required for some time.

Chief executives have a challenge too. If they are in new-economy businesses then they will be discovering that "integration" is displacing

| FIGURE 1 | Binary approach to IT |

New economy portfolio
- New ventures
- Business experiments
- New technology pilots/R&D
- Quick-response fixes

+

Mainstream portfolio
- Infrastructure projects
- Traditional applications
- Rebuilding stable e-commerce applications
- Maintenance and enhancement

"alignment." In driving the shift to the new economy, they may discover that a "binary" approach to IT management may be preferred to a unitary one. "Integration" applies in new business units and "alignment" in the old.

If e-business is the business and if IT strategy cannot be separated from business strategy, the chief executive and technology director need to be partners. This might make the biggest difference of all, not only between those companies who "get it" in the new economy and those who do not, but between those who "make it" and those who do not. For strategic leadership is required as well as new concepts and practices of strategy formulation – and leadership is more effective if it involves more than just the nominal leader.

Further reading

Henderson, J.C. and Venkatraman, N. (1993) "Strategic Alignment: Leveraging Information Technology for Transforming Organizations," *IBM Systems Journal*, 32(1), 4–16.

Earl, M.J. (1993) "Experiences in Strategic Information Systems Planning," *MIS Quarterly*, March, 1–24.

Earl, M.J. and Feeny, D.F. (2000) "How to Be a CEO for the Information Age," *Sloan Management Review*, Winter.

Success flows from
business development

Donald N. Sull is an assistant professor of business administration at Harvard Business School.

Aggressive partnership and acquisition strategies are a feature of business development. **Donald Sull** describes how this is changing the business environment.

Business development has become one of the hottest career options in technology-intensive fields. Recruiters scramble to fill vacancies, and online job boards such as Monster.com, Headhunter.net, and Hotjobs.com list thousands of openings in business development, or "biz dev," as it is known. Twelve percent of Harvard Business School's graduates in 1999 described their first job as business development – more than entered either marketing or general management functions.

The emergence of this role raises important questions. What is it? Why has this function emerged? Is it a fad or an enduring aspect of the economy? Business development managers face a host of more concrete questions. If your business card says business development, what should you do all day? Which candidates are best for business development positions? How should they be evaluated and paid?

What is it?

"Business development isn't any one thing, but covers a multitude of sins," says venture capitalist John Schoch of Alloy Ventures. Many people view business development as a glorified sales position, while others associate the position with corporate planning, mergers and acquisitions, marketing, or account management. While these definitions encompass critical aspects, none alone captures its full breadth.

To see the big picture, it is helpful to imagine business development as a process (*see* Figure 1). The first step consists of establishing the company's business model, although this may already be fixed in established companies. Next, managers identify potential partners who could provide the resources to execute the business model, including customers, suppliers, distributors, collaborators, outsourced services, technology providers, and strategic investors. After identifying these

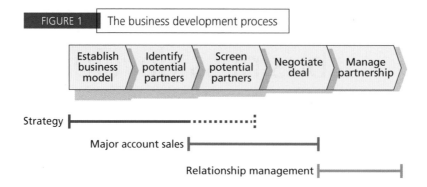

FIGURE 1 | The business development process

Establish business model 〉 Identify potential partners 〉 Screen potential partners 〉 Negotiate deal 〉 Manage partnership

Strategy

Major account sales

Relationship management

partners, the business development team evaluates them against the business model.

Next, the team chooses the most appropriate form of relationship and negotiates terms. Such a relationship might consist of an exploratory strategic investment, a technology licensing agreement, an alliance or joint venture, through to an acquisition. In the final stage, the company manages the partnership or, in the case of an acquisition, integrates the newly purchased enterprise. In many companies, particularly those at an early stage of development, this process may feed back into the company's business model, since new partnerships can create opportunities that spur the company to revise its business plan.

Viewing the whole process helps clarify the business development function. In many companies, the business development group is responsible for only part of the process. If the group focusses primarily on the early stages, it resembles the strategic or corporate planning function. By contrast, business development managers who spend most of their time screening and negotiating deals with customers look a lot like a salesforce, and those focussing on equity investments resemble in-house venture capitalists. Finally, to the extent that business development staff manage on-going partnerships or integrate acquired companies, their role resembles account management, although partners might be suppliers or distributors as well as customers.

Why now?

In established technology companies, such as Hewlett-Packard or Intel, the activities concentrated in business development have always been performed somewhere, but they were scattered throughout the organization. Why, then, have companies chosen to consolidate these activities into a single function? And why now?

While business development undoubtedly owes some of its cachet to management fashion, its rise reflects a profound shift in the nature of competition. Historically, many managers viewed competition as a Hobbesian state in which atomistic companies fought it out in a war of all against all. Corporate managers steeped in this view tried to do everything in-house and saw alliances as an admission of inadequacy. Traditionally, entrepreneurs validated a business model, fine-tuned the technology, and landed major customers before turning to partnerships.

In the past decade, however, managers and entrepreneurs have come to recognize that attempting to do everything in-house costs too much, takes too long and entails too much risk.

The nature of competition has shifted from the war of all against all to competition between fluid networks of complementary companies. While conspicuous in high-tech sectors (consider the Microsoft–Intel–Compaq constellation), networks also dominate competition in other industries such as cars and airlines. Thus, in networked competition, partnerships provide critical ties between companies. The business development function, in turn, centralizes expertise in identifying, evaluating, negotiating, and managing those relationships.

Exemplars

The business development function is still in its infancy and most companies are struggling to discover the best ways to organize and execute their activities. Nonetheless, a few companies, such as Cisco, eBay, Yahoo!, and CNET, have emerged as leaders in business development, and other managers can learn from them.

Clarify the mission

The most effective business development groups have a clear mission that every member can articulate. Cisco's 40-person business development team, for example, is guided by a clear, threefold mission: acquire technology to fuel growth, invest in strategic technology partners, and understand market trends. Unfortunately, Cisco's crisp mission is an exception. Business development in many companies consists of individuals pursuing exciting deals without a clear sense of how these contribute to the company.

Managers can gauge the clarity of focus in a business development group by carrying out a simple exercise. Ask each person in the business development group to write down the business development mission (without consulting any colleagues). Then compare the results. If you find a great deal of variety, you probably need to articulate a mission for the group.

In articulating a mission, it is useful to begin by identifying the stage your company has reached and the associated strategic challenges (*see* Figure 2). In the earliest stage of a venture, the founding team struggles to define a business model. Business development's primary mission at this stage is to explore and evaluate the various ways in which the business model could be implemented and identify possible obstacles.

Once the model has stabilized, the mission of the development group shifts to validating the model by identifying and landing customers, and refining key aspects, such as pricing. While in this phase, the business development group at Iphrase, a US start-up offering dynamic website navigation, evaluated 20 vertical markets such as cars, financial services, and consumer electronics to identify potential customers. It finally validated its business model with a high-profile deal with Charles Schwab.

After validating the business model, the role of business development shifts to identifying and seizing opportunities consistent with the model and screening out deals that would distract from this focus. For example, consider CNET, a company that aggregates information to help people purchase consumer electronics online. Its business development group structures complex

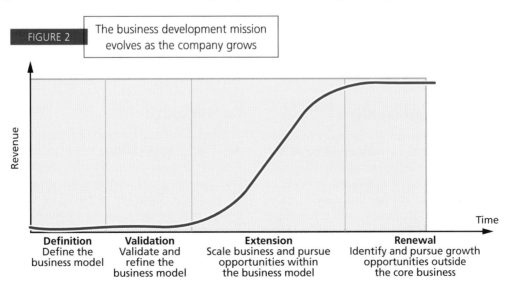

FIGURE 2   The business development mission evolves as the company grows

Revenue / Time

Definition	Validation	Extension	Renewal
Define the business model	Validate and refine the business model	Scale business and pursue opportunities within the business model	Identify and pursue growth opportunities outside the core business

deals with various kinds of partners: advertisers on CNET's website; internet service providers that drive traffic to the website; and companies that offer complementary services such as online storage. All of these partnerships support CNET's core business.

In established companies, the business development mission shifts again. As growth opportunities within the core business slow at such companies as Hewlett-Packard and Intel, business development is charged with identifying and evaluating external opportunities. At Intel, for example, corporate-level business development managers forge strong relationships with customers to increase their use of Intel products and services, while business development managers at the individual business unit level work to develop new initiatives outside the core.

Clearly articulating the business development mission allows managers to hire the right business development people to execute the mission and to tie pay to results. A company validating its business model, for example, might hire a vice-president of business development with detailed knowledge of the chosen market and broad contacts. Pay might be tied to the quality and prestige of early customers and the strength of the resulting relationships.

When a company is expanding with a proven business model, the ideal candidate may resemble a traditional sales representative with experience of selling a complex service to large organizations. Pay might be based on fixed sales quotas. An established company trying to renew itself using business development might favor candidates who have worked in both a start-up and a larger organization.

Apply "triage" to opportunities

One of the greatest challenges faced by business development managers is sorting through the array of relationships they could forge. The business development group in high-profit companies such as CNET, NBCi, or eBay can receive a few hundred unsolicited proposals for partnerships each month, in addition to discussions they initiate. Start-ups are not buried by unsolicited e-mail, but must sort quickly through the huge number of companies they might approach as partners. It is often critical to lock up desirable

partners before competitors do, increasing the need for speed.

To sort rapidly through the large number of potential deals, business development groups adopt a "triage" system. The triage system originated as a speedy method of prioritizing patients that poured into battlefield hospitals. Business development professionals often rely on simple rules of thumb to sort potential relationships and weed out unlikely partners.

At eBay, for example, business development director Gil Penchina uses five rules to screen companies:

- Have I heard of the company?
- Is it a top website as measured by Media Metrix?
- Is it backed by sophisticated venture capitalists?
- Is it in a technology-savvy place?
- Has it been referred by someone I know?

Having done this, the business development team can conduct further analysis, which generally consists of a visit to the company's website to analyze the quality of its customers, management team, partners, and investors. Only if the potential partner appears credible will the company earn a first meeting with eBay. The purpose of this meeting is to size up the potential partner's management team and gauge their level of enthusiasm for a partnership.

This sequence of a rule-based first cut, fast desk research, and an initial meeting provides a series of filters that help eBay's business development team quickly screen out the less promising deals and concentrate on the most promising opportunities.

Learn as you go

A major benefit of centralizing business development is in consolidating strategy making, deal evaluation, negotiation, and relationship management in one group and accumulating knowledge about deals. Creating a business development group may be necessary to consolidate knowledge and foster learning, but it is not always enough. The best business development groups take further steps to capture and reuse lessons learned from experience. For example, eBay's business development group codifies knowledge that it gains from evaluating and negotiating deals as checklists for use in future transactions.

How a business development group is organized also influences how much its members can learn. Consider Cisco. In one year, it completed 25 acquisitions worth $22bn and made 69 equity investments. Based on its experience, Cisco recently reorganized the development group to increase learning.

Historically, the group was organized by transaction type (that is, by acquisition, equity investment, and joint venture). Vice-president Ammar Hanafi believed, however, that critical knowledge about markets was being lost from deal to deal. To capture this knowledge, Hanafi reorganized the business development group into half a dozen teams, each of which focusses on a specific market.

These teams spend time with customers, researchers, and industry experts to understand trends and develop contacts, while working closely with Cisco business unit managers to understand where they see the market moving. The team members build sector expertise and networks, which allow them to identify, screen, and work with potential partners and understand the needs of business unit managers.

The best business development groups also use their standard partnership contract as a mechanism to capture and incorporate lessons from previous deals. For example, eBay's Penchina compares a contract to an intersection: "When there's one accident you put up a stop sign. After a few accidents you hang a traffic light." The company carefully monitors past deals to identify where problems or disagreements have emerged and then flags these items (such as terms and payments, limitations of liability, indemnification, and termination) for close scrutiny and pre-emptive clauses in subsequent contracts.

Business development managers also interview heads of functional areas within eBay to discover what aspects of past deals gave them grief. The accounting department, for example, identified the importance of extending payment terms, while public relations wanted control over announcing the deal. Clauses to cover both were added to later contracts.

While the benefits of many **business partnerships** are often ethereal, the costs are all too real

Manage relationship costs

Some business development managers view partnerships as hunting trophies. The founder of a London-based start-up, for example, proudly explained that his business development group had signed 100 partnership deals in two years. When asked how these added value to his business, he replied that he would figure out how to leverage the relationships later.

While the benefits of many partnerships are often ethereal, the costs are all too real. Business development teams invest time and attention in identifying and evaluating potential partners, and negotiating deals. Nonstandard contracts, for example, are easy for development people to promise, but costly for product teams to deliver. To the extent that relationships are substantive, as opposed to trophy partners, they also require resources to manage the partnership.

The best business development managers use standard contracts and multiple screens to control relationship costs. In some cases, they focus on a certain type of transaction to accumulate expertise in that type of deal. Cisco, for example, now avoids joint ventures, which often entail governance problems, and focusses on equity investments and acquisitions.

Partner to integrate

A common mistake made by novice business development managers is to think that the job is done once the ink dries on the contract. In fact, managing existing relationships often proves the most challenging and time-consuming part of the process.

Managers can improve the odds of a smooth relationship by screening potential partners for compatibility. Cisco's business development team, for example, used the rule of thumb that potential acquisitions should have approximately 75 employees, 75 percent of whom are engineers. Companies with this profile, it turned out, were relatively easy to integrate into Cisco's sales and marketing.

When evaluating potential alliance partners, Hewlett-Packard's managers use structured tools to help them judge compatibility with the company's strong culture. They identify what a potential partner seeks from the relationship and classify those goals as shared, supportable, or incompatible with Hewlett-Packard's objectives. They also draw a matrix with four columns: what Hewlett-Packard would give in the partnership, what it would get, what the partner would give, and what the partner would get. Plotted in rows against these columns are the resources, competencies and risks of each party.

The structure of the business development group can also improve relationship management. Early on, Cisco identified acquisition integration as critical to corporate success and set up a 10-person team to integrate acquired companies. The development group at eBay includes "finders" who identify, evaluate, and negotiate partnerships, and "keepers" who manage these relationships. Managers at eBay believe the group that signs a deal should be responsible for the health of the resulting relationship. When responsibility resides outside the business development group, it is critical to involve the group that will ultimately manage the relationship early in the discussions, and keep them involved.

Conclusion

Historically, people have viewed entrepreneurship as a solo sport. For start-ups it was the lone inventor in a garage. Large corporations, to the extent that they innovated at all, tried to do it all in-house. The success of Silicon Valley, however, has underscored the critical role of networks and relationships in providing the access to information, resources, and guidance that is necessary to pursue opportunities quickly and with acceptable levels of risk.

The business development function is one way to increase a company's ability to seize opportunities. As companies sail into the uncharted waters of networked entrepreneurship, they will look to business development to guide their journey.

I gratefully acknowledge the research assistance of Brian Costello, Jennifer Felch, and Andrew Murphy and the financial support of the Harvard Business School research division.

Further reading

Aiello, R.J. and Watkins, M.D. (2000) "The Fine Art of Friendly Acquisition," *Harvard Business Review*, November.

Doz, Y.L. and Hamel, G. (1998) *Alliance Advantage: The Act of Creating Value Through Partnering*, Cambridge, MA: Harvard Business School Press.

Eisenhardt, K.M. and Sull, D.N. (2001) "Strategy as Simple Rules," *Harvard Business Review*, January.

Demergers:
breaking up is hard to do

Dr Nancy Hubbard is an associate fellow at Templeton College, University of Oxford. She is a director of Hubbard & Associates and consults with KPMG on separation issues.

The number of demergers is likely to increase, says **Nancy Hubbard**. She also sees problems ahead if major issues are not addressed.

Recent years have seen the creation through mergers of corporate giants such as DaimlerChrysler, BP Amoco and AOL/TimeWarner. In future, though, we are likely to see a marked increase in the number and size of demergers. Little research has been done into demergers, but they are increasingly seen as a viable choice. This article will explore the trends, identify differences with mergers, and describe the managerial issues.

Demerging or separation is far more prevalent than most people realize. Forthcoming research by KPMG suggests that up to 30 percent of FTSE 100 companies have been involved in demerging significant portions of their businesses since 1999.

KPMG defines demerger as the disposal of businesses with a capitalization of more than 5 percent of the company's total. While this sounds low, the number of separations in recent years where the percentage has been far greater is significant: British Gas, AstraZeneca, Granada, Cable & Wireless Communications, Hanson, P&O, and Williams, for example. And the trend is set to continue with BT, Kingfisher, and Tomkins considering separating or actually doing so.

There are differences between subsidiary disposals and demergers. The former occur when the shareholder changes to either the management team or other shareholders. Demergers occur when shareholders remain the same but receive shares in new entities. Both disposals and separations, however, share many problems.

Why are so many major companies undergoing demergers while so many others are buying? The activities are inherently related and linked to managers' drive for globalization. To compete in larger markets, companies have striven to gain critical mass, especially in industries with regional or global appeal, such as pharmaceutical, defense, telecommunications, and heavy manufacturing industries.

Merging companies have grown quickly and gained economies of scale accordingly. Many have had to become increasingly specialized, concentrating resources to take a geographically dominant position and achieve considerable cost savings.

Vodafone Mannesmann, for example, aims to be a dominant global player in mobile communications, rather than to dominate the entire telecommunications market. Traditional conglomerates such as Hanson and Tomkins have seen their value to related competitors increase where their suitors know they can achieve considerable cost savings through merging their similar operations.

Even those companies entering into "megamergers" that are unable to achieve the associated cost savings through economies of sale will find themselves vulnerable to the demerger threat. Corporations are relying on survival of the biggest. If they are unable to play the size card they must look to alternatives, including demerger. As long as globalization sits high on corporate agendas, separation will be a compelling solution for many businesses.

Business decisions

There are several important decisions to be made when embarking on a demerger. These serve as the basis for pre-separation planning and are critical to success. If these issues are ignored, the time and resource costs can be considerable.

The exit route

Managers must first understand the intended fates of the separated entities when planning a demerger. The implications for operational systems, for example, differ greatly if one is floating or selling an operation. Millions of pounds can be saved if the separated unit merges into an acquirer's operation rather than implementing systems and processes that the new owner discards. Affected employees also want to know the exit route, especially if another merger might follow the separation.

Order of action

If demerger includes disposing of operations via acquisition, one must ask whether they should be separated and then sold, or sold first and then separated. While this sounds like a "chicken and egg" question, it establishes who is in control during the separation process. The preferred option at present is to announce the exit route partner then work toward separation. Both Cable & Wireless and Granada announced their separating operations' merger partners before the separation. The advantage is that the new partner has an opportunity to shape the separated entity and its systems. This, however, is more complicated for the disposer, because it does not solely control the separation process. Thus, the disposer needs to make binding agreements on how the separation will be handled.

Degree of integration

Demergers are similar to acquisitions: the greater the degree of integration, the more complicated the transaction. Separations are clearly more complex undertakings than a straightforward subsidiary disposal. But understanding why they are more complicated sheds some light on the skills required by either activity. Subsidiary sales, like acquisitions where the two operations are not going to be fully merged, require the disposer to ensure that control and financial systems are robust and in place; this is usually achieved via service and other contractual agreements. Thus overall success in significant subsidiary disposal is governed predominantly by how well one implements financial, legal, and control systems.

True separations, like mergers, are far more difficult and complex. Not only do they encompass the same systems issues as subsidiary disposals, but they also have enormous human complications. Employees previously working side by side may now split into different (and potentially competing) entities. Employee contracts, retraining, redundancy, relocation, retention, roles, and responsibilities, as well as culture and communication, all become separation issues. So, success relies on the resolution of complex human resource issues.

These three decisions, along with the whole host of change and project management issues, form the basis of any separation plan. During separation, however, other issues often come to light, including:

- separation timescales;
- prolonged employee uncertainty;
- related employee issues;
- resourcing and scale;
- partner relationships.

Timescales

There are great differences in the timescales of acquisition and demerger. Acquirers buy a company, then change it, while separations require change before separation. This sounds insignificant but is not. Mergers and acquisitions serve as catalysts for change and generally involve an approximate 100-day "grace period" during which all change is possible.

Separations do not have this luxury; in that respect they resemble change-management programs. During separations, most work is done before the transaction, under the old ownership structure; there is often no urgency for change as time horizons can be so distant. In many separations, work and tension levels increase toward the legal day of separation. Acquisition implementation timescales often slip a few weeks – this is not possible if a company's flotation date is already set.

Separations must also be completed in full before the transaction can take place. The major upheaval surrounding acquisition is the six months after completion; on-going systems implementation, while taking longer, does not retain the emotive turmoil of the earlier phases.

Uncertainty levels

Because of the time a demerger takes, uncertainty can encourage employees to leave. The combination of a prolonged separation with a subsequent merger can create an exodus of the most prized employees unless it is well managed. Levels of uncertainty, however, are affected by the degree of separation – divisional disposals are less complex and cause less uncertainty than full-scale separations. Yet, employees are affected in either case.

One should consider financial inducements aimed at keeping key staff during this period, but this is not enough. The most effective way to retain staff is to have employees involved in the demerger process and to handle that process in a fair way.

Poaching

A major issue during separation is the poaching of staff by demerging parties or those involved after separation. In either case it is normal for a power struggle to ensue, in which important employees are fought over. It is more difficult between demerging parties, as they are likely to know the staff in both organizations; those involved after separation do not usually have that degree of insight.

It is, however, a real problem if the two entities will end up competing with each other – the pool of employees important to both sides is much larger and the potential for discord greater. The advantage lies with the most powerful entity in this bargaining phase, but an agreement of principle regarding key staff will diffuse the situation to some extent. This agreement must be reached early during the separation to ensure it is in place before any rise in tension occurs.

Employees involved in separation and merger in quick succession often "go native" with their new owners – that is, their loyalties transfer from the current employer to the new entity too soon. They begin sharing sensitive information and try to poach colleagues.

This can be problematic if it happens early in the separation, or if the parties end up as competitors. There is a fine line between encouraging co-operation and overdoing co-operation. Communication between the parties and employees, alongside pre-deal agreements, can help.

At senior manager level, the board and head office can both become redundant. Senior employees may jostle for positions in smaller divisional entities, which creates uncertainty in people who should be working to consolidate the companies' futures. Employee anxiety needs managing throughout the process. Defining the top teams, and incentivizing those leaving to continue to perform, can limit political behavior. A transparent and professionally handled separation process, generous redundancy terms, employee support, and communication can assist the wider employee audience.

Resourcing

Large-scale mergers require additional resources to be implemented successfully. Yet, many demerging companies try to staff the separation while simultaneously running the business – a Herculean feat.

Most lean companies don't have the resources and turn to external consultants. For example, one recent demerger saw 115 employees working with 20 consultants. This kind of ratio is common, but calling in experts does not allow the demerging parties to abdicate responsibility. Even when demerging with external help, the corporate team will still do the bulk of work.

Demerging can bring "diseconomies of scale" – the returning of shared systems and people to their respective operations, including information systems, logistics, distribution, purchasing, marketing budgets, and personnel. If production is combined, duplicate and competing production lines must be set up as the businesses are separated.

Adding costs is far harder than taking them out. It is difficult to understand the complexities of an established organization. Systems and process anomalies built up over time mean that any organization operates in a quirky fashion. Processes must be mapped and systems analyzed before those separating can understand what systems and processes are needed in the new scenario.

Separation partners

Unlike acquisitions, there is really no such thing as a hostile separation – at least, not at the beginning. The parties know each other and tend to have good working relationships. The level of co-operation, however, can depend on the exit route – if the entities will become competitors, it won't be long before things become strained.

During this time of co-operation, one should decide the ground rules for dealing with what will inevitably follow. These include agreements covering difficult areas such as dividing intellectual capital, poaching employees, future dealings with customers, contractual service agreements for systems provision, protecting high value sites, co-location issues, and property. It is also important to outline timeframes and how long agreements can continue.

The extent of information sharing also depends on the exit route – competitors are unlikely to share information as freely as noncompetitors. The degree of information sharing should be outlined in principle during planning. It requires a degree of faith that may not be present later.

Finally, there are few genuine mergers because parties are rarely equal. One side usually has the upper hand in dictating the new entity's structure and culture. The same applies to demergers – one side will try to gain the advantage. It can be the head office, the largest or most profitable division, or even an exit partner. It may purloin locations, people, centers of excellence, or intellectual property. Initial agreements will help guard against this, but to some extent it is inevitable.

Conclusion

Demergers are highly complex and emotionally draining. They can easily go wrong. The best defense against a poorly implemented separation is thorough planning. Comprehensive service and agreements in principle, along with frank and open dialog, can ensure mechanisms are in place to deal with conflict. Having enough resources and a professional process is also fundamental to success. If you thought that demerging was just merging in reverse, think again.

The author would like to thank Roberta Carter from KPMG for her invaluable help with this article.

Further reading

Hubbard, N. (2001) *Acquisition: Strategy and Implementation*, Basingstoke: Palgrave.

Global **business**

4

Contents

Introduction to Part 4

It is a little questioned belief of modern society that the world's geographical and economic boundaries are increasingly meaningless in the face of global trade, interlinked financial markets and the communicating power of the internet. Certainly companies are more than ever willing to look beyond their national borders for cheap, reliable or high-quality suppliers, or willing markets for their products and services. However, writers in this part are cautious on the inevitability of a global economy. Alan Rugman argues that trade is not global, but organized regionally. Later, Philip Parker questions the assumption of economic convergence between trading blocs. Other chapters address the cultural issues that come with increased trade, in particular the challenges facing Western and Asian managers as they attempt to find value in their alliances.

The illusion of
the global company

Companies are a long way from becoming global, argues **Alan Rugman**, who sees instead regional groups limited by cultural differences and government regulation.

Alan M. Rugman is Thames Water Fellow of Strategic Management at Templeton College, University of Oxford.

.

Demonstrations in Seattle and Prague have shown that global bodies such as the World Trade Organization are in trouble. Nongovernment groups (NGOs) appear to have checked globalization. However, as this article attempts to show, the widely held image of globalization was nothing more than an illusion.

Far from taking place in a single global market, most business activity by large companies takes place in regional blocs. Strong government regulations and cultural differences divide the world into the triad blocs of North America, the European Union, and Japan. Of the world's largest 500 multinational enterprises, 434 are in the triad, accounting for 90 percent of the world's stock of foreign direct investment.

Globalization

The term "globalization" is much abused and definitions have become too broad. For the past 40 years, globalization has meant the economic integration achieved by the activities of multinational enterprises (MNEs). These have become the engines of economic globalization, engaging in foreign direct investment with a view to international production and sales through networks of subsidiaries and in strategic alliances. The largest 500 MNEs account for 90 percent of the world's stock of foreign direct investment. They also carry out half of all trade, often in the form of intra-company sales between subsidiaries.

Academics outside the study of economics have created their own definitions of globalization. Sociologists such as Anthony Giddens refer to a runaway world in which globalization is broadly defined to include "convergence" of cultural, social, and political life, as well as economic. Political scientists regularly blame globalization for the perceived demise of the power of the state.

Strong regulations and cultural differences divide the world into **triad blocs** for doing business

NGOs see global capitalism as a villain, leading to world income differences, poverty, and the exploitation of poorer nations by unethical MNEs. Business people should be concerned by these viewpoints, none of which is backed up by empirical evidence. Yet, a coalition of anti-globalization NGOs and US labor groups derailed a crucial meeting of the World Trade Organisation (WTO) in Seattle in 1999. MNEs are now viewed by NGOs as "big, bad, and ugly."

Paradoxically, while NGOs believe that MNEs are global and are the only beneficiaries of free trade, in reality the activities of MNEs are regionally based, rather than truly global. Figures indicate that most MNEs are from the "triad" economies of the EU, US, and Japan (*see* Figure 1).

Of the 500 largest MNEs, 434 are from the triad. This picture has been much the same over the past decade. In 1990, for example, 414 came from the triad. As NGOs continue to disrupt vehicles for multilateralism such as the WTO,

the result is to reinforce these regional economic blocs.

The real drivers of globalization are the network managers of these large multinational enterprises. But their business strategies are now regional and responsive to local consumers, rather than global and uniform.

For example, the automobile and specialty chemicals businesses are triad based, they are not global. There is no global car. Instead, over 90 percent of all cars produced in Europe are sold in Europe. Local production and local sales also occur in North America and Japan.

Globalization critics

In his first BBC Reith lecture for 1999, Anthony Giddens painted a vivid portrait of all that is wrong with globalization. He argued that the pace of science, technology, and electronic interchange has increased risk and given people the feeling that they are not in control of their lives. Globalization is said to bear the "strong imprint of American political and economic power." With this statement, Giddens makes the same mistake as anti-MNE writers of the 1970s. They argued that the power of the nation state was being eroded by MNEs. Today, we find governments as strong as ever.

Giddens's views can be contrasted with the research of academic Raymond Vernon. In his work, Vernon found that the power of the nation state was not being eroded by MNEs, but that there was a seesaw of power between governments and companies, determined by the particular circumstances of the times. He predicted a strengthening of the regulatory framework facing MNEs.

The evidence suggests that the nation state remains robust as a regulator of triad-based corporations. Companies in North America and their governments are dealing with changing institutions, but they are also agents of change. The deepening structural interdependence of the world economy has not led to a fall in sovereignty. Governments respond in different ways to corporate activity.

The economic facts indicate that globalization is not entirely new. The world economy has seen

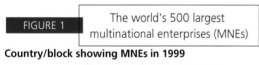

FIGURE 1	The world's 500 largest multinational enterprises (MNEs)

Country/block showing MNEs in 1999

US	179
EU	148
Japan	107
Canada	12
South Korea	12
Switzerland	11
China	10
Australia	7
Brazil	3
Mexico	2
Norway	2
Russia	2
India	1
Malaysia	1
South Africa	1
Taiwan	1
Venezuela	1

Source: Adapted from *Fortune* magazine, "The Fortune Global 500" July 24, 2000 integration in the past, particularly in Victorian times when the British Empire was a hegemony. "Global" economic activity existed in the ancient world; indeed, MNEs are 2,000 years old. Most economic exchange is now regionally based, rather than being global. The extent of internal triad-based trade and investment is not widely understood, and is frequently confused with evidence of globalization.

There is no evidence for globalization, that is, of a system of free trade with fully integrated world markets. Instead, the evidence on the performance and activities of multinational enterprises demonstrates that international business is triad based and triad related. Most of the world's largest 500 multinational enterprises operate in a strong triad home base, with some access to another triad. They organize their production, marketing, and other business activities by regional boundaries.

The future for international business is more of the same. There is no trend toward globalization, but strong evidence of a hardening of triad blocs. Political pressures and NGO activities are reinforcing the triad, not creating a global system. Global governance issues, as at the WTO, are now largely irrelevant to triad issues of accountability and transparency. The latter are particular problems for both the EU and Japan, and not totally resolved in North America.

We have reached the end of globalization. The debate has been wrongly focussed on the power of multinational enterprises. Yet, these operate subject to strong government constraints rather than in a free market. We are now at the beginning of a new debate about multinationals and triad power.

The power of NGOs

One reason for the confusion about the real definition of globalization is the new emphasis on corporate social responsibility put forward by NGOs. Paradoxically, their agendas are consistent with triad-based capitalism. NGOs are opposed to US-driven global capitalism in which US values and products are imposed on the world. In practice, though, business does not operate this way.

Instead, European, North American, and Asian manufacturing and service companies compete viciously for market share, lobbying their governments for shelter and subsidies, and for alliances with NGOs to devalue the reputations of their rivals. The interests of quasi-protectionist corporations and NGOs are often aligned.

For example, environmentalists were a godsend to the US forestry industry when it was challenged by Canadian and European competitors. In the late 1990s, NGOs such as Greenpeace threatened worldwide boycotts of Canadian paper products unless clear cutting of old forests in British Columbia was stopped. At the same time, US forestry companies brought legal actions to reduce imports of Canadian lumber. As a result, the demand for US lumber increased at the expense of Canadian products and the performance of the Canadian industry declined.

Environmental issues, health standards, and safety standards can be twisted by triad-based home companies to keep out more efficient foreign competitors. Managers need to understand the position and power of NGOs.

Apart from the alliances between domestic business and NGOs, there will be an effective corporate response to the accusations of NGOs. The business sector can counter NGO propaganda in several ways. Advocates for business will come from the army of MBAs. In North America, 350,000 students either graduate in business administration or earn MBAs each year. In Britain, more than 100 universities offer MBAs and such programs are expanding across Europe. In Asia, a similar boom is underway. All these graduates want jobs, in consulting, investment banking, corporate management, and so on. As the ethical values of businesses are called into question, legions of MBAs will be articulate defenders of their own self-interest.

Companies will increase spending on their corporate affairs and public relations departments. Every corporation has media spokespeople skilled in presenting the company's viewpoint and in providing industry background that overworked journalists turn to for briefings and information. Most senior executives now receive media training and key members of the senior management team, both at head office and in subsidiaries, are capable of arguing their corner.

In addition, specialist intermediaries, such as consulting firms and public relations firms, can provide briefs, new images, and the personnel to take companies through a suitable change process when they need to be more responsive to stakeholders. Finally, academics provide the rationale for businesses to operate efficiently by studying their activities.

The Prague demonstrations may well have been the high-water mark for the hundreds of NGOs with a self-appointed agenda on the WTO. Bad publicity generated by extremists has undermined the legitimacy of moderate groups. In future, we should expect the NGO movement to split. Groups such as Oxfam and the World Wildlife Fund have long track records in their principal areas and have earned public respect for their work and dedication, so their views will have an impact.

Yet dozens of small NGOs run by a few activists will find it increasingly difficult to capture a mainstream audience. Unless a coalition can be built between them (as the unions did in the past), most small NGOs will fade into insignificance. Their proposals will still be published on the internet, but few will read them. Increasingly, search engines will be aimed at sites that offer research "with credentials." Users will turn to the Oxfam site and a university research site, because these are recognized as authoritative, accountable, and accurate.

The internet

One of the most misleading aspects of the debate about globalization is the two-faced role of communications technology. The internet has the potential to be a global service; at a certain level of wealth, a population can use computers and phone networks to participate in the web. The power of the internet was confirmed when AOL proposed a merger with Time Warner in 2000, linking the world's largest internet service provider with the leading US media group. Such a merger may lead to others between service providers and media/entertainment groups, for example, Yahoo! and Disney.

Yet, while the AOL/Time Warner group will expand its market in North America, and possibly in Europe and Asia, it does not equate to a global business. The internet is a service vehicle for communication and, perhaps, entertainment. It cannot bring people and goods physically together – it can only transmit messages and orders for business goods and services that still need to be delivered locally. Only in the case of media and entertainment will the AOL/Time Warner group be able to co-ordinate worldwide distribution of its news, magazines, and videos.

Although these products are valuable, they cannot match the value of the triad-based car and other manufacturing sectors. So, global entertainment is a possibility, but global business is not.

We are deceived by the publicity generated by pop stars, media events, the growth of US-based pop culture, and related entertainment activities. But these are largely peripheral. We are doubly deceived by the internet. It is not a medium for exchange, nor a product in itself. It is a tool for communication. It does the same job as the telephone and satellite. It provides a global service for local users.

Conclusions

- Globalization is misunderstood – it does not, and has never, existed in terms of a single world market with free trade.
- Triad-based business is the past, current, and future reality.
- Multinational enterprises operate within triad markets and access other triad markets; they have regional, not global, strategies.
- National governments strongly regulate most service sectors, thereby limiting free market forces; the extent of regulation is not decreasing.
- NGOs are influential; however, in the future their lack of accountability and lack of legitimacy will reduce, or at least limit, their influence.
- Neither MNEs nor NGOs will dominate; rather, there will be a complex situation where both exert influence, with minor variations in impact.

Further reading

Giddens, A. (1999) *Runaway World*, London: Profile Books.

Rugman, A.M. (2000) *The End of Globalization*, London: Random House Business Books.

Rugman, A.M. and D'Cruz, J.R. (2000) *Multinationals as Flagship Firms: Regional Business Networks*, Oxford: Oxford University Press.

Rugman, A.M. and Hodgetts, R. (2000) *International Business: A Strategic Management Approach*, London: Pearson Education.

Vernon, R. (1998) *In the Hurricane's Eye*, Boston, MA: Harvard Business School Press.

Cultural answers
to global dilemmas

Fons Trompenaars is founder of Trompenaars Hampden-Turner Intercultural Management Consulting in Amsterdam.

Charles Hampden-Turner is a senior research associate at the Judge Institute, Cambridge University.

Conflicting values are made more acute by cultural differences. Yet **Fons Trompenaars** and **Charles Hampden-Turner** find they can be integrated.

Recent research reveals that the leaders of global corporations are beset by a series of dilemmas. These are pairs of conflicting propositions, each of which clamors for the allegiance of the decision maker. Successful leadership depends on the capacity to integrate such propositions and create strategies that unite both aims.

For example, the leader is expected to set universal rules of applicability, yet treat each culture, or way of working within the company, as a special case of diversity. The leader is expected to originate strategy worthy of Alexander the Great, yet listen attentively to an astonishing variety of inputs. He or she is expected to analyze, yet to create from the resulting mass of statistics a coherent, purposive plan.

Cultures and ideas

No doubt leaders of all companies face such dilemmas. So, what is so special about global companies? The answer is that worldwide operations render these dilemmas more acute, since the values of whole cultures may put varying priorities on one or the other side of a dilemma. In some cultures, for example, stock markets dominate the supply side, in others banks. In some, shareholders own and can dispose of under-performing assets, in others, cross-shareholdings make this much more difficult.

Through a variety of studies and interviews with, among others, 21 chief executives, researchers at the Judge Institute, Anglia Business School, and the Trompenaars-Hampden-Turner Group discovered that "transcultural competence," the capacity to integrate seemingly opposed values, was among the most important skills of the corporate leader. These leaders scored significantly higher on this criterion than a general sample.

Take, for example, the dilemma of globalism against localism. How do leaders reconcile these conflicting imperatives? In several ways. One way, sometimes celebrated as "think global, act local," is to encourage local initiatives, but then globalize information about these activities. Typically, the corporate headquarters has some form of scoreboard monitoring its operations around the world. Any local success could have global implications and might be applicable worldwide. More usually, local adaptations stay local. For example, Shell gave help to pig farmers in the Philippines, which protected its pipelines from sabotage by insurgents.

Another way of integrating cultural diversity is to decentralize "centers of excellence" to those cultures that do the job best and most cheaply. Hence, Motorola has made Bangalore in India its software headquarters, drawing on the skills of some of the world's best software engineers. Sony sources its software in the US. Apple found Singaporeans so good at high-quality computer assembly that they now instruct Apple's factories around the world. The automobile of the future may be designed in Italy, with engines made in Germany, safety systems from Japan, and so on. Global excellence is a synthesis.

Dell Computers

Michael Dell of Dell Computers was a relative latecomer to a maturing industry. Yet he has succeeded in solving one of that industry's major dilemmas: is it possible to serve both a mass market, with all its economies of scale, while focussing on a niche market of customers who have very special needs?

Dell was the first to do both at the same time. It also pioneered direct selling over the internet. Dell sells computers to a wide range of corporate customers, but gives each client "premier pages" on the web, consisting of detailed, private information about the purposes for which computing power is mobilized and how the customer might best use the hardware. Such systems combine confidentiality with transparency. The customer's strategy is confidential, but suppliers have access to inventory levels for just-in-time delivery, without ordering. Never have so many customers received standardized components in so many combinations.

Dell is a good example of the "clicks-and-mortar" businesses even now surviving the decline of dotcom stocks. It harnesses neither the old or new economies alone, but clever combinations of both: high-quality computers enhanced with information supplied by the internet.

McDonald's

An example of how even mass-market suppliers are heeding cultural diversity is illustrated by the experience of McDonald's chairman Jack Greenberg. The Big Mac is so quintessentially American that "McWorld" has become an epithet for the homogenization of world tastes by the US. But Greenberg was to discover that the global popularity of the McDonald's product was increasingly qualified by exceptions.

The international division sustained McDonald's throughout much of the 1990s. Domestic sales were in trouble and it was the company's local adaptations, introduced by franchisees and national co-ordinators, that showed the most sales success, registering 15 years of sustained revenue growth. More importantly, the autonomy first ceded to foreign operators now became the policy of the whole corporation.

When the Indonesian currency collapsed in 1998, potato imports became too expensive. Rice was substituted and later maintained. In Korea, roast pork was substituted for beef, while soy sauce and garlic were added to the bun in much of south-east Asia. Austria introduced "McCafes," a variety of local coffee blends.

When Greenberg examined the sources of recent innovations, he found these had come from regions in the US. The Egg McMuffin had started from local initiatives in San Diego. The Big Mac originated in Pittsburgh. The McFlurry, a soft ice-cream with candy, spread from Florida.

Yet in key respects of quality, cleanliness, speed, and branding, McDonald's will remain uniform. "Decentralization does not mean anarchy," said Greenberg. "Those things aren't negotiable."

Heineken

Another dilemma involves reconciling the self-interest of the corporation with its obligations to customers and community. While free enterprise is by definition self-interested, a crisis can help businesses recognize the importance of social reality. In 1993, when Heineken's bottler mistakenly left ground glass fragments in the bottom of bottles supplied to the plant, chief executive Karel Vuursteen withdrew every bottle in the entire sales area, at a serious loss to Heineken.

It was a difficult decision but the right one. Customers come first. Perhaps not first in economic philosophy, but first in the sequence of those who must be satisfied before profits can flow again. Heineken found, as Johnson & Johnson had before it, that customers accept that accidents and sabotage happen. What really concerns them is how a company behaves in such crises. Does it immediately protect its customers despite serious loss to itself? The sales of both Heineken and Tylenol rose after these incidents.

Lego

The process of innovation creates a tension between the individual and the group. Christian Majgard is marketing director of Danish toy company Lego. In the mid-1990s, he became concerned that, though staff were coming up with a large number of creative ideas, these ideas were not being accepted, shaped, improved, tested, and successfully launched as finished products.

Majgard discovered that whether an innovative idea was accepted depended on the originator's status. Typically, board members supplied ideas and junior staff worked on implementing them. This was doubly disadvantageous because the implementers had no personal stake in the ideas, while the "ideas men" neglected the details of making the innovation viable. There was a fatal schism between the ideal and reality, and ultimately the company's "realists" killed off the ideas.

Majgard made it a rule that anyone championing an idea must fight for it in the team, that the team's criticism be constructive and helpful, and that the whole team, not just the person responsible for the idea, be credited with successful innovations.

He also found that teams with greater diversity of talents and roles were more successful at delivering innovations.

Majgard found that resistance to novelty did not cease, even after the successful launch of a new product. Lego had a "plastic brick culture" because of the celebrated success of its staple product. Even the most successful electronic toy or software game was not embraced as readily as plastic bricks at Lego's headquarters. Deciding to give new businesses autonomy, he put distance between them and corporate headquarters, until they were strong enough to stand up to the traditional culture and modify its values.

All too often, a company's problem is precisely what has made made it successful in the past. It overplays its winning combination and then needs an astute outsider to come in and diagnose the problems.

Club Med

In the 1990s, the French holiday company Club Med was suffering from a surfeit of the strengths that had made it famous: lavish hospitality and conviviality. Those attending Club Med are encouraged to experiment with new identities, reminiscent of old-fashioned shipboard entertainment, in beautiful settings. The organizers facilitated the experience by planning costumed role-playing and creating an ambience of rare experiences.

Villages would compete with each other in cuisine, party giving, and even firework displays. The victims of this grandeur were costs, budgets, and efficiencies. Club Med progressed royally into the red.

The dilemma was that the experience of a dream vacation had got the better of the requirement for counting costs. Philippe Bourguignon took over as chief executive in 1997. Having previously rescued Disneyland in Paris, Bourguignon acted swiftly. Each resort was given responsibility for its profits and losses, and had to stay within its budget. Prices were matched to seasonal demand, with the aim of fuller occupancy and seasons lengthened for the better use of assets. Bookings were streamlined and computerized. Options that were not often chosen were trimmed from the menu of food and activities.

Bourguignon had not only to control costs, but to demonstrate an understanding of Club Med's mission to provide profound experiences. He accordingly added intellectual experiences and artistic appreciation to Club Med's list of offerings. Woodland seminars in the US and an urban resort in Paris for would-be sophisticates broadened the company's range.

Club Med is back in profit, though some people complain that its former élan has been lost. However, most credit Philippe Bourguignon with another historic turnaround. The ambience is still there, but someone is now counting the costs.

Bupa

Val Gooding is chief executive of Bupa, the UK's largest private health insurer and provider. Her dilemma lies between these last two words, "insurer" and "provider." Insurers are neutral, calculating, abstract, legal, and retentive. Providers are comforting, supportive, personal, relational, and compassionate. These values collide at Bupa's call centers, where people who have paid premiums all their lives may eventually seek help. Bupa employees need integrity, care, and calculation in dealing with their customers.

Those staffing the phones must discover within seconds the would-be patient's extent of coverage and arrange for care. Callers are often desperate, sometimes angry. Staff work in groups to give each other support, with "calming rooms" and counselors for those suffering stress. But it is training that provides the "emotional muscle" that staff need.

The approach is unusual. Instead of drilling staff in a form of words, decreeing what they should and should not say, training consists in staff expressing their own family experiences of illness, surgery, bereavement, and bedside vigils. Rather than leaving the "private self" at home and engaging the "work self," everything in the lives of staff that bears on surviving illness is deemed relevant. Those whom trauma and crisis have made emotionally strong tell their stories. When a caller facing bypass surgery needs help, a veteran with such experience is available to counsel.

Gooding seeks to integrate the roles of carer and insurer. It is a difficult task; call operators must identify with frightened customers, but must also know within seconds who the caller is and what his or her insurance covers.

Conclusion

Values are differences. They are not to be summed, but reconciled. Outstanding leaders take apparent opposites and integrate them, so that each value learns from the other, rules grow better through exceptions, and global products spread from a particular locality. These opposites might include rules and exceptions, globalism and localism, mass markets and customized markets, universal types and regional novelties, self-interest and service to customers, individual creativity and group dynamics.

Too often a company overplays its strong suit. The leader should act as a critic of the status quo, restoring balance between, say, dream vacations and paying propositions. We call this capacity "cross-cultural competence," because most of the values involved are weighted differently by different national cultures. Hence, leaders must show respect for all cultures and all values if integration is to be achieved.

The authors can be contacted at info@7d-culture.nl

Culture is of
the essence in Asia

Leo Paul Dana is a visiting professor of entrepreneurship at Insead and former deputy director of the international business MBA program at Nanyang Business School, Singapore.

Even global companies can make major mistakes when dealing with Asian cultures. **Leo Dana** identifies some likely problems.

Business increasingly involves meeting foreign suppliers, employees, distributors, clients, and officials. Each operates in a particular environment, where interactions involve implicit and explicit assumptions. This is a function of the complex belief systems, cultural values, and attitudes that dictate accepted norms.

It is essential, therefore, for people in business to understand cultural differences. Such understanding is not a matter of noting the "different ways" that "those" people have; it is about rooting out the reasons behind these differences. Yet westerners often fail to understand how culture affects enterprise. This article will highlight some important differences between Asian and western business cultures.

Many Asians have mastered the comprehension of western culture and have been highly successful in adapting to it; they have built on the knowledge conveyed to them by a variety of sources. In contrast, westerners seldom have the patience to master an Asian language, let alone one of its cultures. Complex cultural environments require fluency not only in words, but more importantly in understanding what is not said – and this takes time, patience, and dedication. Westerners may argue that time is money and they cannot afford to learn everything it takes before even discussing a deal. In the long term, however, knowledge will pay off.

Many managers report frustrations when doing business in Asia and this is occasionally reflected in Asian business literature. One Chinese author, for example, recommends that Chinese negotiators use delaying tactics in deals with Americans, on the grounds that such delays will often cause them to fluster and encourage them to pay more to secure the deal.

This is a forceful reminder of the western notion that "patience is a virtue." Demonstrating patience and tolerance can speed up negotiations surprisingly; inflexibility and haste may, more often than not, lead

Patience can speed up negotiations; inflexibility and haste may lead to **bad relationships**

to bad relationships, or what the Chinese call *guanxi gao jiang*. In contrast to the short-term focus in the west, Asians often have a longer-range plan.

Cultural difference

In 1980, academic Geert Hofstede suggested that while the principles of leadership, motivation, and decision making may be almost universally applicable, their success depends on the ability of managers to adapt to local culture. He considered four dimensions of culture, formulating a model that has since emerged as a standard way of comparing cultures:

- power distance – the extent to which people accept an unequal distribution of power;
- the extent to which people try to avoid uncertainty;
- the extent to which people stress individualism over collectivism;
- the extent to which people value material goods over quality of life.

In his research, Hofstede found the US to have an individualistic society, with a low power distance and a low need to avoid uncertainty; in contrast, collectivist-oriented societies in Asia scored highly on both these measures.

More recent research suggests that culture makes a difference in the types of motivational factors that influence employees; culture also affects the amount of control people believe they have on their environment. Not only this, but culture affects one's perception of problem recognition, information search, alternatives, choice, and implementation. "Differences are part of life," one may argue, but each of these is a source of potential challenge in business.

The dominant culture in Asian business is that of the Chinese. This is not surprising, since ethnic Chinese are active in business worldwide and are populous in Asian countries.

In Thailand, ethnic Chinese represent 14 percent of the population, but control 90 percent of manufacturing. Likewise, in Ho Chi Minh City, 12 percent of the population is ethnic Chinese, but this group controls half of the local economy. In Indonesia, where the Chinese comprise less than 3 percent of the population, they also control a disproportionate amount of the economy.

In Laos, the Chinese have become highly successful entrepreneurs, partly thanks to the lack of a local entrepreneurial culture. Business activities there are not traditionally associated with high social status. Cultural values, stemming from religious beliefs, emphasize the elimination of desire. Since commerce was perceived as a means to satisfy desire, social forces discouraged enterprise and trade has usually been the role of those with inferior social standing. The communist takeover further discouraged entrepreneurial spirit.

Central to cultural beliefs in Laos is the ultimate goal to extinguish unsatisfied desires. Its doctrine focusses on aspects of existence, including *dukkha* (suffering from unsatisfied desire) and *anicca* (impermanence). Assuming that unsatisfied desires cause suffering, then suffering can be eliminated if its cause (desire) is eliminated. A respectable person, according to this ideology, should not work toward satisfying materialistic desires, but should, rather, strive to eliminate desire itself. When recruiting in Laos, it might be useful to be aware of such social pressures.

Given the widespread influence of Chinese culture, one would think it appropriate for western businesses to take the time to learn something about this culture and how it affects business; yet, even global players have made costly errors. In 1979, Northern Telecom was approached to provide new switching equipment for China. The US communications giant underestimated the importance of "face" and embarrassed Chinese officials by not doing a deal. When the company tried to get a deal with China in 1987, the Chinese officials remembered the slight by Northern Telecom. This time, the tables were turned: although Northern Telecom was eager to do business, the Chinese negotiators were not.

Confucianism, a source of values and beliefs for many Chinese, teaches that people are not equal. To this day, people in China are defined by their role in society and their contribution to it. Status is influenced by relationships and these are attached to implicit duties and obligations. People are viewed as relation-oriented beings, regulated by cardinal relationships that dictate an individual's obligations – *renqing* – toward other people. Observance of proper relationships is essential for the smooth functioning of society.

The idea of *guanxi*

A special relationship, *guanxi*, governs the exchange of favors, usually involving position or rank. It is similar to insurance, in that favors are registered (like premiums) so that benefits may be obtained if and when required. (*Guanxi*, composed of two words – *guan*, meaning "to close up," and *xi*, "to tie up" – expresses the notion of being an insider to a relationship network that involves obligations. *La guanxi* refers to the act of getting on one's good side.)

While western business people usually have a general understanding of this, relatively few westerners realize that the level of one's obligation is determined by one's ability to help – the weaker party expects to receive more, in exchange for less. Furthermore, *guanxi* is not easy for westerners to develop. *Guanxi* is intuitive, rather than rational, and its operation is not limited to business hours.

In the west, relationship marketing – in the pursuit of customer loyalty – involves the fostering of long-term alliances with customers; in a similar fashion, *guanxi* involves building a long-term relationship, based on trust and mutual exchange, to secure customer loyalty and good working relations. *Guanxi* forms a bond among buyers and sellers and between suppliers and producers.

Westerners seeking joint venture partners in China must look for the ideal partner using connections that are maintained through *guanxi*; simultaneously, the foreigner would benefit by linking up with a company that has enough *guanxi* to get things done in China. For companies regulated by legislation such as the US Foreign Corrupt Practices Act, this is not an easy task; difficulty increases if and when a joint venture is established and the venture must maintain the *guanxi* of counterparts in China. Furthermore, it is important to look at the whole, not simply the parts.

Guanxi is of prime importance in Chinese business circles. The west has known contract law since the 1700s; the purpose of such legislation is to give business an assurance that deals will be honored. In the absence of an elaborate contract law, the Chinese have relied on *guanxi* for the same assurance. When a relationship is more valuable than a transaction, then it is likely that the transaction will be smooth. Who would tarnish a relationship for a single transaction? No contract is necessary. The sense of obligation would come from the relationship, rather than a piece of paper.

On the other hand, in the absence of a strong relationship, there exists the possibility that one of the parties might ignore a contract. Although it had 18 years remaining on its lease, McDonald's was evicted from a Beijing site in favor of a newcomer with stronger *guanxi*. In Chinese circles, it is therefore more crucial to monitor a relationship than a transaction. Where a strong relationship exists, problems can always be solved. The long-term benefit of *guanxi* becomes obvious.

During the process of cultivating *guanxi* within business relationships, customer loyalty evolves naturally, while bonds are created with suppliers and with creditors. *Guanxi* rests on the moral premise of *renqing*, as a justification for social exchange. In a Chinese cultural setting, *guanxi* is the norm for carrying on business.

One might argue that western companies also value relationships and that these hold mutual obligations. There is, however, an important difference between the Chinese and western views of relationships. In the west, successful transactions lead to good relationships. In Chinese circles, one builds relationships to initiate transactions; the common belief is that if a relationship is well built, then transactions will follow.

A *guanxi* network – referred to as *guanxi wang* – provides credit as well as opportunities for business. In Singapore, for instance, Chinese

Chinese culture sees **intellectual property** as the result of the achievements of generations

clan associations traditionally provided opportunities to learn about trends in product development, as well as price fluctuations. The associations provided social contacts, training, business ideas, information, concepts, start-up capital, and technical assistance. New knowledge was built on existing knowledge, consistent with the belief that ideas do not belong to anyone, but are to be shared.

More recently, this belief – that ideas can and should be shared – has led to a western concern with the violation of intellectual property rights. Copyright treats intellectual property as the result of an individual's effort, and it is socially acceptable that huge profits can be made from patents, trademarks, and trade secrets. Westerners are worried when they see their technology being taken without payment. In contrast, Chinese culture sees intellectual property as the result of the collective achievements of generations throughout history.

Japanese *wa*

Sharing is also paramount in Japan, as is the concept of harmony, referred to as *wa* in Japanese. Indeed, the appearance of harmony, politeness, co-operation, and conciliatory relationships are social precepts upon which Japanese cultural values are based. Furthermore, *wa* is not necessarily attained by recourse to rational means. Many Japanese develop intuitive skills, which are normally processed in the brain's right hemisphere. In contrast, westerners are conditioned to develop an emphasis on rationality. An understanding of the factors related to *wa* is helpful when doing business in Japan.

North Americans expect a trustworthy person to respond immediately upon being asked a question. A pause inspires mistrust. In contrast, the Japanese are more impressed by an individual who ponders and thinks answers through first. Yet Americans find the resulting periodic silence awkward. Similarly, while Americans accept conflict as inevitable, managers across Japan believe in the concept of *wa*.

During the 1980s, Japanese car manufacturer Mazda and US car maker Chrysler encountered similar economic problems. While the latter reduced its blue-collar workforce by 28 percent and its white-collar staff by 7 percent, the Japanese company's solution was not to fire anyone. Consistent with the notion of promoting harmony, the Japanese managers agreed to a pay decrease of 25 percent. While western companies routinely hire and fire employees, long-term commitments have been the norm in Japan. In this country, individuals were traditionally hired primarily for their potential over the long run, rather than for their skills at the time of appointment.

Corporate decision-making in Japan also relies on harmony. Westerners have sometimes perceived Japanese managers as incompetent or indecisive. If a manager knows what he is doing, thinks the westerner, why does he continually consult his team? In fact, the Japanese tend to resolve issues by consensus rather than by position papers, memos, or the exercise of executive will.

In a typical North American or European meeting, formal agendas dictate the order in which items are discussed, and each item must be resolved prior to proceeding to the next one. The Japanese may prefer to proceed without being confined to a rigid agenda.

This enables them to take a holistic approach, resolving the whole by shifting discussion and nonverbal communication across issues. To most outsiders, this approach may be perceived as unstructured, disruptive, confusing, and frustrating. However, Japanese managers and executives function well in such ambiguity.

An understanding of such differences is a prerequisite to successful business dealings. During negotiations, for instance, westerners expect to focus on problematic issues, such as resolving disagreements. In contrast, the Japanese prefer to discuss areas of agreement, with the expectation that harmony will lead to the resolution of details. This concept of *wa* also explains another statistic: the US has 15 times as many lawyers per capita than Japan.

The Japanese cultural concepts of obligation, indebtedness, and loyalty together reinforce that of harmony. Consequently, verbal agreements are meaningful in Japan, and the need for lawyers is reduced. Instead, the Japanese feel the need to develop personal relationships within business transactions.

Conclusion

Every region has a predominant culture and there are many intricacies intertwined into each one. Just as Europe hosts many different cultures, there is neither one single culture nor one single way of doing business in Asia. The key for those attempting business there is to have patience and to learn as much as possible about what is important to each company, manager, and worker.

Further reading

Dana, L.P. (1999) *Entrepreneurship in Pacific Asia*, Singapore: World Scientific.

Hofstede, G. (1981) *Culture's Consequences: International Differences in Work-Related Values*, London: Sage.

Hofstede, G. (1993) *Cultures and Organizations: Software of the Mind*, London: HarperCollins.

Chinese entrepreneurs
move into the new economy

China has come through the Asian financial crisis and continues to grow. **Pedro Nueno** sees opportunities expanding as financial and banking reforms are put in place.

Dr Pedro Nueno is the Bertran Foundation Professor of Entrepreneurship at IESE Business School. He is vice-chancellor of the International Academy of Management and chairman of the academic council of the China Europe International Business School.

China's integration into the world economy is mirrored by its advances in developing electronic markets. Internet use is growing and the spread of new technology means ever-faster change – faster than most westerners are probably aware. This article outlines the changes in China's economy since the Asian crisis of 1998 and looks at the role of local entrepreneurs in e-business. It then assesses business potential in China, highlighting difficulties and opportunities.

The China Europe International Business School in Shanghai is one of the few places in China that brings together large numbers of English-speaking, knowledgeable, and influential Chinese. In July 2000, a delegation of European politicians and civil servants came to the school for a meeting with Chinese business people.

After the school assembled a few of its alumni to meet the delegation, one introduced himself as follows: "My name is Oliver Hua. I graduated as an MBA in 1998. Then I worked for McKinsey in Shanghai. Recently, I left McKinsey to start Luban.com with a former classmate, two other partners, and the support of a venture capital firm. Luban.com brings buyers and sellers of construction materials together, provides a channel to disseminate and access information, reduces transaction costs in the acquisition of materials and equipment, and improves communication and collaboration among construction project participants."

European visitors were astonished both by such an impressive track record and the presence of such a well-established and sophisticated e-business market in China. "How do you see yourself compared with a European entrepreneur?" somebody asked. "I see myself more like a southern European," was his reply. "I tend to put more emotion in my approach to work. Of course," he added, "as a Chinese, I come from a rich culture that is very different from the European, but in the approach to business problems, I am not so different."

In July, Luban.com, established in Shanghai, attracted one million hits and facilitated transactions worth Rmb25m ($3m). The company generated revenue through commissions, advertising, and fees for membership to the exchange. There are 16,000 web companies in China, many struggling like their western counterparts, but many with a solid business model.

In a report on China, Morgan Stanley noted that the Chinese leaders were committed to speeding up reform. The leadership is watching with interest the development of a Chinese capital market based on a Nasdaq-type exchange, using venture capital and easy access to equity. Many experts agree they want to bring China closer to the US and Europe in the pursuit of new technology and opportunities in the new economy.

Great expectations

Access to the World Trade Organisation (WTO) is the stimulus behind reforms in China. Just as with Spain and Portugal before they joined the European Common Market, or Mexico with the North American Free Trade Agreement, it is understood that membership of the WTO will imply some sacrifice, but there are no doubts it will be worthwhile.

China will have to crack down on counterfeiting and smuggling, as well as reducing tariffs, stamping out corruption, offering better protection for intellectual property, and reducing government subsidies – even if this means letting some state-owned enterprises fail.

The Chinese economy slowed down from a high in 1992 of 14 percent growth, to a low in 1999 of around half that figure. This reflects the impact of the Asian crisis, which China was able to absorb without devaluing the currency. The year 2000 has seen a return to growth. The forecast 8 percent can easily be improved upon. Output will probably have grown by around 12 percent in 2000, as exports and internal consumption increase.

Foreign direct investment seems to be gaining momentum, with growth of more than 20 percent in the first half of 2000, reaching over $20bn. In July and August major investments by

China will have to **reduce subsidies** – even if this means letting some state-owned enterprises fail

Motorola ($1.5bn) and Shell ($4.5bn) were announced, suggesting that the WTO is also a stimulus outside China. Of course, investment contracts do not mean immediate real expenditure and impact on growth, but the trend is clear.

Controls are being placed on counterfeit products, and measures are being taken to reward those who denounce producers of fake products. Border controls are being strengthened to crack down on smuggling. Foreign investors are closer to having access to "A" shares of Chinese companies, and moving toward only one type of share is being considered. Lending by foreign banks is scheduled for two years after entry to the WTO and financial services to the consumer market three years after.

Estimates point to some 80 million "private" business people in China, although this includes many very small businesses or even self-employed farmers or intermediaries. Many collectively owned companies are in fact private enterprises. Adding both categories, their output exceeds that of the state-owned enterprises. Reform of the state sector will imply further privatization. The room for entrepreneurship in China grows much faster than the economy.

New economy in China

The China Internet Information Center, the official internet agency, estimates that 16.9 million people are connected to the web, a quarter of whom are women. Internet Audience Measuring in Asia, a private agency based in Hong Kong, says the figure is closer to 12.3 million, 38 percent of whom are women. Official figures say 16 percent of internet users have made at least one online purchase during the past year. Again, the private agency puts the figure lower, at 5 percent.

Books and computer-related products are the items most frequently bought, with around 30 percent of purchases paid with cash on delivery and 20 percent using credit card. Both agencies put the average age of the Chinese surfer at 30, with an average income of Rmb1,400 a month. Those who have been connected for two or more years have an average monthly income of twice that figure. Internet use grew by a third in the first half of 2000.

A study by Arthur Andersen in China forecast 85 million internet users by 2005, around 35 percent of all Asian users. The same study expects telecom revenues in China to reach $76bn by 2003, 44 percent of all Asia (excluding Japan).

There are more than 300 internet service providers (ISPs) in China. Chinanet, operated by China Telecom, is the largest. Uninet, run by Unicom, the second telephone operator, plans to offer voice and fax services throughout China, and even to introduce a mobile internet service similar to NTT DoCoMo's in Japan. The infrastructure has its "blips," however. For example, Chinanet collapsed completely in June in Shanghai, after several days of severe problems, leaving the city without internet access.

Payment systems

Credit cards are not widely used in China and a lack of standards due to competition between financial institutions is not helping. According to Peggy You, founder of online bookshop Dangdang.com, most customers pay with cash for their orders. Chinapay.com has appeared recently with a solution to the problem in Shanghai by offering a "golden card" secure-payment system.

In 2000 agreements were signed that will help break this bottleneck. The Industrial and Commercial Bank of China signed agreements with eight internet service providers to launch online shopping through the Peony credit card. The bank has issued more than 60 million Peony cards that have handled transactions worth $3bn. The China Finance Certification Authority was established recently under the supervision of the central People's Bank of China to improve the security of internet business deals by certification of internet traders.

Logistics are still a problem. Courier systems in China are in their infancy, although solutions have been found using taxis and mobile phones. The *Shanghai Daily* reported in May 2000 that the second largest taxi operator in Shanghai, Dazhong Transportation, had launched an e-commerce venture providing travel and logistics. Among other services, Dazhong's venture will offer car rental, hotel bookings, event tickets, removals, and conference organization.

Entrepreneurs in China

Since the opening of the Chinese economy in 1978, there has been an explosion of entrepreneurial activity. Intermediaries from Hong Kong, Taiwan, and Singapore sowed the seeds when making deals with state-owned enterprises. As academic Howard Stevenson has said, entrepreneurs are driven by opportunity, not by the resources they control. China is full of opportunity.

Mobilization of external resources is key to entrepreneurs and they tend to be masters at managing networks. Mobilizing external resources through networks fits very well with Chinese culture. Plenty of opportunity, networks, and some clues about how to do it made many new ventures possible.

Money came from a variety of sources – from savings and through creatively engineered loans from state-owned enterprises. Sometimes creativity went across borders and these loans managed to travel to Hong Kong and transform themselves into investments coming back to China. Sometimes foreign intermediaries made loans to Chinese entrepreneurs. In other instances, foreign investment led to joint ventures with Chinese pioneers in private enterprise.

Western venture capital companies based in Hong Kong and Singapore have started to look for entrepreneurial talent in China. Goldman Sachs and Fidelity are reported to have raised $20m to start up Alibaba.com. Founded by Jack Ma, a 35-year-old entrepreneur from Shanghai, Alibaba is an online exchange for medium-sized and small enterprises.

Many entrepreneurs emerged from management positions in state-owned enterprises. But even those who had contact with foreign buyers and local producers often lacked key skills. However, as business schools appeared in Chinese universities, and foreign faculties taught "how to start your own business" courses, a growing number of Chinese became potential entrepreneurs, ready to take advantage of opportunities in their own networks.

Joint ventures and wholly owned foreign subsidiaries have also been a source of entrepreneurs. Armed with management training and local understanding, many people have launched their own initiatives. Mike Tang and David Liu left Dell Computers to form Eachnet.com, an auction site. As in some western companies, they understood that internet activities need telephone and fax support for customers, and established a call center.

Chinese active outside China

Many multinationals followed the obvious reasoning that nobody was in a better position to manage in China than a Chinese who left the country a decade ago, took an MBA in the US or Europe, and became an experienced and successful manager there. Most western companies designed generous compensation packages for ethnic Chinese with western passports. Unfortunately, this assumption turned out to be wrong.

With a few exceptions, Chinese expatriates do not work well in China. They have changed, their country has changed, and the chemistry tends not to work. However, things seem to be different for those who come back as entrepreneurs – and there is a growing flow of them stimulated by the new economy.

According to *China International Business* magazine's July 2000 edition, 35-year-old Wang Chaoyong, chairman of China Equity Advisory, has raised $200m for 15 projects, mostly in the internet sector. Wang Chaoyong is a Chinese with an MBA from Rutgers University and four years of experience as a banker in Morgan Stanley.

Peggy You, also in her mid-thirties, got her MBA from New York University and worked for four years as a merger and acquisitions consult-

Chinese **expatriates** tend not to work well in China, except those who come back as entrepreneurs

ant before returning to China with her husband Li Guoguin to start Dangdang in November 1999. Dangdang is now the biggest bookseller in China stocking more than 200,000 titles, tapping the domestic market and the 70 million-strong Chinese diaspora. Li and You expect Dangdang to be profitable by 2002.

Justin Tang, in his late twenties, also American educated and with experience in Merrill Lynch, claims to have raised tens of millions of dollars to create Asia.com and its subsidiary eLong, with offices in nine Chinese cities to provide product and service information.

Fortunately, in China as elsewhere, there is life beyond the internet, and entrepreneurs find management consulting services an attractive field. This is the case for 34-year-old Zhao Min, a Harvard Business School MBA, founder and chief executive of Sinotrust Business Risk Management.

These entrepreneurs are among the one in ten of the 300,000 Chinese who left the country to study abroad since the opening of the economy but came back. They have been welcomed. Equipped with MBAs and doctorates from Europe and the US, they return with experience and contacts. They have the credibility to raise money and set up business models that have worked overseas and should work in China and the rest of Asia.

Westerners in China

Opportunities exist in China not only for the Chinese but for westerners. Byron Constable and Micah Truman launched Madeforchina.com as early as 1997, and have grown to employ 50 people providing internet and e-commerce services and consultancy. Belgian-born Jan Borgonjon established InterChina, with offices in Beijing and Shanghai, employing Chinese consultants to provide consultancy services to Chinese and western clients in a variety of fields, including internet and telecommunications.

Language and relationships are obstacles for western entrepreneurs. It is difficult to be an entrepreneur through a translator. The respect that the Chinese attach to personal, hierarchy, and family relationships can also create problems. In Europe and the US, choosing a supplier because it is a company located in the town where the purchasing manager was born is seen as bordering on corruption. Offering a discount to a customer who may be a family member would also be difficult to explain.

Western entrepreneurs must be aware of such issues, since they can often be turned into opportunities. Well-managed relationships open doors and networking is a crucial component of an entrepreneur's toolkit. A team of highly qualified Chinese with the right contacts can save a great deal of time.

China's time is now

We may see some Chinese companies fail, just as e-businesses throughout the world are tumbling. The amount of money lost in China, however, will be a fraction of what is written off in the west. Entrepreneurship in China has been, in most cases out of sheer necessity, frugal. But we will see also lots of companies with reasonable revenues. Failures will bring talented people back to an increasingly privatized industrial sector. With internet and entrepreneurial skills, they will be needed to update the operating processes of many companies undergoing rationalization.

Meanwhile, infrastructure keeps improving and competition makes the internet more affordable, while its next generation is ready to be launched. China will join the WTO and this will stimulate a faster reform, opening previously sensitive sectors such as banking and telecommunications to international companies. The changes that will have taken place by 2005 are difficult to imagine. Entrepreneurs would do well to enter the fray now.

Further reading

Dayao, D.L.C (2000) *Asian Business Wisdom*, New York: Wiley.
Roach, S. (2000) *China's Time Is Now*, Morgan Stanley Dean Witter, June 19.

Developing strategy
for a not-so-global village

Philip M. Parker is Eli Lilly Chair Professor of Innovation, Business and Society at Insead.

The idea of global economic convergence has proven to be a myth, making data gathering on emerging markets essential. **Philip Parker** points the way to information sources.

Back in the early 1980s, many argued that a globally standardized strategy was the future. Convergence and standardization went together. Why? Because consumer tastes and preferences were converging across regions, countries, and economies. The idea was that companies should cut costs and conquer the world with global economies of scope, scale, and branding. Geographic differences would disappear as managers focussed on the global village.

If you are still thinking this way, it is time to reconsider. The data are in and standardization is out.

Eighty percent of companies divide the world into three time zones: the Americas (Latin America being run out of Miami or New York); the Asia-Pacific segment, encompassing Beijing, Sydney, and everything between; and the Euro segment (Africa and the Middle East being handled out of London, Paris, Geneva, or Athens). This allows managers to communicate within a segment in business hours.

What are the options? One might consider cultural segments (language, religion, ethnic groupings), economic segments (poor, less poor and affluent), levels of industrialization or similar structures. Yet few regional manager would champion such a strategy for product development, pricing, communications, or supply. Each region would need to depend on and co-ordinate with all others.

Economics tells us that segmentation in either quality or price leads to higher monopolistic profits when one company does it well and others stumble. One would never segment if all consumers or buyers had the same preferences and faced the same suppliers. Arguments to globalize and standardize are based on a belief that markets are converging. Are they?

Convergence

In the 1980s and mid-1990s, managers saw Indonesia, Vietnam, India, Latin America, and, to some extent, Africa as growth markets. It was thought that around half of the planet's population would shortly reach the standards of North America, northern Europe, Japan, Australia, and New Zealand.

Emerging markets were ready to take major products from developed markets and the demand would be explosive. These bad assumptions produced bad results. Companies that planned for convergence paid the price in excess capacity and devalued assets. Was this foreseeable? Yes, but only by accepting three economic regularities: income, consumption and supply divergence; spatial correlation; and physioeconomic forces.

Divergence dynamics

In the 1960s, some economists came to believe economies would converge in the long run. Evidence of convergence is seen, for example, between the economies of European countries after the Second World War and that of the US (as measured in terms of income per capita, car ownership per capita, and so on). When two countries converge to the same or similar level of economic behavior or consumption, this is called "beta" convergence.

Based on theories of diminishing returns, among others, it was felt that highly developed countries would have slow growth rates, whereas poor countries would have high growth rates. Extrapolations over 30 to 50 years suggested that all countries would eventually have similar consumption patterns.

Since the 1970s, however, economists have come to recognize that not all countries are converging. They have also come to recognize that this phenomenon can be traced back over centuries. In fact, there has been a gradual and predictable divergence.

These two forms of convergence are represented in Figure 1. It shows that most economies had similarly low incomes per head before the Industrial Revolution. Academic Simon Kuznets and others have also shown that the average person had a precarious, if not subsistence, standard of living. Things started to change, however, in the sixteenth century, when Europe's income per head began to rise. After the Industrial Revolution began in Britain in the late eighteenth century, the pattern of divergence was large enough to be seen as a nonrandom event. Since the 1800s, rich countries have grown faster than many poor countries, causing global divergence. Today, there are poor and wealthy countries, whereas 500 years ago there were really only poor countries. Beta convergence as conceived in the 1960s has not happened and does

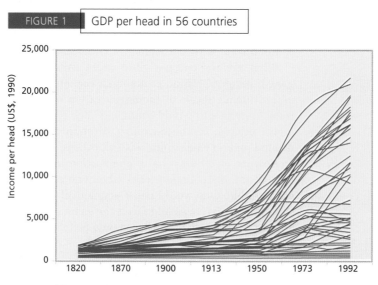

| FIGURE 1 | GDP per head in 56 countries |

Source: Maddison (1995)

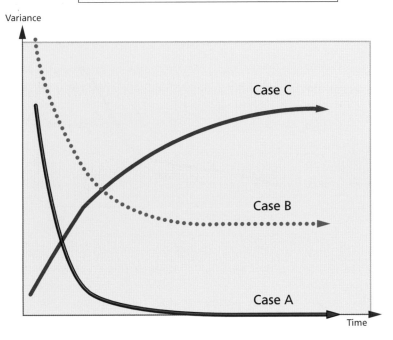

FIGURE 2 | Variance dynamics and conditional convergence

Variance

Case C

Case B

Case A

Time

Source: Maddison (1995)

not appear to be happening.

In the 1980s, a new view of convergence came into vogue, called "sigma convergence" or "conditional convergence." In this view, countries form "convergence clubs." Members of each club converge with each other, but no two clubs will ever look alike.

In mathematical terms, this view holds that worldwide economic behavior converges to a stationary level of "variance" or permanent divergence. Figure 2 illustrates various scenarios within this view. In the case of absolute beta convergence, where all countries converge to the same level of consumption or supply, one will observe variances across countries falling to zero, as in Case A.

This has been shown to be the case for infant mortality, death and birth rates, life expectancy, and literacy. For these development indicators, variances were great 100 years ago, but today are small, with similar absolute levels being reached by all countries.

If variances fall, but do not reach zero, this indicates that countries are not converging in an absolute sense, but that the variance is stabilizing. Shown as Case B, therefore, the world began

with high variance, but this narrows over time. In fact, long-run consumption per head across countries remains divergent. This case is not very common in economic data.

In Case C, the world starts in a convergent state (that is, all countries are equally poor), but over time diverges to a constant level of variance. Case C is observed today for economic behaviors involving consumption of goods and services. Figure 3, for example, plots the mean and variance of income per capita from the country data in Figure 1. Dispersion has increased, while income per capita has also generally increased on average.

Some countries, however, increased consumption dramatically, while others did not. Of the three convergence cases, Case C exists for virtually all economic activity, when measured per capita, irrespective of industry. However, it only exists when considering countries that span different geographic regions. For example, if we examine only countries in the Nordic region, Case A appears. If one adds southern European countries to these data, we observe Case C.

Today, economists are debating the conditions that lead to Case C. Clearly, the long-term

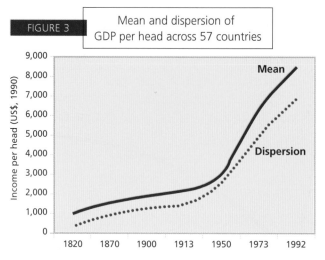

FIGURE 3 Mean and dispersion of GDP per head across 57 countries

Source: Maddison (1995)

dynamics of some countries lead to low levels of income or consumption, while others lead to high levels. What is it that makes a country permanently consume less than others? If we know the factors driving divergence, what are the growth implications for global companies segmenting by country?

Spatial correlation

A telltale sign of factors driving conditional convergence, or beta divergence, is the fact that economic indicators are spatially correlated. In other words, growth dynamics of neighboring countries are not independent. Similarly, the economics of two adjacent locations seem to exhibit beta convergence in the long term – Case A in Figure 2.

This spatial correlation is not symmetric in all directions, however; growth patterns will be more similar among some neighbors than among others. Provided countries have similar political regimes, economic systems, and absolute latitudes, all seem to converge to similar behavior. However, if one takes countries along the same longitude, neighbors are less similar to each other than to countries an equal distance away along the same latitude.

Stated differently, countries of the same absolute latitude and political system have similar growth dynamics. In particular, the farther a country is from the equator (all other factors held constant), the higher its income and con-

sumption per capita in the long run. This is called the "equatorial paradox." Exceptions to this rule are noncapitalist countries such as North Korea, countries extremely rich in resources such as Brunei or Kuwait, or strategic locations such as Singapore and Hong Kong.

The colder countries of the world (whether adjacent neighbors or not) seem to be converging to the same level of economic wealth and consumption. Absolute latitude, in fact, explains some 70 percent of the cross-country variances in income per head, and is the single most important factor explaining economic divergence compared with many other variables. Convergence clubs are, in fact, "climatic clubs." This effect has been increasing since the Second World War, especially as more countries adopt capitalist economic systems.

Why is this? First, it is clear that all value chains end with a consumer. All industrial products are transformed via manufacturing or some other value-enhancing process, and in turn are transformed or distributed to end users. These users consume clothes, housing, food, entertainment, transportation, and other goods (clothes, food, and housing represent between 60 and 95 percent of all things consumed on the planet). Countries that are hot all year round will, in the long term, consume less clothing, food, housing, and energy.

While this view of conditional convergence may seem obtuse, it has secure roots in physics

The colder countries seem to be **converging** to the same level of economic wealth and consumption

and its effects on human physiology. The world is not a set of countries, but climatic zones with varying resource bases and economic regimes.

Physioeconomic forces

Which countries will have faster economic growth in the long term? According to physioeconomics, high growth rates can be expected from countries that currently have low levels of consumption compared with other countries in the same convergence club (that is, countries with similar climates and terrain, or similar natural resources). It is not appropriate, in this view, to compare France with Panama, given that the two countries are not members of the same convergence club. Rather, France should be compared only with countries in its convergence club (such as Germany or the UK), or having similar starting conditions (such as climatic or geographic conditions).

| What to do about it

It appears that having a grasp of supply and demand differences across countries is necessary to divide global markets rationally. Unfortunately, the data to identify these differences are difficult to come by, especially if one needs very specific information across some 200 countries. Going global means research. This section describes how to gather global data and market intelligence on countries outside the top 25 markets by following six steps.

Step 1: Report aggregators

Start with web-based aggregators and directories. These services typically do not publish the reports they sell, but redistribute reports across some 100 publishers. From these, the user can often purchase only the paragraph or chapter of a report of interest. The advantage of these

aggregators is that their studies go beyond Anglo-Saxon markets. A list to start with includes:

www.commercial.ecnext.com

www.marketresearch.com

www.mindbranch.com

http://nlresearch.northernlight.com/market_research.html

www.profound.com

Some of these sites require a subscription, while others can be freely searched. Some allow reports to be downloaded directly.

Some aggregators combine market research data with financial data:

www.hoovers.com

www.tfsd.com

www.multex.com

www.xls.com

All of the above should be searched. In addition, most countries have sites that aggregate or list market research, such as Chinaonline.com. These are too numerous to list here, but are only available for some countries. Add to this list the larger internet book retailers, because these are beginning to list such research on their sites, and e-book sellers, such as Mightywords.com (select business).

Step 2: Global publishers

A number of sources specifically cater to the global intelligence market by supplying research reports, benchmarks, and data across most industries. Examples include:

www.eiu.com

www.euromonitor.com

www.icongroupedition.com (complementary culture data).

Serious business research libraries or business intelligence centers that are global or regional in focus tend to require subscriptions.

Step 3: Public sources

Public bodies are an excellent source of global data, though these cover only general demographic and economic data:

www.worldbank.org (select data)

www.cia.gov (select the world factbook)

www.imf.org (select country information)

www.wri.org (select publications).

Various agencies also sell data, such as the International Telecommunications Union (www.itu.org; select databases).

Step 4: Global references

In addition to market reports and data from the above, much can be gleaned from news sources with a global perspective. These articles will often cover the activities of competitors across countries and are the sources for many of the reports that are for sale above. The following are a good start:

www.economist.com

www.ftdynamo.com

www.factiva.com (Reuters business briefing).

Downloading from these sources may require a corporate subscription.

Step 5: Specialists

The last step involves research specialists and boutiques, not all of which have placed their data or reports with the aggregators, but nevertheless sell global studies. These are typically specialized in a vertical market (such as chemicals or electronics) and have created websites selling their research, such as Strategisgroup.com for telecommunications. Space limitations prevent a full listing here, though these publishers are generally listed as sources in the websites mentioned in Step 1.

Some aggregators focus on particular industries. For example, Allnetresearch.com focusses on internet research and Aktrin.com specializes in furniture.

The last step

The last step of the process, of course, is analyzing and synthesizing data to generate a segmentation strategy. This will probably take a few weeks. The analysis would certainly focus on the similarities between markets, but also their substantial differences. Ignoring time zones, one can quickly surmise, for example, whether a strategy or competitive structure found in the Philippines is likely to arise in a similar fashion in West Africa or Latin America.

Uncovering such wisdom, however, may lead to problems. The hard part becomes matching this wisdom with the situation of your company. You may realize that segmenting by absolute latitude, income per capita, language, or some other measure is the best strategy, but your company is organized by time zone and only a central authority can co-ordinate an alternative approach. What regional manager will volunteer to change the status quo? The steps above will look trivial compared with managing that problem.

Further reading

Kuznets, S. (1971) *Economic Growth of Nations*, Cambridge, MA: Harvard University Press.

Maddison, A. (1995) *Monitoring the World Economy*, Paris: Development Centre Studies, OECD.

Parker, P.M. (2000) *Physioeconomics: The Basis for Long-Run Economic Growth*, Cambridge, MA: MIT Press.

Rothman, T. (1995) *Instant Physics: From Aristotle to Einstein, and Beyond*, New York: Byron Press.

Business and society

5

Contents

Introduction to Part 5

This part deals with ethical and regulatory issues in business. Companies have many motivations for behaving ethically, aside from the truism that it is the right thing to do. In the "war for talent," firms that are not concerned with the moral consequences of their activities may find that the brightest individuals prefer to use their skills elsewhere, and employees may face conflicts between personal beliefs and their workplace roles. Corporate scandals can sometimes be endured, but often they inflict such damage on a company's reputation that the business is severely affected. Later in this part, writers examine the role that corporate governance can play in monitoring managers and assisting when things go awry. Are there standard rules for all companies, or should different rules apply at different stages of a company's growth? Many large businesses are family-owned. What are the ramifications for corporate and shareholder control?

Adding corporate
ethics to the bottom line

Thomas Donaldson examines the logic behind the growth of corporate ethics programs and seeks evidence for their success or failure.

Thomas Donaldson is
Mark O. Winkelman
Professor at the Wharton
School, University of
Pennsylvania.

Corporate ethics programs were like hummingbirds in the 1950s. You didn't see one often and when you did it seemed too delicate to survive. Now, these curiosities have proved their sturdiness, flourishing and migrating steadily from their historical home in Europe and the US to Asia, Africa, and Latin America. Most of the 500 largest corporations in the US now boast a code of ethics, and the proportion among a broader collection of US companies has risen to 80 percent. Similarly, a recent study of FTSE 350 companies and nonquoted companies of equivalent size undertaken by the London Business School and Arthur Andersen showed that 78 percent of the responding companies had a code of conduct, compared with 57 percent three years ago.

In the 1950s, ethics programs were the personal creations of charismatic leaders, such as General Johnson who fashioned Johnson & Johnson's Credo statement; today, they are produced by a wide variety of organizations. They encompass not only written standards of conduct, but internal education schemes, formal agreements on industry standards, ethics offices, social accounting techniques, and social projects.

The popularity of ethics programs raises several questions. Do they deliver what they promise in making companies more ethical? Do they aid companies in achieving traditional performance measures such as return on investment or customer satisfaction? And, should companies institute new programs, or perhaps change the ones they have?

The vogue for ethics programs does not resolve the most common theoretical question asked of business ethics, namely, what counts as ethical? Even the socially screened investment movement that specializes in assessing stocks for ethical characteristics often seems confused. Consider the tendency of such funds to screen out the "sin" stocks of tobacco, alcohol, and firearms. As a result, high-tech stocks, ones unlikely to produce sinning products, have become darlings of such

Ethics schemes have spread, yet no evidence suggests this is the result of a fall in standards

funds. But while Microsoft, for example, will probably never produce wine and so almost always finds itself on the screened funds' lists, it has been found in violation of US antitrust laws, a sin greater in some people's eyes than fermenting grapes.

Ethics programs, however, offer a solution to the question of what is ethical by simply decreeing an answer. It makes little difference to Motorola whether other companies agree or disagree that its principle of "uncompromising integrity" prohibits even small payments in countries where bribery is common. Motorola is content to set the standard for itself.

Similarly, programs created by industries or international organizations decree their own rules, although they often make use of existing standards as templates. The Organization for Economic Co-operation and Development's (OECD) recent prohibitions on companies based in member countries from engaging in foreign bribery were developed through extensive discussion among participating countries, although they contain precepts seen earlier in the US Foreign Corrupt Practices Act.

Corporate ethics programs have spread very widely, yet no evidence suggests this growth is the result of a decline in standards. Studies indicate that between 25 and 60 percent of employees in any given year admit to having seen ethical misbehavior, depending upon the context in which the question is asked.

The ethics boom

What, then, has driven the ethics boom? Likely factors include the stronger focus by the media on corporate conduct, increased government pressure, and the growing maturity of business institutions. Recently, media exposure of labor standards in Asia prompted a cascade of initiatives by companies such as Nike in the US and Puma in Germany.

Moreover, people have seen that companies reeling from media and legal pressures suffer heavy losses. Names in the financial services industry such as Prudential Group, Daiwa Bank, Salomon Brothers, and Kidder Peabody are sobering reminders that these problems can damage both a company's brand and its financial prospects. According to Roy C. Smith and Ingo Walter, financial experts who have analyzed these cases, Prudential Group's fraud at Prudential Securities and Prudential Insurance cost it $1.8bn in fines and settlements; Daiwa Bank's concealment of its trading losses cost it fines and the loss of its US license; Salomon Brothers' government bond auction scandal cost it $500m in fines and settlements and $1bn in market capitalization; and Kidder Peabody's insider-trading scandals and falsification of government bond trades cost it its viability – it was sold by General Electric in 1994 and is now defunct.

Often fines and court judgments take a back seat to the cost in damaged reputations. In the US, the 1994 legal dispute involving the Bankers Trust Company and its sale of derivatives cost it tens of millions in an out-of-court settlement. But more significant was the company's damaged reputation: in a matter of months, its share price halved. And while Royal Dutch/Shell avoided significant legal action for its alleged passivity during the trial and execution of Nigerian environmentalists, the effect on its reputation in the late 1990s was substantial.

Governments, too, have applied increasing pressure on companies, prompting new designs for ethics programs. In 1991, US Federal Sentencing Guidelines offered companies a dramatic incentive to develop formal schemes. The guidelines promise reduced penalties for companies found guilty of criminal conduct as long as they meet requirements for compliance and ethics programs. In turn, compliance-oriented ethics programs, usually with designated ethics officers, have boomed. Both the Ethics Officers Association and the Defense Industry Ethics Initiative have hundreds of members and share best practice for establishing ethics offices, hot lines, code design, web pages, and training programs. Most of the largest 200 companies in the US belong to one or both of these groups.

Finally, many experts argue that the ethics boom stems partly from the maturing of democratic capitalism. With Marxism dead, capitalism must nonetheless face the moral expectations of market participants. Consumers acknowledge the capacity of markets to generate wealth, but interpret the social contract between business and society as involving more than unmitigated profit-mongering.

The limits of law and regulation to cope with corporate ethics became obvious in the past century when consumers saw that regulation inevitably lags behind knowledge inside an industry. For example, governments were powerless to regulate successfully the use of asbestos because knowledge about its carcinogenic effects was held not by regulators outside the industry, but by employees inside it. By the time the law caught up, it was too late. Society expects companies to use their knowledge in a responsible way.

Most economists agree that externally imposed regulation can be invasive and inefficient. Companies, in turn, reason that if they can substitute moral persuasion for inefficient regulation, then they will benefit.

Modern programs

If the ethics programs of 50 years ago resembled a rare bird, today they resemble a Brazilian aviary. They fall into three types:

- code and compliance;
- identity and values;
- social outreach.

Each program has a different goal. Code and compliance programs are the most common and focus on regulating the behavior of employees. These formal documents specify employee behavior in detail and are often written by lawyers. Such codes govern conflict of interest, accepting gifts, anti-competitive behavior, entertaining customers, and so on. Some industries have slowly developed highly specialized compliance programs. For example, the financial services industry has raised compliance nearly on a par with other aspects of corporate management such as human resources, finance, and marketing.

Employees are often asked to sign a document each year indicating that they have read and understood the code. Thus, if the code is broken, it becomes easier to identify and penalize offenders. Motives for such codes are usually starkly self-interested: companies hope to avoid legal and reputational harm by specifying and monitoring behavior.

A variant of compliance programs is the trend toward third-party sponsored codes. The ISO 9000 code (regulated in conjunction with the Council for Economic Priorities), the Japanese ESC 2000 Code, the Caux Roundtable Principles, the Sullivan Corporate Responsible Principles, OECD directives on foreign bribery, and Kofi Annan's recent Global Compact from the United Nations are a few examples. Many such codes attempt to regulate labor standards in factories that supply global companies, as well as to specify standards for other aspects of behavior.

Companies such as Mattel, Levi-Strauss, and Royal Dutch/Shell have developed their own codes. However, increasingly companies find it convenient, if not more efficient, to use third-party resources for monitoring. One example is the work done by the nonprofit, anti-corruption group Transparency International. This group not only publishes yearly rankings of bribe-paying and bribe-taking countries, but has worked with corporations and governments to clean up institutions in host countries.

Identity and values programs, which sometimes exist alongside compliance variants, differ starkly from their counterparts in tone and motivation. They usually draw inspiration from a list of the company's values that emphasizes positive concepts such as integrity, respect for others, teamwork, and service to stakeholders. Not unlike mission statements, values programs aim to express what the corporation stands for, to specify an "identity." Royal Dutch/Shell's "principles" and Johnson & Johnson's Credo are examples. Most very large US corporations possess such programs, and companies in other countries are following suit.

Nonetheless, many corporations launch values programs only to see them wither. In contrast, companies that have been successful in maintaining schemes tend to renew them from time to time and managers use language from values statements to justify business decisions. The tone of values programs is markedly different from compliance codes. They emphasize positive against negative concepts and self-motivation rather than external sanction. The phrasing tends to be in plain language and sometimes even emotional, in contrast to legalistic compliance codes.

Finally, "social outreach" programs, the least common type, emphasize the company's role as a social citizen. Two trends dominate such programs. The first is the "social accounting" movement with its roots in Europe, and the second is the "competency-based" responsibility movement from Europe and the US. Social accounting programs rest on the premise that companies should account for social activities in much the same way as they account for their financial activities.

Recently, a group of 300 global companies called the Global Reporting Initiative (GRI) began formulating standards to improve social reporting. European companies, including BP and the social accounting pioneer Norsk Hydro of Norway, have adopted such programs. To date, social accounting is a legal requirement only in France, where companies with over 300 employees are expected to produce a *bilan social*.

The second form of social outreach emphasizes a corporation's core competency in its attempt to contribute to society. Increasingly, such programs are adopted by companies that want to move beyond writing checks for good causes.

One of the first to use a competency-based program was US pharmaceutical company Merck. Merck startled the world in 1980s when it moved to develop a drug, Mectizan, that would treat the tropical disease river blindness. Because potential users of the drug constituted some of the world's poorest people, no one, including Merck, expected the drug to make a profit. Merck also knew that developing such a drug would cost hundreds of millions of dollars. But relying upon its identity/values tradition of emphasizing the health of the customer as the best means to achieve profit, Merck pushed ahead.

The result was remarkable. Merck reaped a public relations windfall and, even more significant, the World Health Organisation last year announced that river blindness was on the shortlist of diseases officially eradicated. Following Merck's success, peer pressure on other pharmaceutical companies proved intense. Since then, Pfizer has announced a $60m project to eliminate the eye disease trachoma and GlaxoSmithKline has agreed to give away its drug to cure lymphatic filariasis.

Competency-based initiatives have spread. Ericsson developed a project on magnetic pollution; with help from UNICEF, Procter & Gamble is developing Nutri-Delight, a new product that addresses malnutrition in poorer countries; and in 1998 BP agreed to give solar-powered refrigerators to doctors in Zambia for storing malaria vaccines. Danone sponsors employees in Hungary to work with local groups to raise health standards for children.

Such efforts are not without risk. Monsanto applied its scientific expertise in an initiative with the International Rice Institute, groups from Thailand, and the Thai government to educate poor farmers about how to improve crop yields using scientifically engineered seeds and modern chemicals. But Monsanto has since been the target of vigorous criticism in the media, much of it alleging that Monsanto's technology is a hazard to the environment.

Ethics and profits

The motives behind the three kinds of ethics programs vary markedly. A 1999 study by the Conference Board demonstrated that the reasons behind ethics codes are markedly different in different cultures. Codes dominated by considerations of bottom-line success turn out to be far more popular in the US than elsewhere. The study showed that 64 percent of all US codes are dominated by self-interested or "instrumental" motives, while 60 percent of European codes were dominated by "values" concerns.

Despite geographic differences, the Conference Board study demonstrated that increasing numbers of senior managers are involved. About 95 percent of companies formulating ethics codes include contributions from the chief executive, in contrast to 80 percent in 1987;

and 78 percent of company boards of directors in contrast to 21 percent in 1987.

Do better corporate ethics fuel higher profits? This question has been studied for decades with no resolution. A 1999 academic study by Roman, Hayibor, and Agle summarized 52 research projects devoted to corporate ethics and profit. At first sight, the results appear encouraging for corporate ethics program defenders. The authors concluded that 33 studies showed a positive link between corporate ethics and profit, 14 showed no effect or were inconclusive, and only five suggested a negative relationship. Nonetheless, the problems of grappling with the relationship between ethics and profit are huge. They include determining not only what "counts" as a more "ethical" company, but also excluding reputational effects that can follow financial success. It is difficult to know what to conclude. Even if better ethics is good business, the question of whether programs make better ethics remains.

The 2000 National Business Ethics Survey in the US confirmed earlier studies showing that merely having a code of ethics does nothing to improve corporate ethics. Indeed, this study confirmed the trend of earlier pessimistic studies in showing a slight positive correlation between merely having formal ethical standards and poorer ethics – in this instance, poorer ethics being reflected in the percentage of employees who feel pressure to compromise ethics. The picture, however, is different for companies being restructured.

The study showed that when organizations are not in transition, the presence of ethics program elements (such as formal standards, training, and an advice line) is not statistically related to the pressure employees feel to compromise on ethical standards. But when organizations are in transition, pressure to lower ethical standards is significantly higher if formal initiatives are missing.

Evidence is accumulating that ethics programs are more successful when they are seen by employees not as being about compliance, but about values. A 1999 study undertaken by academics Weaver and Trevino showed that when employees construed companies' ethics programs as being oriented toward "values" rather than "compliance," they displayed far more commitment to

Ethics programs are successful when they are seen by employees as being about **values**

the organization, more willingness to deliver bad news, and more willingness to seek advice.

Another study by the same authors strongly suggests that programs fare better when they are "integrated" rather than "decoupled"; in other words, ethics policies fare better when they are integrated with other corporate structures and policies, such as reward policies, and where people who occupy corporate structures are held accountable. In contrast, less successful "decoupled" ethical policies appear to conform to external expectations, while making it easy to insulate much of the organization from those expectations. Hence, companies that attempt to manage ethics without the co-operation of senior managers and without adjusting structures and policies are less likely to succeed.

In line with this finding, a 1992 US study by the Institute of Chartered Financial Analysts of 5,000 people in the financial services industry showed that only 11 percent of financial services managers who witnessed unethical behavior reported their concerns. Clearly, financial services companies need more than a well-constructed compliance mechanism.

Studies support the connection between employee evaluation of their company's ethical behavior and important indicators such as loyalty. The 2000 National Business Ethics Survey undertaken by the Ethics Resource Center in the US indicated that 43 percent of employees who disagree that the head of their organization "sets a good example of ethical business behavior" also feel pressure to compromise ethics standards. But only 8 percent of employees who agree that he or she sets a good example feel ethical pressure.

In a recent KPMG integrity survey, four out of five employees who felt that managers would uphold ethical standards said they would recommend their company to potential recruits; whereas only one in five employees who did not believe managers supported ethical standards would do so. The study also found that four out of five employees who felt management would uphold ethical standards also believed customers would recommend the company to others, while the figure halved for employees who did not have faith in managers' ethical standards.

Conclusion

First, we should get used to ethics programs. The forces that propelled them into being show no signs of abating. Yet not all ethics programs are created equal. Corporate ethics programs can either fit with or conflict with the interests and aims of the corporations that create them.

Companies that wish to define their identity and communicate their values to employees, stockholders, and customers should adopt different programs from ones who simply want to limit legal and public relations problems. Even in the latter case, however, evidence suggests that compliance programs will be more successful when connected to positive values with which employees can empathize. For any ethics programs, furthermore, the evidence is strong that merely having a formal code is not enough. Any such statement must be synchronized with the company's organizational structures, its culture, and its leadership.

Finally, companies aiming for high standards of social citizenship, or aiding society by doing more than just giving money away, require a different kind of program. Current trends for such programs are toward social accounting systems and making creative social use of a company's core competencies.

Further reading

Donaldson, T. (1996) "Values in Tension: Ethics Away from Home," *Harvard Business Review*, 74(5), 48–56.

Donaldson, T. and Dunfee, T. (1999) *Ties that Bind: A Social Contracts Approach to Business Ethics*, Cambridge, MA: Harvard Business School Press.

Dunfee, T.W. and Hess, D. (2000) "The Legitimacy of Direct Corporate Humanitarian Investment," *Business Ethics Quarterly*, 10(1), 95–109.

Paine, L.S. (1994) "Managing for Organizational Integrity," *Harvard Business Review*, 106–17, January–February.

Weaver, G. R. and Trevino, L.K. (1999) "Compliance and Values Oriented Ethics Programs: Influences on Employees' Attitudes and Behavior," *Business Ethics Quarterly*, 9(2), 315–35.

Weaver, G.R., Trevino, L.K. and Cochran, P.L. (1999) "Integrated and Decoupled Corporate Social Performance: Management Commitments, External Pressures, and Corporate Ethics Practices," *Academy of Management Journal*, 42(5).

Legal problems showing
a way to do business

New technologies have led to legal uncertainties, but as lawyers thrash out the issues, **Constance Bagley** sees potential for managers to create value.

Constance E. Bagley is an associate professor of business administration at Harvard Business School and a member of the State Bars of New York and California.

Law has rarely been so important to managers, yet so in flux. Courts and legislatures are struggling to keep up with advances in technology, especially the transformation of the internet from a vehicle for communication among scientists and academics to an engine of global commerce. According to Forrester Research, internet retail sales were $20bn in 2000 and are expected to climb to $130bn by 2004. The *Christian Science Monitor* has reported that commerce between businesses conducted over the internet is even larger: $176bn in 1999 and estimated to increase to $1,300bn by 2003.

A company's most important assets are now often its intangible intellectual property. The market capitalization of Microsoft is based not on its bricks and mortar but on its ability to use copyright law to prevent others from duplicating its software. Amazon.com's strategy of creating a strong brand and a loyal customer base depends on using trademark law to prevent others from using its name, and on laws protecting trade secrets to prevent former employees from using or selling its customer lists. Patents, once primarily a concern of pharmaceutical, chemical, and manufacturing companies, now protect computer software and even business processes, such as Netcentive's use of frequent flyer miles as rewards for consumers buying telephone services or borrowing money.

The recording industry and other entertainment companies are aggressively defending their right under copyright law to prevent unauthorized distribution of music and video on the internet. For example, MP3.com, a US company, had created a database containing hundreds of thousands of copyrighted songs, which users of its internet service could access. In September 2000, Judge Jed Rakoff, sitting in a district court in New York, ordered MP3.com to pay royalties to the owners of the copyrighted music. Rakoff said some companies on the internet had "a misconception that, because their technology is somewhat novel, they are somehow immune from the ordinary application of laws of the United States, including copyright law." On the contrary, Rakoff declared, "the law's domain knows no such limits." As of mid-November 2000, MP3.com had paid more than $150m to settle copyright claims by the five major record labels.

Napster, which makes it possible for millions of users to play and record music that other users have copied on to their computer hard drives, is defending copyright infringement lawsuits by the Recording Industry Association of America, major recording studios, and artists (including such otherwise anti-establishment artists as Metallica). Napster claims that its service is not liable for music its users might have pirated because the service has substantial noninfringing uses, such as legally distributing the work of new and unknown artists who are not represented by traditional record companies.

The US Supreme Court accepted that argument in 1984, when the major movie studios sued Sony Corporation, claiming that its Betamax video recorder contributed to copyright infringement by making it possible for individuals to record and distribute copyrighted films shown on television. The court ruled that "time-shifting," the ability of a person to watch a program at a later time, was a fair use permitted by US copyright law.

Yet the Napster case appears distinguishable. Unlike Sony, which sold a product but had no subsequent relationship with the user, Napster actively facilitates file sharing by permitting users to keep so-called "hot lists" of people with interesting music. In addition, most people use Napster not to access legal copies of the work of unknown artists but to make unauthorized copies of copyrighted songs. Perhaps recognizing its legal vulnerability, Napster agreed in November 2000 to give an equity stake to Bertelsmann in exchange for permission to use its copyrighted music.

Process patents

Amazon and Priceline.com are defending their business process patents for one-click shopping and computerized buyer-driven auctions, respectively. A US federal appeals court surprised many in 1998 when it embraced the patentability of business processes, and courts and legislatures are wrestling with the appropriate scope of these patents.

Critics claim the US Patent and Trademark Office has been too ready to grant patents for processes that are not novel and worthy of protection. For example, some argue that Priceline received a patent for a process that is basically a computerized version of the Dutch auctions that have been used to sell tulips since the sixteenth century. In addition, the completion of the Human Genome Project and the prospect of patents for human genes raise serious public policy questions about what information should belong to every member of the human race and what should be proprietary.

One area that has become more settled is the application of trademark law to internet domain names. Because a domain name is given to whomever registers it first, holders of registered trademarks had to deal with so-called cyber-squatters, who would register names (such as McDonalds.com and Panavision.com), then offer to sell them to the trademark holders.

A flagrant example was one company's use of "candyland.com" as the domain name for a child pornography site when Hasbro held a registered trademark for "Candy Land," which it had used for decades as the name of a children's board game. The US Congress responded by passing laws barring the use of marks that would tarnish or dilute a famous trademark (such as Candy Land) and prohibiting would-be cybersquatters from registering domain names in bad faith. Disputes are increasingly being resolved not by the courts but through arbitration by the World Intellectual Property Organisation.

Companies are aggressively going after former employees suspected of stealing trade secrets. General Motors recovered $100m from Volkswagen plus a promise to buy $5bn of GM parts after a former executive took pricing information with him when he was hired by Volkswagen. Pepsico went further when it sued a former marketing executive who had developed marketing strategies for All Sport and powdered teas. When the executive left Pepsico, he went to

Quaker Oats to work on the marketing of Gatorade and Snapple drinks.

There was no evidence that the executive had taken any written materials with him, or had disclosed any trade secrets to his new employer. Nevertheless, an appeals court barred him from working for Quaker Oats for six months, after concluding that, given his assignment to work on directly competitive products, it was inevitable that he would use or disclose Pepsico trade secrets. A number of other courts in the US have embraced this doctrine of inevitable disclosure.

In the US Justice Department's suit against Microsoft, the parties sharply disagree about the proper role of competition law and judicial intervention when the technology is constantly changing and network effects and high switching costs cause consumers to gravitate to one standard for maximum interoperability.

The convergence of communications, media, and computers makes it increasingly difficult for regulators to define the relevant market and to assess the anti-competitive effects of mergers involving major industry players, such as Time Warner and America Online.

The European Union is wrestling with the proper forum for lawsuits by consumers against people selling goods and services on the internet. Should consumers be able to sue in their home country, or be required to sue in the country where the seller has its principal place of business?

Courts in the US have held that the mere presence of a website accessible in a particular state does not confer personal jurisdiction over the site owner, but are divided over just what activity is enough to give a state's residents the right to haul an out-of-state seller into local courts.

Both the US and EU have adopted laws on electronic commerce. A US law that went into effect in October 2000 gives electronic signatures the same validity as written signatures. This will enable consumers to obtain insurance and loans online. Companies continue to search for cheap yet reliable ways to authenticate digital signatures.

The US Securities and Exchange Commission (SEC) was one of the first agencies to embrace the internet and its use in selling securities and distributing information to investors. The technology enables companies to hold shareholder meetings online and to give individuals access to the analyst conference calls that routinely follow a company's announcement of quarterly earnings.

In September 2000, in an effort to give individuals, especially day traders (who quickly move in and out of stocks), access to the same information available to analysts and institutional investors, the SEC adopted regulations that prohibit companies from selectively disclosing private information to analysts and favored investors but not to the public. Executives fear the new rules will subject them to liability if they have one-on-one conversations with analysts and warn this will reduce the quality of information available to the market.

The global reach of the internet makes it increasingly difficult for countries to regulate information flows across their national borders. For example, France sued Yahoo!, the web search engine and portal, for giving French citizens access to auctions of Nazi paraphernalia clearly prohibited by French law. After court-appointed experts concluded it was feasible to block access to the offending sites for 90 percent of French surfers, the French court ordered Yahoo! to implement a filtering system proposed by the experts within 90 days of its November 20 ruling, or face fines of FFr100,000 for each day it exceeded the deadline.

Germany has been unable to keep Germans from accessing neo-Nazi sites. Unlike pamphlets or books, which can be intercepted by customs at the border, websites are difficult to block. Similarly, efforts by the US Congress to protect children from pornography on the internet have been derailed because of the technological difficulty of keeping pornography from children without infringing adults' freedom of speech.

Managers and law

Given these uncertainties, what are managers to do? The first thing is to get into the game, even if the rules are not clear. For example, even if a manager is not convinced that obtaining a patent will give a company a competitive advantage, it is critical to have a bargaining chip if charged with

Savvy managers know **legal risks** must come into business decisions in the same way as other risks

infringing someone else's patent. It is increasingly common for a company to respond to a charge of patent infringement by denying the infringement and asserting infringement of its own patents. The resolution often involves an agreement whereby each company gives the other the right to use the patented technology.

Second, managers need to understand how the law can minimize risk and create value. Well-drafted representations and warranties in an acquisition agreement can flush out hidden problems and expressly allocate risk to one party. For example, the buyer of a factory could require the seller to disclose all environmental liabilities and to indemnify the buyer for all hazardous waste clean-up costs, even if they result from conditions not known to the seller.

Employers should require employees with access to confidential information to sign written nondisclosure agreements, in which the employee agrees not to use or give out trade secrets. Assignments of inventions can ensure that any copyrightable work or invention conceived of by an employee belongs to the employer.

In some jurisdictions, employers can require staff to sign covenants not to compete. To be enforceable, they must be reasonable as to duration, geographic scope, and range of prohibited activities. Some jurisdictions, such as the state of California and India, refuse to enforce any employee covenants not to compete (except in connection with the sale of a business) on grounds that they unduly restrict individuals' ability to ply their trade. Others, such as France, enforce them only if the former employer agrees to pay the same salary offered by the prospective employer. Yet even a pro-employee jurisdiction like California will enforce a nondisclosure agreement and assignment of inventions.

Because employers face the possibility of suits by former employees for wrongful termination, discrimination, or sexual harassment, many companies require employees to agree to arbitrate all employment disputes. To be enforceable, these agreements must provide a fair way for resolving disputes. For example, in August 2000, the California Supreme Court struck down a clause that limited the employee's available damages, did not require the employer to arbitrate, and required the employee to bear a portion of the costs of arbitration.

Savvy managers understand that legal risks must be factored into business decisions in the same way as other risks, such as currency risks. Often, the manager will need an attorney to explain the options, but unless the attorney advises that an action is illegal, the manager, not the attorney, should decide whether the risk can be reduced and whether the benefits of the deal outweigh that risk.

Finally, managers should realize that legal disputes are inevitable. Indeed, if one is never challenged, it may mean that opportunities to create value are being lost due to an overly conservative legal strategy. Instead of delegating such disputes to attorneys, successful managers realize that every legal dispute is a business problem requiring a business solution. Too often, managers treat the law as a black box and leave it up to the lawyers, rather than taking responsibility for disputes.

Copyright © Constance Bagley 2001

Further reading

Bagley, C.E. (1999) *Managers and the Legal Environment: Strategies for the 21st Century*, Cincinnati, OH: West.

Gleick, J. (2000) "Patently Absurd," *New York Times Magazine*, March 12.

Siedel, G.J. (2000) "Six Forces and the Legal Environment of Business: The Relative Value of Business Law Among Business School Core Courses," *American Business Law Journal*, 37, 717.

Developing the rules
for corporate governance

Standardized rules on corporate governance have been widely promoted. **Colin Mayer** asks whether the same rules can apply to all companies.

Colin Mayer is Peter Moores Professor of Management Studies at the Saïd Business School, Oxford University.

Corporate governance is widely regarded as being concerned with improving shareholder performance. According to this view, corporate governance is all about accountability, boards, disclosure, investor involvement, and so on. There are rules associated with good governance, best expounded by the UK's Cadbury committee and since adopted by numerous organizations, such as the OECD and the World Bank (*see* Box 1).

A large body of evidence supports this perspective. Good regulation of financial markets and good governance of companies promote markets and the financing of companies. This has been analyzed in large-scale comparisons of financial markets around the world. According to this view we are – and should be – converging on strong regulatory and governance rules that protect and promote the interests of investors, in particular minority shareholders. Just swallow a majority of nonexecutives on your boards, relieve yourself of the chairmanship (if you are the chief executive), and subject yourself to regulatory examinations of your pay, performance, and senior managers; then your company will be viewed as being in the healthiest of conditions.

Box 1 **Corporate governance: the key concerns**

- Investor protection
- Managerial accountability
- Transparency
- Shareholder activism
- Incentivizing management

- Disciplining and replacing bad management
- Enhancing corporate performance
- Improving access to capital markets
- Promoting long-term investment
- Encouraging innovation

This raises two questions. First, is there a set of best governance practices? Second, if so, should we all adopt them? On the first question, it is far from clear that the commonly prescribed rules are universally appropriate. For example, nonexecutives are generally thought to provide an important check on management. The Cadbury report argued there should be an increase in the proportion of nonexecutives on the boards of British companies. Evidence from the US supports the view that nonexecutives perform a valuable disciplinary function. A higher proportion of nonexecutives on the boards of US companies is associated with a greater turnover of board members in poorly performing companies.

But in the UK, the opposite is observed: lower turnover of management occurs where nonexecutives occupy a high proportion of board seats in poorly performing companies. The reason for the difference is clear. In the US, directors have strong fiduciary responsibilities to their shareholders, and shareholders can enforce these in the courts, through, for example, class actions. In the UK, fiduciary responsibilities are less clearly defined and rarely enforced through the courts. Consequently, nonexecutives play more of an advisory and supportive role in the boardrooms of British companies.

This illustrates how the legal environment critically affects corporate governance practice. There are other examples. In the UK, unlike the US, nearly all new equity issues by listed companies are made in the form of rights issues that give existing shareholders first rights to subscribe to new issues. This protects shareholders from the risk that their equity will be diluted by new issues priced at a discount and allows them to dictate the terms on which new finance is provided. In particular, shareholders can and do require managerial changes as a precondition for subscribing to equity issues by financially distressed companies.

Regulation and legal factors therefore combine to bias governance toward financial control in the UK and toward board control in the US.

Local differences

Turning to the second question about the adoption of particular governance practices, it is worth noting how far companies are from implementing a single system. In the UK, there is an active takeover market. In hostile bids that are opposed by target management, roughly 90 percent of the directors of the boards of target companies are replaced within two years of the takeover being completed. Even in friendly acquisitions, around half of the boards are replaced within two years. Takeovers are therefore a key mechanism for changing the boards of British companies.

In continental Europe, few companies have been subject to hostile acquisitions. Some people believe that the bids by Olivetti for Telecom Italia and by Vodafone for Mannesmann were precursors to the emergence of an active European market in corporate control. In fact, there are still serious impediments to this.

To begin with, few companies are up for sale on the stock market. Most are closely held by a small number of dominant shareholders. Figure 1 shows how in Austria, Belgium, Germany, and Italy a single shareholder, or block of shareholders with a voting pact, typically commands a majority or near majority of votes in listed companies. By contrast, in the UK, the average largest voting block is around 10 percent of votes – in the US, the average is below the minimum disclosure level of 5 percent.

Second, even where it is possible to secure majority ownership, this does not necessarily confer control. Rules on the nomination and replacement of board members may impede board control by dominant owners. Figure 2 shows the legal structure of one prominent European company, Unilever. Unilever comprises Unilever NV (the Dutch part) and Unilever plc (the UK part). They trade as a single entity. This is achieved through two holding companies, NV Elma and United Holdings Limited, which are held in turn by the Unilever companies and have cross-shareholdings in each other. They in turn hold special shares and deferred stock in Unilever NV and plc respectively.

The significance of these special shares and

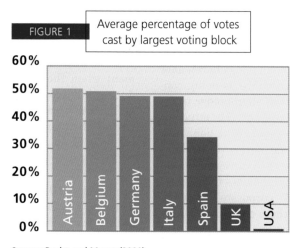

FIGURE 1 · Average percentage of votes cast by largest voting block

Source: Becht and Mayer (2000)

deferred stock is that they nominate people for elections as members of the boards of NV and plc. In other words, elections to the board of Unilever are by two companies owned by Unilever. This is done, according to Unilever's 20F declaration (to the Securities and Exchange Commission), to "ensure unity of management of the Unilever Group."

In the US, devices such as poison-pills, anti-takeover charter provisions, options to issue voting stock to friendly parties, and voting caps can be used to limit the control that external investors exert. Although widely touted as the model for effective shareholder capitalism, a majority of US companies are in fact protected from hostile companies through one or more of these mechanisms.

If there is a single best system of corporate governance, we are therefore a long way from adopting it. Systems of governance differ markedly across countries, and while there may be convergence in financial systems, there is little evidence to date of convergence in governance. And there are probably good reasons why there should not be.

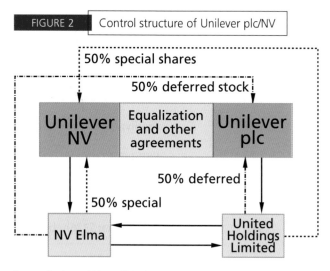

FIGURE 2 · Control structure of Unilever plc/NV

Source: Becht and Mayer (2000)

Governance control

As noted, the conventional view of corporate governance is that it is about enhancing shareholder performance. It views governance as being concerned with the promotion of shareholder interests, and in particular those of the minority, against self-interested managers and dominant shareholders. Why, then, do nearly all systems have devices for protecting the interests of management and dominant shareholders from interference? Have powerful corporate interests captured regulators, or is there a reason for such marked divergences between theory and practice?

The answer is that corporate governance is about more than aligning management and shareholder interests. It is about the control and running of companies – who is in control, for how long, and over what activities.

The way start-up companies in the new economy are financed illustrates this. Start-up companies go through several stages. The first is the seed stage when a concept has to be proven and developed. The second is the start-up phase when products are developed and initial marketing takes place. The company may be less than a year old at this stage. The third is early development when the company is expanding and producing but may well remain unprofitable; it is often less than five years old at this stage. During the fourth stage of expansion it might go public or be sold.

The financing of Amazon.com is a good example (*see* Table 1). The company was initially funded out of Jeff Bezos's savings and some borrowings. The family then invested. Two business angels came in, followed by a larger business angel syndicate. There was a further family investment, followed by a venture capital injection of $8m. A year later the company went public with an initial offering of shares worth $49m.

These stages involve different groups in the running and monitoring of the company. The seed stage is limited to entrepreneurs and immediate families and friends who put up initial financing. In the second and third stages, private

| TABLE 1 | Financing of Amazon.com (1994–9) |

Dates	Share price	Source of funds
1994: July to Nov	$0.0010	**Founder:** Jeff Bezos starts Amazon.com with $10,000; borrows $44,000
1995: Feb to July	$0.1717	**Family:** founder s father and mother invest $245,000
1995: Aug to Dec	$0.1287-0.3333	**Business angels:** two angels invest $54,408
1995–6: Dec to May	$0.3333	**Business angels:** 20 angels invest $937,000
1996: May	$0.3333	**Family:** founder s siblings invest $20,000
1996: June	$2.3417	**Venture capitalists:** two venture capital funds invest $8m
1997: May	$18.00	**IPO:** 3 million shares issued raising $49.1m
1997–8: Dec to May	$52.11	**Bond issue:** $326m bond issue

Source: Van Osnabrugge and Robinson (2000)

investors (angels), sometimes acting in consortia, play an active role in monitoring and managing companies. Venture capitalists may then take the company to the fourth stage, where it is listed or sold off to another company.

At each stage, there is a change in governance and control. It starts with control by an entrepreneur and moves to involving a small number of outside investors, then a small number of institutions, and finally it extends to external control by other companies or investors in the market.

Thereafter, there is a marked difference in the way governance develops. In the UK and US, once a company is listed on the stock market, the original owners sell out rapidly so that after six years a company is typically held by a wide number of owners, with most shares traded on the stock market. In continental Europe, only a small proportion of companies come to the stock market and, in those that do, a majority of the voting shares are retained by the original founders.

There is therefore a significant difference in the evolution of the governance structures of new- and old-economy companies. New-economy companies are characterized by rapidly changing governance structures. Control is transferred in steps from original investors to a large group of outside investors. Old-economy companies have slowly evolving control structures, in which families and other companies retain control over long periods. In old-economy companies, family and corporate owners exert control over long "influence periods"; in new-economy companies, a variety of different groups exert control for short influence periods.

Why is there such a difference in governance structures? The obvious answer is that they are suited to their respective productive activities. Old-economy businesses tend to involve large-scale capital intensive investments, with returns accruing over long periods. New-economy companies require inputs from different parties for comparatively short periods: entrepreneurs developing ideas, managers creating initial products and markets, new managers forging alliances and partnerships, and so on.

The inputs required of old-economy companies have long "realization periods"; those of new-economy companies shorter ones. If new-

Old-economy structures are **too rigid** to accommodate new-economy companies

economy governance structures are employed in old-economy activities, they lead to excessive short-termism. Old-economy structures are too rigid to accommodate new-economy companies.

There is therefore a clear need to match governance structures to different activities. This is not just about new- versus old-economy companies, but also about differences within new- and old-economy sectors. The governance structures required of pharmaceutical companies are different from those of heavy manufacturing industries. Companies undertaking high-risk, innovative investments require different forms of control from those employing more familiar technologies. The former benefit from the markets' ability to absorb risks and to respond rapidly to change. The latter require the closer monitoring, longer-term investment and greater commitments that large, closely involved investors can provide.

There is a more complex and dynamic relationship between ownership structure, governance practice, and companies' competitive advantage than is at first apparent. Different financial systems and governance systems are suited to different types of activities and to companies at different stages of their development. Some systems, most notably the Anglo-American market-based systems, emphasize flexibility in changing control. Others, such as the continental European, provide more continuity and commitment in control. There is no single form of governance that is best for all activities.

Corporate governance is not, as suggested at the beginning, solely concerned with the efficiency with which companies are run and whether they are operated in the interests of shareholders. It is also intimately related to company strategy and lifecycle development. In other words, it is central to understanding the success and failure of companies, and the growth and decline of industries and economies. We are just beginning to understand these relationships.

Further reading

Becht, M. and Mayer, C. (2000) "The Control of Corporate Europe," in F. Barca. and M. Becht, *The Control of Corporate Europe*, Oxford: Oxford University Press.

La Porta, R., Lopes-de-Silanes, F., Shleifer, A. and Vishny, R. (2000) "Investor Protection and Corporate Governance," *Journal of Financial Economics*, 58.

Van Osnabrugge, M. and Robinson, R. (2000) *Angel Investing: Matching Start-up Funds with Start-up Companies*, San Francisco, CA: Jossey-Bass.

The family business
and its governance

Sir Adrian Cadbury was chairman of Cadbury Schweppes from 1975 to 1989 and chairman of the Committee on Financial Aspects of Corporate Governance, the "Cadbury committee," between 1991 and 1995.

Family companies are the dominant business structure, but bring with them special problems as they grow.

Adrian Cadbury identifies clarity in the family's role as the crucial issue.

Family firms form the basic building block for businesses throughout the world. Internationally, they are the dominant form of business organization. One measure of their dominance is the proportion of enterprises that are family-owned rather than registered; this is estimated to range from 75 percent in the UK to more than 95 percent in India, Latin America, and the Far and Middle East.

The way family businesses are governed is therefore crucial to their contribution to national economies as well as to their owners. Governance of a family business is in many ways more complex than that of a company with no family involvement. Family relationships have to be managed in addition to business relationships.

Family businesses come in all shapes and sizes, and experience every kind of success and failure. Some will not reach the stage of forming a board and appointing directors. Others deliberately decide not to grow in order to retain their original pattern of organization. This article focusses on family enterprises that need to formalize their structures to grow, but aim to do so in ways that retain family commitment and promote the business.

Structures

At some stage, a family business will grow beyond the point where there is a close identity between the members of the family managing it and those who share in its ownership. There is then every merit in providing a clear and accepted structural division between governance of the business and the deliberations of the family.

Promoting dialog

It makes sense to encourage all family members with an interest in the

A useful role for family shareholders not involved in running the business is to **protect values**

company to meet regularly. Such gatherings may start by being informal, but there are advantages in moving to a properly constituted council or assembly. This involves deciding who is entitled to membership (for example, should members by marriage who may not own shares be included?) and it is useful to elect someone who can speak for the family, probably the assembly's chairman.

Arguably, family shareholders can be treated like any other shareholders with the opportunity to ask questions and express views at an annual meeting. This, however, weakens the link between family and business, which is what distinguishes the enterprise and should be a source of strength. It also fails to make the most of the advantages that a family forum has to offer.

A family forum provides a means of communication between family and business. Family members can debate issues among themselves and express agreed views through their chairman. In return, family executives can explain the company's plans, policies, and progress. This enables members of the family not in the business to understand the thinking of executives and it is an opportunity to gain support for company strategy. At the same time, the family forum is clearly the accepted link between family and company, rather than approaches by individual family members.

A useful role for family shareholders not involved in running the business is to act as guardians of values. The executives of a family business inevitably have to make changes to maintain its competitive position. The family members outside the business can help them do so in ways that are in line with the company's original philosophy. The obligation on family members, who wish their views to carry weight, is to take the trouble to understand the reasoning behind decisions and to make good use of the information that executives pass on.

The essential point is that there should be no doubt where the power to make decisions lies. It is solely with the executives. The wider family can, however, provide sound counsel through its own forum.

The value of a board

Once they have grown beyond the point where the founder or a family partnership can effectively manage the company, family businesses should establish a board of directors. This is a means of progressing from an organization based on family relationships to one based on business relationships. The structure of a family business in its formative years is likely to be informal and to owe more to past than present needs. Once the business has moved beyond the stage where authority is vested in the founders, it becomes necessary to clarify responsibilities and the process for taking decisions.

Forming a board not only provides a logical structure, but also establishes clear lines of authority and responsibility. This starts with the board, because the board determines which decisions are reserved to it. The board then determines how the powers that it delegates to executives shall be exercised. Introducing order should not be seen as an attempt to impose bureaucratic rules, thereby weakening informal family arrangements that have worked well in the past and stifling creativity. A decision-making structure that is accepted and understood will avoid confusion, lobbying, and wasting time.

An important advantage of having a working board in a family business is that issues of difficulty because of their family implications are more likely to be dealt with, rather than put off. Examples of such issues are the retirement of senior family executives, especially the head of the company, succession within the family, appointment of nonfamily members to the board, and whether to become a publicly quoted company.

The value of outside directors

Nonexecutive directors have a special value for family businesses. One merit of a board of directors is that it provides the ideal way to bring outside advice into a family company's councils. Sharing information, which is power, is a step families may be reluctant to take. Consultants

Box 1 **Forces shaping the family company**

In considering the stages through which family businesses can pass, it may be helpful to draw on my experience at Cadbury, where I spent my working life. The company was founded by my great-grandfather, John Cadbury. He opened a grocer's shop in the center of Birmingham in 1824 and sold tea, coffee, cocoa, patent hops, and mustard. In 1831, he decided to concentrate on the manufacture and marketing of cocoa, founding the firm of Cadbury as owner-manager.

In 1861, his sons Richard and George took over. So the simplest form of business, the owner-manager, gave way to the next simplest, a partnership. When Richard Cadbury died in 1899, the business employed 3,000 people. At that point the business was turned into a private limited liability company, Cadbury Brothers Limited, and a board of directors formed, made up of family members.

The next change came with the merger between Cadbury and Fry in 1919. J.S. Fry & Sons was a family business dating back to 1728 and had been the leading company in the industry. Cadbury overtook Fry in the early 1900s and by then the Fry family had become less directly involved in its management. Few members of the Fry family were in the business and the merger meant that those members of the Cadbury family who were both executives and shareholders were outnumbered by Cadbury and Fry family shareholders who played no part in management.

From this point on, it is understandable that there should have been differences between those in the family who were running the business – whose aims were investment and growth – and those who were owners, but not managers, and primarily concerned with dividend income and the capital value of their holdings. An inevitable point of contention became the price at which shareholdings could be transferred in the absence of an open market for the company's shares.

Diffusion of ownership among the two families as the generations succeeded each other, the increasing proportion of family shareholders whose interests lay outside the company, and the pressures of taxation eventually made the move to a public quotation for the shares irresistible. In 1962, therefore, the business became a publicly quoted company and ceased to be a family business in terms of ownership, although a majority of the board was still made up of members of the family, and the family held more than half the shares. Family shareholders then had an open market for their shares and the directors had to take account of the general interest of a much wider body of shareholders than in the past.

The first nonfamily directors had been appointed in 1943, but when I joined the board in 1958 the company was still effectively owned and managed by the family and all the directors had executive responsibilities within the business. The final change in the structure of the business came with the equal merger of Cadbury and Schweppes in 1969.

The forces that brought about structural changes in the Cadbury business such as growth, family succession, deaths, taxes, an open market for their shares, and amalgamations affect all family businesses.

---

may be brought in to tackle specific issues, but they work to a brief, present their findings, and may or may not be involved in implementation. Their commitment is limited.

Appointing an outside board member means sharing responsibility for the direction of the business with someone who is neither a member of the family nor an executive. It means letting them see the company's books. This may be a major issue for family executives if family members not involved in the business are not privy to this information. Yet there are many advantages in having outside directors on the board.

They can give objective advice on issues relating directly to the family that may be contentious, such as appointments and succession. They are equally well placed to advise on balancing the interests of the company with those of family owners who are not in the business, over issues such as dividend and investment policy, mergers, takeover offers, and whether to become publicly quoted.

Outside directors help counter any allegations of nepotism or self-interest and may be specifically asked to settle the remuneration of the family board members. The advice of outside directors is valuable in itself, because of their experience. Furthermore, it provides assurance to all family members that decisions, with which they may not agree, are made by a board not exclusively composed of relatives.

In my experience, the greatest value of outside directors is in strategy. Having spent my working life in one company, I was aware of how much my thinking was limited by history and experience. Knowledge of the business is vital for strategy, but so is being able to look more widely.

Qualities a board looks for in outside directors are independence and judgment, experience, and commitment to the company. It is independence of mind that helps to resolve conflicts of interest and inspires trust in board decisions. Commitment means they must be able to devote time to their directorial duties.

Keys to success

Family businesses have to strive to be as well managed as the best competitors. The need for a professional approach is arguably even greater than in a nonfamily business. What can family companies do to increase their chances of success, once they are no longer owned and managed by their founders? There are four essential requirements.

Clarity of role

First, they have to think through the present and future relationship between their families and their enterprises. This, in turn, should lead to a clear structure separating the governance of the company from the affairs of the family. Both family executives and family owners have responsibilities to each other. Once appointed, executives alone have the authority to take decisions, while being accountable to those with an ownership stake. Links between family and company should run in both directions, but should be channels of communication, not command.

Members of the family should take the trouble to understand their role. Family owners who are not managers must appoint directors to run the company on their behalf – and then let them get on with the job. Owner/managers need to appreciate that they wear two hats and to be sure that they are wearing the appropriate one when making decisions.

The shareholders of a publicly quoted company do not expect to intervene in its daily management. Nor do they expect to make personal use of the company's facilities. Family owners are in the same position, but may not find it easy to confine themselves to the shareholder role. One reason for this is that family shareholders and directors may be in contact daily, as opposed to the once-a-year rhythm of the general meeting.

An effective board

Second, the continuing success of a family business is best assured if it is headed by an effective board – one with competent, independent-minded, outside directors. Family businesses need to be able to draw on the best independent advice, to complement the strengths that come from the family's expertise and commitment.

The first task of such a board is to clarify the aims of the company. This is a vital aspect of the management of any enterprise, but it is especially important in a family business because, if its members have differing views on the purpose of the business, the stage is set for misunderstanding and dissent. If the board draws up an unequivocal statement of business objectives, owners and managers know where they stand.

Organizational structure

Next, the company structure should be aligned to its purpose, so that the pattern of organization is logical. The chain of command and the decision-making process should be clear. Jobs need to be properly defined and responsibilities allocated; the assignment of tasks should be known inside and outside the business. All of this helps to avoid arguments about the way in which the company is being run and responsibilities shared.

Equality of opportunity

Finally, policies on recruitment and promotion need to be written down and respected. Their importance to family members is self-evident, but they are equally important to others considering whether to enter the business. It is not easy for members of what has been a family business to accept the need to bring in nonfamily executives and to treat them as equals.

Goals of the board

What kind of goals should the boards of family businesses set themselves? The ultimate task of a board has been admirably summarized by the former head of Imperial Chemical Industries, John Harvey-Jones: "The job of the board is all about creating momentum, movement, improvement and direction. If the board is not taking the company purposefully into the future, who is? It is because of the failure of boards to create tomorrow's company out of today's that so many famous names in industry continue to disappear." Achieving that transformation is the challenge for boards of family businesses, determined to build a successful future.

This article is drawn from the brochure *Family Firms and Their Governance: Creating Tomorrow's Company from Today's*, by Sir Adrian Cadbury (Egon Zehnder International, 2000; email: egon_zehnder.lon@ezi.net).

Further reading

Clarke, P. (1972) *Small Businesses: How They Survive and Succeed*, Newton Abbot: David & Charles.

Harvey-Jones, J. (1988) *Making It Happen: Reflections on Leadership*, London: Collins.

Neubauer, F. and Lank, A.G. (1998) *The Family Business: Its Governance or Sustainability*, Basingstoke: Macmillan Business.

The value to be found
in corporate reputation

The public's view of a company not only acts as a reservoir of goodwill, but also boosts the bottom line. **Charles Fombrun** examines how perceptions can be measured.

Charles J. Fombrun is professor of management at the Stern School of Business of New York University and executive director of the Reputation Institute. He is co-founder and editor-in-chief of the quarterly journal *Corporate Reputation Review*.

Company survival and profitability depend on the ability to attract support from four holders of resources: employees, customers, investors, and communities. People must be persuaded to join and work for the company; customers must be induced to buy; investors must be encouraged to supply credit and equity financing; and communities must welcome the company to the neighborhood. Having a good reputation among these resource providers is therefore crucial if a company is to build and sustain a competitive advantage.

Managers try to influence perceptions in many ways. They recruit on college campuses; they invest millions in advertising and sponsorship; they introduce philanthropic programs and community-based initiatives; they involve senior executives in direct conversations with analysts.

These initiatives are successful in so far as they convey the credibility of the company's strategy, boost assessments of its prospects, and generate support from resource holders. In time, favorable perceptions crystallize into the intangible asset of a corporate reputation. These reputations have economic value because they affect a company's bottom line. After describing recent developments in reputation measurement and valuation, this article presents five principles of reputation management that call for closer relationships between practitioners of strategy making, marketing, and communications.

Measurement

A corporate reputation can be good or bad, strong or weak: it describes how people feel about a company based on whatever information (or misinformation) they have, company activities, workplace, past performance, and future prospects. Measuring corporate reputations accurately is crucial if they are to be managed. Unfortunately, many measures of reputation exist, encouraging confusion about a company's reputational assets.

One of the most visible reputation surveys is *Fortune* magazine's annual list of America's most-admired companies. Since 1983, the magazine has asked executives and analysts to rate companies in their own industries on eight attributes: the quality of products and services; innovativeness; value as a long-term investment; financial soundness; ability to attract, develop, and retain talent; community responsibility; use of corporate assets; quality of management. Then there are specialized rankings for working women, for minorities, for those with a social conscience, and for those concerned about the environment.

However, scrutiny of such measures indicates deficiencies in the way they are done that inhibit systematic analysis. Some are arbitrarily performed by private panels and so are not replicable. Some are carried out with private information and so cannot be verified. All rely on idiosyncratic attributes and are devoid of theoretical rationale. The result is a cacophony of incompatible ratings.

Yet it is possible to measure perceptions of companies across industries and with many stakeholder groups. In partnership with research company Harris Interactive and the public relations company Shandwick International, this author held focus groups in the US. People were asked to name companies they liked and respected, as well as companies they didn't like or respect, and asked them why they felt this way. Findings demonstrated that people justify their feelings about companies on one of 20 attributes that were grouped into six categories:

- Emotional appeal: how much the company is liked, admired and respected.
- Products and services: perceptions of the quality, innovation, value, and reliability of the company's products and services.
- Financial performance: perceptions of the company's profitability, prospects, and risk.
- Vision and leadership: how much the company demonstrates a clear vision and strong leadership.

- Workplace environment: perceptions of how well the company is managed, how good it is to work for, and the quality of its employees.
- Social responsibility: perceptions of the company as a good citizen in its dealings with communities, employees, and the environment.

From these, an index was developed to summarize people's perceptions of companies on these 20 attributes – the "reputation quotient" (RQ). In addition, various empirical studies were conducted to benchmark the reputations of companies as seen by different stakeholder segments. The results indicate that RQ is a valid instrument for measuring corporate reputations and can be used to benchmark companies across industries. Various research projects are now underway to verify the technique in different cultural settings. Such a standardized measurement of corporate reputation is necessary if a company's reputational assets are to be managed systematically.

Valuing reputations

Corporate reputation has economic value. Unfortunately, efforts to document this value run up against the fact that a company's reputation is only one of many intangible assets to which investors ascribe value. Isolating a reputation's unique contribution to market capitalization is therefore difficult. Nonetheless, evidence from three sources confirms that reputations have bottom-line financial value.

Crisis effects

The value of corporate reputation is magnified at times of crisis because of the loss of life and assets involved. For instance, Johnson & Johnson's market value fell by $1bn, or 14 percent, after some of its Tylenol bottles were laced with cyanide in 1982. The company took a

Evidence from three sources confirms that **corporate reputations** have bottom-line financial value similar $1bn hit in 1985. Exxon's stock was devalued by $3bn, or 5 percent, in the week after oil gushing from the tanker *Exxon Valdez* fouled Alaska's Prince William Sound in 1989. And Motorola saw its capitalization fall $6bn, or 16 percent, after scientists in 1995 hinted at a link between cell phones and brain cancer.

Clearly, these market losses incorporate investors' expectations of future clean-up costs, legal costs, and reparation costs. They also include anticipated losses from weakened perceptions of the company by customers, employees, and communities.

Over time, some companies recover lost value quickly and the crisis fades. Others experience more extended damage. Research suggests that the difference lies in how the crisis was handled and in how the reputation of the company was beforehand. Good reputations have considerable hidden value as a form of insurance – they act as a "reservoir of goodwill." The insurance value of reputation derives from its ability to buffer well-regarded companies from problems.

Supportive behaviors

Fortunately, most companies are not in crisis. For them, the intrinsic economic value of a corporate reputation lies in its ability to induce supportive behavior from resource holders. The greater resources of a better-regarded company improve its perceived prospects and increase the financial value of the company. These benefits can be described in terms of a value cycle (*see* Figure 1).

The value cycle suggests that a company's market valuation derives from perceptions of future prospects. These perceptions develop from observations of supportive behavior by stakeholders toward the company, such as growth in revenues, growth in employment, or increased visibility. Growth itself demonstrates approval of the company's strategic initiatives and is made possible by more attractive financial valuations.

Financial analyses

Comparing book values with market valuations suggests that the intangible assets of public companies in the US and the UK constitute on average some 55 percent of their market valuations – a proportion that has grown steadily over the past 40 years. These intangibles are made up of intellectual capital such as patents and reputational capital (the strength of the company's stakeholder relationships).

One way of estimating reputational capital is to ask how much a third party might pay to lease a corporate name. Licensing arrangements are actually royalty rates for corporate names. The more a licensee is prepared to pay, the greater must be the drawing power of the company's reputation. Royalties on corporate licenses generally range between 8 and 14 percent of sales. Therefore, one estimate of the value of a company's reputation is the present value of all expected royalty payments over a given period.

Various researchers have sought to quantify the value of reputation. They confirm that large economic premiums are associated with strong

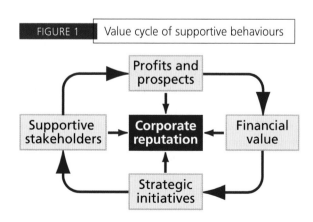

FIGURE 1 Value cycle of supportive behaviours

corporate reputations – although the exact size of the estimate is still in question.

Consider research led by Rajendra Srivastava that compared groups of companies with similar levels of risk and return, but different average reputation scores in 1990. The study showed that a 60 percent difference in reputation score was associated with a 7 percent difference in market value. Since an average company in the study was valued at $3bn, a point difference in reputation score from 6 to 7 on a 10-point scale would be worth an additional $52m in market value.

Another study suggests that reputational capital may generate higher returns. Ervin Black and his colleagues examined reputation scores of companies rated by *Fortune* between 1983 and 1997. They concluded that a one-point difference was associated with $500m in market value.

Five principles

Companies that manage their relationships with resource holders give clues to reputation management. Analysis has identified five principles. They link strategic positioning, brand marketing, organization theory, and corporate communications.

Distinctiveness

Strong reputations result when the companies occupy a distinctive position in the minds of resource holders. Take chip makers Intel and AMD. Both offer comparable products, yet Intel dominates the minds of computer buyers and others. Why? Because Intel owes its reputation, not solely to product quality, but to the "Intel inside" campaign that tried to define Intel as the only quality supplier of components and a guarantor of excellence. Intel made itself distinctive.

A similar process unfolds in all industries. Success in building reputation occurs when companies own an "empty niche." Companies competing in commodity industries are powerful examples of this. For example, oil companies grapple daily with public perceptions of their capacity for polluting. To counter negative images, most companies try to signal their concern for the environment with programs and

Strong reputations arise when companies focus their actions and communications on a core theme

initiatives. In doing so, they run into each other head on.

In an effort to build distinctiveness in the environmental arena, for example, BP Amoco unveiled a new corporate logo. The green and yellow symbol blossoms into a metaphorical flower to convey the tagline "beyond petroleum" and a commitment to environmentally friendly technologies. The strategy is clearly to "own" perceptual space as the world's most environmentally friendly company. Success will depend on the credibility of the claim to stakeholders and on what rivals do in this contested area.

Focus

Reputations tend to improve when companies focus on a core theme. Consider the US medical products group Johnson & Johnson, which is highly ranked on public trust. This is no accident: trustworthiness is a focus of its communications. Its advertising single-mindedly portrays Johnson & Johnson as nurturing and caring, with babies invariably featured (despite baby products representing less than a tenth of the company's portfolio).

Or take top-rated Coca-Cola. All of the company's communications portray a core "devotion to the product" and its integral role in the lives of people. Coca-Cola's dominance is a testament to the merits of focus in the design of reputation programs.

Consistency

Companies should be consistent in actions and communications with all resource holders. In a survey of global companies, better-regarded companies were more likely to orchestrate and integrate initiatives across functions. Companies with weaker reputations suffered from maintaining compartmentalized relationships. Isolated staff in the community relations department manage relationships with community groups; in investor relations with analysts; in advertising departments they counsel on product and corporate positioning; and in human resources, staff typically manage employee communications. Such approaches tend to engender inconsistency. At General Motors, for example, overlapping and conflicting communications emanate from the level of individual brands, stifling the development of stakeholder loyalty to the whole company.

Identity

Strong reputations are built on companies being genuine. In the long run, trying to manipulate external images by relying on advertising and public relations will fail, if this is disconnected from the company's identity. A strong reputation is built from authentic representations of the company to its stakeholders, or what Majken Schultz and her colleagues describe as "self-expressions" in the book *The Expressive Organization*.

In 1996, Royal Dutch/Shell embarked on an ambitious effort to rebuild a corporate reputation that was torn apart by the media following the mishandling of two major crises. The program was rooted in a soul-searching process that required identifying the company's business principles and "core purpose," the values it supports, and behaviors it is willing to endorse. Through focus groups around the world, Shell employees and leaders came to define Shell's core purpose as "helping to make the future a better place." This has since become an anchor for initiatives and communications.

Transparency

Strong corporate reputations develop when companies are transparent in conducting their affairs. Transparency requires communication – a lot of it. Comparing the communications of highly regarded companies against direct rivals who are not so well regarded shows that companies with stronger reputations are more visible in all media. They disclose more information and are more willing to engage stakeholders in dialog. Communications increase the probability that a company is perceived as genuine and credible and so attracts support from stakeholders.

Conclusion

Reputation attracts resources to companies and enables them to operate. Alan Greenspan, Chairman of the US Federal Reserve, appears to agree. As he put it in a speech at Harvard University in June 2000: "In today's world, where ideas are increasingly displacing the physical in the production of economic value, competition for reputation becomes a significant driving force, propelling our economy forward. Manufactured goods often can be evaluated before the completion of a transaction. Service providers, on the other hand, can offer only their reputations."

Corporate reputations are strategic assets. Reputation management is an emerging discipline whose central tenet is that strong reputations result from conveying the genuine, distinctive values and personality of a company. The essence of building reputations does not lie in posturing, spin-doctoring or puffery. Rather, it presents reputation management as a source of competitive advantage – which makes it nothing less than enlightened self-interest.

Further reading

Alsop, R. (1999) "The Best Corporate Reputations in America," *Wall Street Journal*, September 25.

Black, E., Carnes, T. and Richardson, V. (2000) "The Market Valuation of Corporate Reputation," *Corporate Reputation Review*, 3, 31–42.

Fombrun, C.J. (1996) *Reputation: Realizing Value from the Corporate Image*, Cambridge, MA: Harvard Business School Press.

Fombrun, C.J. and Shanley, M. (1990) "What's in a Name? Reputation-Building and Corporate Strategy," *Academy of Management Journal*, 33, 233–58.

Schultz, M., Hatch, M.J. and Larsen, M. (2000) *The Expressive Organization*, Oxford: Oxford University Press.

Srivastava, R.K., McInish, T.H., Wood, R.A. and Capraro, A.J. (1997) "The Value of Corporate Reputation: Evidence from the Equity Markets," *Corporate Reputation Review*, 1, 62–8.

Risk role grows
to enterprise scale

Enterprise risk management provides control over disparate risks in the business environment. **Gerry Dickinson** explains how.

Gerry Dickinson is a professor of international insurance at the City University Business School, London. He is a vice secretary general of the Geneva Association, an international association for the study of insurance economics.

Since the mid-1990s, enterprise risk management has taken root as a concept and as a management function within corporations. Enterprise risk management provides a systematic and integrated approach to managing the total risks that a company faces. Its emergence can be traced to two main causes.

First, following a number of high-profile company failures and preventable large losses, the scope of corporate governance has widened to embrace the risks that a company takes. Directors are now increasingly required to report on internal risk control. This is either through voluntary codes, such as the Turnbull guidelines in the UK, or by legislation, as in Germany through the Control and Transparency in Entities law.

Second, shareholder value models are playing a greater role in strategic planning. Early models paid insufficient attention to risk. Modern versions are based more on shareholder value concepts, which draw their inspiration from finance theory where risk has always played a central role.

Origins of risk management

Risk management as a formal part of decision making within companies can be traced to the late 1940s and early 1950s. There were two earlier strands of practice that have more recently been integrated under the broader concept of enterprise risk management. One of these strands relates to insurance risks.

For many years, companies have been able to transfer certain types of risks to insurance companies. These risks related to natural catastrophes, accidents, and human error or fraud, but as the scope of insurance markets expanded, some types of commercial risks could be transferred, such as credit risks.

The existence of insurance markets led managers to consider alternatives to insurance. Some of these insurable risks could be prevented, or their impact reduced, through loss prevention and control systems, and some could be retained and financed within the company. This led to a broader approach to managing insurable risks.

In the 1970s, companies began to look more closely at how they handled financial risks, such as movements in exchange rates, commodity prices, interest rates, and stock prices. Financial risk management began, as a formal system, at the same time as financial derivative products were developed, for example, financial futures, options, and swaps.

This was no coincidence, because investment banks had developed these financial instruments and their associated markets in part to allow their corporate customers to hedge financial risks. Hence, financial risk management emerged in much the same way as insurance risk management had previously. It was stimulated by the existence of these financial products, which caused managers to consider how much risk should be retained within the company and how much should be offset through these external arrangements.

The existence of financial derivatives also forced companies to consider more carefully the pricing of risks, how risks could be financed internally, and the value of services supplied by investment banks.

Companies also recognized that insurable risks and financial risks should be managed together, since the purchase of insurance and the purchase of derivatives to hedge financial risks performed essentially the same role. This recognition has led to risk-transfer products that combine both types of risk.

An early example of this was the decision by Honeywell in 1997 to take out a contract that combined insurances to cover its property and liability risks with currency options to hedge currency movements on profits from overseas operations.

There was another reason for a more holistic approach to risk management. Contingency planning had been a part of corporate policy for many years, its purpose being to identify those activities that might be threatened by adverse events and to have systems in place to cope with these events. Business continuation management extended the practice of contingency planning by requiring more comprehensive internal systems.

The corporate responses to the Y2K threat provide a recent international example of business continuation management. Both contingency planning and business continuation approaches, however, were limited, since they presupposed that strategic choices had been made and their role was confined to implementation of these strategies.

Measuring enterprise risk

Enterprise risk is the extent to which outcomes from strategy differ from those specified in corporate objectives, or fail to meet these objectives (using a "downside risk" measure). The strategy selected to achieve corporate objectives embodies a certain risk profile, which arises from the activities, processes, and resources chosen to implement strategy.

A range of external and internal factors can cause the outcomes of a company's activities to depart from those set down in its corporate objectives. Some external factors relate to the market in which a company competes, such as new entrants and changing consumer tastes. Other external factors arise from a wider context, such as changes in the economy, changes in capital and financial market conditions, and changes in the political, legal, technological, demographic, and other environments. Most of these are beyond managers' control, although active enterprise risk management requires systems in place to make a company more resilient. Risk management is a dynamic process.

Another set of factors that can cause different outcomes from those planned arise from within the company itself. These are human error, fraud, systems failure, disruption of production, and so on. Such internal causes represent a major part of operational risks.

In assessing the impact of external and internal factors on a company, there must be some simplification to make the task manageable, even with computer modeling. Increasingly, scenario analysis is being used to measure and manage enterprise risk, with support from consultants.

If one measures enterprise risk in terms of corporate objectives, one has a consistent framework of analysis. But there are shareholder value models to consider. Shareholder value models specify that corporate objectives should match those of shareholders. However, shareholder risk can only be determined indirectly, since it depends on how the stock market values the expected riskiness (volatility) of future income streams from the company's activities. When the corporate objectives of a company are fully aligned with those of shareholders, enterprise risk will be close to, if not the same as, the risk perceived in the stock market. Nevertheless, it should be kept in mind that in both competitive product markets and risk-averse stock markets, a corporate strategy with a higher risk profile will tend to have higher rewards: there is a compensation for the lack of predictability.

Retaining and transferring risk

Since the overall risks of an enterprise are an integral part of its corporate strategy, one way of managing these risks is through the choice of corporate strategy. If senior managers consider the risk profile of a particular strategy to be too high, they can change strategy to adopt a lower risk profile. Hence, enterprise risk management must be a top-down process.

Just as other corporate decision-making processes take place in a hierarchical structure, so do risk management decisions. Questions of whether to buy insurance or to hedge financial risks depend on strategic decisions that have already been made. For example, currency risks arise because a company has international activities. Thus, if a company's production is located in a country with a strong currency relative to those countries to which it wishes to export, one way of managing these risks is by relocating production.

Most risks a company faces cannot be insured or hedged, and so they must be retained and financed internally. Other mechanisms exist for reducing risk, apart from buying insurance and hedging with derivatives. Legal mechanisms can be used, for example. Some risks from commercial activities can be restricted through the use of corporate vehicles, using limited liability status.

Large-scale projects and property developments are often structured in this way: the Alyeska Pipeline Service Company was formed in 1970 to build and service the Alaska oil pipeline; and the Olympia & York Canary Wharf Company was formed in 1985 to redevelop part of the Docklands area in London.

Divestment of corporate activities and the outsourcing of operating functions provide other mechanisms for risk transfer. However, unlike insurance, hedging, or legal mechanisms, divestment or outsourcing represents a transfer of commercial activity and not just the risks embedded in these activities.

Decisions on how much insurance is bought, how much of the financial risks are hedged, or the degree of divestment and outsourcing that takes place will be largely determined by a few key considerations. The scale of potential loss or, more precisely, the greater the potential adverse impact on the attainment of corporate objectives, the greater will be managers' preference for risk transfer rather than risk retention.

However, decisions on the balance between risk retention and risk transfer will be related not only to their scale of impact. The degree of information and competence that the company possesses in managing a specific set of risks is also important.

When a company divests or outsources an operation, it does so usually because it considers the recipient to be better equipped and more knowledgeable in managing these activities. For example, outsourcing computer systems to a specialist can reduce risks of technological obsolescence and systems failure, as well as increasing cost-effectiveness. More knowledge and a greater core competence usually means lower risk, since the impact of a risk event often depends on who is managing or controlling the underlying process.

Similarly, in buying insurance or derivative contracts to hedge financial risks, information about the risk is important. Companies will tend to have less information on the underlying probability distributions needed to price insurance risks than will insurance companies, especially if the insurable events are rare. This also applies to pricing financial risks.

Organizational issues

Since enterprise risk management is a top-down process, the chief executive and the senior executive team must determine parameters for policies and organizational structure to ensure its effective implementation. Information must be fed back from those closest to the sources of risk in operating divisions, so that senior managers are well informed when formulating their overall risk policy. In addition, managers must delegate some responsibility to people closest to where the risks are likely to arise, so early action can be taken to prevent a small problem growing.

Because of the complexity of identifying, controlling, and managing risks across a company, specialist expertise is required. A new co-ordinating management role is now emerging – that of the chief risk officer (CRO). The chief risk officer, usually a senior executive and part of the top strategic planning team, may retain a more traditional job title, such as group risk director, even if the responsibilities have widened, but the title chief risk officer is growing in use. Among other companies, Ford, Duke Energy, Koch Industries, Charles Schwab, Fidelity, and Royal Bank of Canada have created such posts.

In addition, the CRO must maintain close links with the chief financial officer (CFO). The financing of risks, whether retained or transferred, rests with the chief financial officer, who will inevitably be a senior executive and will also sit on the main strategic planning committee. The CFO is responsible not only for buying insurance and derivatives, since these decisions fall within the treasury function, but also for the overall financial policy of the company, which includes financing retained risks.

Corporate governance encourages boards of directors to develop more clearly defined risk-audit functions, including an overview of their top management teams. This high-level risk audit is often an additional responsibility for the audit committee of the board of directors. Since executive directors themselves have to be monitored, a nonexecutive director chairs the audit committee to give it the necessary degree of independence. The board has ultimate responsibility for the enterprise risk of the company, being accountable to shareholders and other stakeholders.

In summary, the senior executive committee, including the CEO, CFO, and CRO, will report to the board in setting risk policy, guidelines, and controls. This will be done with input from the audit committee, line managers (through the CRO), and the treasury department (through the CFO).

Conclusion

Enterprise risk management will continue to strengthen its role within strategic planning. Since it has become part of the corporate governance agenda, and because boards of directors and senior managers are now more directly accountable for the risks a company takes, it will likely receive ample financial resources for it to develop fully.

Finally, enterprise risk management also provides a coherent framework within which the insurance and financial risks a company faces can be evaluated and managed.

Further reading

Deloach, J. and Temple, N. (2000) *Enterprise-Wide Risk Management: Strategies for Linking Risk and Opportunity*, London: FT Prentice Hall.

Dickinson, G.M. (1997) "Integrating Insurance and Hedging into the Overall Risk Management of the Firm," *Singapore International Insurance and Actuarial Journal*, 1, August.

Doherty, N.A. (2000) *Integrating Risk Management: Techniques and Strategies for Managing Corporate Risk*, New York: McGraw Hill.

Lam, J. (1999) "Enterprise-Wide Risk Management and the Role of the Chief Risk Officer," *Ivey Business Quarterly*, 3.

Environmental disaster:
not all bad news

Geoffrey Heal is Paul Garrett Professor of Public Policy and Business Responsibility at Columbia Business School.

Pressures from environmental issues are not going to go away, in fact they will increasingly affect the business agenda. **Geoffrey Heal** looks for the benefits.

Environmental issues have become a permanent part of the social, political, and business agenda. Population size is twice what it was only 35 years ago and is likely to double again within three decades. The build-up of atmospheric carbon dioxide has widely reported implications for climate change. Humans now fix more nitrogen than nature and have changed the Earth's nitrogen cycle, with consequences that are seen in poorer water quality worldwide and the growth of "algal blooms," whereby concentrations of microscopic algae poison seawater and kill fish.

The diminution of the Earth's protective ozone layer will remain with us for most of this century, even though the CFC gases used in aerosols and refrigerants are being phased out. These changes, together with destruction of natural habitats by logging and farming, are causing the extinction of many species.

While the consequences for humans are unknown, scientists agree they are likely to be harmful, perhaps seriously so. There will be increasing pressure on economic activities to tread lightly on the Earth and minimize mankind's footprint on the natural environment. This article looks at responses made by the international community and examines some solutions adopted by companies.

First steps

In the past, political responses have often been inadequate in scale and inefficient in structure. For example, vehicle emission controls are inadequate for their purpose and little short of Stalinist in their economic crudeness. One could say much the same of the Endangered Species Act in the US. This is arguably the most important piece of conservation legislation in the US and by far the most controversial. It gives the federal government powers to freeze economic activity on private land where an endangered species has been discovered. These measures rely entirely on command-and-control legislation, with no economic incentives. Economic analysis makes it clear this is usually the most costly of policies.

A more attractive approach is that embodied in the US Clean Air Act of 1990, which introduced a market in sulfur dioxide emissions and harnessed market forces in the cause of environmental policy. It has been a striking success: the costs of removing sulfur from flue gases have dropped to a tenth of their 1990 levels, largely due to the incentives provided for technological innovation.

How does the sulfur dioxide market work? It brings to environmental policy the sophisticated tools of financial engineering now commonplace in financial markets. Companies can buy and sell permits to emit sulfur dioxide: they can also engage in maturity swaps, trade options, and adopt the hedging strategies that option markets make possible. And even companies in compliance can profit from further reducing emissions. As noted, the effect of this act has been to cut greatly the cost of emissions reductions. Similar systems are in use for pollutants such as lead additives.

The 1997 Kyoto Protocol, designed to combat the emission of greenhouse gases, was an attempt to apply this system on a global scale. The essence of these approaches is that they put market prices on previously unpriced natural goods and services. The 1990 Clean Air Act and the Kyoto Protocol put a price on using the atmosphere for disposal of sulfur dioxide and of greenhouse gases respectively. Although the Kyoto Protocol has not yet been implemented, there is already a market in greenhouse gas emission rights, with options and futures trading.

The aim of environmental policies must be a transformation of the way economic activities impinge on the natural world. To the extent that this is successful, no business will be untouched. Thinking about environmental impacts and the effect of environmental policies will become integral to business strategy.

Indeed, several industries are there already.

Companies in power production, transportation, and energy have come to realize, with varying degrees of graciousness, that the natural environment is part of the commercial environment. They have to build this into their product planning at the earliest stages. BP Amoco has made this transformation public in its "beyond petroleum" rebranding; if its performance matches its aspirations, it will gain kudos in the process.

Certainly, businesses do themselves little good by disputing the need for action on environmental issues: they run the risk of becoming the tobacco companies of the twenty-first century. Scientific evidence is compelling. If consumers indicate a desire for a better environment through the political process, businesses may generate a backlash by trying to thwart this. Indeed, in the US they could end up as targets for litigation, as has happened with heavily polluted sites in the Superfund clean-up program.

More generally, consumers in affluent countries have shown a willingness to switch brands in response to perceived differences in social responsibility. Shell, for example, suffered because of its treatment of the disposal of the Brent Spar drilling rig. Recent statements by senior executives at Ford and General Motors have shown awareness of the brand-damaging potential of their fuel-hungry sports utility vehicles, especially when contrasted with Honda and Toyota, which introduced fuel-efficient hybrids just as US rivals were introducing even bigger versions. Brand image and status can be greatly affected by environmental policies.

Impact analysis

Businesses can respond to the focus on environmental issues in several ways. At a minimum, managers should conduct an "environmental audit" of the ways in which the company interacts with its environment.

This begins with a review of all the company's solid wastes, liquid wastes, and gaseous emissions. Managers should then examine the lifecycles of their products, researching where the components of the product end their lives and how the uses of the product affect the environment. Do they lead to wastes or emissions that

Carrying out an **environmental audit** does not force a company to take action immediately

could be reduced by different designs? Could transportation or packaging be reduced? Does the disposal of the product damage the environment?

Companies also need to review the environmental history of their raw materials. For example, are wood products obtained by logging tropical forests? Are minerals extracted in a harmful way? Internal managers will usually be able to conduct such an audit. If not, consultants and environmental specialists can assist.

Carrying out an environmental audit does not force a company to take immediate action on the issues raised, but the company is forewarned and hence forearmed. The sooner an audit is done, the more time there is to respond. Many of the issues raised are unlikely to be anticipated, so time to think strategically and respond carefully could make a great difference to the eventual costs. In fact, it can allow the company to see ways of turning possible problems into profit opportunities.

Potential for profits

Waste products are often inputs for which a company has paid and is not using; reducing them can save costs, at least partially offsetting the costs of waste management. In many cases, materials savings have more than offset the cost of waste reduction and profits have increased. Dow Chemical's US operations in Louisiana averaged a return of 204 percent on investments in energy-saving projects between 1981 and 1993. Other investments in waste management and energy efficiency have yielded returns in excess of 100 percent, far above the usual returns on investments.

In the US, chemical company DuPont has extended the strategy of investing in clean-up operations: it has profited from the expertise that it gained from tackling its own problems by forming a unit to sell clean-up services to other companies. It expects annual revenues of more than $1bn from this business. Forestry products group Weyerhauser has also expanded an internal program into a market offering.

If waste products cannot be reduced, they can be sold. For example, sulfur dioxide is removed from exhaust gases by dissolving it in water, producing sulfuric acid, which can be sold, recovering some of the cleaning costs. Both DuPont and brewer Anheuser-Busch have developed markets for their waste. DuPont sells acid salts once discharged as waste and Anheuser-Busch sells brewery waste as fertilizer.

Heat and power systems have been linked to harness waste. Conventional power stations discard huge amounts of heat at energy levels too low to generate power, but quite hot enough to heat buildings. In combined heat and power systems, power stations sell waste heat to local buildings, significantly improving profitability, removing the need for heating plant in the buildings, and increasing the overall efficiency of fuel. A new generation of industrial parks is building on this principle: Dow's ValuePark in eastern Germany and the Kalundborg industrial ecology park in Denmark are both attempting to link together companies so that wastes from one become inputs to another. Dow is investing $1bn in ValuePark and expects a rate of return of 30 percent.

Recycling components also has profit potential. If components are designed to be recycled and reused, materials costs fall substantially, while the environmental image of the company is raised, as printer manufacturers have found with respect to toner cartridges. Recycled metals are now providing significant cost savings to metal manufacturers: in particular, using recycled aluminum as an input to the production of cans is much cheaper than using ore.

As indicated, the costs of reducing environmental effects may be much less than they first appear and there are sometimes profitable opportunities associated with waste management. There can also be profit opportunities in environmental problems. The growth of market-based environmental management, indeed the introduction of the Kyoto Protocol, presents a great opportunity for investment banks and financial institutions. The resulting markets in environmental financial instruments could provide securities whose movements are uncorrelated with those of stock markets, making them attractive to investors who want to diversify portfolios.

Indeed, the limited market for environmental securities such as earthquake bonds, hurricane bonds, and catastrophe futures already acts in this way for managers of large funds seeking assets that do not follow stock markets.

New energy sources, new power sources for vehicles, and an increasing emphasis on minimal environmental footprints will create new products and markets with no incumbents and opportunities for those who think quickly and differently. BP Amoco is placing bets on solar power sources, Ford and DaimlerChrysler are investing in fuel cells, while Toyota and Honda already have hybrid cars running on a combination of internal combustion engines and electric motors. These changes shake out markets and create opportunities in the supply chain.

Many governments give financial incentives for environmentally friendly innovations. In farming, there are now governmental support systems in the EU and the US related to the provision of environmental goods. The US operates the Conservation Reserve Program; the Tir Cymen system protects parts of South Wales. And the paper and forestry industries stand to gain from new opportunities if the Kyoto Protocol is implemented, through financial rewards for the removal of atmospheric carbon dioxide ("sequestration") by growing trees.

Indeed, the removal of carbon dioxide and other greenhouse gases from the atmosphere could become a significant industry. Linked to concern about climate change is concern about climate volatility. This has led US energy group Enron to create financial products to insure weather risks associated with agricultural production. Enron now sells similar products to power generators at risk from demand fluctuations caused by the weather.

Dow Jones recently launched a Sustainability Group Index, a global index of shares in companies noted for placing weight on environmental and social issues. The associated website (www.sustainability-index.com) includes a simulation of the performance that this index would have had between 1994 and 1999 had it been in operation: it would have beaten Dow's Global Index by a third.

Conclusions

Environmental problems are an integral part of how we live and do business. Responses to them are already shaping strategies in several industries, such as power and transportation. In the future, more and more aspects of business life will be shaped by constraints imposed by our dependence on the environment.

This does not have to be bad news: responding to these constraints provides opportunities. The process of revising business practices to respect the environment can generate new products and markets. Of course, changes are demanding and can be costly, but then, large businesses are familiar with the notion of change.

In general, responding to environmental issues is not complex – for most businesses, it is probably easier than deciding how to respond to the challenges of the internet. A thorough environmental audit provides a starting point, uncovering all points of contact between the organization, its raw materials and products, and the environment.

This can be the basis for uncovering opportunities that help both the company and the environment – waste reduction, sale rather than disposal of by-products, recycling initiatives, and many others. It can help companies do well by doing good – Adam Smith's ultimate justification for the market mechanism.

Further reading

Buchholz, R., Marcus, A., and Post, J. (1992) *Managing Environmental Issues: A Casebook*, Englewood Cliffs, NJ: Prentice Hall.

Hawken, P., Lovins A., and Hunter Lovins, L. (1999) *Natural Capitalism*, London: Little, Brown.

Heal, G. (2000) *Nature and the Marketplace*, Washington DC: Island Press.

Hedstrom, G., Shopley, J., and LeDuc, C. (2000) "Realizing the Sustainable-Development Premium," *Prism*, Arthur D. Little, Q1.

IT comes to the aid of
environmental managers

Dennis A. Rondinelli is the Glaxo Distinguished International Professor of Management at the Kenan-Flagler Business School and director of the Center for Global Business Research at the Frank Hawkins Kenan Institute of Private Enterprise at the University of North Carolina at Chapel Hill.

Environmental information systems began as a way of helping companies cope with mushrooming legislation. Now, their application has spread beyond recognition, says **Dennis Rondinelli.**

Great changes are taking place in the way companies manage the environmental, health, and safety (EH&S) effects of their businesses. Larger companies are using information technology (IT) not just to comply with complex government regulations, but to move beyond compliance to reduce or eliminate hazardous pollutants from their operations. At the same time, small and medium-sized companies are buying software to automate and consolidate EH&S functions that previously had been performed manually in dispersed units and locations.

Multinational companies have advanced from using separate packages for individual functions to integrating their EH&S activities using internet and web-based technologies. Activities such as auditing, permit tracking, emissions monitoring, risk analysis, waste management, training, and cost assessment have all proven ideal subjects for integration. Integrated applications have allowed companies to link environmental information with other business databases; with this capability, they have been able to develop programs for pollution prevention that exceed regulatory needs.

Alcoa, Seagram, and Hewlett-Packard provide good examples. They are installing intranets for ISO 14000 environmental management systems (EMS) in plants around the world.

Dow Chemical and AT&T are using internet systems extensively for EH&S training. AT&T is implementing an "e-EH&S strategy" to break the link between geography and functionality, to collate data and disseminate knowledge. The system tailors and distributes EH&S communications through e-mail and delivers training and awareness messages via websites, as well as electronic and voice mail. Baxter International uses its intranet to link 40,000 employees for similar purposes.

Many companies are also using IT to streamline buying and to trade products that might once have been disposed of as waste. As a result, companies are offering business-to-business (B2B) markets selling goods through virtual "one-stop" shops.

Emerging uses of IT

Interest in environmental IT has spawned a new industry for hardware, software, and services. Companies can manage EH&S functions using software incorporating environmental monitoring and reporting functions for corporate intranets and extranets (intranets that can be accessed by external parties) and web-based software that allows them to develop, implement, and maintain their EMS at multiple sites across national borders.

A survey by the BTI consulting group found that the environmental IT industry had grown to nearly $5bn worldwide by 1998. The sector is growing at about 35 percent a year and is expected to reach $13bn by 2003. This industry is still highly fragmented, with large numbers of environmental and information consulting firms (largely in the US, Canada, and Europe) providing a variety of products and services. Entry into the market is still relatively easy for start-ups that combine environmental expertise with information technology skills.

Not surprisingly, the primary users of IT are chemical, pharmaceutical, oil, primary metal, electric utility, forest products, automotive, and high-technology manufacturing companies, which account for almost 80 percent of environmental spending. Companies in these industries are moving quickly from software for specific activities such as air emissions monitoring, to software that integrates diverse EH&S functions with other programs such as enterprise resource planning (ERP).

Large corporations are also switching from generic software to web-based and intranet environmental management systems customized to corporate needs and integrated with operations and financial databases. A customized enterprise-wide EMS can cost between $3m and $25m.

Regulations

Managers in North America and western Europe first turned to software for help with increasingly complex EH&S regulations. In the US, the number of federal, state, and local environmental regulations rose from 2,000 in 1970 to 100,000 at the end of the 1990s. Even well-staffed EH&S departments in large corporations find it difficult to keep pace with the frequent and numerous changes in air, water, solid waste, and hazardous-materials regulations, to obtain requisite permits, and to respond with timely data and reports. Manual data collection and reporting became especially burdensome for small and medium-sized companies.

Environmental consulting firms responded by offering software with detailed information on federal regulations enforced by the US Environmental Protection Agency, transport department, and Occupational Safety and Health Administration. Using such software, companies can quickly and easily access regulations on hazardous materials, transport, workplace safety, hazardous waste, toxic substances, and the requirements of clean air and water acts, and can receive timely updates on regulatory changes.

Similarly, modular software makes it easier to track regulations, audit operations, and report on changes to keep the company in regulatory compliance. Also, software can create material safety data sheets (MSDS) identifying chemical components of inputs from suppliers and finished goods for customers. The programs produce incoming and outgoing hazardous-materials labels, and generate reports, worksheets, and lists that can be linked to an inventory system.

Other programs help companies carry out specific regulatory compliance and environmental management functions such as emissions management, dispersion modeling, waste-water management, and energy analysis. Software allows companies to perform automatic risk analysis and auditing functions, list pollution sources, manage environmental costs, and offer training to employees.

Integrating EH&S

Since the mid-1990s, corporations have been adopting multi-function environmental compliance programs that co-ordinate environmental tasks and integrate EH&S information with other business databases. Union Carbide uses a networked program to consolidate its 200 different environmental reporting systems into one central system that can be accessed by 4,000 users at 27 sites. The software links EH&S information with Union Carbide's ERP initiative and SAP R/3 software for logistics management. The system consists of air, water, waste, and inventory modules that give users access to information via the internet.

As a result, Union Carbide can make management practices consistent across sites, automate waste labeling, and reconcile manifests for waste containers. IT makes it easier for managers to streamline compliance activities, track accountability, delegate tasks, and generate reports.

By bridging "information islands," these intranets permit EH&S staff to share data. Integrated systems allow companies to streamline operations, track operating improvements, cut costs, and eliminate inefficiencies.

Some companies are developing their own systems. Stanley Works, the toolmaker, is using an intranet that "rolls up" EH&S data from spreadsheets at 40 sites to consolidate scores and weighting parameters and organize information needed for environmental and safety reports.

Managers can use Stanley's system to track health and safety incidents, manage MSDS requirements, co-ordinate waste reduction, and generate EH&S updates. Teams at various sites input data continuously, providing headquarters with current information. The system gives all sites access to shared information. Stanley's EH&S manager points out that "critical safety performance reports that used to take weeks to create manually will now be available automatically throughout the organization whenever they are needed, by mere virtue of the plants inputting their data."

Web-based networks

Because more companies are adopting environmental management systems based on international standards, such as ISO 14001 or the European Eco-Management and Audit Scheme (EMAS), companies are rapidly adopting software and web-based applications that organize all elements of an EMS. These information systems allow companies to prepare for ISO 14001

Critical safety reports that used to take weeks to create will now be available automatically

and maintain their documentation. By 1999, more than 8,000 organizations in 72 countries had formal certification under ISO 14001. Most of these are in Europe and Japan, but more than 850 organizations were certified in the US by mid-2000.

Ford and General Motors are redefining their EMS around ISO 14001 as a common framework for manufacturing plants worldwide. General Motors expects all plants to have third-party certified EMS by 2002. Ford is pushing its plants and suppliers to gain certification. Many other corporations, including Procter & Gamble, use ISO 14001 guidelines to improve systems without formally certifying.

More comprehensive information systems are emerging to help international corporations create customized web-based systems for standardizing their EMS to ISO 14001 guidelines. Seagram and its Universal Studios and Polygram Records companies adopted an internet-based system to provide a structure for its worldwide facilities to meet ISO 14001 and EMAS registration, and to manage EH&S documentation and reporting. Xerox developed its own network-based software, EcoWorx, to streamline and manage its ISO 14001-certified programs. The system stores, tracks, and manages all EMS documentation, as well as generating the required reports.

Alcoa is using Solution Foundry's EMSolution to link EH&S management systems in its 24 business units at 215 operating locations in 31 countries. This is based on Microsoft Office applications that are accessed through a web browser. Alcoa installed the system at seven of its US plants by mid-2000 and will eventually expand it to Europe, Asia, and Latin America. The seamlessly linked electronic management structure can be integrated with existing EH&S systems. It provides 15 customized system procedures derived from ISO 14001 guidelines and 13 system tools to run the company's EMS.

Systems procedures identify environmental aspects along with legal, company, and other environmental requirements. They allow Alcoa to set and track objectives and establish EH&S structures and roles. In addition, companies can put training and other programs on the system.

Alcoa's IT system allows its facilities to meet ISO 14001 needs by controlling EMS documents and operational procedures; disseminating emergency procedures; monitoring environmental performance; tracking nonconformance remedial action; managing records and audits; reviewing and updating the EMS. Alcoa plants and corporate headquarters use template-based tools to document, track, and manage EH&S functions.

Patrick Atkins, Alcoa's director of environmental affairs, became enthusiastic about the web system "when we realized the advantage of an individual plant not having to have everything related to its EH&S system on its own server – or duplicating paper and storing it somewhere."

The system helps plant managers prepare for ISO 14001 by ensuring that all elements of the EMS are in place. It assists them in managing the prodigious documentation that certification requires and helps them implement the EMS after it is certified. Because the system links managers to federal, state, and local regulations, they can also keep up with regulatory changes and automatically generate reports required by agencies in different states, localities, and countries.

B2B marketplaces

As e-commerce expands, managers are paying more attention to the potential for using B2B networks for buying equipment, supplies, and services. Corporations that have seen the advantages of B2B networks for organizing supply chains and rationalizing procurement in manufacturing also tend to see their advantages for obtaining their environmental products and services and, increasingly, for trading or selling "waste" materials.

Pratt & Whitney, General Motors, and Reichhold Chemical are some of the major companies taking part in a pilot project run by

Companies are using e-marketplaces to trade used assets and waste that might have ended up in landfills

Blue292, a B2B e-marketplace for EH&S products and services. The project helps companies streamline their sourcing and environmental project management. It bundles products, equipment, and supplies with analytical services and uses the internet to reduce the time and cost of procurement.

The exchange also gives environmental product and service suppliers strong visibility with potential customers around the world.

According to Phillip Coop, president of EnSafe, an environmental consulting and engineering company, joining the e-marketplace alliance "helped us eliminate process costs and identify inefficiencies in our procurement system. This will provide direct benefits to our customers in terms of lower costs . . . and our improved ability to focus on finding solutions to design and engineering challenges."

GTE Supply, Ford, and many companies in the chemical industry are using e-marketplaces to trade, transfer, or sell excess inventory, used assets, and "waste" materials that might have ended up in landfills. E-commerce companies such as TradeOut, AssetTrade, and Ubid are helping with this. Manufacturers such as Dow and Eastman have set up their own internet marketplaces and other companies are using electronic trading firms such as Chemconnect, CheMatch, and e-Chemicals. Forrester Research reports that the online market for excess materials in the chemical industry is expected to reach $128bn in the US by 2003.

IT, an expanding tool

These EH&S trends are likely to spread rapidly from North America and Europe. E-commerce ventures continue to enter the industry and existing providers are rolling out new products that meet the growing environmental management needs of both large and small businesses. The industry grows as more companies discover the benefits.

The advantages of IT for environmental management are substantial. Seagram is typical in reporting that IT allowed it to halve its EMS development time, implement programs more quickly, improve communications, and save time and money in compliance reporting. Xerox, Ford, Seagram, and others claim IT allows more effective information dissemination, shorter cycle times on report production, more consistent measurement of environmental impacts, and streamlined documentation control.

Xerox found such impressive productivity gains in EH&S management that it made its software available to its customers. Union Carbide, Alcoa, and Stanley Works all point to the relative ease with which IT allows them to integrate EMS among sites worldwide with operational, management, and financial systems.

Managers must, of course, carefully choose IT solutions that are compatible with their overall objectives, resources, and reporting requirements. They should plan for system installation and testing over several years, for adaptation of existing databases and for extensive employee training. An EMS is likely to generate new data needs and managers should plan how to disseminate information the system produces.

As information technologies develop and as firms find additional uses for them in managing their environmental impacts, they create market forces that encourage technology providers to develop yet more information products and services. This "virtuous cycle" of technological innovation and creative application is likely to keep the environmental IT industry growing rapidly over the next decade.

Further reading

BTI Consulting Group (1999) *Market Opportunities in the Environmental Management Information Systems Market*, Boston, MA: BTI Consulting Group.

Gilbert, J.B. (1999) "Selecting Software for Environmental Compliance," *Chemical Engineering*, September, 127–30.

International Organization for Standardization (1999) *The ISO Survey of ISO 9000 and ISO 14000 Certificates: Eight Cycle – 1998*, Geneva: ISO.

Lee, S.A. (2000) *Point, Click, Manage: Business Meets the Environment – Online*, Woodstock, GA: The Solution Foundry.

Makower, J. (2000) "EH&S.com: How Companies Harness Web Power to Educate Employees on the Environment," *The Green Business Letter*, August.

Salwen, P. (1998) "The Intranet Edge: Online Information Systems are Opening a New Era," *Occupational Health and Safety*, May, 114–16.

Xerox Corporation (1999) *1999 Environment, Health and Safety Progress Report*, Webster, NY: Xerox.

Venture philanthropy:
effective or meddling?

New economy millionaires have found their own way to fund good deeds. **Rachel Croson** weighs the pros and cons of their approach.

Rachel Croson is associate professor of operations and information manage-ment at the Wharton School of the University of Pennsylvania.

Recently, a *Harvard Business Review* article introduced "venture philanthropy" to the business world. The term has since become a buzzword in nonprofit organizations in the US, (along with "strategic philanthropy," "e-philanthropy," and "social entrepreneurship"). Hundreds of groups claim to be using the principles of venture philan-thropy and a 1999 White House conference on philanthropy included a session outlining its philosophies. There are many definitions of ven-ture philanthropy; this article describes the principles and their pros and cons.

Box 1 Venture philanthropy organizations

Echoing Green	www.echoinggreen.org
Morino Institute	www.morino.org
New Schools Venture Fund	www.newshools.org
Peninsula Community Foundation	www.pcf.org
Roberts Enterprise Development Fund	www.redf.org
Robin Hood Foundation	www.robinhood.org
Silicon Valley Social Venture Fund	www.siliconvalleygives.org
Social Venture Partners	
Seattle (original)	www.svpseattle.org
Austin	www.asvp.org
Dallas	www.dvsp.org
Denver	www.svpdenver.org
Arizona	www.svpaz.org
San Francisco	WWW.svpbay.org
The Entrepreneurs' Foundation	www/the-ef.org
Urban Enterprise Fund	www.urbanenterprise.org

The innovation of venture philanthropy is to apply methods from venture capital to philanthropy. Like venture capitalists, venture philanthropists actively seek out funding opportunities and approach these with an eye toward managing and balancing their (charitable) portfolios. Venture philanthropy departs from more traditional approaches in two ways: how projects are chosen and how they are managed. Within each of these areas, concepts from venture capital have been applied.

Choosing projects

Traditional philanthropy is based on a "pull" process of funding. Philanthropists have money, indicate their interest in some particular area, and receive requests for funding that they process. Thus, funding is pulled from its source by nonprofit organizations.

In contrast, venture philanthropists use a push process, whereby they identify an area and particular charities they think would benefit from funding. So, funding is pushed from its source to the nonprofit organization.

For example, the Morino Institute, a venture philanthropy fund, does not accept unsolicited grant proposals. Instead, staff or sponsors identify groups they would like to fund and that fit with the institute's mission. In other venture philanthropy bodies, charities wishing to be funded send a letter describing themselves and their goals. The philanthropists then solicit a grant proposal if they are interested in providing funding.

Venture philanthropy's supporters argue that identifying worthy, but perhaps overlooked, groups is an important innovation. The process increases the pool of groups that are funded and provides money for the nonprofit equivalent of "start-ups." Skeptics argue this limits the scope of funded organizations rather than increasing it, claiming it leads to an "in-group" of funded charities, which happen to be familiar to the venture philanthropist.

Risk/portfolio management

A second difference between venture philan-thropy and the traditional kind is the use of risk or portfolio management. With venture capital, funds are provided for many businesses, only a few of which are expected to survive. In venture philanthropy, the parallel is increasing the proportion of start-ups to well-entrenched charities. Echoing Green, a venture philanthropist with a focus on social entrepreneurship, for example, claims it "invests in entrepreneurs' projects at an early stage, before most funders are willing to do so."

Beyond simply balancing a portfolio between start-ups and established groups, venture philanthropists spend a great deal of time and resources identifying how and where their resources would be placed most effectively. For example, a fixed investment in Aids research will be more productive when accompanied by a program of Aids education in schools or by television commercials. Thus, venture philanthropists can effect more social change for their money by diversifying their "portfolios" of charitable assets; by using multiple channels, limited resources can have larger impacts.

Supporters argue that by creating a portfolio of more and less risky groups, the venture philanthropist can increase the chances of success. By diversifying the risk of investment, the philanthropist can do more with less. Similarly, by identifying complementary attributes of charities in the funding portfolio, more social benefits can be achieved with less money. For example, funding Aids research and Aids education together yields more social change than funding either for twice as much.

However, skeptics argue that while in the venture capital world the success of one business can fund the failure of another, in the philanthropic world these outputs are not so interchangeable. An additional concern is that this strategy spreads funding too thinly; overdiversifying contributions may mean that no given nonprofit group has sufficient resources to achieve its goals.

Managing projects

As with choosing projects, the different approach of venture philanthropy raises new issues in terms of the way projects are managed.

Length of grants

Venture philanthropy calls for larger and longer-term grants than normal. While the first grant will be for one year, renewals of three to five years are likely. The description of grant funding by another venture philanthropic body, the Robin Hood Foundation, says: "Nearly 75 percent of the organizations supported by Robin Hood have been receiving our support for more than five years."

Supporters argue that longer and larger grants free up managers of recipients from the need for fundraising, allowing them to get on with the business of doing good. Skeptics argue that more, smaller grants can have larger impacts than fewer, larger grants. (This links with the discussion on risk management.)

Performance measures

More controversially, venture philanthropists focus on performance measures. In a 1999 article, Michael Porter and Mark Kramer wrote: "Non-profits operate without the discipline of the bottom line in the delivery of services . . . as a result, they lack strong incentives to measure and manage their performance." Terms such as social return on investment (SROI) are often used to highlight to nonprofit groups the types of results venture philanthropists want to see. Although conventional philanthropists also look at efficiency measures (such as percentage of grants spent on overhead), performance measures used by venture philanthropists are likely to be outcome specific.

For example, the Urban Enterprise Fund has specified its goal as providing employment opportunities for individuals with economic disadvantages. It assesses effectiveness by measuring the number of new workers a given organization has introduced to the labor force.

Supporters argue that by measuring performance, venture philanthropists ensure that recipients focus on what really matters. The addition of structure and measurement techniques helps nonprofit groups compare different uses of funding in a sensible and structured way.

Skeptics, however, argue that goals are difficult or impossible to measure. For example, consider the funding of an art museum. The natural measure of success (attendance) may not capture the extent to which the museum contributes to a city's wellbeing, including increased tourism, civic pride, and education. This aspect of venture philanthropy has also found critics in the nonprofit world, who argue that new donors do not always understand what charities do and how they do it, and try to impose their own (profit-oriented) values.

A final, related concern about firm goals is that nonprofit groups may be forced to sacrifice long-term aims to meet short-term deadlines and ensure continued funding. This concern is not unique to venture philanthropy, but venture philanthropy's focus on measurable and deliverable goals makes it more pressing.

Extent of involvement

A final (and controversial) difference between venture and traditional philanthropy is how involved the philanthropic organization is in the day-to-day management of the nonprofit group. In traditional philanthropy, the recipient submits periodic reports on progress. Venture philanthropists, in contrast, become deeply involved in the nonprofit group, sitting on boards, offering advice, and helping to find resources. Paul Brainerd, founder of Social Venture Partners, writes that his organization provides not just financial resources but also "connections in the community . . . advice and counsel, such as how to find the right person for your marketing department, assist with financial issues or answer legal questions." New Schools, another venture philanthropy fund, offers its grantees services such as "matching board members, recruiting management team members, consulting and linking education entrepreneurs to a powerful network of peers and new economy resources."

For supporters, this type of input is seen as very valuable, particularly for charities just starting out. Furthermore, by making the most of the skills of its members, venture philanthropists can provide services that are more valuable (and scarcer) than money. These services can increase the productivity of the recipient, making donations more effective.

However, skeptics express concern that this type of involvement might have unanticipated consequences, including steering the nonprofit group toward the goals of the philanthropist and away from its core competencies, so reducing the group's ability to raise funding from other sources. When advice comes with funding, recipients often feel obliged to agree to keep the money coming. Accusations of "micromanaging" and "arrogance" are often leveled at donors who suggest new organizational forms or marketing campaigns for well-established charitable groups.

How new is it?

It should be noted that these concepts are not new to philanthropy. Many traditional philanthropic organizations started a move from "pull" to "push" funding and were thinking of their grants as "portfolios" long before 1997. Also, the move to longer, larger grants reflects a trend rather than a revolutionary idea. The insistence on measurable outcomes is newer and more controversial; it has advantages, but relies on identifying the appropriate measure.

The most productive and, perhaps, revolutionary idea is the principle of active involvement. Skeptics are correct in that forced involvement as a condition of funding can be dangerous. However, involvement requested by the recipient can be effective. When venture philanthropists provide management expertise, consulting advice, or transport, which are cheap to provide but more valuable than cash for the recipient, they create value, rather than simply engaging in a straight transfer.

Again, this idea is not new; it is the basis for volunteerism common in the nonprofit world. The Service Corps of Retired Executives in the US has been voluntarily offering advice and management expertise to start-up businesses and nonprofit groups since 1964; the UK charity Voluntary Services Overseas has sent graduates and professionals around the world since 1958. Venture philanthropy's innovation is to link this type of in-kind assistance with funding.

A final opportunity, which venture philanthropy seems to have overlooked, yet which also has the potential for increased effectiveness, is the idea of benchmarking.

Philanthropic organizations have a bird's eye view of the landscape. They fund many charities and so can identify potential partners, document best practices, and provide a forum to enhance communication between charities working toward the same goal. For example, the Pew Charitable Trusts' Center on Global Climate Change brings together researchers, encourages them to share best practice, and serves as a clearing house for research. Such cross-fertilization, so useful in business, also seems a natural step for the nonprofit world.

The future

There is one contrast between traditional and venture philanthropic organizations that remains implicit in most discussions of this new trend: the donors. Most venture philanthropists were founded and are run by successful representatives of the new economy, who have earned substantial wealth earlier in their lives than in any previous generation.

These people want to contribute actively to society. They are not content to write a check – they want to offer expertise, skills, and energies as well as money. Venture philanthropy provides this opportunity and, by doing so, may induce a younger generation to contribute. Even if none of the principles of venture philanthropy survives, introducing this generation to the joys of giving will have a lasting impact.

Mark Kramer has highlighted the extent of commitment that venture capitalists exhibit for their companies. "Venture capitalists use every ounce of leverage they have to make their companies succeed. Other deals are held out as bait, favors are called in, personal connections of investors and directors are called upon, investment banks are pressured, senior managers are recruited, courted and promised support." He concludes: "For the venture-capital model to work in the non-profit world, a foundation must be willing to put itself on the line for its grantees."

Although Kramer counts himself as a skeptic, this conclusion is one with which venture philanthropists are likely to agree. When this does happen, the venture philanthropy model will indeed work.

Further reading

Kramer, M. (1999) "Venture Capital and Philanthropy: A Bad Fit," *The Chronicle of Philanthropy*, April.

Letts, C.W., Ryan, W., and Grossman, A. (1997) "Virtuous Capital: What Foundations Can Learn from Venture Capitalists," *Harvard Business Review*, January.

Porter, M.E. and Kramer, M.R. (1999) "Philanthropy's New Agenda: Creating Value," *Harvard Business Review*, November.

The organization and **human resources**

6

Contents

Introduction to Part 6

Managers readily assent to the suggestion that a company's people are its greatest asset, yet what does this cliché suggest about the ideal structures of an organization, the processes and policies that guide people within it, and the means of encouraging creativity and innovation? The topic of human resource management answers these questions and is discussed in this part. A company's HR policies cover a great range of issues, such as recruitment, employee retention, motivation, corporate values, leadership, legal issues, stress management, career development and training. In examining these and other questions, this part assesses the human challenges facing the modern organization, and offers a variety of solutions.

Business moves
beyond bureaucracy

Bureaucracies allowed people with knowledge to control ignorant workers. Now, says **Jonas Ridderstråle**, new structures are needed as knowledge spreads.

Jonas Ridderstråle is an assistant professor at the Center for Advanced Studies in Leadership, Stockholm School of Economics.

Balance sheets have faithfully recorded the value of companies for more than 500 years, yet they fail to capture the value of many modern companies. Value today is more likely to lie in knowledge, people, and brands than property, plant, and equipment. While knowledge has always been critical to business, digitization, deregulation, and globalization dramatically amplify its economic value.

Knowledge dispersion

In many industries competition has become transnational. A recent study by McKinsey showed that some 20 percent of world output is open to global competition. In 30 years, the forecast suggests a level of 80 percent. As part of this trend, knowledge is spreading more evenly. The second largest center for software development is not in the US or Europe. It is in Bangalore, India, where 140,000 IT engineers are challenging the hegemony of the west.

Some companies, particularly those combining knowledge from many fields, realize that demand and supply are not always closely located. For instance, Finnish mobile phone company Nokia needs to be aware of the latest trends in design, yet the world's trendsetters do not all live near Helsinki. Therefore, it sends people to King's Road in London and Venice Beach in Los Angeles to pick up the latest signals. The knowledge required to develop a competitive customer offering is increasingly dispersed.

Knowledge diversity

Products and services are becoming more complex. First, it is more difficult to separate the two. In the car industry, developing and launching a vehicle requires a combination of mechanics, electronics, design, manufacturing, marketing, and finance skills. The product itself is becoming a platform for delivering services. A single company may not have to do everything, but the process still needs to be co-ordinated.

Second, we see more products being turned into multi-technology offerings. Nokia's Communicator is part mobile phone and part computer, and Sony's digital Mavica combines digital imaging and computer technology. Often, the result of such developments is increased convergence.

Third, the main routes to product creation – where a product is either developed by engineers or demanded by marketers – are being combined in cross-functional efforts in which technological and market knowledge is combined. In Japan, for example, parallel development projects in which marketing and technology specialists work side by side are widespread.

Fourth, increased diversity is not limited to technologies, industries, and the need for cross-functional collaboration, but also encompasses people possessing these skills. In Silicon Valley, for instance, traditional "minority groups" in business, such as women, immigrants, and people below 35, are over-represented as compared with traditional US companies.

Knowledge depth

Knowledge develops cumulatively. The number of US patents awarded each year has increased by 70 percent in the past decade. Since the early 1960s, the number of MBAs graduating in the US has increased by 1,500 percent. In 1967, two MBA programs existed in the UK and now there are 130. When the US Army fought the Vietnam War, only 15 percent of the men had a college degree. During the Desert Storm campaign, 99.3 percent of the soldiers were graduates.

Spending on executive education is rising. For instance, Motorola employees get 40 days of training per year. In addition, the distribution of competence is no longer concentrated among senior managers, and knowledge workers may be found on every level. At Federal Express, front-line employees and second-level managers must attend 10 weeks of training in the first year. As a result, in many industries the knowledge required to develop a competitive customer offering is increasing in depth.

Knowledge durability

Knowledge tends to lose its value quickly. The expected "lifetime" of consumer electronics products in Japan is less than three months. In response, companies are forced to cut development time and increase the frequency of product launches. At Hewlett-Packard, most revenues stem from products that did not exist a year before. Disney chief executive Michael Eisner has claimed his company introduces a new product, such as a CD, video, or T-shirt, every five minutes.

Manufacturing processes are also accelerating. Mexican cement company Cemex has invested $200m in a customer information system to meet a 20-minute delivery window with 98 percent accuracy. In 1998, the company had a 35 percent profit margin compared with an industry average of 21 percent.

Corporate response

To create new customer offerings, knowledge must often be combined and re-combined across geographical, organizational, technological, and institutional borders; for example, in the form of joint ventures or strategic alliances. This is a challenge, especially as the time available to do it is decreasing. Developing a competitive knowledge system is the first step. To speed up the process from knowledge to action, companies have to develop organizational solutions that use corporate creativity to the full.

The hallmark of a large company in the past century was hierarchy. Yet, hierarchy rests on principles that are at odds with the new strategic requirements. High-performing organizations have responded to increasingly complex knowledge systems by developing organizational solutions that are not centered around hierarchy. Specifically, there are four ways in which companies depart from the traditional bureaucratic model.

Flat

Historically, companies have handled greater complexity by increasing the division of labor and specialization, leading to a hierarchy. Henry

Ford's assembly line is an example. But in a company with a more sophisticated knowledge system, quick decisions need to be taken near to where critical knowledge resides, geographically as well as organizationally. This needs a more decentralized and flatter structure. Chrysler, for instance, has increased the span of control from 20 people per manager in the 1980s to 50. It aims to reach 100.

There are two ways to flatten a company. The first is to reduce layers from the top, while raising the lower levels by increased training and education. The second way is to remove layers of middle management. Western economies have preferred the second approach. However, it carries a risk: companies may come to rely on "seniles" managing "juveniles." Often the most relevant experience resides with middle managers; they are in better touch with operations than those at the top and more confident and pragmatic than those below. Intelligent organizations make use of their skills as a value-adding link between the top and the bottom. Indeed, many Japanese companies talk about "middle-up-down" processes rather than "bottom-up" or "top-down" processes.

Flexible

Bureaucracies derive strength from being efficient at repetitive tasks where processes are rationalized and routinized. But today's changing circumstances do not allow companies to use a single structure. Not only that, there is less potential for planning and rationalization because opportunities may demand that knowledge be assembled across the boundaries of a traditional organization chart. If boundary-spanning projects become the main vehicles for action, people will have less permanent places in the hierarchy. They must be able to move across both functional and geographical borders.

A hierarchy divides people into those who think and those who do; the former group positioned at the top, the latter at the bottom. In reality, however, we know that many opportunities (and problems) in a company occur horizontally – across functions, business areas, divisions, or countries. Moreover, there is little room for suppliers and customers in a vertical system – in theory, at least, they sit outside the company. Such a system is no longer appropriate when, for instance, IBM links no less than 12,000 suppliers to its network. Knowing how, what, and where no longer suffice if you do not also know "who."

Smart

In a bureaucracy, a manager is supposed to know who knows whom, who knows what, who knows how, and who knows where. Modern companies need to give every employee the same level of familiarity with personnel and capabilities. "If only we knew what we knew," an executive at Hewlett-Packard once remarked. Without knowing what the company knows, managers cannot exploit current knowledge or create new knowledge. Expansion also increases the chance that problems and solutions may be uncoupled. This is also true for awareness of resources outside the company. Leaders must convert companies from places with islands of creativity into learning organizations, controlling the learning process.

Successful companies appear to be systematic in managing their assets. Their knowledge management architecture includes the development of a detailed inventory of core competencies and "core competents," the people who make competencies happen. This system is set up so that managers can inform themselves as needed.

Tribal

Bureaucratic control and co-ordination are based on legal authority and formal rules. However, in a complex knowledge system conditions change so fast that formalized procedures become too rigid. Knowledge may be located in the periphery, where little formal authority resides, but rapid action is still required. Experts in various fields need to know the general direction from those in charge, but they themselves will often be sufficiently skilled to take the best decisions. Thus, as the system increases in complexity, it becomes more important for managers to share principles to ensure co-ordination.

These "lowest common denominators" can be anything from shared ownership and rewards, to culture, vision, and values. We see shared ownership at such diverse companies as Dell,

Starbucks, and General Electric, where over 20,000 employees own stock options, compared with 200 during the 1980s. These principles provide common ground. Such companies evolve into "tribes." Within each tribe, norms and values are similar, though other attributes may differ. The process of developing tribal qualities starts with recruitment. "We hire attitudes," says Herb Kelleher at Southwest Airlines. People can easily add to their knowledge, but it may be less easy to change attitudes

Multiple structures

The theologian Pseudo-Dionysius introduced the word "hierarchy" 1,500 years ago. Dionysius's hierarchy was a celestial structure of heaven and hell, which in turn comprised three separate, and balanced, parts: knowledge, action and position. Remembering this three-point system can be useful when contemplating organizations. Letting the positional structure dominate will result in a bureaucracy. If action drives the entire system, the design resembles a project-oriented adhocracy. Finally, if knowledge is the only organizing principle, we are left with a meritocracy.

For companies with more simplistic knowledge systems, the three structures overlap in a way that indeed makes the positional structure a reasonable proxy for the others. In other words, the chief executive or headquarters may control most of the critical skills and relationships with external parties, and is thus well placed to take all relevant decisions, while subsidiaries can be relegated to minor roles of implementation.

In economist Max Weber's ideal bureaucracy, position was granted according to technical competence, and corporate relationships were based on authority and subordination. Since most people were uneducated, it was said, they could only handle simple jobs, so companies needed complex structures. In the past, when only the few had access to higher education, position and knowledge were indeed correlated. This no longer holds true.

When the knowledge system of a company increases in complexity, the positional structure must still be clear to all staff (not necessarily from the viewpoint of senior managers). Overall

structure is given a more symbolic role. It becomes a home to which people can return, a map of units and people.

In this structure, resources are transferred from units in the positional structure to temporary and boundary-spanning projects with increased organizational clout. These projects work as flexible and dynamic processes where competencies are combined and re-combined. To prevent structures from drifting apart, a structure of shared norms, values, and visions is used to co-ordinate the organizational tribe. In effect, you are someone; you do something; you know something; and you have a reason to come to work.

One might ask, isn't this already the case in organizations? Indeed it is, the only difference being that intelligent companies let it be reflected in how they are organized and managed.

Undoubtedly, the need to transform both the nature of knowledge systems and the organizational arrangements to manage them poses a challenge for business leaders. It may be wise to recall the words of Peter Drucker: "One cannot manage change. One can only be ahead of it." Companies must invest in shaping their own future. Postponing the creation of a competitive knowledge system and a matching organizational design until you are forced to change only increases the likelihood of becoming rather than making history.

The author wishes to express his debt to the late Professor Gunnar Hedlund, who was instrumental in the development of the ideas in the article.

Further reading

Chandler, A.D., Jr (1962) *Strategy and Structure*, Cambridge, MA: MIT Press.

Morgan, G. (1998) *Images of Organisation*, London: Sage.

Nonaka, I. and Takeuchi, H. (1995) *The Knowledge-Creating Company: How Japanese Companies Create the Dynamics of Innovation*, New York: Oxford University Press.

Ridderstråle, J. and Nordström, K.A. (2000) *Funky Business*, London: Financial Times Prentice Hall.

Change: success
is all in the detail

Employees may embrace change or resist it. **Joel Brockner** suggests that paying a little extra attention can make all the difference – and contribute directly to the bottom line.

Joel Brockner is Philip Hettleman Professor of Business at Columbia Business School.

The only constant is change – it may be an old adage, but it is more applicable today than ever before. In response to environments that are shifting rapidly, organizations have made many strategic and operational changes, including mergers and acquisitions, technologies, downsizing, relocation, re-engineering, and restructuring, to name a few.

Moreover, the nature of the change process itself has changed. Not long ago organizations would embark upon a major change effort, followed by a relatively lengthy steady-state period, then initiate another major change and so on. Now, organizations initiate multiple changes simultaneously. Three-quarters of mid- to upper-level managers report that their organizations are undertaking two or more change initiatives at a time. Nearly all say the time between major change efforts has shrunk dramatically, in some cases disappearing.

The stakes associated with organizational change have never been greater. However, change initiatives vary considerably in how well they are managed. Sometimes employees embrace change. They respond with high levels of productivity and morale, thereby enabling the organization to move forward. In other instances, employees respond with cynicism ("flavor of the month") or other forms of resistance and in so doing threaten the viability of the organization.

Managers need to know what factors affect employees' response to change, in particular, the factors they can control. These will determine their success in the role of change agents. Note that the term "change agent" is defined broadly. It is not simply the chief executive or top management team, but all managers who help plan and implement change.

Employees' reactions

How employees react to change depends upon the content (or the "what") of the change and the process (or the "how") of the change.

Change content

Understandably, employees worry about what effects any change will have on them personally. Will their pay fall? Will their career prospects be brighter? Is work likely to become more interesting? Will their personal status be lower? In short, people want to know whether they will be better off or worse off. Naturally, they are far more likely to embrace change if they feel it will make them better off.

As important as this is, it is not advisable for change agents to devote all of their energies to convincing employees how they will be better off. In some cases, they will be worse off; in other cases, the benefits may be uncertain. Furthermore, although employees are more likely to accept change if they believe that they will be handsomely compensated, it simply may not be economically feasible.

The change process

Employees' reactions are also determined by the procedures used by change agents. An important factor is whether employees are given an opportunity to affect the process. In general, people are more likely to embrace change if they have had input into the process, rather than if decisions were imposed. Having said that, several studies have shown that the effect of employee input varies. In cultures where it is customary to expect decisions to be made by authority figures (such as Hong Kong, Mexico, China, and Turkey), it is unlikely that employee input will help them embrace change. The opposite is true in cultures (such as Costa Rica, Germany, and the US) in which people expect or want to have input.

Communication issues reign supreme in a change process. In many organizations, the need for change may not be widely shared. This is especially so after a long history of success (for example, IBM in the years prior to the arrival of Louis Gerstner). Change agents need to carry a sense of urgency to organizations that may be suffering from complacency, so that initiatives are introduced proactively rather than reactively. Of course, communication goes well beyond this. A clear, feasible, and engaging vision must be proposed, along with a rationale of how the change will move the organization closer to that vision. Details about the "who, what, where, when, and how" of the change need to be provided.

In addition, it is necessary to communicate aspects of the work environment that will not be changing. Note that giving out information only once may not get the message across. Important information should be sent at least three times, preferably in different ways, such as e-mail, memos, videos, or at meetings.

Perhaps even more importantly, employees' interpretations and reactions need to be monitored. The atmosphere in which change is introduced is fraught with uncertainty, confusion, and stress. Consequently, the agents' intended messages may not be the ones recipients actually hear. Unless change agents make efforts to learn how their intended messages were received, they will not be able to determine if the message that was heard matched the one intended. For example, Eastman Kodak conducts pilot tests of communications during times of change. Prior to rolling out information to many employees, managers ask small groups for their reactions. This enables the company to adjust communications, so they are more likely to be interpreted as intended.

Another important factor is the length of advance notice employers provide. Consider the case of downsizing. Twenty years ago, employers in the US gave employees a week's notice of being laid off. Conventional wisdom was that the quicker people left, the better. While there clearly are instances in which this makes sense, it is often the case that layoffs are implemented with too little notice. To deal with the problem of employers making sudden announcements, the US government passed a law requiring employers to provide advance notice of at least 60 days whenever a plant closure or large-scale redundancy was planned.

In short, it is critical for organizations to pay attention to how they manage change. The results of many recent studies provide evidence of three reasons to do so. First, if the process is managed well, then employees are more likely to accept change. Second, if the process is managed well, then employees' reactions will be less dependent on the perceived content of the change. In other words, whether employees believe that they will be better or worse off will have relatively little effect, provided they believe the process was handled well.

A study by academic John Schaubroeck illustrates this second point. He studied the effects of a temporary pay freeze on two groups of workers. While the pay freeze was identical for both groups, the change process differed dramatically. In one group the reasons for the freeze were clearly explained. In contrast, the second group did not receive an adequate explanation. The perceived content of the change depended on how much economic hardship the pay freeze posed to employees. While the pay freeze was objectively identical, some employees said it created more hardship than others. Thus, while no one was better off, some people were more worse off than others. One might expect employees to be more resistant if the freeze created more hardship for them. In fact, this was only the case for the group where the change process was not handled well. For the group who had the better experience of the change process, there was no relationship between the degree of economic hardship and employees' resistance to the pay freeze.

Cost-effectiveness

A third reason to handle the change process well is that it is usually cost-effective to do so. The financial costs of many aspects of a well-managed change process (for example, involving employees, frequent communications, providing ample notice, and treating people with dignity and respect) are often relatively low. However, the positive effects of a well-managed change process on the bottom line may be considerable. Consider these three examples.

Researcher Jerald Greenberg examined reactions to a pay cut in a manufacturing company. He found that employees were more likely to

The positive effects of a well-managed **change process** on the bottom line may be considerable

steal tools, equipment, and office supplies relative to another group in which no pay cut was introduced. A third group of employees also had to endure the pay cut, but in this case the process of introducing the change was handled well. In a meeting that took about 90 minutes, the president of the organization sympathetically explained why the pay cut was necessary, how it would enable the organization to move forward and carefully, and considerately answered questions about the change. Greenberg found that the rate of theft was half as much in this third group, relative to the group who received the same pay cut but for whom the process of change was not handled as well.

In a second study, Greenberg and Allan Lind investigated employees' decisions to file a wrongful termination lawsuit against their former employers after being laid off or fired. The legal costs of defending such suits are considerable. (In a 1988 study by the Rand Corporation, they were found to be on average $80,000 a suit.) The most important predictor of whether employees went to law was the perceived fairness of the termination process. Among those who perceived the process to be highly fair, only 1 percent filed a suit. Among those who perceived the process to be highly unfair, the figure was 17 percent. Given that legal costs are likely to have risen since 1988, a conservative estimate of savings by handling the termination process fairly rather than unfairly is on average $12,800 (16 percent of $80,000) for each person made redundant. Employees' perceptions of the fairness of the termination process were based on factors such as how respectful managers were in delivering the news, the completeness of the explanation of why they were losing their job, and the employer's honesty. While it is difficult to attach a cost to these factors, it is no doubt less than $12,800.

To soften the blow of layoffs, organizations often provide assistance packages, including severance pay and support in finding jobs. The costs of doing this can be high. Such help not only influences those who are laid off; people left in the company appreciate it as well. In general, the more those kept on believe the package to be generous, the greater their productivity and morale. However, the effect of the generosity of the package on retained staff depends upon how well the layoff process was handled in other, more intangible ways. When "survivors" felt the organization provided ample notice and that the reasons had been well explained, the perceived generosity of the package was less likely to affect their productivity and morale.

The common theme in these examples is that many important aspects of a well-managed change process are not financially costly. And yet they can affect employees' reactions to change in ways that directly relate to the bottom line. The cost-effectiveness of a well-managed change process is reminiscent of a thesis about the economics of trust by academic John Whitney. He suggests that when employees do not trust one another, the organization must construct costly controls to ensure compliance. Put differently, companies can reap huge productivity gains by creating cultures in which employees trust one another. The management of organizational change is perhaps the main arena in which cultures of trust are created, maintained, or destroyed. Well-managed procedures for planning and implementing change instill employees' trust in their supervisors and in each other, which will be cost-effective both in the context of the change initiative and future policies and practices.

Change is not cost free

While the financial costs of many aspects of a well-managed change process are low, the process is not cost free. Costs may not be financial, but, rather, reflected in the demands on the time and energy of the change agents. Involving employees takes time, something change agents are likely to find in short supply. Moreover, change agents need to be psychologically available to employees. This means change agents will be exposed to the painful emotions that

Another reason for **employee resistance** is their ability, actual or perceived, to change

employees experience. It is little wonder, then, that change agents may feel the urge to withdraw from employees. As strong as this urge may be, this is precisely when change agents need to bite the bullet and stay in contact.

While certain aspects of well-managed change cost little financially, others have more of a price tag. Until now it has been implied that employees resist change based on a lack of desire to cooperate. After all, if the process is handled poorly, employees will hardly be inspired to embrace the change. Another reason for employee resistance is their lack of ability (actual or perceived) to change. It is one thing to tell people what they need to do differently. It is quite another to provide them with the tools, information, and training necessary to do so.

US conglomerate General Electric under Jack Welch and aircraft parts manufacturer Allied Signal under Larry Bossidy have both done masterful jobs of introducing quality initiatives. To support these initiatives, the organizations provided training for everyone, including senior managers. Training to give people the ability to do things differently costs money. However, in the long run, such activities are likely to be more cost-effective than change programs that fail to account for how the process is handled.

In conclusion, as daunting as the challenge of change is, the underlying message to change agents is one of hopefulness and optimism. While successful organizational change typically requires great physical and emotional energy, the actions advocated here are within the grasp of most change agents. Moreover, those who pay attention to how they handle the process are likely to provide their organizations with a sustainable source of competitive advantage.

Further reading

Brockner, J. and Wiesenfeld, B.M. (1996) "An Integrative Framework for Explaining Reactions to Decisions: Interactive Effects of Outcomes and Procedures," *Psychological Bulletin*, 120, 189–208.

Greenberg, J. (1990) "Employee Theft as a Reaction to Underpayment Inequity: The Hidden Costs of Pay Cuts," *Journal of Applied Psychology*, 75, 561–8.

Jick, T. (1994) "Managing Change," in, E.G.C. Collins and M.A. Devanna (eds), *The New Portable MBA*, New York: Wiley.

Lind, E.A. and Greenberg, J. (forthcoming) "The Winding Road from Employee to Complainant: Situational and Psychological Determinants of Wrongful Termination Claims," *Administrative Science Quarterly*.

Schaubroeck, J., May, D.R., and Brown, F.W. (1994) "Procedural Justice Explanations and Employee Reactions to Economic Hardship," *Journal of Applied Psychology*, 79, 455–60.

Making sharing
good for all

Angel Cabrera is professor of organizational behavior and human resources and the director of the human resources faculty at Instituto de Empresa in Madrid. His research focusses on knowledge management and strategic human resource management.

Sharing knowledge may be good for a company, but the same may not be true for individuals. This is just one of the issues that needs to be addressed to make knowledge management work, says **Angel Cabrera**.

Underlying the concept of knowledge management systems is the simple aim of making the best use of the collective human knowledge and talent of an organization. Systems try to encourage individuals to be creative and investigative, to share their knowledge and ideas, and to apply ideas from other people, as well as their own.

It is a concept that has come of age, with 62 percent of leading organizations in Europe and the US reporting that they have, or are setting up, a knowledge management system, according to a KPMG survey in 2000.

In theory, knowledge management initiatives can be very diverse, from information technology projects, to organizational structures, to human resource policies. In practice, KPMG found that systems are five times more likely to be led by an information technology department than by human resources or operations. In fact, most knowledge management initiatives are built around an intranet, database, or group software that allow people to communicate, share ideas, and engage in discussions.

For example, Accenture's knowledge management system is based on a Lotus Notes database that allows thousands of consultants around the world to exchange experiences, methods, and tools. The system provides electronic mail and adds the ability to navigate easily through specialized databases and to post contributions to the database.

Consultants are encouraged to add developments from their own projects to the knowledge repositories, and are invited to participate in knowledge-building dialogs across the company. Participation is voluntary and there are no explicit sanctions for not contributing.

This type of knowledge-sharing system, which has been widely adopted by consulting companies and is moving into other industries, is called a "knowledge repository" or "discretionary database."

The strong focus on information technology in most knowledge management initiatives has perhaps overshadowed the importance of human issues. Technology may provide a useful tool, but knowledge has more to do with brains than with bits. When the KPMG survey asked companies about the most important problems they were facing in implementing knowledge management initiatives, only 7 percent mentioned technical problems. The rest were more worried about people not using the system because of communication problems (20 percent); difficulties integrating the system with work (19 percent); lack of time to use the system (18 percent); lack of training (15 percent); and lack of benefits (13 percent).

Knowledge exchanges are complex social processes bringing significant costs and benefits to all parties. To ensure that investment in knowledge management yields the desired effects, we need to understand the social and psychological dynamics of knowledge transactions and try to build an organizational environment that takes them into consideration.

Knowledge-sharing dilemmas

To illustrate this, consider the choice faced by a sales executive in a telecommunications equipment manufacturer who, by working closely with a cellular phone client, has developed a valuable understanding of the client's needs. The executive's company has an intranet knowledge repository to help sales, production, and research personnel share knowledge and discuss ideas about products. With relatively little effort, the executive could post a report on the knowledge repository. The posting could perhaps initiate a discussion with research staff about new trends, and it could give salespeople from other divisions hints about how to introduce their products to the client.

While these outcomes carry a clear value for the company, it may not be such a good idea from a personal standpoint. Writing and posting the report would take time that might be invested in more profitable tasks – sharing knowledge does not yield commission. Even if we disregard the time issue, sharing knowledge may dilute an individual's competitive edge within the organization. If bonus and promotion decisions are

It may be naïve to expect people to **share ideas** just by installing technology to make it possible

primarily based on sales, the last thing a sales executive might want to do is to help others.

The situation can be even worse if the organization is, say, making people redundant: would you share knowledge that might save your job? In organizations where knowledge is a source of personal power, it may be naïve to expect people to share ideas just by installing technology to make it possible.

The choice faced by an individual in such a situation is known to sociologists as a social dilemma. In such a dilemma, individual rationality (behavior guided exclusively by individual payoffs) leads to collective irrationality. Consider, for example, a group of herders sharing a pasture. For each herder, there is a benefit in having as many cows as possible on grazing land, but if all herders followed suit, the land would be damaged to the point where no one would benefit. This situation, known as the "tragedy of the commons," constitutes a dilemma because individual attempts to maximize payoff result in collective damage.

The social dilemma that best represents the dynamics of a knowledge repository is probably the so-called public good dilemma. A public good is a shared resource from which every member of a group may benefit irrespective of whether they personally contribute to its provision. Since access to the public good is not restricted to contributors, there is a temptation for individuals to "free-ride," that is, to enjoy the resource without contributing to its provision. After all, not co-operating yields the best individual result regardless of what everyone else does. If everyone else co-operates and I do not, I enjoy the good for free. If no one else or very few others co-operate, I will be saving a wasted contribution.

Most people in a public good dilemma would prefer to enjoy the good and pay their individual contribution, rather than not enjoy the good and save the cost. The problem is that there is no guarantee of contribution; if there were, most people would gladly contribute. This is where the dilemma resides: if everyone acts "rationally" from an individual standpoint, no one would co-operate, and everyone would suffer the consequences. Furthermore, once an unco-operative equilibrium is reached, there is no individual incentive to break it, so the group gets trapped behind a "social fence" that prevents the group benefitting from co-operation.

A knowledge repository creates a public good dilemma among employees for the same reasons. If everyone contributes to the repository with ideas, everyone has the chance to improve performance by learning from others. However, the knowledge repository is accessible irrespective of any contribution, which creates an individual incentive not to contribute. As in most public good situations, it only takes a few participants to free-ride for the entire group to get trapped in an unco-operative equilibrium, thus sending investments in knowledge management technology down the drain.

How to skip over the social fence

Existence of a social dilemma does not imply that all public goods will be undersupplied. There are many examples of successful public goods in society and plenty of examples of successful knowledge sharing in organizations. These examples have helped social researchers understand the circumstances under which co-operation is more likely to take place. This research may help organizations devise interventions that will help them skip over the social fence and create co-operative environments where knowledge management systems are likely to succeed.

There are three conditions under which social co-operation is more likely to take place. The first concerns the cost of individual contributions. The less costly it is for people to contribute to the common good, the less likely they will be to withhold their contributions. The second condition has to do with the perceived effect of contributing. The more clearly people can see the impact of their contributions, the more motivated they are to make the effort. The third condition has to do with the size and composition of the group. Smaller groups, for example, tend to

enact social pressure mechanisms that foster co-operation. Each of these three conditions suggests specific interventions, most of which have been proven to work with public good dilemmas.

Reducing the cost of contributing

The most straightforward way to reduce the cost of sharing knowledge is to provide adequate resources to do so. These resources may include well-designed technology as well as time. However, the major cost incurred by a knowledge contributor is the dilution of personal competitive edge and the vulnerability created by revealing a personal insight. To compensate for this, it is important for organizations to revise their appraisal and incentive systems by incorporating an assessment of each person's contributions to the knowledge repositories. IBM, for example, requires a minimum level of contributions before anyone is considered for promotion.

Group incentives such as stock options may also help reduce the perceptions of cost by making everyone a beneficiary of everyone else's performance. These incentives reduce the value of hoarding knowledge, because revealing a personal insight can contribute to overall performance and, consequently, to collective rewards.

Increasing efficacy

Human behavior is determined to a great extent by outcome expectations. People will generally choose to act if their action is likely to have a positive outcome. So someone will be more inclined to make a personal contribution if it will clearly add value to the shared resource. Knowledge management technology can play an important role in increasing contributors' perceptions of adding value by setting up feedback mechanisms about their contributions. For instance, a knowledge exchange system could inform contributors of the number of "hits" by readers on their contributions. Or it could allow readers to send back comments on other people's contributions. Anything that helps individuals know what effect their contributions are having will raise the overall level of contributions.

To guarantee a minimum level of quality in the knowledge repository, thus increasing individual perceptions of impact, some organizations are experimenting with editorial filters. These may include reviews by subject matter experts or knowledge managers as well as by peers.

Managing group size and composition

The effect of group size on participation rates is not straightforward. On the one hand, there needs to be a minimum number of potential contributors for the repository to be worth anyone's while. If the number of contributors falls short of that threshold, the value drawn from the repository may not be enough to compensate individual efforts, and group members may be better off not wasting their time formalizing their knowledge exchanges. However, just as small groups may not constitute the best ground for organizational knowledge exchange, having too large a group may bring other problems. As groups become larger, individuals may perceive that their contributions do not make a difference. Also, as group size grows, it becomes more difficult to monitor and sanction individual participation, and the informal mechanisms of social pressure tend to lose their power.

Research shows that the likelihood of co-operation increases when interactions among participants are frequent and durable; participants are easily identifiable; and there is sufficient information available on each individual's actions. If it is likely that the individuals will not interact again, or if the identity of other participants is unknown and there are no records of past interactions, there will be an incentive for individuals to free-ride because there will be no way to make people accountable. Although technology can help promote these social accountability mechanisms, the effectiveness of social control may be hindered by group size.

In summary, knowledge communities need to be large enough to provide an enriching exchange of knowledge, yet not so large that people will lose their sense of community. The larger the community, the greater efforts will need to be taken to keep people involved.

When setting up knowledge communities, we also need to pay attention to group composition. In every organization people have varying levels of expertise and backgrounds. Whereas interdisciplinary communities may yield useful and creative exchanges, wide variation in terms of level of expertise may be harmful; among other reasons because experts may not find it useful or challenging enough to interact with novices.

Conclusions

In an era when competition is based more on what an organization knows rather than on what it owns, managers face the challenge of creating environments that foster knowledge creation and diffusion. Information technologists have developed tools that enable individuals to exchange insights across time and distance barriers. However, technology is just one ingredient in implementing a knowledge management system. More important than technology is a social environment that encourages knowledge creation and sharing.

While the value of sharing knowledge may seem obvious to managers, not sharing may be the safest option for employees. Research on social dilemmas reveals why co-operation may be hard to elicit and provides hints on how to make it more likely.

Organizations must tackle three problems to make knowledge sharing a reality. First, they need to recognize and reduce the costs of revealing personal knowledge. Second, they need to devise mechanisms by which individuals can see the effects of their contributions. Finally, they need to manage the size and composition of knowledge communities. In some cases, these solutions may impose design constraints on technology. But more often than not, solutions will take the form of organizational and human resource interventions.

Further reading

Davenport, T.H. and Prusak, L. (1997) *Working Knowledge: How Organizations Manage What They Know*, Cambridge, MA: Harvard Business School Press.

Kollock, P. (1998) "Social Dilemmas: The Anatomy of Co-operation," *Annual Review of Sociology*, 24, 183–205.

KPMG Knowledge Management Survey 2000, www.kpmgconsulting.com/kpmgsite/service/km/survey2000.html.

Turning knowledge
into business advantage

Susan E. Jackson is a professor of human resource management at the School of Management and Labor Relations, Rutgers University.

Randall S. Schuler is a professor of human resource management and director of the Center for Global Strategic Human Resource Management at the School of Management and Labor Relations, Rutgers University.

The true measure of a learning organization is the ability to translate new knowledge into new ways of doing business, say **Susan Jackson** and **Randall Schuler**.

What factors distinguish learning companies from other companies? In this article we argue that they combine an ability to manage knowledge with an ability to change continuously so as to improve their effectiveness. Knowledge is needed for learning, but is not sufficient. What companies also need is the capacity to translate knowledge into new ways of doing business.

For individuals, learning implies that a person changes in some way. Similarly, organizational learning implies change – in management philosophies and practices, organizational culture, and procedures. Innovation and change are never-ending processes that become routine. For example, at Southwest Airlines, when clerks suggested doing away with tickets, chief executive Herb Kelleher encouraged them to experiment on selected routes. Long before other airlines adopted electronic ticketing, Southwest Airlines was using it to reduce costs and loading times.

For many companies, knowledge resources and learning capabilities are ways of gaining sustainable competitive advantage. Figure 1 shows the acronym "Learn," which summarizes the principles. Each principle is explained in the following sections.

Leverage

Knowledge and learning capabilities are sources of competitive advantage when they add value and contribute to the company's ability to satisfy its stakeholders, including customers, employees, the community, and shareholders. Customers may seek goods and services that are low in cost, high in quality, and/or unique.

Successful companies use learning to understand customers better and give them more of what they want. The US search engine Yahoo!, for example, receives thousands of comments and suggestions from users who are eager for sites that suit their needs. Employees at Yahoo! constantly experiment to improve their site and so satisfy more customers.

Employees understand that their own value in the labor market increases if they improve their knowledge and skills. Companies that offer opportunities for self-improvement therefore benefit by attracting and retaining the best talent.

Communities and governments are concerned that companies contribute to the wellbeing of their citizens. Learning organizations therefore understand that their chances of success are improved when they share knowledge with the community and work to help develop the intellectual capital of citizens. Dow Chemical supports 26 advisory panels that address issues of importance to the community. In addition to sponsoring local activities, these panels work as partners to community organizations. They share their expertise to assist the community in planning for, training for, and implementing responses to emergencies.

Owners and shareholders invest money in companies in the hope of eventual profit. Learning organizations address their concerns by evaluating the value of their knowledge management and learning practices. Siemens University, for example, put the value of new solutions to business problems that were developed through its management education courses in 2000 at $11m. Ford Motor Company estimates the value to date of its five-year-old best practices replication process at $11bn.

Embed

The value of a company's knowledge resources and learning capabilities depends on how diffi-cult they are for competitors to imitate or replace. A learning culture that is embedded in a company's strategy and management practices is very difficult to imitate.

Eclecticism in environment, information, perspectives, and experiences is the catalyst of creativity. In learning organizations, employees form multidisciplinary teams. To encourage the free flow of ideas, these teams may be formed only as needed for projects, or they may be more enduring "communities of practice" that serve as forums for discussion.

Flat, open, and team-based structures often go hand in hand with a philosophy of empowerment, which places responsibility on employees for identifying and solving problems. This should not be equated with multiplying employees' responsibilities, nor with imposing formal objectives on every team effort. In fact, doing so may stifle the types of serendipitous exchange that lead to innovation.

Learning organizations encourage informal interactions that cross a company's boundaries. Even office layout can make a difference. At Viant, a consulting firm in Boston, the open-plan office includes plenty of informal meeting space near intersections where people are likely to bump into each other.

Beyond these internal initiatives, many learning organizations develop a network of alliances with suppliers, customers, and even competitors to gain new knowledge. In the US, International Sematech is an example of a multilateral alliance that supports learning through collaborative research. Through joint participation, 13 semiconductor manufacturers from seven countries share knowledge and expertise in ways that ultimately influence the entire industry.

Network structures maximize links among organizations. Such links can improve the organization's understanding of problems that lie beyond its own boundaries as well as motivate other members in the network to share knowledge and expertise in order to find creative solutions.

When a bottle maker learned how to recycle plastic, it recognized the commercial opportunities of the technology. Subsequent discussions with suppliers, customers, and competitors about a collaborative venture eventually helped all the partners realize that the idea would require substantial investment in research and development. Out of this, a collaborative research network was born. Each company paid toward the research at a university and participated in quarterly board meetings. The research output – the learning – became the venture's property and all interested parties were assured licensing rights for a nominal fee.

If knowledge resources and learning capabilities are recognized as essential to implementing company strategy, management practices ought to be oriented toward maximizing them. In reality, many managers believe these issues can be addressed by merely investing in technology and training. Experience with knowledge management technology often is the best antidote to such naïvety. For most organizations, transforming the human elements of the organization proves to be the most important. In this respect, Figure 2 lists the variety of management practices that may need adjusting.

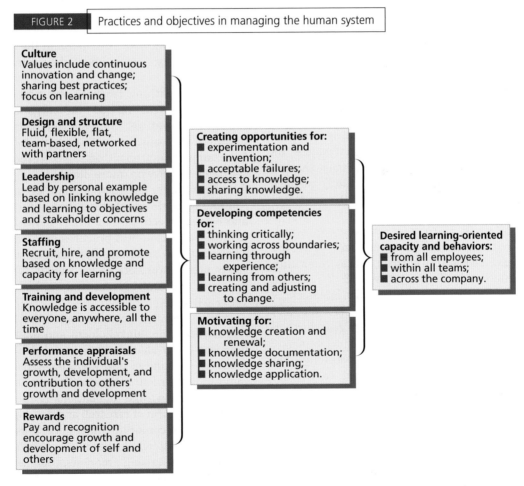

FIGURE 2   Practices and objectives in managing the human system

Culture
Values include continuous innovation and change; sharing best practices; focus on learning

Design and structure
Fluid, flexible, flat, team-based, networked with partners

Leadership
Lead by personal example based on linking knowledge and learning to objectives and stakeholder concerns

Staffing
Recruit, hire, and promote based on knowledge and capacity for learning

Training and development
Knowledge is accessible to everyone, anywhere, all the time

Performance appraisals
Assess the individual's growth, development, and contribution to others' growth and development

Rewards
Pay and recognition encourage growth and development of self and others

Creating opportunities for:
■ experimentation and invention;
■ acceptable failures;
■ access to knowledge;
■ sharing knowledge.

Developing competencies for:
■ thinking critically;
■ working across boundaries;
■ learning through experience;
■ learning from others;
■ creating and adjusting to change.

Motivating for:
■ knowledge creation and renewal;
■ knowledge documentation;
■ knowledge sharing;
■ knowledge application.

Desired learning-oriented capacity and behaviors:
■ from all employees;
■ within all teams;
■ across the company.

Copyright: S.E. Jackson and R.S. Schuler, 2001

Accessible

Whether one approaches knowledge and learning from the perspective of technology, human resources, or production, two objectives must be achieved: learning opportunities must be widely accessible and widely accessed. Putting a rich store of knowledge at everyone's fingertips is of little value if no one is motivated to access it. Conversely, instilling an appreciation of the value of knowledge and learning is of little use if the knowledge or opportunities for learning are difficult to access.

Explicit knowledge, which can be articulated and codified, is the easiest to make accessible. Indeed, the ease of making it accessible can create problems, in particular that of information overload. People will stop using a system if searches yield inaccurate, out-of-date, or low-value knowledge. At KPMG, an editorial board checks the validity of knowledge in the company's tax knowledge system. It also evaluates submissions. Of 6,000 annual submissions, only about one in 10 adds sufficient value to justify retention.

Many companies are turning to electronically delivered training as a way of improving accessibility. Cisco Systems is among the leaders. Its employees have electronic access to more than 40 hours of material. To encourage staff, modules are designed to be completed in 20 minutes or less.

KPMG and Cisco illustrate ways in which knowledge and learning systems can be designed to attract people to use them. Other companies use different methods. At Ernst & Young, the performance review system includes assessments of knowledge capturing, archiving, sharing, and use. Royal Bank Financial Group goes further, offering $25,000 for suggestions.

Such practices can improve accessibility and access. However, even in the best companies, most explicit knowledge never appears in documents or databases. It must be accessed through the people who possess it. In addition, much implicit knowledge becomes available only through social interaction with relevant experts – employees, customers, and competitors.

For this reason, learning organizations invest in creating face-to-face opportunities for learning and knowledge sharing as well as information technologies. Meetings around the water cooler are encouraged rather than discouraged. Social events, mentoring, classroom-based workshops, conferences, and community service are all seen as forums for implicit knowledge sharing and learning.

Renew

Learning organizations understand that much knowledge dates quickly or, if it remains valid, soon becomes a commodity. To ensure that business decisions reflect the latest, rare knowledge, learning organizations aggressively scan both the external and internal environments for information. They obtain information about how customers are reacting to current goods and services, how employees feel about working for the organization, their reputation in the community, and analysts' views about their competitive strength.

Used thoughtfully, feedback about how stakeholders are reacting to the organization's activities serves as a basis for continuous improvement. At accountants Deloitte & Touche, for example, data about employee turnover led the firm to develop more flexible and family-friendly practices designed to retain key talent.

Finding and transferring best practices is another approach to renewing knowledge. At Colgate-Palmolive, best practices are spread and adapted to new situations by managers who routinely accept transfers to unfamiliar functions, divisions, and countries en route to higher-level positions.

While learning organizations must gather information from stakeholders and enable best practices to be shared, such knowledge seldom produces the kind of new knowledge that drives radical innovation. Organizations must also renew the knowledge foundations of their businesses in the form of research and development.

Motorola's corporate university uses action learning to help employees create knowledge. A course on assessing markets, for example, required managers to visit bankers, officials, and business people in Latin America to practice their new skills. In the process, managers gained much of the first-hand knowledge they needed to implement the company's strategies in the region.

Siemens University also uses action learning to renew and regenerate knowledge. Its in-house corporate training gives responsibility for solving real business problems to analysts and engineers from around the world, who work together in "student" teams. Students share their analyses with business units and debate the benefits and costs of their plans.

Measurement

Intangible assets, such as knowledge and learning, account for a large part of a company's value. Yet traditional performance indicators provide little to guide investment in knowledge and learning. Recognizing this, Leif Edvinsson developed a management model at Swedish financial services group Skandia built around the concept of intellectual capital. Consultants now offer help to companies when assessing their knowledge resources and learning capabilities.

A standardized approach to measurement may help thinking about the value of knowledge and learning. However, every company has unique and complex relationships governing its knowledge resources, so the best approaches are tailored for each one. Measurement systems might:

- track employee competencies and development activities;
- assess learning;
- audit processes and databases;
- survey staff about their perceptions of a company's learning culture;
- assess the extent to which outsiders seek knowledge from staff.

Turning the learning organization from a concept into a source of competitive advantage requires organizational transformation. This demands resources and leadership commitment. Although change often unfolds in fits and starts, organizations can learn to improve. To judge improvement, an organization needs to know where it started and where it is now. Systematic measurement makes assessing improvement possible.

Further reading

Becker, B.E., Huselid, M.A., and Ulrich, D. (2001) *The HR Scorecard: Linking People, Strategy, and Performance*, Boston, MA: Harvard Business School Press.

Doz, Y.L. and Hamel, G. (1998) *Alliance Advantage: The Art of Creating Value Through Partnering*, Boston, MA: Harvard Business School Press.

Edvinsson, L. and Malone, M.S. (1997) *Intellectual Capital: Realizing Your Company's True Value by Finding its Hidden Brainpower*, New York: HarperBusiness.

Jackson, S.E. and Schuler, R.S. (2000) *Managing Human Resources: A Partnership Perspective*, Cincinnati: South-Western.

Storey, J. (2001) *Human Resource Management: A Critical Text*, London: Thomson Learning.

Recruitment makes
the most of the digital era

Peter Cappelli is George W. Taylor Professor of Management at the Wharton School of the University of Pennsylvania. He is also director of the Center for Human Resources.

Monika Hamori is a doctoral student at the Wharton School of the University of Pennsylvania.

Technology and corporate restructuring are driving changes in recruitment practices. **Peter Cappelli** and **Monika Hamori** set out the issues.

Employers show increasing willingness to restructure their companies by hiring experienced staff with different skills and abilities. Furthermore, as labor markets tighten, staff are increasingly willing to move and retention has become a problem. The result is that revenues of corporate recruiters have tripled in five years.

The phenomenon of more open labor markets and greater hiring from the outside is new. As outside hiring increases, employee turnover rises and many countries are experiencing tight labor markets.

Surveys suggest younger workers have much less interest in spending a lifetime with a single employer, which was the model for the previous generation. Yet lifetime employment was not always the case, even for large companies. In the US and Japan it is relatively new, existing for not much more than a few generations. However, for most people, it seems as though the typical job, especially at large employers, has been for life. With lifetime employment, the task for employers was to find good entry-level candidates and develop them. Hiring was an entry-level problem and fending off applicants was often harder than finding good ones.

New era

Pressure to respond faster to markets has persuaded employers they cannot restructure without hiring experienced workers from outside. A better understanding of intellectual capital has helped persuade employers that the best people can be worth an order of magnitude more than average ones.

The shift toward hiring experienced workers creates new challenges, beginning with the fact that the experienced candidates that most recruiters want are not applying for jobs. The best candidates are likely to be good workers who are happy where they are; at least some of the candidates who apply for jobs may be problem workers who are searching because they need to find a new job.

Finding applicants who are not looking to move requires new techniques. "Passive" candidates may not have curriculum vitae, so their skills must be assessed in other ways, often subtly and without their knowledge.

Here, recruiting is increasingly moving toward marketing. It has come to rely on customer profiling tools such as behavioral profiles, which identify what the targetted group does for fun and focusses marketing on those areas. Cisco Systems, for example, has sponsored pool tournaments, bike races, and other events that software engineers attend.

Other tools include market analyses, which identify companies that have the employees your company would like to hire. Contemporary practices go as far as placing advertisements about job openings in the car parks of companies that have announced restructuring.

In responding to these trends, the goal is to think about job candidates as if they were customers. Rather than wait for jobs to become vacant, companies run long-term campaigns to develop a steady stream of applicants.

Developments online

The development responsible for moving recruiting in the direction of marketing has been online recruiting. Websites represent three of the top five sources of information for job seekers in the US. Ninety percent of large US companies recruit online and recruiting services are booming – $2.5bn in revenues in 2000, $600m in start-up money in each of the last two years, and estimates that online recruiting revenues will be $30bn in five years. Job boards, where employers can post vacancies and applicants can post curriculum vitae, are common. There are 5,000 in the US alone.

What drives the interest in online recruiting is efficiency. Costs are about 5 percent of print recruiting and estimates suggest hiring time can be cut by two-thirds. Speed comes through automating and simplifying the hiring process with management systems that take applications in a standardized form over the internet, screen them and track their source, monitor where the applicant stands in the process, and calculate how long it took to get the job filled. These systems automate recruitment, make it possible to outsource some aspects, and create potentially powerful databases about applicants.

Recruiting costs are further reduced because experienced, passive candidates can be found without using expensive corporate recruiters. Estimates suggest there may be 30 million curriculum vitae on the internet. Experienced online recruiters can pull up thousands of results with any skill set or from most large employers, none of whom has applied for a job.

Recruiters can sometimes "flip a URL," which means follow a link on a curriculum vitae back to a company's intranet and download employee directories or other information such as company awards. Referral.com pays participants for confidential leads and references about fellow workers who might be interested in moving. On job boards such as Monster.com, recruiters can find millions of profiles, most of people who are not actively looking for a job.

Also, many people are looking for jobs on the internet. At Monster, for example, four million people search for jobs each Monday, the peak day for searches. Online services give access to unprecedented levels of information that helps shift power in the employment relationship to employees.

Vault.com and Wetfeet.com in the US offer inside information about what jobs are like in specific companies as well as insights into what they ask at interview. Salarysource.com offers customized data on compensation by job and location, through which employees can quickly benchmark salaries. Careerzone.com provides career management advice.

Online techniques change the way companies recruit and that begins with a positive image at their website. Sophisticated companies are building a human resources "brand" by tying recruitment advertising in with product advertising. Fidelity Investment discovered that its reputation in financial services was identified by almost 70 percent of respondents as a reason for seeking and accepting employment with the company.

One survey has found that 20 percent of job

applications were prompted by the company's product advertisements. Recruiting increasingly relies on much larger product marketing campaigns as a way to attract candidates and get them to the company's website, where sophisticated and cost-effective recruiting can take place. Hewlett-Packard has abandoned most print advertising for jobs and pursues approaches designed to bring applicants to its website.

Some companies list workplace awards on their websites, along with information about helping employees to balance work and family life. Once at the website, attempts are made to get viewers to apply for jobs. Technology companies, for example, match recruitment banner advertising to web pages viewers have chosen. J.P. Morgan runs an interactive, game-like program on which college graduates begin their applications.

Selection and screening

Having attracted applicants, the next step is to get better at sorting them out. Most companies now ask screening questions about, say, willingness to move or start dates, as a way to weed out less serious applicants. Others have become much more sophisticated. Brainbench.com provides skill tests and some companies have developed their own. Allstate Insurance, for example, screens applicants online with selection tests that feature instant feedback. Pricewaterhouse-Coopers has one of the more sophisticated online tests.

The risk of more complicated applications is that they may cause many applicants to go elsewhere. One study found that 46 percent of those who began online applications did not complete them. That may be a good thing for sifting serious applicants.

Except for convenience, however, there is nothing magical about online tests and they are only as good as the content that goes into them. When it comes to the validity or predictive power of selection techniques, one of the reliable techniques is also the most popular: unstructured, sequential interviews by managers. Structuring interviews and using common questions improve effectiveness enormously. In terms of written tests, cognitive and ability tests do well in their predictive validity.

Much of what is known about employee selection is based on experience with entry-level applicants; the challenge is to develop more effective ways to assess experienced candidates. Making sense of an applicant's prior experiences is a long-standing concern. Employers use this approach when they search for candidates who have done similar jobs at another employer. The harder, but more valuable, task is to find whether applicants can succeed in a different job. This is where skills tests have become important. The US education department estimates there are 5,000 organizations that certify skills. Employers are also rediscovering assessment centers that simulate work tasks.

Selling the job

The last step in the process is selling the job to the applicant and closing the deal. After decades of slack labor markets, this skill has atrophied. Online recruiting has made the problem worse by making it relatively easy for recruiters to find qualified applicants rather than trying to hire a few good ones. Some companies have begun to send recruiters to sales training to learn how to persuade applicants to take jobs.

Because recruiting reflects employers' characteristics, improved activities may make it easier to sell jobs to applicants. More personable and informed recruiters lead to better outcomes, as does more detailed information about the job. Applicants prefer assessments that are job related and do not seem to mind tough interview questions that clearly relate to jobs. They have a much less positive response to integrity tests, personality inventories, and drug testing, however. Interviews can also serve as a selling technique.

Finally, applicants want to find out how they are doing quickly – in tight labor markets, recruiters risk losing good applicants if they cannot respond promptly. As noted earlier, online screening offers instant feedback and many companies do one-day interviewing, notifying the applicant of the decision on the same day.

More generally, the traditional model of looking for applicants who fit predetermined and narrowly defined jobs is giving way to a more complicated model. As specific job tasks are becoming more transient, new competencies such as flexibility, personality, and the potential to innovate are becoming important. These developments are pushing organizations to focus on competency-based selection – key skills, aptitudes, and behaviors that lead to high performance in most jobs. Research shows that where jobs require problem solving, innovation, and autonomy, intelligence and personality traits prove better predictors of performance.

Employee retention

With so many companies interested in hiring passive candidates, it is impossible to defend completely against outside hiring. Managing employee retention therefore begins with accepting that the task is to shape who leaves and when they go.

Managing turnover in this way requires employers to have a realistic understanding of how important it is to keep different employees. That, in turn, requires more accurate assessments of competence and performance than most organizations are capable of doing. The next step is to use that information by focussing on employees who are most important to keep. Here, compensation is the mechanism of choice.

Bonuses payable after an employee has been with the organization for a particular period have become common retention devices. At US brokers Prudential Securities, bonuses are not given out across the board, even to employees with the same job title.

Perhaps the most successful ways to retain staff exploit social relationships. People tend to stay in organizations where they have built up strong ties to fellow workers. Teamwork, employee involvement, and social activities at the workplace create relationships that most employees would like to retain and that competitors cannot duplicate.

Following the principle that the best retention devices are ones that competitors cannot easily copy, the key issue for employers is to offer an attractive "employee value proposition." In some cases, it is opportunity. McKinsey & Company has adapted to the tight labor market by offering associates more interesting jobs than in the past and promoting the best ones faster.

Even companies in declining industries have been able to offer opportunities, such as the fact that management teams will soon be retiring, so creating openings for younger managers. Nortel has decided that the best way to keep people is to develop an internal online job board to create an open labor market.

Other approaches help companies to live with higher staff turnover rates. One mechanism is to improve retention on jobs that are more difficult to fill. At United Parcel Service, when a driver quits, training a replacement is expensive. The problem was traced to the difficult task of loading trucks at the start of a run. When the company assigned loading to a new group of workers, job retention of drivers improved dramatically. The turnover in the loading jobs was astronomical, at up to 400 percent a year, but those jobs were easy to fill.

Conclusion

The pressure to respond to changing markets by restructuring companies has led to outside hiring as the means to reshape competencies inside companies. The interest in outside hiring, in turn, is driving retention problems. Companies may have to get better at recruiting and retaining staff or lose out to competitors. In the process of doing so, employers are raising the stakes for human resources. Employees are benefitting from these developments, as are human resource managers, whose ability to manage recruiting and retention will make them increasingly influential.

Further reading

Cappelli, P. (1999) *The New Deal at Work: Managing the Market Driven Workforce*, Cambridge, MA: Harvard Business School Press.

Morgan, R.B. and Smith, J.E. (1996) *Staffing the New Workplace: Selecting and Promoting for Quality Improvement*, Milwaukee WI: Amer Society for Quality; Riverwoods, IL: CCH Incorporated.

Articles by recruiters: www.erexchange.com/articles.

The anchors that
dictate our careers

Edgar H. Schein is Sloan Fellows Professor of Management Emeritus at MIT Sloan School of Management.

In times of job uncertainty, people must be aware of what drives their career decisions. **Edgar Schein** describes the concept of career anchors.

Global competitiveness has led most industries to re-examine their concepts of productivity, efficiency, and costs. As is painfully evident, most companies have responded with something akin to downsizing or, as they prefer to say, "rightsizing."

These corporate efforts at restructuring have resulted in massive layoffs and a fundamental change in the attitude of organizations toward staff. Whereas the concept of lifetime employment and building long-term relationships with employees was, at one time, the preferred way to structure human resource policies, few organizations are willing now to promise a lifetime career.

Instead, the concept of "employability" security has grown (as opposed to employment security). This means the company owes people enough training and development so that if they are laid off, they will have a chance to develop their career in another company. At the same time, some organizations have come to believe that their human resources are critical, but they are finding it harder to figure out how to hold on to the people they need in a climate where career responsibility has shifted to the individual.

This shift has made it much more important for people to become acquainted with what I have called their "career anchor."

When employees face being made redundant or are offered an insecure contract, their self-esteem is threatened and their self-concept of what they are good at is challenged. It is often at this time that they have a chance to discover their career anchor, and it is no accident that organizations have begun to use the career anchor exercise as part of their outplacement services.

What, then, is a "career anchor" and how does one assess it? As people go through education and early job history, they acquire information about themselves in three basic areas. First, they discover their true motives and needs. Sometimes people know what career they want to pursue from childhood, but it is more typical that with each job they discover aspects that they want and don't want. Their motives become clearer with each new educational and work experience.

Second, they discover the talents and skills they possess. Unless locked into a very limited work situation, people find they are good at some things and less good at others. They discover that they enjoy being competent, so they tend to enhance skills and drop areas where they feel incompetent. For this reason, it is important early in their career to experience many different kinds of work. Only through such variety can people get a good sense of their talents and skills.

Third, they discover their values through the feeling of comfort or discomfort they have in various work situations. They may not be aware of having democratic values until they meet a particularly autocratic boss or a rigid bureaucratic organization. Or they may discover they cannot work for a company that produces a product of which they disapprove, even if the job is excellent. Or they may seek out organizations that allow them to exercise their values, as when a person with strong environmental values decides to work for Greenpeace or the Sierra Club.

The career anchor is the evolving self-image that includes these self-perceptions of motives, skills, and values. The more life and work experience people have had, the stronger their sense of who they are, hence the stronger the anchor. Why an anchor as the metaphor? Because people reported that when work assignments did not fit their self-image, they did not like it and felt "pulled back" into a "safe harbor."

Most jobs and careers allow people to meet a variety of needs and exercise a variety of skills. The "anchor" can then be thought of as those elements of the self-image that people would not give up if they were forced to make a choice. For example, someone who wants to be an engineer and a manager can go through many career stages practicing both. However, suppose that at one point he or she has to choose between running a division, with the emphasis on management, or becoming the chief technical officer, which would emphasize the engineering skill. At that point the person needs to know what his or her career anchor is to be able to choose wisely.

Types of career anchor

Career anchors fall into eight general categories. The important point is that, depending on what one's anchor is, one will want very different things from a career. Four of the anchor categories revolve around a dominant motive or need.

Autonomy/independence

People in this category have discovered that above all else they need to feel free and on their own in what they do. Some traditional jobs allow a great deal of this kind of freedom, but often these people opt for self-employment or for jobs that are highly autonomous. They can be freelance consultants, teachers, independent small business people, field salespeople, and so on.

Security/stability

At the other extreme to autonomy, people anchored in the security category need to design their career around the goal of achieving long-range stability and security. They feel that they can relax once they have achieved a position of career success and stability that allows them the feeling of "having made it." They are less concerned with the exact type of work and more concerned with a feeling of security.

Entrepreneurial creativity

For some people, the need to be personally creative in building something larger than themselves is the dominant need. They define themselves by their ability to create their own enterprise and they measure themselves by the enterprise and its success. This need is so strong that they may tolerate many failures in their career in the search for that ultimate success.

Pure challenge

Some people discover that what they need above all else is a sense of challenge, of insurmountable obstacles, or powerful opponents against whom they can compete.

These people define themselves less by the type of work they do and more by the sheer joy of competing or winning out over obstacles or strong opponents. If a company does not provide ever more difficult challenges, these people will leave to search other further challenges.

In addition to these anchor categories based on motive, two anchors revolve around a dominant sense of what one is competent at.

Technical/functional competence

People with this career anchor define themselves by their competence in a certain knowledge base, skill, or "craft", and continue to look for ever more challenge in that specific area of competence.

This kind of person wants to become the world's "best" salesperson, engineer, mechanic, surgeon, or whatever. The biggest problem for people with this anchor is that they tend to be pulled into generalist and managerial jobs in which they may fail and which they will hate.

General managerial competence

These individuals define themselves by their ability to manage other people, to integrate functions, and to be responsible for an entire unit or organization.

They measure their career progress by climbing to ever higher positions of responsibility in the company. They want to be able to attribute the success of their organization or project to their own managerial capabilities based on analytical skills, interpersonal and group skills, and the emotional capacity to deal with high levels of responsibility.

Each of the final two career anchors revolves around specific value issues.

Service or dedication

People with this anchor define themselves by their commitment to some deep value that the occupation permits them to express, such as teaching, environmentalism, human resource management, medicine, and so on. It is their value system that determines the kind of work and kind of organization that they will seek.

Lifestyle

This anchor is in a certain sense not specifically related to the career, but to valuing the integration of work and family issues. It did not surface in research 30 years ago, but is increasingly prevalent today. People with this anchor have decided that their working career must be integrated with family and personal values in such a way that the total lifestyle fits their personality and family situation.

Some of them will organize their work around the career of a spouse, or in terms of geographic area in which they want to live, or in terms of issues such as the area where they want their children to grow up or go to school.

Changing anchors is rare

Do anchors change as life circumstances change? Career concerns change, but anchors, once recognized and experienced, do not. For example, while sending children through college someone may take a job that pays more but is less in line with the anchor. Does this mean they have switched to the security anchor? No, it merely means that for a short time they are doing something that they do not entirely enjoy and that they will change as soon as the opportunity arises.

The only thing that would change an anchor is a life experience that provides new information about someone's motives, competencies, and values. This happens rarely once one is past the age of 30. What is more striking is that once one has identified what one wants and is good at, and has incorporated that into one's self-concept, this becomes very stable. People may change jobs, organizations, even careers, but the career anchor tends to remain the same.

Occasionally people encounter experiences that reveal new motives and skills that had not been called into play, but have always been present. Once external circumstances reveal them, they become incorporated into the self-image as well. The career anchor then becomes more differentiated and complex, but rarely would people switch from one category to another.

For example, a person in our research sample who seemed to have a technical functional anchor started in the computer consulting business. Then, he went into law when an inheritance permitted him to go back to law school. However, he discovered that computer-related law was not a viable career and eventually settled into a small town practice where his technical skills play out in various computerized processes he has invented to deal with property, divorce, and other law-related issues.

As he reflects back on his career, it is evident that what he has always valued most and what has not changed at all is his need to be challenged in his area of computer competence.

Another way anchors evolve is in terms of the opportunities or constraints that the later stages of life present. If people are successful and economically secure, concerns for autonomy grow. Many early retirees decide that instead of seeking another job in a company they will develop a business of their own, often with a spouse. This is not so much an entrepreneurial effort as an effort to be more on one's own, to gain autonomy and self-determination.

Self-insight

In times of transition, such as today's new economy, people need to discover their career anchors to decide certain things: what industry to pursue, what job level to seek or settle for, what functional and interpersonal skills to highlight in the search for the next job, and how to assess career potential. In more stable times people could remain unaware of their career anchors, but if more choices have to be made, it becomes more important to know what one's inner priorities are, for example, what one would not want to give up.

Discovering career anchors is not difficult. It is based on doing a good educational and job history with careful thought about why each decision along the way was made. The anchor emerges out of the pattern of answers to the "why" question. This is best done in an interview.

It is not important to fit into one of the eight categories above. What is important is to get a sense of what a person's motives, skills, and values are so priorities can be identified in making job and life choices. People cannot take responsibility for their career if they do not know what the inner drivers of that career are.

Further reading

Barth, T.J. (1993) "Career Anchor Theory," *Review of Public Personnel Administration*, 13(4), 27–42.

Durcan, J. and Oates, D. (1996) *Career Paths for the 21st Century*, London: Century Business Press.

Nordvik, H. (1991) "Work Activity and Career Goals in Holland's and Schein's Theories of Vocational Personalities and Career Anchors," *Journal of Vocational Behavior*, 38, 165–78.

Schein, E.H. (1993) *Career Anchors*, San Francisco, CA: Jossey-Bass.

Careers, work, and life:
ways of finding a better balance

Cary L. Cooper is BUPA
Professor of
Organizational Psychology
and Health at Manchester
School of Management
and deputy vice-
chancellor at UMIST.

Executives need ways of managing the stress created by longer working hours, for themselves and their employees. **Cary Cooper** outlines some options for more flexible ways of working.

Each decade tends to have defining characteristics. The 1960s were known for innovation and challenges to established social norms; industrial strife dominated the 1970s; the 1980s were characterized by "enterprise culture," strategic alliances, and privatization; and in the 1990s a short-term contract culture arose, with outsourcing, downsizing, and long working hours.

One effect of the 1990s shift is that European work cultures are beginning to be "Americanized," first in the UK and then throughout the continent of Europe. The American work culture has many characteristics, but the three most relevant to this article are leaner organizations, intrinsic job insecurity, and a longer working hours culture. This trend, toward what is euphemistically called the "flexible workforce," found a European foothold in the UK.

The UK had led the way in privatizing the public sector in the 1980s, when its companies reduced their workforces substantially during the recession of the late 1980s and early 1990s. They outsourced many corporate functions as the country's recession lifted in the early 1990s, faster than in the rest of Europe.

However, this Americanized scenario is beginning to have an adverse effect on employee attitudes and behavior. In a recent Institute of Management/UMIST Quality of Working Life survey of 5,000 UK managers (from directors to junior managers), it was found that the changes toward downsizing, outsourcing, delayering, and the like had led to substantially increased job insecurity, lower morale, the erosion of motivation, and, most important of all, a decline in loyalty to the organization. Although changes were perceived to have raised corporate profitability and productivity, decision making was slower and the organization was deemed by managers to have lost the right mix of human resource skills and experience.

Long working hours

A more worrying feature of this trend was that it showed an increase in working hours, adversely affecting the health and wellbeing of managers and their families. In the 1999 survey, 81 percent of executives worked more than 40 hours a week; 32 percent more than 50 hours; and 10 percent more than 60 hours. A substantial minority of interviewees also worked frequently at the weekends.

In addition, whereas 32 percent of these executives in 1998 felt that their employer expected them to put in these hours, by 1999 this rose to 58 percent. What is disturbing about this is managers' perception of the damage inflicted on them and their families: 71 percent of these executives reported that longer working hours damaged their health; 86 percent that it adversely affected their relationship with their children; 79 percent that it damaged their relationship with their partner; and 68 percent that long hours reduced their productivity.

It was also interesting that there was no difference between directors and junior managers in terms of the damage caused – both suffered in equal measure.

Job insecurity

Since the Industrial Revolution, few white-collar and professional workers in the UK have experienced high levels of job insecurity. Even blue-collar workers who were laid off in manufacturing industries were frequently re-employed when times got better. Can people cope with permanent job insecurity, without the security and continuity of organizational structures that in the past also provided training, development, and careers?

The 1995 European survey by International Survey Research of 400 companies representing 8 million workers showed a substantial decline in perceived job security between 1985 and 1995 in most European countries. Britain showed the worse decline in employee satisfaction in terms of job security, dropping from 70 percent who were satisfied (in terms of security) in 1985,

down to 48 percent by 1995, and stabilizing at this low level in the 2000 survey.

How will this trend affect employees? Can companies continue to demand commitment from employees to whom they don't commit? What will a culture of long hours do to the two-earner family, which is the majority family in the UK? The economy may be doing well, but levels of job insecurity and dissatisfaction are high and growing. Developing and maintaining a "feel-good" factor at work is not just about profits. In a civilized society it should be concerned with quality of life, which includes such issues as hours of work, family time, achievable workloads, control over one's career, and job security.

Flexible working

Some of these work–life balance issues may be tackled by giving people greater control over their working lives – which means more flexible working. There are many ways to help meet employee needs and minimize the negative effects of some changes in the workplace. In the book *Balancing Your Career, Family and Life*, seven are identified.

Flexitime

Flexitime is a system that permits variable times of arrival and departure within limits set by managers. A specified number of hours have to be completed during a given period, but the times of work can be altered. Usually, but not always, there is a core period during which everyone must be in the office. This does not create more time for family and home life, but it does give workers slightly more control over their lives, enabling them to balance different demands.

The benefits vary depending on the system used. Academics Sheila Kamerman and Alfred Khan describe four different types of flexitime, from the least to the most flexible:

- Flexitour: staff choose start and end times, but must keep within a schedule they select and work the same number of hours a day.
- Gliding time: this is similar to flexitour, except employees may vary the time they start and finish.

- Variable day: employees can vary the number of hours worked each day, providing they are present for a minimum core period.
- Mariflex: daily hours can be varied as desired. Employees do not have to be present for a core period.

Systems allowing maximum flexibility enable employees to opt for arrangements such as a compressed working week. This involves working for 10 or more hours on three or four days. This would benefit commuting couples. Parents of young children can use this method to help manage childcare.

Flexiplace

Helpful companies can be flexible about where, as well as when, staff work. Employees may be able to work at home or spread their workload between home and office. Many different types of work are amenable to flexiplace, including financial services, design, and information technology. The limits of flexible locations are set by the need for contact with clients and customers, and the need for equipment.

In some cases, clients may be prepared to visit a person's home rather than a central workplace. Transferring equipment to the home may not be practical, but many kinds of equipment are now portable.

The growth of telecommuting has come about partly in response to the need to retain experienced staff, especially women who have taken maternity leave. Working from home is not a solution to childcare – substitute childcare is still necessary. However, it can give more flexibility and benefits partners who work in different locations. It is a possible solution to relocation problems.

Introducing homeworking involves investment in computers and other equipment, but can be cost-effective in the long term. Apart from saving the expense of training new staff, telecommuting will reduce investment in office space and increase efficiency by reducing commuting time. It may also have a positive impact on pollution, transport, and the environment.

However, homeworkers may feel isolated and cease to think of themselves as members of the larger organization. This effect can be reduced

Companies need to question the view that only **full-time** employees are serious about their careers

by providing homeworkers with a shared desk or space for occasional office-based work, by regular meetings, and by arranging social events.

Some managers cannot trust anyone they cannot see. Often they fear losing control when employees are not physically present. One solution lies in training and encouraging managers to realize that they will be able to supervise more people more efficiently, while at the same time responding to employees' needs.

Part-time work

Part-time working has often been limited to low-status jobs, with restrictions on benefits, training, and promotion. Organizations now need to question the view that only employees who work full-time are serious about their careers. When both spouses are employed, one or both can afford to work part-time when their children are young or while they have other family commitments. However, highly trained individuals are unlikely to be satisfied with dead-end jobs in which their skills are underused. More part-time jobs are needed with career opportunities, which take account of family and professional needs.

Job sharing

If full-time attendance is essential, companies can consider job sharing. The popularity of job sharing is growing for positions in management and elsewhere, in local authorities, banks, retail chain stores, firms of solicitors, and other types of organization. Employers see advantages in terms of retaining skilled and experienced staff. It is also recognized that working part-time allows people to stay fresh, energetic, and creative during the hours worked, and there is evidence of greater productivity among job sharers.

V-time

Voluntary reduced time (V-time) is a system that allows full-time employees to reduce working hours for a specific period, with a corresponding reduction in salary. It differs from the usual concept of part-time work in that it is temporary, with a guaranteed opportunity to return to full-time employment. Usually the schedule remains in force for a designated period, perhaps six months or a year, to allow employees and employers to try the new arrangement with the assurance that the commitment can be renegotiated or ended after this period. Employee benefits are maintained during the period of reduced work, which may be a regular event, such as shorter days or weeks, or as a block of time, perhaps during school holidays.

V-time is useful for creating opportunities to balance work with other responsibilities and may be used by employees for gaining new skills or responding to a health problem.

Sabbaticals

Opportunities can also be created by sabbaticals, which are increasingly offered by large and small companies alike to staff with a certain level of service. Arrangements are usually made to cover absences by creating an opportunity for a trainee, or reorganizing colleagues' responsibilities to share the work. This provides other employees with the chance to take on more responsibility, which can contribute to personal and career development. Sabbaticals may be used for working with supplier companies to understand their problems, for further education, working in local or national government, to care for sick relatives, and so on.

Career break schemes

Maternity and paternity leave will not be sufficient leave for all parents – some prefer to spend more time with their infants. Realizing that breaks for childcare are usually temporary, some organizations have taken steps to accommodate a longer career break. Re-entry and retainer schemes allow certain employees to interrupt their usual working arrangements for a number of years, after which they can return with no loss of seniority.

The employee is usually expected to undertake at least two weeks' paid relief work for the company during each year of absence and is provided with regular information packs and a refresher course for returners.

The scheme may permit one five-year break or two shorter breaks, each starting from the end of statutory maternity leave. Many women prefer two shorter breaks that enable them to return to work between the births of their children. Ideally, the choice of one long or two short breaks can be left to the employee. Career breaks are open, in principle, to men and women, although in practice they tend to be taken by women. Organizations permitting two short career breaks could encourage the sharing of these between the two parents.

The benefits of operating a career break include:

- ensuring participants stay in touch with their work, maintaining confidence and expertise;
- attracting young women with talent and ambition, because they are no longer forced to choose between family and career;
- ensuring investment in training is not lost;
- enabling employment later with a minimum of retraining.

The practicalities

More and more companies are introducing innovative work–life balance programs. The following two examples are drawn from the UK government booklet, *Creating a Work–Life Balance*.

One of the most comprehensive programs among larger companies is the Lloyds TSB work options scheme. Launched by the bank in early 1999, the program is open to 78,000 employees in the UK and abroad. Individual employees negotiate the work–life balance that suits them and their work. The individual initiates the request, but has to provide a business case and details of how the change would work in practice. The proposal is then discussed and refined with a line manager.

The scheme has a wide range of options and "as long as there is no negative impact on the business, the request is likely to be approved by the line manager," according to the government report. Staff surveys show a positive response to the scheme. Around 95 percent of applications are approved and nearly one in five male employees has used the program.

Elsewhere, Dutton Engineering manufactures stainless steel and mild steel enclosures for electronics, and employs about 50 employees. It has introduced a contract of 1,770 hours a year: staff can work to customer demand and, when this is slack, take time off. Managers refer to "quality hours": when a customer has immediate needs these are fulfilled and when employees are not needed they can go home. Staff use computers to keep in touch and are encouraged during slack periods to spend time with families and pursue outside interests.

Conclusion

The social anthropologist Studs Terkel once wrote: "Work is about a search for daily meaning as well as daily bread, for recognition as well as cash, for astonishment rather than torpor, in short, for a sort of life rather than a Monday to Friday sort of dying." At the beginning of a new century, employers should reflect on where they are going and what that might mean for employees and society. In short, they should try to live up to their often espoused but rarely implemented belief: people are the most valuable asset.

Further reading

Cooper, C. and Lewis, S. (1997) *Balancing Your Career, Family and Life*, London: Kogan Page.

Department for Education and Employment (2000) *Creating a Work–Life Balance: A Good Practice Guide for Employers*, London: DfEE.

Kamerman, S. and Khan, A. (1987) *The Responsive Workplace*, New York: Columbia University Press.

Terkel, S. (1977) *Working*, London: Penguin.

Managing to take
the stress out of pressure

The effects of stress are resulting in more court cases by staff against companies. **Lyn van Oudtshoorn** shows how managers can prevent this happening.

Dr Lyn van Oudtshoorn is a director of Powercalm Ltd, a consultancy specializing in organizational pressure and performance management.

You may already subscribe to the view that intellectual capital is your company's greatest asset. You may also accept that a happy, healthy workforce translates directly into higher productivity and better customer service. Can we assume, then, that your organization already has the stress issue well under control? Not necessarily.

Despite the common experience of mounting pressure in our working culture, surprisingly few organizations are tackling the problem in a systematic way, either because the costs are regarded as high, or the subject is in its infancy. Indeed, the canons of best practice are still being laid down. Yet principles and guidelines are beginning to emerge.

Stress principles

Stress begins with the "adrenalin rush" we feel at times of high arousal. The evolutionary purpose of the "fight or flight" response is survival and it remains entirely appropriate in situations of acute threat. However, in the face of chronic, low-level threat (in other words, worry), the body reacts in the same way, but without the same opportunities to discharge the energy it generates. This is stored as a tension that slowly eats away at our levels of resilience, our capability and, ultimately, our health.

Stress manifests itself in a variety of ways. The early warning signals might include disturbed sleep, sudden weight gain or loss, headaches, impaired judgment, or making silly, uncharacteristic mistakes. When the warnings are ignored, more serious consequences can include damage to the immune or cardiovascular systems, depression, or breakdown.

Organizational life abounds with opportunities for excessive pressure, from autocratic or chaotic management styles, to work overload or constant change. Though this field is still being debated, there are accepted principles of stress management.

Forget the notion that stress can be good for you. A dictionary definition of stress is: "oppression, hardship, adversity, affliction; a force acting on or within a body or structure and tending to deform it." By definition, therefore, stress is a bad thing. There is an important distinction, however, between stress and pressure. Pressure is the agent; stress is the effect of too much or too little pressure. The right amount of the right sort of pressure is essential to proper functioning, and being stretched from time to time is a precondition for professional and personal growth. Yet if we are overstretched, we experience strain and can tip over into exhaustion.

This is as true for corporations as it is for individuals, and herein lies the challenge. The right amount of the right sort of pressure is a dynamic thing, a continuous balancing act. What is true today may not be so tomorrow. The solution must therefore be flexible and sustainable.

Managers experience less stress than those they manage. The Whitehall research study, conducted by University College London, tracked 28,000 civil servants over 30 years. Taking into account variables such as diet and smoking habits, researchers demonstrated that the closer people get to positions of real power, and therefore control over their own lives, the smaller their chances of dying from cardiovascular disease. Conversely, the lower down the hierarchy an employee is, the greater the risk of heart disease.

This is equally true of actual and perceived control, demonstrating further that habits of thought predispose us to reacting in particular ways to situations, even when they may not be genuinely threatening. So, the ability to change perspectives is a powerful ally against excessive pressure.

Treating the symptoms is not a cure. In the 1980s and early 1990s, managers wanting to tackle stress would buy in an employee assistance program (EAP) and hope for the best. An EAP is an external agency that organizations use to outsource the counseling role. Any more radical measures still lay in uncharted water. In fact, the role of tertiary care should be minimal: what really matters is addressing the sources of strain.

The literature on workplace health has long

The role of **tertiary care** should be minimal: what really matters is addressing the sources of strain

advocated a three-tier approach to prevention, where the environment in which a person works is given at least as much attention as its effects on individual employees. This was applied to stress management in the 1980s by academics such as Tom Cox, Cary Cooper, and Larry Murphy. The UK's Health and Safety Executive (HSE) endorsed this structure in the early 1990s with its publication of Cox's reports on workplace stress, which are now regarded internationally as the framework around which an effective pressure management policy should be built.

The primary level of intervention looks at corporate culture, policies, management, and working practices, with a view to removing hazards or reducing employees' exposure to them. In the context of pressure management, this might include improving job design, introducing flexible working hours, rationalizing goals, reducing excessive working hours, enhancing skills and so on.

The secondary level is to improve the organization's and employees' ability to recognize and deal with risks as they arise. Like the primary level, it is proactive and includes training in managing pressure. The tertiary level is reactive, providing help for the walking wounded in coping with and recovering from problems that have already occurred.

Risk assessment and intervention are continuous and inseparable. To develop a program of intervention, companies must first work out where undue pressure is occurring and why. There are several ways of assessing the risks and they can be assessed either before or during a program of intervention.

Diagnostic tools are available, including the Occupational Stress Indicator (OSI) developed by academics Cary Cooper and Stephen Williams, and the Pressure Management Indicator (PMI) developed by Williams. These take the form of questionnaires, completed by a target group of

Managers should not try to **quantify stress** precisely, since this can distract from more important issues

employees and analyzed statistically. There are also conversationally based risk assessment approaches, such as work analysis interviews advocated by the HSE. These have the advantage of flexibility, so they can be tailored to the needs of a particular group and organization. They also cost less.

Sophisticated diagnostic tools can provide an insight into organizational pressures. However, any tool used just once can only provide a snapshot. Unless there is a way of assessing risk embedded in the system over time, there is a good chance a new hazard will be missed. Managers should not try to quantify stress too precisely, since this can distract from managing more important issues. Ideally, the on-going risk assessment arises out of the intervention process and is specific to an organization.

Top-level support is critical. Stress is a subject of fear for people. Without strong leadership from the very top, few managers will risk supporting a program of intervention. The process needs to be controlled by line managers if it is to be taken seriously, but they should be supported by other functions such as organization development, human resources, or occupational health. Safety is a good reason for top-level support. Another is that an effective program will throw up organizational issues that need to be dealt with at the policy level.

Practical issues

The case studies in Boxes 1 and 2 show how companies are dealing with the issue of stress and are putting these principles into practice. Lessons can be drawn from each of these programs in the way they:

- focus on primary and secondary levels of intervention, while still providing help at a tertiary level;
- are aimed at good management practice, rather than focussing on stress in a narrow sense;

Box 1 **Glaxo Wellcome case study**

Glaxo Wellcome (now GlaxoSmithKline) launched its global mental wellbeing policy in 1996, recognizing that stress was a significant hazard and that a healthy corporate attitude was a major contributor to business goals. It wanted an analytical and preventive approach, in keeping with its scientific business. Beyond that, each operating company was free to implement the policy in the way that best suited its culture.

Around the same time, Glaxo Wellcome's research and development division in the UK launched a behavioral competence framework, setting the criteria for behaviors relating to (among others) decision making, leadership, and teamworking, against which managers would be appraised. The essence of the program is that managers are coached to assess the risk of stress to their teams, to prioritize the most important stress factors, and

to look at measures to control them. They use a simple, informal system that was designed in-house. Analysis is carried out through group discussion of primary stress factors, which are contributed anonymously in writing by team members. Actions to control them are agreed and recorded at the meeting. The cost is low because the demands of the training and implementation are minimal. Managers' training takes only two hours. The program was run at the highest level, which helped circumvent potential resistance lower down the company.

Support for individuals trying to cope with pressure takes the form of workshops, counseling via in-house provision and EAP, and an information pack. The aim throughout is to help employees achieve a balance between the acknowledged demands of working in a high-pressure industry and their ability to cope.

Box 2 **Unipart case study**

The motor industry has faced intense global competition and corporate change, with obvious effects on the workforce. The Unipart Group of Companies (UGC) embarked on a wellbeing program in the early 1990s with a view to preventing stress, rather than finding a cure. The company looked at ways to improve and maintain the physical fitness of its staff. A gym and health center were established alongside the existing occupational health provision. Then in the mid-1990s, attention moved to the causes of pressure and stress.

Counselors were recruited to provide support. The take-up rate provided a measure against which the program could be evaluated and showed which issues needed to be addressed. Individuals were offered pressure management workshops and team workshops were customized for managers.

The innovative part of UGC's approach was a third phase called the pressure mentor network. The company selected certain people to be a "first port of call" for anyone showing signs of stress. At such times, people need to put things back into perspective, often simply by talking it through. These mentors are not counselors, but fellow employees. They are selected across the boundaries of rank, gender, and age, and represent a cross-section of employees. They are trained to recognize the symptoms of stress, to understand situations they are likely to encounter, and in the use of first-stage helping skills.

In addition, they need a clear understanding of the limits of their role and to have support at hand. Their training is continuous and they are supervised and rehearsed in procedures.

Structured feedback is fed back to the primary level, where policy issues can be addressed.

- cascade through every level in the organization, making no assumptions about where stress might arise;
- incorporate risk assessment;
- are backed by the chief executive.

The benefits that accrue reach further than simply avoiding litigation. However, the rising number of compensation claims is a legitimate concern. It is apposite to ask how an organization can ensure it does not become the target of litigation and, if this does happen, how a company can demonstrate that it takes its duty of care seriously.

It should be noted that stress is not recognized as a medical condition and that distress is not sufficient grounds for bringing a case to court. There are no "stress cases" in the sense that somebody has successfully sued an organization for inflicting stress. Legal cases must hinge on other complaints or events.

Briefly, the burden of proof lies with claimants, who must prove that:

- they are suffering from a recognizable medical condition and that it has been brought about by circumstances at work;

- the condition was foreseeable;
- adequate steps to alleviate their situation were not taken.

In the UK, the classic case that illustrates these points is *Walker v Northumberland County Council*. Mr Walker, a social worker, had a psychiatric breakdown (a recognizable medical condition) and had to retire on medical grounds. He had suffered a breakdown already as a result of increased workload and had told his employers he was struggling (a foreseeable situation). However, his workload had not decreased, nor had he been given resources that would have enabled him to cope, despite having been promised these (an inadequate response).

This was the first case to be declared a "stress case" in England and Wales, but many previous examples could have been so labeled. Employees are taking their employers to court and winning such cases in increasing numbers.

Either of the programs described here would provide evidence of an employer diligently pursuing its duty of care. More importantly, it would vastly increase the chances of an employer becoming aware of a potentially dangerous situation and provide an opportunity to address it in a constructive way. Most importantly of all, where raised awareness and skill levels permeate a corporate culture, such situations are far less likely to arise.

Conclusion

Many managers still operate on the assumption that the best way of getting the job done is to apply pressure without ceasing. This has the unfortunate consequence of appearing to be true in the short term. Not only is it unsustainable in the longer term, but it betrays a fundamental misunderstanding of the psychology of motivation.

A workplace where everyone strives because they are fired up by the satisfactions of their job is an achievable goal. Addressing the issue of stress is a good place to start.

Further reading

Cox, T., Griffiths, A., and Auty, A. (1998) *Work Stress: Advice on its Prevention and Management*, London: Loss Prevention Council, by fax at +44 (0)207 902 5301.

Cox, T., Griffiths, A and Auty, A., (1998) *Work Stress: A Brief Guide for Line Managers*, London: Loss Prevention Council, by fax at +44 (0)207 902 5301.

Earnshaw, J. and Cooper, C. (2001) *Stress and Employer Liability*, London: Chartered Institute of Personnel and Development.

Marmot, M. et al. (1991) "Health Inequalities among British Civil Servants" (The Whitehall II study), *The Lancet*, 337, 1387–93, or www.ucl.ac.uk/ epidemiology/ white/white.html.

Sapolsky, R.M. (1998) *Why Zebras Don't Get Ulcers*, New York: WH Freeman.

New face in the top team:
how to ensure a good fit

Andrew Kakabadse is a professor of management development and deputy director of Cranfield School of Management.

Financial performance is not the only way of judging senior executives and new board members. **Andrew Kakabadse** outlines the issues on the selection agenda.

During a recent "away day," the chief executive of a US financial institution congratulated his team on its progress in gaining market share. Contribution to group profits had risen by more than 49 percent during the previous 18 months. Yet he was also prompted to comment that unless this rate of success was maintained, he might find himself forced out of the organization. The reason? The demanding style adopted by the chief executive and his team went against the grain of the board's traditional culture.

The success of the chief executive's strategy was not in question. The issue was instead one of approach and philosophy. The board saw a good fit with the organizational culture as equally important to a high performance rating.

Executive turnover and succession are becoming ever more prominent business issues. Meeting the demands of critical investors, maintaining and enhancing stock price at a level that provides the value shareholders seek, while satisfying the expectations of customers, is a balancing act that a number of senior executives have not been able to maintain.

In addition, the growing influence of other stakeholders, such as the media, pressure groups, and politicians, makes chief executives more likely to be labeled scapegoats in times of trouble. The unfortunate Gerald Corbett of UK's Railtrack was supported by his board after the Hatfield train crash that killed four people, but not by his political masters, and became one of the casualties who could not satisfy the full range of stakeholder demands.

The importance of succession is well recognized by corporations. Will the new chief executive make a difference? Will shareholders lose confidence with the change of top manager? Can processes be introduced to enable the corporation to get the right people in place at the right time, so minimizing the traumas that inevitably arise from executive turnover? Or, can formal mechanisms ever be expected to ensure a successful process of succession? Research instead suggests that managers need to deal sensitively with the dynamics of each succession, irrespective of the effort put into personnel planning.

Cranfield School of Management has conducted studies into leadership performance and succession dynamics, examining more than 11,000 organizations in 14 countries. The results emphasize that five critical considerations require attention:

- respecting context;
- effectively managing the dynamics of top teams;
- being realistic about the transition experience;
- hiring headhunters who challenge applicants;
- establishing a cadre platform.

Context

An important conclusion that has emerged from these studies is that defining the core value proposition of the corporation is a challenging experience for senior managers. No single proposition is likely fully to represent the spread of competencies and activities within the company.

Many factors require reconciliation: the historical reasons for the structure of the organization, the nature of the product and service portfolio, the degree of regional spread, the level of investment in particular processes and activities, and the attention paid to reducing costs. In response, the chief executive needs to establish a clear vision and persuade the top team to accept that vision. Part of this process requires the team to reach conclusions as to how the corporate center will relate to the operating businesses. Will the interactions be based on a philosophy of partnership or one of control, or will the center/operating business relationship simply be a reflection of the personality of the chief executive?

Particular patterns of interaction between the center and the rest of the organization are already likely to have been established. For instance, the enterprise may be pursuing an economy-of-scale strategy, centralizing functions and applying the disciplines of cost management

across the company. Alternatively, the company may be concentrating on customer service, which requires the devolution of authority and a shared philosophy of common purpose.

Either of these strategies may be distorted by the peculiarities of the chief executive's personality. For any new incumbent, it takes time to distinguish the business logic driving the organization from the personality of their predecessor. Although the successor may accurately identify the parts of the predecessor's contribution that should be carried forward into the future, it is unwise to assume that influential stakeholders will share this analysis. What customers and other stakeholders value may conflict with shareholders' expectations.

Succession tends to bring out these tacit issues. The talented executive will spot them and manage them. For the less perceptive, their effective integration into the company is likely to be heavily influenced by the chairman. Sound chairmen, so often the calming voice in controversial issues, also act as the mentor of the newly appointed chief executive, providing guidance as to what is workable and what is best left until a later date. Less able chairmen often end up acting as the chief executive, thus placing themselves in confrontation with the new appointee, usually leading to the departure of one or the other.

The top team

A particularly important determinant of successful executive succession is the orientation of the members of the top team. Who is in the top team, however, varies from one organization to the next. The top team could consist of the board. In other organizations, the top team could be the board and members of the senior management committee. Alternatively, the top team could consist of executive directors and general managers who are charged with driving through a mix of strategies that will determine the competitive edge of the enterprise – perhaps 90 or so people.

Just as there is no ideal size for the top team, there is equally no ideal way of working. Debate could be open, inhibited, or unpleasant. In fact, the Cranfield surveys conclude that, on average, more than a third of corporations have directors who find themselves unable or unwilling to agree upon and pursue a shared vision for the enterprise. Not surprisingly, commitments are broken and only the less important matters are implemented properly.

Attempts to introduce new ways of working without considering the reactions of those on the team can lead to further problems. The Cranfield studies highlight that more than 65 percent of companies have senior managers who shy away from debating crucial but sensitive issues concerning the running of the enterprise, often because powerful individuals on the team are unwilling to debate any difficult issues.

In short, the human resources department should not try to establish procedures for succession without attempting to get the culture "right." If discussions are inhibited and the wrong choices are made, staff and lower-level managers, suppliers, and shareholders witness a continuous turnaround of senior managers, and lose confidence in the organization.

Transition

For the new appointee, the transition can be challenging. Research into the experiences of senior executives shows that for 55 percent of the executive population, the learning curve averages out at about 30 months. Not that it takes 30 months to stop making mistakes – no one would survive in a senior job if that were the case. The learning is contextual. What does it take to fit into the organization? Is fitting in the same as making a positive contribution? What is core to the business? What attitudes and modes of working, established in the previous job, need to be set aside so that new ways can be learned?

During the transition phase, relationships are made or damaged. The new entrant may inspire and raise expectations. Equally, their early behavior may be seen as "out of step" with the organization, they may be judged critically and see their credibility damaged.

The new executive must identify what is relevant in the many agendas that confront him or her – this confirms in the minds of others whether the correct choice has been made. Poor timing and insensitive judgment, even when the

Insensitive judgment and **poor timing**, even when the decision is right, may lead to an early departure

decision is right, may lead to the early departure of a senior executive. Learning must take place in real time, since there is no opportunity for rehearsal. Even the best selection procedures may be for nothing if inadequate attention is given to transitional learning.

Professional search

Executive succession is increasingly being handled by professional search agencies. Some headhunters take down personal and job-related details and then chase an endless series of contacts to identify a suitable complement of candidates. Nowadays, more thoughtful headhunters attempt first to understand the culture of the client's organization, to determine the gap between statement and reality. They spend time with the chairman, chief executive, and other influential directors, and gather enough information to construct and negotiate a realistic brief.

This allows them to work out how the organization functions and so determine what are the appropriate attributes needed by prospective candidates. The search can then focus on identifying those who exhibit the necessary leadership capabilities and track record.

The Cranfield studies highlight that for many customers and financial analysts, organizations do not differentiate themselves sufficiently from their competitors in terms of their product portfolio, service quality, brand, and image. At the level of the individual director, being functionally skilled and technically competent no longer makes a difference.

What characteristics mark out a powerful human resources director, or a chief information officer? It is someone who accurately considers the business circumstances of the company and applies his or her skills and experience in ways that will induce different ways of working. These will ultimately result in competitive advantage.

Thus, the unit of analysis for assessing performance contribution in executive selection is capabilities. The executive search question should be: "How capable is the individual of applying skills and competencies in a way that will make a difference in this company today?"

Those senior managers whose experience and capabilities meet the contextual requirements of their prospective new organization are also more likely to negotiate a motivating remuneration package. A well-conducted search process, which explores the dynamics of the organization as well as the attributes of the candidate, allows both parties to have a clear understanding of each other.

On this basis, both can readily agree on what the job is worth and what the individual needs to do to contribute. Such honesty, reflected in pay arrangements, helps the company retain good executives.

The accomplished headhunter has one additional service to provide: post-selection mentoring. The best possible candidate may have been selected, but sometimes the transitional phase can mean that the "right person" leaves prematurely – for example, the chairman may have controlling rather than coaching instincts. Coaching for success is as important during the post-selection phase as it is at any other time in the senior executive experience.

Cadre platform

For many years, the UK brewer Bass has identified its potential future leaders by the names on the "chairman's list." The brainchild of chairman Sir Ian Prosser, the list represents the cadre of Bass. Chairman's list managers are the accomplished high flyers. They are expected to share the philosophy of the organization, consistently promote best practice, and behave according to the company's core values.

Although the chairman's list represents the next generation of leaders, only some will be selected for the top jobs. Despite competing against each other as well as against outsiders for senior positions, chairman's list managers responsibly perform as the present and future

Allowing for the dynamics of top teams leads to better outcomes in **executive succession**

backbone of the organization.

Adopting the cadre concept for succession planning allows managers who display leadership potential to be further developed. Such development may take the form of challenging external programs or tailored executive education. Whatever the nature of formal development, being a member of an elite group stretches people by forcing them to confront difficult issues with their colleagues. Cadre-driven succession planning not only enables capable individuals to come forward to be chosen for key positions, but allows a whole generation of managers to be groomed for senior levels of accountability, irrespective of the role they will ultimately hold.

Conclusion

Human resource planning processes can identify a cadre population to provide that extra edge to the management of an organization. Evidence also shows that taking account of the context of an appointment and the dynamics of top teams leads to better outcomes in executive succession. Identifying, selecting, and establishing successful applicants in key positions requires managers to treat each succession case as unique.

Managers must be honest about what is happening in the organization, about who are the people driving the enterprise, and about what a newcomer will really experience when entering the company. Capable managers are in high demand and their retention is crucial. The selection experience and transition into the organization will greatly influence their long-term impressions. Well-managed processes of selection make for good executive choice.

Further reading

Kakabadse, A.P. (2000) "From Individual to Team to Cadre: Tracking Leadership for the Third Millennium," *Strategic Change*, 9(5), 5–16.

Patching, K. and Chatham, R. (2000) *Corporate Politics for IT Managers: How to Get Streetwise*, London: Butterworth-Heinemann.

Tyson, S. and York, A. (2000) *Essentials of Human Resource Management*, London: Butterworth-Heinemann.

Mentoring and
coaching at the top

Managers are never too senior to stop learning. **David Clutterbuck** advises on choosing mentors, coaches and counselors for top executives.

David Clutterbuck is visiting professor at Sheffield Business School and a founder director of the European Mentoring Center. He leads Clutterbuck Associates, a mentoring consultancy, and is chairman of employee communication company the ITEM Group.

Most chief executives have had a mentor at some point in their careers. Such mentors would offer their learning and support, act as sounding boards when there were difficult choices to make, or goad them into tackling issues they might otherwise have avoided. As young managers, they were grateful for learning acquired in this way, recognizing it as a gift between generations for which there is little obvious reciprocation, other than to pass it on in return. One study estimates that 80 percent of chief executives had such a relationship at an early stage in their careers.

However, it has been much less common for executives and directors to continue this kind of learning once they reach or approach the top. Instead they have assumed that the time has come for them to become the mentor and – by inference – that their own need for learning and personal support is past. For this reason, both coaching and mentoring programs in western companies have been focussed on relatively junior employees, or on a cadre of high flyers.

In the past decade, however, much has changed. Mentoring and coaching have become important at all levels. Companies have become increasingly involved in mentoring within the broader community. And managers at the top have had to rethink their own attitudes to learning. A number of trends have combined to bring the latter about.

Among them are increased complexity and rapid change, which mean that people who stop learning become less and less useful. Skills gained early in a career are insufficient and the potential to make costly mistakes through ignorance has risen. Second, the large numbers of MBAs and other academically educated employees puts older executives at a disadvantage, especially in the area of strategy. Finally, there is the increasing use of performance measurement, often against a competency framework, which exposes weaknesses. Where top executives avoid being measured (though expecting it of everyone else), they may become negative role models for learning, with predictable results on the behavior of others.

The problem for executives is that the most accessible ways of learning are impractical. Taking a substantial break to attend a business school is difficult to arrange and potentially fatal politically – much change can take place during an executive's absence. In general, executives have less and less time to be taught; they require instead highly focussed opportunities to learn.

Even if there is time to attend short courses lasting a few weeks, the executive is likely to find that these only partially meet his or her needs. Executives typically learn best when the content and process are directly relevant to issues they face. At lower levels in the organization, training can be delivered using computer-aided learning processes, but these are insufficiently customized for the executive, who needs to address specific issues and circumstances.

The rise of executive coaching and mentoring has been driven by the need for a more accessible, relevant, pragmatic source of learning – one that sets out less to deliver new knowledge than to help executives do some or all of the following:

- recognize learning needs and respond to them;
- access previous learning and experience to develop new responses, tactics, and strategies;
- manage careers and development of personal competencies;
- develop self-awareness and informed self-confidence.

This combination of learning and support is difficult to find within normal organizational structures (although it is a defining characteristic of effective line management). Executive mentors and, to a lesser extent, executive coaches provide islands of stability to which executives can turn, whether they need to be challenged and stretched, or simply find a means of discussing issues.

Coaches, mentors, and counsellors

Coaching and mentoring tend to be used synonymously, but the terms describe distinct roles. Coaching is concerned primarily with perform-

ance and the development of definable skills. It usually starts with the learning goal already identified, if not by the executive, then by an influential third party. It will typically be a short-term relationship. Coaches often offer direct feedback, based on observation of the executive in practice – something executive mentors almost never do, not least because they are not in a position to observe in this way.

The most effective coaches share with mentors the capability to help the learner develop the skills of listening to and observing themselves, which leads to much faster acquisition of skills and modification of behavior. Coaches also share with mentors the role of critical friend – confronting executives with truths no one else feels able to address with them. Whereas the coach is more likely to approach these issues through direct feedback, the mentor will tend to approach them through questioning processes that force the executive to recognize problems for themselves.

Mentoring is usually a longer-term relationship and is more concerned with helping the executive determine what goals to pursue and why. It seeks to build wisdom – the ability to apply skills, knowledge, and experience in new situations and to new problems. It provides a way for the executive to explore approaches. One chief executive describes it as "my chance to think out loud." Mentoring sits somewhere between coaching and counseling, with counseling being directed at helping the individual overcome specific psychological barriers to performance or helping them deal with dysfunctional behavior.

In practice, these boundaries may become blurred as, for example, a coach becomes drawn into helping an executive think through whether a proposed job move will help their long-term goals, or a mentor invites an executive to work with them on a project, to learn by observation. In selecting a learning partner it is therefore important to define where the executive's needs lie. It doesn't help that agencies providing professional coaches or mentors are not consistent in the definitions they apply. Executives seeking this kind of help (or the human resource managers arranging it on their behalf) should question exactly what sort of process the provider

TABLE 1 Checklist: What do executives need?

Type of need	Appropriate help
Develop skills to perform better in the current job	Coaching Mentoring
Build and implement a career development plan	Career counseling Mentoring
Learn to cope with or overcome psychological barriers to performance	Counseling
Manage a major transition (such as a first assignment overseas or a first board appointment)	Mentoring
Acquire a sounding board/ source of challenge for personal/business development	Mentoring
Help in applying knowledge or skills learnt externally (such as at a business school)	Coaching Mentoring

expects to use and treat with skepticism anyone who claims to operate across the spectrum. Table 1 provides a checklist for distinguishing these roles.

It is also important to recognize that effective executive learners have relatively wide learning nets – in other words, they know people in a variety of positions and with a variety of expertise upon whom they can draw for advice and support. Part of the role of the mentor may be to help people develop and extend their nets. It is increasingly common for an executive to have both a coach and a mentor, or more than one mentor, each focussing on a different aspect of their development portfolio. Some may be external professionals; others may be peers inside or outside the company, or academics, or close family. One of the signs of learning maturity is the ability to access multiple sources of learning.

Range of issues

The complexity of business and personal issues that may arise in a mentoring relationship makes it important to create a focus for issues of priority. One way of achieving such a focus is for the executive to maintain a diary of events that have particularly pleased or frustrated them.

This provides a rich source of issues, especially when patterns begin to emerge between events. (For example, one chief executive recognized that many of the problem issues related to lack of clarity of role between himself and his chairperson. Once identified, the issue could be tackled directly.)

The following are common dilemmas that executives bring to the mentoring relationship:

■ How do I stimulate constructive challenge from my peers and people below me?

■ How do I achieve through influence, rather than command?

■ How do I continue to learn when most of the knowledge I need to acquire is based on intuition?

■ How do I obtain sufficient contextual understanding of disciplines I have little experience of?

■ How do I become a director? A chief executive? A chairman?

■ How do I get my team to behave the way I want them to?

■ What do I do with an inherited team I don't respect?

■ How much should I ask my family to sacrifice for the sake of my job?

■ How do I motivate people for a task I have no enthusiasm for myself?

In most cases, executives have the answer within them; they just haven't worked it out yet. The mentor works with them patiently, helping them to see the issue from different perspectives, to develop alternatives ways of modeling what is happening and what could happen, and to assess the options against criteria the learner develops for him or herself.

Building a learning alliance

The most powerful coaching and mentoring partnerships achieve a balance between getting on well enough to develop a strong rapport and having sufficient difference of experience to generate a potential for learning. Learning relationships at this level also demand specific attributes and skills on the part of both partners.

Executives need to explore difficult, sometimes painful issues. Part of an initial verbal contract might be that chief executives expect to feel uncomfortable sometimes. They must also accept responsibility for preparing for sessions and thinking issues through to some extent before discussing them. Many mentoring sessions begin as sounding-board sessions, before delving deeper. Studies in Scandinavia and elsewhere suggest that the most effective mentoring relationships are those where the executive is highly proactive and the mentor relatively reactive.

It also helps if executives are prepared to "learn by teaching." Practicing coaching and mentoring skills on other people makes them more responsive to being on the receiving end. It can also make them more critical of poor coaching – as a general rule, if executives feel the coach or mentor is being manipulative or predictable, it is because they are inadequate in the role.

Executive coaches and mentors also need to examine their motivations, behaviors, and competencies. Perhaps the most difficult lesson to learn is that one's own store of expertise and experience is like the nuclear option – a stockpile that is rarely used, but that informs and influences the process. The mentor's wisdom is what enables him or her to ask the questions that stimulate executives to develop their own wisdom.

Selection

In selecting mentors for owner-managers of companies, it is surprising how many people are rejected. Many applicants are drawn into the role by a desire to avoid thinking about their own issues, and therefore see the issues of the person they were supposed to help only in terms of their own. Others may have held many positions in large companies, but none where the buck truly stopped – and therefore lack both experience and credibility.

Defining the competencies of an executive coach or mentor is not easy, because the need will vary according to the situation. However, common attributes are:

- Self-awareness: important in developing and using rapport, and in recognizing the boundaries of one's capability to help.

- Behavioral awareness: having a good understanding of how and why others behave as they do.
- Business or professional savvy: at one level, "been there, seen it, done it," but also having a reputation for good judgment.
- Sense of proportion: the ability to place issues in a broader context.
- Communication skills: especially an ability to listen and to use anecdotes to illustrate learning points.
- Conceptual modeling: having a broad portfolio of models to help the executive analyze and understand interactions; being able to evolve new models as part of the dialog.
- Commitment to their own learning: a role model for learning.
- Commitment to developing others: having a genuine interest and pleasure in their achievements.
- Strong skills of relationship management: from building rapport to helping the learner maintain a constant focus on important goals.
- Goal clarity: the ability to help people sort out what they want to achieve and why, and to develop practical plans for getting there.

As the amount of executive coaching and mentoring increases, there will be further moves to improve the consistency of quality. In the UK, for example, there are national standards for mentoring, although there has been insufficient time for them to be widely applied. At the end of the day, however, it is the executive's responsibility to understand and articulate what they require of a coach or mentor. A chief executive gets the mentor he or she deserves.

Further reading

Clutterbuck, D. and Megginson, D. (1999) *Mentoring Executives and Directors*, Oxford: Butterworth-Heinemann.

Crawford, D. et al. (2000) *Mentoring – Draft Occupational Standards*, Women's Development Programs, University of North London, Spring.

Rajan, A. (1996) *Leading People*, London: Cilntec and Create.

Beyond Sloan: trust is
at the core of corporate values

Manfred F.R. Kets de Vries
is Clinical Professor of
Leadership Development
and Raoul de Vitry
d'Avaucourt Professor of
Human Resource
Management at Insead.

Technocrats no longer rule and hierarchies are dead.

Manfred Kets de Vries finds common traits at the heart of

the best companies.

During the industrial age, corporations such as General Motors were the archetypes for organizations and leadership. Alfred Sloan's *My Years with General Motors* became a bible for generations of business leaders. The book was an ode to the pyramidal structure, the hierarchical organization, staff departments, top-down decision making, and position power. It heralded a period when functional and divisional structures prevailed. Technocrats ruled and consumer needs were often sidelined. Bureaucratic leaders had credibility and were viable in an age of stability and continuity.

These concepts became less relevant as we entered a period of increased discontinuity. Corporations faced a multitude of destabilizing economic and social factors in the past two decades. Demographic shifts took place. An explosion in information and communication technology began to transform business activity. After the fall of the Iron Curtain, eastern Europe and Russia underwent dramatic economic and social change. The euro was launched as a monetary unit, affecting the financial and economic arrangements of participating and neighboring European countries.

During this period many companies restructured and large industries consolidated through mergers, acquisitions, and strategic alliances on a global scale. In the new environment, the former archetypes of management no longer worked. Top-down decision making created autocratic leadership, a bureaucratic culture, bloated corporate headquarters, and rigid, irrelevant policies and procedures. Many of these organizations became more inward looking, obsessed by power politics, neglectful of outside constituencies, customers, and the competition. Given the increasing irrelevance of the model provided by Sloan, what should replace it in the twenty-first century?

The self-renewing organization

One way of answering this question is to consider *Fortune 500* magazine's listing of the most admired companies in the US. Since 1983 (the date the list started), a number of companies have made it to the top many times. They include Merck, Procter & Gamble, Coca-Cola, Johnson & Johnson, Wal-Mart, 3M, Hewlett-Packard, Microsoft, Intel, and General Electric. What makes them different? Is there something special about their leadership and organizational practices?

Broadly, they know how to reinvent and renew themselves, and they recognize when to deal with changes in the business environment. They also know how to select, develop, and retain people who make a difference. And these people are distinguished by their possession of a common set of values, which are set out below.

First, these companies are permeated by the perception that people are treated fairly: trust is a critical part of the equation. There exists a strong relationship between the effectiveness of a leader and the degree to which people trust him or her. With trust comes candor, the willingness of people to speak their minds. When people are reluctant to discuss their ideas and thoughts openly, realism disappears, and the quality of decision making deteriorates. In healthy organizations, employees have a healthy disrespect for their superiors.

Second, successful organizations are good at building teams and exploiting teamwork. People need to be able to work in teams; they need to subordinate their own agenda to the wellbeing of the group. Further, organizations need to foster diversity, which entails respect for the individual and makes group decision making more creative. Such organizations also empower their employees. Decision-making power is pushed to the lowest level at which a competent decision can be made. To foster such a process, managers should operate with minimal secrecy.

Customer focus is the third core value. Employees realize that their most important constituency is their customers. Another value is the spirit of competition: having the desire to win. Focussing on achievement helps to create excitement and momentum. Further, no organization can survive without fostering creativity and encouraging innovation among employees. In these companies, an executive's mistakes do not put a permanent black mark on his or her career. On the contrary, senior managers realize that people who don't make mistakes don't accomplish anything.

There is a rule of management that states: "What isn't measured doesn't get done," the implication being that everything should be accounted for. The corollary is that managers should use benchmarking inside and outside the company to deter tunnel vision and the emergence of the not-invented-here syndrome, or any arrogance about the success of the organization on the part of employees. To forestall hubris, the best companies foster an attitude that welcomes change. Those who resist change will not fare well.

Leaders of self-renewing organizations are keenly aware of the need to develop employees and so invest in training and development. They create a learning environment, which allows them to tap the creative abilities of staff. A primary role of a leader is to act as teacher or coach, able to foster other leaders throughout the organization. Distributed leadership, which is not confined to the top of the organization, is essential.

Creating successful organizations

Apart from possessing a set of values that creates the right conditions for high performance, is there something more going on in the best companies? Do they touch upon a deeper layer of human functioning that causes people to make an extra effort? Several concepts from psychology throw some light on this.

When psychotherapists talk about helping people to live up to their full potential (which is the essence of their discipline), they want them to gain insights into their own goals and motivations; to understand better their strengths and weaknesses; and to prevent them from engaging in self-destructive activities.

The emphasis is on widening choice, which

enables people to choose more freely, instead of being led by forces of which they are unaware.

Motivational need systems

Motivational need systems are the systems on which such choice is based. They drive people to behave and act the way they do. These need systems become "wired" at infancy and continue throughout life, but are altered by the forces of age, learning, and maturation.

One motivational need system regulates physiological needs for food, water, sleep, and breathing. Another handles needs for sensual enjoyment and (later) sexual excitement. Another still deals with the need to respond to specific situations perceived as threatening, through antagonism or withdrawal. Although these systems will influence work, two other motivational need systems are of particular interest for life in organizations: attachment/affiliation and exploration/assertion.

The search for relationships is an essential human trait. The need for attachment concerns the process of engagement with another human being, the universal experience of wanting to be close to others. It also relates to the pleasure of sharing and affirmation. When this need for intimate engagement is extrapolated to groups, the desire to enjoy intimacy can be described as a need for affiliation. Both attachment and affiliation serve an emotional balancing role by confirming the person's self-worth and contributing to self-esteem.

The need for exploration, closely associated with cognition and learning, affects the ability to play and to work. This need is manifested soon after birth, and opportunities for exploration continue into adulthood. Closely tied to the need for exploration is the need for self-assertion, the need to be able to choose. Playful exploration and manipulation of the environment in response to exploratory-assertive motivation produce a sense of effectiveness and competence, of autonomy, initiative, and industry. Because striving, competing, and seeking mastery are motivating forces of human personality, exercising assertiveness (following preferences, acting in a determined manner) is a form of affirmation.

Organizational culture and personal needs

Leaders who want to get the best out of their people create an ambience where people feel inspired to give their best. Managers need to pay attention to motivational need systems. First, they must ensure these personal needs are congruent with the organization's objectives. Such a sense of congruence will give people a feeling of control over their lives and a belief that their actions make a difference. This is what empowerment is all about.

Companies that get the best out of their people are characterized by a set of higher values than those listed earlier. As mentioned, attachment, affiliation, and exploration provide a powerful underlying motive in human behavior; so the first such value is a feeling of community, a sense of belonging to the company. The second value contributes a sense of fun, of enjoyment. These feelings can be enhanced in several ways, such as by organizational structure or specific practices. A sense of belonging will help create a cohesive culture. Furthermore, people who have fun together stay together. Such values contribute to the emergence of distributed leadership.

Organizations that enhance ways for staff to relate to each other are the ones where senior executives obtain vicarious pleasure in coaching younger executives and feel proud of the accomplishments of others. The experience of developing and caring for others can be a source of creativity and, indeed, continuity, by seeing one's efforts continue through the work of successors.

If these basic motivational need systems can be presented in the context of transcending one's own personal needs, for example by improving the quality of life, helping people, or contributing to society, the impact can be extremely powerful. People like to work in organizations that provide a sense of meaning. These are the kinds of places where people put their imagination and creativity to work and have a feeling of involvement and concentration in whatever they are doing. As one CEO said: "People work for money but die for a cause."

Conclusion

The challenge for leaders is to create corporations that possess these qualities. Working in such organizations is an antidote to stress, enhances the imagination, and contributes to a more fulfilling life. Such companies help employees maintain an effective balance between personal and organizational life, and give time for self-examination. Crucially, they will be able to turn continuous and discontinuous change to their advantage. These are the organizations we need to strive for in the twenty-first century.

Further reading

Bass, B.M. (1990) *Bass & Stogdill's Handbook of Leadership: Theory, Research, and Applications*, New York: Free Press, 3rd edn.

Csikszentmihalyi, M. (1990) *Flow: The Psychology of Optimal Experience*, New York: Harper and Row.

Kets de Vries, M.F.R. and Florent-Treacy, E. (1999) *The New Global Leaders: Percy Barnevik, Richard Branson, and David Simon and the Remaking of International Business*, San Francisco, CA: Jossey-Bass.

Sloan, A.P. (1964) *My Years with General Motors*, Garden City, NY: Doubleday.

Building companies
founded on people

Inspiration for most people is not found in balance sheets, but in a search for meaning. **Lynda Gratton** shows how to bring people values to the fore.

Lynda Gratton is an associate professor of organizational behavior at London Business School and dean of the MBA program.

Some say that a company's people are its main source of sustainable competitive advantage. For many companies, it is their only source. Employees' innovation and determination create and build new products, their enthusiasm and insight deliver outstanding customer care, and their knowledge and wisdom solve seemingly intractable problems. The realization of this simple fact has had a profound effect on the nature of organizations. This article explores how managers can respond.

In the early 1900s, corporations were founded on their ability to access finance. Those who could fund their ideas and create profitable businesses gained market share. The historical dominance of financial capital has left its mark on the frameworks of modern organizations, in the constant measurement of financial resources, and in the reporting of financial assets.

Access to capital no longer brings sustainable competitive advantage. And since the average length of a patent is nine months, technological breakthroughs have only a limited value.

There is growing awareness that competitive advantage is created by people. Companies see a shift from financial and technological capital to human capital, which in turn affects the way those organizations are designed and work is created.

This shift takes us to a basic philosophical question: "If people are at the heart of competitive advantage, how are they different from financial or technological capital?" It is an important question, because it informs the debate about how we can create organizations in which people are excited, motivated, and inspired.

The answer can be found in three tenets of humanness. These tenets frame the way we look at organizations and the way in which we can put people at the heart of corporate purpose. They are at the core of any organization in which the talent of employees can grow and flourish.

The three tenets

We operate in time

Large companies are skilled at raising capital quickly and easily. They can also make changes in technology in a matter of weeks or months. The human beings within those companies, however, take much longer to change their work practices, culture, and organizations. The skills and motivation of the workforce cannot be quickly transformed; they are subject to the universal pace of human development.

Our attitude to time is unique. We are profoundly embedded in time, and we operate in time, with our memories of the past, our perceptions of the present, and our aspirations for the future. The past is always with us and must be acknowledged and linked with our hopes for the present.

Carla Fiorina, chief executive of Hewlett-Packard, demonstrates this when she recreates the dynamic entrepreneurial beginnings of the company – the "garage" in which Hewlett-Packard was born.

Alongside our memories of the past come what management writer Arie de Geus has called "memories of the future," captured in our daydreams and the vignettes we paint to think through our options and the way we would like to see our lives develop. These can become the impetus for creating engaging visions about ourselves and about our organizations. To deny the past and to fail to build on individual dreams of the future is to create an organization without hopes or aspirations.

The search for meaning

The second fundamental aspect of the human condition is the search for meaning: meaning in our lives and work. We are not simply passive recipients of data from outside. Rather, we actively engage with life. As individuals and collectively, we strive to create meaning. We yearn to be part of something significant and to achieve things that are consistent with our sense of self.

Work plays a crucial part in creating this meaning. We seek meaning in our work, try to understand the purpose of the organization and select companies with the same values as our own. In its recent rebranding exercise, BP implicitly recognized this. The company has refashioned its image from that of a conventional oil company to one that is deeper, more meaningful and resonant, captured in the phrase "beyond petroleum." Building shareholder value may meet the needs of investors, but it does little to excite or inspire those who have invested their personal human capital in an organization.

We have a soul

We are not simply machines, programmed to deliver results in a rational and predetermined way. We have hopes and fears, we laugh, cry, and dream. The emotional side of the organization involves trust and commitment, inspiration and exhilaration. Organizations that can justifiably lay claim to having a soul are those that acknowledge and support human dignity, and put fairness and justice high on the corporate agenda.

Since the advent of mass production, work has been designed primarily for efficiency and productivity: tasks were divided into easily replicable parts; quality was assured through constant monitoring; and as a consequence, much of the working day was spent in repetitive activity. Now, this has changed. The growth of electronic commerce has placed an emphasis on innovation and entrepreneurship rather than cost cutting. Individuals feel a growing sense of autonomy and freedom, and are faced with a wider variety of working opportunities.

People and process

Companies can now design the structure of work to meet the desires and aspirations of employees. What do such companies look like? Most attempts to describe them emphasize observable facets, such as the lounge-like qualities of advertising agencies, the stock option schemes of internet companies, or the sabbatical arrangements of biotechnology companies.

These are all instances of work being designed around people and as such are important symbols of this new ethos. But they are only symbols. More profound is the broad context of work, how decisions are made, how power is shared, and who is engaged in decisions about the future: in other words, the question of process. The nature of this process will distinguish those companies truly able to capture the potential energy of their employees. Articulating broad strategic goals is important, but creating the energy, determination, and inspiration to deliver these goals is what separates great companies from the also-rans. Companies that are adept at putting people at the center of their corporate purpose engage in a specific set of processes, which are outlined below.

Build a guiding coalition

A company can realign itself around a clear business goal only when it succeeds in engaging its people in that goal, particularly younger employees. The journey from present to future is driven by shared hopes and dreams. It begins in building guiding coalitions of people from different areas of the company and of different ages.

Nortel Networks, for instance, assembled groups from its European companies to consider and debate the future of the business. In these coalitions the younger people offered radical ideas, while more experienced employees brought sponsorship and resources. In such processes, diversity – of age, gender, nationality, and functional experience – is often responsible for ultimate success.

Imagine the future

The main function of these coalitions is to debate how a company might be transformed. Too much corporate time is spent considering the next small step. Engaging visions are only formed when people place themselves in a future scenario and look back at the present. Recall that we operate in time and on a personal level we dream of possibilities: a company may engage in these dreams or stay firmly in the present, but individuals will continue to dream.

When they debate a company's future, people paint a picture of the company's values and aspirations, and discuss how the organization could be structured. In many cases these discussions have been important and moving experiences for team members. Freed from short-term financial constraints, they find themselves able to imagine an ideal future. In this respect, their strategic capability cannot be measured by the quality or quantity of strategic documentation, but rather by the richness and depth of their debate. People become engaged through discussion and the application of imagination, not through looking at policy statements.

The creation of a shared vision lies at the heart of a people-centered strategy. It should not be a one-off activity, but a way of thinking and conversing, of creating excitement, of building a shared agenda. It involves hard conversations about what is important and how collective dreams can become a reality.

Understand capabilities

Dreaming is necessary, but not sufficient. If a company wishes to move from the rhetoric of aspiration to the reality of delivering, it must look openly at the capabilities of the business and its people, and must measure the gap separating vision from reality. Without such insights, which may be painful, plans are unlikely to succeed.

Too often, executives have a limited understanding of the reality of the organizations they manage. They certainly understand the financial base and products, but rarely do they monitor or acknowledge the human capital of the business.

They do not have their finger on the pulse of "emotional capital" – employees' level of commitment, excitement, and inspiration. They fail to understand the "social capital," which is the depth and breadth of networks and propensity for knowledge sharing and arbitrage. And they do not monitor "intellectual capital," the means of creating and accumulating valuable knowledge.

At 3M and Hewlett-Packard, the systematic monitoring of employee behavior and attitudes, processes, and values is used to assess the state of the organization. How does such monitoring take place? Through employee surveys, focus groups, and coffee mornings, and the assimilation of individual performance data and collegiate and peer-based feedback.

Map the system

How often have the dreams of a company's future

run out of steam when presented on a flipchart in the manner of a shopping list? Such an approach, suggesting that the world contains orderly sequences of action and descriptions, will always be deeply dissatisfying. Humans have a propensity to search for underlying themes, to see contradictions, and to visualize cause and effect – to create a map of the system. Shopping lists fail because they do not take account of this complexity.

Some companies acknowledge this view. They analyze the business not as a series of unrelated factors or items, but rather as a dynamic system with themes of value and process, and loops of cause and effect. This systems approach allows managers to construct a map of the current and future organization, showing how those individuals within it will view it. Such a map describes how the parts can be constructed as a meaningful whole.

This search for meaning involves the active interpretation of events, the search for coherence and integration. Organizations are dynamic systems. Each part – whether the group's structure, the company's processes, or its values – is perceived as a whole by individual employees. To understand these relationships we need to model how the elements of this system work. The discipline of systems thinking and complexity theory provides tools and techniques to do this. The aim is a visual description of several things: the major themes of individual behavior, values, and processes; their alignment to the business goal; and how these processes can be designed to be mutually reinforcing.

Model the dynamics of the vision

Most companies model what they perceive as their key assets, such as financial assets or structural assets. However, few model the human side of the business: the behaviors, knowledge, values, processes, and structures. The speed and agility needed to reinvigorate competitive formulae require that managers develop such models. It will not be sufficient to blunder through designing processes or structures and then await the outcomes. Managers need to anticipate how human elements can reinforce each other and the business goal, and foresee consequences that will destroy the desired outcomes.

For example, managers at Philips Lighting had established a reward process focussed on individual creativity and innovation. In the process of creating a systems map, the team realized that this process was at odds with their broad business goal of fast-reacting, cross-functional teams. The team also had an opportunity to model the dynamics of the system over a five-year period by describing the forces that would be operating for and against the changes they had envisaged. This enabled them to judge the impact of processes and values over time, and thus anticipate and plan for any obstacles.

Bridge into action

There is no great strategy; there is only great execution. The challenge of management is to move from ideas and maps to action. The success of this transition rests on how well managers understand their people and the right way to build a high-performance organization. The three tenets suggest that key factors are the close involvement of people in the business, communication and involvement of all in the vision, and the creation of processes that together reinforce business goals.

Building fair and just practices is a critical aspect of the third tenet. Justice and fairness, as perceived by employees, means the dignity and consideration with which people are treated as changes in the process and structures are rolled out. As we enter an era where business models will change rapidly, so the human side of the business will have to remain flexible and adaptive.

Further reading

Argyris, C. (1977) "Double Loop Learning in Organizations," *Harvard Business Review*, 55(5), 115–25.

De Geus, A. (1999) *The Living Company: Growth, Learning and Longevity in Business*, London: Nicholas Brealey.

Folger and Cropanzano (1998) *Organisational Justice and Human Resource Management*, London: Sage.

Gratton, L. (2000) *Living Strategy: Putting People at the Heart of Corporate Purpose*, London: FT Prentice Hall.

Gratton, L., Hailey, V.H., Stiles, P., and Truss, C. (1999) *Strategic Human Resource Management: Corporate Rhetoric and Human Reality*, Oxford: Oxford University Press.

Pfeffer, J. (1994) *Competitive Advantage through People: Unleashing the Power of the Workforce*, Cambridge, MA: Harvard Business School Press.

Senge, P. (1990) *The Fifth Discipline: The Art and Practice of the Learning Organisation*, London: Century Business.

Skills of **management**

7

Contents

Introduction to Part 7

General managers need a repertoire of skills in order to get the best out of those they manage and create real value for the organization. some, such as selling and appraising, may be taught in business schools or at internal training sessions. Others may be difficult to impart in a structured seminar and depend much more on a steady accumulation of experience and judgement. In this part writers discuss both kinds, looking in particular at negotiation, teamwork, communications, leadership and clarity in business writing.

Interests, value, and
the art of the best deal

James K. Sebenius is Gordon Donaldson Professor of Business Administration at Harvard Business School and a principal of Lax Sebenius LLC. With David Lax he co-wrote the forthcoming *3-D Negotiation™: Dealmaking for the Long Term.*

David A. Lax is a principal in Lax Sebenius LLC and co-heads Summa Capital Management.

Managers should negotiate to create value as well as to claim it. **James Sebenius** and **David Lax** offer a strategy for making deals that can lead the other party to choose what you want.

Behind the headlines that trumpet the mega-deals, internal and external negotiation has become a way of life for managers. Whenever interests or perceptions differ and parties depend on one another for results, the need for negotiation arises. Yet what is its essence? Haggling? Building relationships? Carving up an economic pie? Expanding it? There is truth in each of these, but, in essence, I am an effective negotiator if I can persuade you to say yes, and mean it, to a proposal that also meets all my real interests. And why should you say yes? Because the deal meets your real interests better than your best no-deal option. So my problem is to shape your perceived choice, of deal versus no-deal, so that what you choose in your own interest is also what I want. Paraphrasing Italian diplomat Daniele Vare, negotiation is "the art of letting them have your way (for their reasons)."

This principle can be read as a recipe for manipulation. Understood more deeply, it offers the key to jointly creating and claiming value in a sustainable way. To do this most effectively, you should map the full set of involved parties; assess the full set of your and their real interests; appraise each side's no-deal options; and, finally, solve the joint problem of crafting a deal for all that is better than any of the no-deal options.

Step 1: Draw a deal diagram

This may seem obvious: in the simplest negotiation, two principals negotiate. Yet your deal diagram should include potentially complicating parties such as lawyers, bankers, and other agents. While there may be a single negotiator for the other side, you should be alert for internal factions with different interests; they may be deal blockers or internal champions of your proposal. Anglo-Saxon companies attempting acquisitions in Germany, for example, have been stymied by the unexpected importance of the management board (*Vorstand*) as well as the supervisory board (*Aufsichtsrat*) and unions under the potent policy of "co-determination." The crucial first step is to map all parties in the context of their decision process – and don't forget to include influential players in your own internal negotiations.

When pharmaceutical giants Glaxo and SmithKline Beecham announced a merger in 1998, investors increased the combined firm's market capitalization by $20bn. Yet despite early agreement on executive positions in the combined company, internal disagreement about management control and position sank the deal and the $20bn evaporated. (Logic ultimately drove the two back together again, but only after nearly two years.) This episode confirms two related lessons. First, while the overall economics of a deal are generally necessary, they are often not sufficient. Second, map potentially influential internal players; don't lose sight of their interests or capacity to affect the deal. What is "rational" for the whole may not be so for the parts.

Step 2: Assess interests

Your interests in a negotiation are whatever you care about that is at stake in the process. The best negotiators are clear on their ultimate interests and those of the other side. They also know their trade-offs among lesser interests and are remarkably flexible and creative on the means.

Assess the full set of interests at stake – yours and theirs – including relationships, the process itself, and the "social contract." Negotiations generally address tangible factors such as price, timing, and specifications. Yet, as Felix Rohatyn, former managing partner of Lazard Freres, and a veteran of making deals, observed: "Most deals are 50 percent emotion and 50 percent economics." Crucial interests are often intangible and subjective: the character of the negotiating process, the effect on trust and your reputation, and so on.

When working out longer-term arrangements, it is relationships, rather than transactions, that can be the predominant negotiating interests in much of Latin America, southern Europe, and

southern Asia. Deal-oriented North Americans, northern Europeans, and Australians often come to grief by underestimating the strength of this relational interest in such cross-border encounters.

Similarly, in setting up a new venture, for example, negotiators tend to focus on the economic contract: equity splits, governance, and so on. Yet, often implicitly and often poorly, the parties also negotiate a "social contract," or the "spirit of a deal." Beyond trust and a good working relationship, the social contract includes expectations about the nature, extent, and duration of the venture, about process, about the way unforeseen events will be handled, and so on. Some negotiators fail to develop positive social contracts that reinforce valuable economic contracts; as with other interests, the "hard" can drive out the "soft." Scurrying to check the founding documents when conflicts occur can signal a badly negotiated social contract.

Probe negotiating positions to understand deeper interests. Issues are on the table for explicit agreement. Positions are your stands on the issues. Interests are underlying concerns that would be affected by resolution. Positions on issues affect underlying interests, but need not be identical. For example, an issue in taking a job may be salary, on which your position may be a demand for $90,000. Yet, while your interests reflected in that salary demand include purchasing power, they may also involve status, or needs that could be met in ways other than money.

Positional bargaining envisions a dance of positions, which ideally converges to agreement. Interest-driven bargaining sees the process primarily as a reconciliation of underlying interests: you have one set of interests, I have another, and through joint problem solving we should be able to agree. For example, environmentalists and farmers endlessly battled a US power company over whether to build a dam (the issue). Their positions: "absolutely yes" and "no way." Yet incompatible positions masked compatible interests. The farmers were worried about reduced water flow below the dam, the environmentalists were focussed on the downstream habitat of the endangered whooping crane, and the power company needed results and a greener image. They devised a better agreement than continuing court warfare: a smaller dam built on a fast track, stream flow guarantees, downstream habitat protection, and a trust fund to enhance whooping crane habitats elsewhere.

Too much emphasis on positions – What's your position? Here's mine! – often drives negotiation toward a risky, ritual dance that does not meet the parties' fundamental concerns. Learning about and reconciling the full set of interests requires patience, researching the other side, many questions, and real listening.

Step 3: Assess your Batnas

Our Harvard colleagues Roger Fisher and Bill Ury coined the acronym Batna, or "best alternative to negotiated agreement," to describe the course of action you would take if the proposed deal were not possible. Your Batna may involve anything from walking away, to approaching another supplier, to bombing Serbia. The value of your Batna to you sets the threshold of the full set of your interests that any acceptable agreement must exceed. This is also true for the other side. As such, Batnas imply the existence or absence of a zone of possible agreement, and determine its location.

Not only should you assess your own Batna, you should carefully analyze that of the other side. In one instance, a British company hoped to sell a poorly performing division for a bit more than its depreciated asset value of $7m to one of two potential buyers known to be fierce rivals. Each might be induced to see its Batna not as failing to buy a relatively unprofitable business, but as a hated rival snatching a prize away. So their advisers designed a strategy to ensure that each suitor knew the other was looking, and never to let either buyer say they were not interested. Following this, the division was sold for $45m.

Consider improving your Batna; be careful not to worsen it. Not only do Batnas define the minimum conditions for a deal, but they also enhance the ability to "walk away," a factor often associated with negotiating influence. The better your Batna appears both to you and to the other party, the more credible your threat to walk away. Instead of further refining your tactics at the

table, you should sometimes act away from the table to improve your Batna.

Steve Holtzman, chief business officer for Millenium Pharmaceuticals, did a string of deals from the company's founding in 1993 to a value of $1.4bn. He said: "Whenever we feel there's a possibility of a deal with someone, we immediately call six other people. It drives you nuts, trying to juggle them all, but it will change the perception on the other side of the table, number one. Number two, it will change your self-perception. If you believe that there are other people who are interested, your bluff is no longer a bluff, it's real."

Step 4: Solve the joint problem

Here is your basic negotiation problem: by the choice of agreement or no agreement, how can you best advance the full set of your interests? The other party's problem is a mirror image of yours: by the choice of agreement or no agreement, how can they best advance the full set of their interests? Since they will say yes for their reasons, not yours, agreement means joint problem solving: addressing their problem as a means to solving your own. In this sense, effective negotiators are "selfish altruists." An associate of Rupert Murdoch remarked that, as a buyer, Murdoch "understands the seller – and, whatever the guy's trying to do, he crafts his offer that way. He is able to see what the person most wants out of the deal."

Understand and shape how they see their basic negotiation problem. To change the other side's mind, you need to know their mind; "putting yourself in the other party's shoes" is venerable but good advice. Then, with them, you can try to build what Bill Ury calls a "golden bridge" from where they now are to where you want them to go. This is generally more promising than shoving them toward your destination.

Tough negotiators sometimes dismiss the other side's concerns: "That's their problem. Let them handle it." This attitude can undercut your capacity to influence their problem, as they see it, in your interest. Early in a career of making deals at Cisco Systems, Mike Volpi's "outward confidence" was mistaken for arrogance and he

Many people assume their interests are the **opposite** of yours, rather than different

had trouble completing proposed deals. Many acquisitions later, a colleague said: "The most important part of [Volpi's] development is that he learned power doesn't come from telling people you are powerful. He went from being a guy driving the deal from his side of the table to the guy who understood the deal from the other side."

Even in tough dealings, this perspective is useful. A multinational company was engaged in a contentious, highly publicized negotiation with a shareholder and joint venture partner. Despite a reputation of near invincibility, research revealed he had not in fact "won" all such battles but had an acute interest in maintaining that perception. The multinational firm therefore offered a deal that kept the essential substance for itself, but gave the shareholder the appearance of victory (while making sure the shareholder saw his Batna as a very public loss).

Solve the joint problem by "creating value." The important issue here is to create value in a sustainable way as well as merely "claiming value." To do this, search beyond common ground for differences among the parties as the ingredients for value creation. By "claiming value," we mean the process of dividing the pie. By "creating value," we mean the vital process for simultaneously increasing the worth of the agreement to each side. The trick is to recognize and manage the tension between co-operative actions needed to create value and competitive ones to claim it.

Barriers to value creation seem to be hard-wired: many people equate negotiation with value claiming. They simply assume their interests to be the opposite of yours – rather than different and potentially compatible. If the pie is fixed, of course, the enterprise truly is one of claiming value (zero-sum or win–lose), in which my gain is your loss. Psychologists have discovered this "fixed pie" bias to be pervasive. For example, in one survey of 5,000 subjects in 32

negotiating studies, participants failed to see compatible issues fully half of the time. In real-world terms, this means unknowingly leaving value uncreated, or both sides walking away from money on the table.

When Egypt and Israel were negotiating over the Sinai, their positions were incompatible. Deeply probing behind those positions, however, negotiators exploited a vital difference of underlying interest: the Israelis cared more about security, while the Egyptians were more concerned about territory. The solution was to establish a demilitarized zone under the Egyptian flag.

Even where the issue is economic, finding differences can break a deadlock. A small technology company and its investors, demanding a high price, were stuck in negotiation with a large strategic acquirer that was adamant about paying much less. The acquirer was willing to pay the asking price, but was very concerned about sharply raising price expectations in a fast-moving industry sector where it planned to make more acquisitions. The solution was for the two sides to agree a modest cash purchase price initially, which was widely publicized, with complex contingencies that virtually guaranteed a higher price later.

To solve the joint problem, employ a "3D" approach, including actions "away from the table." "One-dimensional" negotiation is the most familiar image: an interpersonal process involving persuasion, cultural sensitivity, crafting offers, and so on. Two-dimensional negotiation moves from interpersonal process to the substance of value creation: "deal crafting" or the logic of devising and structuring agreements that create sustainable value. Yet these two dimensions are limited: when the parties engage in a face-to-face process of creating and claiming value over a given agenda, much of the die is cast.

The best negotiators play a wider, 3D game. With the potential value to be created as their guiding beacon, they act as entrepreneurs. They envision the most promising architecture and act, often away from the table, to effect it. They get the right parties to the table, in the right order, to deal with the right issues, at the right time, by the right process, and facing the right Batnas. 3D negotiators not only play the game as given, they are masters at setting it up and changing it to maximize the results.

In summary, seeing negotiation as a 3D joint problem is a reminder that solving the other party's problem is very much part of solving your own. Having done a deal diagram and having assessed the full set of interests and Batnas, your strategy is to shape how they see their basic problem such that, for their reasons, they choose what you want. The goal is to create and claim sustainable value. Superb deal makers instinctively understand François de Callières, an eighteenth-century commentator, when he described a negotiation master as possessing "the supreme art of making every man offer him as a gift that which it was his chief design to secure."

An extended version of this article with sources can be found at: Sebenius, J. (2000), "Dealmaking Essentials," item 2-800-443, http://www.hbsp.harvard.edu.

Further reading

Bazerman, M. and Neale, M. (1992) *Negotiating Rationally*, New York: Free Press.

Lax, D. and Sebenius, J. (1986) *The Manager as Negotiator*, New York: Free Press.

Raiffa, H. (1982) *Art and Science of Negotiation*, Cambridge, MA: Harvard University Press.

Ury, W. (1993) *Getting Past No*, New York: Bantam.

Putting the team
into top management

Companies are awash with tales of senior managers not talking to their chief executives. **Donald Hambrick** examines how to get top managers working well together.

Donald C. Hambrick is
Samuel Bronfman
Professor of Democratic
Business Enterprise at
Columbia University
Graduate School of
Business.

Two years had passed since my last visit to Richard, the chief executive of a large financial services firm. After our hellos, it quickly became clear that things had gone sour for him and the company in that time: "We were riding high, doing so well. Then we hit a wall. Competitors started offering attractive bundled products to major customers; they started serving global accounts in an integrated way; and they beat us in developing electronic offerings. I'm embarrassed at how long it took us to figure out what was happening, and I'm angry at myself and my team for being unable to develop and deliver our responses."

Worse still, attempts to tackle things had failed: "Whenever I try to get my top executives together to wrestle with these challenges, invariably one or more of the division presidents will argue that they're each aggressively dealing with them in their own units. But these problems call for company-wide action, not piecemeal initiatives. Frankly, I think we're paying a big price for the autonomy we've granted senior executives. They're each running their own fiefdoms. We can't get our act together."

Regrettably, Richard's situation is not unique. He has no real top management team. Even though he calls his executive group a "team," it has few team properties. And he is paying for it. When marketplace opportunities or threats call for co-ordination and unity of action, a company with a fragmented senior group will usually suffer dearly, as had Richard's.

The expression "top management team" is a misnomer for the groups that exist at the apex of many firms (*see* Box 1). Many such groups are simply constellations of executive talent: individuals who rarely come together (and then usually for perfunctory information exchange), who rarely collaborate, and who focus almost entirely on their own part of the enterprise. Senior executives often sing the praises of teamwork at lower levels, but when it comes to themselves, they

The term "top management team" entered the academic literature in about 1980 and is widely used. This focus on top teams represents an important advance in thinking about executive leadership, since the management of an enterprise is typically a shared activity, extending well beyond the chief executive.

Top management team does not necessarily imply a formalized arrangement with a committee or co-executive, such as the office of the chief executive. Most commonly, it refers simply to the relatively small group of most influential executives at the apex of an organization. In interviews, company heads tend to define their top teams as the executives who report directly; typically a group of eight, with a range of five to fifteen. In an average team, about half the members are line executives respon-sible for business sectors or markets; the others are responsible for company-wide support, service, or external activities.

Senior teams are responsible both for formulating responses to the environment and for implementing them. They are bombarded with information, much of it ambiguous and unstructured, often contradictory. It is this information overload that makes a focus on top teams so important, both for executives and academics. Because strategic stimuli are so open to perceptual filtering and interpretation, the characteristics of the top team (biases, blinkers, aptitudes, and interpersonal dynamics) determine the decisions made. Thus, the chief executive who wants to improve the company's performance and fitness for the future will be determined to improve the caliber and functioning of the top team.

often exhibit aloofness and blinkered perspectives.

The problem of fragmentation at the top can be traced to a variety of factors. In some companies, chief executives are resistant to teamwork at the top level, fearing either that it amounts to an abdication of their leadership role, or that it runs counter to their company culture of unit accountability and initiative. What these executives do not understand is that an effective top management team greatly extends the capabilities of the chief executive; it rarely dilutes them. A well-functioning top team is an important complement to, not the antithesis of, business unit drive.

The meaning of teamwork

In an era requiring corporate coherence, companies have to orchestrate their activities at the highest levels, not just operations. They must promptly identify and diagnose the need for periodic company-wide changes and be able to execute those changes. Companies can do this only if their top executive groups have team properties, particularly what I call "behavioral integration."

Behavioral integration is urgently needed in the upper echelons. It describes the degree to which the senior management group engages in a mutual and collective way. It has three elements: the quantity and quality (richness, accuracy, timeliness) of information exchange among executives; collaborative behavior; and joint decision making. That is, a behaviorally integrated top management group – a real team – shares information, resources, and decisions.

Having a top management group with these properties does not mean management by parliamentary body. It does not rule out having a strong chief executive, although it does rule out having one who serves as the broker or mediator in all senior executive interchanges or who attempts to formulate major changes alone. Also, behavioral integration doesn't rule out entrepreneurship by business units, although it does reject disjointed initiatives or those that are at cross-purposes to the bigger picture. In fact, because many executives seem so skeptical about teamwork at the top, it is useful to specify what behavioral integration is not.

It is not likemindedness. Top executives should have differing experiences and perspectives. Behavioral integration capitalizes on differences by providing forums of exchange and debate, not "groupthink" (see Box 2). Nor is such behavior the same as interpersonal appeal or friendship. Although outright antipathy among executives is harmful, chumminess is rare and is

Box 2 **Groupthink: management cohesiveness gone bad**

Fragmentation isn't the only problem of senior executive groups. Another, "groupthink," has been widely documented. While the fragmented group is reluctant to convene around a discussion table, the team suffering from groupthink is only too eager to meet, nod, and agree in unison.

Groupthink refers to an excessive likemindedness and striving for unanimity that can develop in some highly cohesive groups.

It can be difficult for a team leader to identify (at least until decisions prove to be unsound) because such groups are so harmonious, amicable, and seem to run smoothly. But the symptoms are unmistakable: frequent references to the firm's invulnerability and competitors' ineptitude; aggressive pressure on dissenting members; and discussions that are one-sided and reaffirming.

Groupthink tends to occur when group members have very similar experiences and frames of reference, particularly when they all have relatively long tenures in the group. A company head who dislikes conflict or who punishes dissenters also creates the conditions for groupthink.

The chief executive's own behavior is the linchpin in avoiding groupthink. He or she must continually invite critical evaluation and debate. In addition, group members should be charged with periodically discussing the group's deliberations with trusted associates in their own units and relaying reactions. Sometimes, outsiders should be invited to group meetings and expressly encouraged to challenge the views and momentum of the group.

---

not necessary for integration. Finally, behavioral integration does not demand endless meetings. Some face-to-face contact is necessary, but extreme amounts are not.

What can be done?

If you believe your senior executive group needs to become more of a team, what should you do? Research suggests some promising initiatives. First, be sure the group has a clear identity. The group should have a name, even something as straightforward as executive committee or policy group. Membership needs to be clearly conveyed, not to establish an elite, but to allow members to identify with the team and to understand they are a part of it.

Second, assign real work to the group. If the group only convenes to share information or to review other people's work, there can be no sense of team commitment or energy. The senior group needs to roll up its sleeves and take on substantive tasks. Appropriate tasks include those that deal with company-wide marketplace challenges. Another job for the group to take on is retooling the company's performance management system (its evaluation, measurement, and incentive processes). One of the chief executive's key tasks is to look for suitable company-wide

issues the group can tackle.

Third, be sure the group meets often enough to feel like a team. This is not as often as some people might expect. Once a month for half a day is usually sufficient. (If team members are located around the world, quarterly meetings plus video conferencing can suffice.) The group should have at least a couple of two-day meetings away from the office each year, at which difficult issues can be tackled in depth. In the process, familiarity and trust will be reinforced.

Fourth, pull executives out of their parochial zones. For instance, consider giving unit heads additional responsibilities for company-wide endeavors. These "overlay" assignments can be temporary (such as heading up an e-commerce taskforce) or more continuous (overseeing a staff or support unit).

Another initiative, increasingly being used, is to rotate executives selectively, requiring them to take their experience and perspective to a new setting within the company. The objective, again, is to develop a senior team of executives with a company-wide perspective. For instance, Jorma Ollila, chief executive of Nokia, rotated several of his top executives about a year ago as a way of keeping them fresh and focussed on company-wide opportunities.

Fifth, be sure executives have an incentive to be concerned about the whole. At least a third of incentive compensation should be tied to overall company performance. And a third of every executive's annual incentive reward should be paid in company stock or options. These are precisely the initiatives Louis Gerstner took at IBM to overcome the parochial behavior of executives who had almost all of their pay riding on how well their units – and only their units – performed. Nothing is worse than asking executives to devote their efforts to the team, but then rewarding them only for their own unit's performance.

Finally, the chief executive must set the tone. He or she must convey and reinforce norms of openness and constructive candor in the team. The chief executive must ensure disagreement and minority views are not penalized and, above all, that healthy, sometimes heated, debate never becomes personal.

Implementing change

An integrated senior team is crucial not only to diagnosing the company's situation and formulating large-scale change, but also to implementing change. In fact, senior managers' attitudes and conduct always make the difference between successful and unsuccessful corporate transformation. Top executives particularly have an essential, and often overlooked, role as leading advocates of change.

In any large-scale organizational change, employees have four essential questions in their minds. Why do we have to change? Why is this the right change? Why do you think this organization can handle the change? What are you going to do to help me through the change?

Answering these questions is a central challenge for leadership. However, the selling effort cannot succeed as a one-person endeavor. This is a job not just for the chief executive but for the whole top team. Tragically, the greatest obstacles in the internal effort to sell change are often the chief executive's own direct lieutenants – precisely the people who are supposed to lead the change. If even just one of these executives gives mixed signals to his or her department, the change effort may be doomed. Corporate transitions can succeed only if all the top executives commit themselves to convincing others of the

wisdom and feasibility of the company's new direction.

Jack Welch's early days as head of General Electric provide an illustration. Once he had assembled a group of senior executives who agreed with important new themes (such as, "We will only be number one or two, or else we will sell it, fix it, or close it" and "We believe in openness and candor"), the entire senior management group was sent to visit operations around the world and spread the message. Each of these executives spent several months doing this. It was critically important, of course, that the themes were reinforced by substantive actions, such as resource allocation, rewards, and staffing. But the role of the entire senior management team in mounting a unified campaign in support of the new direction was key to the transition GE experienced.

Conclusion

Like all resources, an effective senior team requires investment and time to develop. A team cannot be produced on command, particularly in a crisis. Therefore, the business head who wants more teamwork at the top must start today. Then, when a major market shift occurs, the top team will be able to comprehend and interpret the shift, formulate a strategic response, and implement it.

Further reading

Hambrick, D.C. (1995) "Fragmentation and the Other Problems CEOs Have With Their Top Management Teams," *California Management Review*, 37(34).

Hambrick, D.C., Nadler, D.A., and Tushman, M.L. (eds) (1998) *Navigating Change: How CEOs, Top Teams, and Boards Steer Transformation*, Cambridge, MA: Harvard Business School Press.

Janis, I.L., and Mann, L. (1977) *Decision Making*, New York: Free Press.

Katzenbach, J.R. (1998) *Teams at the Top*, Cambridge, MA: Harvard Business School Press.

Nadler, D.A., Spencer, J.L., and Associates (1998) *Executive Teams*, San Francisco, CA: Jossey-Bass.

How to say the right
thing in the right way

Gerry Griffin is a corporate communications trainer and consultant. He is a regular speaker and tutor at London Business School. He can be contacted at gerry@redmarketing.co.uk

Every comment from major companies is likely to be picked over by journalists and analysts. **Gerry Griffin** provides a step-by-step guide to communications strategy.

August Busch III, head of Anheuser Busch, the world's largest brewer, once ended his section of an annual report with a single exhortation: "Sell more beer." Unfortunately, this command overrode the company's commitment to protecting natural habitats, aluminum recycling and other activities, voiced elsewhere in the report. Baldly stated, Busch's advice appeared self-interested and overly product-focussed.

It raises an important issue: how do the activities of a company and the ways in which they are presented influence sales activity? Was Busch stating the unvarnished truth, or was his message and how it was communicated actually likely to damage sales?

How senior managers communicate corporate messages is of increasing importance. Indeed, everything they say is a corporate message, dissected and analyzed by a range of audiences. What they communicate has a direct effect on the bottom line. Consider how the Body Shop's stance on animal testing and fair trading has helped to differentiate its products from those of other cosmetic retailers. Anita Roddick, the company's founder, is unlikely to call for Body Shop employees to "sell more moisturizer." Indeed, she says: "I can't take moisture cream too seriously – what interests me is the revolutionary way trade can be used as an instrument for change."

Corporate communication can look to and shape the future. It can take up indirect or long-term topics to create or maintain sales, for example by lobbying regulatory authorities to permit use of genetically modified foodstuffs.

Some dismiss corporate communication as mere tactical maneuvering. Some argue that a company needs to be more than just the sum of its sales and marketing parts; that a company must offer more than just employment, tax revenue, and, of course, its goods or services.

Academic Sumantra Ghoshal has argued that corporations create social value. To see them merely as vehicles for shareholder value is blinkered: "Amid a general decline in the authority of other institutions – political parties, churches, the community, even the family unit – corporations have emerged as the most influential institutions of modern society; not only in creating and distributing a large part of its wealth, but also providing a social context for most of its people, thereby acting as a source of individual satisfaction and social succour."

Thus, if a company is to communicate effectively, it must have a clear sense of what it is as an entity. In this sense, corporate communications should be applied common sense.

Objectives

The starting point for corporate communications is the area that needs most attention: setting out the objectives of the business. A snapshot of most activity would contain some or all of the following: donorship to charities or artistic foundations; corporate advertising; initiatives with nongovernmental organizations, such as Friends of the Earth; meetings with analysts; local community initiatives.

If a company is unsure how its business interests are being served by any of these activities, then both the activity and any communications surrounding it are likely to lack rigor. In poorly communicating companies, explanations range from the traditional ("We're doing it because we've always done it") to patronage ("The chairman thinks it's a good idea") and philanthropy ("It's a good cause").

It may well be a good cause. But there are many good causes and selection must be based on rigorous criteria. Formulating a clear objective takes good leadership; to implement and assess it takes good management.

Often, managers both fail to communicate the business objectives and are poor examples of communication in action. Management consultancy SKAI believes that when leaders communicate badly it is because they:

■ abdicate responsibility to the corporate communications department;

■ blandly give out the "corporate" message, offering nothing of themselves in either content or delivery;

■ talk at too high a level, which rarely works internally;

■ sanitize their words;

■ don't have a decision-making process on making information available, therefore never get information out in a timely manner.

At a company-wide level, corporate communications require staff to have a clear picture of what they are trying to achieve as a business. A consistent message should be delivered through credible channels and timed for maximum impact. The company must:

■ acknowledge business objectives;

■ define the type of organization (what is the corporate culture?);

■ decide what it expects to gain from communicating either its corporate values or its corporate activities.

The last point is where experience pays off. The expectations of the communicator need to be managed alongside those of the audience: executives will never solve problems with a few well-chosen words, and there will always be divergence between what a company says and what it does.

How, then, should a corporate communications plan be created?

The beginning

Corporate communications should express the essence of an organization. Sadly, most campaigns start off with little knowledge of how the business objective is being served by the activity – and with an idealized version of where the company wants to be. This can lead to bland, sanitized, and ultimately irrelevant acts of corporate communication, which we see all around us each day.

Managers should know what makes the company tick, since this will imbue corporate communication with a credible sense of what it is trying to achieve. The words may be perfect, but if they are undermined by contrary words spoken elsewhere or by the company's behavior, the

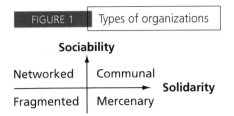

FIGURE 1 — Types of organizations

Sociability

Networked | Communal

Fragmented | Mercenary

Solidarity

communication will be of little value.

Academics Rob Goffee and Gareth Jones have presented a way for managers to chart where their organizations stand with regard to two main criteria: sociability and solidarity. Sociability is "a measure of friendliness among members of a community. People do kind things for each other because they want to – no strings attached."

By contrast, "solidarity is based not so much on the heart as the mind. These relationships are based on common tasks ... and clearly understood shared goals that benefit all the involved parties, whether they personally like each other or not."

Using these principles, Goffee and Jones have divided organizations into four main types: networked, communal, fragmented, and mercenary (*see* Figure 1).

So, for example, a technology company that aims to build and market an innovation might be a mercenary organization – it will not have much in the way of mutual support networks within the business, but will have strong teams driven toward common business goals. The top right-hand quadrant (communal) is where many organizations aspire to be (Hewlett-Packard is an example). The authors warn communal organizations to beware of smugness and complacency.

In finding an effective starting point for corporate communications, managers should remember that the whole organization (salespeople, call-center operators, reception, security, accounts, engineers, and so on) communicates values every day to a vast network of audiences.

In the old economy, there were a few points of contact regulating information between the inside and outside of the organization, such as media spokespeople, analyst liaison officers, and personnel managers. The neat distinction between what lies inside and outside an organi-

zation is now becoming more difficult to make. The proliferation of the internet, e-mail, and supplier portals makes it easier for the outside world to interact continuously with people at all levels in the organization.

Building a plan

Let us consider how a corporate communications plan can be managed, using the example of a bottling plant. Figure 2 is loosely based on a planning chart used by communications consultancy Burson-Marsteller.

Step 1: Business objective. Increase capacity at facility by 50 percent.

Step 2: Corporate culture. This is expressed as the way in which the specific facility operates. How has it interacted with its surrounding community? What are industrial relations like? What is the dominant culture (in terms of sociability and solidarity)?

Step 3: Review business actions. The expansion requires a host of business actions. Considerations include:

- investment decisions;
- planning applications (the facility needs to be expanded on to a field used by local residents, though the land is owned by the business);
- tendering processes;
- project management teams;
- construction;
- disruption of working patterns;
- increased noise and dust;
- increased employment;
- modification of timetable in which stock is collected and materials delivered (because of greater volume).

Step 4: Identify where communications can have a significant impact. Take the last point from Step 3. In the fictional plant, collecting stock and delivering are based on an 18-hour rotation: 6 am to 12 pm. The facility is in the middle of a residential area. The new distribution timetable is for 24-hour delivery and collection, with lorries filled with empty bottles rattling over speed ramps, past sleeping residents. This needs careful handling.

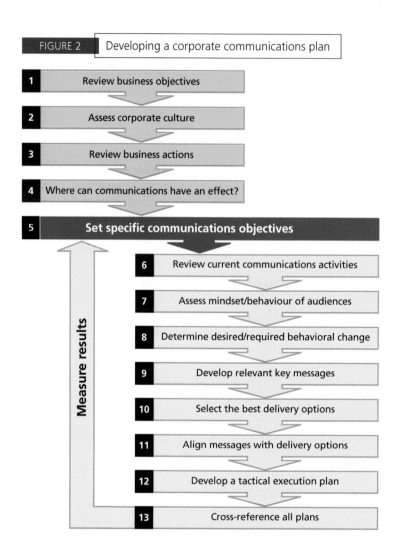

FIGURE 2   Developing a corporate communications plan

1. Review business objectives
2. Assess corporate culture
3. Review business actions
4. Where can communications have an effect?
5. **Set specific communications objectives**

Measure results

6. Review current communications activities
7. Assess mindset/behaviour of audiences
8. Determine desired/required behavioral change
9. Develop relevant key messages
10. Select the best delivery options
11. Align messages with delivery options
12. Develop a tactical execution plan
13. Cross-reference all plans

Step 5: Set communication objectives. This would include expediting planning approval and minimizing negative reaction from community groups at the stages of planning application, construction, and operation.

Step 6: Assess current communication activities. What is the business doing locally? Examples might include sponsoring a local football team, funding conservation, and so on. The fewer "wheels" that need reinventing, the better.

Step 7: Assess the mindset and behavior of people involved. Start with the local community, planning officials, employees who live locally, employees generally, media, the financial community. Be realistic – some independent research may be needed to set your bearings properly.

Step 8: Determine required mindset/behavior change. Any strong negative views of the company need to be improved or marginalized. If 24-hour distribution is not negotiable, for example, what could be done to keep the affected audience on board? Where there are positive views, they should be marshaled in the company's defense, such as the value as a local employer and tax-payer.

Step 9: Develop key messages. These are the essence of your stance. They are also designed to move an audience (as in Step 8). In the case of the local stance on taxation (probably aimed at planning officials), the message might be: "Without expansion, the plant will not be competitive, so endangering jobs [and taxes]."

Step 10: Select the best delivery options. When you need to identify, recruit, educate, and mobilize third parties to speak on your behalf, do you contact people directly in open meetings or by letter, or generically, through the media?

Step 11: Align messages with delivery options. Make sure the right people are set up to give the right messages. Local managers are often best for dealing with local issues. Press officers need to be trained. Third parties need to be given information and support materials.

Step 12: Develop a tactical plan. Timing is particularly important here – making sure you get the right messages to the right audiences through the right channels. For example, there is little point delivering the right message to the planning officials too late to have an effect.

Step 13: Make sure the plan is consistent with other plans, particularly timelines. You need to get messages out as swiftly as possible – ahead of the rumor mill. You also need to be consistent in words and deeds.

Conclusion

Corporate communications is a way in which the corporate essence is expressed and consolidated. Used well, it can encourage transparency and build confidence that the business is doing what it says and saying what it does.

Further reading

Burson-Marsteller: www.bm.com/insights/

Ghoshal, S. and Bartlett, C.A. (1999) *The Individualized Corporation*, London: William Heinemann.

Goffee, R. and Jones, G. (2000) *The Character of a Corporation*, London: HarperBusiness.

How to groom the
leaders of the future

Michael Useem describes the attributes of leadership and looks to examples among companies and individuals for ways of developing the essential qualities.

Michael Useem is William and Jacalyn Egan Professor of Management at the Wharton School, University of Pennsylvania, and director of the Wharton Center for Leadership and Change.

For management writer Peter Drucker, leadership is having followers who "do the right thing." For political historian James MacGregor Burns, leadership is a "calling." For US president Abraham Lincoln, leadership is appealing to the "better angels of our nature." Leadership is also a matter of making a difference. It entails changing a failed strategy or revamping a languishing organization. It requires us to make an active choice among many plausible alternatives, and it depends on bringing others along, on mobilizing them to get the job done.

Leadership is at its best when the vision is strategic, the voice persuasive, and the results tangible. In the study of leadership, an exact definition is not essential, but guiding concepts are needed. The concepts should be general enough to apply to many situations, but specific enough to have tangible implications for what we do. Four frameworks are particularly valuable for company leadership. Their focus is on the individual capacities that have the greatest impact in the broadest circumstances.

The three-part story

Leaders such as Martin Luther King, Margaret Thatcher, Pope John XXIII, Eleanor Roosevelt, Alfred Sloan, and Nelson Mandela had an immense affect on society. Our experience in the present century will long reflect what they achieved in the past century. What is the common thread that explains their legacy?

For academic Howard Gardner, the answer lies in their consistent use of a three-part account. Whether with a few supporters or in front of a nation, great leaders consistently offer their vision of both what should be and how it should be achieved. Moreover, they always include a third element: all honor to the people who will build that future.

Nelson Mandela, for instance, demonstrated this kind of leadership by declaring that the people of South Africa would create a multiracial, democratic nation; they would do so through the peaceful transformation of South Africa; and both the black and white people of South Africa would get them there.

The teachable point of view

During nearly two decades at the helm of General Electric, Jack Welch built one of the leading producers of everything from toaster ovens and jet engines to television programs and financial services. He transformed a company worth $12bn in 1981 to one valued at $560bn today.

When asked to reveal the secret of his success, Welch says it is certainly not knowing which alloys to use in engines nor which shows to broadcast on Mondays. It is, rather, knowing how to pick the right leaders for making those products and then ensuring that the chosen ones master their growing responsibilities and changing markets. And for this, argues academic Noel Tichy, you must have a "teachable point of view," a message that defines what you want the company to achieve and how it will do so, and both must be conveyed in a form that others can readily learn and teach in turn.

The other intellect

Many managers will have known brilliant colleagues who had every answer but no respect. Cognitive intelligence is a prerequisite for most responsible positions, whether a Nasa flight director or an investment bank manager. What distinguishes the people who move up to those positions is a capacity that writer Daniel Goleman has called emotional intelligence. It amounts to the following: if you are self-aware and self-regulating, empathetic and compassionate, and skilled at bringing out the best in people around you, you will hear what you need to know and inspire what they need to do.

The 70-percent solution

Some institutions are notorious for deplorable leadership; others are legendary for their excellence at the top. The US Marine Corps is

> A **vision is a picture** of where you want to go, how you want to get there and why anybody should follow

renowned for its leadership abilities and offers insights into what is essential in business. The Marine Corps prepares its commanders to:

- seek a "70-percent" solution rather than a 100-percent consensus;
- avoid indecisiveness, a fatal flaw that is worse than no decision;
- clearly explain a decision's objectives and then allow subordinates to work out the details;
- tolerate and even encourage mistakes when they generate better performance next time;
- prepare everybody to lead, including those in the front line.

Business writer David Freedman and former McKinsey consultants Jon Katzenbach and Jason Santamaria argue that although companies march to different drummers, their leaders will do well to adapt the best of what the Marines have already discovered.

Leadership changes

Without John F. Kennedy's persuasively articulated vision, human beings would not have walked on the moon in 1969. A powerful vision is a precondition for leading a company or country at any time. It is a persuasive picture of where you want to go, how you want to get there, and why anybody should follow.

Herb Kelleher formed Southwest Airlines in 1971 to make flying affordable and the company profitable, and that vision has guided the company ever since. The airline still has some of the lowest ticket rates and highest profit rates in the business, reporting a net income of $474m in 1999 on revenue of $4.7bn.

Not only should chief executives articulate a strong vision, but they must do so in the face of new pressures: intensified competition and less time in which to achieve goals. Before AT&T's deregulation in 1984, for example, the chief executive was virtually assured of last year's earnings plus 6 percent in the following year. The current chief executive, Michael Armstrong, is not even assured of his job next year. Professional investors and stock analysts are turning up the heat and the internet is requiring rapid-fire action. Wall Street and the City expect people at the top to understand where the market is going, pick a strategy for succeeding in it, and rally a reluctant workforce to master it. Michael Armstrong has to reduce costs and create innovation, but money managers and stock analysts also expect him to divine and shape his future better and faster than anybody else in business.

Vision and strategy are therefore essential, but they have been joined by new critical capabilities.

Leading out

As companies increasingly outsource services, use joint ventures, and construct strategic alliances, they require managers who can lead out, not just down. In other words, the skill of sending work downward to subordinates is being supplemented by a talent for arranging work with partners. Such lateral leadership is essential for achieving results when you have no authority to guarantee them. And managers are requiring more of that every year: recent surveys of managers report annual outsourcing expenditures growing by 15 percent or more.

Consider a senior US manager in a telecommunications company who was responsible for developing outsourcing contracts worth $1bn for information services. Company executives told him that cutting service costs and reducing management distraction were the purpose and left him to identify which services could be outsourced. He then had to contract the right outside partners to provide the services and convince skeptical internal managers that the deal would deliver what they wanted.

Lateral leadership requires strategic thinking to understand when and how to collaborate for competitive advantage; deal making to secure the right arrangements with outside companies and ensure they provide quality service; partner-

> If done in an unsubtle way, **upward leadership** may prove little more than a career-shortening move

ship governing to oversee and develop the collaborative contract; and change management to spearhead new ways of doing business despite internal resistance.

Leading up

As companies have decentralized authority, they have put a premium on a manager's capacity to muster support from above as well as below. Managers must be able to lead their own bosses. If superiors lack data, managers should ensure they receive what is needed.

Consider a brokerage manager who could see the potential of the internet, but whose boss and board remained skeptical. He labored to persuade them that online trading would come to dominate the trading market, even though it meant cannibalizing their existing franchise and incurring momentary losses. He prevailed, and his company became one of the industry's largest.

Upward leadership depends upon followers who are ready to speak out, solve problems, and fill the breach. But it must also be executed with subtlety and verve. If done in an unsubtle way, it may prove little more than a career-shortening move for those who try it. Yet, the middle manager who fails to handle things firmly may never be noticed by the very senior managers who are most in need of help.

Moving fast

The widespread adoption of the web has increased the availability of information to buyers and sellers and reduced the costs of transactions between them. Whether building a new internet company or an online capacity in an established enterprise, acting decisively can be essential in quickly changing markets. So too is an ability to revamp the business model and redeploy assets to take advantage of competitive changes before others do.

Consider eBay, the world's largest online auction site. It was the first mover in its market, and when Amazon.com and others subsequently began competing in the auction market, chief executive Meg Whitman incorporated some of their features – such as password retrieval and fraud insurance – on eBay's website. She also added new features, such as a way for buyers to look for items in their own city and to be notified when an item they desired became available for bid. Today eBay has attracted 16 million registered users and holds 90 percent of the online auction market. Whitman's swift actions helped create a market valuation of $14bn.

How to build leadership

Some managers have a head start in acquiring leadership capacities, but everyone can improve. It is a learned capacity, albeit one that for many proves very difficult to master.

A first step for building leadership is to identify those whose leadership skills will need to be developed during the years ahead. Senior executives may decide it is only the managers of major operations who should be included, but they may conclude instead that it should be virtually everybody with responsibility. Middle managers will probably want to involve anyone reporting to them.

Managers can begin by engaging those closest to them in a leadership debate, and asking them to do the same with their associates. They can discuss their moments of both success and setback; ask them to synthesize lessons from their own leadership experiences; provide them with personal coaching and individual mentoring; and change the business culture so they can make decisions without acute fear of failure.

An explicit leadership development program may also help. Abbott Laboratories, a $13bn revenue US healthcare manufacturer with 57,000 employees, brings groups of 35 high-performing, high-potential directors and vice-presidents together for three weeks of leadership development over nine months. Participants examine the leader's role and responsibilities at Abbott, they consider alternative leadership approaches, and they receive feedback on their own leadership style and impact.

DuPont, with revenues of $27bn and 94,000 employees, has created its own "knowledge intensity university," a set of programs for training managers in how to identify expansion strategies, create a culture of urgency, and allocate resources to encourage rapid growth.

One program for top executives of product divisions and global businesses is designed to help them identify the best methods for bolstering business. A second program for top management teams helps them specify, test, and implement the best "growth engines" for business. Both programs include week-long learning events with an intensive focus on strategic alliances, e-commerce, and change leadership.

Ford Motor Company has annual sales of $162bn and employs 365,000 people. To accelerate the formation of its future leaders, it runs a "new business leader" program for 2,000 managers every year. Participant teams identify ideas that could help transform the company's way of doing business, design a course of action for implementing the best proposals, and develop a "teachable point of view" for advocating them.

Instilling leadership

One of the most effective ways of instilling leadership in such programs is to examine what other leaders have done in times of crisis. By looking at others' experiences, managers can better anticipate what they should do when faced with leadership challenges. This teaches strategic thinking and how to act decisively.

It can be particularly powerful to walk historic battlefields or recall critical decisions. Jon Krakauer's *Into Thin Air*, for example, describes how two climbing groups, simultaneously nearing the summit of Everest, were hit by a violent storm. It is useful to ask what went right – and why so many things went so terribly wrong – for the leaders of the two teams as they desperately sought safety.

Eight climbers (including both team leaders) never found shelter. In asking how their decisions might have gone differently, how their leadership mattered, and what we might do to reach our own summits more safely, we can deepen our own commitment to preparing ahead and instilling responsibility for when it is really needed.

The British explorer Ernest Shackleton's journey to the Antarctic presents another useful illustration of leadership in a crisis. Shackleton set out in December 1914 with a team of 28. His ship became trapped in ice and although it appeared that everyone was doomed, Shackleton's exceptional perseverance, ingenuity, and leadership led them all to be rescued 21 months later. In *Leading at the Edge*, Dennis Perkins suggests several enduring lessons to be taken from Shackleton's saga:

■ *Keep sight of the ultimate goal but focus on interim objectives.* Shackleton was driven by the safety and survival of his men. When morale plummeted at one point, Shackleton organized a trek to cross 314 miles of ice floe to an old food cache. The trek failed, but the collective endeavor restored the crew's life-sustaining spirits.

■ *Engender optimism.* As a way of maintaining morale, Shackleton openly planned the team's next expedition – to Alaska.

■ *Minimize your perquisites.* Ten of the 28 castaways were forced to use inadequate sleeping bags after the ship sank. Shackleton assigned these bags by lottery, except for one that he assigned to himself.

■ *Risk nothing needlessly, bet everything when essential.* When Shackleton's marooned crew finally reached an inhospitable island at the edge of the Antarctic, they stood on land for the first time in 497 days. Yet the island offered no respite. The nearest help, South Georgia Island, still lay 800 miles across one of the most daunting oceans in the world. With few navigational aids, Shackleton set out with five others in a 22-foot craft. Eighteen days later, in one of the greatest feats of steerage and survival ever, he landed their tiny boat on South Georgia.

Further reading

Freedman, D.H. (2000) *Corps Business*, New York: HarperBusiness.

Gardner, H. (1995) *Leading Minds: An Anatomy of Leadership*, New York: Basic Books.

Gardner, J. (1993) *On Leadership*, New York: Free Press.

Goleman, D.P. (1997) *Emotional Intelligence*, New York: Bantam.

Katzenbach, J.R. and Santamaria, J.A. (1999) "Firing Up the Front Line," *Harvard Business Review*, May–June.

Krakauer, J. (1997) *Into Thin Air*, New York: Villard/Random House.

Perkins, D.N.T., with Holtman, M.P., Kessler, P.R., and McCarty, C. (2000) *Leading at the Edge*, New York: American Management Association.

Tichy, N.M. (1997) *The Leadership Engine*, New York: HarperBusiness.

Useem, M. (1998) *The Leadership Moment*, New York: Times Books/Random House.

The key to clear writing
is in the introduction

Writing reports need not mean nights of lost sleep. Keep the reader in mind and focus on being sure what question you want to answer, says **Barbara Minto**.

Barbara Minto is an independent consultant and author of *The Minto Pyramid Principle: Logic in Writing, Thinking and Problem Solving.*

One of the least pleasant aspects of a manager's job is the need to put ideas down in writing. A letter or memo is generally not a problem, but many managers groan inwardly when required to write a thick report, a lengthy slide presentation, or a detailed explanation of why or how to go in a certain direction. They shudder at the likelihood of late nights and many rewrites.

Some executives, on the other hand, are able with apparent ease to produce documents that are clear, crisp, and compelling every time. Their secret is that they spend most of their writing time thinking through the introduction.

This insight often comes as a surprise to people who consistently write introductions by simply writing the heading "Introduction" (or "Background," or sometimes "Purpose" or "Agenda," or even "Executive summary") and then producing a list of the sections like this:

Introduction

This memorandum describes the project team approach to identifying and achieving significant profit improvements. It is organized in six sections, as follows:

1 Background
2 Principles of the team's approach
3 What project work is
4 How the program is organized
5 Unique benefits and results
6 Prerequisites for success

Here, the writer expects readers to take in, without preparation, a string of topics rather than a set of ideas, and arrogantly assumes they will easily grasp their significance and want to read on – which of course

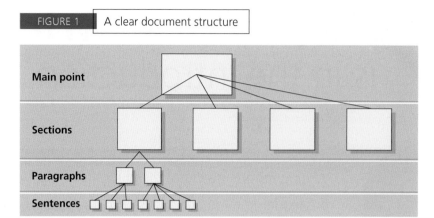

FIGURE 1 A clear document structure

Main point

Sections

Paragraphs

Sentences

they won't. At the same time, the writer is denied the discipline that makes him or her discover and state precisely what points are to be made.

In fact, a good introduction is the most important element in ensuring clarity in any document. Its function is not just to set out the gist of the thinking, but to direct and speed the task of writing for the author. Thus, 90 percent of the thinking in putting together a document takes place in writing the introduction.

This article looks at how the introduction serves the document, and shows how the process of developing it is the key to clear writing.

Why an introduction?

The introduction exists to remind the reader of the question the document is meant to answer. To see why that makes sense, we have to look at what a clearly structured document looks like. A clearly structured document groups together sentences into paragraphs, paragraphs into sections, and sections under a single summary thought, as shown in Figure 1.

Ideas go in the boxes. An idea raises a question in the reader's mind because the writer is saying something the reader doesn't know – that is, the writer's thinking. (People don't read business documents to find out what they already know, they only read to find out what they don't know.) If you present the ideas in a pyramid form, you automatically create a question–answer dialog with the reader.

The top (main) point will make a statement that raises a question that will be answered on the line below, as in Figure 2. The writer then continues to raise and answer questions down the pyramid, until the point is reached where there are no more questions logically in the reader's mind.

For this to work, the point at the top of the pyramid must be the right one for the reader. Once this point is identified, though, the rest of the document is dictated. The only way to ensure that the point at the top is right for the reader is to direct it toward answering a question that already exists in the readers' minds – or that would exist or should exist if they thought for a minute about what they already knows.

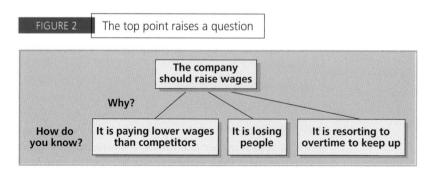

FIGURE 2 The top point raises a question

The company should raise wages

Why?

How do you know?

It is paying lower wages than competitors

It is losing people

It is resorting to overtime to keep up

The writer should begin with a story about the subject of the document. And it should be a **"good" story**

People will read the document only because they need to know what it says, and that will apply only if they have a question in their minds that they expect the document to answer. The purpose of the introduction is to remind both writer and reader of the question, so the writer can proceed confidently to give the answer.

Now, clearly, the question does not come out of thin air. It has to come from what the reader already knows about the subject of the document. The introduction, therefore, is meant to review that knowledge for the reader and in the process prompt the question the writer wants to answer. At the same time, of course, the writer is convinced that the answer will be relevant and welcome.

What, then, is the most efficient way to go about prompting the reader to ask the right question? It is by telling a story.

Why a story?

Telling a story guarantees that the reader will pay attention to what is said. As noted earlier, the readers do not read for pleasure. They read because they must. Nor does the reader come with a mind ready to receive what is written. The reader brings instead a jumble of unrelated thoughts, most of which are on other subjects, and all of which are far more interesting than anything the writer might say.

Thus, the writer should begin with a story about the subject of the document. And it should be a "good" story, which will keep the reader's attention. Every good story must have a beginning, a middle, and an end. That is, it establishes a situation, introduces a complication that leads to a question, and then offers a resolution. For example:

Situation. Boy meets girl and falls madly in love.
Complication. Rival comes along and takes girl away.

Question. What should boy do?
Resolution. Boy punches rival and keeps girl (or girl punches rival and keeps boy).

As applied to an introduction, the situation will remind the reader of some generally stable state of affairs that existed before a complication occurred that has led to the question. The question will be the reader's question and the resolution will be the point at the top of the pyramid. Here is a typical example, told in the same skeletal way as the love story above:

Situation. The bank's customer knowledge database shows us areas where profit is nil, growth can be encouraged, and costs should be cut.
Complication. These insights point to ways in which the bank should change the way it does things.
Question. How should it change the way it does things?

As can be seen, the story structure allows the writer to move the reader effortlessly from nodding in agreement, to raising the question, to taking in the answer. It also enables the writer to tell readers things with which they will agree (the facts of the past), before saying things with which they may disagree (the writer's thinking, as embodied in the pyramid). The early pleasure makes readers more receptive to the later pain, so to speak.

Looked at in a different way, the story-like review of the past enables the writer to make sure that readers are "standing in the same place" before taking them by the hand and leading them through the reasoning. It gives a clear focus for the point at the top of the pyramid, and a means of judging in advance that the report is conveying the right message in the most direct way.

Bringing the reader to "stand in the same place" need not be a lengthy process, as can be seen in the following examples. How much is said beyond these skeletons is a matter of style, but style should not affect the storyline.

Situation A. The new lead-generating system has been set up to enable the field salesforce to spend more time selling and less time prospecting. Expect it to generate 10,000 warm leads a week.
Complication. Phase two, which is building the

new consumer development center, is set to start next week. But before you turn the first spade, you want to make sure that your investment and return will be what you originally planned, and that you should in fact go ahead.

Question. Should we?

Situation B. Combining UK and European computer systems on a common platform involves integrating a large number of individual hardware and software components in a very short time, using 12 separate teams.

Complication. To minimize risk and prevent adverse impact on the business, we intend to conduct co-ordinated testing.

Question. How will it work?

Situation C. As we know, our objective for next year is extremely ambitious – to increase growth in the domestic market by 15 percent.

Complication. As we also know, major barriers to growth in this market exist.

Question. What should our strategy be to ensure we achieve our objective?

There is no place in this structure for headings that say introduction or background, particularly at the very beginning. Headings are meant to separate sections, but since there is no text preceding the introduction from which you want to separate it, there is no need for a heading. And telling the story is giving the background.

So far, this article has discussed the way in which the structure of situation, complication, and question pulls the reader into wanting to read the document. But its real value is for the writer. In determining the question the document is meant to answer, the writer is led to discover what the message must be. Indeed, writers cannot be certain of the message until they know the question.

Unfortunately, people tend not to know precisely what they think until they have been forced to say it out loud or write it down. This is what makes writing difficult. In addition, our brains are capable of generating an infinite number of points that could be written down. To select the right points for a particular document, one must know the question it is meant to answer.

Once the question is known, generating the right points is easy. The question demands an answer, which becomes the point at the top of the pyramid. The answer raises a new question in the reader's mind, which the writer must answer on the next line, continuing to raise and answer questions down the pyramid.

However, the validity of the pyramid hinges on getting the original question right. And that means using the situation–complication–question structure of the introduction to ferret it out.

How does it work?

Step one in the process is to focus on the subject of the document. Draw a box that represents the box at the top of the pyramid, and write the subject in it. Then, visualize the readers and state roughly the question you think you want to answer for them about the subject. If you were writing about the bank's new customer knowledge database, for example, you might begin with Figure 3.

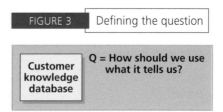

FIGURE 3 | Defining the question

You now have a focus for your thinking. Your mind is ready to review what the reader knows and so confirm the question.

How do you know what the reader knows? Begin by making a statement about the topic that you think the reader will agree is true. This step works as a check on your thinking. If you do not want to start by making a statement about the topic, it suggests you are starting in the wrong place or have the wrong subject.

Describing the situation reminds the reader of some established truth about the subject, usually that a specific activity or set of events has taken place. Whether the reader actually "knows" that these events took place is not too important. All you need to be able to judge is that the statement will be accepted. In other words, reading it should not raise any questions. When there are many readers, all of them must be able to accept what you say as true and all must want the answer to the same question.

Complications

The "complication" is not the same as a problem, although it may be one. It is simply the complication in the story being told, which creates the tension that triggers the question. In the bank example, the complication is: "The insights from the customer service database point to ways in which the bank should change the way it does things." It is less a problem than an indication that change is required, triggering the question: "How should we change?" How does the complication trigger the question? Using the previously "established truth" about the subject as its starting point, the complication explains what happened next in the story that inevitably led to the question. "What happened next" is usually one of four types of thing, leading to one of four generic questions, as shown in Figure 4. In the previous examples of introductions, each question falls into one of these categories.

Readers' questions

The reader does not determine the question. The writer does. The writer did the thinking and is the one with the message to communicate. The reader cannot know in advance what that message will be. The writer's job, in reviewing the past, is to determine what the reader should want to know, and therefore what the writer should be planning to say.

In the bank example, we expect readers to ask how the bank should change, because that's what they should want to know, given a review of the facts. It is also what we have learned the document should be structured to tell them.

However, sometimes the writers will know in advance the message to communicate, and so have to make readers ask for the information they want to give them (in other words, to "plant" the question).

Suppose you are writing to a group of people to tell them to do something and they do not know you will be writing. The introductory structure might be like this:

Situation. As you know, at the field sales meeting in July, we will be teaching you how to present the new space management program to supermarket chains.
Complication. To customize the presentation for each region, we need information in advance about one of your problem chains.
Question. (How do I give you the information?)

This review of what the readers know (the situation) and will agree is true (the complication) forces them to ask the question you want to answer.

There will also be situations in which you could envisage several questions. Consider the following options:

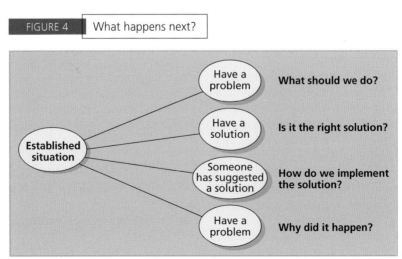

FIGURE 4   What happens next?

Option 1

Situation. Increased oil prices due to recent developments in the Middle East have brought about the likelihood of reduced earnings for Alpha.

Complication. To mitigate the earnings decline, Alpha has indicated that it plans to reduce operating costs (versus its original forecast) by $10m.

Question. Will that be enough to stem the earnings decline?

Option 2

Situation. Given the expectation of reduced earnings, Alpha has indicated that it plans to reduce operating costs by $10m.

Complication. However, raw material and variable operating costs are not easily controllable in the short term, and are likely to increase if oil prices rise.

Question. Where should we look for the $10m reduction?

Option 3

Situation. Alpha has indicated that it plans to reduce operating costs by $10m. However, because raw material and variable operating costs are not easily controllable in the short term, the reductions cannot come from that area.

Complication. In that case they will have to come from the fixed cost area.

Question. Is it possible to cut fixed costs that much?

The "right" question to answer depends on your assessment of what the reader already knows.

Final presentation

The final form of the introduction should contain the information in the situation, the complication, the question (stated or implied), the answer, and the next level of thinking. In that way, the introduction plays another vital role for the reader, because it gives a summary of the entire message of the document in the first 30 seconds of reading. An introduction for the Alpha example is given in Box 1.

This kind of introduction is not only easy to read, but accomplishes exactly what executives say they yearn for – to have the entire thinking reduced to one sheet of paper. Given the clear statement of points at the beginning, it does not really matter how long the rest of the document becomes. The reader has got the message right at the start.

Writing the introduction to a document requires an immense amount of concentrated thinking. Imposing a heading such as "Introduction" or "Background" does nothing to help. What does help the process is the knowledge that any document written to communicate thinking must be structured to answer a question in the reader's mind.

The introduction tells the story of how the question arose, and at the same time directs the writer to produce the kinds of ideas appropriate to the readers. And, when it finally appears on the page, it serves to summarize the entire document.

Box 1 **Alpha introduction**

Increased oil prices due to the recent developments in the Middle East have brought about the likelihood of reduced earnings for Alpha. To mitigate the earnings decline, Alpha has indicated that it plans to reduce operating costs (versus its original forecast) by $10m during the next financial year. Since raw material and variable operating costs are not easily controllable over the short term, and are likely to increase with higher oil prices, the cost reductions will have to come from fixed costs.

Alpha is not certain that it is realistic to expect such large reductions to be available in that area. Consequently, you asked us to determine whether it is realistic to cut $10m from fixed costs. We have concluded it is possible by:

- Holding selling, general, and administrative costs to last year's level.

- Cutting contract and outside services by 5 percent.

- Controlling nonplant operating and processing supplies.

Further reading

Hayakawa, S.I. (1949) *Language in Thought and Action*, New York: Harcourt Brace.

Minto, B. (1995) *The Minto Pyramid Principle*, London: Minto International.

Zelazny, G. (2000) *Say it with Presentations*, New York: McGraw-Hill.

Marketing

8

Contents

Introduction to Part 8

Marketing is concerned with the interaction of the company (or its products and services) with the customer. Among other things this includes the nature of the product, its price, the point of sale, and how the company and its wares are presented in advertising and promotional material. However, marketing has grown in complexity as opportunities for new kinds of interaction have appeared, and marketers have more opportunities to collect and analyse data than ever before. This part begins with the central topic of branding, before covering segmentation, integrated marketing campaigns, pricing, experiential marketing and retailing. Finally, writers examine the future for the sales team, and best practices for marketing in emerging markets.

The essence of building
an effective brand

Kamran Kashani is a professor of marketing at IMD, Lausanne.

Turning a name into a unique consumer experience requires a determined strategy over time. **Kamran Kashani** proposes a framework to follow.

The role of brands and their contribution to business performance have been a source of controversy over the years. In the mid-1990s, following the rise of private labels in fast-moving consumer goods industries, many were quick to announce the decline and fall of brands such as Coca-Cola, Marlboro, and Gillette.

However, those predictions were premature. By the end of the decade not only had most of the fallen brands recovered, but a number of non-consumer goods and service companies had joined the club of sophisticated brand builders.

Who would have thought, for instance, that Intel – an industrial label for a semiconductor chip that computer users do not see, touch, smell, or taste – was on its way to becoming one of the world's most recognized and valuable brand names? Intel's management, with a keen eye on the growing number of first-time PC buyers, saw the potential for creating and then protecting a highly differentiated branded position in an increasingly commodity-like market for semiconductor chips.

Intel's success, confirmed by the premium prices PC customers are willing to pay for a product with an Intel sticker, has been an inspiration for many raw material and component manufacturers. Like Intel, they seek ways of enhancing their competitive position through the effective use of their brands.

The controversy surrounding brands was reignited most recently with the rise of electronic commerce. Once again, many predicted the decline of brands. They argued that brands had little to contribute in internet markets, where price transparency is the rule. As experience accumulated, however, skeptics were again proved wrong.

While products and prices can be compared endlessly, internet consumers are nonetheless sticking to a few established sites with recognized names – such as Amazon.com and Charles Schwab, and even old-economy labels such as Barnes & Noble and IBM.

Critics argued brands had little to contribute in **internet markets**; they were proved wrong

The realization that brands are just as important online as offline has encouraged many e-commerce companies to invest heavily in advertising. At the height of the dotcom frenzy, many e-commerce start-ups spent sums several times their sales revenues in an attempt to establish a dominant presence in the internet's crowded market space.

The logic of brands

What explains the persistence and growth of brands in both the old and new economy, and the endemic skepticism about their role? What is the enduring logic of brands? A closer analysis of Intel's campaign may provide some answers.

In the early 1990s, a court gave Intel's rival AMD the right to copy the company's microchips – an unforeseen byproduct of a licensing agreement between them. Managers were faced with the challenge of finding new ways of differentiating Intel's chips from those produced by its competition. Competing on price was not an appealing option. Branding computer chips itself was a new idea, but reaching the consumer with a brand statement was totally unconventional, especially in an industry where differentiation had always been fought on technical superiority. After all, the skeptics argued, Intel's customers were PC makers, not PC users. Why should the consumers care about the brand of a component inside their PC?

However, Intel's managers understood the psychology of a growing number of first-time PC buyers who wanted reassurance that their investment in a computer was a safe one. The "intel inside" sticker on each PC communicated quality and power – exactly what the consumers needed. All the company's press and broadcast advertisements emphasized the brand values of assured quality and high-tech power. Intel's brand was to stand for a safe choice.

The message fell on receptive consumer ears, but consumers were not the only beneficiaries of Intel's logic. Intel had also recognized that many lesser-known manufacturers would be interested in buying the company's premium-priced microchip and displaying the Intel logo on their products and advertising. While the brand on the computer, often an IBM clone, might not be well known, consumers had no difficulty recognizing the Intel sticker that had come to represent assured quality and computing power.

Sales benefits

Market research indicated that consumers were willing to pay a premium for PCs containing Intel's chip. Intel decided to offer the PC makers a rebate on chip purchases, to be spent on advertising that displayed the Intel logo. It was an offer clone makers could not refuse. By the late 1990s, even big names such as IBM and Hewlett-Packard had joined the bandwagon. Intel's logo appeared on the computers of more than 1,600 manufacturers and its chips held a 75 percent market share.

Intel's campaign also led to benefits for PC retailers. Consumer preference for the brand increased stock turnover for computers carrying the company's logo. It also raised margins. The computer retail trade thus shared in the payoffs from a well-recognized brand.

As Intel's example shows, the logic of brands can be compelling across the value chain. Effective brands facilitate consumer choice, provide retailers with added incentives, and help differentiate a company's products or services.

In the final analysis, though, a brand-differentiated business must produce higher returns or else the branding exercise is futile. The good news for such businesses is that strong brands do confer such superior returns. For example, Interbrand, a company that specializes in valuing brands, places Intel among the world's four most valuable brand names (after Coca-Cola, Microsoft, and IBM) and estimates the brand to be worth nearly $40bn. This is the highest value ever seen for an ingredient brand; it is proof that when fully understood and exploited, brands have tangible payoffs.

FIGURE 1 | Brand building: decisions and actions

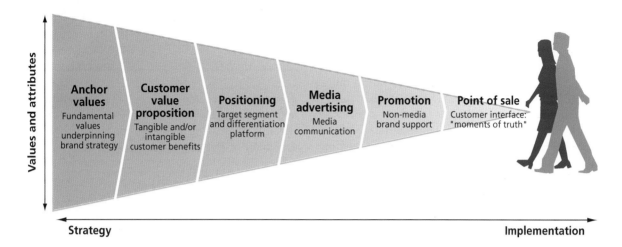

Brand building: the process

What turns a name into a great brand? There are no simple answers to this, but an important principle underlies all attempts at creating brands. Strong brands do not just happen; they are built over time through a deliberate management process involving strategic decisions and corresponding actions. The quality of this process can make all the difference between a desirable brand and the also-rans.

Figure 1 shows the elements of brand building. The process elements are depicted along two dimensions: strategy implementation on the horizontal axis, and the values and attributes dimension along the vertical one. The wedge itself consists of six decision and action elements: anchor values, customer value proposition, positioning, media advertising, promotion, and point of sale. These elements define the strategic and operational imperatives of a given brand; they provide a structured blueprint for building a brand.

Anchor values

Every brand needs to be based on values and attributes that are permanent, purposeful, and fundamental to its strategy. Anchor values give depth of meaning to an otherwise inert name and, in so doing, provide a strategic ambition and direction to the brand.

For example, when Ericsson launched its cellular phones, managers decided on 10 anchor values: simplicity, dependability, independence, co-operation, ambition, fulfillment, innovation, social interaction, up-to-date, accomplishment.

These values were to inspire everything the company did, from choice of technology and design to how the brand communicated to its target consumers. They were also meant to reflect the unique corporate attributes of Ericsson, a 120-year-old telecommunications company that believes in human interaction above cold technology.

Anchor values can be thought of as genetic codes for everything that might relate to a brand, not just its communication. Deciding on these values is the first step toward defining a long-term brand strategy.

Customer value proposition

Second, managers should define what anchor values would mean for the customer. This element, referred to as customer value proposition (CVP), is about translating general anchor values into specific statements on the benefits that drive the buying decision. Simplicity of design and use, a tangible functional benefit, is part of Ericsson's CVP for its mobile phones.

Nondifferentiated products and services cannot credibly rely on such tangible and functional benefits as drivers of consumer choice. Their CVPs should be based on less tangible, more emotional, or aspirational propositions. "The Pepsi generation," for example, was a CVP for younger drinkers who saw themselves as belonging to an up-and-coming generation with new habits and lifestyles.

CVP is inspired by anchor values but is more targetted toward benefits that are highly regarded by customers. Like the security associated with Intel's chips, CVP gives customers reasons to seek the brand. An effective CVP is based on deep insights into customer needs and behavior; it adds a customer-led trajectory to brand strategy.

Positioning

The third element in brand building consists of two decisions: one concerning target segments, the other a differentiation platform. Together, they define a brand's positioning.

Segment definition identifies customers for whom the anchor values are most relevant and whose wishes are best addressed by the brand's CVP. They also constitute the target for future brand building. For example, Nescafé's redefined strategy targets consumers who welcome new ways of drinking coffee and are willing to "open up" to the idea of a good cup of instant coffee. Not all coffee drinkers fall into this definition. For Intel, the target segment was the first-time PC buyer who wanted a safe choice. Knowledgeable computer buffs were not part of Intel's target group.

The second decision concerning a differentiation platform attempts to answer the question: "Why this brand?" Unlike CVP, which is focussed on customer benefits, differentiation is about how a brand is different. For Sony, what differentiates its brand is the excitement embedded in its products, a streamlined but intelligent simplicity that often hides a complex technology. Accordingly, when the company uses a label saying "It's a Sony," it tries to communicate the essence of its differentiation: that the product is simpler on the outside, more sophisticated on the inside, and, as a consequence, more fun to use.

Anchor values, customer value propositions, and positioning constitute the three strategic elements of brand building. They set in place clear

Anchor values, customer value propositions and positioning are the **strategic elements** of brand-building

guidelines for management implementation; actions that consistently convey the brand values through the use of media, promotional schemes, and point-of-sale customer interaction.

Media advertising

The most visible part of brand strategy implementation is advertising. Huge sums are spent each year on print, outdoor, TV, radio, and website advertising. But, to the dismay of brand builders, most spending is wasted because advertisements either do not reach the target audiences or, when they do, they fail to leave lasting impressions. Two factors contribute to this problem: clutter and decay.

Clutter results from the average consumer being exposed to an estimated 200 to 300 commercial messages a day. The challenge for an advertiser is to cut through this clutter. The brand builder faces a second factor, decay, which means that most of the message is forgotten minutes later.

Clutter and decay put special demands on media communication, where often the largest resources are spent. It remains an advertiser's challenge to relate in a more intimate way with target customers, not only for the brand message to be better noticed, but also to leave a longer-lasting impression. These aims were behind Nescafé's recent "open up" international television campaign. This uses unusual people and situations to stand out from other coffee advertisements and to convey the essence of its brand message for drinkers of roast and ground coffee – open yourself up to a new experience, that of instant coffee.

Promotion

Not all great brands are built on the back of high-budget mass advertising. Promotion can be even more effective. Consider, for example, the

Body Shop, the pre-eminent retailer for cosmetics and personal care products. The founder's philosophy of doing business precludes the use of advertising along with, among others, excessive packaging and animal testing. Yet the Body Shop's unorthodox promotional schemes, including sponsorship of social activism and environmental causes, have greatly contributed to the brand's success among progressive and affluent youth. Other examples of promotional activities include Swatch's sponsorship of sports events and Harley-Davidson's owners' clubs.

The ever-rising cost of advertising, media clutter, and the emergence of highly targetted promotional vehicles have contributed to the increasing reliance on nonmedia promotions. Effective promotions create synergies with other marketing vehicles and support the brand strategy. Accordingly, any promotional activity that fails this test must be avoided, as it risks diluting, or even conflicting with, the brand's anchor values.

Point of sale

The final element in the brand-building process, at the sharp end of the wedge, involves activities affecting the customer experience at the point of sale. These are "moments of truth," when decisions are made for or against buying a given brand. In supermarkets, where brands reach out from the crowded shelves for attention, the point-of-sale experience may be as short as three seconds. Availability and location on the shelf, packaging, and the words and images on the product are all factors that shape a customer's experience and choices at the point of sale, in seconds.

The importance of the point of sale is not limited to bricks-and-mortar businesses. The customer interface on a website can also be a determining factor, affecting the outcome of a given online transaction. Evidence suggests that the rate of "online drop-outs" (shoppers who considered buying online but decided against it) is directly related to the customer's experience on the website. Research shows that the simplicity and convenience of a site are crucial to repeat shopping and customer loyalty.

Where personal selling is part of the buying experience, as is the case for many industrial products and services, the point-of-sale interaction can have an overwhelming impact on brand values as they are experienced by the customer.

Consider Hilti, a manufacturer of construction power tools and fastener systems with a 7,500-strong direct salesforce. These salespeople communicate Hilti's CVP of superior product quality and end-user service to customers around the world. For Hilti, every day represents nearly 70,000 customer contacts, each offering an opportunity to create a branded customer experience.

From the rigorous training of field salespeople to their unified appearance (including a bright red hardhat and toolkit) and well-programmed sales pitch, managers make a conscious effort to use every interaction to reinforce Hilti's brand values. The company knows that no other communication vehicle can be as powerful as the customer experience.

As important as customer interface tends to be at the point of sale, it is often left out of the brand-building process, given over to chance and possibly to divergent localized actions. McDonald's has well understood the importance of customer experience in its fast-food outlets. Its speedy service, friendly atmosphere, and cleanliness are as much a part of McDonald's brand values as are its consistent food quality and family orientation.

At the sharp end of the brand-building wedge, where strategy is finally translated into a specific customer interface, it is the experience that speaks louder than commercial words. Accordingly, it is important to ensure that every moment of truth leads to a reinforcement of what the brand stands for and, as such, to a uniquely branded customer experience.

Beyond the talk

While the above brand-building model highlights important process decisions and actions, a brand-builder's ultimate aim should be one of establishing and managing a relationship with the customer – a task far more complex than following a decision guide. Effective brands evoke a trusting relationship, which is reinforced with every customer transaction.

Trust in brands, as in any relationship, comes from consistency and continuity. On consistency, every customer experience with the product or service must reaffirm and reinforce the values it communicates. Anything short of this is cause for distrust and termination of the relationship. Consistency puts a special demand on managers to question the fit between every brand-related action and the core values of strategy.

Continuity is critical because strong brand relationships are only built over a long time. (Awareness may be built quickly, but this does not constitute a relationship. It takes accumulated positive experience for people to bond closely with brands.) Shifting brand values and irregular investments in communication, both signs of erratic management priorities, are two culprits that lead to a discontinuous relationship. Customers reward those brands that stand for continuity and invest for the long term.

Further reading

Aaker, D.A. (1996) *Building Strong Brands*, New York: Free Press.

Carpenter, P. (2000) *eBrands*, Boston, MA: Harvard Business School Press.

Kapferer, J.-N. (ed.) (1997) *Strategic Brand Management*, London: Kogan Page.

Kashani, K. (2000) "Brands that Grow: The Compelling Logic of Innovation," *European Business Forum*, Autumn, 35–40.

Reichheld, F.F. and Schefter, P. (2000) "E-Loyalty: Your Secret Weapon on the Web," *Harvard Business Review*, July, 105–13.

Ries, A. and Ries, L. (1998) *The 22 Immutable Laws of Branding*, New York: HarperBusiness.

Ward, S., Light, L., and Goldstine, J. (1999) "What High-Tech Managers Need to Know About Brands," *Harvard Business Review*, July, 85–95.

Turn your customers
into advocates

Get to know your customers well and you not only develop loyalty, but they will extoll the virtues of your products, says **Barbara Kahn**.

Barbara Kahn is Dorothy Silberberg Professor of Marketing at the Wharton School of the University of Pennsylvania.

Banks have traditionally treated retail customers identically: "Deposit your money and you get a check book." Yet when banks began to collect data that allowed them to compute profitability for each customer, there were marked differences. Some kept a lot of money in their checking accounts and rarely accessed it or, if they did, withdrew the cash through automatic machines. These customers were very profitable. Others kept low balances and made frequent withdrawals, often through contact with tellers. Such customers ended up costing the bank more, and were not profitable. Identifying profitability helped banks devise strategies to suit different types of customers.

Customer portfolio management

The analysis banks used to track profitability was customer portfolio management. It is a technique that has proved useful for many businesses – those dealing with both consumer and business markets. To determine which customers were most valuable, banks had to allocate revenues and costs at the customer level. Although revenues had traditionally been allocated at the customer level (banks always knew who had the most money in their accounts), it was not typical to treat costs in this way. In banks, as in most companies, costs were handled at the product or operations level.

By allocating costs to each customer, banks were able to find out which customers were most profitable. It then became easier to devote resources and time to the most profitable customers. While revenues were known to follow an 80/20 law, so that 80 percent of revenues were generated by 20 percent of customers, costs can follow a 90/10 law, so 90 percent of costs are generated by 10 percent of "whiny" customers. If you reduce the costs of serving customers whose business does not

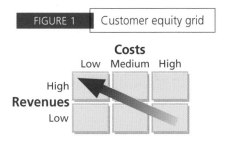

FIGURE 1 | Customer equity grid

Costs

Low Medium High

High
Revenues
Low

warrant additional attention, and spend more time serving customers whose business does, the overall customer portfolio can become more profitable.

The trick is to figure out how to allocate costs to each customer. Costs can vary by units (such as inventory, physical handling, cost of goods sold). They can vary at the transaction level (order processing, shipping, order frequency costs); or at the relationship level (maintaining an account, contact time, service costs). There are also selling and maintenance costs (promotional mailings, free samples) and enterprise-level costs (warehousing). These costs need to be assigned as appropriate to each customer. When costs are broken down and compared with revenues from each customer, profitability can be computed.

This profitability determines the asset value of the customer relationship, or the customer equity. One way to think about customer equity is to create a grid with revenues (high/low) on the vertical axis and customer costs (low/medium/high) on the horizontal. Customers can be designated to one of the boxes on the grid and profitability assessed (*see* Figure 1).

When customers are designated in a portfolio system, management goals become clear. With unprofitable customers in the lower-right box, managers need to do three things. First, reduce the costs of dealing with them, for example by encouraging electronic banking. Second, increase the revenues generated, perhaps through fees for services or price increases. Finally, consider ending the relationship, although this is frequently an undesirable or unethical solution.

The problem with profitable customers in the upper-left box is retaining them, because they will attract the attention of your competitors.

Building customer relationships may be the answer to both types of problem.

Relationship marketing

Relationship marketing is grounded in the idea of establishing a learning relationship with customers. At the lower end, building a relationship can create cross-selling opportunities that may make the overall relationship profitable. For example, some retail banks have tried selling credit cards to less profitable customers. With valuable customers, customer relationship management may make them more loyal and willing to invest additional funds. In banking, these high-end relationships are often managed through private bankers, whose goals are not only to increase customer satisfaction and retention, but also to cross-sell and bring in investment.

In determining which customers are worth the cost of long-term relationships, it is useful to consider their lifetime value. This depends on:

- current profitability computed at the customer level;
- the propensity of those customers to stay loyal;
- expected revenues and costs of servicing such customers over the lifetime of the relationship.

Building relationships makes most sense for customers whose lifetime value to the company is the highest. Thus, building relationships should focus on customers who are currently the most profitable, likely to be the most profitable in the future, or likely to remain with the company for the foreseeable future and have acceptable levels of profitability.

Relationship goals

The goal of relationship management is to increase customer satisfaction and to minimize any problems. By engaging in "smarter" relationships, a company can learn customers' preferences and develop trust. Every contact point with the customer can be seen as an chance to record information and learn preferences. Complaints and errors must be recorded, not just fixed and forgotten. Contact with customers in every medium, whether over the internet, through a call center, or through personal contact, is recorded and centralized.

Many companies are beginning to achieve this goal by using customer relationship management (CRM) software. Data, once collected and centralized, can be used to customize service. In addition, the database can be analyzed to detect patterns that can suggest better ways to serve customers in general. A key aspect of this dialog is to learn and record preferences. There are two ways to determine customers' preferences: transparently and collaboratively.

Learn transparently

Discovering preferences transparently means that the marketer learns the customers' needs without actually involving them. For example, the Ritz Carlton hotel makes a point of observing the choices that guests make and recording them. If a guest requests extra pillows, then extra pillows will be provided every time that person visits. At upmarket retailers, personal shoppers will record customers' preferences in sizes, styles, brands, colors, and price ranges and notify them when new merchandize appears or help them choose accessories.

With increased use of the internet, companies have more opportunities to learn customers' preferences and behavior transparently. Information that can be easily collected includes:

- words used in search engines to find your site: these can help understand how to categorize your services;
- source of visit (search engine, other sites, directory sites, portals, banner advertising, and so on);
- individual customer measures such as number of monthly visits; time spent per visit and search patterns; orders from site; conversion (from visitor to purchaser); spending per order; spending per visit.

Learn preferences collaboratively

When marketers learn customers' preferences collaboratively, they engage in dialog to help customers articulate their needs and identify how to meet those needs. Ultimately, this method should result in an ideal product, but this can take time.

The goal of the marketer in learning preferences collaboratively is to determine a way to maximize learning without frustrating customers. Again, the web can be useful with online questionnaires and forms.

Permission marketing can also be used. This involves asking customers for permission to gather personalized information or to contact them in the future. Finally, collaborative filtering is effective for learning customers' preferences and helping them choose items they may enjoy. The book retailer Amazon.com uses this approach. The company tracks customers' preferences and purchase patterns, matches them with those of similar customers, and recommends other products based on purchases by similar customers.

When customers collaborate with marketers, the customers are also learning their own preferences. Customers can thus have more control and ensure they get what they want. A product designed with the customer is by definition not wrong, so having a customer collaborate on discovering his or her own needs encourages the customer to commit. Finally, just being part of the process seems to increase satisfaction. Levi-Strauss found this to be the case with customized jeans. Customers were more likely to be satisfied with the final product if they actually tried on a pair of jeans (although this wasn't necessary in the process).

Learning helps cross-selling

One advantage of learning a customer's preferences is that the company then has a record that can be used to cross-sell other products or services. For example, if a customer used personal finance software, such as Quicken, then a marketer could (as a service) offer to provide credit card information in that format. This information would be useful to the customer for financial planning and would provide a rich information bank for the marketer.

As well as helping the customer to control his or her finances, the marketer (with permission, of course) could learn about the customer's recent purchases. For example, if a customer began buying children's clothing, the marketer could propose related goods; or if plane tickets were bought, hotels could be suggested.

Other customer histories can help the marketer. For example, health organizations could keep a record of incidents and patient lifestyles that might suggest diagnostic testing and treatments. Insurance companies, such as USAA, which has traditionally focussed on military officers and their families, already do this. USAA follows marriages, births, and other life-changing patterns so it can advise customers on changing needs. By responding to these patterns, USAA increases revenues by selling more insurance and financial services. Furthermore, it increases customer satisfaction and loyalty by monitoring and adapting to their needs.

Marketers need to be careful with this information and build a relationship based on trust. Some businesses have natural advantages: people are more likely to trust a doctor or a bank than a supermarket. However, if relationships can be built and if the marketer provides valuable suggestions, the customer is likely to be loyal. It is easier for a customer to stay with a trusted company than to switch to another.

Conclusion

By learning customer preferences and focussing on long-term relationships, managers can provide products and services that fit customers' needs. They can also do this in a way that ensures loyalty. If a company earns a customer's trust and if, as a result of that trust, customers share strategic information about their preferences and needs, it will be difficult for competitors to duplicate the relationship.

As relationships develop, customers will tend to buy more from the company. Further, the more a customer buys, the more likely he or she will be to buy from that company again. This virtuous circle is reinforced, because the more a customer buys from the trusted company, the less likely he or she is to turn to another supplier. Finally, the regular customer is more likely to switch to a premium product or service.

The ultimate reward in managing customized relationships will come if a company can transform customers into advocates. A recent example has been among Palm Pilot owners. The Palm Pilot, a pocket organizer, can be customized and so has fanatical supporters. Owners are willing to submit their names and preferences, to be on mailing lists, and are frequent visitors to the company's web pages. In addition, these loyal customers extoll the virtues of the product to potential buyers.

Although price strategies may be effective in the short term, they rarely come out best in the long run. A better strategy to transform customers into advocates is to try to meet the needs of each customer more precisely. Learning customers' preferences can not only help meet their needs better than the competition, but can also help marketers forge an enduring relationship.

Further reading

Gordon, I. (1997) *Relationship Marketing*, Chichester: Wiley.

Peppers, D. and Rogers, M. (1996) *The One-to-One Future*, London: Piatkus.

Wayland, R. and Cole, P. (1997) *Customer Connections*, Boston, MA: Harvard Business School Press.

Segmentation: making
sure the customer fits

Venkatesh Shankar is
Ralph J. Tyser Fellow of
Marketing at the
Robert H. Smith School
of Business, University
of Maryland.

Selling the right product to the right customers is the essence of marketing. **Venkatesh Shankar** discusses examples and explains their underlying strategies.

Markets continue to become more competitive all over the world. In an environment marked by heightened competition and fragmented markets, how does an organization win out against its competitors? Segmenting the market correctly and targetting the right customers are vital to a company's success.

What is segmentation? It is the process of dividing the total market into groups or segments of customers with similar needs or preferences. Segmentation precedes targetting, when a company chooses the best segments for its products or services.

Companies use segmentation for several reasons. First, different groups of customers have different needs and preferences. Second, one product or brand cannot be all things to all people. Third, segmentation allows a company's marketing mix (its brand, product, price, advertising, sales promotion, and distribution channels) to be more closely aligned to customers' needs, so improving the ways in which it uses resources. In particular, segmentation allows a marketer to offer products at different prices consistent with the price sensitivities of different segments.

Segmentation

The first step in segmentation is to identify the bases or dimensions of segmentation – the factors that drive customer needs. These can be identified by carrying out a survey of a representative sample of customers.

For example, when faced with declining sales and profits in 1995, Exxon Mobil (then Mobil) undertook a large-scale segmentation exercise. It identified its segmentation dimensions as convenience (ease of finding a petrol station), price sensitivity, and additional benefits (such as the ability to purchase snacks, beverages, and other groceries).

The second step is to determine the preference of each type of customer for each dimension. One customer may need a high level of convenience, desire additional benefits, and not be concerned by prices; another's preferences may be completely different.

The third step is to group customers into segments based on similarities in the identified dimensions. Customer A could be part of Segment 1 and Customer B could be part of Segment 2. Exxon Mobil unearthed five segments, which it labeled "road warriors," "true blues," "generation F3" (fuel, food, and fast), "homebodies," and "price shoppers."

The final step is to develop descriptive profiles of each segment that aid targetting. Such customer profiles typically include demographic, psychographic, attitudinal, and behavioral information. Exxon Mobil found that road warriors earn $75,000-plus, drive long distances, prefer full service, and like to snack while driving. True blues typically earn $60,000 and $75,000, prefer self-service, and have a limited need for buying other items in the petrol station. Similarly, generation F3, homebodies, and price shoppers differ from one another and the other segments in demographic, psychographic, and behavioral characteristics (see Table 1).

Dimensions, preferences, and the classification of segments can be determined in many ways. So what constitutes a good segmentation exercise? It should have the following characteristics:

■ *Measurement*: are the segments measurable? Can we count the number of customers?

■ *Size*: are the segments large enough in revenues and profits to justify the marketing and manufacturing investments?

■ *Access*: can segments be reached by marketing mix elements?

■ *Action*: does the organization have the ability to take action based on the results of the segmentation scheme?

How detailed should a good segmentation scheme be? The answer will depend on the costs and benefits involved. Because a need- or preference-based segmentation exercise is costly and

| TABLE 1 | Segmentation by Exxon Mobil |

Segment	Convenience	Price sensitivity	Additional benefits
Road warriors	High	Low	High
True blues	Low	Low	Medium
Generation F3	Medium	Low	High
Homebodies	High	Medium	Low
Price shoppers	Low	High	Low

takes time, companies look to segment the market using "surrogate variables" for segmentation. These include demographic, geographic, psychographic, and behavioral variables. Box 1 shows some of these variables for business-to-consumer markets; Box 2 gives the same for business-to-business markets. Managers can use these checklists to guide their segmentation exercises.

Targetting

Targetting consists of evaluating the attractiveness to the company of each segment and selecting on the basis of this evaluation. Some use the "3C" framework below to assess attractiveness. For each segment identified in the exercise above, marketers should ask the following questions:

■ *Customer*: is the segment large enough in revenues and profits? Is the growth potential high?

■ *Competitor*: are there any unmet needs of customers? What is the intensity of competition? What are the barriers to entering the segment?

■ *Company*: are the segment needs consistent with the company's objectives? Does the company have the capabilities to satisfy the needs of the segment?

Depending on the answers to these questions, four types of targetting strategy are possible.

Undifferentiated

When a company decides to offer the same product to several segments or the entire market, it follows an undifferentiated marketing strategy. For a long time, Hershey Foods used this strategy in the confectionery market. In the computer industry, Microsoft follows it for its Office software.

Box 1 **Segmentation variables for business-to-consumer markets**

Demographic variables

Age	Occupation
Sex	Family size
Race	Family lifecycle
Ethnicity	Religion
Income	Education

Geographic variables

Region
Urban/rural
City size
County size
Climate

Psychographic variables

Lifestyle
Personality
Social class

Behavioral variables

Benefits desired
Purchase frequency
Usage occasion
Brand loyalty
Attitude toward brand
Price sensitivity

An undifferentiated strategy is appropriate when:

- the market is young or growing;
- maximizing market share is a critical objective;
- customer needs do not vary substantially across the segments;
- brand equity is high;
- price points are not significantly different across the segments;

- the costs of offering different products or brands for different segments outweigh the incremental returns on them;
- customers can "opt in" to versions of the same product.

Differentiated

When a company offers different products or brands to different segments, it adopts a differentiated marketing strategy. For example,

Box 2 **Segmentation variables for business-to-business markets**

Benefits desired from product

Product performance
Durability
Economy
Ease of use

Benefits derived from vendor

Delivery
Service
Reputation
Convenience

Organizational characteristics

Location
Size, (sales, employees)
Industry group
Years in business
Financial position

Behavioral characteristics

Frequency of purchase
Quantity purchased
Type of purchase
(new, modified repeat, straight repeat)
Purchasing approach
Price sensitivity

Marriott Hotels offers the Ritz Carlton brand for luxury-conscious travelers, the Marriott brand for quality-conscious travelers, and the Courtyard brand for travelers on a budget. Similarly, Intel offers the Pentium IV chip to high-end PC makers and the Celeron chip to low-end PC makers.

A differentiated strategy is most effective when:

- segments are significantly different in preferences and desired price levels;
- brand perceptions are different across segments;
- the market is in late growth or maturity stages;
- there are several competitive offerings in the market.

Personalized

This strategy is a special case of differentiated marketing strategy in which a marketer targets customers by addressing them as individually as possible. The most common way to do this is by mass customization, whereby customers in each segment are further divided into a few subgroups and offered a choice of a selected number of variations in the product or service.

True "one-to-one marketing" means that each customer is offered a different product using a particular marketing mix. However, it is rarely done. The costs of personalization are too high, production and service too constrained, and there is a lack of perceived need for a completely customized product.

However, the internet has enabled companies to target much smaller groups. For example, Dell Computers allows customers in each segment (educational institutions, small businesses, individuals, and so on) to choose their own configuration of computer from a range of options. In the service industry, the concept of MyYahoo.com offered by Yahoo! and other content-related internet services such as Excite and AOL are examples of a personalized marketing strategy.

The internet's customization potential should not be taken as a guarantee of success. Failures abound. For example, Garden.com, which offered a high level of personalization on its site, recently closed. Similarly, Musicmaker.com, which allows listeners to choose their mix of songs on its website and create their own CDs, is struggling to stay afloat.

A major reason for the problems of such companies with highly personalized targetting strategies is that they could not convert their personalization efforts and potential into extracting a sustainable price premium from their customers and growing their customer bases.

A personalized marketing strategy should be adopted when:

- the company has the ability to customize its offerings;
- the product category suits personalization;
- the company can offer customized value and command a higher price with personalization;
- lifetime values are very different across customers;
- personalization can differentiate a company from its competitors.

Concentrated or niche

Concentrated or niche strategies consist of targetting just one segment and offering one brand to customers in that segment. In the confectionery market, Godiva is an example of niche targetting, since it focusses on the specialty, premium niche segment. In the UK airline industry, EasyJet targets the price-sensitive segment. In the car industry, Volvo goes for safety-conscious consumers.

A niche strategy approach is recommended when:

- there is a strong unmet need in a distinct segment;
- revenues or margins in that segment are attractive;
- the needs of such a segment fit squarely with company objectives and capabilities;
- focussing on multiple segments poses the risk of diluting company credentials and spreading its resources too thinly.

Strategy in practice

Using the results of its 3C framework, Exxon Mobil decided to pursue an undifferentiated strategy. It targetted three segments: road war-

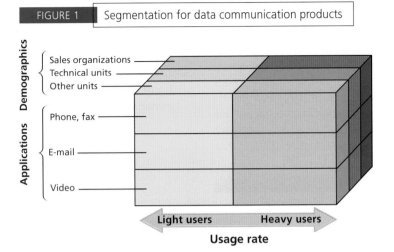

FIGURE 1   Segmentation for data communication products

Demographics
- Sales organizations
- Technical units
- Other units

Applications
- Phone, fax
- E-mail
- Video

Light users   Heavy users

Usage rate

riors, true blues, and generation F3. Stations were redesigned to include a shop, more full-service pumps and attendants, and a mechanism for faster service using a card called "Speedpass."

The company wanted to capture a large market share. Collectively, these segments represented about 59 percent of the market. The company allowed customers to "opt in" for full-service convenience or additional purchases at the store. Thanks mainly to its segmentation and targetting, Exxon Mobil achieved substantial results – increases of $800m in revenues and 30 cents in earnings per share over two years.

An example of business-to-business targetting is shown in Figure 1. In this example, a company such as British Telecommunications (BT) may use the following dimensions to segment the market: demographics, applications, and usage rate. The demographics dimension is defined on three levels: by sales organizations, technical units, and other units. The applications dimension consists of three levels: phone/fax, e-mail, and video. The usage dimension comprises two levels, heavy and light.

The combination of these levels leads to 18 possible segments. BT can evaluate the attractiveness of each segment using the 3C framework and come up with its target segments.

International issues

Typically, a company with a presence in several countries will treat each country like a single market with an appropriate segmentation scheme. Some segments, however, may share characteristics across countries, presenting global marketers with both opportunities and challenges. For example, the target segment for Citibank's platinum Visa card is similar in many countries. This allows the company to use resources more efficiently. A global marketer's challenge is to identify common segments, target them, and market to them.

In some cases, the same product or brand may be targetted at different segments in different countries. Holiday Inn focusses on higher-bracket travelers in Asia, but basic travelers in North America. A troubling issue with such differential targetting is that Holiday Inn may confuse customers and prospects traveling in both North America and Asia.

It has tried to overcome this problem by inventing sub-brands. For example, upmarket hotels in Asia are branded Crowne Plaza Holiday Inn, while some economy hotels in the US are branded Holiday Inn Express.

Heineken beer faces a similar issue. In the Netherlands Heineken is targetted at the mass market, whereas in Belgium it is focussed on a higher-income audience. Because information travels quickly between the Netherlands and Belgium, the company faces an additional challenge – how to maintain its different targetting positions in these countries.

Conclusion

Successful marketers are those who can divide the market into valid segments, take aim at the appropriate customer segments, and shoot with the right weapons in the marketing mix. Global marketers must also be able to exploit the opportunities and surmount the challenges of globalization. By following a systematic approach, they will be better prepared to conquer their markets.

Further reading

Peppers, D. and Rogers, M. (1993) *One-to-One Future*, New York: Doubleday.

Shankar, V. (2001) "Personalization in the New Digital Environment," working paper, University of Maryland.

Integration as the
way ahead for marketing

Mark Ritson is an assistant
professor of marketing at
London Business School.

The glamorous world of advertising is losing out to
other forms of marketing. **Mark Ritson** charts the rise
of integrated marketing communications.

Advertising once occupied a prime position in the marketing mix. It
was an "above the line" business – an agency could charge clients
a commission based on the value of press and television space bookings
of between 10 and 15 percent for its work. "Below the line" referred to
less glamorous formats, such as direct marketing and sales promotions,
which were fee based. Each form branched out on its own with separate
industry bodies, different forms of remuneration, and different ways of
evaluating the effects on consumers.

In the 1990s, however, various forces began to undermine the accepted norms. Corporate managers became frustrated with an advertising
industry that continued to raise the cost of campaigns as the number of
commercial minutes per hour of television increased, so dramatically
raising their total costs.

Clients also demanded better data on cost-effectiveness. Although
advertising has a demonstrable effect on consumer awareness, this does
not always result in an immediate, measurable effect on sales. In the
case of car advertising, for example, it could be years before a campaign
altered consumers' buying behavior. Indeed, a strength of advertising is
that it can build enduring connections that go beyond simply encouraging the consumer to buy the product immediately. In contrast, sales promotion and direct marketing can affect sales and demonstrate this
clearly. A coupon promotion has a direct cost and all managers need to
do is identify sales levels before and after the promotion to calculate a
break-even figure.

Another factor in the growth of other forms of marketing was the
increasing emphasis on relationship marketing. Managers became
aware that existing customers were far more receptive, lucrative, and
less expensive to target than new consumers. Many marketers realized
they could use very focussed lists of particular target segments or, later,
the internet's targetted user groups to sell more goods and build long-

Managers became aware that **existing customers** were far more receptive than new consumers

term relationships through direct marketing. Rather than advertising to all consumers as if they were first-time prospects, marketers increasingly reached out to existing markets in a more cost-effective way.

Perhaps the most important explanation for the rise of other forms of marketing communication was a growing awareness that synergy could be realized between different formats. It is not hard to see why. Ten percent of an advertising budget spent on public relations activities that promote a new advertising campaign might generate higher levels of awareness for the campaign. Names collected from a sales promotion competition could be used for direct marketing. Consumers who were interested in a brand could be sent direct mail promoting the brand's website.

Integrated marketing

We have entered the era of integrated marketing communications (IMC). Managers can combine approaches and allow brands to speak with a single voice across all media formats. At every point of contact with the brand, consumers see the same messages.

Yet integration has not been easy to achieve. Differences in each industry made it almost impossible to bring together communications to serve a single brand client. A brand manager might be able to gather agencies to work on a brand, but turf wars would break out. The PR company might threaten to walk out because the advertising agency was doing its job; or the direct marketing company might feel undervalued compared with other partners.

Major agencies consolidated to offer a complete package. WPP, Omnicom, and Interpublic grew up during the 1990s with the goal of buying independent companies across a spectrum of industries. By doing so, they could offer integrated marketing.

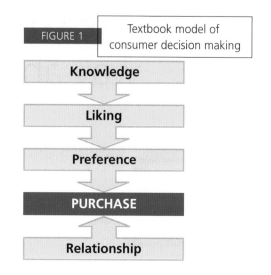

FIGURE 1 — Textbook model of consumer decision making

Knowledge → Liking → Preference → **PURCHASE** ← Relationship

In the past few years, however, companies have realized that the only people who can integrate so many disparate formats into the service of their brands are brand managers. The new breed of brand manager is fluent with the main forms of marketing and can bring them together. There are four steps in integrated marketing.

Step 1: Understanding consumers

Like other marketing activities, IMC begins with the consumer. It is crucial for a brand manager to understand that decision making is not a formulaic sequence that all consumers progress through on their way to a unilateral purchase stage. Figure 1 represents a classic decision-making sequence. Such century-old textbook models are meant to illustrate every consumer decision-making process in general and none in particular.

Reality is never so simple. Good brand managers appreciate that they must use both quantitative and qualitative research to reveal the steps that consumers go through to buy a particular brand. There are no generic models. The actual steps in a particular decision-making model cannot be guessed at, but come from extensive immersion in the consumer's world.

One of the best places to begin this research is to ask recent purchasers to describe the "story" of their purchase: from knowing nothing about the brand to buying it. After only a few of these stories, a pattern of decision making will emerge.

Of course, there may not be a single sequence. Recognizing multiple target segments for a brand carries an assumption of multiple decision-making sequences. Yet isolating these decision-making sequences is the first step in planning an IMC campaign.

Step 2: Zero-based budgetting

IMC is based on identifying the actions that consumers follow in making a purchase, then using different tools to target this sequence. At the outset of an IMC campaign, a brand manager does not know how much money will be necessary, nor where that money should be spent.

Too many budgets are set in an arbitrary way, or are calculated using a crude advertising-to-sales ratio (typically 5 to 10 percent of expected revenue). Both approaches have obvious faults and should be avoided.

The best way of assigning budgets is by zero-based budgetting. The brand manager first needs to assess the range of activities to be carried out. Typically, these estimates can be provided by the client's marketing communications agency. Next, a calculation is made of the effects that must take place with respect to the consumer to take them through a decision-making sequence and into purchase and repurchase.

The secret of this process is not to separate the act of purchase from the other equally essential stages in any consumer's decision making. One cannot happen without the other.

Finally, a manager can submit a budget that contains both an overall figure and a breakdown of where money should be spent. If this budget is rejected, the manager must try to find another way to achieve the same effect for less. Taking what you can get from senior managers and spending it is not an option for an IMC approach. Indeed, the first step in zero-based budgetting is to decline a budget that is not strategically derived in favor of an approach based on consumer research.

Step 3: Selecting the mix

There are five main types of marketing communication, each with its strengths and weaknesses (see Figure 2). Just as a toolbox contains tools for different tasks, the IMC mix will contain marketing methods whose relevance depends on the brand in question and the decision-making steps of target consumers.

Each activity has advantages and disadvantages. Advertising plays an essential part in most IMC campaigns because of its national impact and its role in building strong brands. Advertising is the classic brand-building tool because it can associate a brand with a range of cultural icons that become imbued with the brand itself. The Belgian beer Stella Artois becomes "reassuringly expensive" and continental in style because of its advertising. Similarly, the British beer Boddingtons has used its extensive advertising budget to communicate a Northern, adventurous quality.

Advertising has drawbacks. It is relatively weak at "closing the sale" and forcing purchase. It is also not the most effective way of forming

| FIGURE 2 | Suitable areas for different IMC tools |

	Awareness	Knowledge	Liking	Preference	PURCHASE	Relationship
Advertising	National advertising campaigns			Brand building with cultural associations		
Public relations	Pre-launch and launch of new products	Third-party reviews and information				
Direct marketing					Ordering through catalogs and telemarketing	Building relationships with direct mail
Internet		Unlimited information source				User groups and specialty websites
Sales promotion				Immediate preference gained from offer	Encouraging sale/trial	

relationships with consumers over time. Advertising is a tool for mass audiences and does not allow for the subtleties of relationship marketing.

Public relations is typically less expensive than other tools, yet for the right product it can be highly effective. PR comes into its own before and during the launch of a brand. It is an old marketing adage, but the minute a product goes on sale it is yesterday's news. PR is a tool for generating "buzz" about the brand through mainstream media.

The US launch of the new Volkswagen Beetle in 1998 demonstrated the power of PR. Volkswagen had several well-placed stories in the press and used support media such as video news releases, which were made available to the media for free. It was able to establish the car in the minds of potential customers without spending anything on advertising.

PR can also be invaluable for brands that involve technical information or that depend on third-party review for their ultimate success.

The central problem with PR is the loss of control brand managers face in using it. No matter how well a story is positioned, the target media have the freedom to decide if they will use the story and how they will frame it. However, the barrier to increased use of PR is client ignorance. Most European managers do not realize the cost-effective nature of PR or have not seen the contribution it can make, particularly to product launches.

Spending on direct marketing has grown faster than spending on other forms of communication, year on year, for most of the past 15 years. With the evolution of complex data archiving and mining systems, and the increasing amount of data available, direct marketing has become much more effective.

In particular, when a company already has the names, addresses, and buying behavior of its customers (such as companies in the hotel or airline industries), it has greater opportunities for building strong, personalized relationships with them. Northwest Airlines, for example, uses its database of frequent fliers to provide the best customers with special offers from partner organizations and updates on air miles. Importantly, it tailors the kinds of offer made to

The internet can instantly transform itself from a promotional tool to a **sales site**

the consumer based on his or her flying history with the airline.

The key to direct marketing is its testability. It is possible to mail out 500 pieces of direct mail and, from that sample, derive an estimate of how many returns a company could expect from a national mailing and decide if the campaign would be worthwhile.

Unfortunately, the popularity of direct marketing has created problems. European and North American consumers have been bombarded with junk mail and unsolicited telephone calls. Many people now throw away unopened letters that they recognize as direct marketing.

The main advantage of the internet as a form of marketing communication is its ability to deliver large amounts of information. This ability, combined with its speed, is unprecedented. Consumers now consult the internet for purchases that demand research before a commitment is made. What is more, the internet can instantly transform itself from a promotional tool to a sales site.

It is important, however, to remember that for many products the internet remains irrelevant. People still want to squeeze their bananas before buying. Similarly, it is easy to forget that many market segments are not accessible. Nonetheless, brands such as Dell and BMW have benefitted from a strong, integrated web presence.

Finally, sales promotions have continued to be popular. Perhaps the most important factor is that the day a promotion opens, it affects sales. It can be used to protect a market or to steal market share from a competitor and encourage people to switch brands. Supermarket group Tesco has run coupon offers in which consumers' past shopping behaviors dictate the coupons they are sent.

A concern with sales promotions is that they may turn brands into commodities. Advertising encourages consumers to buy a brand because of associations and meanings, whereas promotions remind consumers to buy for commodity reasons: because it is cheaper, or it contains a third more.

Many sales promotions, however, are able to build brand equity while encouraging trial and purchase. Suntan lotion maker Hawaiian Tropic, for example, has had great success with competitions to win trips to Hawaii: the offer encourages purchase and builds brand equity simultaneously.

Stage 4: Continual review

Finally, to embrace IMC is also to acknowledge that as markets evolve, so must managers adapt strategies. The final stage of any IMC campaign should therefore be a return to the customer: only by continuing to collect and interpret customer data can the brand manager determine the campaign's impact. The goal here is to avoid the annual cycle of budgetting and planning. Instead, market segments and their behavior must guide when a marketing strategy is formulated and executed.

Conclusion

We are likely to see an end to some traditional approaches. The old model of "advertising and promotions," where a manager was given a budget and spent half of it on advertising and kept the rest for promotions, now has no place in the industry. The main barrier to moving toward IMC is the reluctance of clients and agencies to embrace change.

To prepare for this challenge, it is important to remember that despite the complexity of IMC approaches and terminology, the principles could not be simpler. The marketing manager faced with the challenge of building brands in the twenty-first century must adopt IMC. The opportunity to have more impact on more consumers for less money means it will become an essential element in the brave new world of marketing.

Further reading

Burnett, J. and Moriarty, S. (1997) *An Introduction to Marketing Communications*, London: FT Prentice Hall.

Schultz, D.E., Tannenbaum, S.I., and Lauterborn, R.F. (1994) *The New Marketing Paradigm: Integrated Marketing Communications*, The National Textbook Company.

The brave new
world of pricing

Garrett J. van Ryzin is professor of management science at Columbia Business School.

The web is just the latest in a long line of mechanisms for setting market prices. Online companies ignore the history of price discipline in the airline industry at their peril, says **Garrett van Ryzin**.

Once, businesses and consumers appeared content with simple list prices, punctuated with an occasional sale. Today, the internet is producing a tidal wave of pricing innovations. Dynamic pricing, auctions, reverse auctions, guaranteed-purchase contracts, and high-tech versions of haggling are spreading like a virus through the new economy. Research company Jupiter Communications projects that business-to-consumer online sales via auctions will reach $4.5bn by 2004, an increase of 45 percent a year, while sales via other pricing models will increase 70 percent a year, reaching $7bn by 2004.

While it is tempting to attribute this innovation to the web, in many ways its genesis can be traced back over 20 years to the deregulation of US airlines. Faced with intense competition, highly seasonal demand, diverse segments of customers, and the flexibility offered by the world's first truly "electronically distributed" product (an airline reservation), pricing practices of airlines rapidly evolved to an unmatched state of sophistication. Thanks to the internet, these same forces are at work in other industries.

So, what is in store for pricing practices? Will the emerging "Wild West" of pricing be a permanent feature, or will these practices collapse? If high-tech pricing is here to stay, how can companies position themselves to deal with the changes?

Pricing principles

Pricing has never been as simple as portrayed in the classical theory of supply and demand. Here's the standard story from Samuelson's *Economics*: "If more is wanted of any good, say, shoes, a flood of new orders will be given for it. This will cause its price to rise and more to be produced. On the other hand, what if more of a commodity – such as tea

– becomes available than people want to buy at the last-quoted market price? Then its price will be marked down by competition. At the lower price people will drink more tea, and producers will no longer produce quite so much. Thus, equilibrium of supply and demand will be restored."

It is hard to quibble with this reasoning. Indeed, nothing about the new economy has really changed the logic. But such a description is a little like explaining to an adolescent that they will eventually pair up with a mutually compatible mate. In the aggregate, this is certainly true; but it suppresses certain complexities about the underlying process.

As with mates, so it goes with buyers and sellers. In the aggregate, they do come together at something approximating a market-clearing price. But exactly how they find each other and exactly which prices they eventually agree on is far from clear. In fairness to Professor Samuelson, the theory of pricing goes well beyond the explanation above. At the same time, the exact mechanisms behind market prices are often overlooked.

One notable exception is auction theory. Here, economic theory and business practice have found a happy marriage. Auctions provide a simple yet powerful way to uncover market-clearing prices. They have proved their effectiveness over centuries, for everything from government bonds to tulips to fine art.

Why do auctions work? Consider a single seller and a group of potential buyers. The seller has a notion of a minimum acceptable price (the reserve price); each buyer has some notion of a maximum price to pay. However, no party knows the price thresholds of others; this information is "private." Moreover, buyers and sellers are self-interested and will reveal private information only if it is to their benefit.

Call Buyer 1 the one who is willing to pay most, Buyer 2 the one willing to pay the second most, and so on. The market will clear at any price between that which Buyer 2 and Buyer 1 are willing to pay, provided it is higher than the seller's reserve. At any price between these two, Buyer 1 is the only one willing to purchase. We are left with one buyer and one seller; supply equals demand and the market clears.

But how do we find Buyer 1? Auctions provide one mechanism. For example, in ascending price auctions, a low price is announced and buyers are given the opportunity to accept. The price is increased until only Buyer 1 is left. By definition, the resulting price is a market-clearing one. A descending price, or Dutch, auction works the other way. In the Aalsmeer and Naaldwijk flower markets in Holland, a high price is announced and then decreased. The first buyer to accept the price ("hit the panic button") gets the item. Again, a price is discovered at which our seller is matched with the buyer willing to pay most – Buyer 1.

But auctions are only one way to match buyers and sellers. Another is bilateral bargaining, better known as haggling. A buyer and seller, having some knowledge of the market, enter into unstructured negotiation to find a mutually acceptable price. If negotiation succeeds, an exchange is made; otherwise, both try again with another party. Through a series of negotiations, the market is cleared.

The most familiar mechanism to consumers is fixed-price lists. Sellers announce a price at which they are willing to sell: potential customers take it or leave it. Buyers examine the products and price lists of sellers over time and make a decision about when and from whom to buy. Sellers adjust price lists and buyers purchase over time until, again, the market clears.

In the aggregate, all these mechanisms accomplish roughly the same task: they uncover prices at which buyers and suppliers are matched. It is even plausible that, in the aggregate, over the long run and on average, the prices produced by these mechanisms are, approximately, the ones predicted by classical economic theory. However, such general statements are cold comfort to participants in this turbulent game of matching supply with demand. The trick for them is to deftly surf the market. And that is where technology comes in.

A grand experiment

The internet has produced a rash of experiments with pricing. Why? Simply, it either makes new mechanisms feasible or allows old mechanisms to

> The web either makes **new price mechanisms** feasible or allows old mechanisms to be applied in new ways

be applied in new contexts. Both hold the promise of improved markets for buyers and sellers.

One new online mechanism is Priceline.com's "buyer-driven conditional purchase offer," which has a US patent. The entire company is based on founder Jay Walker's vision of turning the usual buyer–seller relationship on its head. Rather than having sellers set list prices, buyers declare what they are willing to pay. Priceline collects these buyers and their guaranteed willingness to pay, and presents them to sellers as a take-it-or-leave-it offer. This is a form of "demand aggregation."

Another demand aggregation mechanism is Mercata.com's patented "group purchase" system, where prices fall dynamically as more people agree to buy a product. These price drops are generated according to seller-specified volume discounts that reflect margin targets, acquisition costs, and economies of scale.

The internet also makes traditional mechanisms, such as auctions, work in new ways. Although auctions are simple and effective, they require simultaneous participation by all buyers and sellers. Product information has to be available to buyers, prices must be announced, buyer responses collected, and new prices disseminated. Previously, such co-ordination required the presence of participants. The web allows these same functions to be conducted remotely.

The result is that auctions are now feasible in many businesses. Antique dealers, for example, are now as likely to operate with an internet connection to a trading site such as eBay as with a store front for tourists.

List pricing has also been invigorated. In the bricks-and-mortar world, changing prices meant new advertising, sending out catalogs, and retagging merchandize on shelves. However, online sellers can change product offerings and prices by updating a web page.

Moreover, pricing can be customized for each visitor. The prospect of making price changes so easily, together with the ability to make offers to individual customers, has stimulated interest in dynamic, real-time pricing as a turbocharged version of list pricing. Buyers are still presented with a take-it-or-leave-it offer, but these offers can be continually updated based on unsold stock, competitive prices, and customer characteristics. Carrie Johnson, an analyst at research company Forrester, has called this "personalized pricing."

Even the ancient practice of haggling has resurfaced on the web. A technology developed by Hagglezone.com provides automated bilateral bargaining. You even get to select a "haggler" – characters that include dialog, poses, mood, and biographical profiles.

One size fits all?

Of course, simply because a mechanism is feasible doesn't mean it is effective or desirable. Some mechanisms require more work of buyers. Take auctions. For some they're entertaining, for others a hassle. For example, imagine the appeal of having to participate in an auction for every item on your grocery list. Similarly, haggling with an electronic counterpart over a printer cartridge probably requires more work than most of us would tolerate. In contrast, list pricing offers the advantage that busy (or lazy) buyers can simply click on and buy a product at a price they like, but it may not always be the best price.

Another factor is time. Auctions are effective because they bring together competing buyers. This helps ferret out those willing to pay most. But this makes them undesirable if either buyers want to buy or sellers want to sell at different times. Similarly, demand aggregation mechanisms, like those of Priceline and Mercata, typically involve delays as prospective sellers are sought or a critical volume of buyers is reached. In contrast, with haggling and list pricing, buyers can close a deal on the spot.

Some mechanisms also create their own risks. For example, with airline tickets, Priceline buyers take their chances on important details such as airline, arrival time, and connections. As a

Given enough **discounting rope**, companies were as likely to hang themselves as not

result, risk-averse buyers are apt to offer low prices, or avoid buying.

Auctions impose different risks. A buyer uncertain about the value of an item may underbid or overbid. This might be fine if winners paid their average bid, but more likely, they win precisely when they overestimate an item's value. This produces the so-called winner's curse, in which successful bidders tend to regret their purchases. With haggling, the other party might know more about the market for printer cartridges than you and corner you into a high price.

Lessons from airline pricing

Where is the sense in all this innovation in pricing? What impact will it have? It's probably too early to say, but one can glean some insights by examining a similar "pricing revolution" that occurred 20 years ago in the US airline industry.

Beginning with the Airline Deregulation Act of 1978, the US Civil Aviation Board (CAB) loosened control of airline prices, which had been strictly regulated based on standardized costs and profitability targets.

The effect was like throwing jet fuel on the fire of airline competition. It resulted in a rash of pricing innovations: "peanuts fares," "super-saver fares," "simple saver fares," and "jackpot fares." Such fares offered consumers the chance to travel on routes at up to 70 percent less than the regulation-era coach fares.

Product competition increased as well. New, low-cost airlines entered the market. Established carriers were free to change schedules and service without CAB approval. Freedom had created unprecedented competition and innovation.

But even more dramatic than these visible changes were those taking place in airline management. Thanks to spectacular failures such as People Express, the industry quickly learned

that, given enough discounting "rope," companies were as likely to hang themselves as not. So discounting had to be controlled.

In response, the airlines imposed targetted restrictions such as advance-purchase requirements, Saturday-night stay requirements, and nonrefundability. These aimed to make purchasing a discount ticket less convenient (or even impossible) for the less price-sensitive – and very profitable – business segment.

But such crude controls alone were not sufficient. In parallel, airlines began scouring the data from their huge mainframe reservations systems to analyze patterns of usage by departure. Applied mathematicians, previously employed to handle the complexities of fleet planning and flight scheduling, were assigned to build statistical and optimization models to calculate the precise number of discount seats to sell on every departure. Teams of business analysts with revenue responsibility were then deployed to oversee the model recommendations and monitor booking activity in each market – like so many stock market traders hovered over their terminals.

After 20 years, these practices – referred to as "revenue management" – are now critical to running a successful airline. Most airlines have departments of business analysts and technical staff devoted to revenue management. An industry of consulting and software vendors has grown up to provide the necessary technical infrastructure. United Airlines even uses one of the few IBM "Big Blue" supercomputers in commercial application to run its revenue management models. Robert Crandall, the colorful former head of American Airlines, counts revenue management among the three most important innovations in his industry (the other two being frequent flyer programs and hub-and-spoke networks).

The seas ahead

What parallels to today's environment can be drawn from this experience? Like US airlines in 1978, today's internet businesses are facing intense competition from established companies and new entrants alike. Like travel agents in the

Airlines have business analysts and technical staff devoted to **revenue management**

1970s, lunchtime internet shoppers scour real-time pricing information from multiple sellers before buying. And like airlines in the post-deregulation era, internet retailers today are grappling with an array of pricing initiatives.

While the analogy is not perfect, the parallels suggest some important lessons for today's internet retailers. The first is the need for control. Just as airlines found that indiscriminate discounting was fatal, internet retailers are finding that indiscriminate use of auctions, aggregate buying, haggling, and dynamic pricing pose as many risks as rewards. In response, they will need strategies to segment consumers and target them with appropriate pricing, just as the airlines imposed well-crafted restrictions on discounted fares. For example, the very characteristics of these new mechanisms – the work required of consumers, the timing constraints and delays, the associated risk – can help form the basis for an effective segmentation strategy.

The second lesson is the need for sophisticated tactics to manage pricing. As consumers arm themselves with search engines, price comparison sites, and intelligent agents, so too must business arm itself with systems and practices to support real-time responsiveness to market forces. As with the airlines, this is likely to require significant effort to develop data sources, models, and systems to support the tactical responses required. And like airlines, internet retailers may need to reorganize themselves, putting pricing in the hands of analysts who have the information and authority to respond to market forces daily – or even hourly.

Indeed, these parallels are far from theoretical. Airlines have been in the vanguard of many of the new-economy pricing practices. Sales of airline tickets already generate the largest revenue and profits for Priceline and many airlines use these ticket auctions to sell distressed inventory on selected flights.

This is hardly surprising given the industry's history. On the infrastructure side, technology is converging as well: Manugistics, a supplier of supply chain management (SCM) software to the consumer products and durable goods industries, recently announced plans to acquire Talus Solutions, a revenue management consultancy and software vendor. Other major revenue management vendors, PROS Strategic Solutions and Sabre Decision Technologies, could soon find themselves in the sights of SCM competitors such as SAP, i2, and Oracle in response. If this convergence of infrastructure companies continues, airline pricing technology will rapidly spread to other industries.

Are most businesses prepared for these changes? Clearly not. For some, this will matter little. Businesses with stable markets, extremely strong brands, and simple product economics – luxury goods manufacturers, for example – may float atop the turbulent surf. It's even possible that many of these new pricing technologies will ultimately find a home only in fringe channels – to unload occasional excess inventory or outdated merchandize, for example. Even eBay has announced a startling "innovation": a new format where people can buy at fixed prices!

But complacency would be a mistake. Businesses in highly volatile markets, with strong competition and complex production constraints – for example, consumer electronics, computers, clothing, toys, cars, transportation, and energy, to name a few – will continue to face price volatility. And the new pricing mechanisms will increase it. Such companies risk being outmaneuvered should rivals arm themselves with sophisticated, high-tech pricing practices. If only as a hedge, prudent companies should develop the ability to respond.

Further reading

Columbia Business School's Deming Center, Revenue Process Optimization Initiative, sponsors research and seminars on revenue process optimization: www.demingcenter.com.

Cross, R.B. (1998) *Revenue Management: Hard-Core Tactics for Market Domination*, New York: Broadway Books.

Johnson, C. (2000) *Pricing Gets Personal*, Forrester.

McGill, J. and van Ryzin, G.J. (1999) "Revenue Management: Research Overview and Prospects," *Transportation Science*, 33, 233–56.

Nagle, T.T. and Holden, R.K. (1995) *The Strategy and Tactics of Pricing: A Guide to Profitable Decision Making*, New York: Prentice Hall.

Samuelson, P.A. (1976) *Economics*, New York: McGraw-Hill.

Marketers seeking
sense in sensibility

Bernd H. Schmitt is a professor of business at Columbia Business School and founder and executive director of the Center on Global Brand Leadership.

Forget the features, how do consumers experience your product? That's central to the idea of experiential marketing. **Bernd Schmitt** looks at the pioneers who are making it work.

Companies in many industries are turning away from their traditional marketing practices that focus purely on features and benefits. Experiential marketing focusses on enriching customers' sensory, emotional, and intellectual experiences when they use a product, shop for it, browse the web, or engage in any other marketing-related activity.

Consider Apple Computer. From 1996 to 1998, it grossly underperformed the US stock market. But now Apple is back, and its stock has outperformed the Standard & Poor's 500 over the past three years, despite a drop of 52 percent at the end of September 2000.

This turnaround was not achieved with better products in a functional sense. While other computer makers continued to compete on processing speed, memory, and hard disk space, Apple differentiated its products by introducing vibrant color into the world of beige and grey computers. Products such as the iMac, the iBook, and the G4 appeared in "indigo," "ruby," "sage," "graphite," and "snow." Rather than presenting a boring list of features and benefits, Apple commercials persuaded with 1960s music themes. Computer have become playful: "Collect all five," one advertisement proclaimed.

Or think about the success of Sephora perfume and cosmetics stores. LVMH, the luxury goods group that owns Sephora, has 300 stores in 180 cities. Sales growth is three times that of the average department store. Sephora has revamped the way people buy cosmetics through its unusual selling concept and experiential shops. Dramatic lighting and color schemes, museum-like displays of fragrance bottles, and many other nonfunctional elements make up the unique look and feel of Sephora stores.

In 2000, Singapore Airlines rolled out an upgrade of services, promising "more than ever, a great way to fly." The focus is not just on timely and convenient schedules. As the airline's 1999 annual report says, the company focusses on "all aspects of the travel experience" in all classes.

There are numerous examples of experiential marketing. Volkswagen's new Beetle has an unusual shape, a nostalgic advertising campaign – and a flower vase on the dashboard. W, a hotel chain in the US owned by Starwood Hotels, provides a contemporary atmosphere for its Generation-X target segment that is entirely different from the fast and functional style of most business hotels. Campaigns for chip maker Intel, management consultancy Accenture, and some industrial products concentrate on the experience of the product or service.

In these examples, functional features and attributes, rational persuasive appeals, or quality and price tell only part of the story. In each case, some nonfunctional component – the bright colors of Apple's computers, the shape of the Beetle, or the exotic atmosphere aboard Singapore Airlines – becomes the starting point for creating an entire experience for the customer that differentiates the product.

What has caused this shift? In most categories, features and benefits, price and quality are easy to match. Customers take them for granted. These are important for a good product, but they often do not differentiate the offer. What customers want are products, communications, and marketing campaigns that dazzle their senses, touch their hearts, and stimulate their minds. They need to be able to relate to these things and incorporate them into their lifestyles. In short, they want an experience.

Joseph Pine and James Gilmore of consultancy Strategic Horizons have proposed four stages in economic value: commodities, goods, services, and experiences. They argue: "As services, like goods before them, become commoditized … experiences have emerged as the next step in the progression of economic value. From now on, leading-edge companies – whether they sell to consumers or businesses – will find the next competitive battlefield lies in staging experiences."

Comparisons

Unfortunately, traditional marketing offers little guidance for capitalizing on the emerging experiential economy. It presents an engineering-

driven, rational, analytical view of customers, products, and competition. Its methods were developed in response to the industrial age and the early stages of the consumer society, not the information, branding, and communications revolution companies face today.

Traditional marketing has three main characteristics. First, it focusses on features and benefits. Marketers – and product designers – assume that customers weigh functional features in terms of their importance, trade off features by comparing them, and select the product with the highest overall utility.

Second, in traditional marketing, competition occurs primarily within narrowly defined product categories – the battleground of product and brand managers. In this world, McDonald's competes against Burger King and Wendy's (but not Pizza Hut or Starbucks). Similarly, Chanel fragrances compete against Dior fragrances (and not against those offered by a mass-market retailer like Gap).

Third, traditional marketing views customers as making rational decisions. Customers go through several rational problem-solving steps and presumably engage in a series of thoughtful and reasoned actions.

In contrast to this narrow focus on features and benefits, experiential marketing focusses on customer experiences. Experiences occur as a result of encountering, undergoing, or living through things. They provide sensory, emotional, cognitive, behavioral, and relational values that supplement functional values. Moreover, experiential marketers do not think in terms of narrowly defined categories. Instead, they consider the entire consumption situation.

Experiential marketers do not market shampoo, shaving cream, or blow dryers. They consider "grooming in the bathroom" and wonder what products fit this consumption situation, how to design such products to make them appealing, and how to package and communicate the

> # Traditional marketing offers little guidance for capitalizing on the **experiential economy**

consumption experience. Finally, for an experiential marketer, customers are driven by impulse and emotions as well as logic.

Traditional marketers and experiential marketers also differ in their methodological approaches. Traditional marketers use established methods of social science research such as surveys, perceptual maps, or conjoint analyses. These methods are precise and statistically reliable. Yet they often fail to provide true insight because they are administered in an artificial setting and are cumbersome for the respondent to complete.

In contrast, the methods and tools of an experiential marketer are diverse. Experiential marketing is not bound to one methodological ideology; it is eclectic.

Some methods may be analytical and quantitative (such as eye-movement studies for measuring the sensory impact of communications). Others may be more intuitive and qualitative (such as brain-focussing techniques used for understanding creative thinking). They may be verbal, taking the traditional format of a focus group, in-depth interview, or questionnaire. Or they may be visual, engaging customers to create a visual image of the brand. Methods and tools may be administered in an artificial environment or in the place of consumption, such as a bar.

Guiding experiences

Gathering information through such methods means customer experiences have become something that marketers can guide, shape, and manage. This raises some questions. First, what kinds of experiences can be provided for customers; and, second, how can these experiences actually be delivered?

To address the first question, many companies have found it useful to distinguish between different types of experience that result in five distinct approaches.

Sense marketing appeals through sight, sound, touch, taste, and smell. Sense marketing differentiates companies and their products through a unique sensory style and aesthetics.

Starbucks coffee stores provide a good example. Through a combination of organic and manufactured components, smooth and natural-tone surfaces, white-track lighting and distinctive visual merchandising for each coffee, Starbucks creates the atmosphere of a modern coffee house. As Howard Schultz, chief executive of Starbucks, put it: Starbucks is about "reinventing the coffee experience."

Feel marketing appeals to customers' inner feelings and emotions. It aims to create affective experiences that range from mildly positive

---

Box 1 Websites fail to deliver a satisfactory experience

Websites are important for experiential marketing. As an article in the *McKinsey Quarterly* said: "On the World-Wide Web, the brand is the experience and the experience is the brand." Many companies have their third- or fourth-generation websites, yet many still fail to deliver.

"Technologists often forget the general user. Technology is only as good as the user experience," Linus Torvalds, inventor of the Linux operating system, said at the 2000 Linux World conference.

According to research company Forrester, 75 percent of consumers visit a website again because of its content and 66 percent return because of ease of use. Yet some sites look like little more than corporate brochures. Moreover, they do not take advantage of the web's strength: the interlinked nature that invites browsing, interactivity, and customization.

Just as bad are sites that are full of animation and sound, but short on information value. They are slow and require plug-ins that many users do not have and may not bother to install.

Then there are the e-commerce sites that fail to deliver an efficient transaction – or the product. In a study of internet shopping, Accenture found that 64 percent of shoppers said the desired gift was out of stock and 40 percent said it was not delivered on time.

Companies need to understand how to deliver a better online experience – and how this experience can change as we move to online access via mobile phones and digital devices.

moods linked to a brand (for a noninvolving, nondurable grocery brand, for example) to strong emotions of joy and pride (for example, for a consumer durable, technology, or social marketing campaign). Hallmark provides a quintessential example of feel marketing: from its greeting cards to its 150 new Creations stores in the US to its revamped website.

For feel marketing to work, a close understanding is needed of what stimuli and situations trigger certain emotions, as well as the willingness of the consumer to engage in the process. As many companies have realized, it is difficult to create successful feel campaigns on an international scale because both the emotion-inducing stimuli and the willingness to empathize in a given situation differ from culture to culture.

Think marketing appeals to the intellect with the objective of creating cognitive, problem-solving experiences that engage customers creatively. Successful think marketing is surprising, intriguing, and at times even provocative (Benetton campaigns, for example). Think campaigns are commonly used for new-technology products. A good example is Microsoft's "Where do you want to go today?".

Act marketing enriches customers' lives either by targetting their bodily experiences, or by showing them alternative ways of doing things (for example, in business-to-business and industrial markets), alternative lifestyles and interactions. Changes in lifestyle and behavior are often motivational and inspirational in nature and work best by providing role models (such as movie stars or athletes). Nike's "Just do it" has become a classic of act marketing.

Relate marketing contains aspects of the four other experiential approaches. However, relate marketing expands beyond the individual's personal, private feelings, thus relating the individual to something outside his or her private state by including group appeal. The US motorcycle maker Harley-Davidson is clearly a relate brand. From the bikes themselves to Harley merchandise and tattoos on the bodies of enthusiasts (who cut across all social groups), consumers see Harley as a part of their identity.

Experiential appeals rarely result in only one type of experience. Many successful corporations combine the five experiences to broaden the experiential appeal. Ideally, marketers should strive to create integrated experiences that possess qualities from all five categories.

How can marketers provide such experiences? They can focus on "experience providers," which include communications, visual and verbal identity, product presence, co-branding, spatial environments, people, and websites.

Leading companies manage these experience providers in three ways:

- coherently (that is, in an integrated way);
- consistently over time;
- by paying attention to detail.

The marketing of Absolut vodka, the Swedish brand that is estimated to account for more than 10 percent of the profits from Seagram's spirits business, has met all three aspects.

Absolut campaigns are managed coherently. Whether you encounter the brand in an advertisement, on a website, or on the shelves of a bar, one element always stands out: the bottle shape. The campaign is also managed consistently over time: the same Absolut advertising concept (with the bottle shape in the center of the advertisement and the term Absolut underneath followed by one other word) has been running for almost 20 years. Finally, the campaign pays attention to the details; for example, running original and relevant local campaigns in each new city where the brand is marketed.

Experiential marketing not only provides a new set of concepts and techniques. It is, strictly speaking, not just an approach. It is also a new way of conducting business and, as such, works best when the whole company is oriented toward managing the customer experience.

What is needed to build the experience-oriented company is not a new organizational chart but a new spirit that pervades the entire culture. An organization that is serious about experiential marketing places an emphasis on creativity and innovation. It views the creativity and innovation displayed by employees as its intellectual capital, and considers the hiring and experiential growth of its employees as a key human resource requirement.

Such a culture is rare. For example, even if an organization is market oriented (that is, it pays attention to customer needs and competition, works cross-functionally, collects market information, disseminates the information, and acts on it), it is not necessarily experience oriented.

Many market-oriented organizations are focussed on functions and strategic planning. They lack the culture to promote creativity and innovation. Increasingly, organizations are recognizing the limitations of traditional culture and are cultivating a more entrepreneurial, innovative spirit. Even large corporations are trying to emulate the speed and energy of the "garage" start-up; an example is Hewlett Packard's initiative to reinvent the company from the ground up.

Conclusion

Traditional marketing has provided a valuable set of strategies, implementation tools, and methodologies for the industrial and early stages of the consumer age. Now we have entered the branding and information

age, it is necessary to shift attention from an approach based on features and benefits to one featuring customer experiences. Managers need to consider new concepts and, most of all, new approaches within the organization to capitalize on the opportunities offered by experiential marketing.

Further reading

Dayal, S., Landesberg, H., and Zeisser, M. (2000) "Building Digital Brands," *McKinsey Quarterly*, Spring.

Pine, J., II and Gilmore, J. (1998) "Welcome to the Experience Economy," *Harvard Business Review*, July/August.

Schmitt, B.H. (1999) *Experiential Marketing*, New York: Free Press.

Schultz, H. and Yang, D.J. (1997) *Put Your Heart Into It*, New York: Hyperion.

Retailing wakes up
late to global ambitions

Jonathan Reynolds is director of the Oxford Institute of Retail Management at Templeton College, University of Oxford, and a lecturer in marketing at the Saïd Business School.

For a mature industry, retailing is facing some testing times. **Jonathan Reynolds** finds there is work to do in expanding globally and through new channels.

The past two years have been uncertain ones for retailers, in supposedly stable and mature markets. It was not always thus. Marketers and economists used to regard retailers as mere ciphers in the distribution channel, smoothing the flow of goods and services between suppliers and consumers. In practice, of course, not only have retailers always been active agents in their own right within the supply chain, but they have also come to represent a significant proportion of a mature economy's gross domestic product and employment base. For example, retailing and wholesaling comprised some 34 percent of the European Union's enterprises and employed 18 percent of the EU's labor force in 1999.

Retailers are closer to the consumer than supplier companies. This has two implications. First, retailers are better placed to gather information on consumers and customers than organizations further back in the supply chain. Second, this data gathering puts them in a better position to communicate effectively with consumers and to develop winning strategies in their markets. Hence, many retail brands have flourished and in some cases eclipsed those of supplier companies, becoming icons in their own right.

Yet many of these certainties have been called into question. A retailer's position in the consumer front line has not always been an advantage: assumptions about consumers have often proved to be complacent or mistaken. Consumers have become increasingly smart and market conscious. The psychology of purchasing and consumption has been difficult to predict. As a result, many commentators now see a change in the way the sector is perceived by consumers.

In part, this has been a response to increasing consumer pressure, as customers have become better informed and more able to differentiate among stores. E-commerce has also added to price transparency and price deflation in sectors such as electrical goods.

Box 1 **Retail: past and future**

The role of the retailer is that of an intermediary. Retailers source goods designed to appeal to groups of consumers and that achieve a profitable trade-off between price and quality. To do this, the retailer has traditionally required suitable stores, buying power through expertise or scale, and an intimate knowledge of consumer needs. The role requires skills in operations management and attention to detail. Better retailers have cultivated brand positioning – over and above the branding of products sold – that adds to their appeal to consumers.

The arrival of new, international retail formats (a combination of physical store and market positioning) has increased the speed, efficiency, and need for responsiveness within many retail markets. Consider, for example, the growth of "fast fashion" operators in the UK such as Zara and H&M in relation to more traditional operators such as C&A and Marks & Spencer.

The notion of the internet as an efficient marketplace may be a myth for consumers, but it will have a role in creating new models of intermediation. The internet also allows retailers to find new channels to consumers, and so challenge shop-based retailers.

In the UK, the most successful retailers are now those that focus on value, rather than just price. Companies such as Matalan, H&M, Peacocks, Asda, Argos, and Iceland have tapped into consumers' concern with value for money. At the upper end of the market, specialty or variety stores such as Selfridges and Next have also been doing well, as have luxury retailers offering international brands. But those organizations that have traditionally served the mass middle market or who have failed to revive flagging store formats, such as Marks & Spencer, J. Sainsbury, BhS, and Arcadia, have seen their margins coming under considerable pressure. Those retailers stuck in the middle will be forced to reinvent themselves.

European retailers have global ambitions, judging by the merger of Carrefour and Promodès, which displaced Metro and emerged as Europe's largest retailer. US players such as Wal-Mart and Gap have also continued to impress with their determination to remain competitive, although they have met setbacks outside their home territory. At the same time, regulators have taken a closer interest in retailing, which has served to bridle global ambitions. A result of these trends, together with the once-feared growth of e-commerce (and the rhetoric surrounding it), is that transformational change can no longer be avoided.

Two growth strategies are especially attractive for retailers: globalization and the exploitation of electronic channels to market. Yet, paradoxically, these two opportunities are also among the biggest risks faced by even the largest retail businesses.

Global challenge

The 1990s proved to be the most active decade for retail globalization to date. Many of the biggest retailers, such as Carrefour-Promodès and Marks & Spencer, ambitiously expanded their operations across continents. Others, such as Wal-Mart, Ahold, Tesco, Kingfisher, and Delhaize, have become "retail engineers," transferring know-how and systems from country to country as well as store formats. Global markets are attractive to retailers. They generated $11,000bn in sales in 1999 and offer opportunities to escape small, low-growth or saturated domestic markets, while providing potential scale economies in buying, learning opportunities, and a balanced portfolio of stores capable of withstanding isolated economic cycles.

Retail companies have also performed well when compared with other sectors. In the annual *Fortune* global 500 survey, three groups of retailers are represented: food and drug stores, general merchandisers, and specialist retailers. Over a relatively short time, this group's representation among the world's largest companies has increased (though it fell back slightly in 1999). Between 1996 and 1998, the numbers of retailers in the top 500 increased from 46 to 56, their share

| TABLE 1 | Levels of globalization by industry |

Industry	FA/TA (%)*
Tobacco	78.38
Soap	55.66
Chemicals	50.07
Computers	40.85
Pharmaceuticals	40.21
Automotive	35.37
Electronics	34.68
Banking	28.58
Retailing	26.28
Aerospace	24.07

* FA/TA = foreign assets/total assets

Source: Templeton Global Performance Database 2000

of revenues from 7.8 to 9.9 percent, their share of profits from 4.6 to 6.5 percent, and their share of assets from 0.8 to 1.6 percent.

Yet this evidence should not blind us to the realization that retailers have come relatively late to globalization. Of the 27 different industry segments represented in the Templeton Global Performance Index 2000, retail ranks near the bottom (21st place) in terms of levels of globalization (*see* Table 1). Whereas the 20 retailers in the index have 26 percent of their assets in foreign markets, the average for all companies is 36 percent.

Further, regulators have given mixed messages to retailers aspiring to global status. Competition authorities face dilemmas in many regions. In Europe, there is a need to shore up the competitiveness of the whole region while defending the interests of suppliers and local consumers. In the US, one of the challenges for policy makers is to understand better the changing nature of retailing, where increasingly scrambled merchandising makes effective comparisons and calculations of market power using traditional techniques difficult. There has been a hardening stance toward market concentration by the Federal Trade Commission.

What empirical evidence do we have for the

success of particular types of global retail strategy? The work of Charles Waldman at Insead on international operations of retailing, offers several explanations for failure:

- inadequacy of the retail format for the host country's consumers;
- difficulties in providing economic support to overseas ventures;
- insufficient attention to integrated decision making.

Nevertheless, determined and thoughtful internationalists have achieved considerable success in carefully selected markets.

New channels

In 1998–99, during the rise of the dotcom companies, it was fashionable to bemoan the extent to which established retailers (often disparagingly called "legacy businesses") had tended to back away from investments in new channels to market. The window of opportunity, it was suggested, was closing. Research conducted by the Boston Consulting Group, for example, found that US companies concentrating solely on the business-to-consumer market already had a 20 percent share of that market in Europe. The researchers were particularly critical of legacy businesses, which had focussed on national markets for electronic commerce growth, while the new entrants had been able to develop increasingly pan-European businesses. As discussed above, most European and North American retail businesses are largely nationally oriented. The internet-based US retailers still tend to think of Europe as a single, undifferentiated market.

International retailers, however, are showing a more aggressive approach to e-business, which is linked to their concerns over growth through consolidation and has already begun to affect their business structures. Academic Karl Moore suggests that while there is a variety of organizational forms, most will tend to converge on an integrated model over the next two to three years as businesses overcome mismatches in culture and outlook. These structural changes have accompanied a number of strategic initiatives in relation to the supply chain.

Analysts and commentators have been in gen-

Australian retailer Coles Myer's attempt to consolidate its four years' experience with internet retailing has proved instructive. E.colesmyer was to be a division of the parent group, rather than as a stand-alone venture. This was despite lessons learned from the independent treatment of its computer retailer Harris Technology. Analysts were not impressed. They pointed to the tiny scale of Coles' online business compared with the parent; to the unwieldy nature of its existing general-purpose portal; and to the reactive nature of the strategy.

Around the same time, French retailer Carrefour announced an @carrefour internet arm. This would involve spending nearly $1bn on a free web portal extended to 15 countries by 2003, with broadband and mobile channels added eventually. Canal+ Technologies was announced as a partner. Investors were not impressed, and the share price fell by 11 percent.

It did not help that the announcement was made at the same time as profits growth for the overall business proved lower than expected. But the Carrefour plan was short on detail and came as commentators were casting doubts on the value of broad-based portal business models (rather than niche portals). In the Carrefour model, these portals (such as travel) would follow. Carrefour has since announced that it will scale down its ambitions.

---

eral more supportive of another feature of strategic realignment in respect of electronic channels to market: the business-to-business exchanges now emerging between retail buyers and suppliers.

B2B marketplaces have become increasingly fashionable vehicles for investment and development among retailers, even if some are not quite sure what they comprise. Single, industry-wide exchanges have achieved cost savings for participants: these have been so important that businesses normally in competition have been apparently happy to suspend traditional rivalry to achieve mutual benefit. Such exchanges particularly favor those sectors where concentration is high and there are relatively few buyers.

Retailing, where supply chain efficiencies are highly prized (particularly in the grocery sector), is nevertheless not as highly concentrated as other B2B markets and there is less logic for mutual buying pacts that suppress competitive instincts. Again, this is partly because until recently retailers were shielded from the pressures of globalization faced by other industries.

In short, established retailers are making efforts to become international multi-channel operators, partly by taking stakes in internet businesses. Such relationships are likely to proliferate as internet start-ups continue to stretch their resources. But are such moves overdue? Are they essentially defensive or offensive strategies? Investors' reactions suggest they will not be satisfied by rhetorical announcements.

It is also clear that purely structural or organizational announcements in the absence of justifiable strategic objectives and milestones are likely to be viewed as inadequate. Taking a strategic approach to e-commerce is proving as problematic for the world's biggest retailers as for anyone else.

Conclusion

Retailers have always faced disruptive influences on their businesses. There will be enormous pressures on their margins in the years ahead. The winners will be those that continue to impose a professional and ruthless discipline on supply chains and possess both the financial resources and willingness to innovate. They must be able to take risks in delivering what consumers will value in both domestic, new geographic, and new channel markets. There are likely to be precious few winners.

Further reading

Berman, B. and Evans, J.R. (1997) *Retail Management*, London: Prentice Hall.

Corstjens, M. and Corstjens, J. (1999) *Store Wars*, Chichester: Wiley.

Gestrin, M., Knight, R., and Rugman, A. (2000) *Templeton Global Performance Index*, Oxford: Templeton College.

The drivers that
make sales teams tick

Every salesforce wants to improve its results.
Andris Zoltners explains how productivity drivers can be used by managers to prioritize changes.

Andris Zoltners is a professor of marketing at the Kellogg Graduate School of Management, Northwestern University. He is a founder and managing director of ZS Associates, a sales and marketing consulting firm.

Any salesforce can improve its results by 5 to 10 percent. Good salesforces rework their strategy and sales process when confronted with circumstances such as customer consolidation, new product and market opportunities, technological innovation, and aggressive competitive moves. The best salesforces establish processes that enable them to fine-tune their performance even when the environment does not require it.

Salesforce issues

Major salesforce issues, challenges, and concerns fall into two categories: alpha and beta concerns. Alpha concerns require immediate attention. They might include: "Customers are consolidating and our selling model no longer works"; "Technology is changing our product line and the way we need to sell"; "Competitors are attacking our most profitable segments"; "How do we build a salesforce for our new product line?"

Beta concerns are daily, familiar productivity issues: "How do we retain our best people?"; "How do we increase the skills and capabilities of our salespeople?"; "How do we motivate salespeople?"; "How good is our salary and bonus plan?" Box 1 provides a more complete list of contemporary salesforce concerns.

Alpha concerns threaten the entire organization. The salesforce must evolve or else perish at the hands of a more nimble competitor. Beta concerns are more insidious. Nothing needs to be done immediately and managers are likely to say: "Let's do what we did last year – it worked then, didn't it?" However, Beta concerns should never be taken lightly. They are today's oversights that will become problems tomorrow.

How do salesforce executives go about addressing these challenges

Box 1a **Examples of alpha concerns**

CUSTOMERS

How does the salesforce react to:

- a buying process change?
- market consolidation?
- increased customer sophistication?
- global customers?
- a market segmenting into transactional and consultative buyers
- price pressure?

COMPETITION

How does the salesforce react to:

- global competitors?
- rapid commodification?
- larger competitors?
- global customers?
- more aggressive competitors?
- price pressure?

ENVIRONMENT

How does the salesforce react to:

- High-velocity changes?
- growing markets?
- stagnant markets?
- dying markets?
- deregulation?
- technology?
- internet?
- tight labor markets?

STRATEGIC SHIFTS

- Develop a start-up salesforce
- Merge existing salesforces
- Implement a new go-to-market strategy
- Launch new products successfully
- Enter new markets successfully
- Redesign the selling process

Box 1b **Examples of beta concerns**

PERFORMANCE

- Missing the sales, profit, market share goal
- Salespeople and/or managers lack motivation/lack critical competences/are plateaued/are leaving the company
- Salesforce effort allocation is inappropriate
- Salesforce is not sized correctly

- Compensation plan is not paying for performance
- Hiring the wrong people
- Salesforce lacks tools and data
- Sales and marketing are fighting again

and concerns? The answer is a decision framework. This is based on identifying a set of salesforce productivity drivers that reveal what changes must be made to address salesforce challenges and concerns (*see* Box 2).

Productivity drivers

Salesforce productivity drivers are made up of the decisions sales managers make and the

processes they use that directly affect all parts of the selling organization. They fall into four categories.

Sales research includes the results of data collection and analysis that enable the organization to understand better customer-buying behavior and to segment, prioritize and target specific markets.

The salesforce investment and organization category covers decisions on the appropriate size for the salesforce, the best organizational struc-

Box 2 Sales force productivity drivers

SALES RESEARCH
- Market understanding define needs
- Market segmentation
- Market assessment
- Market prioritization
- Market targetting

INVESTMENT & ORGANIZATION
- Size
- Structure
- Deployment such as product/market/activity
- Territory alignment
- Sales and marketing co-ordination

PEOPLE
- Selling competencies
- Recruiting

- Training
- Promotion
- Coaching
- Supervision
- Motivation
- Evaluation
- Progression

SALES SYSTEM
- Compensation
- Incentives
- Benefits
- Provide data such as lead generation and targetting
- Provide tools such as precision selling and automation
- Provide processes such as strategic selling, mentoring, partnering, consultative selling

---

ture, the best deployment of resources across products, markets, and activities, and the right alignment of sales territories. These are of most interest to senior managers.

The people category includes selection (recruitment and promotion), training and development, coaching and supervision, defining and assessing selling competencies, motivation programs, and personnel evaluation and progression systems.

Decisions about these factors strongly affect the interaction between the salesforce and the customer. The person the customer sees is the result of hiring, training, and the "success" atmosphere that the sales manager creates and fosters. These decisions have the greatest impact on sales success.

The sales systems category includes management decisions that directly affect the efficiency, effectiveness, and job satisfaction of salespeople and hence affect customers indirectly. Compensation, incentives, benefits, salesforce data, tools, and other productivity enhancement programs are included.

How can these productivity drivers help managers resolve the problems of a salesforce? A large global paper and packaging company provides a good illustration. The retention of its best salespeople was a major concern, because personnel turnover rates in some of the divisions were as high as 40 percent a year.

Studying the salesforce productivity drivers gave managers several hypotheses:

- The company was hiring people with the wrong profile.
- Training was not appropriate.
- Salespeople were not bonding with the company because the sales manager was not providing sufficient coaching and recognition.
- The compensation program was underpaying compared with the marketplace.
- Sales territories were not aligned to provide equal opportunity for everyone.
- The company did not provide the tools to reduce tedious administrative work and identify high-opportunity prospects.

Box 3 **Best-practice insights**

RECRUITMENT

- Interviewing alone will not reveal the best candidates; it is wise to observe the behaviour the candidate will need to succeed in the job
- Success profiles should be developed to guide the search
- Success profiles can differ by product, market and over time
- Assign the best people to recruiting

TRAINING

- Rapid prototyping works
- Individual training has advantages over group training
- Action learning is more effective than passive learning
- Training modules should be structured around real business problems
- The internet creates opportunities for delivering information-based training

Any one or all of these could help solve the turnover problem.

In another example, a pharmaceutical company was faced with launching several new products within a year. The company also wanted to protect its strong existing products. It turned to the salesforce productivity drivers to establish options for developing its salesforce strategy.

Results suggested several options for addressing the dual problems. The company could increase its salesforce size to support its dual objectives. It could restructure parts of its salesforce to create one or more specialty teams to gain access to "hard-to-see" physicians. It could identify the early adopters and influencers to help salespeople deploy their time in the most effective way during the launch. It could develop an incentive program to create both excitement for the new products and a commitment to attaining established sales goals for the existing product portfolio.

Challenges and concerns arise regularly for every salesforce. Returning to the categories of alpha and beta concerns, different change processes should be used to tackle each kind of concern. The immediacy of alpha issues often requires surgery, while persistent beta issues call for a good exercise routine.

The alpha change process

The alpha change process contains three steps.

Step 1: Identify the drivers

Study the salesforce productivity drivers to determine which are the salient drivers. The most pressing need for the pharmaceutical company in the above example is to resize and restructure its salesforce. It will lose millions if the launches are not successful or if it fails to support the existing brands.

Step 2: Identify best practices

Investigate best practices and best processes for addressing the salesforce productivity drivers identified in Step 1. There are various ways of determining best practices. The salesforce represents a large investment for many companies. Consequently, many companies try to determine the most effective way to manage their salesforces and they frequently share their successes with noncompeting companies in other industries. Benchmarking current practices across industries is one method for identifying best practices.

Consulting firms are another source for best-practice insights. Some conduct hundreds of salesforce studies every year covering a wide range of issues, and so have a good grasp of the most effective practices. Academic studies that integrate theory with practice can also throw light on the best practices of salesforces.

Companies that borrow from all three sources usually have a good picture of the best practices for each of their critical salesforce productivity drivers. Box 3 provides several best-practice

FIGURE 1   The competency / impact mix

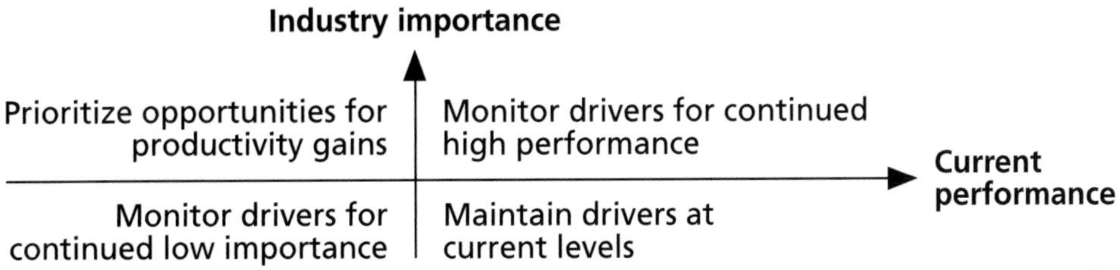

Industry importance

Prioritize opportunities for productivity gains	Monitor drivers for continued high performance
Monitor drivers for continued low importance	Maintain drivers at current levels

Current performance

insights for two of the drivers, recruitment and training.

Step 3: Implementation

Decide on the salesforce driver changes and implement them quickly – successful salesforces are quick salesforces.

Companies need to be careful not simply to select those drivers that pose no threat. The most commonly selected drivers are training and compensation. They are safe. More training or a better bonus plan threaten no one. More often than not, other productivity drivers need to be addressed before considering training and compensation. How easily does a selling organization come to the realization that its main problem is an ineffective first-line sales management team?

The beta change process

It can be difficult to generate enthusiasm for the pursuit of greater productivity when a company is consistently achieving its sales targets. Yet improving even some productivity drivers can increase sales by 5 to 10 percent. For many companies, the impact will be significantly greater.

The beta change process is a productivity hunt. It has three steps.

Step 1: Assess and prioritize

Beta concerns must first be diagnosed, measured, and prioritized. The salesforce productivity drivers need to be evaluated periodically. Two measures of these productivity drivers have proven to be useful: competency and impact. First, each decision or process is evaluated in terms of how good or how competent the selling organization is at that decision or process.

Second, each decision or process is evaluated in terms of the impact the decision or process has on the selling organization's ability to succeed.

An assessment and prioritization grid can be developed, with performance and importance rated on the axes from high to low. Each driver should be analyzed with regard to its position on the grid (*see* Figure 1). This provides a valuable tool to assess the status of the salesforce productivity drivers:

- Drivers in the "low importance, high performance" quadrant can be maintained at current levels for the time being.

- Drivers in the "high importance, high performance" quadrant need to be monitored closely to ensure their performance stays high.

- Those that fall in the "low importance, low performance" category can be monitored in case the importance of the driver increases over time.

- Top priority goes to productivity drivers with low performance and high importance for salesforce success. These areas present the greatest opportunity for productivity gains.

The matrix requires measurement of both the impact and the current competency of relevant salesforce productivity drivers. Methods for this type of measurement have been scrutinized and continue to improve as more selling organizations adopt this approach.

Both quantitative and qualitative measures have been used to assess competency and impact. There are many quantitative measures, but territory-level analysis has proven to be useful for many of the sales productivity drivers:

- If salespeople do not allocate their time effectively, they need to improve their targetting.

- If high performers are underpaid and low performers are overpaid, the compensation scheme will need to be revisited.
- If some sales territories have significant workload and others do not have enough work to keep the salesperson busy, the sales territories need rebalancing.

Consider the example of the distribution of salespeople for a cosmetics company. The workload, expressed in hours of face-to-face time required to cover all of the accounts in each territory, was calculated for each person. The results showed that the workload ranged from 375 to 1,980 hours across the total salesforce of 205 people. The ideal workload had already been estimated at 1,000 hours a year for each salesperson. Allowing a 15 percent variation either way, anyone having more than 1,150 hours of workload could not adequately cover all accounts in the territory. Anyone with fewer than 850 hours of workload had too little to do.

The company was not using its resources appropriately, because 65 territories were too large and 55 were too small. This misalignment would cost the company millions each year.

Step 2: Action plan

Improvements in the salesforce productivity drivers fall into two categories: "quick win" opportunities and long-term initiatives. Realigning the sales territories for the cosmetics company above is an example of a "quick-win" initiative. Longer-term initiatives might include developing a retention plan for the paper and packaging company that would include recruiting, sales manager selection, a sales-assistant program to relieve the administrative burden, and an enhanced recognition program. Any action plan must balance short-term wins and long-term initiatives. The plan needs a statement of objectives, specific action items, anticipated results, and a timeline.

Step 3: Implement and track

The action plan needs to be implemented and the results tracked. This year's results serve as input into next year's assessment and salesforce driver prioritization.

Current practice

Companies have used the alpha process for years. It is a necessary process for dealing with urgent needs. Implementation of the beta process is more limited but increasing. A needs assessment and prioritization every two years seem most appropriate.

Conclusion

Salesforces constantly face weighty issues and challenges. Some of these threaten the ability to compete. Others are opportunistic and challenge competitive advantage well into the future.

The salesforce productivity drivers provide a company with a list of decisions and processes that address the most pressing concerns of its salespeople. Salesforce executives can look to the list of drivers to discern which ones can remedy their immediate concerns.

Companies seeking constant and consistent improvement in their sales performance can prioritize those drivers that will be most effective. Every salesforce has an opportunity to increase its sales by performing better on one or more of these criteria.

Further reading

Churchill, G.A., Ford, N.M., and Walker, O.C. (eds) (1999) *Sales Force Management*, New York: Irwin/McGraw-Hill.

Rackham, N. and DeVincentis, J.R. (1998) *Rethinking the Sales Force*, New York: McGraw-Hill.

Zoltners, A., Sinha, P., and Zoltners, G. (2001) *The Complete Guide to Accelerating Sales Force Performance*, New York: Amacom.

The new language
of emerging markets

Niraj Dawar is associate professor of marketing and Walter A. Thompson Faculty Fellow at the Richard Ivey School of Business, University of Western Ontario, Canada.

Amitava Chattopadhyay is the L'Oréal Chaired Professor of Marketing, Innovation and Creativity at Insead.

Billions of customers in China and India are a tempting prospect for multinationals, but reaching them can be difficult. **Niraj Dawar** and **Amitava Chattopadhyay** discuss why.

Lured by the prospect of a billion breakfast eaters, Kellogg, the US cereals giant, ventured into India in the mid-1990s. Three years later, sales stood at an unimpressive $10m. Indian consumers were not sold on breakfast cereals. Most consumers either prepared breakfast every morning or grabbed some biscuits with tea at a local roadside stall. Advertising positions common in the west, such as the convenience of breakfast cereals, did not resonate with the mass market in India. People who did find the convenience appealing were unable to afford the price.

These results led the company to re-examine its approach. In 1999, Kellogg changed its marketing by introducing breakfast biscuits under the Chocos brand. At Rs5 ($0.10) for a 50g pack and with extensive distribution that includes roadside tea stalls, they are targetted at the mass market and expected to sell in large volumes.

Like Kellogg, many multinationals have rushed into emerging markets agog at the billions of consumers liberated from planned economies and protectionist barriers. But there is a growing realization that these consumers have not reciprocated the multinationals' embrace. Local competitors are stronger than expected and competition for the top tier of the market is fierce as multinationals compete for the same pie.

Local managers of global companies now realize that the 3 to 5 percent of consumers in emerging markets who have global preferences and purchasing power no longer suffice as the target market. Instead, they must delve deeper into the local consumer base to deliver on the promise of tapping into billion-consumer markets.

Most multinationals have resisted targetting the local consumer. They have argued that the mass market in a single emerging economy is not large enough to justify localization. Further, multinational managers rationalize, emerging market consumers are becoming more like their developed counterparts. Thus, the multinational is better off offering global products and waiting for consumers to evolve toward these.

These are powerful arguments. However, that emerging markets are considered small is a self-fulfilling prophecy. Products transplanted from affluent markets only appeal to an elite, which is no more than 5 percent of the market. Delving into the population base to establish mass-market positions creates the economies of scale necessary to justify localization. And localization along factors common across emerging markets allows costs to be spread over much larger volumes. Emerging market veterans such as Unilever and Colgate Palmolive have amply demonstrated the viability of mass markets in emerging economies, as well as the benefits of rapidly transferring knowledge gained in one emerging market to others.

The second argument, that emerging market consumers are becoming more like their affluent market counterparts, is true if one focusses on the income gap. But the rate of change is not as rapid as some contend. In most emerging markets, the mass market will remain poor well beyond the planning horizons of most multinationals. Further, even as they grow more affluent, it is far from certain that Chinese and Indian consumers' preferences will converge with those of Europeans or Americans.

Standard marketing strategies must be questioned in emerging markets, but lessons can be drawn from companies that have designed programs from the ground up. These can be analyzed using some of the pillars of marketing: segmentation, product, price, distribution, and communication.

Segmentation

Multinationals bring to emerging markets not just their products, technology, and skills, but also, implicitly, their understanding of market structures from developed-country contexts. This knowledge base often encourages assumptions that are at odds with reality in emerging markets. At the root of the mismatch are assumptions about segmentation. Fine-grained segmentation only works if the costs of segmentation are low and the returns are high. Take the example of soap. In developed markets, hundreds of brands offer finely differentiated benefits on dimensions such as fragrance, freshness, skin type, naturalness, softness, gentleness, and lather.

Such segmentation is expensive in terms of product development, branding, and distribution costs. These costs are justified if consumers are able and willing to pay for specialized products. But the mass market in emerging economies is unable to afford this. Segments are far coarser. In Indonesia, 88 percent of the market is classified as "regular" soap, with another 11 percent accounted for by deodorant soap, and the remaining 1 percent moisturising soap. The average price of soap in Indonesia is less than a third of that in the US.

Low wages mean that time has a low opportunity cost. Thus, labor-saving benefits, which are fundamental to ready-to-eat foods, new formats for washing powder, shampoo–conditioner combinations, and household appliances, are unlikely to sell well in undeveloped markets.

While the opportunity cost of time is low for most consumers, it is high for a small but significant segment. For this small segment, products that save labor might be attractive. However, segmenting the market by cost of time is not useful, because time can be bought. In other words, richer consumers substitute others' time for their own, and the market for time savings is served through inexpensive services rather than products. Premium-priced, non-stick cookware from DuPont has little appeal if consumers who can afford it rely on hired help for cooking and cleaning. In China, DuPont has struggled to raise market share beyond 2 percent.

This does not mean the products are not viable, but rather that they need to be positioned differently. For example, fast food is popular not because it is fast, but because it is trendy. Similarly, washing machines may not have much appeal as labor-saving devices when potential consumers are used to hiring people to do laundry by hand. But the machines can be positioned as reliable (hired help is often not), or on performance. These benefits complement rather than compete with labor. Sometimes consumers will both buy a washing machine and hire someone to work it.

Product

Some local and international companies have demonstrated that well-targetted, indigenously developed, and locally produced products can yield profits in mass markets. One lesson is that practices in developed markets, such as rapid product development, continuous product innovation, and accelerated obsolescence, do not work well in emerging markets.

Here, consumers dislike products that evolve too rapidly, making their recent purchases obsolete. Instead, consumers need basic, functional, long-lasting products. Volkswagen's Beetle was the largest-selling car in Brazil long after it had been phased out in affluent markets and despite assaults by car makers with newer models. It was known to be a dependable workhorse with readily available and inexpensive spare parts.

Low levels of income also mean that the cost of time for the consumer is low and, therefore, a company's cost of creating some of the benefits of a product is higher than their value to consumers. Since consumers can substitute their time for the benefit at a lower opportunity cost, engaging consumers' energy as a substitute for including benefits can allow companies to market a product at a price affordable to the mass market. For example, in its early efforts in emerging markets Whirlpool made little headway with highly priced, automatic washing machines. Only after it introduced cheaper twin-tub machines that used consumers' labor did its sales take off. Interestingly, Whirlpool had to acquire the "obsolete" technology from Korea.

Price

Prices need to be set in the context of local consumers' purchasing power, rather than in relation to international standards. Purchasing power parity (PPP) exchange rates estimate the value of a currency in terms of the basket of goods that it buys (compared with the cost of a similar basket in a reference country and currency) rather than in terms of the existing market exchange rates. By this measure, most emerging market currencies are severely undervalued relative to developed country currencies, meaning they buy more than one would expect from the exchange rate.

International companies are attracted to many emerging markets precisely because of the size of the market in PPP terms. One company found that in China, for example, the number of consumers in the $10,000 to $40,000 income range is less than 3 million at market exchange rates, but over 80 million at PPP rates. But companies often fail to recognize that this market is only accessible if product prices are established relative to local purchasing power, rather than by converting international prices at market exchange rates.

In other words, companies need to work back from PPP numbers when pricing products. Using exchange rates translates into overpriced products, making them accessible only to the wealthiest consumers. For example, the PPP of the renminbi in China is around 4 to the US dollar, while the market exchange rate is more than RMB8 to the dollar. A product that sells in the US for $10 will be priced using the market exchange rate at RMB80. In reverse PPP terms, this is the equivalent of pricing the product at $20. Clearly, expectations of large PPP-based markets are incompatible with prices based on exchange rates.

Thus, strategies that favor thin margins and large volumes tend to succeed. Pricing needs to dominate marketing, and drive product, packaging, distribution, and communication decisions. Unilever's Lifebuoy soap, popular in Africa, India, and Indonesia, is priced low and made using inexpensive local ingredients and packaging. By volume, Lifebuoy is the world's largest-selling brand of soap.

Multinationals, stuck with international pricing strategies, often resort to price promotions to capture volumes. Such promotions can yield dramatic, if temporary, sales increases. These large-volume increases reveal a potentially sizeable market that remains untapped, just below the actual price points. To generate sustainable volume sales, a permanent product entry at the lower price is required. Thus, Gallo, the Italian rice and pasta maker, introduced the Nobleza Gaucha brand in Argentina to capture volumes with razor-thin margins, while maintaining the price premium of its flagship Gallo brand.

Failure to capture volume segments leaves an opportunity for local companies, as Unilever discovered in the Indian detergent market. Nirma, an initially ignored local brand, went on to topple Unilever's Surf from its dominant position.

Distribution

In contrast to concentrated retailers and distribution in developed markets, the trade in emerging markets is fragmented. While chains such as Ahold, Carrefour, Nanz, Metro, and Wal-Mart operate in many emerging markets, they have yet to develop a retail format with mass appeal. Overall, chain stores account for less than 3 percent by value of retail markets in China and India.

Multinationals sometimes rely on these chains as their primary channel, but it is unlikely that chains will provide access to mass markets. High population density, small homes with little space for storage, lack of refrigeration, and low car ownership mean consumers buy daily and locally. As a result, retail outlet density is very high. These conditions prevent retail formats of developed countries from delivering products economically. Therefore, foreign retailers cannot be the pillar of mass-market distribution.

At the same time, using small, independent stores poses a challenge to international companies because they lack the expertise to deal with a fragmented trade. It is estimated that there are 9 million small, independently owned grocery shops in China, which have limited working capital and typically occupy fewer than 300 square feet. To access even the first tier of these outlets, and to establish a brand presence, companies need large, dedicated salesforces and a lot of capital.

Beyond the first tier of retail outlets, many companies use multiple levels of wholesalers and distributors to capture shelf space one store at a time. This many-layered distribution channel puts a large distance between mass markets (especially rural markets) and manufacturers, impeding learning and marketing adaptation. Notwithstanding the challenges, some international companies have successfully developed distribution systems. Unilever's network in India, which provides it with a formidable barrier to entry, serves 800,000 retail outlets directly and relies on wholesalers and distributors to reach another 3.5 million.

Despite being fragmented, shops have considerable power. Store formats do not allow consumers to browse. Typically, the consumer deals directly with the shopkeeper (often the owner), whose advice carries weight. The owner's relationship with consumers is based on an understanding of their buying habits and is often cemented when the retailer extends credit. These relationships give trade outlets tremendous clout in recommending brands, making trade marketing an essential element of any manufacturer's program.

Building relationships with a fragmented trade requires an understanding of their interests. For example, it is counterproductive to push inventory on them because most have little working capital. Rather, successful manufacturers develop new revenue activities for the retailer.

United Phosphorous (UPL), an Indian crop protection company, is a good example. It realized that farmers were not using pesticide, or were applying it inappropriately due to a lack of equipment. The cost of pumps and dispensers (up to $3,000) placed it out of reach of small farmers and rural retailers. So, UPL arranged for bank loans for rural retailers to buy the equipment and demonstrated to these retailers the revenue possibilities from renting the equipment to farmers. The result was an added revenue stream for retailers and additional sales of pesticides for UPL.

Communication

Mass media, the mainstay of communication in developed markets, are less effective in emerging markets. Large populations in rural areas are dispersed across vast distances in small, isolated groups, with limited access to broadcast media. There may be many languages and varying levels of illiteracy. To overcome these challenges, Unilever pioneered video vans. These vans tour villages screening films in the local language, interspersed with advertising for Unilever prod-

In Asia, the cost per customer of **door-to-door sales** was lower than inserts in magazines

ucts. The company also demonstrates products, because instructions on the pack may not be read by consumers who are either illiterate or do not understand the dialect.

Reliance on mass media is also ineffective because of shopping patterns. Consumers in emerging markets shop daily, which gives them 365 chances a year to switch brands. Attempting to encourage repeat purchase by reaching buyers during the short purchase cycle, by showing point-of-sale advertising, and by marketing heavily to retailers, is indispensable. This requires significant changes in western-style campaigns. For example, outdoor advertising accounts for 7 percent of media expenditure in India, but only 0.8 percent in the US.

Last, but not least, reliance on mass media in developed markets is based on television and press advertising, being less expensive than face-to-face contact. But in emerging markets, the face-to-face method has always been more economical. When Citibank launched its credit card in Asia, it found that the cost per customer of door-to-door sales was lower than magazine inserts, direct mail, and application forms placed on sales counters. Personal selling also delivers more customized and interactive messages. This is important at an early stage in a product's lifecycle and leads to better conversion rates than, say, television advertising.

Conclusion

Consumers in emerging economies will remain an elusive target unless multinationals develop value propositions that appeal to the mass market. These companies should understand that mass markets in emerging countries are unlike markets they have traditionally served. Behavior is molded by low incomes. Consumers are unlikely to respond to marketing transplanted from developed markets.

Instead, marketing needs to be built locally. Yet such a strategy challenges marketing practices and the tensions that arise can be painful. Perhaps one way of justifying the pain is to abandon country-focussed strategies and consider an emerging market strategy. This approach highlights the common features of emerging markets and their real size. Thus it enables accurate assessment of the costs and benefits of localization.

Further reading

Dawar, N. and Frost, T. (1999) "Competing with Giants: Survival Strategies for Emerging Market Companies," *Harvard Business Review*, March–April, 119–29.

Dawar, N. and Ramachandran, J. (1999) "Defending Turf: Marketing Strategies for Emerging Market Companies," in R. Batra (ed.), *Marketing Issues in Transitional Economies*, Dordrecht: Kluwer Academic Publishers, 225–34.

Prahalad C.K. and Lieberthal, K. (1998) "The End of Corporate Imperialism," *Harvard Business Review*, July–August, 68–79.

Finance and **accounting**

9

Contents

Introduction to Part 9

Finance lies at the heart of business, since it is concerned with the value of the business and its operations. In universities and business schools it is a recognized academic discipline and its practitioners have developed complex theories to explain its workings, backed by empirical evidence. This part presents the principles of finance and accounting. Authors explain the basic structure of the annual report, and assess the various means of valuing a company? What is the nature of cost management? What can the market reveal about a company? Should internet or high-tech companies be treated differently when managers are valuing them? Finally, writers examine the options for executive compensation, and describe the technical requirements of the accounts department in a fast-growing company.

How to read
those annual reports

Accounting principles are the same the world over, but financial reports can still be a challenge. **Peter Knutson** goes back to basics to take the struggle out of the numbers.

Peter H. Knutson is associate professor emeritus of accounting at the Wharton School, University of Pennsylvania, and a Sloan fellow in the Wharton Financial Institutions Center.

The annual report of your company has arrived with a thud. Now, what do you do with it? You have avoided learning accounting and the little they did teach you has long been forgotten. Yet the annual report contains financial statements and you need to find out what they say. This article addresses the needs of both those who answer to this description and others who wish to refresh their knowledge of accounting at a basic level.

The equation

The basic accounting equation is:

$$\text{Assets} = \text{Liabilities} + \text{Owners' equity}$$

The terminology may vary around the world, but the notion is constant. That is, the economic resources (assets) of an enterprise are equal to the claims of those who provide the resources: creditors (liabilities) and owners (owners' equities). To understand accounting, think of:

$$A = L + OE$$

In its basic form, accounting is the process of measuring and reporting an enterprise's assets and liabilities, owners' equity being the difference between the two.

Defining assets

Assets are defined as an enterprise's economic resources. However, in accounting, there are restraints on reporting their value. A business can report an asset only when it exists. That is the case where the enterprise:

- expects the asset to cause its future net cash flows to increase;
- has already done what is needed to be entitled to benefit from the asset;
- has the ability to obtain benefits and keep others from accessing them.

That definition means the valuation of assets is done in retrospect. For example, a company that signs a contract to build a dam will be better off in an economic sense when the contract is signed. However, the assets arising under that contract will be recognized in the financial statements only when the work is done.

Most assets are recorded at their purchase price until events prove the value has changed. Enhancements of value are validated by exchanges between the company and outsiders. Exchanges virtually always involve changing the form of an asset. For example, at the time of a sale, stocks (inventories) are converted into debtors (receivables). Decreases in value are recorded when they occur. Because decreases frequently occur without a transaction with an outsider, recording and reporting them can be subjective.

Defining liabilities and equity

Liabilities are present obligations either to convey assets, or to render services to someone in the future as a result of past transactions. Therefore, the first step in liability measurement is to test for the existence of liabilities.

Most liabilities are payable in cash. They are reported at those amounts, and reduced to their present value by discounting amounts due more than one year in the future. Usually, the discount rate is the one in effect when the liability was incurred. The value of many liabilities can only be estimated. For example, consider the liabilities of an insurance company for claims on any losses that have not yet been reported.

Liabilities that will be satisfied by providing services can be easy to measure. Examples include royalties, rents, subscriptions, ticket sales, and so on, received in advance. The price of these has been established and either they have been performed or they have not – hence, the liability exists only for unperformed services. In contrast, measuring the cost of other obligations,

Assets arising **under a contract** are recognized in the financial statements only when the work is done

such as warranties or life-long healthcare for retired employees, can be very difficult. They are reported as estimates, which is better than nothing at all.

Owners' equity poses no problems. It is the excess of assets over liabilities. Therefore, it depends on how assets and liabilities are measured.

Financial reports

A financial report includes three major financial statements plus additional disclosures necessary for completeness. These disclosures are often called "footnotes," but are more accurately called "notes to the financial statements." The three major financial statements are:

- Balance sheet, sometimes called the "statement of financial position."
- Income statement, sometimes called the "profit and loss statement" or the "earnings statement."
- Statement of cash flows.

Also, although it is not considered a major statement, most corporate financial reports include a statement of changes in shareholders' equity.

The balance sheet

The balance sheet is a listing of, on one side, all the enterprise's assets. The other side is an organized listing of liabilities, plus the owners' equity. It forms the basic accounting equation for an enterprise, hence its name.

Assets are presented on the balance sheet in order of liquidity. The first category is current assets, which comprises cash and assets that will be turned into cash (such as stocks and debtors) within one year or the current operating cycle, if greater. The current operating cycle is the period that it takes for cash to be converted into stocks (inventory), into debtors (accounts receivable), and back into cash again. Other categories include:

- property, plant, and equipment: the long-term tangible assets;
- investments: holdings of financial instruments and other long-term assets being held for purposes other than productive activities;
- intangible assets: patents, copyrights, leasehold improvements, and others, including goodwill.

There may also be a category called other assets, for assets that managers are unable or unwilling to categorize.

Liabilities are classified between current liabilities, those payable within the period used to define current assets, and all other liabilities, which are called noncurrent liabilities. Noncurrent liabilities are frequently subclassified as long-term debt (the amounts owing in the form of long-term financial instruments such as bonds and mortgages) and other noncurrent liabilities.

For corporate enterprises, shareholders' equity is classified as paid-in capital, the amounts received as investments by the owners; retained earnings, the cumulative amount of earnings reinvested in the company; and treasury stock, a deduction for the cumulative amount paid by the company to buy back its shares. Given the complexity of the transactions, the owners' equity section of a balance sheet may be complicated and confusing.

Income statement and cash flows

These two statements are dynamic, in contrast to the static nature of the balance sheet. The balance sheet tells us where we are. The income statement and statement of cash flows say how we arrived there. They cover the period between two balance sheets. (The accounting period is one year, but publicly owned companies report more frequently.) The relative value of these two statements is often debated, but a company must be both profitable and liquid to survive.

The income statement lists first the revenues of the enterprise. Revenues are the gross increase in company value from selling goods and services to customers. Expenses are deducted from revenues to obtain the profit or income of the enterprise. They make up the gross decrease in company value from the production and delivery of goods and services to customers. Expenses are the costs incurred to earn the revenues.

The concept of business income was defined by the economist J.R. Hicks as the amount a company could distribute to its owners without decreasing its capital. That definition means that every change in asset or liability valuation, other than transactions with the owners, affects the amount of periodic income.

In the US, certain of those changes are not reported on the income statement, but are held in owners' equity, waiting to appear on the income statements of one or more later periods. However, US corporations are required to include them in a supplementary income number called comprehensive income. In the UK, the profit and loss (income) statement includes only operating items, but is supplemented by the statement of total recognized gains and losses (STRGL), known affectionately as "the struggle."

The statement of cash flows presents gross cash flows, both positive and negative, classified as operating cash flows; investing cash flows; and financing cash flows. Operating flows are the cash flows relating to income statement items: collections from customers, payments to suppliers, employees, utilities, and so on. The format in which operating cash flows are presented usually does not show the flows directly. Instead, the presentation usually starts with the net income number, followed by a list of the items that caused income to be different from cash flow from operations (increases in debtors and stocks, depreciation, changes in accrued liabilities, and so on). That presentation ends with the net cash flow from operating activities.

Investing cash flows are the payments and receipts from buying property, plant, and equipment; disposing of plant assets; buying other businesses; selling subsidiaries; and buying and selling financial instruments for investment.

Financing cash flows comprise the transactions by which the enterprise raises capital. These include borrowing; debt repayments (although interest paid is an operating cash flow); proceeds from issuing share capital (capital stock); dividend payments; and amounts paid to buy back shares.

Using statements

The next article points out the pitfalls of using accounting numbers to measure rates of return. In short, limitations arise because financial statements focus on the past and do not record values that exist but have not been validated by a transaction. In addition, many costs that add value are recorded as expenses rather than as assets, because it is too difficult to extract the value-adding part and in many cases the value created has little direct relation to the cost incurred.

Take, for example, research by a drug company. Much is spent on projects that fail, whereas successful products may have value many times the cost of development. Therefore, research and development costs are treated as expenses in the period they are incurred as an expediency. Many other costs receive similar treatment.

Despite the limitations of accounting numbers, much good use can be made of them. For example, within an enterprise, comparisons can be made over time, and period-by-period changes will divulge information because each period's numbers will have been prepared in a comparable way. Comparisons between enterprises require greater care, but are useful when companies within a sector use comparable accounting. In the absence of comparable accounting, analysts make adjustments, using information in the financial statement notes, to enhance comparability. Period-by-period comparisons are called time-series analyzes. Comparisons across different enterprises are called cross-sectional analyzes.

Financial statement analysis employs many methods, including:

- common-size statements;
- percentage-change analysis;
- financial ratio analysis.

A common-size balance sheet is one where each asset, liability, and owners' equity account is presented as a percentage of total assets. It allows the analyst to compare financial structures of different companies, or of a single company over time, as if they were of equal size. It permits a focus on the array of assets deployed

by each company in each period and the various financing sources for those assets. Its strength is in enabling comparisons.

A common-size income statement sets total revenues or sales equal to 100 percent and expresses each of the remaining income statement lines as a percentage of revenues (sales). As with the balance sheet, it also facilitates cross-sectional and time-series analysis by holding size constant and focussing on proportions.

Percentage change is strictly a time-series analysis, but also can be applied cross-sectionally. It first computes the change in a balance sheet or income statement item by deducting the previous period amount from the current amount. The change is then divided by the previous amount and expressed as a percentage. The percentage change in individual items can be compared with the change in a control item, such as total assets or revenues. The strength of this technique is that it quickly identifies areas needing further attention.

Financial ratios are used to measure liquidity, efficiency, solvency, and profitability. Note that a ratio is calculated by dividing one accounting number by another, thereby possibly magnifying the effects of uncertainties in the numbers. Furthermore, all ratio analysis is relative, among enterprises and over time. There are no absolutes! Ratio examples include:

- *Current ratio.* This liquidity ratio is calculated by dividing current assets by current liabilities. It measures the ability to pay bills.

- *Stock (inventory) turnover.* This efficiency ratio is calculated by dividing the period's cost of goods sold by the average stocks (inventory) held during the period. It shows how many times stocks are sold during the year. The average number of days' stock held during the year may be computed by dividing 365 by the turnover.

- *Times interest earned.* This is a solvency ratio computed by dividing the income before interest and taxes (income available to cover interest) by the interest expense for the year. It is a rough measure of the ability to service debt.

- *Return on equity.* This useful profitability ratio is calculated by dividing the net income by the average owners' equity during the period. Many analysts use this ratio as a starting point, proceeding from there to disaggregate it into various components in their search for explanations of why results have varied.

What can change?

There are several developments that could change the nature of financial statements. Two are of particular interest now: internationalization and fair value accounting.

The International Accounting Standards Committee (IASC) was formed in 1973 to harmonize standards around the world. In 1995, the IASC agreed with the International Organisation of Securities Commissioners (IOSCO) to complete a set of core standards by 1999.

The core standards have been completed and in 1999 IOSCO recommended that its members allow multinational issuers to use 30 IASC standards in cross-border offerings and listings. In February 2000, the US Securities and Exchange Commission (SEC) asked interested parties to comment on issues arising if the SEC were to allow foreign registrants to use IASC accounting in filings with the SEC without reconciliation to US accounting principles.

It is too early to predict what the SEC might do. However, the prospect is for an increase in the number of foreign enterprises issuing securities in the US and listing them on US exchanges.

Second is the issue of financial reports relying on historic cost for asset valuation. Recently, bodies that set accounting standards have proposed changes that would report changes in the value of financial instruments in the period they occurred, not when they were realized by disposal. Perhaps the greatest impetus for fair value accounting is an international working group of standards bodies established by the IASC. It includes several national accounting standard setters and its work is near completion. Given that the group has a broad membership, its conclusions are likely to become world standards.

Conclusion

The basic concepts of accounting are simple: A = L + OE. However, they are seldom easy to apply. Accounting measurements require a trade-off between reliability (of historic cost) and relevance (the strongest argument for fair value). Accounting should represent the economic reality it seeks to depict in numbers. It should be free from bias that would favor either the buyer or seller of a security. Accounting and financial reports yield useful information, but must be read with care. Finally, accounting provides vital information for efficient markets, which would collapse without financial reports.

Further reading

Anthony, R.N. and Pearlman, L.K. (1999) *Essentials of Accounting*, Reading, MA: Addison-Wesley. On CD-Rom, by Ivy Software, www.cstone.net/~ivysoft.

Mulford, C.W. and Comiskey, E.E. (1996) *Financial Warnings*, New York: Wiley.

Murray, D., Neumann, B., and Elgers, P. (2000) *Using Financial Accounting: An Introduction*, Cincinnati: South-Western College Publishing.

Schoenebeck, K.P. (2001) *Interpreting and Analyzing Financial Statements*, Englewood Cliffs, NJ: Prentice-Hall.

Tracy, J.A. (2001) *Accounting for Dummies*, IDG Books.

Weil, R.L. (1998) *Accounting: the Language of Business*, Sun Lakes, AZ: Thomas Horton.

Value metrics:
use with care

Chris Higson is a professor of accounting at London Business School.

Using accounting rates of return as a measure of value is simple in theory, but tricky in practice. **Chris Higson** explains the issues and adds a note of caution.

Accounting rates of return on capital are used to measure economic return in business and to identify whether companies are creating or destroying value. Investors use accounting returns to rank companies when selecting stocks. Value-based management has encouraged companies to use accounting returns for measuring performance and in compensation schemes for managers. Regulators and competition authorities use accounting returns to identify excess profits.

In all these applications, accounting returns are being used as value metrics in the sense that they are being compared, explicitly or implicitly, to the cost of capital. This is a stern test of accounting data and in this article the reliability of accounting returns as value metrics is discussed.

We can see why, in principle, an accounting rate of return on capital measures economic return by recalling some basic investment theory. An activity creates value when it is expected to produce cash flows with a higher value than if the resources were put to their next best use. Assume the resources are assets and capital is not rationed (so the activity is not competing for funds against other projects). Then, the test of value creation is whether the value of the expected cash flows from using the assets, discounted at the company's cost of capital, is greater than the cost of the assets.

If a company buys £10m of assets today and uses them to generate a cash flow worth £12m today, it has created £2m of value. In the language of capital budgetting, the investment has a net present value (NPV) of £2m. Equivalently, value is created when the expected cash flows net of investment have a yield or internal rate of return (IRR) that is greater than the cost of capital.

Since there is a close relationship between value and return, we can judge economic performance in either way, by examining the quantity of value created, or by comparing a rate of return to the cost of capital.

(Note that NPV and IRR are equivalent ways of thinking about economic performance apart from cases when internal rates of return are ambiguous. These cases are explored in standard finance texts.)

The widget project

My grandmother has provided £10,000. On January 1, I will rent a room, buy a widget press for £8,000, and invest £2,000 in an inventory of widget blanks. I will trade for a year, making and selling widgets. I expect to receive cash from customers of £15,000 and to spend another £6,000 for widget blanks and £2,000 for rent. I estimate the machine could be sold for £5,000 at the end of the year.

At the end of the year, therefore, I will be left with a machine worth £5,000, no inventory, and receivables of £1,500 from customers who have yet to pay. Is the project worth doing? Note that my grandmother got the money by selling some of her equities and these equities were expected to return 8 percent on average, so 8 percent is the opportunity cost of the capital used in the project.

Using the techniques of capital budgetting, we would appraise the project by calculating its IRR and its NPV. As is conventional (though crude), we assume all revenues are collected as cash, and expenses paid in cash, at the end of the year (date 1), apart from the investment, which is made at the beginning of the year (date 0). Also assume the machine can be sold, and the outstanding receivables collected, on the last day of the year, and there is no tax. Table 1 shows a discounted cash flow (DCF) analysis for the widget project.

For a single-period project, the IRR is easy to calculate as follows:

$$(13,500/10,000) - 1 = 0.35 = 35\%$$

The present value of the future cash flow is given by:

$$13,500/(1 + 8\%) = 12,500$$

So, the NPV of the project, the present value of expected cash flows less the initial investment, is £2,500. On either criterion, the project is worth

TABLE 1	DCF analysis of the widget project

Project cash flows are:

	Date 0	Date 1
Investment in machine and inventory	(10,000)	
Operating cash flow (15,000 – 6,000 – 2,000)		7,000
Realize the assets (machine, 5,000, receivables, 1,500)		6,500
	(10,000)	13,500

TABLE 2	Accounting analysis of the widget project

Revenue:		
paid in cash during year	15,000	
outstanding at year end	1,500	16,500
Cost of materials:		
paid during year	6,000	
outstanding at year end	2,000	(8,000)
Rent		(2,000)
Depreciation of machine		(3,000)
Operating profit		3,500

My balance sheets are:

	Date 0	Date 1
Cash		7,000
Receivables		1,500
Inventory	2,000	
Machine	8,000	5,000
	10,000	13,500
Equity – invested	10,000	10,000
– retained profit		3,500
	10,000	13,500

doing: the IRR of 35 percent is above the 8 percent cost of capital and the NPV is positive.

How would this project have looked in accounting terms? Profit would be calculated as shown in Table 2.

My accounting return on capital, measured using beginning capital, is:

$$(3,500/10,000) = 35\%$$

So, accounting return on capital and IRR give the same answer.

The price to book ratio is the accounting equivalent of NPV. Imagine that my simple project above were traded on the stock market. Its market capitalization at January 1 would be the market's evaluation (present value) of future cash flows, precisely what we valued at £12,500. Price to book is NPV expressed as a ratio:

$$12,500/10,000 = 1.25$$

Importance of taxes

The company must pay corporation tax on its income, so the company's cost of capital, which is the investors' required return, relates to income after corporate taxes. For comparison with the cost of capital, we need an after-tax measure of return on capital. Consider two traditional measures of accounting return on capital. Operating return is operating profit (before interest paid and tax) divided by operating assets. It is an enterprise-level measure of return in the sense that operating assets are financed by both equity and loans. The return to investors is measured by return on equity, which is earnings (after interest paid and tax) divided by equity shareholders' funds.

Since earnings are after tax, return on equity can be benchmarked against the cost of equity capital. However, to find an enterprise-level return on capital (which in this case will be benchmarked against WACC, the weighted average of the costs of the loan and equity capital), we will need to calculate an after-tax operating return. A moment's thought suggests that this will not be entirely straightforward. We need a measure that is pre-interest paid, but after tax, which is not the order of things in the income statement. The problem is that the tax reported in the income statement contains tax paid on operating profit but also the tax paid on other

income, less tax saved on interest payments. We resolve this by calculating net operating profit after tax (NOPAT), where T is the corporate tax rate, as:

$$\text{NOPAT} = \text{Operating profit} - \text{Tax} + \\ (\text{Net interest paid} \times \text{T})$$

We can also get at NOPAT by working up from profit after tax:

$$\text{NOPAT} = \text{Profit after tax} + \text{Net interest} \\ \text{paid} \times (\text{I} - \text{T})$$

We then have:

$$\text{After-tax operating return} = \text{NOPAT}/ \\ (\text{Operating assets})$$

Take the example of Brigand & Co, which has the following data:

Operating profit	100
Interest received	10
Interest paid	(30)
Profit before tax	80
Tax	25
Earnings	55

Brigand has average operating assets of 500. The local corporate tax rate (T) is 35 percent. To find NOPAT, which is operating profit after tax, we need to know the tax on the operating profit. The actual tax paid is 25, but this reflects the fact that the company got a tax deduction at 35 percent on its net interest payments of 20, a deduction of 7. So, tax on operating profit must have been:

$$25 + 7 = 32$$

and NOPAT is:

$$100 - 32 = 68$$

Though the statutory tax rate is 35 percent, Brigand's effective tax rate is not 35 percent and 32 is not 35 percent of 100. Taxable profit reflects the various allowances (and disallowables) in the tax code, carried-forward losses, investment tax credits, and so forth. The NOPAT calculation reasonably assumes that interest paid (received) is deducted (taxed) at the marginal, statutory, rate and that the tax breaks that reduce the effective tax rate relate to operating profit.

An alternative way of getting NOPAT is from the bottom up, working back from earnings. NOPAT is profit after tax plus interest paid, net of the tax shelter on interest. In Brigand's case, this is $20 - 7 = 13$. So:

$$NOPAT = 55 + 13 = 68$$

Brigand's after-tax operating return is thus:

$$68/500 = 13.6 \text{ percent}$$

Internalizing the cost of capital

In the Brigand example, if the WACC was 8 percent, we would conclude that after-tax operating return of 13.6 percent reflected superior performance. The difference between return and cost of capital is called spread. Brigand's spread was 5.6 percent.

The same data can be presented in a different way. If we make a charge against NOPAT for the cost of using capital as operating assets during the year, the surplus is residual income.

$$\text{Residual income} = \text{NOPAT} - \\ (\text{Operating assets} \times \text{WACC})$$

Brigand had a NOPAT of 68 and assets of 500. Its WACC is 8 percent, so its residual income is:

$$68 - (500 \times 8\%) = 28$$

Residual income is also known as economic value added (EVA) and economic profit. The term "EVA" was coined by a consulting firm, Stern Stewart. Its version of EVA also incorporates a number of accounting adjustments, designed to correct shortcomings of actual accounting.

Great claims are made for residual income measures, but the statement that a company has positive residual income is logically identical to saying it is earning a return greater than its cost of capital. Both metrics hold the same information. In simple terms, when we ask if a company is earning a return greater than the cost of capital, we are asking whether:

$$\text{Profit/Capital} > \text{WACC}$$

Multiplying both sides by capital, the question becomes whether:

$$\text{Profit} > \text{Capital} \times \text{WACC}$$

Moving the right-hand side over to the left recasts the question in terms of whether residual income is positive:

$$\text{Profit} - (\text{Capital} \times \text{WACC}) > 0$$

Data integrity

In the simple world of the widget project, it is easy to see why accounting returns and price to book gave the same answer as IRR and NPV. View each year in the life of a company as an investment project. The company starts with a stock of assets and has earnings during the year, some of which are distributed as dividend (that is, cash flow to investors) and the rest are retained, increasing assets. The fundamental accounting identity is:

$$\text{Earnings} \equiv (\text{Dividend} + \text{Increase in assets})$$

For a one-period project the IRR is:

$$\text{IRR} = (\text{Cash flow} + \text{Increase in assets})/ \\ \text{Opening assets}$$

So, the accounting return measured on the opening assets of the company will be identical to the IRR:

$$\text{IRR} = \text{Earnings/Opening assets}$$

In practice, the reliability of an accounting measure of return as a value metric depends crucially on the accounting. In capital budgetting, we know that NPV or IRR will only be correctly measured if the assets committed at the outset are measured at their opportunity costs, all incremental cash flows over the project life are identified, and the recovery of any assets that remain at the end is included at their opportunity cost. By analogy, for accounting to have the data integrity of capital budgetting, three things are needed.

First, the accounting identity has actually to hold, so that all balance sheet changes pass through earnings. Earnings must be comprehensive or, in current parlance, "clean-surplus." Second, the balance sheet needs to be complete in that it records all the assets and claims over which property rights have been established. Third, these assets and claims need to be valued at opportunity cost.

In practice, accounting rarely meets this ideal and, though practicing analysts and consultants make adjustments to the reported numbers, the goal remains elusive. There are three problem areas.

Comprehensive income

The traditional role of the income statement is to describe profit from operations. But, for example, part of the return that a company delivers to its investors may take the form of unrealized holding gains on assets such as real estate. These may not be recognized, but even when they are, they will rarely be passed through the income statement. Earnings will not be comprehensive if key balance sheet changes, such as gains and losses on foreign exchange and gains and losses on revaluation, are taken direct to reserves in the balance sheet rather than passed through earnings.

Balance sheet completeness

There are two main reasons why the balance sheet may be an incomplete list of a company's assets and claims.

First, under the historic cost convention of accounting, assets will only be recorded if they were acquired in a transaction rather than as windfalls. Moreover, conservatism dictates that managers should write off the costs of building intangible assets such as brands, human capital, and research and development (R&D) as they are incurred, rather than carry them in the balance sheet. As a result, balance sheets usually do not carry the intangible assets of the company. One modest exception, which may be capitalized, is a rather limited class of expenditure on applied R&D of products with a known market and which can reasonably be expected to be profitable. Acquired, rather than home-grown, intangible assets are sometimes carried, though these are never subsequently revalued.

It is common practice in calculating value metrics to capitalize R&D expenditure, but not other intangible-building expenditure. Companies that grow by takeover may make very large investments in goodwill, which is the difference between the cost of an acquired company and the identifiable (in terms of balance sheet recognition) assets acquired. Internationally, the goodwill asset is amortized over widely varying periods. Hence, accounting returns look very different between companies that grow organically and those that grow by acquisition, and also between acquirers in different countries.

Second, the company may have written contracts to keep assets off the balance sheet. Companies write operating lease contracts to shift tangible fixed assets, and the corresponding liabilities, off the balance sheet. Factoring the sales ledger, or using consigned inventory, may keep current assets off balance sheet. Analysts commonly capitalize operating leases to enhance the completeness of the balance sheet, but such devices are hard for outsiders to observe and there is usually no attempt to adjust for them.

Balance sheet values

Though the balance sheet is usually complete in tangible fixed assets, by default fixed assets are carried at their historic costs that, particularly for long-lived assets such as land and buildings, may bear little relation to current values. Internationally, revaluation of fixed assets is either not permitted, as in the US, or has unfavorable tax consequences, as in much of Europe. In the Netherlands and the UK, where revaluation is allowed, it is found predominantly in property-rich sectors such as hotels and drinks, where it is occasional and partial – not all asset classes are necessarily revalued. Though acquired, rather than built, intellectual property assets are sometimes carried in the balance sheet, these are never subsequently revalued. It is not common for analysts to attempt to re-express fixed assets in current prices.

Current assets and liabilities are more likely to approximate current values. As short-life assets, they are carried at reasonably current prices and have to be written down to realizable value when this falls below cost. Deviations from current value occur when accounting standards permit or encourage "hidden reserves" in the form of undervalued assets. One example is the use of LIFO (last in, first out) for inventory valuation in the US; another is the excessive write-down of receivables by making general provisions that is common in some continental European countries.

Conclusion

The reliability of a value metric depends crucially on how the accounting is done. To provide the data integrity of capital budgetting, profits would need to be measured comprehensively and the balance sheet would have to measure the opportunity cost of all company assets and liabilities. These balance sheet requirements are very difficult to achieve in practice, so comparisons with the cost of capital need to be treated with caution.

Further reading

Edwards, J.S.S., Kay, J.A., and Mayer, C.P. (1987) *The Economic Analysis of Accounting Profitability*, Oxford: Oxford University Press.

Higson, C. (1995) *Business Finance*, Oxford: Butterworths.

A bigger yardstick for
company performance

Christopher D. Ittner is
associate professor of
accounting at the
Wharton School of the
University of Pennsylvania.

David F. Larcker is Ernst &
Young Professor of
Accounting at the
Wharton School of the
University of Pennsylvania.

Financial data has limitations as a measure of company
performance. Other measures such as quality may be better
at forecasting, but can be difficult to implement, say
Christopher Ittner and **David Larcker**.

Choosing performance measures is a challenge. Performance measurement systems play a key role in developing strategy, evaluating
the achievement of organizational objectives, and compensating managers. Yet many managers feel traditional financially oriented systems
no longer work adequately. A recent survey of US financial services
companies found most were not satisfied with their measurement systems. They believed there was too much emphasis on financial measures such as earnings and accounting returns, and little emphasis on
drivers of value such as customer and employee satisfaction, innovation, and quality.

In response, companies are implementing new performance measurement systems. A third of financial services companies, for example,
made a major change in their performance measurement system during
the past two years and 39 percent plan a major change within two
years.

Inadequacies in financial performance measures have led to innovations ranging from nonfinancial indicators of "intangible assets" and
"intellectual capital" to "balanced scorecards" of integrated financial
and nonfinancial measures. This article discusses the advantages and
disadvantages of nonfinancial performance measures and offers suggestions for implementation.

Advantages

Nonfinancial measures offer four clear advantages over measurement
systems based on financial data. The first of these is a closer link to
long-term organizational strategies. Financial evaluation systems
generally focus on annual or short-term performance against accounting
yardsticks. They do not deal with progress relative to customer

requirements or competitors, nor other non-financial objectives that may be important in achieving profitability, competitive strength, and longer-term strategic goals. For example, new product development or expanding organizational capabilities may be important strategic goals, but may hinder short-term accounting performance.

By supplementing accounting measures with nonfinancial data about strategic performance and implementation of strategic plans, companies can communicate objectives and provide incentives for managers to address long-term strategy.

Second, critics of traditional measures argue that drivers of success in many industries are "intangible assets" such as intellectual capital and customer loyalty, rather than the "hard assets" allowed on to balance sheets. Although it is difficult to quantify intangible assets in financial terms, nonfinancial data can provide indirect, quantitative indicators of a firm's intangible assets.

One study examined the ability of nonfinancial indicators of "intangible assets" to explain differences in US companies' stock market values. It found that measures related to innovation, management capability, employee relations, quality, and brand value explained a significant proportion of a company's value, even allowing for accounting assets and liabilities. By excluding these intangible assets, financially oriented measurement can encourage managers to make poor, even harmful, decisions.

Third, nonfinancial measures can be better indicators of future financial performance. Even when the ultimate goal is maximizing financial performance, current financial measures may not capture long-term benefits from decisions made now. Consider, for example, investments in research and development or customer satisfaction programs. Under US accounting rules, research and development expenditures and marketing costs must be charged for in the period they are incurred, so reducing profits. But successful research improves future profits if it can be brought to market.

Similarly, investments in customer satisfaction can improve subsequent economic performance by increasing revenues and loyalty of existing customers, attracting new customers, and reducing transaction costs. Nonfinancial data can offer the missing link between these beneficial activities and financial results by providing forward-looking information on accounting or stock performance. For example, interim research results or customer indices may offer an indication of future cash flows that would not be captured otherwise.

Finally, the choice of measures should be based on providing information about managerial actions and the level of "noise" in the measures. Noise refers to changes in the performance measure that are beyond the control of the manager or organization, ranging from changes in the economy to luck (good or bad). Managers must be aware of how much success is due to their actions or they will not have the signals they need to maximize their effect on performance. Because many nonfinancial measures are less susceptible to external noise than accounting measures, their use may improve managers' performance by providing more precise evaluation of their actions. This also lowers the risk imposed on managers when determining pay.

Disadvantages

Although there are many advantages to nonfinancial performance measures, they are not without drawbacks. Research has identified five primary limitations. Time and cost have been problems for some companies. They have found that the costs of a system that tracks a large number of financial and nonfinancial measures can be greater than its benefits. Development can consume considerable time and expense, not least of which is selling the system to skeptical employees who have learned to operate under existing rules. A greater number of diverse performance measures frequently requires significant investment in information systems to draw information from multiple (and often incompatible) databases.

Evaluating performance using multiple measures that can conflict in the short term can also be time-consuming. One bank that adopted a performance evaluation system using multiple accounting and nonfinancial measures saw the time required for area directors to evaluate branch managers increase from less than one day per quarter to six days.

Bureaucracies can cause the measurement process to degenerate into mechanistic exercises that add little to reaching strategic goals. For example, shortly after becoming the first US company to win Japan's prestigious Deming Prize for quality improvement, Florida Power and Light found that employees believed the company's quality improvement process placed too much emphasis on reporting, presenting, and discussing a myriad of quality indicators. They felt this deprived them of time that could be better spent serving customers. The company responded by eliminating most quality reviews, reducing the number of indicators tracked, and minimizing reports and meetings.

The second drawback is that, unlike accounting measures, nonfinancial data are measured in many ways: there is no common denominator. Evaluating performance or making trade-offs between attributes is difficult when some are denominated in time, some in quantities or percentages, and some in arbitrary ways.

Many companies attempt to overcome this by rating each performance measure in terms of its strategic importance (from, say, not important to extremely important) and then evaluating overall performance based on a weighted average of the measures. Others assign arbitrary weightings to the various goals. One major car manufacturer, for example, structures executive bonuses so: 40 percent is based on warranty repairs per 100 vehicles sold; 20 percent on customer satisfaction surveys; 20 percent on market share; and 20 percent on accounting performance (pre-tax earnings). However, like all subjective assessments, these methods can lead to considerable error.

Lack of causal links is a third issue. Many companies adopt nonfinancial measures without articulating the relations between the measures or verifying that they have a bearing on accounting and stock price performance. Unknown or unverified causal links create two problems when evaluating performance: incorrect measures focus attention on the wrong objectives, and improvements cannot be linked to later outcomes. Xerox, for example, spent millions of dollars on customer surveys, under the assumption that improvements in satisfaction translated into better financial performance. Later analysis found no such association. As a result, Xerox shifted to a customer loyalty measure that was found to be a leading indicator of financial performance.

The lack of an explicit casual model of the relations between measures also contributes to difficulties in evaluating their relative importance. Without knowing the size and timing of associations among measures, companies find it difficult to make decisions or measure success based on them.

Fourth on the list of problems with nonfinancial measures is lack of statistical reliability – whether a measure actually represents what it purports to represent, rather than random "measurement error." Many nonfinancial data such as satisfaction measures are based on surveys with few respondents and few questions. These measures generally exhibit poor statistical reliability, reducing their ability to discriminate superior performance or predict future financial results.

Finally, although financial measures are unlikely to capture fully the many dimensions of organizational performance, implementing an evaluation system with too many measures can lead to "measurement disintegration." This occurs when an overabundance of measures dilutes the effect of the measurement process. Managers chase a variety of measures simultaneously, while achieving little gain in the main drivers of success.

Selecting measures

Once managers have determined that the expected benefits from nonfinancial data outweigh the costs, three steps can be used to select and implement appropriate measures.

Understand value drivers

The starting point is understanding a company's value drivers: the factors that create stakeholder value. Once known, these factors determine which measures contribute to long-term success and so how to translate corporate objectives into measures that guide managers' actions.

While this seems intuitive, experience indicates that companies do a poor job determining and articulating these drivers. Managers tend to use one of three methods to identify value drivers, the most common being intuition. However, executives' rankings of value drivers may not reflect their true importance. For example, many executives rate environmental performance and quality as relatively unimportant drivers of long-term financial performance. In contrast, statistical analyzes indicate these dimensions are strongly associated with a company's market value.

A second method is to use standard classifications such as financial, internal business process, customer, learning, and growth categories. While these may be appropriate, other nonfinancial dimensions may be more important, depending on the organization's strategy, competitive environment, and objectives. Moreover, these categories do little to help determine weightings for each dimension.

Perhaps the most sophisticated method of determining value drivers is statistical analysis of the leading and lagging indicators of financial performance. The resulting "causal business model" can help determine which measures predict future financial performance and can assist in assigning weightings to measures based on the strength of the statistical relation. Unfortunately, relatively few companies develop such causal business models when selecting their performance measures.

Review consistencies

Most companies track hundreds, if not thousands, of nonfinancial measures in their day-to-day operations. To avoid "reinventing the wheel," an inventory of current measures should be made. Once measures have been documented, their value for performance measurement can be assessed. The issue at this stage is the extent to which current measures are aligned with the company's strategies and value drivers. One method for assessing this alignment is "gap analysis." Gap analysis requires managers to rank performance measures on at least two dimensions: their importance to strategic objectives and the importance currently placed on them.

Our survey of 148 US financial services companies found significant "measurement gaps" for many nonfinancial measures (see Figure 1). For example, 72 percent of companies said customer-related performance was an extremely important driver of long-term success, against 31 percent who chose short-term financial performance. However, the quality of short-term financial measurement is considerably better than measurement of customer satisfaction. Similar disparities exist for nonfinancial measures related to

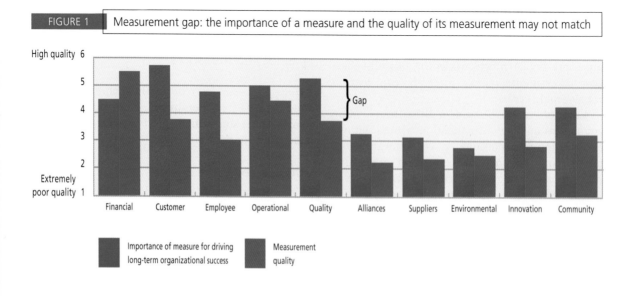

| FIGURE 1 | Measurement gap: the importance of a measure and the quality of its measurement may not match

The **choice** of performance measures has a substantial effect on employees' careers and pay

employee performance, operational results, quality, alliances, supplier relations, innovation, community, and the environment. More important, stock market and long-term accounting performance are both higher when these measurement gaps are smaller.

Integrate measures

Finally, after measures are chosen, they must become an integral part of reporting and performance evaluation if they are to affect employee behavior and organizational performance. This is not easy. Since the choice of performance measures has a substantial impact on employees' careers and pay, controversy is bound to emerge no matter how appropriate the measures. Many companies have failed to benefit from nonfinancial performance measures through being reluctant to take this step.

Conclusions

Although nonfinancial measures are increasingly important in decision making and performance evaluation, companies should not simply copy measures used by others. The choice of measures must be linked to factors such as corporate strategy, value drivers, organizational objectives, and the competitive environment. In addition, companies should remember that performance measurement choice is a dynamic process – measures may be appropriate today, but the system needs to be continually reassessed as strategies and competitive environments evolve.

Further reading

Baum, G. et al. (2000) "Introducing the New Value Creation Index," *Forbes ASAP*, April 3, 140–3.

Ittner, C. and Larker, D. (1998) "Are Nonfinancial Measures Leading Indicators of Financial Performance?" *Journal of Accounting Research*, supplement, 1–35.

Costs count in
the strategic agenda

Anthony Hopwood is
Peter Moores Director of
the Saïd Business School,
Oxford University.

Managing costs is about more than making cuts, argues **Anthony Hopwood**. Financial skills need to spread beyond the accounts department to all managers.

Costs have always been a strategic consideration in corporate affairs, and never more so than today. Strategically efficient companies can go beyond the mere identification of costs and focus on ways to change cost structures to serve wider corporate objectives. This is much harder than many off-the-shelf packages sold by consultants and accountants would have managers believe. It is at the heart of top-level management.

Consider the sourcing activities of a global US-owned clothing retailer. Having taken goods from the Philippines for several years, it became aware of lower prices in China. By putting pressure on its Philippine source to match the Chinese prices, it at first forced the manufacturer to bear the reduced margins itself. But over time, the pressures from China eliminated all profit potential for the Philippine supplier. As a result, the supplier switched to become a purchasing agent, sourcing the retailer's needs itself from another country.

When the supplier began to source from Laos, it introduced a cost level even lower than the Chinese. Yet this is not the end of the process. Rather than creating an equilibrium at a lower price, the competitive process is more than likely to introduce continued cost reduction into the system. This is driven by increasing end-market competition, pressures for profit, and a radical shift in cost structure away from product costs and toward the cost of brand creation and maintenance. Cost consciousness has become an agent for change in its own right.

Such pressures are at work in even the most traditional industries. Consider a major UK producer of building supplies. It was recently bought by a US competitor that was primarily interested in expanding market share. The company intends to close down UK manufacturing (which is easier to do than it is in continental Europe) and use the increased efficiency of transportation to source low-cost supplies from eastern Europe instead.

Every sector of business could provide comparable examples. Competition and globalization have introduced a new momentum into cost management. Costs are now of strategic significance in a more intensive way. And the resulting pressures are radically changing the geographies of production and distribution, patterns of outsourcing, and the mobilization of information flows. They are also driving cross-border mergers and acquisitions, which are transforming industries in Europe and Asia.

Strategic cost

If it is easy to identify why cost management has become a strategic issue for global industries, it is not so simple to write blueprints for how companies should adapt cost management practices in the light of new strategic imperatives. Many of the commercial solutions that have appeared in the last decade, such as activity-based costing (ABC) and the balanced scorecard approach, are oversimplified treatments of a complex and dynamic management challenge.

However, some principles of strategic cost management have emerged. First, managers must try to mold their costs to fit medium- and longer-term corporate objectives. Rather than taking existing costs as a baseline, companies need to shape the costs that they incur. The primary purpose of cost management is not merely to count costs, as has historically been the case, but to manage them in a proactive way.

Second, successful cost management is an interdisciplinary and multi-functional activity, not something that can be safely left to corporate bean-counters alone. It should draw on the insights of engineers, production managers, design experts, distributors, financial specialists, and many others. Cutting-edge cost management draws on wide expertise to identify and then act on those factors that can radically shift where and how costs are incurred.

Consider, for example, the ways in which consumer electrical and electronic equipment is now designed. Today these involve complex design processes, which, while they might result in higher variable costs for individual components, nevertheless produce lower overall costs when they are configured and employed together.

Third, it accords a new role and status to the business of cost calculation. Instead of the static, periodic, and company-wide accounting of the past, the need now is for specific and localized activity that is repeated time and time again as different options are considered and evaluated. The role of cost calculation now is creative rather than reactive. It suggests changes, as well as evaluating those already made. In large part, this new remit has bypassed the traditional domains of the accountant, and is increasingly carried out by departmental or general managers.

Finally, calculations required to measure and transform costs at a strategic level tend to be neither technically complex nor bureaucratic in nature. *Ad hoc* estimates of broad economic differences often prove to be the catalysts that mobilize major changes in sourcing policy, for example. Given the rapid pace of changes in this area, traditional costing systems have proved to be too inflexible to provide the necessary responses. This is an area where it pays to be roughly right rather than precisely wrong – a state of affairs that has troubling implications for many accountants, whose skills tend to be of a specific rather than a visionary nature.

Accountancy's reply

Accountants have tried to respond to these challenges. Strategic cost accounting (or strategic management accounting) is now a distinct category in the sales manuals of consultancy firms. But it remains a broad and ambiguous label, which covers a variety of technical fads and gimmicks. Too much emphasis has been placed on specifying new standardized systems of accounting for costs. These undoubtedly create new weapons for corporate financial bureaucrats to deploy, but probably do little to assist top managers with strategic options.

Rather than observing new organizational practices and learning from them, consultants and accountants have mostly opted to design new futures for themselves, which maintain the rigidity of the past rather than exploit the potential technology provides for more flexible decision making. Nowhere is this better illustrated than in the fashion for activity-based costing and the balanced scorecard. They have been cleverly sold as new innovations with immense strategic potential, when in practice they are nothing of the sort.

For enterprises wanting to be strategic in the face of intense competition, modifying the bureaucracy of performance reporting, which is what these techniques really amount to, is a poor substitute for genuine processes of organizational insight, learning, and adaptation.

These costing approaches originated in the US defense and aerospace industries, where a cost-plus culture has long been the norm. Traditional methods of allocating costs had begun to lose their legitimacy, as more capital-intensive technologies produced ever-higher allocation rates. There was a genuine interest in a more legitimate costing bureaucracy. Although now forgotten, the new costing movement emerged in this highly specific setting, from where it has been applied to many sectors to which it is less obviously appropriate.

Going strategic

The key to understanding what is required is to realize that continual analysis is more important than once-and-for-all systems, that expertise is dispersed rather than concentrated in any single organization or occupation and, most crucial of all, that successful strategic cost management is about finding ways to transform costs rather than merely identifying them. Within these broad principles, more specific comments can be made.

Sharing costing expertise

Evidence suggests it is important to spread knowledge of the principles of cost accounting as widely as possible. Rather than being a monopoly of accountants, all managers need to understand what costs are and how they are calculated. Basic economic understanding is more important than complex accounting techniques. People need to understand cost variability, the sensitivity of cost to changes in timescale, opportunity cost, and so on. Calculating skills are important, but only to the extent that they allow people to engage in *ad hoc* assessments of options as they occur.

Basic economic understanding is more important than **complex accounting** techniques

Sharing the language of costs

Just as important as calculating costs is the ability of an organization to think and talk the language of costs. Indeed, talking costs down can be as effective a basis for action as the most sophisticated technical calculations. One major retail multinational has successfully created a culture in which cost now features in almost every sentence of management discussion about the business, even though the costing system in the company itself is still simple and old-fashioned. The cutting edge of costing is talk, not system. Good talk works because it leads to good action. In this company, a powerful rhetoric of costing and a wide awareness of its principles has had more impact than many sophisticated systems in other companies.

Sharing responsibility for costs

Acting on costs rather than merely revealing them requires the shared expertise of most management functions and departments. Product and process design is crucial, along with an insight into the operation of markets. Expertise from production engineering, distribution, and logistics is important. The financial expert is invariably needed for these discussions, but more as a facilitator than as a leader or a source of original inspiration. Multi-skilled working parties and temporary project teams are the best way to realize cost management.

Localized action

The days of the company-wide cost initiative, when head offices sent out instructions for across-the-board cuts, are over. Serious cost management these days occurs on specific sites, on specific product lines and as a result of redesigning components, distribution channels, and so on. It is a highly localized endeavor, whether at the top or the bottom of the company. It has to engage the energies and enthusiasms of particular managers working in specific settings. Indeed, viewed in such a way, cost management requires positive energies, whilst cost cutting generates negative feelings. The two are completely different.

Comparisons and benchmarking

While insights can generate significant changes in costs, in many cases costs can best be managed by providing comparative and benchmarking information in both a routine and *ad hoc* way. What are competitors' prices and costs? What can be gauged of competitors' cost structures? Are they differentially sensitive to changes in volume or relative input prices?

Where possible, every effort should be made to incorporate such information into regular patterns of reporting. Industry surveys, consultancy reports, and trade press analyses can assist this. Otherwise, companies should undertake detailed analyses of the likely cost breakdown of competitors' products or services, the anticipated cost consequences of new technologies and new methods of organization, and the cost implications of variations in product attributes and differential levels of service.

Not all costs are to be avoided

Cost increases are sometimes advantageous! Invariably, the emphasis of traditional cost management has been on cost reduction. Given the increasing intensity of competition, this is understandable. But strategic analyses of cost can sometimes suggest cost increases, or at least changes in the overall structure of costs, such as an increase in direct costs that nevertheless produces a reduction in overall costs. It is precisely in such circumstances that looking at costs strategically is important. In a world of short-term gains, getting costs down is imperative. But when consideration of the medium- and longer-term implications of differential product or service positioning is possible, the costs of product or service enhancement, improved quality, and rebranding can all be considered. In these cases, managers should think carefully about how higher costs may feed through into higher revenues, or costs in one area result in disproportionately lower costs in other areas.

Routine systems do not provide a foundation for **highly specific** changes in plans and operations

Financial controls still matter

Although particular emphasis has been placed here on *ad hoc*, specific, and localized cost analysis, this should not be taken to imply that routine overall financial control is no longer needed. Studies of successful innovative decision making in highly uncertain environments have shown that a backbone of serious, regular financial control remains essential. It provides the context against which organizational expectations can be formulated, a way for managers to learn, and a prompt for discussions about improvement.

Invariably, routine systems do not provide a foundation for highly specific changes in plans and operations. That is where informed action comes in. But they do provide the foundation for a uniform and well-understood language of financial action.

Regrettably, there are few comprehensive studies of successful cost management. Exhortation has ruled the day and systematic evidence is thin on the ground. But one recent comparative study of financial control in British and Finnish hospitals supports most of the above guidelines. In the UK hospitals, financial control has been placed in the hands of accountants. The function is now carried out by an army of specialist financial calculators.

Large budgets have also been spent on systems consultants in the UK, even though the resulting financial systems have made the organizations more complex. Where success is deemed to have been achieved, it is judged in terms of overall cuts and savings, rather than by reference to changes in the way health management is organized. Celebrations focus on 5 percent savings rather than the introduction of new approaches to healthcare.

In Finnish hospitals, in contrast, accountants no longer have a monopoly over cost management. In many cases, medical specialists have taken on the task of financial management, as well as that of healthcare. Because they accept the overall aims of financial efficiency and containment, rather than going to war over budget cuts imposed from outside, doctors are now actively engaged in their own localized actions to improve the way resources are used. Rather than sitting on the edge of medical management, financial expertise is permeating medical practice.

Observations of successful industrial and commercial practice suggest that it is just such an intermingling of knowledge that has the greatest potential to change the cost structure of operations. Rather than intensifying functional conflict, a strategy of localized, specific and collaborative action on costs is increasingly seen as the way to manage costs strategically – transforming costs as part of a wider process of informed and directed corporate change.

Further reading

Ahrens, T. (1999) *Contrasting Involvements: A Study of Management Accounting Practices in Britain and Germany*, Newark, NJ: Harwood Academic Publishers.

Johnson, H.T. and Kaplan, R.S. (1987) *Relevance Lost: The Rise and Fall of Management Accounting*, Boston, MA: Harvard Business School Press.

Jönsson, S. (1996) *Accounting for Improvement*, Oxford: Pergamon.

Jönsson, S. and A. Grönlund (1988) "Life with a Subcontractor: New Technology and Management Accounting," *Accounting, Organizations and Society*, 513–34.

Kaplan, R.S. and Cooper, R. (1998) *Cost and Effect: Using Integrated Cost Systems to Drive Profitability and Performance*, Boston, MA: Harvard Business School Press.

Oldman, A. and Tomkins, C. (1999) *Cost Management and Its Interplay with Business Strategy and Context*, Aldershot: Ashgate.

The secrets hidden
in market prices

Markets distill information in a way that managers can easily use and prices includes data that are not publicly available, explains **Lisa Meulbroek**.

Lisa Meulbroek is an associate professor of finance at Harvard Business School.

When asked why financial markets exist, a manager might describe them as an arena where individuals and businesses trade financial assets. Through trading, corporations raise capital and redistribute risk among investors. The manager might add that debt markets supply cash to the company; equity markets both supply cash and allow risk sharing by dispersing the company's risk among shareholders; and derivatives markets allow a company to retain some risks and shed others.

Such a depiction would be accurate, but incomplete. Financial markets have another function, which extends beyond the realm of the financial specialist to the general corporate manager. In short, stock market prices provide information that enables those managers to operate the company on behalf of its dispersed and changing owners.

This article describes how managers can extract information from market prices. Using this information, the manager can better allocate capital among the company's various products or divisions and more accurately evaluate corporate performance.

Financial markets

Economists have long recognized the role financial markets have played in the foundation of the modern corporation. As the economist Irving Fisher demonstrated in the early part of the twentieth century, with a relatively small amount of market information, the manager is able to choose investments that are optimal for shareholders, without needing to know the individual preferences of those shareholders.

To identify such investments, managers can use interest rate and price information from financial markets. This information represents the returns that can be earned elsewhere in the economy. Managers can then compare the company's investment possibilities to the returns from other investments, selecting projects that are expected to outperform those other investments.

Indeed, this market information alone yields exactly the same set of investment decisions as would a poll of each of the company's shareholders about their preferred investments (a poll that would, of course, be totally impractical, if for no other reason than the ever-shifting composition of those shareholders). Thus, market information enables managers to operate a corporation efficiently for dispersed and changing owners.

Since Fisher's time, financial innovation has led to the development of liquid markets for a broad set of financial instruments. This innovation has, in turn, produced richer information, enhancing managers' ability to make decisions on behalf of shareholders, which will maximize value.

Treasury bond markets provide information about the return investors require to borrow and lend funds (a major element in the company's cost of capital). Prices of the recently introduced inflation-indexed treasury securities, along with the prices of the older nominal treasury bonds, can also be used to estimate economy-wide inflation.

Similarly, current and historic stock market prices yield information on the premium investors require for bearing risk (another essential component in the company's cost-of-capital calculations) and the ever-expanding derivatives markets based upon those stocks, stock indices, and other assets allow managers to extract even more information. For instance, current prices in option markets provide information about the anticipated uncertainty and volatility in the future price levels of individual stocks, the overall stock market, interest rates, exchange rates, and commodities (such as heating oil, cattle, or corn).

Likewise, futures and forward markets in commodities reveal market expectations about the availability of those commodities and the profitability of storing them for future use. As a consequence, even managers of companies that may never transact in derivatives markets may well benefit from understanding how to use price information from those markets.

Information need

One might ask why managers need information from the market. Professional managers, after all, have both specialized experience and access to private and proprietary information about the company's processes and technology. The answer is twofold.

First, while managers clearly are better informed than other market participants in some ways, there are many types of information they may not have. As Figure 1 shows, one would not expect managers to have special expertise in predicting inflation, interest and exchange rates, oil prices, or other relevant variables.

Furthermore, although managers have superior knowledge about their own company, the same will not be true of competitors.

The value of a paper manufacturer's capital

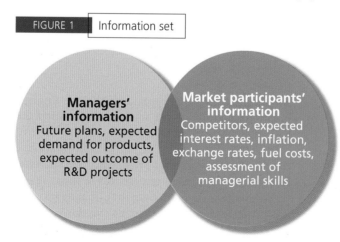

FIGURE 1	Information set

Managers' information
Future plans, expected demand for products, expected outcome of R&D projects

Market participants' information
Competitors, expected interest rates, inflation, exchange rates, fuel costs, assessment of managerial skills

expenditure plan, for instance, is entwined with the expansion plans of its competitors. Paper and pulp prices are cyclical, depending heavily on industry capacity. Extra capacity leads to lower prices and smaller profits. To decide whether to go ahead with capital expenditure, a manager would like to know both competitors' plans and the future demand for paper and pulp.

Spot and futures markets in paper and pulp can help managers estimate future capacity and demand. Moreover, the price of options on pulp and paper will reflect how volatile prices are expected to be, which may help managers determine the risk of expenditure. A good manager, therefore, will seek to extract information from market prices to supplement private knowledge of the company.

A second reason why even well-informed managers need market information lies in the role such information plays in selecting projects that maximize shareholder value. A manager deciding whether to proceed with a proposed investment may believe that the investment offers an attractive return, but such an opportunity must always be evaluated against other uses of capital.

So, while managers may know about opportunities in their own companies, they cannot have the same awareness about the countless opportunities in the wider economy. Indeed, such opportunities will vary, making comparison with every potential investment impossible.

Managers can address this problem by using market rates. These rates reflect, in compact form, the returns available from investments with similar levels of risk. By comparing the returns expected on the proposed investment to the returns offered for other investments with like risk, the manager can evaluate whether the proposal represents the best use of shareholders' capital. In this fashion, the market system assists in directing the flow of capital to the most efficient users of that capital.

Harvesting data

Market information can be useful in many ways, its precise application depending on both the type of market and the model used to extract information from market prices.

For instance, consider a bank that is thinking about acquiring another bank. The target bank's value to the bidder comprises two elements: the current value of the target (the "stand-alone" value) and the value of any cost savings or other benefits from the merger. Suppose the managers of the bidding bank are able to estimate the expected savings. To calculate the value of the target bank, the managers must also estimate the stand-alone value of the target. (The stand-alone value and the cost savings together give the maximum the bidder can afford.) Perhaps the stand-alone value of the target bank depends on the value of its loan portfolio or the status of its off-balance-sheet hedging operations, neither one of which will be entirely transparent to outsiders.

Hence, the bidding managers have a firm idea of the likely savings, but only a rough estimate of the value of the target's current operations.

In such a case, one might argue that the market value of the target provides the bidding managers with the best estimate of the value of the target's current operations. They can use this price to form the foundation of their bid, as it encompasses the market's "consensus" estimate of the target's stand-alone value, rather than the truncated information available to the bidders.

Equity prices can be used in other ways to help managers make decisions – they can help managers gauge company and executive performance, derive measures of company risk, and make valuations based on multiples.

Corporate debt markets

Perhaps less well understood are the uses of prices from corporate debt markets. For a company that borrows funds at the aggregate corporate level, but allocates capital across many businesses, debt prices are essential for allocating capital and assessing the performance of its businesses. Thus, a corporate parent that borrows on behalf of its subsidiaries, but is more creditworthy than those subsidiaries, uses its superior asset base to secure loans on more favorable terms than the subsidiaries could alone obtain. Just as a corporate parent charges its subsidiary for a transfer of machinery, it must also charge the subsidiary for this value transfer created by the parent's implicit credit guarantee.

So, to allocate the company's capital correctly among its businesses, as well as assess the performance of those businesses, the parent must account for the subsidiary's use of the parent's superior asset base. By using information from the bond market, managers can make such corrections.

To illustrate this, consider a bricks-and-mortar corporate parent with an internet-based subsidiary that is less creditworthy than the parent. Let's assume that the funding for that dotcom subsidiary comes from its parent. Viewed on its own, the dotcom venture is both risky and highly levered: it has $100m in assets and debt with a current market value of $98m. The difference represents the dotcom's equity value of $2m. If the dotcom were to issue debt itself, rather than depend on the corporate parent for funding, its debt would have a much lower market value, perhaps $91m. This is because, without the backing of the corporate parent, creditors are exposed to greater risk.

If the dotcom performs poorly, investors cannot turn to the corporate parent to repay the dotcom's debt. This below-investment-grade debt would sell for, say, $91m in the bond market. The $7m difference between the parent-issued debt and the dotcom issue is the value of the corporate parent's implicit guarantee of the dotcom's debt. This guarantee represents additional equity from the parent and must be accounted for in any performance evaluation.

Suppose the corporate parent evaluates the dotcom's performance using a return-on-equity measure, with a "hurdle rate" of 15 percent (that is, a return of 15 percent indicates a performance that compensates for the capital used by the subsidiary) and the dotcom's earnings are $1m. If the corporate parent's $7m guarantee were ignored, the dotcom's return on equity appears to be 50 percent (which is calculated by dividing the $1m earnings by the subsidiary's $2m equity base).

Such a performance would, of course, far exceed the benchmark of 15 percent. Indeed, based on this, the parent ought to devote greater resources to the dotcom and reward its managers for their superior performance. But using information from the debt market produces a very different conclusion. The true return on equity is not 50 percent, but 11 percent. If the dotcom's equity base is properly measured, it comes to $9m, not $2m, due to the corporate parent's "transfer" of its $7m implicit guarantee. The difference derived from the market prices of the debt reflects the parent's true contribution to the subsidiary and with this $7m correction, the subsidiary is underperforming the benchmark rate of return, not exceeding it.

Derivatives markets

Beyond the stock and bond markets lies the broad terrain of derivatives markets, which include exchange-traded as well as customized futures, options, and swaps. Derivatives are based upon underlying assets such as individual stocks, commodities, currencies, interest rates, indices, weather, and even internet bandwidth.

To illustrate the use of information from derivatives markets, consider a car company that is contemplating building an assembly plant. The company must decide whether to build a plant devoted exclusively to executive saloons or a plant whose output can be easily switched between models. If consumer demand for saloons remains steady, both the initial outlay and the subsequent assembly cost per car will be less if the company builds the plant tailored for saloons. Doing so forgoes the flexibility of switching production to other models, but such flexibility is only valuable if consumers begin favoring those models.

Likewise, the managers of the car maker know that if consumer demand for saloons changes frequently, the company would be better off building the flexible plant. Still, the managers are unsure how variable consumer demand must be to justify the higher cost of the flexible plant.

Suppose they determine that consumer demand is linked to oil prices and the state of the economy. When oil prices are high, consumers buy fewer cars and smaller cars. When oil prices are low, consumers buy more cars, indulging in large executive saloons. The probability that consumer tastes will change rests on the probability that oil prices change. By providing information about expected fluctuations in oil prices, derivatives markets give managers guidance about which factory to build.

Market prices incorporate public information and some **private information** from trading by managers

To extract such information, managers must first quantify the relationship between oil prices and consumer demand. Using historical data, they might create a statistical model that lets them predict, for example, how many more saloons would be sold if oil prices dropped by 10 percent. This knowledge, combined with an estimate of how volatile oil prices are likely to be, allows managers to forecast the range of future demand.

The prices of option contracts on oil enable just such a forecast by providing information about expected future volatility of oil prices. To calculate this, the manager uses an option-pricing model. Volatility is, after all, a direct input into the option-pricing model: options are worth more when the underlying asset is volatile. So, one can reverse this calculation: given an option price, one can estimate the volatility necessary to justify that price. Managers can then map this estimate into an estimate of future consumer demand volatility. Finally, the probability of shifting demand determines how valuable manufacturing flexibility is likely to be.

Aggregating data

The extent to which managers should rely on market prices depends upon the range and accuracy of that information. Because market prices represent the aggregation of many information sources, it is often difficult to determine exactly which pieces of information any single price reflects. Posed in terms of the dilemma faced by the managers in the pulp and paper concern, will spot and futures from pulp and paper markets reflect publicly announced capital expenditure plans by their competitors? Will those prices also reflect the private expenditure plans of all competitors, whether announced or not?

In general, market prices incorporate most public information and some private information. Private information comes from trading by informed market participants. These might include the managers themselves, who are permitted to trade (subject to insider trading restrictions) in both the US and the UK if they report such actions to regulators.

Studies suggest that the amount of information in prices can be significant. More than that, even the most casual market observers will report that stock prices can move dramatically before news of mergers and other events becomes public. These sizeable pre-announcement movements further support the notion that prices incorporate private information.

Market reactions

Since market prices tend to reflect most public information, as well as some private information, the market reaction to a managerial decision has the potential to offer managers an informed assessment of that decision.

Consider, for example, Quaker Oats' 1994 acquisition of Snapple Beverages. Quaker Oats, maker of Gatorade sports drink, announced its purchase of Snapple Beverages, a maker of fruit juices and ice teas, for $1.7bn. After the announcement, Quaker Oats' stock price fell by 9.9 percent, a drop amounting to more than $1bn in Quaker's market value. The price did not rebound in subsequent trading.

Quaker explained to analysts that it hoped to gain distribution and other synergies from buying Snapple. Quaker Oats distributed Gatorade through traditional supermarkets; Snapple distributed mostly through other stores. Quaker's managers expected each brand to bolster the other's weaker distribution channel.

Quaker's attempts to explain these expected synergies did not change the market's response. Ultimately, Quaker's managers concluded that the market response was incorrect and stemmed from a misunderstanding of the distribution synergies to be gained. They moved ahead with the merger. Unfortunately, the expected synergies never materialized. Quaker later sold Snapple to Triarc Companies for $300m, much less than its $1.7bn purchase price.

Managers must make their own **judgments** about how much weight to give to the market

This example underscores both the potential value of the market's response to managers' decisions and the complexities managers face in interpreting that reaction. Managers who believe, after careful re-examination, that a fall in the stock price is unwarranted might choose to disclose information they believe has been overlooked by investors.

Of course, concerns over proprietary information may sometimes limit such disclosures, making the loss in shareholder value a (presumably temporary) cost of maintaining secrecy. If prices fail to rebound even after additional information is released, as in the Quaker example, managers may want to reconsider their own assessment.

Ultimately, managers must make their own judgments about how much weight to give to the market. These will be based upon an understanding of what information market prices are likely to incorporate and how such information can be best extracted. Ironically, one indication of the formidable nature of this task comes from the performance of financial asset managers. That these professional money managers as a group so seldom outperform the market suggests the difficulty in determining whether market prices already reflect the information upon which their investment decisions are based.

In the end, however, the value of market information does not rest upon its ability to incorporate private information. Indeed, even if market prices reflected only publicly available information, managers would still have much to gain by using those prices. That is, as collectors and aggregators of information, market prices are a low-cost way for managers to estimate important variables, especially in areas unrelated to their managerial expertise.

So, a manager needing an estimate of future inflation can extract that information from market prices of inflation-indexed treasury securities and conventional treasury bonds, rather than devote time to developing macroeconomic forecasting skills. Even the US Federal Reserve relies on such market "forecasts" when it uses the volatility implied by government bond option prices as an indicator of the degree of uncertainty about future interest rates.

Conclusion

The development of global financial markets has greatly expanded the information that managers can extract from market prices. This allows managers to make more accurate forecasts at a lower cost.

Even managers well informed about their own businesses can profit from the market's distillation of a vast array of data. Although, in theory, managers could collect and analyze the information themselves, in practice this would overwhelm even large organizations. Moreover, markets incorporate information that would otherwise be unavailable. So, skillful managers will take advantage of information embedded in market price to improve their ability to allocate capital, make investment decisions, and evaluate performance.

Further reading

Bodie, Z. and Merton, R.C. (2000) *Finance*, Englewood Cliffs, NJ: Prentice Hall.

Crane, D.B., Froot, K.A., Mason, S.P., Perold, A.F., Merton, R.C., Bodie, Z., Sirri, E.R., and Tufano, P. (1995) *The Global Financial System*, Boston, MA: Harvard Business School Press.

Meulbroek, L.K. (1992) "An Empirical Analysis of Illegal Insider Trading," *Journal of Finance*, XLVII(5).

Untangling the values
of web companies

Sunil Gupta is Meyer Feldberg Professor of Business at Columbia Business School.

Donald Lehmann is George E. Warren Professor of Business at Columbia Business School.

The rise of web companies has thrown traditional methods of corporate valuation into turmoil. **Sunil Gupta** and **Donald Lehmann** describe an approach based on the potential value of customers.

Recent turbulence in stock markets and the high valuation of internet companies have perplexed many people, including financial experts. A few years ago it would have been hard to imagine a situation in which a company such as General Motors would have a market value of $32bn, while web companies such as Yahoo! and AOL could be worth $31bn and $115bn respectively. Such extraordinary valuations seem to defy traditional valuation methods. This article presents a different way of valuing companies, based on one of their most important assets: customers and the future growth of their customer base.

There are three traditional approaches to valuation. The first is the discounted cash flow (DCF) analysis, where a company's future cash flows are discounted at a risk-adjusted discount rate to derive an estimate of value. The second is the economic profit approach, where a company's value equals its invested capital plus the present value of projected economic profits. The third is a relative valuation method, where the value of a company is based on the pricing of comparable companies relative to earnings (that is, its price/earnings ratio), cash flows, book value, or revenues.

Why are these methods difficult to apply to the new economy? Most internet companies have negative earnings but high growth potential. It is hard to define a price/earnings ratio for these or comparable companies when all of them have negative earnings. Similarly, the DCF approach needs a forecast of future cash flows and an estimate of terminal value. However, when companies accrue losses for several years, historical data is unlikely to provide positive cash flow projections in the future. Estimates of terminal value and economic profit are equally problematic for internet companies.

Customer-based valuation

For most companies, the customer base is a crucial asset. Internet companies as well as financial analysts frequently discuss the number of customers, the growth rate of the customer base and even market capitalization per customer. Research demonstrates that customer-based measures correlate highly with the market value of these companies.

The premise for customer-based valuation is simple – if the long-term value of a customer can be assessed and an estimate made of the growth in customer numbers, the company's customer base can be valued. To the extent that customers are important assets for the company, this approach would capture a large portion of the company's overall value.

Let us introduce a concept called the lifetime value (LV) of a customer. The LV of a customer is the present value of all future profits that the company can generate from that customer. This analysis is similar to that of discounted cash flow analysis, with one difference – customer retention or loyalty is built into the calculations of the LV. Formally, assuming a constant margin and retention rate,

$$LV = \text{(Annual gross margin per customer)}$$
$$\div (1 + \text{Discount rate} - \text{Retention rate})$$
$$= \text{Annual gross margin per customer}$$
$$\times \text{Margin multiple}$$

In other words, to convert annual gross margin into LV, we multiply margin by a factor that we call margin multiple. This multiple depends on the customer retention rate and is equal to:

$$1/(1 + \text{Discount rate} - \text{Retention rate})$$

The discount rate is the cost of capital. The retention rate (a measure of loyalty) is the percentage of customers retained over a year; it is estimated from market research or the company's customer database. Table 1 shows that the margin multiple for most companies ranges from 1.8 to 5.0. The higher the retention rate and the lower the discount rate, the higher the margin multiple.

TABLE 1   Variation in margin multiple

Retention rate %	Discount rate %			
	10	12	14	16
60	2.00	1.92	1.85	1.79
70	2.50	2.38	2.27	2.17
80	3.33	3.13	2.94	2.78
90	5.00	4.55	4.17	3.85

Economics of customer acquisition

Lifetime value is useful for assessing the economics of customer acquisition. For example, does it make sense for internet broker E*Trade to spend an average of $250 to acquire a new customer? Or, what is the maximum E*Trade should be willing to spend to acquire a new customer?

E*Trade's financial and annual reports show that at the end of June 2000, the annual margin per customer was about $325. Assuming a discount rate of 12 percent and a retention rate of 90 percent, the LV of an E*Trade customer comes out as $1,477, which is the maximum E*Trade should be willing to spend on a customer. With its current acquisition cost (AC) of $250 per customer, the net lifetime value (NLV) of an E*Trade customer is LV less AC, or $1,227.

Note that the LV is very sensitive to the retention rate. For example, if the retention rate for E*Trade's customer is only 80 percent, the LV of its customers falls from $1,477 to $1,015. NLV helps managers both estimate the value of customers and companies and manage the sources of this value.

Once we know the LV of a customer and the current number of customers, we get an idea of the value of this customer base. For example,

What is the **maximum** an online company should be willing to spend to acquire a new customer?

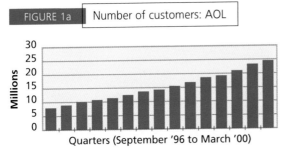

FIGURE 1a — Number of customers: AOL

Millions (y-axis: 0, 5, 10, 15, 20, 25, 30)

Quarters (September '96 to March '00)

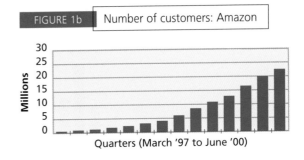

FIGURE 1b — Number of customers: Amazon

Millions (y-axis: 0, 5, 10, 15, 20, 25, 30)

Quarters (March '97 to June '00)

Source: Company annual reports and 10K reports

with a LV of about $1,000 (assuming an 80 per-
cent retention rate) and a base of 2.9 million customers as of June 30 2000, the value of
E*Trade's customers is $2.9bn. However, this
static analysis ignores future changes in the
number of customers, acquisition costs, and margin per customer. (Acquisition costs have not
been included in this calculation since E*Trade
has already incurred this cost for current customers. However, acquisition costs for customers
acquired in the future should be explicitly incorporated.) Figures 1 to 3 show these changes over
time for AOL and Amazon.

In the early stages of development, many
internet companies experience exponential
growth in their customer base. However, such
growth cannot be sustained. Marketing
researchers have developed models to study and
forecast how innovations diffuse through the
population. In cases where there is little information, such as the first few quarters of a company's operations, average estimates from

similar companies can be used as starting points
in a statistical analysis.

For example, we estimate that while AOL is
likely to increase its current customer base of 25
million customers to 117 million, Amazon's current customer base of 22.5 million customers is
likely to grow to only 29 million or 30 million
customers. These estimates are based purely on
historical data and should be adjusted based on
an understanding of the industry and companies.

Two opposing forces affect customer acquisition costs in future. If a company builds strong
brand recognition and a large mass of customers,
it often finds it easier to attract more customers
and can drive down acquisition costs. However,
as a company acquires more and more customers, it gets increasingly harder and more
expensive to acquire new customers who are not
immediately attracted to that company. Further,
competition usually intensifies, driving acquisition costs higher. For example, the acquisition
cost per customer for Ameritrade, an online

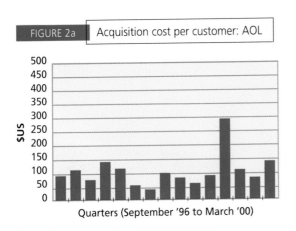

FIGURE 2a — Acquisition cost per customer: AOL

$US (y-axis: 0, 50, 100, 150, 200, 250, 300, 350, 400, 450, 500)

Quarters (September '96 to March '00)

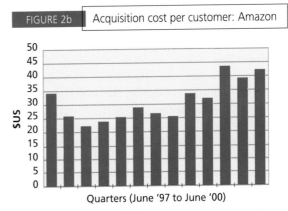

FIGURE 2b — Acquisition cost per customer: Amazon

$US (y-axis: 0, 5, 10, 15, 20, 25, 30, 35, 40, 45, 50)

Quarters (June '97 to June '00)

Source: Company annual reports and 10K reports
Note: Acquisition costs are estimated as total marketing and selling expenses divided by the number of new customers

FIGURE 3a	Quarterly margin per customer: AOL

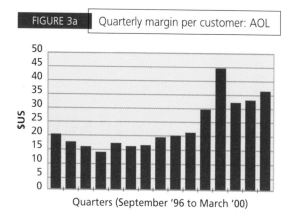

Quarters (September '96 to March '00)

FIGURE 3b	Quarterly margin per customer: Amazon

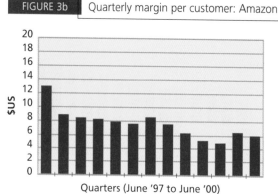

Quarters (June '97 to June '00)

Source: Company annual reports and 10K reports
Note: Margins per customer are gross margins for the firm divided by the number of customers

While the **average margin** per customer increased for AOL, it declined for Amazon

brokerage, increased dramatically from $157 in the third quarter of 1999 to $451 in the fourth quarter.

The profit margin per customer is also driven by two opposing factors. On the positive side, the longer a customer stays with the company, the more profitable that customer becomes. This improvement comes from the reduced cost of serving the customer, the ability to charge higher prices due to customer loyalty, and the company's ability to cross-sell other products. On the negative side, as a company acquires more marginal customers, the profit for an average customer declines. The net impact of these two factors may either increase or reduce average margin per customer over time. For example, Figure 3 shows that while the average margin per customer increased for AOL, it declined for Amazon.

As a simple illustration, we show how these factors affect customer-based valuations of AOL and Amazon. Assuming no changes in average margins and acquisition costs from their most recent estimates (given in Figures 2 and 3), Table 2 shows how the value of Amazon and AOL customers changes with the discount and

retention rates. Note two things. First, the customer retention rate, typically 70 to 80 percent, has a greater impact on overall value than discount rate. Second, customer-based value for both Amazon and AOL is significantly lower than their current market value (as of November 14 2000, Amazon's market capitalization was $9.9bn and AOL's was $115bn).

Although it is possible that these stocks are overvalued, there are at least two aspects

TABLE 2	Customer-based value of Amazon and AOL in $USbn

Amazon

Retention rate %	Discount rate %	
	12	14
70	1.90	1.80
80	2.60	2.40

AOL

Retention rate %	Discount rate %	
	12	14
70	13.3	12.3
80	21.6	19.8

TABLE 3 | Value of AOL customers $USbn

Retention rate %	Increase in margin %	
	10	20
70	15.5	17.8
80	24.7	27.7

Retention rate %	Increase in acquisition cost %	
	10	20
70	12.4	11.6
80	20.7	19.8

that the customer-based approach does not capture:

- the value of other assets;
- an option value where companies may add businesses to improve margins (such as Amazon selling cars or AOL going into television).

Considerable judgment is needed in estimating either this option value or in assessing how margins may change in the future when companies exercise these options. As an illustration, assuming a discount rate of 12 percent, Table 3 shows the changes in this value for AOL with changes in margins and changes in acquisition costs. These tables again highlight the importance of customer retention.

Valuing traditional companies

The customer-based approach can also be used to value companies where traditional valuation methods work well. Consider Capital One, a US company that offers credit cards and financial services. As of June 30 2000, the company had 27.1 million customers with an annual margin per customer of $34 and an acquisition cost of $117. Based on our forecasts, we estimate that

TABLE 4 | Customer-based value for Capital One in $USbn

Retention rate %	Discount rate %		
	10	12	14
60	9.9	9.6	9.2
70	13.9	13.3	12.6
80	20.5	19.2	18.0

Capital One will add another 28.5 million customers in the future. Assuming no change in margins and acquisition costs in the future, the company's customer-based value for various levels of retention and discount rate ranges from $9.2bn to $20.5bn (see Table 4). The market value for Capital One as of November 14 2000 was $11.1bn.

Conclusion

One of the main advantages of this approach is that it highlights the drivers of value and their impact on customer and therefore company value. For example, our analysis suggests that customer retention is a key driver of overall value. Yet most internet companies have focussed on customer acquisition without heeding the quality of customers they were attracting. Of course, no method is perfect and this is also true for the customer-based valuation approach, which is only as good as its forecasts. Further, the method focusses on only one asset – the customers. Still, it appears that this customer-based method adds both predictive value and insights to traditional valuation methods.

Further reading

Koller, T., Murrin, J., and Copeland, T. (2000) *Valuation: Measuring and Managing the Value of Companies*, New York: Wiley.

Reichheld, F.F. (1996) *The Loyalty Effect: The Hidden Force Behind Growth, Profits, and Lasting Value*, Boston, MA: Harvard Business School Press.

Economic value added:
the missing link

Managers may be capable of superior performance, but are they delivering? Linking incentives to EVA provides an answer, says **David Young**.

S. David Young is a professor at Insead. His research interests include value-based management, economic value added, and executive compensation.

The move toward value-based management in large corporations is based on two assumptions. The first is that the main aim of any business in a market economy is to maximize shareholder value. The second is that markets are too competitive for companies to create such value by accident. They must plan for it. And that means having the right culture, systems, and processes in place so managers make decisions in ways that deliver better returns to shareholders.

At the very least, corporate functions must be informed by value-based thinking – planning, capital allocation, operating budgets, performance measurement, incentive compensation, and corporate communication. Economic value added, or EVA, is a tool for achieving this. EVA measures performance, but its uses extend further. When implemented properly, and especially if tied to management compensation, it is a powerful way to promote shareholder value.

What is EVA?

EVA is a measure of profit, but not the accounting profit we are accustomed to seeing in a corporate profit and loss statement. Rather, it is profit as economists define it. The difference between the two is simple. Both are measured net of operating expenses; they differ in the treatment of capital costs. While accountants (and, hence, P&Ls) recognize only explicit, out-of-pocket costs, such as the interest paid to bankers, EVA recognizes all capital costs, including the opportunity cost of shareholder funds. It is based on a century-old idea of the English economist Alfred Marshall: for investors to earn true economic profits, sales must be sufficient to cover all costs, including operating expenses (such as labor and materials) and capital charges. Such economic profits are the basis of value creation.

In fact, it is easy to prove mathematically that the value of any business must equal its net assets (the sum of fixed assets, cash, and net working capital) plus the present (in other words, discounted) value of future EVAs. Therefore, as capital market expectations of corporate EVA increase, so too do share prices. Companies can thus use EVA targets to motivate managers to deliver the financial results capital markets want. This approach is especially useful for executives one or two levels below top management, who have little direct influence over share price and for whom stock options are less effective.

The case of SPX

SPX is a large US auto parts and industrial products company. It was a chronic underperformer in the early 1990s, with low profits and a languishing share price. After John Blystone took over as chief executive in 1995, the company ushered in a series of actions designed to reverse its poor performance. The company's 1995 annual report proclaimed: "One of the most important of these actions has been the decision to move ahead as quickly as possible to implement EVA." Formal adoption took place at the end of 1995, and by the end of the following year a dramatic improvement in performance was evident.

Senior managers were put on an EVA bonus plan. Within a year, 4,700 managers were in the program, including nonexecutive directors. By 1999, SPX was transformed into an EVA company, with a positive effect on the share price. When EVA was implemented, SPX's share price was under $16. Recently (and within five years of implementation), it was selling for $180. What did SPX do to achieve this turnaround, and how was it able to sustain the momentum to continue delivering improvements after adopting EVA?

What makes this company's experience instructive is that it was able to create a culture that put value creation at the center of management systems. As the company explained in its 1998 annual report: "EVA is the foundation of everything we do ... It is a common language, a mindset, and the way we do business."

EVA's most important contribution to the turnaround was its central role in management compensation. The actions taken by SPX to improve performance were neither unusual nor dramatic. Any good executive knows what they are. The key lesson of the SPX experience, however, is not whether managers are capable of delivering superior performance, but whether they are motivated to do so.

What value-driven managers do

So, what exactly have SPX and other EVA companies done to improve financial performance and deliver superior returns to shareholders? The clues can be seen in the definition of EVA. EVA equals after-tax operating profit minus capital costs, with capital costs equal to net assets multiplied by the weighted average cost of capital (or Wacc). When operating profit is divided by net assets, it yields a measure called Rona, or return on net assets. The difference between Rona and the Wacc, or the "EVA spread," multiplied by net assets, equals EVA:

$$\text{EVA} = (\text{Rona} - \text{Wacc}) \times \text{Net assets}$$

Assuming other variables stay constant, EVA increases when Rona increases; or Wacc decreases; or net assets increase (assuming profitable growth); or net assets decrease (in the case of money-losing assets). Evidence from EVA adopters shows several ways to achieve improvements.

Increasing asset turnover. Herman Miller, a US office furniture manufacturer, cut inventories by 24 percent in two years while sales increased 38 percent. It also cut its days of receivables (that is, the money owed by customers) from 45 in 1992 to 30 in 1997. The cut in receivables is especially interesting because the impetus for this came from operating managers, not the accountants.

As one observer explains: "When they went on EVA and began focussing on capital costs like receivables, Miller employees in the divisions attacked the late payment problem on their own and discovered that the cause of overdue receivables was incomplete orders. When an order arrived missing a piece or two, the customer would withhold all payments until the last items arrived. So the 'Millerites' got receivables down by speeding up production of missing items and making sure shipments were complete as well as on time. The result: improvements in EVA and customer satisfaction."

SPX also witnessed dramatic improvements in asset efficiency. In the year after adopting EVA, inventories were cut by 15 percent, despite higher sales. To improve performance, the company focussed its operating units on quality and operating excellence. One such unit began a next-day delivery policy that helped it to achieve market leadership. Such efficiencies, combined with sourcing initiatives, caused a 12.5 percent improvement in operating profit in 1997 (the second year after EVA was implemented).

Disposing of unprofitable businesses. Armstrong, a US plastics and floor products company, sold one of its largest divisions when it concluded the company was incapable of producing a cost-of-capital return on the $338m selling price. In the case of SPX, several divested businesses were profitable, but strategic reviews revealed the businesses were worth more to others and therefore should be sold.

Of course, well-managed companies have always done this, but EVA-based compensation systems create stronger incentives for managers to seek such opportunities.

Repairing assets. Many companies discover that managers on EVA incentive plans are more likely to overhaul existing assets than request capital to buy new ones. Also, when additional capacity is required, managers are more likely to acquire used assets. This practice has proven popular with trucks and forklift trucks. Internet-based secondary markets in capital goods have made this easier.

Structuring deals that require less capital. Before it adopted EVA, Armstrong insisted on having a controlling stake in any acquisition. After adoption, the company began to define the minimum amount of capital it could put into a deal and still get what it wanted.

US paper and paper products manufacturer Boise Cascade had a similar goal in mind when it changed the way it sourced raw materials. Before EVA, the company relied on contracts where it paid in advance for the right to cut timber over a

specified period, usually one to three years. The practice, known as "timber under contracts," protected the company from price swings, but because of the up-front payment, it also tied up capital. Capital charges imposed by EVA showed that the price protection offered by the timber contracts was more expensive than previously thought. As a result, managers began negotiating harder with landowners and entered into fewer contracts.

Increasing leverage. Most managers tend to "underlever" their businesses, which means they rely too much on equity finance and not enough on debt. As a result, companies do not use valuable tax shields that can increase after-tax cash flows available to shareholders. EVA changes that, because when managers are charged for capital, they have powerful incentives to design capital structures that minimize Wacc. For the underlevered company, this means taking on debt, which is precisely what many companies have done after adopting EVA.

Investing in profitable growth. SPX acquired a fire protection company in 1999 to provide its life-safety systems business with additional products for growth in Canada. The acquisition of Advanced Performance Technology in that same year expanded SPX's traditional focus on automatic transmission filters to other filtration applications. Contrary to popular myth, the capital charge imposed by EVA does not discourage investment that creates value, as long as care is taken in the design of EVA bonus plans, which are discussed below.

Delivering superior value

Three of the above actions (increasing asset turnover, repairing assets, and structuring deals with less capital) increase EVA through improvements in Rona. Disposing of unprofitable businesses increases EVA, provided that improvements in the spread between Rona and Wacc are greater than the reduction in net assets. Increasing leverage increases EVA by reducing Wacc, assuming that the company is underlevered when it begins taking on more debt. Investing is profitable, and increases EVA, as long as the Rona on the investment exceeds the Wacc.

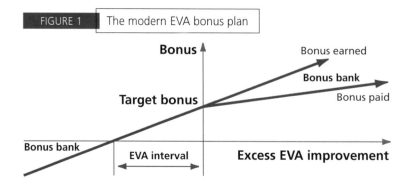

FIGURE 1 The modern EVA bonus plan

These examples show that when managers are evaluated and paid on the basis of EVA, they are more likely than their counterparts in other companies to make the sort of operating, investing, and financing decisions that deliver superior value to shareholders.

EVA compensation

EVA bonus plans don't just motivate managers to think about current EVA. If they did, managers would focus entirely on short-term performance at the expense of the future. Value-creating investments might be avoided because their immediate effects on EVA are negative. The solution is to give managers a direct economic stake in future EVA, not just the current period. Figure 1 shows how such an approach can work.

Remember that the value of the company (that is, the value of debt and equity) equals net assets plus the present value of future EVAs. This means that the market capitalization of a company's shares is based on expectations of future EVA performance. Share price increases when these expectations are exceeded.

This insight yields the first principle of EVA-linked compensation: the key performance measure is not EVA itself, but excess improvement. To derive this measure, companies must first set targets based on market expectations. Then, a target bonus, usually stated as a percentage of salary, is paid if the target level of EVA improvement derived from the company's share price is earned.

Note, however, that the payout is not capped.

This is the second basic principle of EVA-linked compensation. If manager and shareholder interests are to be aligned, management pay should more closely resemble payouts received by owners.

As a result, there is no ceiling on the EVA bonus, but there is also a downside. The bonus earned in any year is the sum of the target bonus plus a fixed percentage of excess EVA improvement (which can be positive or negative). This bonus is credited to a bonus bank, and the bonus bank balance, rather than the current year bonus earned, determines the payout.

Typically, the payout rule for the bonus bank is the full bonus bank balance (if positive), up to the target bonus, plus one-third of the bank balance in excess of the target bonus. When the bonus bank is negative (which is possible if underperformance is great enough), no bonus is paid. The EVA interval shown in the figure determines the sensitivity of the bonus earned to excess EVA improvement, and is chosen by senior managers based on the degree of upside potential and downside risk they wish to inject into the plan.

The bonus bank component adds a critical dimension to the scheme by extending managerial planning horizons beyond the short term. The bank allows for a negative bonus, wiping out at least a portion of EVA bonuses earned in previous years. This practice forces managers to think not only about what they need to do in the short term to boost performance, but also what they must do to increase it in future years. Otherwise, part of the bonuses they earn in the current year might be forfeited. In other words, the bonus bank provides medium-term incen-

EVA can provide value creation **incentives** for managers of divisions, not just top executives

tives for value creation, in addition to the short-term incentives from annual payouts. Stock options add to the EVA bonus plan by providing long-term incentives.

Is EVA appropriate?

All companies can benefit from the shareholder value perspective and the value-creating incentives offered by EVA, but some are more likely to benefit than others (*see* Table 1).

An important part of EVA is that it can provide value-creation incentives for divisional managers, not just for top executives. This suggests that companies with autonomous business units benefit more than companies that operate as one large unit. Also, matrix organizations tend to derive fewer benefits because of the difficulty of establishing accountability.

Companies with substantial shared resources are less likely to benefit from EVA. For example, if common manufacturing facilities or sales staff serve multiple business units, and if these units

are not forced to "buy" this capacity, investment accountability, EVA measurement, and management incentives can be undermined.

Another difference between successful and unsuccessful users is that the former rely on strong managerial wealth incentives tied to business unit performance. The latter tend to place heavier emphasis on stock options. Successful EVA companies use stock options, but recognize that the strongest incentives for divisional managers come from measures based on divisional performance, not corporate measures such as stock price. Unsuccessful users are also more inclined to exercise discretion in paying managers. In other words, they override the bonus plan, probably because of low tolerance for differences in business unit compensation.

In successful EVA users, the chief executive is an enthusiastic advocate, whereas in unsuccessful users, the CEO may not have realized what he or she signed up for. Maybe the CEO thought EVA was what the markets wanted. Or perhaps there was a failure to appreciate the effort needed for full implementation. As a result, implementation is erratic.

Another feature of successful users is that they try to establish and maintain accountability for business unit heads. This, in turn, requires that these managers stay put for extended periods. In unsuccessful adopters, job tenure for business unit managers is short. This difference

| TABLE 1 | Profile of successful and unsuccessful EVA users |

Successful users	Unsuccessful users
■ Autonomous business units	■ One large business unit
	■ Matrix organization
	■ Substantial shared resources
■ Strong managerial wealth incentives tied to business unit performance	■ Excessivee emphasis on stock options
	■ Discretionary approach to compensation
■ CEO is an enthusiastic advocate	■ CEO dosen't realize what he/she signed up for
■ Business unit heads stay put	■ Short-term tenure for business unit heads

is crucial because if managers move around, there is no long-term accountability. Without accountability, deferred compensation is not possible. Deferred compensation, in the form of a bonus bank, plays a critical role in ensuring the EVA bonus plan forces managers to think beyond the current year.

EVA is no panacea, and it is no substitute for sound corporate strategies. But when EVA is at the center of a company's performance measurement system, and when management bonuses are linked, alignment between the interests of managers and shareholders improves. The effect is that when managers make important decisions, they are more likely to do so in ways that deliver superior returns for shareholders.

Further reading

Ehrbar, A. (1998) *EVA: The Real Key to Creating Wealth*, Chichester: Wiley.

Young, S.D. and O'Byrne, S.F. (2000) *EVA® and Value Based Management: A Practical Guide to Implementation*, New York: McGraw-Hill.

Paying executives in
shareholders' interests

In theory, managers run companies in shareholders' interests. **Rajesh Aggarwal** examines how the theory can be better tied to corporate practice.

Rajesh K. Aggarwal is an associate professor of business administration at the Tuck School of Business at Dartmouth College.

Modern finance theory holds that the proper objective of managers is to run the company in shareholders' interests. But managers, with effective control over the company, can make decisions and take actions that serve their own interests instead. The best way to ensure they act in the interests of shareholders is to tie their compensation to the company's performance. Recent experience has borne this out: top executive compensation and stock prices have both increased dramatically.

However, the increase in executive compensation has sparked debate about whether such compensation is excessive, especially when average workers' incomes have been relatively stagnant. While there may well be serious issues associated with the widening gap, this article looks at what matters for company efficiency and the shareholders. Do executive compensation packages provide appropriate incentives to managers, thereby aligning their interests with those of shareholders?

Components

To understand how incentives might be created, the components of executive compensation must first be understood. As an example, consider the compensation for IBM's five highest-paid executives for the fiscal year 1999 (Table 1).

The short-term components of total annual compensation are mainly salary and bonus. Annual salary is fixed in advance and is not seen generally as a performance incentive. The exception to this is that future increases in salary may in part be determined by current company performance. In any event, the present value of current and future increases in salary and bonuses is just a part of total incentives.

Annual bonuses are typically tied to accounting measures of company performance, such as return on (book) equity (ROE), return on assets

TABLE 1 | Executive compensation, IBM, financial year 1999

Name	Title	Salary ($)	Bonus ($)	Other annual ($)	Restricted stock granted ($)	Stock options granted ($)	LTIP ($)	All other comp. ($)	Total annual comp. ($)
L.V. Gerstner, Jr.	Chmn. & CEO	2,000,000	7,200,000	66,376	0	0	5,250,717	285,000	14,802,093
J.M. Thompson	Sr VP	662,500	900,000	5,122	0	3,890,899	3,029,530	49,875	8,537,926
S.J. Palmisano	Sr VP	575,000	775,000	0	6,312,500	3,890,899	2,019,686	44,250	13,617,335
L.R. Ricciardi	Sr VP & gen. couns.	500,000	725,000	276	0	3,112,720	2,524,608	40,500	6,903,104
N.M. Donofrio	Sr VP	550,000	650,000	729	0	2,334,540	3,029,530	36,000	6,600,799

Source: S & P CompuStat ExecuComp

(ROA), return on investment (ROI), or economic value added (EVA). Other measures include subjective reports by board members or superiors for middle managers and targets established by the board. These targets can include investment, product or plant quality, market share, growth rates for income or sales, strategic objectives (such as expansion into new lines of business or restructuring of old businesses), and performance relative to competitors.

While short-term compensation does carry some incentive features (especially in regard to the bonus component), it is typically not linked to company performance in the form of stock returns. Salary provides the executive with a minimum level of income prior to any performance standards or targets being met, while bonuses typically reflect how well the company or executive has met specific objectives established by the board. Long-term components of compensation are much more strongly linked to stock returns.

In Table 1, the salary and bonus paid to chairman and chief executive Louis Gerstner stand out. The short-term components of his annual compensation are worth roughly six times those of the other IBM executives. The size of Mr. Gerstner's bonus is perhaps a reflection of the fact that while bonuses are usually set objectively according to predetermined standards, there is also room for discretion in making bonus payments. His bonus was large enough to keep him as the highest-paid executive in 1999, even though he received no stock options.

The long-term components of total annual compensation are grants of restricted stock, grants of stock options, long-term incentive plan payouts (LTIP), and all other compensation. All other compensation typically includes "gross-ups" to cover for tax liabilities, perquisites, preferential discounts on stock purchases, contributions to benefit plans, and severance payments. Other compensation is usually relatively unimportant.

Restricted stock grants are only paid if the executive remains with the company for a specified time, typically five years. This has two implications. First, the executive has a strong incentive to stay with the company to benefit from the grant. Second, because the stock cannot be sold during the specified period, part of the compensation is tied to company performance during that time. Restricted stock grants clearly align an executive's interests with those of shareholders. Still, the use of restricted stock grants has declined and the use of stock option grants has supplanted them as an incentive mechanism.

Stock options have become the primary mechanism through which managers are given incentives. A stock option gives the manager the right, but not the obligation, to purchase a share of the company's stock for a predetermined price (the exercise price) on or before a specified date. Most stock options are granted "at the money," which means the exercise price is set at the stock price on the day of the grant.

A typical stock option grant has a life of 10 years and becomes available according to a schedule; for example, 10 percent of an option grant every six months, so that the full grant is due over five years with another five years to maturity.

Since stock prices tend to increase, over time

most stock options will move into the money, meaning that the current stock price is greater than the exercise price, which was set months ago.

Clearly, stock options are tied to the company's stock price. As a result, they usually do a good job of aligning managers' interests with those of shareholders, especially as options move into the money.

Most executives who receive stock options in the US do so in the form of nonqualified options. Under US regulations, these have no tax implications at the time of issue. When the option is exercised, the executive pays tax on the difference between the stock price and the exercise price at the ordinary income tax rate.

The US company deducts the difference between the stock price and the exercise price as compensation expense. If the executive later sells the stock, the executive pays tax (at the capital gains tax rate) on the difference between the sale price and the market price at exercise of the option. Because the company is able to deduct the difference between the stock price at exercise and the predetermined exercise price as compensation expense, nonqualified options are preferable from the perspective of company taxation.

Favorable tax treatment is a significant part of the explanation for the dramatic increase in use of stock options. Favorable accounting treatment also enters into it. For the most part, stock options never show up on accounting statements. In the US, companies are required to disclose grants of stock options, but are not required to take an accounting charge for them if the options are granted at or out of the money. As a result, stock options are an excellent way of providing managers with deferred compensation without incurring an accounting liability.

Looking at Table 1, while Mr. Gerstner received no new option grants in 1999, the other executives received substantial grants. Mr. Gerstner received a grant of new options in 1997 worth $82m, which propelled him into the top 25 highest-paid chief executives in the US that year, with a total of almost $91m in compensation.

The last component of compensation is the long-term incentive plan (LTIP). These plans are similar to bonuses but are awarded for performance over several years. For example, an LTIP may be triggered if ROA is at least 15 percent for three consecutive years.

In general, LTIPs are not that important from year to year because they occur only when a long-term target is met. For IBM in 1999, however, LTIPs were important for all five executives. As is clear from the table, IBM's five highest-paid executives were well compensated, with significant amounts related to performance.

Trends

The dominant theme in the public debate about executive compensation is the soaring pay packages of chief executives. By 1999, according to the magazine *Business Week*, the average compensation package of a US chief executive, including bonuses and stock options, was 475 times that of the average blue-collar worker. However, this statistic is misleading for several reasons.

Table 2 summarizes compensation for 13,109 executives at 1,500 publicly traded US companies from 1993 to 1997. For each company, data are reported for the top five executives ranked annually by salary and bonus.

While the sums paid to chief executives are substantial, they are not as large as is often portrayed in the media. The average US manufacturing worker made about $28,800 in 1997, so the median chief executive's total annual compensation was 52 times that of the average worker.

Although the figures are not strictly comparable, contrast this multiple with the 475 times claimed by *Business Week* for 1999. The magazine focussed on the compensation packages of chief executives at the largest companies, which are not representative of all companies. The average chief executive is paid much less than the highest flyers.

The sums paid to executives are a fraction of the monetary value of executives' stock and option holdings, especially for chief executives. In terms of monetary values, stock holdings are more important for chief executives and executives with oversight authority than are option holdings, while the converse is true for executives in "divisional" and "neither" categories (*see* footnote to Table 2). This may be partly because

TABLE 2

TABLE 2 Median executive compensation by job classification, 1993–7

	Chief executive	Oversight executives	Divisional executives	Neither (such as vice presidents)
Total annual compensation (in 1997 dollars)	1,494,000	847,000	605,000	555,000
Long-term components of total annual compensation (in 1997 dollars)	543,000	296,000	190,000	170,000
Holdings of stock (in 1997 dollars)	5,801,000	1,079,000	422,000	475,000
Holdings of options (in 1997 dollars)	2,218,000	887,000	583,000	578,000

Source: Aggarwal and Samwick (2000)

Classification categories: chief executives; executives with oversight authority for the company (such as the chief operating officer or chief financial officer); executives with divisional responsibility (such as division or subsidiary chiefs, executives in charge of a specific product line or geographical area, and executives with specific production related responsibilities); and executives with neither oversight authority nor divisional responsibility (for example, vice presidents with no other information given).

chief executives and executives with oversight are more likely to include company founders who typically have large equity positions and may not participate in option programs (for example, Bill Gates of Microsoft).

In summary, stock and option holdings provide the bulk of incentives for all executives. However, comparisons of levels of compensation or values of holdings do not say much about the strength of incentives or how well-aligned managers' interests are with those of shareholders. How is compensation translated into incentives?

Incentive power

A measure of how much executive compensation depends on company performance is given by calculating pay–performance sensitivities (PPS) based on stock returns.

The PPS from stock is the fraction of the total equity outstanding held by the executive. The PPS from options is the number of shares on which options are written divided by the total number of shares outstanding multiplied by an adjustment for the probability that the option will finish in the money.

From 1993 to 1997, the median stock and option PPS for chief executives in US companies was 1.28 percent. That is, the chief executive's holdings of stock and options was 1.28 percent of the total equity outstanding in the company. The PPS is often reported as the money that accrues to an executive from a $1,000 increase in shareholder wealth.

At the median, then, the value of a chief executive's stock and option holdings increases by $12.80 for every $1,000 increase in shareholder wealth. If the other four executives in the top management team are included, at the median, the value of the top management team's stock and option holdings increases by $30.80 for every $1,000 increase in the wealth of shareholders.

Given the financial returns generated by publicly traded companies in the US, these pay–performance sensitivities constitute substantial incentives for executives.

Figures 1 and 2 illustrate the evolution of the use of stock and options as incentive devices from 1993 to 1997. While pay–performance sensitivities from stock holdings have remained relatively constant, pay–performance sensitivities from options have shown a dramatic increase, more than doubling for chief executives.

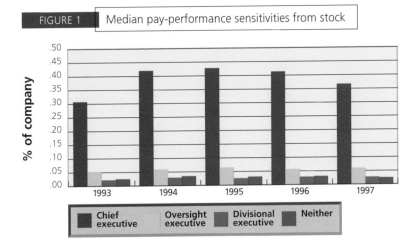

FIGURE 1 Median pay-performance sensitivities from stock

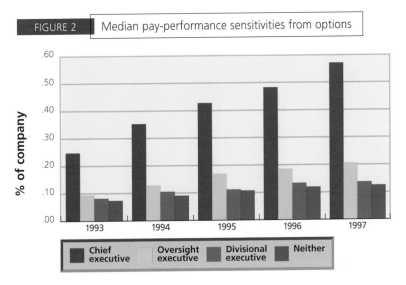

FIGURE 2 Median pay-performance sensitivities from options

The same is true for executives with oversight authority. While the pay–performance sensitivities from options have shown large increases for executives with divisional responsibility and executives with neither responsibility, these increases have not been as large as the increases for chief executives and executives with oversight authority.

At the median, all four groups of executives have greater pay–performance sensitivities from options than they do from stock (even though for chief executives and oversight executives, the dollar value of stock holdings is greater than that of options). Once again, this reflects the fact that options have become the incentive device of choice for most companies in the US.

Conclusion

The importance of incentives for executives has increased in recent years, with most of the increase in the 1990s attributable to the use of stock options. While other components of compensation are important, holdings of stock and stock options are best at aligning managers' interests with those of the shareholders. Because stock option grants are such a large component of soaring executive pay, much of this phenomenon can in fact be attributed to a better alignment of managers' and shareholders' interests over the past decade.

Further reading

Aggarwal, R.K. and Samwick, A.A. (2000) "Performance Incentives within Firms: The Effect of Managerial Responsibility," working paper available at http://mba.tuck.dartmouth.edu/pages/faculty/raj.aggarwal/perf0001.pdf.

Business Week (2000) "Executive Pay: Special Report," Business Week, April 17.

Hall, B.J. and Liebman, J.B. (1998) "Are CEOs Really Paid Like Bureaucrats?" Quarterly Journal of Economics, 113(3), 653–91.

Jensen, M. and Murphy, K.J. (1990) "Performance Pay and Top Management Incentives," Journal of Political Economy, 98, 225–64.

Murphy, K.J. (1999) "Executive Compensation," in O. Ashenfelter, and D. Card (eds), Handbook of Labor Economics, Vol. 3B, Amsterdam: North Holland.

Integrating finance
systems at Microsoft

Brent Callinicos is treasurer of Microsoft Corporation.

Jeanne Mendez is director of global cash management and treasury operations at Microsoft Corporation.

With cash turnover of $100bn, Microsoft's treasury department still relied on retyping data. **Brent Callinicos** and **Jeanne Mendez** explain how integration worked for them.

Since its founding in 1975, Microsoft has managed treasury department functions centrally from its headquarters in the US. The treasury department is responsible for the management and investment of the company's worldwide assets, all foreign exchange trading and hedging, subsidiary funding for local expenses, corporate finance functions related to strategic equity investments, and buying back Microsoft stock.

The company has undergone tremendous growth, the pace of which has provided ample challenges for the treasury department. A decade ago, the company's revenues were just over $1.1bn and total cash and short-term assets on the balance sheet were $450m. There were few foreign exchange positions and little investment portfolio activity; the treasury department consisted of five people.

By mid-1996, managers recognized that development of the department's business processes and systems had been outpaced by the company's growth. Cash balances exceeded $7bn and the department managed thousands of foreign exchange hedge positions and had begun to use derivatives for risk management. Annual cash turnover exceeded $100bn. And this growth was expected to continue. Indeed, by June 2000, annual revenues had reached $23bn and total cash balances exceeded $20bn, in addition to a strategic equity portfolio of $17bn. Foreign exchange exposure ranged between $4bn and $6bn, actively managed through five distinct hedging programs. The group was responsible for 1,500 cash and custody accounts around the world.

As the 1996 financial year ended, the department was using many different *ad hoc* systems tools, which had been developed independently, on various technologies, and without significant integration. Further, system maintenance was complicated by numerous patches on legacy systems.

The department did use a portfolio management system for its fixed income portfolio (Princeton Financial's PAM), but much of the rest of the department's work was done on spreadsheets. The department relied on Excel excessively for analytical functionality and data storage, maintaining hundreds of different files, some of which exceeded 15MB. Attached to these spreadsheets were more than 300 links to external sources of market data.

Managers were concerned about controls over data and manual transaction processing. A decentralized approach to data entry and storage resulted in duplication and inconsistency in data across groups, and when data needed transferring between groups it had to be retyped. For treasury staff to remain confident in the integrity of the data, they had to spend many hours on reconciliation – rather than doing the strategic planning and analysis that would add value to the company.

The Gibraltar project

After a four-month analysis project in 1996, Microsoft developed a plan for an improved and integrated treasury system, called the "Gibraltar project." It was expected to deliver improved security and control, financial risk management, a single point of data entry without retyping, online reporting, integrated system-based checks and balances, and a seamless integration of many different tools. The company chose to build all system solutions on Microsoft technology.

The treasury department also anticipated the need to make changes in business processes, including the creation of a dedicated treasury controller's group responsible for accounting entries, compliance monitoring, and confirmations of trades. One of the first responsibilities of this group was to review treasury processes and recommend improvements to control guidelines. Security procedures around all treasury transactions, including foreign exchange trading, wire transfers, and investment decisions, were strengthened. The department also defined team functions strictly and segregated duties more clearly. These changes were made before selecting any department-wide system, but with an eye toward their inclusion in any future solutions.

This review of all the department's business processes made it easier for teams to identify system needs and solutions. To aid in the analysis, the department and its colleagues in finance's information technology group (FIT) created process-flow maps and placed them on the walls of the department's hallways for months at a time, allowing impromptu discussion and modification by employees.

To improve data integrity and the distribution of information within and outside the department, the department set up a central data warehouse, internally called MST (Microsoft treasury), using Microsoft's SQL server database architecture and Pace software from Eagle Development Group, which was customized. Aggregating all treasury data in MST reduced the unreliability and inconsistency of various data in disconnected systems and spreadsheets. The tool is also a robust reporting engine, allowing treasury staff and senior managers to view data at various levels of detail and in different formats through user-driven changes to reporting criteria.

Many levels of detail in any given report are available through a single mouse click. So, for example, the director or one of the traders from the portfolio management group can pull up a consolidated holding report at the group's morning meeting and within seconds obtain specific information about a single security or company in those holdings. At the same time, other people can review details from the same source.

MST also uses links to external, market-related data that is essential for making financial decisions, and archives much of that data for historical perspectives. Treasury staff and senior managers use it to review and analyze financial data, including portfolio holdings, credit-reporting guidelines, portfolio performance metrics, counter-party exposures, position analyses, cash balances, and transactions. This information is often available in real time and via the web.

Since its inception three years ago, MST has improved efficiency and allowed treasury staff to focus on financial analysis and decision making rather than on data management. One example of this is the ability to check performance of the portfolio management group internally: it has reduced the time taken to report on results by two weeks.

Treasury transactions

The Gibraltar project also aimed to implement an integrated treasury transaction system, with the ability to initiate and account for transactions across the portfolio, foreign exchange, cash management, and treasury controller's groups.

In the first half of 1997, the team evaluated 30 solutions from outside vendors, yet concluded that no single tool would meet all the company's needs. It decided that the portfolio management group would continue to use PAM and a separate solution was to be found for foreign exchange and cash management needs.

Half a dozen vendors demonstrated products to the treasury department. Two were short-listed and each spent a week in the company's headquarters in Redmond. The department provided both vendors with scripts representing a typical week. The process maps mentioned above were critical in creating these scripts. Recognizing that no two treasury departments operate identically or have the same needs, this approach helped to ensure the team could assess whether a product really was suitable, rather than being sold only on the product's strengths by sales representatives or vendor references.

In fall 1997, the department selected the Integra-T package from Integrity Treasury Solutions and began work on implementation, configuration, and enhancement. It is important to note, however, that the department avoided custom solutions, recognizing that future support is hampered by major customization.

With its interfaces, front-end analytic tools, and reporting through MST, Integra-T is the core component of the overall treasury transaction system (TTS). The system, which is fully compliant with the department's segregation of duties and other control policies, allows staff to perform a range of tasks: transaction input, revaluation of trading positions, real-time pre-trade compliance monitoring, cash flow and exposure forecasts, trade confirmation and settlement, cash balance and transaction reporting, bank account reconciliation, wire transfer initiation, and the automated posting of transactions to the company's SAP general ledger system.

Using more than 500 scheduled daily jobs, the system receives real-time data of market information from sources such as Bloomberg and Reuters, as well as detailed banking data from Microsoft's global banking partners. It passes funds transfer information automatically to banking systems. This is managed by a software package (Sys*Admiral from Tidal Software). Any exceptions are reported automatically, so the package allows processing to take place 24 hours a day, seven days a week, without support from IT staff. Data capture and creation by TTS are reported through MST, providing consistent methodology and flexibility across the department.

The system has proven its worth since August 1998. The department can point to improved controls, systemic audit trails and compliance reporting, a single source of bank data, MST reporting, and the automated creation of accounting entries. It also achieved one of its primary goals: staff input data just once. Foreign exchange traders, for example, enter their data through a trade interface. That data is passed automatically to the cash management group for settlement and then to the treasury controller's group for online review before being posted to the SAP general ledger. The groups have eliminated e-mails, paper reports, and Post-it notes for these processes, greatly enhancing controls and efficiency.

Gains have also been made by linking additional external processes to the system. For example, the corporate accounting department creates monthly reports of payments owed to and from subsidiaries. Each month, this process creates hundreds of payments, all to be made within two days. The treasury and accounting departments created an automated process for passing this data from SAP into the treasury transaction system, using pre-formatted wire transfer instructions as well as default accounting entries for all the payments. Doing so virtually eliminated the manual entry previously required and reduced the time needed to perform these functions by more than 20 hours every month.

Risk reduction

Perhaps the most important, objective of the Gibraltar project was to improve understanding, monitoring, mitigating, and reporting of financial risks taken by the treasury department. In all companies, the treasury department is expected to increase return on capital while controlling risk. No treasurer wants to be the subject of a newspaper article that ascribes company losses to an inadequate assessment of risk. With that in mind, Microsoft's policy is to engage only in risk management activities that it can understand, measure, and monitor internally.

In 1996, different groups in the department used independent risk-monitoring tools, but there was no method of aggregating and reporting on risk seamlessly and uniformly. The team researched best practices and decided to adopt several approaches, including value-at-risk (VAR) and stress testing as complementary risk-measurement methodologies, each measuring different types of market risks. VAR is used to provide senior managers with an aggregate view of likely outcomes of financial transactions, whereas stress testing attempts to identify scenarios that would create worst-case results.

Over the next year, the department formulated a risk management system called FinRisk. It comprised two packages: TotalRisk (from Barra Redpoint) and an internally developed tool called IRMA (Internal Risk Management Application). In addition, treasury uses the Raroc service from Banker's Trust for monthly validation of risk assessments. Using more than one system has advantages: first, it is more thorough; second, it provides a back-up should any system become unavailable; and third it allows staff to validate across systems, which helps check data integrity.

As an aggregated system, FinRisk is an integrated platform that analyzes data from many sources, including MST, as well as external data feeds. It allows the group to model scenarios, on historical as well as hypothetical bases, before executing transactions. FinRisk allows for desktop, web-based reporting and analysis of consolidated risk data across asset classes and groups, as well as risk metrics by department, group, and individual portfolios, and provides senior managers with a single source of critical risk data.

The FinRisk project has also established a "culture of risk" within the treasury department. Today, individual portfolio managers can know in advance what a particular trade will do to Microsoft's overall risk.

Conclusion

Building tools with the goal of integration has brought numerous benefits: integrated risk management, intuitive and integrated workflow processes, improved data integrity, the elimination of data redundancy and reconciliation, online reporting, reduction of manual tasks and paper-based reporting, and better controls.

Microsoft's treasury department may have an advantage in its access to strong IT support. However, it is believed that the critical component of success with the Gibraltar project has been the emphasis on working with fully integrated data and processes and with intuitive and relevant software tools. These tools can be created separately or at different times, but if their creators bear in mind their ultimate integration with existing systems, workflow can be made seamless and efficiency greatly enhanced. This is a philosophy that can be usefully adopted by treasury departments around the world.

Production
and operations

10

Contents

The essence of service lies in focus 465

Rogelio Oliva, Harvard Business School

Service operations differ from manufacturing in several respects: people, not physical products, are fundamental to services; a service is labor intensive and is produced and consumed at the same time.

Introduction to Part 10

The techniques of production and operations have seen remarkable advances in recent years. Concerned with the transformation of raw materials into finished products and their distribute to customers, the subject has been revolutionized by the possibilities of electronic automation and the internet. In this part, authors ask what area of this revolution is likely to fizzle out, and what will endure. They examine the history of production management, and outline the best ways of using research and development to create value. Enterprise resource systems are described and assessed, and the distinctions between product and services operations is made explicit and relevant.

All change in the second
supply chain revolution

Supply chains face fundamental change because of electronic commerce. Early automation wrought a similar upheaval. **Morris Cohen** and **Vipul Agrawal** foresee consequences, not just for companies, but the structure of whole industries.

Morris A. Cohen is Matsushita Professor of Manufacturing and Logistics at the Wharton School of the University of Pennsylvania. He can be contacted at cohen@wharton.upenn.edu

Vipul Agrawal is chief operating officer at MCA Solutions LLC. He was assistant professor of operations management at the Leonard H. Stern School at New York University. He is at agrawal@mcasolutions.com

Technological innovation opens the door to new business models, and such models eventually lead managers to develop new processes for matching demand with supply. As a result, changes occur in the nature of the supply chain governing a company's relationships with its suppliers, distributors, and customers. In turn, this leads to major shifts in the competitive structure of industries.

Many argue that the effects of e-commerce on supply chain management typify this process and will overturn accepted business models. Before discussing the effect of e-business, we should note that it is not the first time the supply chain has undergone a revolution. The first occurred at the turn of the nineteenth century and formed the model for manufacturing and distribution throughout the twentieth century. It is instructive to examine this revolution in more detail.

The first revolution

Between 1870 and 1917, a massive reorganization of the economies of developed nations took place. Commerce had been characterized by small companies that operated within a limited geographic space and focussed on a thin slice of the value chain. During this period these companies were replaced by large, vertically integrated corporations. Decisions about the allocation of resources that ensured the matching of supply with demand throughout the value chain were removed from the marketplace and placed in the hands of managers. Indeed, as the economist Alfred Chandler put it, the "invisible" hand of market allocation was replaced by the "visible" hand of decision making by corporate managers.

The switch from market allocation to corporate allocation was based on a simple economic reality. The cost of allocation of resources within the company became lower than the cost of using the market. Those who recognized this fact developed business models that took advantage of the opportunity by expanding and integrating operations within the company. The primary areas where changes took place were in the production and distribution of goods, that is, the supply chain.

What were the technologies that enabled the movement to the "visible hand" to take place? The most important were the introduction of continental railroad and telegraph systems and the arrival of high-speed, continuous-process production machinery. By 1870 it became possible in developed countries to ship goods and to communicate from coast to coast. For the first time, continental markets could be accessed, both for the supply of raw materials and the distribution of finished products. The scale and complexity of business increased, requiring the invention of management skills such as scheduling, accounting, and co-ordination across many interacting locations.

Soon, mass distributors appeared. These companies used national rail networks to make fast, reliable, low-cost deliveries. Heavy use of such infrastructure gave them a high stock turnover for a high volume of goods. The successful distributors set up networks of retail chains and commodity dealerships and came to dominate their regional markets.

The success of mass distributors was based on "economies of speed," whereby a company internalized a high volume of market transactions. The increase in transaction volume led to high stock turnover, which in turn led to rapid cash flow. This cash flow then enabled companies to buy raw materials in large quantities at lower costs, with lower credit cost terms, and thus to self-finance expansion. The economies of speed supported the growth of market share because mass distributors were able to offer more variety at a lower cost to their consumers.

A second class of technological innovation introduced at the end of the nineteenth century was high-speed, continuous-process manufacturing equipment. This technology made the most of economies of scale. An illuminating example is the Bonsack machine invented for making cigarettes. In 1881, Mr. Duke of North Carolina

The first supply chain revolution was based on **integration** of mass production with mass distribution

acquired the first of these machines in the US. It was capable of producing 70,000 cigarettes a day (as opposed to a maximum of 3,000 a day for the manual rolling of cigars). Fifteen of these machines could saturate the entire US market.

Consequently, Duke and his American Tobacco Company had to develop aggressive advertising techniques to persuade consumers to try this new product. Similar developments occurred in other process industries, such as the Diamond Match Company, which adopted comparable high-speed manufacturing technology, and Quaker Oats, which introduced gradual reduction roller flour mills in 1870 to yield another new product (in this case, breakfast cereal).

Process technology led to a new type of supply chain. National manufacturing corporations integrated with companies further down the chain to control distribution and marketing, because the current methods and channels could not handle the high output from their machines. These corporations also integrated with suppliers to manage (in terms of both quality and availability) the unprecedented flow of raw materials required to feed the newly mechanized processes.

In some cases, cartels formed (such as Duke with cigarettes and Diamond Match with matches) and it was necessary to stimulate demand through advertising to absorb the large volume of new products. Finally, networks of branch sales offices were built to handle the wholesaler function needed to co-ordinate distribution in regional markets. The first movers built empires by financing expansion internally, thus retaining ownership. Integrated production and distribution also acted as a barrier to entry.

The first supply chain revolution was based on integration of mass production with mass distribution. The business model used economies of speed and scale to provide first movers with an advantage that led to high concentration and unprecedented value. Crucially, the flow of mate-

Box 1 **The effect of the supply chain**

How does the evolution of supply chains relate to changes in an industry's competitive structure? The history of the personal computer industry provides a revealing illustration of this relationship. In the early 1980s IBM adopted a bold strategy for the design and production of this new product. It outsourced two key components, the operating system and the central processing unit, to Microsoft and Intel respectively. This "supply chain" decision was made at a time when most discounted the potential of the personal computer to overtake the mainframe as the dominant product.

When IBM made this decision, computers were highly integrated products produced in an industry that was essentially vertical. An IBM computer consisted of specialized components that could not be used in any competing product. The design, production, delivery, and after-sales support of components, as well as the assembly of the final product, all took place in premises owned and managed by IBM. Other market leaders in the computer industry, such as DEC and Unisys, had similar structures.

IBM's seemingly innocuous outsourcing decisions coincided with a fundamental upheaval in the industry. IBM let Intel and Microsoft in. Product design shifted from integral (components are designed only for a specific product and assembled by a single company) to modular (components can be used in a variety of products and have standard interfaces). As a result, components could be supplied by different vendors; the industry moved from a vertical to a horizontal structure.

Another type of supply chain occurred in the computer industry about 10 years later. In the 1990s Michael Dell began building computers to order in his college dormitory in Texas. Each customer could specify a configuration. This meant components could be procured and assembled by Dell with lower cost and shorter lead times than "make to stock" companies because the product design was modular and the industry was horizontal. This simple supply chain strategy is known as the "Dell direct model." It is characterized by low inventory (that is, less than seven days), high profit margins, and a very high return on assets.

Since lifecycles for computers are short, one of the major costs of storing components is obsolescence. The mass customization process of the Dell model reduces this cost. Through its direct sales channel, Dell can shift a customer's demand to a configuration with a higher margin and better availability. It might present a choice between a rapid response for components that are in stock (and perhaps more expensive) and a delay for fulfilling the configuration initially requested with components that are unavailable but on order.

Dell's rapid response and lean asset base are supported by a supplier network that can place components at its assembly plants in Austin, Texas, within minutes of the order being made. These "revolver" distribution centers support just-in-time production. Dell's volume is sufficient inducement for most suppliers to absorb the capital costs and risks associated with supporting Dell's supply structure.

Recently Dell has shifted much of its sales to the internet and these sales have risen to more than $30m a day. Purchases made on the internet have substantially higher margins and reduced costs. Customers make fewer telephone calls (one call, as opposed to five). The original call center sales model also was limited due to the cost (in time) of providing information to customers. Sales staff have incentives to maximize the margin dollars earned per minute of contact time. They will thus act to conclude a sale with a choice that may not reflect the customer's willingness to pay for higher-margin components. On the internet, the indecisive customer can surf without limit and may end up buying a more expensive configuration.

What are the lessons we can learn from the PC industry? First, changes in the architecture of computers coincided with a shift in supply-chain strategy and a reorganization of the industry. These changes allowed Michael Dell to create the Dell direct model. Second, e-commerce can lead to lower costs, enhanced service, and higher profit margins. Thus, the computer industry is an early example of the revolutionary change other industries are now going through.

rial from its raw stages through the manufacturing, distribution, and retail stages was controlled by managers, not by markets. This internal control reduced transaction and information costs and led to more efficient use of capital and labor.

The resulting lower unit cost supported a larger market share and higher cash flow, and reduced the cost of capital. By 1917 the revolution was over and many industries in the US and Europe were controlled by large, integrated corporations.

The second revolution

We believe a second supply chain revolution is underway, fueled by the internet and business-to-business commerce. It began some time in the past decade and has yet to run its course. The seeds of this revolution were sown in the 1990s, the "golden age" of supply chain management. During this period companies experimented with novel supply chain strategies. For example, under postponement, companies created finished products as close as possible to the point of customer demand. Another development, mass customization, involved producing customized products on a scale and at a cost comparable to the mass production of standardized products. Their success was based on the introduction of mechanisms that reduced uncertainty and non-productive delays, enabled information to be shared, and co-ordinated decision-making throughout the supply chain.

Let us now consider an ideal situation in which information, material flow, product attributes, and decision-making realize the full potential of e-commerce technologies. Information flows in this ideal world will be accurate, rich, and instantaneous. Information, moreover, will be based on all supply chain transactions (retail to raw material) and will be visible throughout the chain. The internet will reduce search and price discovery costs to a minimum.

Goods will flow directly between suppliers and end customers, controlled by just-in-time shipment. In this environment, the cost of changing suppliers will be zero. Products will become more customized. Companies might also be able to develop economies of scale in production by adopting automated flexible manufacturing processes.

How realistic is this picture of the future? The technologies that can make it happen exist, along with the profit incentives for companies that can build such supply chains. The combination of unlimited information, computing power, and capacity will make it possible for managers to match supply with demand on a global scale.

Innovative supply chain structures are rapidly emerging. These incorporate expanded access to "e-sources" of supply, which use web-based exchanges and hubs, interactive trading mechanisms and advanced optimization, and matching algorithms to link customers with suppliers for individual transactions. Consequently, the dream of always providing the right product to the right customer at the right time and place and at the right price will very likely become a reality.

Since we are in the midst of the second supply revolution, predictions about its final result must be tempered. Companies are already adopting a range of new supply chain structures and competitive strategies. It is naïve to think that one size will fit all or that any firm will restrict itself to a single structure for all of its transactions. Above all, new supply chains must provide diversity and flexibility. The structure of industry, however, will not remain static. Just as in the first supply chain revolution at the turn of the last century, the implications for corporate organization and industry structure are profound. Their effects will be felt far beyond the present advances in supply chain management.

Look to the process
for a better product

Production techniques have revolutionized product manufacturing. **Roy Westbrook** looks at recent progress and what is to come from automation and robotics.

Roy Westbrook is a fellow of St Hugh's College and lecturer in management studies at the Saïd School of Business, Oxford University.

Production operations management is the systematic creation and delivery of products to customers. Most things you buy, from the clothes you are wearing to the book you are reading, started out as some kind of raw material, which has been processed, finished, packaged, and delivered. It is the job of production operations to deliver the products every day, on time, at the right cost and quality.

This requires a systematic process to transform the input resources of materials, information, staff, and equipment into outputs of goods – thus the production operation typically accounts for 80 percent of business costs. If operations are too costly compared with rivals, the business eventually fails. If quality is poor or delivery times too long, customers will go elsewhere. Hence the operation, the value-adding part of a business, is the heartbeat of a corporation.

Types of process

In production operations there are four main types of process, characterized by the range or variety of products made and the volume required for each production or customer order. For a company making a wide range of unique products the appropriate process will be jobbing. A jobbing operation designs and makes items to customer order, in very low volumes, and one or a few staff do it all – examples would be bespoke furniture or handmade shoes. The variety of such operations, which never make quite the same thing twice, means that repetitive mass production cannot be used and skill levels are high. Hence, costs and prices are high too.

As volumes increase and more items are repeated, batch manufacturing becomes appropriate. Here there is still the flexible equipment used in jobbing, but machines produce longer runs of items and then are reset for the next product. This is the most common type of operation, covering such industries as printing and clothing. As volumes increase further and the range of items made narrows, a company may use a line operation, with sequenced workstations repeating short-cycle tasks and producing quite complex products (for example, consumer electronics) comparatively cheaply. In Japan, production lines are ubiquitous – Yamaha even makes grand pianos on a line operation. When volumes are very large, a line may be automated, as with cars.

Finally, a commodity product produced in vast quantities requires a continuous flow process, such as a paper mill or oil refinery. These processes need large capital investment but little labor, so their scale, level of automation, and ability to run continuously lead to very low unit costs – essential for commodities. In practice, companies develop processes that mix the virtues of different types.

Toshiba's Ome plant makes laptops and other computing equipment on a manual assembly line. But the line can make as few as 20 of the same item before changing to another product. This is possible because the line is linked by computer to the planning and engineering functions. At each workstation on the line a screen displays a drawing of and instructions for the model being worked on. As the model changes, so does the screen, allowing a line to be used for small batches and thus greater variety.

Materials flow

Although only one type of operation is called continuous flow, in practice most types, even those employing several discrete stages, aspire to continuous flow. Moving materials swiftly through processing reduces cost – fewer handling and storage charges, lower inventory, lower work-in-progress levels (reducing control problems), and shorter lead times. This is the principal lesson from the Japanese "just-in-time" (JIT) method of production, perhaps the greatest innovation in manufacturing methods since the moving assembly line.

The JIT approach was pioneered in the 1970s at the Toyota motor company, which is still its best exponent. (In Japan, JIT is often called "TPS," for Toyota production system.) The principle of just-in-time is implied by its name: the satisfying of demand as it arises, so there is neither the waste of having finished goods waiting in store for an order that may never come, nor the unresponsiveness of making a customer wait. Elimination of waste and responsiveness are pillars of JIT. When this idea is applied through the production chain and beyond to suppliers, we approach continuous flow, each process demanding materials from its supplier and receiving them at once. Materials are pulled through the supply chain ultimately by customer request – hence the term "pull" systems. The idea is not to hold more than the minimum inventory and to make just what is needed when it is asked for and not before.

For Toyota, this has meant small trucks delivering similar parts in small batches eight times per shift – bringing just enough for the next hour's production and delivering it straight to the assembly line, not via goods inwards inspection. Another Japanese carmaker, Nissan, illustrates the process of synchronized manufacturing. As each car enters production at its UK Washington plant, a coding tag triggers a message to Sommer Albert, a carpet maker 3 km away, ordering one of 120 variations of carpet and interior trim for that vehicle. At Sommer the correct material is selected, trimmed, and put on a truck in the same sequence as the cars on the line. The delivery is made straight to the line.

This highly responsive, low-stock system reversed the western notion of protecting production from disruption in supplies by holding "buffer" stock. The Japanese notion is to eliminate buffers and solve the problems being buffered against – unreliable suppliers, machine breakdowns, labor inefficiencies, defective material, and so on. The result is a dramatic fall in costs, since the removal of such problems and of the inventory that masked them refocusses the operation entirely on adding value. This has been dubbed "lean production."

Yet for the true world-class manufacturer the journey never ends – there are always costs to be squeezed out or improvements to be made. In Japan this is attributed to the notion of *kaizen* or continuous improvement. In September 2000,

Hiroshi Okuda, chairman of Toyota, announced a 30 percent cost reduction in the Yaris model and plans for similar improvement in other products. Part of these savings will come from the online purchasing systems that most automotive companies are setting up, but much will still depend on continuous improvement of the JIT system.

A key technique associated with JIT is set-up time reduction. Here again, a tenet of western manufacturing was overturned – the idea that because several hours were lost resetting equipment to make a different part, the cost of that lost time needed to be spread over many subsequent units of production. This meant long production runs of the same item, many more than were needed immediately. These items remained in stock, sometimes becoming obsolescent.

For Toyota the key lay in reducing machine changeover time to a few minutes, so the economics of long runs no longer applied. What was a parameter within which manufacturers worked became a problem to be solved. Turning parameters (something one has to live with) into problems (to be solved) is the main reason why JIT has been revolutionary.

Since the 1980s no company in large-scale repetitive manufacturing has been untouched by these ideas and operational competitiveness has depended on the degree to which they have adopted JIT and lean production. At cosmetics company L'Oréal, for example, one improvement project reduced machine changeover time on the hair-colorant line from two hours to eight minutes. This in turn permitted a reduction in batch size from 30,000 to 2,000. The economic production of such small batches gives a company the flexibility to respond to market need just-in-time.

Mass customization

The next phase of manufacturing development seems likely to be the spread of mass customization – the production of customized items, but at close to mass-market availability and pricing. Here the classic case is National Bicycle in Japan, which has developed a system to make custom-built bicycles for about 15 percent more

---

The next stage in manufacturing seems likely to be the spread of **mass customization**

---

than the price of a top-of-the-range mass-produced machine. The customer is measured in the shop on a special frame and chooses style, color, brakes, tires, pedals, and so on, right down to the script for his or her name to be painted on the finished bike (11 million potential variations).

These details are faxed through to the plant and entered into the host computer, which generates bar code instructions for the tube cutting machine, painting robots, and other processes. Each unique bicycle is delivered two weeks after order. (In fact, this is a marketing ploy: the company can build it in a week, but claims "it's such a special product we feel it's right to wait a fortnight").

Levi-Strauss and other companies in the US are doing the same with jeans, shoes, T-shirts, and golf clubs. The attraction for the manufacturer is the Toyota principle: you sell the car, then you build it, so avoiding the risk of inventory exposure to obsolescence or falling sales. In a world of increasingly diverse markets and ever smaller and discriminating market segments within them, the appeal is clear. With customers searching for products that exactly meet their tastes, pressure will grow for operations to become more agile to satisfy those needs at an acceptable cost.

Quality revolution

Such operations depend on consistent component quality. Once manufacturers have removed buffer stocks, defective supplies will stop production. Similarly, in a world of very small batches or even one-piece flow, the next item has to be perfect if production is to continue. Thus JIT and lean production have been accompanied by a revolution in quality management. Once again the location was Japan, but the ideas were American.

After the Second World War, US experts in

Box 1 The elements of TQM

- Commitment of top management to a change program, which they lead personally.

- Involvement of everyone in the company, not only production personnel or quality professionals.

- Formation of teams to work, usually without managerial direction, on quality improvement and cost reduction.

- Development of solutions to problems using a rigorous procedure. In Japan and elsewhere this will usually be Deming's "plan–do–check–act" or PDCA cycle.

- Collection and use of data to establish true defect rates and causes, using standard techniques.

- A focus on the "cost of quality" model, whereby increased resources devoted to prevention reduce appraisal and failure costs, so that quality increases but overall costs fall.

- Education and training in quality tools and techniques.

- Organizational culture change, placing quality at the center of operations rather than as an adjunct to them.

quality control, including Joseph Juran and W. Edwards Deming, taught the Japanese statistical quality control and other techniques for eliminating the variations that cause problems. So effectively were these applied that Japanese products rapidly reversed their reputation for poor quality and gained market share from western manufacturers in market after market. Soon many companies were going to Japan to relearn what had seemingly been forgotten.

What they found was not just a set of techniques but a whole system of quality management – even a philosophy – that has been labeled total quality management (TQM). The elements vary, but most accounts will contain the items in Box 1. Not every program was an unqualified success, however, and by the mid-1990s TQM had even been discredited in some quarters. It was too often regarded as a "quick fix" by companies, or seen as a *smorgasbord* from which to select dishes, rather than as tough medicine to be swallowed whole.

Some companies owed their success or survival to quality initiatives. Ford in the 1980s made a turnaround by following the nostrums of Deming, according to chief executive Don Peterson. Motorola became famous for its "Six Sigma quality" campaign, which implied a defect rate of only 3.4 defective parts per million. This became a slogan for others, such as General Electric's Jack Welch, who set a corporate goal of "becoming, by the year 2000, a Six Sigma quality company, which means a company that produces

virtually defect-free products, services and transactions."

If quality initiatives as change programs have disappeared from the management agenda, this is surely because they are now seen as essential. Also, the role once played by proselytizers such as Deming has been taken over by awards, institutions, and standards, such as the Malcolm Baldrige award in the US, ISO 9000, and the European Foundation for Quality Management.

Technology

As the examples of National Bicycle and Toshiba show, technology can transform manufacturing. The key factor is linking information technology to processing technology, which began with numerical control (NC) machines in the 1950s and led to flexible manufacturing systems (FMS) in the 1980s. NC machines received instructions from cards or punched tape and later became computer-controlled (CNC) machines. FMS links machines together, usually with automatic tool change and workpiece transfer. As well as the obvious benefit, to the company at least, of lowering costs by replacing labor, such systems offer stricter conformance to component specifications, potentially enhancing quality. They can also be linked to the design function: computer-aided design outputs can be converted into instructions for computer-aided manufacture, widely known as CAD/CAM. The internet has allowed these links to ignore geography – drawings and instructions can be sent anywhere to be turned into products, creating a virtual factory.

The use of robots to perform human tasks in manufacturing is another example of linking process and information technology. Robots have become almost universal in volume car plants, where they are used especially for such difficult or dirty tasks as welding body parts and spray painting. However, their use in other sectors – and in different countries – varies widely. In 1998 the UK had about 10,000 robots in its factories, 19 for every 10,000 persons employed (a measure known as robot density). The US had 77,000 (density 42) and Japan had 413,000 (density 277). At Fanuc's robot-making plant on the slopes of Mount Etna one can see robots building robots.

Both cost and quality benefits are offered by robotics and the latter is critical in electronics. Certain areas of a semiconductor plant need to be 1,000 times cleaner than a hospital operating theater, so some tasks are carried out by robots in a vacuum. In disk drive assembly, the work is easier for robots than people. Matsushita Kotobuki Electronics (MKE) make Quantum's disk drives at an automated facility where 400 people and 150 robots produce 50,000 units a day. Quantum's main competitor is Seagate, which makes a similar number in Singapore and Taiwan, with few robots and 25,000 people.

As the last example shows, automation remains a choice rather than an imperative. But this will change as the price of equipment falls (and wages rise). The factory of the future is already with us – all the elements are at a late stage of development, at least in showpiece plants. The last phase is to bring it all together, making high quality, attractively priced, customized goods in highly automated lean-production units. That is twenty-first-century manufacturing.

Further reading

Hill, T. (2000) *Operations Management*, Basingstoke: Macmillan.

Slack, N., Chambers, S., and Johnston, R. (2000) *Operations Management*, London: Financial Times Management.

The way forward
for operations strategy

David F. Pyke is a professor of business administration at the Tuck School of Business at Dartmouth College.

Making sense of the many innovations in operations management is difficult. **David Pyke** sets out a framework for deciding priorities.

Japanese manufacturing success, particularly in cars and consumer electronics, was the topic of business debate in the early 1980s. Just-in-time (JIT) manufacturing and total quality management (TQM) became everyday terms. As a result, managers realized that the operations process could be a source of competitive advantage and that, if it were ignored, it could damage a company.

More recently, companies have realized that improvements in their market position from streamlining operations are limited by supply chains. They are beginning to emphasize supply chain management (SCM), including inventory, production, procurement, product development, and relationships with customers and suppliers. Is supply chain management another buzzword soon to fade away? How does a manager make sense of JIT, TQM, and SCM, not to mention time-based competition and other hot topics? This article develops a framework to put these trends in context.

Three-level strategy

Operations strategy has three levels: mission, objectives, and management levers (see Figure 1). However, operations should be integrated with other strategy areas, including marketing, finance, and human resources. Nevertheless, sometimes one function should take precedence over others. For example, one company went through a painful period of not responding to customers in a long-term effort to improve customer satisfaction. This was because the operations group needed to develop the ability to manufacture high-quality items in large volumes. To avoid disruptions during the process, customer desires were neglected and marketing personnel were frustrated. In the long term, however, customers were delighted.

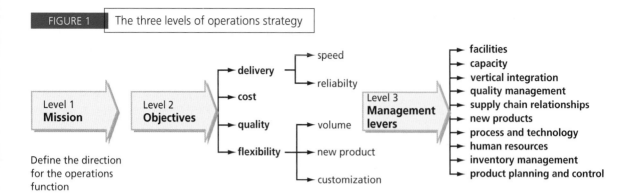

FIGURE 1   The three levels of operations strategy

Level 1
Mission

Define the direction
for the operations
function

Level 2
Objectives

→ delivery → speed
→ reliabilty

→ cost

→ quality → volume

→ flexibility → new product
→ customization

Level 3
**Management
levers**

→ facilities
→ capacity
→ vertical integration
→ quality management
→ supply chain relationships
→ new products
→ process and technology
→ human resources
→ inventory management
→ product planning and control

Mission

The operations mission defines a direction. McDonald's, for example, uses four terms for its operational mission: quality, cleanliness, service, and value. The annual report in 1988, more than 30 years after defining those terms, still devoted a page to each. Because the mission should not change significantly over time, the statement is often vague. Otherwise, it would have to be reworded frequently. Employees need to know there is a consistent direction for the company.

A sleepy statement of direction, resembling that of other companies, would make it difficult to attract employees. Therefore, a mission statement should try to convey the excitement of top managers and proclaim the excellence of the company.

Objectives

If the mission is vague, it is difficult to know whether it has been achieved. So the next level of strategy, operations objectives, provides measurable goals. For more than 20 years, companies have used four objectives for this: cost, quality, delivery, and flexibility.

Objectives must be defined carefully, clearly measurable, and ranked. Some terms are often used loosely: quality at McDonald's restaurants is different from quality at a five-star restaurant, which is very different from quality in a hospital. Objectives should be measurable so managers know whether they are meeting their goals. It is perhaps desirable to use more than one measure

for each objective (for instance, warranty cost and parts-per-million defective for quality).

Objectives should be ranked so managers can prioritize them. The manager of a high-volume manufacturing line stressed that cost was more important than delivery. When questioned, however, he noted he had sometimes gone over budget by using overtime to meet a deadline. In other words, his behavior indicated delivery was more important. Discussions with senior managers helped clarify that delivery was indeed more important.

In the 1970s, many people in operations thought cost and quality were incompatible, as were delivery and flexibility. More recent experience, however, suggests cost and quality are complements, not opposites. Warranty, prevention, and detection costs decrease as quality improves. Rework and congestion on the factory floor also decrease, thereby reducing costs. In addition, rapid delivery of customized products is now possible. This is especially true with technologies such as flexible automation, electronic data interchange, and the web. Most companies have instances, however, in which trade-offs must be made. Therefore, although combined improvements are possible, objectives should be ranked.

The first objective, cost, can be considered in one of three categories: low, competitive, or premium. In a low-cost environment, such as discount retailing, the goal is to have the lowest cost. Companies aiming for competitive costs do not necessarily strive for the cheapest products, but rather want to be competitive with most rivals. Some companies produce prototypes or have a unique product for which they can charge a premium; hence, cost is less important. Cost measures include price per unit, inventory turns, and labor hours per unit. In the US, low cost tended to be the primary objective of manufacturing companies from the 1950s to the mid-1970s.

The quality objective rose to the fore in the mid-1970s with the inroads made by Japanese products. In particular, the car industry felt the effects of high-quality Japanese products. Quality can be defined by understanding which of its multiple dimensions are important. An article by David Garvin describes eight dimensions of quality: performance, conformance, reliability, durability, serviceability, features, aesthetics, and perceived quality. Quality measures include parts-per-million defective, returns, satisfaction survey results, warranty costs, and so on.

Third, delivery can be defined by speed and reliability. For instance, some companies compete on delivering within 24 hours. Others take longer, but assure customers that goods will be delivered reliably within a quoted time. Some companies rank delivery last. Prototype printed circuit boards, for instance, may be completely customized and, therefore, require long delivery times. Measures for delivery include the percentage on time, time from request to receipt, percentage out of stock, and so on.

The fourth objective is flexibility, which has three dimensions: volume, new product, and product mix/customization. Volume flexibility is the ability to adjust for seasonal variations. It is particularly important for fashion clothing. New product flexibility is the speed and frequency with which products are brought from concept to market. Western car makers have made great strides in new product flexibility. A niche car allows a company to enter profitable, low-volume markets quickly. This flexibility is impossible if development time is eight years, as was traditionally the case. Japanese manufacturers, on the other hand, halved this time, which was then matched by Chrysler and Ford. Once again, however, Toyota has raised the bar by introducing the Ipsum in just 15 months.

Product mix/customization flexibility is the ability to offer a range of products. This may simply mean the catalog contains many items, or

it may mean the company can develop customized products. Many machine tool companies produce a single product for a given customer and never make that product again.

Some have argued that delivery and flexibility are the most important objectives because cost-cutting and quality programs have leveled the playing field in these areas. Such companies then compete with rapid introduction of new products and rapid delivery. "Time-based competition" has been used to describe this.

Finally, note that objectives are dynamic. For instance, as a new product begins full-scale production, the company may emphasize flexibility to design changes and delivery so market share is not lost. As the design stabilizes, the emphasis may change toward quality and cost.

Management levers

Although the operations objectives provide measurable goals, they do not indicate how a company should pursue those goals. Ten management levers provide the tactical steps necessary to achieve the goals: facilities, capacity, vertical integration, quality management, supply chain relationships, new products, process and technology, human resources, inventory management, and production planning and scheduling.

Interestingly, in the late 1970s researchers did not include quality management, supply chain relationships, new products, and human resources as management levers. Today, these are critical and new levers will be introduced. The categories for operations objectives, on the other hand, have not changed.

Facilities decisions concern the location and focus of factories and distribution centers. Are several required? Does each facility perform all functions or is one focussed on a market, process, or product? Many companies have a parent plant responsible for oddball parts and new product introduction. When products reach high-volume manufacture, they are moved to a plant where efforts are focussed on excellence.

Decisions on capacity expansion interact with location decisions. For instance, some companies set limits on the number of employees at any location, to encourage teamwork. As demand

Many companies are eliminating functional areas and organizing by business processes. For instance, a major company recently re-engineered in a way that redefined roles to be more responsive to customers. A common re-engineering approach is to replace the operations, logistics, and marketing functions with teams focussed on process.

One team may be devoted to generating demand, while another tackles fulfilling demand. The team working on generating demand performs tasks traditionally done by marketing, but may carry out other functions, including product development. The fulfillment team often looks like the manufacturing or operations function, but may include logistics, sales, and marketing as well.

The idea is to align organizational structure with the processes used to satisfy customers. Barriers between functions are removed, so the company can meet customer orders in a more seamless way.

grows, expansion at the site would violate the limit, so a new plant must be found. One US textile maker had expanding sales in Europe. When capacity at its factory could no longer meet demand, managers had to determine whether to expand near the same site, elsewhere in the US, or in Europe. The decision was to build in eastern Germany to lower transport costs and import duties and to exploit government tax breaks.

Make/buy decisions are at the heart of vertical integration. Some companies make components, perform final assembly, and distribute their products. Others focus on design and assembly, relying on suppliers for components and distribution. Facilities, capacity, and vertical integration decisions are made for the long term because of the investment needed.

The tools and techniques used to achieve quality goals comprise the quality management lever. This lever is distinct from the quality objective in that the objective provides the definition and measurable targets, while the lever specifies the means to achieve the targets. Quality management includes such things as statistical process control (SPC), Taguchi methods, and quality circles. Note that different definitions of quality may dictate different procedures.

The supply chain relationships lever focusses on dealings with suppliers and customers. These take different forms. For instance, General Electric has a "trading process network" that involves putting part specifications on the internet so suppliers can bid. These "virtual markets" are growing. Other companies maintain strategic alliances with a few suppliers or customers.

Some supply chain initiatives, such as vendor-managed inventory (VMI), involve restructuring supply chain relationships, often reducing the number of suppliers and encouraging digital communication.

The procedures and structures behind new product introduction are the core of the new products lever. Most companies use multifunctional teams of design engineers, marketing personnel, manufacturing managers, and production line workers. The new products lever specifies reporting relationships as well as procedures for setting development milestones.

The process and technology category encompasses the choice of a production process and the level of automation. The product–process matrix, which analyzes product characteristics with production processes, is useful for evaluating choices.

Human resources involves the selection and motivation of people. The inventory management lever encompasses decisions regarding purchasing, distribution, and logistics, and specifically addresses when and how much to order. Finally, production planning and scheduling focus on controlling and planning production.

Conclusion

First, researchers and practitioners keep introducing terms that describe some aspect of management. An example is supply chain management. The supply chain relationships lever, of course, pertains to supply chain management, but so too do inventory management, production planning and scheduling, vertical integration, and new products. Occasionally it is necessary to introduce a new lever to focus attention on important issues.

Second, the policies in place for each of the 10 levers should be consistent, not only with the operation's objectives but among themselves. If there are inconsistencies, managers should make changes. For example, many companies pursued quality without changing incentives, so workers were rewarded for the volume of output regardless of quality. In other words, quality objectives were inconsistent with human resources policies. Reward systems had to be changed to support quality goals.

Finally, in auditing manufacturing strategy, managers should understand distinctive competences at the detailed level of management levers. These competences should inform objectives, mission, and business strategy. Thus, information flows from strategy to levers and back.

Further reading

Fine, C. and Hax, A. (1985) "Manufacturing Strategy: A Methodology and an Illustration," *Interfaces*, 15(6), 28–46.

Garvin, D.A. (1987) "Competing on the Eight Dimensions of Quality," *Harvard Business Review*, November–December, 101–9.

Hayes, R. and Wheelwright, S. (1979) "The Dynamics of Process–Product Life Cycles," *Harvard Business Review*, 57(2), 127–36.

Silver, E.A., Pyke, D.F., and Peterson, R. (1998) *Inventory Management and Production Planning and Scheduling*, New York: Wiley.

Enterprise systems:
not an easy fit

M. Lynne Markus is a
chaired professor of
electronic business in the
faculty of business at City
University of Hong Kong.

The track record of enterprise systems is mixed and in some cases they have contributed to disaster. **Lynne Markus** analyzes the pitfalls and the potential of integrated software.

To a technology watcher, one of the most interesting recent developments has been enterprise systems. These commercial software packages integrate transaction data and business processes throughout an organization. Enterprise systems (ES) include enterprise resource planning (ERP) packages and related software such as planning, sales automation, and customer relationship management.

In the 1990s, companies that had previously developed their own systems began buying "integrated" offerings. Market researchers began tracking vendors and offering advice to would-be buyers. A handful of vendors came to dominate the market and investors followed the high flyers such as SAP, Oracle, Peoplesoft, and Baan.

Today, these enterprise systems command less attention. The focus has shifted to e-commerce and enterprise systems "extensions," such as customer relationship management and supply chain management. But billions have been spent on enterprise systems and spending continues. It is therefore worthwhile to ask what the fuss was all about. What was gained? What developments can we expect?

Characteristics

Enterprise systems have characteristics that set them apart from custom legacy systems and traditional packages, such as accounting software (*see* Table 1).

Applications integration

Perhaps the most important characteristic of enterprise systems is "integration." Traditional programs were designed for a single task: accounting, inventory control, manufacturing control, human resources, and so on. The reasons are several: limited processing capacity,

447

TABLE 1 | Comparing enterprise systems with traditional methods

	Legacy software	Traditional packages	Enterprise systems
Integration?	Systems usually developed in a stand-alone way; integration can be achieved at a price	Most applications are stand-alone; integration can be achieved at a price	Process support is built around a common database and common data structures
Package?	No: adopting organization is responsible for maintenance	Vendor will support package unless adopting organization has modified it	Vendor will provide support unless adopting organization has made changes
Tailored?	Highly tailored to needs of organization	Designed to fit the typical organization in large market segments	Can be configured to fit a wide variety of needs; industry-specific versions exist, but some needs cannot yet be met
Best practices?	Custom software is designed to fit existing or desired organization process, which may or may not be best practice	Traditional packages are generally designed to fit the way most organizations do things	Enterprise systems have normative practices built into the software; using the software without modification may require organizational change

difficulty amassing expertise in several areas, and, quite simply, the absence of a perceived need for cross-functional integration.

Gradually, however, the disadvantages of non-integrated systems became clear. One problem concerned management information. Executives knew that somewhere in their information systems enough data was captured to answer any query. But when they asked for reports analyzing data in different ways, they were told that these requests, if possible to satisfy at all, required expensive and time-consuming new programming.

Another common problem involved customer information. Many companies organized themselves by product lines and built systems in the same way. When someone finally asked, "How many customers for product X also buy Y?" or "Why don't we send customers a single bill?" the answer was, "Our systems won't do that."

Information on product availability was a problem. In a global economy, customers wanted to specify order delivery exactly, regardless of where parts were made. But suppliers lacked integrated information about inventories and deliveries to do this. These problems fueled demand for enterprise systems. Sadly, enterprise systems imperfectly met these needs. Today, the same needs fuel demand for data warehousing and mining solutions and the e-commerce extensions of ERP systems.

Packaged software

A second important feature of enterprise systems is that they are "packages." Unlike custom programs, they are commercial products from independent software vendors.

This gives them two advantages. The first is reduced development time and risk, because packages have already been shown to work. This was a big inducement to buy ES, because many companies had major disappointments in the early 1990s when they tried to convert main-frame systems to client–server architecture. After years of frustration and untold expense, many businesses quietly canceled conversion projects, until the Y2K problem forced change.

Packages, once scorned by large corporations, were seen as a viable alternative to in-house development. They were also consistent with moves to outsource noncore processes. When the Y2K scare hit its peak, ES vendors already had client–server versions and ES adoption boomed.

A second advantage of software packages is that the adopter can benefit from vendors' research and development. Companies spend huge sums on maintaining and developing existing systems. Changing needs require constant fiddling with business systems, but this costly activity is seen as a necessary evil, not as a strategic activity. So it is now high on the list of things to outsource. ES adopters expect a stream of new features and much lower maintenance costs.

Built-in best practice

A third characteristic of enterprise systems is that they are configurable – up to a point. One attribute that has always reduced the attraction of software packages is that they are not custom built. Instead, they support standard ways of performing "common" activities in a "typical" business. Companies with specialized needs are stuck with an unpalatable choice: change the way they do business, work around the software (such as doing some things manually), or modify the package (strongly discouraged by vendors).

But by the mid-1990s many companies were ready to change business processes. Re-engineering promised great improvements from streamlining processes. When it came to putting the new processes in place, however, legacy systems proved a stumbling block. Modifying them to support new processes required unacceptable time, cost, and risk. So, many solid re-engineering ideas were shelved – until these companies began adopting enterprise systems.

For their part, vendors made conflicting claims about enterprise software's role in re-engineering. First, ES packages were "configurable" to support varied process flows. Earlier business applications were relatively inflexible, so adapting them often meant modifying the package, against all advice. By contrast, enterprise systems are structured around tables of parameters that adopters can set to make the software conform to a wide range of business practices. Thus, enterprise systems promised to provide the benefits of "standard" packages and the bespoke nature of custom software.

The vendors' second claim was that enterprise software embodied "best practices." Working with the vendors on software development were academics noted for expertise in inventory management and other business concepts. Further, the vendors worked with so-called best practice companies. Adopters would benefit, it was claimed, from advanced knowledge about how processes should be done.

In short, the re-engineering trend led businesses to expect process change and enterprise systems were seen as the way to support it.

Successful adopters of enterprise systems cite various benefits. Some claim enterprise systems have provided support for globalization strategies, to provide "one face to the customer" or to know their inventory is "available to promise." Others cite benefits such as reduced operating costs of a client–server environment, lower software maintenance costs, the ability to expand without exhausting capacity, and a response to the Y2K problem (*see* Box 1).

Problems of ES

The benefits of enterprise systems are based on the assumption that adopters will replace their legacy information systems. Otherwise, for example, some applications will never be integrated. But completely replacing systems is an enormous undertaking. Projects can be very costly (costs of more than $500m have been reported) and take years to complete.

Further, they are not all successful; for example, Fox-Meyer Drug, the fourth-largest US drug wholesaler, went bankrupt owing to a botched implementation. Problems can be summarized in three categories:

- lack of alignment between technology and business needs;

- difficulties implementing and upgrading enterprise software;
- inability to support all business needs with enterprise software.

In addition, many ES adopters have not attempted full replacement of their legacy systems. Therefore, they miss out on those benefits that can only be delivered by a total system solution.

Business misalignment

Despite enterprise systems' strong business rationale, many companies have viewed ES largely in technical terms. In the best case, this results in limited benefits. In the worst case, it results in failure.

Since installing ES involves replacing systems, it is easy to view them as technology replacement projects. However, technology replacement decisions do not get the same scrutiny as new technology investment decisions, so opportunities may be missed. For example, one company expected no business benefits from its enterprise system, because the system was replacing one with severe capacity restraints. This company could have achieved far more if it had used ES implementation as an opportunity to improve business processes.

Business involvement in IT projects is a critical success factor. By contrast, failing to see ES initiatives as business projects can result in technically successful projects that do not accomplish business goals. For example, enterprise systems only provide global inventory if they are configured to do so. Some multinationals have allowed divisions to implement ES independently. Without common part numbering or consistent pricing, these companies are not able to achieve

"available to promise" capability or a consistent customer interface.

Implementation difficulties

As noted, ES implementation represents a significant departure from historical approaches. Early on, lack of deep knowledge about enterprise software and effective implementation approaches contributed to implementation difficulties. But the problems have continued, despite an accumulation of knowledge and expertise.

The reason is that enterprise systems involve trade-offs between business and systems change. In some cases, organizations avoid difficult business process changes by "tailoring" an enterprise system to fit current operations. In other cases, they reduce tailoring time, cost, and risk by changing organizational behavior. It is rarely possible to avoid both business change and systems tailoring. Neither is easy to do.

Organizational change can provoke resistance, so careful attention to human and organizational concerns is essential. Yet companies consistently underestimate the effort required. When training and support are insufficient, human errors run rife and people lack the knowledge to recover from them.

The technical aspects of enterprise systems implementation have proven more difficult than anticipated. In the first place, whereas the ES software is internally integrated, it is not integrated with the platform (hardware, database software, and telecommunications) on which it runs. Designing an appropriate platform has proven difficult for many ES adopters, because knowledge is spread among many specialists and companies. Adopters reported having to upgrade processors and memory or to replace database software several times before platforms worked.

Second, for many reasons, few companies have attempted to replace legacy systems fully. Consequently, to achieve the benefits of "integration," they have had to develop custom interfaces between enterprise and legacy systems. Doing so is expensive, time consuming, and risky.

Third, few adopters have found it possible to tailor enterprise systems to their needs entirely through configuration. Whether because software lacks functionality, implementers lack knowledge of that functionality, or companies are unwilling to change practices, many companies have modified the ES software. In some cases this has caused system failure and problems with upgrading.

Functional deficiencies

The earliest releases of enterprise packages were developed for generic organizations (usually manufacturing) and not customized for different industries. Most ES packages now come in industry-specific "flavors," but the degree of fit may still be low.

For example, a company with several plants making discrete parts may buy a version of the software tailored for those plants, only to find it doesn't fit a continuous process plant. Thus organizations may consider modifying the package, despite the problems.

The marketplace has responded to this with third-party, bolt-on packages. The success of these depends on relations between ES vendors and third parties. It also depends on the uniqueness of a company's need.

Further, despite vendors' promises and adopters' unrealistic expectations, enterprise systems have proven deficient in addressing the business needs that fueled their adoption: decision support and integrated customer and product availability information. To address these needs, ES adopters have added "extension" products for data warehousing and mining, customer relationship management, and supply chain management. Naturally, these have greatly increased costs.

Conclusion

The difficulties of ES implementation are great. Many adopters do not achieve expected rewards or do so at much greater cost than anticipated. Few companies implement enterprise systems as the vendors predicted and enterprise systems alone have not provided everything adopters need.

Consequently, companies adapt enterprise systems. There is now substantial interest in the technologies of integration, called "enterprise application integration"; whether they fulfill their promise is a trend to watch.

Enterprise systems have evolved from custom business software. The question is whether ES will follow the historical trajectory of increasing integration and close fit with unique business requirements – or whether ES will take off on a new path of disintegration, standardized shared services, and external management.

Further reading

Davenport, T.H. (2000) *Mission Critical: Realizing the Value of Enterprise Systems*, Boston, MA: Harvard Business School Press.

Markus, M.L. (2000) "Paradigm Shifts: E-Business and Business/Systems Integration," *Communications of the AIS*, 4(10), http://cais.aisnet.org.

R&D stuctures to keep
the focus on products

Rajesh Nellore is head of strategic planning in group global purchasing at Electrolux AB. He was formerly a senior research scientist in the technology management group of General Motors Corporation.

Great technical ideas can end up as corporate white elephants without a customer voice in the research division. **Rajesh Nellore** suggests some ways forward.

Research and development (R&D) is the generation and application of scientific knowledge to create a product or its component parts. It may also include the development of the manufacturing process for the product. Projects can last many years – Lusec, a drug designed to alleviate stomach ulcers, for example, was 20 years in development. By contrast, when the software industry modifies its products, the time for R&D may only be two to three months. So it is important to understand the different components of R&D when making comparisons between different industries and drawing conclusions about how it should be managed.

In the 1920s, companies began separating "long-range research" and "advanced product engineering." Long-range research is not directly related to a particular product and its applications may be unclear. For example, in the 1920s General Motors created the "copper-cooled" engine, which used air driven over copper fins by a fan to keep the engine from overheating. This was not designed for any particular product, it was simply conceived as a radical new technology.

Advanced product engineering, by contrast, is directed at specific products and the results can be used on other product lines – advances made in the design of one car engine might also be used in another. Advanced product engineering generates product-specific concepts, but these must be matched with other concepts that together constitute the final product.

In many companies there is a further department, called product engineering or release engineering (*see* Figure 1). Product engineers certify each part for use in the final product. In the motor industry, product engineers take concepts from different advanced engineering groups and adapt them for products. Product engineering is a separate function in, for example, General Motors and Swedish truck maker Scania.

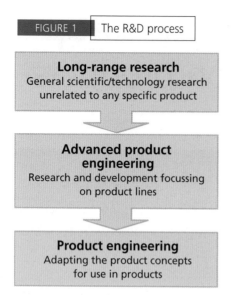

FIGURE 1   The R&D process

Long-range research
General scientific/technology research unrelated to any specific product

Advanced product engineering
Research and development focussing on product lines

Product engineering
Adapting the product concepts for use in products

Some companies are too small to afford separate product engineering departments. Here, the advanced product engineering department also performs the product engineering function. This is also common in industries where the rate of innovation is low and the emphasis is more on developing existing knowledge.

Divisions of R&D

For most of the last century, R&D referred to long-range research. In theory, a department would create a technology, then hand it over to an advanced engineering group for application in products – what was called a "phased hand-out." General Motors continues this tradition, with its R&D team devoted to long-range research.

However, many companies felt that separating R&D from product development could create problems, because the long-range research team was detached from the concerns of customers. The copper-cooled engine, for example, failed because it was not designed with a final product in mind.

Some companies have tried to solve this problem by maintaining the freedom of long-range research, but placing it alongside advanced product engineering under the umbrella of R&D. "Pure" ideas are developed alongside product

applications. Managers can sense changes in the market and in technologies and implement them more quickly in consumer products.

Scania has followed this approach. Long-range research engineers and advanced product engineers report to the same managers, so they are able to focus on technologies with the greatest potential to be realized in the market. There is no phased hand-out of concepts, but advanced product engineers test ideas as they are produced by the long-range research team. This means long-range research engineers can discuss ideas and be influenced by the advanced product engineering staff on the applicability of their research as it takes place.

Rolls-Royce seeks the same result in a different way. It has a central research organization (the long-range research team), which in turn has appointed technology specialists within business units such as civil engines, military engines, and so on. These people provide the connection between long-term research and market feasibility. R&D and advanced product engineering do not report to the same manager, but are co-ordinated through these specialists.

In general, new technologies should be developed to a certain level, then kept on hold until managers have demonstrated market acceptance. The Swedish company Volvo Aero has defined 10 levels for technology development in R&D (*see* Box 1).

Marketing input

A perennial problem of managing R&D is how to incorporate marketing departments in decisions on product development. Marketing input or the "voice of the customer" needs to be brought into the R&D process. However, in the approaches discussed so far there is no point where such data can be communicated. Ideally, it would happen at every stage of the process. Few companies have the resources to implement such a system, however. If integration is difficult between research teams and product engineers, it is even more so between researchers, engineers, and marketers.

One solution is for a single manager to have responsibility for communicating marketing

Swedish company Volvo Aero has defined 10 levels for technology development in R&D

1. Basic principles defined
2. Technical concept formulated
3. Analytical proof of concept presented
4. Component validated in laboratory conditions

5. Component validated in real conditions
6. Subsystem validated in laboratory systems
7. Subsystem validated in real systems
8. Prototype built
9. Prototype tested and validated for production
10. Continuous validation for a defined period

A problem with R&D is how to bring marketing departments into **decisions** about products

---

information to the long-range research team, advanced product engineering team, and product engineering teams – all of which constitute the R&D department. Product engineering is the "nuts and bolts" of manufacturing and involves close communication with, and feedback from, customers about products. With an integrated system, decisions about product termination, product enhancements, and new products will be made with a view to the core capabilities and limitations of the company.

This approach often works well for projects that span different areas of technology. One such project is the Connect system being introduced by Italian car maker Fiat. Each car will contain a computer system that provides on-board navigation, as well as internet access and operator assistance. Fiat must be sure of the future needs and desires of customers when designing the Connect system, so it has encouraged and organized close contact between long-range research, advanced engineering, and product engineering teams.

This relationship has enabled Fiat to phase the introduction of Connect into all its on-board systems. In other words, irrespective of the car they buy, consumers will be offered any type of service that the system can provide. Some may wish to spend less on the car and more on the navigation capabilities and operator services.

Suppliers as well as manufacturers can benefit from this approach. For example, defense industry supplier Raytheon has used its long-range research, advanced product engineering, and product engineering teams to extend its "night vision" technology for civil applications. The consumer version is a heat detector that warns drivers of upcoming obstacles on the road – beyond the range of headlamps. General Motors has introduced the technology in its Cadillac line.

Products and planning

Adapting a new technology to real products in all their minor or major variations is a formidable challenge. For example, a radio approved for installation on an Opel Corsa would need to be adapted for a Pontiac, even though both cars are produced by the same company. In general, the more hand-over phases there are between R&D departments, the greater will be the difference between planned and final products. It is also possible to make another generalization: with a phased hand-out, problems met in the adaptation phase by the vehicle engineering department will rarely be communicated to advanced product engineering or R&D for incorporation into future work.

A leading European car maker with separate departments for long-range research, advanced product engineering, and product engineering was preparing to export its cars to the US. In the US people often use a cup holder in their cars. Product engineers therefore installed the holder as an after-market option. Since sales were slack, product engineers asked the advanced product engineering department to incorporate the cup holder in the dashboard.

The more hand-overs there are, the greater the difference will be between **planned and final** products

After some delay, the cup holder was available in a standard size. Unfortunately, cup sizes changed soon afterwards and the new holder was the wrong size. The long-range research department therefore got involved, developing a flexible cup holder that could adapt to different sizes. The system of phased hand-over between R&D departments failed – the car maker expended far greater resources than if R&D been involved from the start.

The source of ideas

Companies no longer develop technologies completely in-house, but use outside suppliers for ideas and new technologies. Therefore, managing R&D involves not only the generation of ideas internally but also their external sourcing.

Companies tackle this in different ways. Nissan holds workshops where suppliers are encouraged to give technological presentations in the light of its product plans.

Electrolux classifies its suppliers in five ways: visionary, associate, mature, child, and contractual. Contractual suppliers are those whose goods are purchased by catalog. Child suppliers are given detailed specifications of what is needed and are consulted and monitored. Mature suppliers are allowed to start work after receiving rough specifications, such as a component's dimensions, weight, tolerances, and so on. Visionary and associate suppliers are expected to engage in R&D on their own, the difference being that visionary suppliers have a more established relationship with Electrolux – sometimes as long as 15 years.

BMW also classifies suppliers and has different expectations of them. It recognizes that all suppliers can provide ideas for R&D and therefore channels those ideas through a supplier innovation agency based in its German purchasing headquarters.

In general, the selection process for R&D ideas should be resolutely neutral. Undue interference should not be exerted by any particular department or those favoring certain suppliers.

Once ideas have been selected, they need to be prioritized and budgets allocated. Budget provisions are often not made (or the decision process made difficult) for ideas that have turned out to be very successful later. If there is no organized budget for long-term research, engineers and scientists may use other means to get ideas developed – by working with suppliers not approved internally or simply by leaving the company.

Value creation

Supplier innovations offer companies different opportunities for value creation. Innovations could be of "threshold value," which means the same technology is available elsewhere. Innovation in the glass industry is a good example. Glass suppliers for the automotive industry have to offer safety glass or complex shapes in glass simply to remain competitive – it is a minimum threshold of innovation for them.

"Incremental value" represents minor modifications to existing technology, such as new foam compositions for seats. "Known value" incorporates technology that is known but does not yet exist in the market, such as in-car information systems. "Breakthrough value" refers to a technology that is genuinely unknown, such as the night vision mentioned earlier.

Depending upon the type of value creation and the required capability of the manufacturer, decisions can be taken at different levels. Breakthrough value creation that requires new manufacturing capabilities may need a decision-making process that involves senior managers. Rigid decision-making may be considered for technological enhancements to existing capabilities for threshold or incremental value creation.

A supplier might also offer a technology that requires a new capability, yet offers only an incremental value creation for the customer. Such "opportunity-centered" decision-making entails sophisticated relationships between manufacturer and supplier, and requires the most seasoned technology evaluators.

Conclusion

Research and development needs to encompass three functions – long-term research, advanced product engineering, and product engineering. Product concepts should have a wide scope within this framework, from "intelligent" refrigerators, to embedded internet access and enabling technologies such as new fuel cells. All three functions should be organized under a single manager.

Yet R&D should also be brand-driven and customer-focussed. If Saab places safety high on its list of brand values, then it must focus on that area. R&D is becoming a core competence in many corporations, driven by the forces of competition, customer input, internal creativity, and supplier innovations. R&D is a challenging and rewarding activity, which brings enduring value to organizations that are capable of managing it rigorously and creatively.

Further reading

Mitchell, G.R. and Hamilton, W.F. (1998) "Managing R&D as a Strategic Option," *Research and Technology Management*, May/June.

Nellore, R and Soderquist, K. (2000) "Portfolio Approaches: The Missing Link to Specifications," *Long Range Planning*, April.

Nellore, R. and Soderquist, K. (2000) "Strategic Outsourcing through Specifications," *Omega*, 28, October.

Sloan, A.P., Jr. (1941) *Adventures of a White Collar Man*, New York: Doubleday, Doran & Co.

Sloan, A.P., Jr. (1963) *My Years with General Motors*, New York: Doubleday.

Measures of
success for R&D teams

Christoph H. Loch is an associate professor of technology management at Insead.

U.A. Staffan Tapper is an R&D manager and consultant. He is associated with Wits Graduate School of Business, Johannesburg.

Christoph Loch and **Staffan Tapper** suggest a practical framework for linking results from R&D activity to company strategies.

Despite the high costs and importance of research and development (R&D), many companies struggle to determine how well R&D is doing. Evaluating results by financial criteria has not provided an answer. In fact, companies using only financial measures in R&D funding decisions perform worse than those using qualitative criteria.

Companies have used nonfinancial measures: time to market (Toyota can develop a car in 18 months); product sales ratio (3M derives 35 percent of sales from products less than three years old); and R&D intensity (Pfizer has the highest R&D ratio at 19 percent of sales). However, such ratios cannot be compared across strategies and industries. For example, intensity is lower for a generic drug company than for top research companies, as they compete in different ways.

Moreover, R&D itself makes performance measurement difficult. A third of R&D managers believe it is impossible to measure R&D because:

- effort is not directly observable;
- incentives to invest in risky projects may be low because managers cannot "own" the benefits, and results are often so delayed they no longer affect the manager's career;
- there is great uncertainty: a product may fail for unforeseeable reasons.

Bill Hewlett, co-founder of Hewlett-Packard, once said: "What you cannot measure, you cannot manage. What gets measured gets done." Does this mean R&D cannot be managed? In this article, we propose it is possible to develop effectiveness measures that reflect both the strategic mission and the characteristic uncertainty of R&D.

Measurement

R&D performance measurement has four main functions: alignment and prioritization, evaluation and incentives, operational control, and learning and improvement. Consider a trip in a car. At first glance, performance seems straightforward: time needed, safety, and fuel used. However, it may not be so simple. Table 1 shows three trips with different purposes – a truck delivery, a race, and a family drive.

Alignment and prioritization

Performance measures focus the attention of the organization on mission and strategy. The mission for the truck driver is reliable delivery on time. In the race, safety is a concern, but not as much as for the truck: winning requires taking risks. For the Sunday family drive, time is no issue at all. What matters is enjoying the process of the ride. The mission determines which actions to take and it drives appropriate evaluation, control, and learning measures.

Evaluation and incentives

Performance measures often aim to evaluate individuals. In the example, the truck driver can be evaluated on fuel efficiency and keeping to schedule because he can affect the outcome. However, if the trip occurs in a congested area, the schedule must contain a buffer, or the driver cannot be held accountable for keeping to it. Likewise, the racing driver may be the best in the world, but still come in last if the engine does not perform.

In the context of R&D, this suggests that project performance should be measured as either output or process, depending on project risk. For routine projects, teams can influence outputs and so be held responsible for them. Moreover, multiple measures can force the manager to balance factors, rather than pursue a single goal.

In a project with high uncertainty, however, output measures are not under the control of the researcher and are thus inappropriate as evaluative measures, except to reward success. Therefore, the researcher should receive rewards based on the quality of the research process.

Even if process measures are preferable for projects, output must be measured and tracked. A racing driver may not be responsible for the result of a single race, but performance over a season does reflect his abilities. Similarly, risks of individual projects can be "averaged out" at the aggregate level of the department. A department

---

| TABLE 1 | Evaluating the performance of different car trips |

Type of trip	COMMODITY DELIVERY	MOTOR RACE	SUNDAY DRIVE
Key stakeholder	**TRUCK OWNER**	**RACE TEAM AND DRIVER**	**DRIVER AND FAMILY**
Mission: alignment and prioritization	Deliver reliably, on time, and at low cost	Complete distance in minimum time	Fill time, have fun
Operational control measures (in addition to steering and braking)	Distance made versus plan Respect speed limits Obstacles (traffic, road blocks)	Speed Engine revolutions (rpm) Position in race Tire condition, weather	Distance from home Obstacles (traffic jams) Proximity of attraction (e.g. bar) Weather
Evaluation measures (incentives)	Cost On-time performance Safety (accidents, traffic fines)	Lap speed Ability to overtake Safety (no accidents) Strategy (e.g. refueling)	Attractiveness of road and places visited Flexibility to stop Safety (accidents)
Learning and improvement measures	Route conditions Traffic conditions Natural stopping points Routes allowing return freight	Mechanical performance Mechanical failure reasons Competitors' race strategies	Traffic conditions Attractiveness of route Conversation during trip How to keep children entertained

head can influence output by improving processes and allocating more resources to a good portfolio.

Operational control

Many changes occur during an R&D project, making continuous feedback an essential part of the process. In the car trip, feedback must be immediate to allow the car to stay on the road – the driver needs to react instantly when a car ahead brakes. Similarly, operational measures must be tracked for R&D projects to stay on course. Schedules, milestones, and budgets are typical factors, but additional measures can help the department react faster, such as competitive factors, organizational support, technical capability, or new market demands.

Learning and improvement

To learn from projects, the R&D team needs a process by which data can be collected, results analyzed, and causes identified. This is similar to total quality management, which ensures quality in production processes.

GemStone research

The measurement framework can be illustrated with the example of GemStone, a medium-sized diamond producer. Mining diamonds requires sophisticated technology. Typically, 1,000 tonnes of rock yield 100g of high-quality diamonds. Rocks are crushed and the diamonds picked out. If rocks remain too large, diamonds may go undetected. If crushing is too fine, large diamonds are damaged. Technology can reduce these losses.

The research department exhibited three performance measurement difficulties to a high degree: nonobservability, uncertainty, and long delays. R&D managers could not describe their output to senior managers, nor could they argue for a specified research expense. So the annual budget was usually the previous year's plus inflation (or less). While operating units recognized past successes, they could not judge current work. This left nagging doubts as to whether research was subsidized by the rest of the company. The research department decided to devel-op R&D measures to become better connected to the company.

Business strategy and research

Figure 1 shows how GemStone linked its business strategy with its R&D strategies. The strategy can be characterized by the five questions at the top: what do we sell, to whom, how (with what core competencies and processes), why (what is the value proposition to the customers and its competitive advantage), and what are major threats in the environment (such as artificial diamonds)?

As GemStone does not produce diamonds, but finds them; innovation is solely concerned with new processes, not new products. Thus key contributions from R&D concern the costs and yields of business processes. Based on the strategy, the research group identified four types of contribution:

- Technology demonstrations, that is, proof of feasibility and potential, with working prototypes, process instructions, or technical reports demonstrating a principle.

- Breakthrough concepts, such as finding diamonds using X-rays.

- Being a knowledge repository for the company about diamond production. This may include training staff for technical services.

- Building a reputation for technology outside the company, through conferences, publications, and so on.

The above analysis led the research group to create programs with a clear rationale and relevance to the company's strategy. It also allowed researchers to form ideas of how they might contribute to the business. The group was then able to formulate performance measures that reflected the strategic mission and the work to be done, including risks.

Performance measures

Performance measures can be plotted as a spider chart (see Figure 2). The "output" is divided into four categories: new technology, technical support, knowledge repository, and process quality. Measures are operational and are derived from

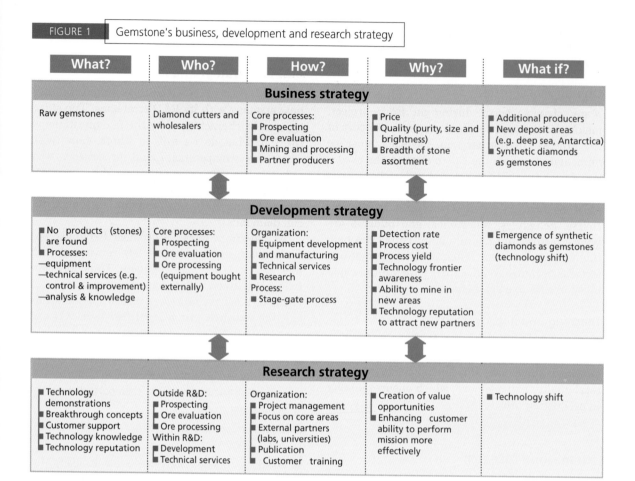

FIGURE 1 Gemstone's business, development and research strategy

What? | **Who?** | **How?** | **Why?** | **What if?**

Business strategy

What?	Who?	How?	Why?	What if?
Raw gemstones	Diamond cutters and wholesalers	Core processes: ■ Prospecting ■ Ore evaluation ■ Mining and processing ■ Partner producers	■ Price ■ Quality (purity, size and brightness) ■ Breadth of stone assortment	■ Additional producers ■ New deposit areas (e.g. deep sea, Antarctica) ■ Synthetic diamonds as gemstones

Development strategy

■ No products (stones) are found ■ Processes: —equipment —technical services (e.g. control & improvement) —analysis & knowledge	Core processes: ■ Prospecting ■ Ore evaluation ■ Ore processing (equipment bought externally)	Organization: ■ Equipment development and manufacturing ■ Technical services ■ Research Process: ■ Stage-gate process	■ Detection rate ■ Process cost ■ Process yield ■ Technology frontier awareness ■ Ability to mine in new areas ■ Technology reputation to attract new partners	■ Emergence of synthetic diamonds as gemstones (technology shift)

Research strategy

■ Technology demonstrations ■ Breakthrough concepts ■ Customer support ■ Technology knowledge ■ Technology reputation	Outside R&D: ■ Prospecting ■ Ore evaluation ■ Ore processing Within R&D: ■ Development ■ Technical services	Organization: ■ Project management ■ Focus on core areas ■ External partners (labs, universities) ■ Publication ■ Customer training	■ Creation of value opportunities ■ Enhancing customer ability to perform mission more effectively	■ Technology shift

company strategy. Also, they capture the trade-offs of R&D. For example, the number of equipment technologies is counted, but also the level of innovation and maturity of their transfer.

New technologies are by definition more risky than support activities for internal customers. Similarly, knowledge repository activities are intangible (it is hard to measure their direct usefulness). Therefore, process measures are more important for new technology and knowledge repository projects than for support.

The research team agreed to set a risk-adjusted balance between output and process measures for each case. In risky projects, output should result in reward if the researcher succeeds, but no punishment when the project fails. At the same time, the researcher should be responsible for conducting the project professionally – sloppy execution is not to be encouraged.

The benefits

There are various benefits in this approach, such as empowerment, managerial integration, prioritization, and benchmarking.

R&D employees had the opportunity to give themselves a process for diagnosis and improvement rather than having a system imposed. This creates an atmosphere of trust, in which researchers are treated and behave as professionals rather than order takers. Researchers can never be fully monitored, because their work

Measures to assess performance **educate** researchers about business needs and strategy

FIGURE 2 | Performance measures for GemStone's research group

is idiosyncratic and complex. But just like racing drivers, researchers can give themselves "best practice" procedures that increase the chances of success.

Performance measures also allow ideas to rise up from operational levels. They educate researchers about business needs and help them think strategically. Although measures are set by senior managers, they help researchers justify an idea in relation to the business, or express how a new idea might address strategy. Thus they become a communication tool between managers and researchers, boosting motivation and creativity.

The framework allows research to be prioritized. Estimating the value and contribution of research projects builds a better intuition for the difficult and nonquantifiable process of project evaluation. This allows managers to set priorities and construct an effective R&D portfolio.

The framework tells managers where to

benchmark. Benchmarking creates insights and learning only on measures that are used for similar reasons in both organizations. For example, a company that pursues an aggressive policy of generating revenues from licenses must have different goals for patent generation than GemStone, which wants to be seen as competent in technology. In the context of the performance measures, benchmarks can be truly comparable.

Conclusion

In the past, researchers at GemStone wanted to move out of research to develop and sell the machines they had invented, because this was the only way they could gain recognition. Now, the new measures allow researchers to understand better their unique role within the company and to focus on it. Senior executives, having helped develop the measures, are gradually accepting that R&D furthers company objectives. As a result, the measures have led to significant productivity gains in a short time.

The GemStone example concerns applied research. Measurement is harder in basic research, which relies on peer reviews and patenting activity. Yet the key is active engagement between top managers and R&D managers. Our studies suggest R&D staff can direct their creativity toward business strategies without having to give up ideas that are slightly "off." Once strategies are clear, progress can be assessed and the idea that unconventional ideas might complement strategy can be discussed, rather than dismissed out of hand.

Further reading

Hauser, J. (1998) "Research, Development and Engineering Metrics," *Management Science*, 44 (12/2), 1670–89.

Kaplan, R.S. and Norton, D.P. (1996) *The Balanced Scorecard*, Boston, MA: Harvard Business School Press.

Markides, C.C. (1999) "A Dynamic View of Strategy," *Sloan Management Review*, Spring, 55–63.

Terwiesch, C., Loch, C.H., and Niederkofler, M. (1998) "When Product Development Performance Makes a Difference: A Statistical Analysis in the Electronics Industry," *Journal of Product Innovation Management*, 15(1), 3–15.

The essence of
service lies in focus

Rogelio Oliva is an
assistant professor of
business administration at
Harvard Business School.

Many companies are expanding into services in the search for higher margins, but customer satisfaction appears to be falling. **Rogelio Oliva** identifies the traits needed for success.

Companies have become very good at managing manufacturing systems: they know how to balance production lines and how to optimize stock reorder points and logistics. Services management represents a different challenge, but some aspects of manufacturing models can be used to improve performance. Managers can, for example, determine the number of staff to ensure that clients will not wait for too long, find the ideal location for service facilities, and set prices that maximize revenues.

Yet despite advances in technology and manufacturing, poor service proliferates. The media increasingly focus on poorly run service operations and, even during a booming economy, companies seem incapable of getting services right: the US customer satisfaction index for services fell from 74.4 in 1994 to 69.4 in 1999.

Nature of services

By definition, services cannot implement all the techniques of manufacturing. Services differ in important respects. At one level, the servers (employees) and the elements being processed (customers) are human – with psychological attributes, perceptions, and expectations – as opposed to passive machines and parts.

There is a fundamental difference in how value is created. Manufacturing transforms raw materials into products. In this model, value is captured in the output of the transformation process, that is, the finished good. It makes sense to maximize output and to do things in the most efficient way.

Service, in contrast, is an "act done for the benefit of another." Value is created by the interaction of server and consumer (the process itself). Whether value is created can be assessed only by the consumer, and

> **Service capacity** is set not only by the number of employees, but by their attitudes, effort, and stamina

maximizing output (the number of transactions) does not have the same implications as in manufacturing.

Let us explore the ramifications of this difference. First, service organizations generate value through the delivery of an intangible (the interaction). Intangible services are difficult to describe and it is likewise difficult for customers to specify what they expect. For instance, try defining "good service attributes" from a travel agent. Soon you will realize that the list of attributes depends on the purpose of the trip, the circumstances, the time spent in search of the most economical option, and your preferences.

Quality can only be evaluated by comparing customers' expectations with their perception of the service. Consequently, customers do not evaluate service quality solely in terms of the outcome of the interaction; they also consider the process. Service quality thus encompasses all aspects of service delivery and is difficult to assess and to communicate.

Second, production and consumption are inseparable. That is, server and consumer have to be available at the same time for the transaction to take place. This leaves no room for a "finished goods inventory" as a buffer from variations in demand, so excess capacity is "perishable" because revenues cannot be recovered later.

The inseparability of production and consumption also means there is no time buffer during which quality can be assessed and, if necessary, improved. All operations take place in front of the customer and errors need rectifying immediately. Provision of the service is the "moment of truth."

Further, services brings employees and customers physically and psychologically close. Customers' perceptions are not only affected by the conditions under which the service is delivered, but also by employees' attitudes. Similarly, employees' attitudes toward their jobs are influenced by customers' attitudes toward the service.

Finally, services are labor-intensive. Service employees play a dominant role in a process in which value is added by personal exchange between consumer and provider. So, service capacity is determined not only by the number of employees, but by their skills, attitudes, efforts and stamina. The customized effect of personal interaction between customers and servers means that productivity gains through capital substitution in high-contact services are difficult to achieve. Despite investment in technology, improvements in service productivity lag behind manufacturing.

Yet not all services are intangible, inseparable, and labor intensive. For example, airlines provide a tangible service (transportation) and are not too labor intensive because the interactions with service personnel represent a fraction of their value. By contrast, legal counsel is a pure service in which the product is intangible (advice) and the direct worker is part of the service, making the service inseparable and labor intensive.

In summary, in service settings, interactions between social and technical systems create another level of complexity that limits the usefulness of manufacturing models. Study of service organizations requires an understanding of the social systems that produce and consume the service, as well as the characteristics of the delivery system. Service organizations should be designed and managed in a way that builds on the unique characteristics of services, or at least attempts to minimize the negative aspects of these characteristics.

Leverage

Researchers at Harvard Business School have identified a set of relationships that service organizations seem to exploit when managing their operations, called the "service profit chain." Two ideas that underpin this model are considered below.

First, in a setting where value is created through the interaction between customers and employees, there are significant advantages of learning curves. The more experience a customer (or employee) has with a service, the easier it is for the employee to provide the service. In a study attempting to identify the drivers for profitability for service organizations, academics Frederick Reichheld and Earl Sasser found that companies with higher customer loyalty enjoy higher profitability and that loyal customers become more profitable over time.

The benefits of loyal customers are many. The obvious one is that loyal customers yield a continuous source of revenue and savings on customer acquisition costs. While organizations spend a lot of time looking at their acquisition rates, few focus as closely on how long they retain customers.

A simple calculation can shed light on the value of customer loyalty and how to offset the average customer acquisition cost (the cost of attracting new customers, divided by the number of new customers attracted in a set time). Dividing this cost by the margin obtained from each customer per month yields the minimum period you need to retain a customer in order to make a profit.

Take the example of Iusacell, a mobile phone operator in Mexico. To establish a large user base, and in response to intense competition, Iusacell launched an aggressive campaign to attract new customers. The cost of acquiring each customer was, on average, $1,000.

These customers, lured by similarly aggressive competitors, were switching to other providers after an average of 17 months. Since Iusacell's profits were $35 a month from each customer, the average value of each customer was a loss of $405. More aggressive promotion would have little effect on profitability, so the company concentrated on retention.

The real benefit of loyalty, however, lies in the tendency of long-term customers to buy products and services with higher margins, and the potential of each satisfied customer to bring in new clients. For example, my internet service has no qualms in giving me a free month of access for every new customer that joins as a result of my recommendation. Not only does the promotion recognize my efforts, but the lifetime value of a customer is much higher than the acquisition cost (a month's fee).

The same loyalty effects help reduce cost

Organizations spend more time looking at how to **acquire customers** than how to retain them

when applied to employees. Experienced employees are more productive than novices. They know the company's processes and resources, and, more importantly, they know the customers. Further, they can help by selling related services more effectively, selecting and training new employees, and assisting in customer retention.

Although the economics of loyalty could be used to manage any business, the framework particularly suits services. Customers (or employees) are loyal if satisfied; that is, it is necessary to match or surpass their expectations of service in order to discourage their search for an alternative. This is no secret. But what does is take to satisfy customers?

According to academics Valarie Zeithaml, A. Parasuraman, and Leonard Berry, the principal determinant of service quality is reliability. That is, that the organization delivers what it promises. At this point, the second idea from the service profit chain comes into play: focus.

Focus aims to reduce variability introduced by clients who have subjective expectations and standards, and employees with varying skill sets. According to academic James Heskett, focus is achieved by producing a limited set of service "products" and aligning these to a specific market segment. Concentrating on one customer need through consistent delivery not only makes it easier to communicate what the service organization delivers, but also allows managers to streamline delivery to focus only on what is required by the customer. Heskett found that successful service organizations have either market focus or operational focus, and that those with both were very strong competitors.

Southwest Airlines (SWA) in the US has had 28 profitable years. It has grown at 15 percent every year since 1974 and its arrival record and customer satisfaction rating lead the industry. Furthermore, it charges half the price of other airlines for many of the same trips.

SWA has a limited offer: it does not support

transfers with other carriers, provides no meals, and seats cannot be booked. Instead, SWA has selected as its target market the "road warriors" – frequent travelers who have to cover short distances and could drive. Because it is a short trip, this passenger does not require meals, nor a connection to other airlines. He or she is more interested in convenience and flexibility for the return trip. Thus SWA establishes frequent departures between city pairs and a ticket can be used on any scheduled flight. Boarding passes are distributed on a first-come-first-to-board basis, and since passengers generally do not have much luggage and there are no booked seats, boarding is much faster than on other airlines. No company delivers as much value to the traveler in this segment as SWA.

How can the concept of focus help with employee retention? SWA's highly specific process allowed it to identify attitudes and skills that were desirable in flight attendants. It has developed selection processes that identify those attitudes and training to develop skills for the job.

SWA does not pay above-market salaries, yet is regarded as one of the best companies to work for and has the lowest employee turnover of any airline. It achieves this by developing a culture and environment that are valued by its employees. In a way, it has carefully segmented the labor market to ensure it attracts employees who enjoy the kind of work offered.

Notice that both ideas presented here (focus and economics of loyalty), though developed to better serve and profit from customers, can be applied to service employees. Nowhere is the saying "employees are the most valuable asset of the organization" more true than in the service industry. Successful service organizations treat employees like customers.

Integration

Management literature advises manufacturers to integrate support services into core offerings as a way of extending revenues. There are several reasons: services help to differentiate products; customers will pay for services because of the complexity of products; downsizing has created more flexible firms and narrower definitions of core competencies.

Further, services, because they are difficult to imitate, have higher margins, and revenues are more resistant to variations in the business cycle. Manufacturers have advantages in providing services for their own products: low customer acquisition cost; low knowledge acquisition cost (full information on product design and maintenance is available); and low capital requirements (manufacturing facilities can produce spare parts). It is not surprising to see companies such as Xerox and Hewlett-Packard aiming to become service providers.

The literature is less helpful on how this integration should be achieved. The transition from manufacturing to services is a challenge: services need different structures and processes. There are three ways in which manufacturers need to change:

- Metrics: from throughput and efficiency metrics that govern manufacturing to metrics reflecting the value created in service interaction.
- Knowledge management: from centralized knowledge centers (design labs) and products that are intrinsic recipients of that knowledge (a car or a printer) to service centers that require extrinsic knowledge.
- Economic model: from a one-off purchase to a long-term relationship with a continuous revenue stream.

What makes the transition difficult is the clash between the norms of a manufacturer and what is required for good service. This clash was captured in the words of a German manager: "It is difficult for an engineer who has designed a multimillion-dollar piece of equipment to get excited about a contract worth $100,000 for cleaning it." If a manufacturer succeeds through quality and the excellence of its processes, incentives and systems will aim to develop this excellence. The values and processes to excel in services take second place.

Manufacturers handle these difficulties by creating a separate service organization with its own culture, norms, and values. Although this diffuses the cultural clash, manufacturers are still challenged: the service business diverts resources from manufacturing and it is not easy to manage the tightly coupled businesses.

Also, increasing the quality and scope of the service offering might extend the product's life, so reducing replacement sales. Similarly, improving the product might reduce revenues to the service wing. Sorting out the trade-offs between competing business models and replicating successful practices will be a major challenge for services management.

Further reading

Heskett, J. (1986) *Managing in the Service Economy*, Boston, MA: Harvard Business School Press.

Heskett, J., Sasser, W., and Schlesinger, L. (1997) *The Service Profit Chain*, New York: Free Press.

Reichheld, F. and Teal, T. (1996) *The Loyalty Effect*, Boston, MA: Harvard Business School Press.

Zeithaml, V.A., Parasuraman, A., and Berry, L.L. (1990) *Delivering Quality Service: Balancing Customer Perceptions and Expectations*, New York: Free Press.

Business-minds

For who to read, what to know and where to go in the world of business, visit us at www.business-minds.com. here you can find out more about the people and ideas that can make you and your business more effective.

Subject index

futurizing 110
stimulants 111
threats 111
underestimating developing technologies 52
see also information technology
telecommuting 247
think marketing 348
third-party sponsored ethics codes 165
time 272
total quality management (TQM) 438, 441
toy exchanges 92
trade secrets 170–1
trademark law 169, 170
training 218
transcultural competence 135–6
transparency 189
Treasury bond market 398
treasury departments 421–4
triage system 118
tribalism 219–20
trust 268
trusteeship 14

uncertainty 5–10
underwriters 47–8
undifferentiated marketing strategy 328–9
unions 21

valuation of companies
    for business plans 36–7
    IPOs (initial public offerings) 48, 49–50
    for mergers and acquisitions 86–7, 399
    web companies 403–7
value creation 28, 34, 86, 94–5, 284, 456
value cycle of supportive behaviours 187
value drivers 387–8

values-based ethics programs 165–6
venture capitalists 7, 30, 42, 43
venture managers 57–61
    business proposition development 57–8
    checking market acceptance 59
    controling costs 59
    coping with uncertainty 58
    early warning systems 60
    and failed ventures 60
    framing the challenge 58–9
    killer deals 59
    and skills deficiencies 59–60
venture philanthropy 205–8
    active involvement 208
    choice of project 206
    grant funding 207
    performance measures 207
    portfolio management 206
    risk management 206
video vans 364–5
vision 273, 274
voluntary reduced time (V–time) 247–8

wa 142–3
waste management 197
web-enabling existing operations 106–7
websites *see* e-commerce; internet
work culture 245
work structure 272–3
work-life balance 248–9
worker rights 18
working hours 246
wrongful termination lawsuits 223

zero-based budgeting 335

Organization index

L'Oréal 437
Lotus 83
Luban.com 145–6
Lucent 106
LVMH 345

McDonald's 136, 321, 346, 442
McKinsey 217, 240
Madeforchina.com 148
Mannesmann 69, 174
Manugistics 343
Marks & Spencer 352
Marlboro 317
Marriott Hotels 70, 330
Mars 77
Matalan 352
Matsushita 439
Mattel 165
Mazda 142
Mercata.com 341
Merck 166, 268
Merger and Acquisition Consulting 11
Metro 352, 364
Microsoft 29, 51, 54, 69, 72, 81, 164, 169, 171, 268, 318, 328, 348, 421–4, 433
Mightywords.com 155
Millenium Pharmaceuticals 283
Monsanto 166
Monster.com 52, 115, 238
Motorola 55, 136, 146, 164, 218, 234, 438
MP3.com 169–70
Musicmaker.com 330

Nanz 364
Napster 170
National Bicycle 437
National Westminster Bank 69
NationsBank 88, 89
NBCi 118
Nestlé 77
Netcentive 169
Netscape 69, 81
New Schools 207
Next 352
Nike 164, 348
Nippon Telephone and Telegraph 11
Nissan 11, 436, 456
Nokia 217, 218
Norsk Hydro 166
Nortel Networks 106, 240, 273
Northern Telecom 140
Northwest Airlines 336
NTT DoCoMo 147

OECD (Organization for Economic Co-operation and Development) 164
Olivetti 174
Olympia & York Canary Wharf Company 193
Omnicom 334
Oracle 81, 84, 106, 343, 447

Oxfam 132

P&O 121
Peacocks 352
People Express 342
People's Bank of China 147
Peoplesoft 447
Pepsico 170–1
Pew Charitable Trust 208
Pfizer 166, 459
Philips 77, 274
Polygram Records 201
Pratt & Whitney 202
Priceline.com 58, 170, 341
PricewaterhouseCoopers 239
Procter & Gamble 69, 166, 201, 268
Promodès 352
PROS Strategic Solutions 343
Prudential Group 164, 240
Puma 164

Quaker Oats 171, 401, 432
Quantum 439
Quicken 325

Railtrack 257
Rand Corporation 223
Raytheon 455
Reichhold Chemicals 202
Ritz Carlton 325, 330
Robin Hood Foundation 207
Roche 55
Rolls-Royce 454
Royal Bank of Canada 194
Royal Bank Financial Group 234
Royal Bank of Scotland 69
Royal Dutch/Shell 54, 77, 136, 146, 164, 165, 189, 196

Sabre Decision Technologies 343
Safeguard Scientifics 55
Sainsbury 352
Sakura Bank 11
Salarysource.com 238
Salomon Brothers 164
SAP 343, 423, 447
Sara Lee 77
Saturn 55
Scania 453, 454
Schwab 51, 55, 194, 317
SCO 54
Seagate 70
Seagram 199, 201, 203
SEC 171
Securities and Exchange Commission (SEC) 45–9, 377
Selfridges 352
Sephora 345
Service corps of Retired Executives 208
Shandwick International 186
Shell 54, 77, 136, 146, 164, 165, 189, 196
Shoei Corporation 11

Siemens 77, 232, 235
Singapore Airlines 345, 346
Sinotrust Business Risk Management 148
SKAI 292
Skandia 110, 235
SmithKline Beecham 282
Snapple Beverages 401
Social Venture Partners 207
Sommer Albert 436
Sony 11, 136, 170, 218
Southwest Airlines 29, 231, 298, 467–8
SPX 410–12
Stanley Works 201, 203
Starbucks 220, 347
Starwood Hotels 346
Stella Artois 335
Strategic Horizons 346
Strategisgroup.com 156
Sumitomo Bank 11
Sun Microsystems 81, 84, 89, 106
Swatch 321
Symantec 86, 89

Talus Solutions 343
Telecom Italia 174
Telefonica 79
Tesco 336, 352
Thermo Electron 55
3M 27, 77, 268, 273, 459
Tidal Software 423
Time Warner 121, 132, 171
Tomkins 121, 122
Toshiba 81, 436
Toyota 196, 198, 436–7, 459
Toys R Us 72
TradeOut 202
Transparency International 165
Trump 70

Ubid 202
Unicom 147

Unilever 77, 174–5, 362, 363, 364
Uninet 147
Union Carbide 200–1, 203
Unipart 254
Unisys 433
United Airlines 342
United Parcel Service 240
United Phosphorous (UPL) 364
Universal Studios 201
University College London 252
UniversityAngels.com 42
Urban Enterprise Fund 207
USA Today 53
USAA 326

Vault.com 238
Viant 232
Virgin Atlantic 29
Vodafone 69, 122, 174
Volkswagen 170, 336, 346, 363
Voluntary Services Overseas 208
Volvo 78, 79, 455

W 346
Wal-Mart 71, 92, 268, 352, 364
Webvan 49
Wetfeet.com 238
Weyerhauser 197
Whirlpool 363
Williams 121
World Trade Organization 129, 146
World Wildlife Fund 132
WPP 334

Xerox 53–4, 58, 82, 84, 201, 203, 387, 468
Yahoo! 117, 132, 171, 231–2, 330, 403

Yamaha 57, 436

Zara 352

Name index